D1275845

THE UNITED STATES CONGRESS:

A BIBLIOGRAPHY

Robert U. Goehlert
and
John R. Sayre

THE FREE PRESS
A Division of Macmillan Publishing Co., Inc.
NEW YORK

Collier Macmillan Publishers
LONDON

606006

The Free Press
A Division of Macmillan Publishing Co., Inc.
866 Third Avenue, New York, N.Y. 10022

Collier Macmillan Canada, Inc.

Library of Congress Catalog Card Number: 81-19526

Printed in the United States of America

printing number
1 2 3 4 5 6 7 8 9 10

Library of Congress Cataloging in Publication Data

Goehlert, Robert U.
   The United States Congress.

   1. United States. Congress—Bibliography. I. Sayre, John R. II. Title.
Z7165.U5G575   (JK1061)   016.32873   81-19526
ISBN 0-02-911900-6   AACR2

JK
1061
.Z9
G626
1982

Contents

Introduction

Our aim in compiling this volume was to produce a comprehensive bibliography on the United States Congress. While a wealth of material has been written about the Congress, no such bibliography has previously been published as a guide to the literature. In order to provide a guide to the broad spectrum of sources and fill the need for an extensive bibliography on the Congress, we conducted a systematic search of the literature. The bibliography is designed to assist both the general reader and serious students and scholars.

The primary focus of this bibliography is on the history, development and the legislative process of Congress, not with national politics and government policy in general. Consequently, secondary and peripheral materials on the federal government, foreign affairs, campaigns and current events are not included. Our aim was to include all scholarly research material published in English over the last two hundred years. Those who desire to find more general information about specific events and issues and the day-to-day activities of Congress should explore the primary documents of Congress, newspaper accounts and the voluminous material indexed in *Reader's Guide to Periodical Literature*. Also, though some biographical material is included in the bibliography, as a rule biographies are excluded. The authors have simultaneously been compiling a companion volume to this work, which will include all scholarly materials written about all members of Congress past and present.

The bibliography includes books, edited volumes, original essays in compilations, journal articles, research notes and review essays, dissertations, theses and selected U.S. documents. In the case of books which have been revised or issued in new editions, we have cited the last edition. For edited volumes and compilations of essays which have been issued in new editions, we cited every original essay regardless of the edition in which it was published. If a dissertation was published as a commercial monograph, only the latter citation is provided. If an article on the same topic as the author's dissertation has appeared, both citations are provided for the sake of accessibility. While many of the monographs included in the bibliography have been reprinted, the original publisher and date is given. The reason for using the original publishing information and not the reprint date is to provide users with the time frame in which a work was published. U.S. documents and articles from *National Journal* and *Congressional Quarterly Weekly Report* were chosen on a selective basis. The choice of documents and articles from these two weekly journals was to provide continuity and coverage on topics for which little has been written, as well as to illustrate the kinds of materials available from those sources. There is a vast number of U.S. documents concerning the Congress. Those interested in pursuing additional documents should use Congressional Information Service's *CIS/Index, CIS/U.S. Serial Set Index, CIS/U.S. Congressional Committee Prints Index* and the forthcoming *CIS/U.S. Congressional Committee Hearings Index. Public Affairs Information Service Bulletin* also selectively indexes major U.S. documents dealing with Congress. *National Journal* and *Congressional Quarterly Weekly Report*, both invaluable journals for the student and serious researcher of Congress, are indexed quarterly and annually. With the exception of the dissertations, theses and reports of the Congressional Research Service cited in the bibliography, the bibliography includes only published materials, assuring easy accessibility of the materials listed. Consequently, the bibliography does not include conference papers and other typescript volumes. Most of the dissertations and theses, though not all, are available from University Microfilms on microfilm or xerography. Reports of the Congressional Research Service, though they are distributed on a limited basis, were included because of their uniform excellence. Many CRS reports have been microfilmed and indexed by University Publications of America in a series entitled *Major Studies and Issue Briefs of the Congressional Research Service*. This microfilm series, containing hundreds of studies, is available in many large academic, law and public libraries. As many CRS studies and reports are printed in some form by the U.S. Government Printing Office, usually in committee hearings or prints, they are in the public domain and are often available at depository libraries. The CRS reports printed in committee hearings and prints are indexed in *CIS/Index*. Also, the Congressional Research Service began publishing in 1978 a listing of *CRS Studies in the Public Domain*.

One of our goals is compiling the bibliography was to include materials from all subject disciplines in the humanities, social sciences and law. In order to be as comprehensive as possible, we searched thirty-six indexes and abstracting services. These indexes are listed in Appendix A. The dissertations cited were found in *Comprehensive Dissertation Index* and *Dissertation Abstracts International*; the theses were found in *Masters Abstracts*. To identify books on Congress we searched various sets of the *National Union Catalog, Books in Print, American Book Publishing Record, Cumulative Book Index, Publishers Weekly, Public Affairs Information Service Bulletin* and the *Universal Reference System, Political Science Series*. We also checked numerous bibliographies on Congress published in books or articles. These were identified by using *Bibliographic Index*.

The bibliography is classified according to fourteen major topics: (1) History and Development of Congress, (2) Congressional Process, (3) Reform of Congress, (4) Powers of Congress, (5) Congressional Investigations, (6) Foreign Affairs, (7) Committees, (8) Legislative Analysis, (9) Legislative Case Studies, (10) Leadership in Congress, (11) Pressures on Congress, (12) Congress and the Electorate, (13) Congressmen and (14) Support and Housing of Congress. There is a complete author index and extensive subject index. While the entries are not annotated, the Table of Contents and Subject Index can be used to locate information. The Table of Contents indicates the overall organization of the bibliography and facilitates easy access to major topics. The Subject Index can be used to locate materials on major topics and subtopics appearing throughout the bibliography, as well as specific individuals, laws, cases, events and subjects. The authors devised their own Subject Index, in which they attempted to use both general headings and terms found in the literature on Congress. The Subject Index contains extensive see references and cross references to assist the user. Also, under numerous main headings we have indicated the span of entry numbers which pertain to a broad category. Additionally, many entry numbers in the Subject Index are followed by the Congress or time period for which that item pertains. These are in parentheses after the item number, i.e. 2504 (91st Cong.) or 1742 (*1950–58*).

Though this bibliography is by no means definitive, it is hoped that it will prove useful to those interested in Congress and promote more intensive research and attention to aspects of Congressional studies that have not been fully treated in the existing literature.

Robert U. Goehlert
John R. Sayre

Appendix A.
Indexes Searched

ABC POL SCI
America: History and Life
Architectural Periodicals Index
Art Index
Australian Public Affairs Information Service
British Humanities Index
Business Periodicals Index
Combined Retrospective Index to Journals in History
Combined Retrospective Index to Journals in Political Science
Current Contents: Social and Behavioral Science
Education Index
Environment Abstracts
Environment Index
Historical Abstracts
Human Resources Abstracts
Humanities Index
Index to Legal Periodicals
Index to Periodical Articles Related to Law
Index to U.S. Government Periodicals
International Bibliography of the Social Sciences: Political Science
International Political Science Abstracts
Legal Resource Index
Psychological Abstracts
Public Affairs Information Service Bulletin
Quarterly Strategic Bibliography
Religion Index One
Sage Public Administration Abstracts
Sage Urban Studies Abstracts
Selected Rand Abstracts
Social Sciences Citation Index
Social Sciences Index
Sociological Abstracts
United States Political Science Documents
Urban Affairs Abstracts
Women's Studies Abstracts
Writings on American History

I. History and Development of Congress

The Study of Congress

General Studies

1. Acheson, Dean G. *A Citizen Looks at Congress.* New York: Harper, 1957.

2. Bailey, Stephen K. *Congress in the Seventies.* 2d. ed. New York: St. Martin's Press, 1970.

3. Bailey, Stephen K. *The New Congress.* New York: St. Martin's Press, 1966.

4. Bailey, Stephen K. and Samuel, Howard D. *Congress at Work.* New York: Holt, 1952.

5. Barry, David S. *Forty Years in Washington.* Boston: Little, Brown, 1924.

6. Bates, Ernest S. *The Story of Congress, 1789-1935.* New York: Harper, 1936.

7. Beard, Charles A. "Congress as Power." In his *The Republic: Conversations on Fundamentals,* pp. 192-206. New York: Viking Press, 1943.

8. Bouchey, L. Francis. "The Case for Congressional Government." *New Guard* 13 (Nov. 1973): 6-9.

9. Boykin, Edward C. *The Wit and Wisdom of Congress.* New York: Funk and Wagnalls, 1961.

10. Brogan, D. W. "The Wayward Child: Congress." *Parliamentary Affairs* 3 (Winter 1949): 84-93.

11. Bryant, Beverly B. "Perspectives on Congress: An Analysis of Approaches Used by Political Scientists." Ph.D. dissertation, Arizona State University, 1971.

12. Burnham, James. *Congress and the American Tradition.* Chicago: Regnery, 1959.

13. Cater, Douglass. "Congress." In his *Power in Washington: A Critical Look at Today's Struggle to Govern in the Nation's Capital,* pp. 117-176. New York: Random House, 1964.

14. Chelf, Carl P. *Congress in the American System.* Chicago: Nelson-Hall, 1977.

15. Clark, Joseph S. *Congress: The Sapless Branch.* New York: Harper and Row, 1964.

16. "Congress Remains Divided on Question of Federal Role." *Congressional Quarterly Weekly Report* 20 (Dec. 28, 1962): 2290-2295.

17. "Congress Sharply Divided on Question of Federal Role." *Congressional Quarterly Weekly Report* 19 (Oct. 20, 1961): 1751-1763.

18. Congressional Quarterly. *Congress and the Nation, 1945-1964.* Washington: Congressional Quarterly, 1969.

19. Congressional Quarterly. *Congress and the Nation, 1965-1968.* Washington: Congressional Quarterly, 1969.

20. Congressional Quarterly. *Congress and the Nation, 1969-1972.* Washington: Congressional Quarterly, 1973.

21. Congressional Quarterly. *Congress and the Nation, 1973-1976.* Washington: Congressional Quarterly, 1977.

22. Congressional Quarterly. *Guide to Congress of the United States: Origins, History and Procedure.* 2d. ed. Washington: Congressional Quarterly, 1976.

23. Congressional Quarterly. *Inside Congress.* Washington: Congressional Quarterly, 1979.

24. Congressional Quarterly. *Origins and Development of Congress.* Washington: Congressional Quarterly, 1976.

25. Congressional Quarterly. *Powers of Congress.* Washington: Congressional Quarterly, 1976.

26. Cooper, Joseph. "Congress in Organizational perspective." In *Congress Reconsidered,* eds. Lawrence C. Dodd and Bruce J. Oppenheimer, pp. 140-159. New York: Praeger, 1977.

27. Dale, Edwin L. "The Imperial Congress." *Across the Board* 15 (Nov. 1978): 37-39, 42-43.

28. Davidson, Roger H. and Kovenock, David M. "The Catfish and the Fisherman: Congress and Prescriptive Political Science." *American Behavioral Scientist* 10 (June 1967): 23-27.

29. Davidson, Roger H. and Oleszek, Walter J. *Congress Against Itself.* Bloomington: Indiana University Press, 1977.

30. De Grazia, Alfred, ed. *Congress: The First Branch of Government.* Garden City, N.Y.: Doubleday Anchor Books, 1967.

31. De Santis, Vincent P. "The Historical Growth of Congress." *Current History* 27 (Oct. 1954): 193-200.

32. Dexter, Lewis A. *The Sociology and Politics of Congress.* Chicago: Rand McNally, 1969.

33. Dodd, Lawrence C. *Congress and Public Policy.* Morristown, N.J.: General Learning Press, 1975.

34. Dodd, Lawrence C. "Congress and the Quest for Power." In *Congress Reconsidered,* eds. Lawrence C. Dodd and Bruce I. Oppenheimer, pp. 269-307. New York: Praeger 1977.

35. Dodd, Lawrence C. and Oppenheimer, Bruce I., eds. *Congress Reconsidered.* New York: Praeger Publishers, 1977.

36. Dodd, Lawrence C. and Schott, Richard L. *Congress and the Administrative State.* New York: Wiley, 1979.

37. Dry, Murray. "Congress." In *Founding Principles of American Government: Two Hundred Years of Democracy on Trial,* eds. George J. Graham and Scarlett G. Graham, pp. 223-257. Bloomington: Indiana University Press, 1977.

38. Eliot, Thomas H. "In Defense of Congress." *Common Sense* 10 (Dec. 1941): 372-373.

39. Elsbree, Hugh L. "The Political Scientist and the Congress." *Public Policy* 10 (1960); 332-340.

40. Eulau, Heinz and Abramowitz, Alan I. "Recent Research on Congress in a Democratic Perspective." *Political Science Reviewer* 2 (Fall 1972): 1-38.

41. Feulner, Edwin J. and Schuettinger, Robert L. "Liberalism and Compromise in the U.S. Congress." *Il Politico* 41 (1976): 652-665.

42. Fiorina, Morris P. *Congress: Keystone of the Washington Establishment.* New Haven: Yale University Press, 1977.

43. Fleming, James S. "Political Conditions for a Liberal Congress." Ph.D. dissertation, University of Arizona, 1971.

44. Galloway, George B. *Congress at the Crossroads.* New York: Crowell, 1953.

45. Garfield, James A. "A Century of Congress." *Atlantic Monthly* 40 (July 1877): 49-64.

46. Geigle, Ray A. and Hartjens, Peter G. *Representation in the United States Congress, 1973.* Rev. ed. Washington: American Political Science Association, 1975.

47. Gibert, Stephen P. "Congress: The First Branch of Government?" *Public Administration Review* 27 (June 1967): 178-189.

48. Goetcheus, Vernon M. and Mansfield, Harvey C. "Innovations and Trends in the Study of American Politics." *American Academy of Political and Social Science, Annals* 391 (Sept. 1970): 177-187.

49. Green, Mark J. with Michael Calabrose. *Who Runs Congress.* 3rd ed., rev. and updated. New York: Viking, 1979.

50. Griffith, Ernest S. and Valeo, Francis R. *Congress: Its Contemporary Role.* 5th ed. New York: New York University Press, 1975.

51. Haass, Richard. *Congressional Power: Implications for American Security Policy.* London: International Institute for Strategic Studies, 1979.

52. Haines, Lynn. *Your Congress.* Washington: National Voters League, 1915.

53. Hinckley, Barbara. *Stability and Change in Congress.* 2d. ed. New York: Harper and Row, 1978.

54. Holt, Marjorie, ed. *The Case Against the Reckless Congress.* Ottawa, Ill.: Green Hill Publishers, 1976.

55. Huitt, Ralph K. "Congress: Retrospect and Prospect." *Journal of Politics* 38 (Aug. 1976): 209-227.

56. Huitt, Ralph K. "Congress: The Durable Partner." In *Lawmakers in a Changing World,* ed. Frank Elke, pp. 9-29. Englewood Cliffs, N.J.: Prentice-Hall, 1966.

57. Huitt, Ralph K. and Peabody, Robert L. *Congress: Two Decades of Analysis.* New York: Harper and Row, 1969.

58. Humphrey, Hubert H. "A Tribute to the Congress." In *The Senate Institution,* ed. Nathaniel S. Preston, pp. 3-6. New York: Van Nostrand Reinhold, 1969.

59. Huntington, Samuel P. "Congressional Responses to the Twentieth Century." In *The Congress and America's Future,* ed. David B. Truman, pp. 5-31. Englewood Cliffs, N.J.: Prentice-Hall, 1965.

60. Hurst, James W. *The Growth of American Law: The Law Makers.* Boston, Little, Brown, 1950.

61. Jewell, Malcolm E. "New Perspectives on the Congress: A Review Article." *Legislative Studies Quarterly* 2 (Feb. 1977): 77-91.

62. Jones, Rochelle and Woll, Peter. *The Private World of Congress.* New York: Free Press, 1979.

63. Josephy, Alvin M. *The American Heritage History of the Congress of the United States.* New York: American Heritage Publishing Co., 1975.

64. Josephy, Alvin M. *On the Hill: A History of the American Congress from 1789 to the Present.* New York: Simon and Schuster, 1979.

65. Keating, Kenneth B. *Government of the People.* Cleveland: World Publishing Co., 1964.

66. Keefe, William J. *Congress and the American People* Englewood Cliffs, N.J.: Prentice-Hall, 1980.

67. Kefauver, Estes and Levin, Jack. *A Twentieth Century Congress.* New York: Essential Books, 1952.

68. Lahr, Raymond M. and Theis, J. William. *Congress: Power and Purpose on Capitol Hill.* Boston: Allyn and Bacon, 1967.

69. Lowi, Theodore J. and Ripley, Randall B. *Legislative Politics U.S.A.* 3d. ed. Boston: Little, Brown, 1973.

70. Luce, Robert. *Congress: An Explanation.* Cambridge, Mass.: Harvard University Press, 1926.

71. Luce, Robert. *Legislative Assemblies: Their Framework, Make-Up, Character, Characteristics, Habits, and Manners.* Boston: Houghton Mifflin, 1924.

72. Luce, Robert. *Legislative Problems: Development, Status, and Trend of the Treatment and Exercise of Lawmaking Power.* Boston: Houghton Mifflin, 1935.

73. McCall, Samuel W. *The Business of Congress.* New York: Columbia University Press, 1911.

74. Merriam, Rae L.M. 'The Rise of Northern Democracy in the U.S. Congress." Master's thesis, University of Texas at Austin, 1978.

75. Miller, Arthur S. "The Changing Role of Congress." *American Bar Association Journal* 50 (July 1964): 687-689.

76. Miller, Vernon X. "Something About Congress." *Loyola Law Review* 4 (June 1948): 137-148.

77. Moore, Joseph W. *The American Congress: A History of National Legislation and Political Events, 1774-1895.* New York: Harper and Brothers, 1895.

78. Moran, Thomas F. *The Rise and Development of the Bicameral System in America.* Baltimore: Johns Hopkins University Press, 1895.

79. Muchow, David J. *The Vanishing Congress: Where Has All the Power Gone.* Washington: North American International, 1976.

80. Murphy, Thomas P. *The New Politics Congress.* Lexington, Mass.: Lexington Books, 1974.

81. Newman, William J. and Gibbs, Hubert. "American Congressman's Independence." *Fortnightly* 179 (May 1953): 301-307.

82. Orfield, Gary. *Congressional Power: Congress and Social Change.* New York: Harcourt Brace Jovanovich, 1975.

83. Ornstein, Norman J., ed. *Congress in Change: Evolution and Change.* New York: Praeger, 1975.

84. Page, Benjamin I. "Cooling the Legislative Tea." In *American Politics and Public Policy,* eds. Walter Dean Burnham and Martha W. Weinberg, pp. 171-187. Cambridge, Mass.: M.I.T. Press, 1978.

85. Parker, Glenn R. "A Note on the Impact and Salience of Congress." *American Politics Quarterly* 4 (Oct. 1976): 413-421.

86. Peabody, Robert L. "Research on Congress: A Coming of Age." In *Congress: Two Decades of Analysis,* by Ralph K. Huitt and Robert L. Peabody, pp. 3-73. New York: Harper and Row, 1969.

87. Pennock, J. Roland. "Another Legislative Typology." *Journal of Politics* 41 (Nov. 1979): 1206-1213.

88. Phillips, William G. "Congress: A Study in Political Realities." *American Federationist* 68 (Feb. 1961): 12-17.

89. Phillips, William G. "The United States Congress." *Freedom and Union* 16 (May 1961): 12-15.

90. Riegle, Donald W. and Armbrister, Trevor. *O Congress.* Garden City, N.Y.: Doubleday, 1972.

91. Rieselbach, Leroy N. "Congress as a Political System." In his *Congressional System: Notes and Readings,* pp. 1-27. Belmont, Calif.: Wadsworth, 1970.

92. Rieselbach, Leroy N. *Congressional Politics.* New York: McGraw-Hill, 1973.

93. Rieselbach, Leroy N. *The Congressional System: Notes and Readings.* 2d ed. North Scituate, Mass.: Duxbury Press, 1979.

94. Rieselbach, Leroy N., ed. *The Congressional System: Notes and Readings.* Belmont, Calif.: Wadsworth, 1970.

95. Robinson, Armstead L. "The Politics of Reconstruction." *Wilson Quarterly* 2 (Spring 1978): 107-123.

96. Roche, John P. and Levy, Leonard W. *The Congress.* New York: Harcourt, Brace, and World, 1964.

97. Rogers, Lindsay. "Congressional Government." In *Encyclopedia of the Social Sciences,* vol. 4, pp. 201-203. New York: Macmillan, 1931.

98. Saloma, John S. *Congress and the New Politics.* Boston: Little, Brown, 1969.

99. Schwab, Larry M. *Changing Patterns of Congressional Politics.* New York: Van Nostrand, 1980.

100. Settle, T. S. "Why I Respect and Admire the Congress of the United States." *Federal Bar Association Journal* 3 (Nov. 1937): 113-116.

101. Snow, Freeman. "A Defense of Congressional Government." In *American Historical Association, Papers* 4 (1890): 309-328.

102. Thomas, Norman C. and Lamb, Karl A. *Congress: Politics and Practice.* New York: Random House, 1964.

103. Thompson, Walter. *Federal Centralization: A Study and Criticism of the Expanding Scope of Congressional Legislation.* New York: Harcourt Brace, 1923.

104. Tidmarch, Charles M. "Exploring the Cave on the Hill: Alternative Approaches to Understanding Congress." *American Politics Quarterly* 2 (Oct. 1974): 450-460.

105. Truman, David B., ed. *The Congress and America's Future.* Englewood Cliffs, N.J.: Prentice-Hall, 1973.

106. *Twelve Studies on the Organization of Congress.* Washington: American Enterprise Institute for Public Policy Research, 1966.

107. Vinyard, Dale. *Congress.* New York: Scribner, 1968.

108. Vogler, David J. *The Politics of Congress.* 2d ed. Boston: Allyn and Bacon, 1977.

109. Willoughby, William F. *Principles of Legislative Organization and Administration.* Washington: The Brookings Institution, 1934.

110. Wilson, Woodrow. *Congressional Government.* Boston: Houghton Mifflin, 1888.

111. Wise, Sidney and Schier, Richard F. *Studies on Congress.* New York: Crowell, 1969.

112. Wolfinger, Raymond E., ed. *Readings on Congress.* Englewood Cliffs, N.J.: Prentice-Hall, 1971.

113. Worthley, John A. *Public Administration and Legislatures: Examinations and Exploration.* Chicago: Nelson Hall, 1976.

114. Young, Roland A. *The American Congress.* New York: Harper and Row, 1958.

115. Young, Roland A. *This Is Congress.* 2d ed. New York: A. A. Knopf, 1946.

116. Young, Roland A. "Woodrow Wilson's *Congressional Government* Reconsidered." In *The Philosophy and Policies of Woodrow Wilson,* ed. Earl Latham, pp. 201-213. Chicago: University of Chicago Press, 1958.

The Legislative Process

117. Adams, Samuel H. "The Joke's on You: How Your Chosen Representatives Work the Joker Game on Legislation." *American Magazine* 70 (May 1910): 51-59.

118. Berman, Daniel M. *In Congress Assembled: The Legislative Process in the National Government.* New York: Macmillan, 1964.

119. Bibby, John F. and Davidson, Roger H. *Studies in the Legislative Process on Capitol Hill.* 2d ed. Hinsdale, Ill.: Dryden, 1972.

120. Borchardt, Kurt. *Towards a Theory of Legislative Compromise.* Cambridge, Mass.: Program on Information Technologies and Public Policy, Harvard University, 1976.

121. Chamberlin, Joseph p. *Legislative Process: National and State.* New York: Appleton-Century, 1936.

122. Cushing, Luther S. *Elements of the Law and Practice of Legislative Assemblies in the United States of America.* South Hackensack, N.J.: Rothman Reprints, 1971.

123. Harris, Joseph P. *Congress and the Legislative Process.* 2d ed. New York: McGraw-Hill, 1972.

124. Jewell, Malcolm E. and Patterson, Samuel C. *The Legislative Process in the United States.* 2d ed. New York: Random House, 1973.

125. Keefe, William J. and Ogul, Morris S. *The American Legislative Process: Congress and the States.* 4th ed. Englewood Cliffs, N.J.: Prentice-Hall, 1977.

126. Lewak, Ben. *The Social Studies Student Investigates the Legislative Process.* New York: R. Rosen Press, 1977.

127. Polsby, Nelson W. "Legislatures." In *Government Institutions and Processes, Handbook of Political Science 5,* eds. Fred I. Greenstein and Nelson W. Polsby, pp. 257-319. Reading, Mass.: Addison-Wesley, 1975.

128. Radler, Don. *How Congress Works.* New York: Signet, 1976.

129. Reinsch, Paul S. *American Legislatures and Legislative Methods.* New York: The Century Company, 1907.

130. Riddick, Floyd M. *The United States Congress: Organization and Procedure.* Manassas, Va.: National Capitol Publishers, 1949.

131. Ripley, Randall B. *Congress: Process and Policy.* 2d ed. New York: Norton, 1978.

132. Van Der Slik, Jack R. *American Legislative Processes.* New York: Crowell, 1977.

Job of a Congressman

133. Bailey, Stephen K. and Samuel, Howard D. "A Day in the Life of a Senator; the Congressional Office: 1952." *Commentary* 13 (May 1952): 433-441.

134. Boyd, James. "Legislate? Who, Me? What Happens to a Senator's Day." *Washington Monthly* 1 (Feb. 1969): 44-53.

135. Boyd, James. "A Senator's Day." In *Inside the System,* 2d ed., eds. Charles Peters and John Rothchild, pp. 99-112. New York: Praeger, 1973.

136. Clapp, Charles L. *The Congressman: His Work as He Sees It.* Washington: Brookings Institution, 1963.

137. Davidson, Roger H. *The Role of the Congressmen.* New York: Pegasus, 1969.

138. Evins, Joe L. *Understanding Congress.* New York: Clarkson N. Potter, 1963.

139. Flynn, John T. *Meet Your Congress.* Garden City, N.Y.: Doubleday, 1944.

140. Groennings, Sven and Hawley., Jonathan P., eds. *To Be a Congressman: The Promise and the Power.* Washington: Acropolis Books, 1973.

141. Matthews, Donald R. *U.S. Senators and Their World.* Chapel Hill: University of North Carolina Press, 1960.

142. Oehlert, Benjamin H. "Congress: A Soft, Easy Job; Address February 7, 1967." *Vital Speeches* 33 (15 May 1967): 472-475.

143. Pepper, George W. *In the Senate.* Philadelphia: University of Pennsylvania Press, 1930.

144. Tacheron, Donald G. and Udall, Morris K. *The Job of the Congressman: An Introduction to Service in the U.S. House of Representatives.* 2d ed. Indianapolis: Bobbs-Merrill, 1970.

145. Torrey, Volta. *You and Your Congress.* New York: William Morrow, 1944.

146. Wright, James C. *You and Your Congressman.* rev. ed. New York: Putnam, 1976.

Comparative Studies of Congress

147. Bradshaw, Kenneth and Pring, David. *Parliament and Congress147.* London: Constable, 1972.

148. Galloway, George B. *Congress and Parliament, Their Organization and Operation in the U.S. and the U.K.* Washington: National Planning Association, 1955.

149. Harsch, Joseph C. "Congress or Parliament, Which?" *New York Times Magazine,* 20 March 1960, pp. 37, 65, 67-68.

150. Herbert, Hilary A. "The House of Representatives and the House of Commons." *North American Review* 158 (Mar. 1894): 257-269.

151. James, Robert R. "A Squalid Charade? Perils of Parliament and Congress." *Encounter* 39 (Dec. 1972): 74-76.

152. Kim, Haingja. "A Comparative Study of the U.S. House of Representatives and the National Assembly of Korea: A Cross-Cultural Study Focusing on Role Analysis of Female Politicians." Ph.D. dissertation, University of Hawaii, 1975.

153. Kornberg, Allan. *Legislatures in Comparative Perspective.* New York: McKay, 1973.

154. Kornberg, Allan and Musof, Lloyd D., eds. *Legislatures in Developmental Perspective.* Durham, N. C.: Duke University Press, 1970.

155. Kornberg, Allan and Thomas, Norman C. "The Political Socialization of National Legislative Elites in the United States and Canada." *Journal of Politics* 27 (Nov. 1965): 761-765.

156. Kornberg, Allan and Thomas, Norman C. "Representative Democracy and Political Elites in Canada and the United States." *Parliamentary Affairs* 19 (Winter 1965-1966): 91-102.

157. Lees, John D. and Shaw, Malcolm. *Committees in Legislatures: A Comparative Analysis.* Durham, N. C.: Duke University Press, 1979.

158. Loewenberg, Gerhard and Patterson, Samuel C. *Comparing Legislatures.* Boston: Little, Brown, 1979.

159. Low, A. Maurice. "Legislative Procedure in Two Anglo-Saxon Countries." *American Political Science Review* 8 (Feb. 1914): 148-154.

160. Mezey, Michael L. *Comparative Legislatures.* Durham, N. C.: Duke University Press, 1979.

161. Russett, Bruce M. "International Communication and Legislative Behavior: The Senate and the House of Commons." *Journal of Conflict Resolution* 6 (Dec. 1962): 291-307.

162. Schwarz, John E. and Shaw, L. Earl. *The United States Congress in Comparative Perspective.* Hinsdale, Ill.: Dryden, Press, 1976.

163. Shaw, Malcolm. "Parliament and Congress. *Parliamentarian* 50 (April 1969): 83-91.

164. Siva Dharma Sastry, B. *A Comparative Study of the Speaker: India, Britain, and the U.S.A.* New Delhi: Sterling, 1978.

165. Steffani, Winfried. "Congress and Bundestag." In *Comparative Political Parties: Selected Readings,* ed. Andrew J. Milnor, pp. 288-309. New York: Thomas Y. Crowell, 1969.

166. Stephens, David. "The Private Member of Parliament Under the British, French and U.S. Congressional Systems of Government." *Journal of Constitutional and Parliamentary Information* 105 (1976): 1-28.

167. Thomas, Norman C. and Kornberg, Allan. "The Purposive Roles of Canadian and American Legislators: Some Comparisons." *Political Science* 17 (Sept. 1965): 36-50.

168. Wheater, Stanley B. "Parliamentary Rhetoric: The American Congress and the House of Commons Compared." *Parliamentary Affairs* 28 (Winter 1974-1975): 8-21.

Congress and the Constitution

169. Albertsworth, Edwin F. "Extra-Constitutional Government." *Kentucky Law Journal* 20 (Nov. 1931): 18-46.

170. Alfange, Dean. "Congressional Power and Constitutional Limitations." *Journal of Public Law* 18 (1969): 103-134.

171. Andrews, William G., comp. *Coordinate Magistrates: Constitutional Law by Congress and President.* New York: Van Nostrand Reinhold, 1969.

172. Barber, Satirios A. *The Constitution and the Delegation of Congressional Power.* Chicago: University of Chicago Press, 1975.

173. Beedle, Thelma G. "When and Under What Circumstances is Congressional Legislation Violative of the Tenth Amendment of the Constitution of the United States?" *Nebraska Law Bulletin* 11 (May 1933): 484-498.

174. Brown, Douglas W. "The Proposal to Give Congress the Power to Nullify the Constitution." *American Law Review* 57 (Mar.-April 1923): 161-181.

175. "Congressional Power Under the Appointments Clause After *Buckley v. Vales.*" *Michigan Law Review* 75 (Jan. 1977): 627-648.

176. Dean, Benjamin S. "The Betrayal of a Sacred Trust." *Lawyer and Banker* 24 (May-June 1931): 122-137.

177. Dillon, Conley. "American Constitution Review: Are We Preparing for the Twenty-First Century?" *World Affairs* 140 (Summer 1977): 5-24.

178. Durham, James A. "Congress, the Constitution, and, Crosskey." *Indiana Law Journal* 29 (Spring 1954): 355-366.

179. Evans, Medford. "Congress and the Constitution." *American Opinion* 21 (July 1978): 25-32, 133-136.

180. Fisher, Louis. "Flouting the Constitution." *Center Magazine* 10 (Nov. 1977): 13-19.

181. Garrison, Lloyd K. "Form of Constitutional Amendment." *American Labor Legislation Review* 27 (Mar. 1937): 11-16.

182. Goodnow, Frank J. "The Legislative Power of Congress Under the Judicial Article of the Constitution." *Political Science Quarterly* 25 (Dec. 1910): 577-608.

183. Hackett, Frank W. "Changing the Constitution." *Yale Law Journal* 24 (June 1915): 649-662.

184. Hettinger, H. Russell. "Representative Government, the Constitution and the Case for the Informing Function of Congress." *Journal of Contemporary Law* 3 (Spring 1977): 278-292.

185. Kaye, David. "Congressional Papers and Judicial Subpoenas." *UCLA Law Review* 23 (Oct. 1975): 57-76.

186. Kaye, David. "Congressional Papers, Judicial Subpoenas and the Constitution." *UCLA Law Review* 24 (Feb. 1977): 523-580.

187. Lacy, Donald P. and Martin, Phillip L. "Amending the Constitution: The Bottleneck in Judiciary Committees." *Harvard Journal on Legislation* 9 (May 1972): 666-693.

188. Lenroot, Irvine L. "Congress and the Constitution." *Marquette Law Review* 7 (1922-1923): 181-191.

189. McQuillin, Eugene. "Should the Congress Rule?" *Central Law Journal* 96 (Aug. 1923): 259-265.

190. Mikva, Abner J. and Lundy, Joseph R. "Ninety-first Congress and the Constitution." *University of Chicago Law Review* 38 (Spring 1971): 449-499.

191. Morgan, Donald G. *Congress and the Constitution: A Study of Responsibility.* Cambridge, Mass.: Harvard University Press, 1966.

192. Nedelsky, Jennifer R. "Property and the Framers of the United States Constitution: A Study of the Political Thought of James Madison, Gouverneur Morris, and James Wilson." Ph.D. dissertation, University of Chicago, 1977.

193. Richberg, Donald R. "Social Welfare and the Constitution." *American Labor Legislation Review* 27 (Mar. 1937): 5-10.

194. Smith, D. "Has Congress Power to Call Conventions in the States to Consider Constitutional Amendments?" *Kansas Bar Association Journal* 2 (Aug. 1933): 1-7.

195. "Twenty-Fifth Amendment Proposals Aired in Senate Hearings; Association Position Favors No Change." *American Bar Association Journal* 61 (May 1975): 599-605.

196. U. S. Congress. House. Banking, Finance, and Urban Affairs Committee. *Looking Toward the Constitutional Bicentennial: A Proposed Amendment to Permit Members of Congress to Serve in Key Executive Branch Offices.* 96th Congress. Washington: GPO, 1980.

197. Vold, Lauriz. "The Supreme Court, Congress and the Constitution." *Quarterly Journal of the University of North Dakota* 15 (May 1925): 314-359.

198. Wheeler, Wayne B. "Two-Thirds of Congress." *Law Notes* 22 (Feb. 1919): 220.

199. Williams, George H. "Article V of the Constitution." *Constitutional Review* 12 (April 1928): 69-83.

History of Congress

1774–1789 Continental Congress

200. Ammerman, David L. "Annapolis and the First Continental Congress: A Note on the Committee System in Revolutionary America." *Maryland Historical Magazine* 66 (Summer 1971): 169-180.

201. Ammerman, David L. "The First Continental Congress and the Coming of the American Revolution." Ph.D. dissertation, Cornell University, 1966.

202. Ashton, Rick J. "The Loyalist Congressmen of New York." *New York Historical Society Quarterly* 60 (July-Oct. 1976): 95-106.

203. Bacon, William J. *The Continental Congress: Some of Its Actors and Their Doing, with the Results Thereof.* Utica, N.Y.: E. H. Roberts, 1881.

204. Becker, Carl. "Election of Delegates from New York to the Second Continental Congress." *American Historical Review* 9 (Oct. 1903): 66-85.

205. Berkhofer, Robert F. "Jefferson, the Ordinance of 1784, and the Origins of the American Territorial System." *William and Mary Quarterly* 29 (April 1972): 231-262.

206. Betz, Israel H. "The Continental Congress at York, Pennsylvania, 1777-1778." *Pennsylvania-German* 7 (Mar. 1906): 64-68.

207. Bevan, Edith R. "The Continental Congress in Baltimore, Dec. 20, 1776-Feb. 27. 1777." *Maryland Historical Magazine* 42 (Mar. 1947): 21-28.

208. Black, Henry C. "Continental Congress." *Constitutional Review* 6 (July 1922): 148-164.

209. Bourguignon, Henry J. "The First Federal Court: The History of the Continental Congress' Committees on Appeal and Its Court of Appeals in Cases of Capture, 1775-1787." Ph.D. dissertation, University of Michigan, 1968.

210. Brown, Richard D. "The Founding Fathers of 1776 and 1787: A Collective View." *William and Mary Quarterly* 33 (July 1976): 465-480.

211. Burnett, Edmund C. "The Committee of the States, 1784." *American Historical Association, Annual Report*, 1913, vol. 1, 141-158.

212. Burnett, Edmund C. *The Continental Congress.* New York: W. W. Norton, 1941.

213. Burnett, Edmund C. "The Continental Congress and Agricultural Supplies." *Agricultural History* 2 (July 1928): 111-128.

214. Burnett, Edmund C. "The 'More Perfect Union': The Continental Congress Seeks a Formula." *Catholic Historical Review* 24 (April 1938): 1-29.

215. Burnett, Edmund C. "Our Union of States in the Making: Achievements of the Continental Congress." *World Affairs* 98 (Sept. 1935): 148-160.

216. Burnett, Edmund C., ed. *Letters of Members of the Continental Congress.* 8 vols. Gloucester, Mass.: P. Smith, 1963.

217. Coleman, Edward M. "The History of the Third Session of the Second Continental Congress, December 20, 1776 to February 27, 1777." Ph.D. dissertation, University of Southern California, 1941.

218. Coleman, John M. "How 'Continental' Was the Continental Congress: The Thirteen Colonies and the Rest of North America." *History Today* 18 (Aug. 1968): 540-550.

219. Collier, Christopher. *Connecticut in the Continental Congress.* Chester, Conn.: Pequot Press, 1973.

220. Collins, Varnum L. *The Continental Congress at Princeton.* Princeton, N.J.: The University Library, 1908.

221. Cometti, Elizabeth. "The Civil Servants of the Revolutionary Period." *Pennsylvania Magazine of History and Biography* 75 (April 1951): 159-169.

222. Dutcher, George M. "The Rise of Republican Government in the United States." *Political Science Quarterly* 55 (June 1940): 199-216.

223. Ferguson, Elmer J. "Business, Government, and Congressional Investigation in the Revolution." *William and Mary Quarterly* 16 (July 1959): 293-318.

224. Ford, Paul L. "The Association of the First Congress." *Political Science Quarterly* 6 (Dec. 1891): 613-624.

225. Fowler, James H. "The Breakdown of Congressional Authority: A Study of the Relations Between the Continental Congress and the States, 1780-1783." Ph.D. dissertation, Oklahoma State University, 1977.

226. Garver, Frank H. "Attendance at the First Continental Congress." *American Historical Association, Pacific Coast Branch, Proceedings* 25. Washington, 1930, 21-40.

227. Garver, Frank H. "Transition from the Continental Congress to the Congress of the Confederation." *Pacific Historical Review* 1 (June 1932): 221-234.

228. Gerlach, Larry R. "Connecticut, the Continental Congress, and the Independence of Vermont, 1777-1782." *Vermont History* 34 (July 1966): 188-193.

229. Gerlach, Larry R. "A Delegation of Steady Habit: The Connecticut Representatives to the Continental Congress, 1774-1789." *Connecticut Historical Society Bulletin* 32 (April 1967): 33-39.

230. Gerlach, Larry R. "Firmness and Prudence: Connecticut, the Continental Congress, and the National Domain, 1776-1786." *Connecticut Historical Society Bulletin* 31 (July 1966): 65-75.

231. Gerlach, Larry R. "Toward 'A More perfect Union': Connecticut, the Continental Congress and the Constitutional Convention." *Connecticut Historical Society Bulletin* 34 (July 1969): 65-78.

232. Head, John M. "A Time to Rend: The Members of the Continental Congress and the Decision for American Independence, 1774-1776." Ph.D. dissertation, Brown University, 1966.

233. Henderson, H. James. "Constitutionalists and Republicans in the Continental Congress, 1778-1786." *Pennsylvania History* 36 (April 1969): 119-144.

234. Henderson, H. James. *Party Politics in the Continental Congress.* New York: McGraw-Hill, 1974.

235. Jensen, Merrill. "The Idea of a National Government During the American Revolution." *Political Science Quarterly* 58 (Sept. 1943): 356-379.

236. Jones, Charles C. *Biographical Sketches of the Delegates from Georgia to the Continental Congress.* Boston: Houghton Mifflin, 1891.

237. Klingelhofer, Herbert E. "The Presidents of the United States in Congress Assembled." *Manuscripts* 28 (Winter 1976): 2-14.

238. Klingelhofer, Herbert E. "The Presidents of the United States in Congress Assembled. The 'Millionaire' Presidents: Randolph, Middleton, Hancock, and Laurens." *Manuscripts* 28 (Spring 1976): 83-96.

239. Klingelhofer, Herbert E. "The Presidents of the United States in Congress Assembled. The Middle Presidents: Jay, Huntington, McKean, Hanson, and Boudinot." *Manuscripts* 28 (Summer 1976): 171-187.

240. Klingelhofer, Herbert E. "The Presidents of the United States in Congress Assembled. The Post-War Presidents: Lee, Gorham, St. Clair, and Griffin." *Manuscripts* 28 (Fall 1976): 255-271.

241. Lord, Clifton L. *The Atlas of Congressional Roll Calls for the Continental Congresses, 1777-1781.* Cooperstown, N.Y.: New York State Historical Association, 1943.

242. Lundin, Robert A. "A History of the Second Session of the Second Continental Congress." Ph.D. dissertation, University of Southern California, 1942.

243. Marsh, Esbon R. "A History of the First Session of the Second Continental Congress." Ph.D. dissertation, University of Southern California, 1940.

244. Meigs, Cornelia L. *The Violent Men: A Study of Human Relations in the First American Congress.* New York: Macmillan, 1949.

245. Mevers, Frank C. "Congress and the Navy: The Establishment and Administration of the American Revolutionary Navy by the Continental Congress, 1775-1784." Ph.D. dissertation, University of North Carolina at Chapel Hill, 1972.

246. Miller, William B. "Presbyterian Signers of the Declaration of Independence." *Presbyterian Historical Society Journal* 36 (Sept. 1958): 139-179.

247. Montross, Lynn. *The Reluctant Rebels: The Story of the Continental Congress.* New York: Harper and Brothers, 1950.

248. Morgan, David T. *North Carolinians in the Continental Congress.* Winston-Salem, N.C.: J. F. Blair, 1976.

249. Morgan, David T. and Schmidt, William J. "From Economic Sanctions to Political Separation: The North Carolina Delegation to the Continental Congress, 1774-1776." *North Carolina Historical Review* 52 (July 1975): 215-234.

250. Morgan, Edmund S. "The Political Establishments of the United States, 1784." *William and Mary Quarterly* 23 (April 1966): 286-308.

251. Mullett, Charles F. "Imperial Ideas at the First Continental Congress." *Southwestern Social Science Quarterly* 12 (Dec. 1931): 238-244.

252. Munroe, John A. "Nonresident Representation in the Continental Congress: The Delaware Delegation of 1782." *William and Mary Quarterly* 9 (April 1952): 166-190.

253. Oaks, Robert F. "Philadelphia Merchants and the First Continental Congress." *Pennsylvania History* 40 (April 1973): 149-166.

254. Onuf, Peter. "Toward Federalism: Virginia, Congress and the Western Lands." *William and Mary Quarterly* 34 (July 1977): 353-374.

255. Park, Edwards. "200 Years Ago This Month: Colonies Choose Members for Their Fateful Congress." *Smithsonian* 5 (July 1974): 20-21.

256. Pavlovsky, Arnold M. " 'Between Hawk and Buzzard': Congress as Perceived by Its Members, 1775-1783." *Pennsylvania Magazine of History and Biography* 101 (July 1977): 349-364.

257. Platt, John D. R. *The Continental Congress in the New York City Hall, 1785-1788: Background and Evaluation Study.* Washington: U.S. Office of Archeology and Historic Preservation, 1969.

258. Proctor, Donald J. "From Insurrection to Independence: The Continental Congress and the Military Launching of the American Revolution." Ph.D. dissertation, University of Southern California, 1965.

259. Prowell, George. *Continental Congress at York, Pennsylvania and York County in the Revolution.* York, Pa.: York Printing Co., 1914.

260. Rakove, Jack N. *The Beginnings of National Politics: An Interpretive History of the Continental Congress.* New York: A. A. Knopf, 1979.

261. Reed, John F. "The Immortal Fifty-Six: The Public Services of the Signers of the Declaration of Independence." *Historical Society of Montgomery County, Pa., Bulletin* 20 (Spring 1976): 103-180.

262. Robinson, S. M. "God and the Continental Congress." *Christianity Today* 1 (Feb. 1957): 3-5.

263. Rolater, Frederick S. "The Continental Congress: A Study in the Origin of American Public Administration, 1774–1781." Ph.D. dissertation, University of Southern California, 1970.

264. Rossie, Jonathan G. "The Politics of Command: The Continental Congress and Its Generals." Ph.D. dissertation, University of Wisconsin, 1966.

265. Royer, Helen E. "The Role of the Continental Congress in the Prosecution of the American Revolution in Pennsylvania." Ph.D. dissertation, Pennsylvania State University, 1960.

266. Ryan, Frank W. "The Role of South Carolina in the First Continental Congress." *South Carolina Historical Magazine* 60 (July 1959): 147-153.

267. Ryden, George H. *Delaware: First State in the Union.* Wilmington: Delaware Tercentenary Commission, 1938.

268. Sanders, Jennings B. *The Evolution of Executive Departments of the Continental Congress, 1774-1789.* Chapel Hill: University of North Carolina Press, 1935.

269. Sanders, Jennings B. *The Presidency of the Continental Congress, 1774-1789: A Study in American Institutional History.* Chicago, 1930.

270. Schmidt, William J. "The North Carolina Delegates in the Continental Congress." Ph.D. dissertation, University of North Carolina at Chapel Hill, 1968.

271. Small, Albion W. "The Beginnings of American Nationality: The Constitutional Relations Between the Continental Congress and the Colonies and States from 1774 to 1789." Ph.D. dissertation, Johns Hopkins University, 1889.

272. Smelser, Marshall. *Congress Founds the Navy, 1787-1798.* Notre Dame, Ind.: University of Notre Dame Press, 1959.

273. Smith, Paul H., ed. *Letters of Delegates to Congress, 1774-1789.* Washington: Library of Congress, 1976.

274. Staples, William R. *Rhode Island in the Continental Congress, 1765-1790.* Providence, R.I.: Providence Press Co., 1870.

275. Storch, Neil T. "Congressional Politics and Diplomacy, 1775-1783." Ph.D. dissertation, University of Wisconsin, 1969.

276. Taplin, Winn L. "The Vermont Problem in the Continental Congress and in Interstate Relations, 1776-1787." Ph.D. dissertation, University of Michigan, 1956.

277. Teeter, Dwight L. "A Legacy of Expression: Philadelphia Newspapers and Congress During the War for Independence, 1775-1783." Ph.D. dissertation, University of Wisconsin, 1966.

278. Wood, George C. *Congressional Control of Foreign Relations During the American Revolution, 1774-1789.* Allentown, Pa.: H. R. Haas, 1919.

1789–1809   *Formative Years*

279. Bowling, Kenneth R. "Politics in the First Congress, 1789-1791." Ph.D. dissertation, University of Wisconsin, 1968.

280. Brown, Everett S., ed. *William Plumers' Memorandum of Proceeding in the United States Senate, 1803-1807.* New York: Macmillan, 1923.

281. Childs, James B. " 'Disappeared in the Wings of Oblivion':The Story of the United States House of Representatives Printed Documents at the First Session of the First Congress, New York, 1789." *Papers of the Bibliographic Society of America* 58 (2nd. Quar. 1964): 91-132.

282. Childs, James. B. "The Story of the United States Senate Documents, 1st Congress, 1st Session, New York, 1789." *Papers of the Bibliographical Society of America* 56 (2d. Quar. 1962): 175-194.

283. Colegrove, Kenneth W. "The Early History of State Instructions to Members of Congress." Ph.D. dissertation, Harvard University, 1915.

284. Cunningham, Noble E. *Circular Letters of Congressmen to their Constituents, 1789-1829.* Chapel Hill: University of North Carolina Press, 1978.

285. Cunningham, Noble E. *The Process of Government Under Jefferson.* Princeton, N.J.: Princeton University Press, 1978.

286. Dearmont, Nelson S. "Federalist Attitudes Toward Governmental Secrecy in the Age of Jefferson." *Historian* 37 (Feb. 1975): 222-240.

287. Dearmont, Nelson S. "Secrecy in Government: The Public Debate in Congress During the Formative Years of the American Republic." Ph.D. dissertation, City University of New York, 1975.

288. Dennison, George M. "An Empire of Liberty: Congressional Attitudes Toward Popular Sovereignty in the Territories, 1787-1867." *Maryland Historian* 6 (Spring 1975): 19-40.

289. DePauw, Linda G., ed. *Senate Executive Journal and Related Documents: United States 1st Congress, 1789-1791.* Baltimore: Johns Hopkins University Press, 1974.

290. Fribourg, Marjorie G. *The U.S. Congress: Men Who Steered Its Course, 1789-1867.* Philadelphia: M. Smith Co., 1972.

291. Galloway, George B. "Precedents Established in the First Congress." *Western Political Quarterly* 11 (Sept. 1958): 454-468.

292. Gilpatrick, D. H. "North Carolina Congressional Elections, 1803-1810." *North Carolina Historical Review* 10 (July 1933): 168-185.

293. Harlow, Ralph V. *The History of Legislative Methods in the Period Before 1825.* New Haven, Conn.: Yale University Press, 1917.

294. Henderson, H. James. "Congressional Factionalism and the Attempt to Recall Benjamin Franklin." *William and Mary Quarterly* 27 (April 1970): 246-267.

295. Jordan, Daniel P. "Politicians and Property: Taxable Holdings of Early Western Virginia Congressmen, 1801-1825." *West Virginia History* 37 (Jan. 1976): 122-126.

296. Jordan, Daniel P. "Virginia Congressmen, 1801-1825." Ph.D. dissertation, University of Virginia, 1970.

297. Kenyon, Cecelia M. "Men of Little Faith: The Anti-Federalists on the Nature of Representative Government." *William and Mary Quarterly* 12 (Jan. 1955): 3-43.

298. Lacy, Alexander B. "Jefferson and Congress: Congressional Method and Politics, 1801-1809." Ph.D. dissertation, University of Virginia, 1964.

299. Lansing, Mrs. Robert. "The First Congress." *Daughters of the American Revolution Magazine* 48 (May 1916): 317-321.

300. Long, Everett L. "Jefferson and Congress: A Study of the Jeffersonian Legislative System, 1801-1809." Ph.D. dissertation, University of Missouri at Columbia, 1966.

301. McCluggage, Robert W. "The Senate and Indian Land Titles, 1800-1825." *Western Historical Quarterly* 4 (Oct. 1970): 415-425.

302. Maclay, William. *Sketches of Debate in the First Senate of the United States in 1789-90-91.* Harrisburg, Pa.: Lane S. Hart, 1880.

303. McPherson, Elizabeth G. "Reports of the Debates of the House of Representatives During the First Congress, 1789-1791." *Quarterly Journal of Speech* 30 (Feb. 1944): 64-71.

304. Marks, Henry S. "Proceedings of the First Florida Congressional Delegation." *Florida Historical Quarterly* 44 (Jan. 1966): 205-211.

305. O'Dwyer, Margaret M. "French Diplomat's View of Congress, 1790." *William and Mary Quarterly* 21 (July 1964): 408-444.

306. Tinling, M. "Thomas Lloyd's Reports of the First Federal Congress." *William and Mary Quarterly* 18 (Oct. 1961): 519-545.

307. Venza, James R. "Federalists in Congress, 1800-1812." Ph.D. dissertation, Vanderbilt University, 1967.

308. Williams, Robert P., ed. *The First Congress, March 4, 1789–March 3, 1791: A Compilation of Significant Debates.* New York: Exposition Press, 1970.

309. Winston, Sheldon. "West Virginia's First Delegation to Congress." *West Virginia History* 29 (July 1968): 274-277.

310. Young, James. S. *The Washington Community, 1800-1828.* New York: Columbia University Press, 1966.

1809–1828   Rise of Congress

311. Barlow, William R. "Congress During the War of 1812." Ph.D. dissertation, Ohio State University, 1961.

312. Barlow, William R. "Ohio's Congressmen and the War of 1812." *Ohio History* 72 (July 1963): 175-194.

313. Bogue, Allen G. and Marlaire, Mark P. "Of Mess and Men: The Boardinghouse and Congressional Voting, 1821-1842." *American Journal of Political Science* 19 (May 1975): 207-230.

314. Detweiler, Philip F. "Congressional Debate on Slavery and the Declaration of Independence, 1819-1821." *American Historical Review* 63 (April 1958): 598-616.

315. Lacy, Eric R. "First District Congressmen and Slavery Issues, 1820-1861." Master's thesis, East Tennessee State University, 1960.

316. Selby, Paul O. "Missouri's 268 Congressmen, 1821-1960." *Missouri Historical Review* 57 (April 1963): 285-290.

317. Smith, Carlton B. "Congressional Attitudes Toward Military Preparedness During the Monroe Administration." *Military Affairs* 40 (Feb. 1976): 22-25.

318. Wilson, Major L. "An Analysis of the Ideas of Liberty and Union as Used by Members of Congress and the Presidents from 1812 to 1861." Ph.D. dissertation, University of Kansas, 1964.

1828–1860   Age of Jackson

319. Bentham, Jeremy. "Anti-Senatica, An Attack on the U.S. Senate, sent by Jeremy Bentham to Andrew Jackson, President of the United States." *Smith College Studies in History* 11 (July 1926): 209-267.

320. Burg, Maclyn P. "The Careers of 109 Southern Whig Congressional Leaders in the Years Following Their Party's Collapse." Ph.D. dissertation, University of Washington, 1971.

321. Campbell, Mary R. "Tennessee's Congressional Delegation in the Sectional Crisis of 1859-1860." *Tennessee Historical Quarterly* 19 (Dec. 1960): 348-371.

322. Cobun, Frank E. "Educational Level of the Jacksonians." *History of Education Quarterly* 7 (Winter 1967): 515-520.

323. Hart, Charles R. D. "Congressmen and the Expansion of Slavery into the Territories: A Study in Attitudes, 1846-1861." Ph.D. dissertation, University of Washington, 1965.

324. Henry, Milton. "Summary of Tennessee Representation in Congress from 1845 to 1861." *Tennessee Historical Quarterly* 10 (June 1951): 140-148.

325. Huff, Carolyn B. "The Politics of Idealism: The Political Abolutionists of Ohio in Congress, 1840-1866." Ph.D. dissertation, University of North Carolina at Chapel Hill, 1969.

326. Irwin, Ramon L. "Congressional Debates of James K. Polk's Administration: A Study in Factualism." Ph.D. dissertation, University of Minnesota, 1947.

327. Lacy, Eric R. "Crossroads in the Highlands: First District Congressmen and the Age of Jackson." *East Tennessee Historical Society's Publications* 37 (1965): 23-30.

328. Parsons, Lynn H. "Censuring Old Man Eloquet: Foreign Policy and Disunion, 1842." *Capitol Studies* 3 (Fall 1975): 89-106.

329. Sadler, Richard W. "The Impact of the Slavery Question on the Whig Party in Congress, 1843-1854." Ph.D. dissertation, University of Utah, 1969.

330. Sefton, James E. "Black Slaves, Red Masters, White Middlemen: A Congressional Debate of 1852." *Florida Historical Quarterly* 51 (Oct. 1972): 113-128.

331. Silbey, Joel H. "The Slavery-Extension Controversy and Illinois Congressmen, 1846-50." *Journal of the Illinois State Historical Society* 58 (Winter 1965): 378-395.

332. Tusa, Frank J. "Congressional Politics in the Secession Crisis, 1859-1861." Ph.D. dissertation, Pennsylvania State University, 1975.

333. Walton, Brian G. "Georgia's Biennial Legislatures, 1840-1860, and Their Elections to the U.S. Senate." *Georgia Historical Quarterly* 61 (Summer 1977): 140-155.

334. Yarwood, Dean L. "Congress in Crisis: A System Analysis of the Senate During the Decade Prior to the Civil War." Ph.D. dissertation, University of Illinois at Urbana-Champaign, 1966.

335. Yarwood, Dean L. "Legislative Persistence: A Comparison of the United States Senate in 1850 and 1860." *Midwest Journal of Politics* 11 (May 1967): 193-211.

1860–1877   Civil War and Reconstruction

336. Anderson, Eric D. "Race and Politics in North Carolina, 1872-1901: The 'Black Second' Congressional District." Ph.D. dissertation, University of Chicago, 1978.

337. Atchley, Lucy E. "The Attitude of the Tennessee Members of Congress on the Tariff Question, 1865-1894." Master's thesis, University of Tennessee, 1937.

338. Avillo, Philip J. "Phaton Radicals: Texas Republicans in Congress, 1870-1873." *Southwestern Historical Quarterly* 77 (April 1974): 431-444.

339. Avillo, Philip J. "Slave State Republicans in Congress, 1861-1877." Ph.D. dissertation, University of Arizona, 1975.

340. Bailey, Thomas A. "Party Irregularity in the Senate of the United States, 1869-1901." *Southwestern Political and Social Science Quarterly* 11 (Mar. 1931): 355-376.

341. Barnes, William H. *History of the Thirty-Ninth Congress of the United States.* New York: Harper, 1868.

342. Bayless, Robert W. "The Attitude of West Virginia Senators and Congressmen Toward Reconstruction, 1863-1871." Master's thesis, West Virginia University, 1947.

343. Benedict, Michael L. *A Compromise of Principle: Congressional Republicans and Reconstruction, 1863-1869343.* New York: Norton, 1974.

344. Bowers, Claude G. *The Tragic Era.* Boston: Houghton Mifflin, 1929.

345. Boykin, Edward C. *Congress and the Civil War.* New York: McBride, 1955.

346. Brock, William R. *An American Crisis: Congress and the Reconstruction, 1865-1867.* New York: St. Martin's Press, 1963.

347. Chadsey, Charles E. "The Struggle Between President Johnson and Congress over Reconstruction." Ph.D. dissertation, Columbia University, 1896.

348. Cooper, Constance J. "Tennessee Returns to Congress." *Tennessee Historical Quarterly* 37 (Spring 1978): 49-62.

349. Currie, James T. "The Beginnings of Congressional Reconstruction in Mississippi." *Journal of Mississippi History* 35 (Aug. 1973): 267-286.

350. Curry, Leonard P. "Congressional Democrats: 1861-1863." *Civil War History* 12 (Sept. 1966): 213-229.

351. Dippie, Brian W. "What Will Congress Do About It? The Congressional Reaction to the Little Big Horn Disaster." *North Dakota History* 37 (Summer 1970): 161-189.

352. Fischer, Leroy H. "Lincoln's First Congress." *Illinois History* 15 (Feb. 1962): 101-102.

353. Folmar, John K. "Reaction to Reconstruction: Pennsylvania Republicans in the Forty-Second Congress, 1871-1873." *Western Pennsylvania Historical Magazine* 61 (July 1978): 203-220.

354. Gambill, Edward L. "Who Were the Senate Radicals?" *Civil War History* 11 (Sept. 1965): 237-244.

355. Goldwater, Barry M. "Congressional Policy in Indian Affairs in Arizona, 1871-1886." *Views on the Military History of the Indian-Spanish-American Southwest, 1598-1886.* 1976. pp. 180-187.

356. Hart, Charles R. D. "Why Lincoln Said 'No': Congressional Attitudes on Slavery Expansion, 1860-1861." *Social Science Quarterly* 49 (Dec. 1968): 732-741.

357. Hood, James L. "For the Union: Kentucky's Unconditional Unionist Congressmen and the Development of the Republican Party in Kentucky, 1863-1865." *Register of the Kentucky Historical Society* 76 (July 1978): 197-215.

358. Hume, Richard L. "The Membership of the Virginia Constitutional Convention of 1867-1868: A Study of the Beginnings of Congressional Reconstruction in the Upper South." *Virginia Magazine of History and Biography* 86 (Oct. 1978): 461-484.

359. Jordan, Daniel P. "Mississippi's Antebellum Congressmen: A Collective Biography." *Journal of Mississippi History* 38 (May 1976): 157-182.

360. Josephson, Matthew. *The Politicos: 1865-1896.* New York: Harcourt, Brace, 1938.

361. Kendrick, Benjamin B. "Journal of the Joint Committee of Fifteen on Reconstruction, 39th Congress, 1865-1867." Ph.D. dissertation, Columbia University, 1915.

362. Kendrick, Benjamin B. "The Journal of the Joint Committee of Fifteen on Reconstruction, 39th Congress, 1866-1867." *South Atlantic Quarterly* 14 (April 1915): 186-188.

363. Knox, Clinton E. "The Possibilities of Compromise in the Senate Committee of Thirteen and the Responsibility for Failure." *Journal of Negro History* 17 (Oct. 1932): 437-465.

364. Kolchin, Peter. "Scalawags, Carpetbaggers, and Reconstruction: A Quantitative Look at Southern Congressional Politics, 1868-1872." *Journal of Southern History* 45 (Feb. 1979): 63-76.

365. Lerche, Charles O. "Congressional Interpretations of the Guarantee of a Republican Form of Government During Reconstruction." *Journal of Southern History* 15 (May 1949): 192-211.

366. Oliver, David L. "The Contribution of Kentucky to Lincoln's Fourth of July Session of Congress, 1861." *Register of the Kentucky Historical Society* 60 (April 1962): 134-142.

367. Perman, Michael. "The South and Congress's Reconstruction Policy, 1866-67." *Journal of American Studies* 4 (Feb. 1971): 181-200.

368. Quimby, Rollin W. "Congress and the Civil War Chaplaincy." *Civil War History* 10 (Sept. 1964): 246-259.

369. Robertson, John B. "Lincoln and Congress." Ph.D. dissertation, University of Wisconsin, 1966.

370. Russ, William A. "Congressional Disfranchisement, 1866-1898." Ph.D. dissertation, University of Chicago, 1934.

371. Russ, William A. "The Struggle Between President Lincoln and Congress over Disfranchisement of Rebels." *Susquehanna University Studies* 3 (Mar. 1948): 221-243.

372. Seip, Terry L. "Southern Representatives and Economic Measures During Reconstruction: A Quantitative and Analytical Study." Ph.D. dissertation, Louisiana State University, 1974.

373. Simon, John Y. "Congress Under Lincoln, 1861-1863." Ph.D. dissertation, Harvard University, 1961.

374. Smith, Gerald W. "West Virginia Congressional Opinion on the Tariff, 1865-1895." *West Virginia History* 23 (Jan. 1962): 106-138, 224-230.

375. Sprunger, Keith L. "Cold Water Congressmen: The Congressional Temperance Society Before the Civil War." *Historian* 27 (Aug. 1965): 498-515.

376. Sutherland, Keith. "The Structure of Congress as a Factor in the Legislative Crisis of 1860." *Mid-America* 51 (Oct. 1969): 244-259.

377. Tarrant, Catherine M. "A Writ of Liberty or a Covenant with Hell: Habeas Corpus in the War Congresses, 1861-1867." Ph.D. dissertation, Rice University, 1972.

378. Tarson, Theodore L. "Congressional Concepts of Competition, 1865-1890." Ph.D. dissertation, Yale University, 1962.

1877–1896   Gilded Age and Party Government

379. Dunn, Arthur W. *From Harrison to Harding: A Personal Narrative, Covering a Third of a Century, 1888-1921;* 2 vols. New York: Putnam's, 1922.

380. Hill, John L. "Congress and Representative Institutions in the United Provinces, 1886-1901." Ph.D. dissertation, Duke University, 1967.

381. Lodge, Henry C. "The Coming Congress." *North American Review* 149 (Sept. 1889): 293-301.

382. Morrison, Paul W. "The Position of the Senators from North Dakota on Isolation, 1889-1920." Ph.D. dissertation, University of Colorado, 1954.

383. Peck, Harry T. *Twenty Years of the Republic, 1885-1905.* New York: Dodd, Mead, 1913.

384. Reid, G. W. "Four in Black: North Carolina's Black Congressmen: 1874-1901." *Journal of Negro History* 64 (Summer 1979): 229-243.

1896–1921   Progressivism and Reform

385. Abrams, Richard M. "Woodrow Wilson and the Southern Congressmen, 1913-1916." *Journal of Southern History* 22 (Nov. 1956): 417-437.

386. Allen, Howard W., Clausen, Aage R., and Clubb, Jerome M. "Political Reform and Negro Rights in the Senate, 1909-1915." *Journal of Southern History* 37 (May 1971): 191-212.

387. Block, Robert H. "Southern Congressmen and Wilson's Call for Repeal of the Panama Canal Tolls Exemption." *Southern Studies* 17 (Spring 1978): 91-100.

388. Damiani, Brian P. "Advocates of Empire: William McKinley, the Senate and American Expansion, 1898-1899." Ph.D. dissertation, University of Delaware, 1978.

389. Grant, Philip A. "Missourians in Congress, 1916-1920." *Bulletin of the Missouri Historical Society* 34 (April 1978): 151-156.

390. Grant, Philip A. "Tennesseans in the 63rd Congress, 1913-1915." *Tennessee Historical Quarterly* 29 (Fall 1970): 278-286.

391. Grantham, Dewey W. "Southern Congressional Leaders and the New Freedom 1913-1917." *Journal of Southern History* 13 (Nov. 1947): 439-459.

392. Grantham, Dewey W. "Texas Congressional Leaders and the New Freedom, 1913-1917." *Southwestern Historical Quarterly* 53 (July 1949): 35-48.

393. Grinder, Robert D. "Progressives, Conservaties, and Imperialism: Another Look at the Senate Republicans, 1913-1917." *North Dakota Quarterly* 41 (Autumn 1973): 28-39.

394. Kendrick, Jack E. "Alabama Congressmen in the Wilson Administration." *Alabama Review* 24 (Oct. 1971): 243-260.

395. Kirwin, Harry W. "The United States and the Revolutionary Disintegration of Congress, 1919-1925." Ph.D. dissertation, Fordham University, 1949.

396. Leake, James M. "Four Years of Congress." *American Political Science Review* 11 (May 1917): 252-283.

397. Link, Arthur S. *Wilson: The New Freedom.* Princeton, N.J.: Princeton University Press, 1956.

398. Livermore, Seward W. *Politics is Adjourned: Woodrow Wilson and the War Congress, 1916-1918.* Middletown, Conn.: Wesleyan University Press, 1966.

399. Merrill, Horace S. and Merrill, Marion G. *The Republican Command, 1897-1913.* Lexington: University Press of Kentucky, 1971.

400. Meyer, Karl. "The Politics of Loyalty: From LaFollette to McCarthy in Wisconsin, 1918-1952." Ph.D. dissertation, Princeton University, 1956.

401. Neuberger, Richard L. "Progressives in Congress." *Common Sense* 11 (Mar. 1942): 83-86.

402. Newby, I. A. "States' Rights and Southern Congressmen During World War I." *Phylon* 24 (Spring 1963): 34-50.

403. Olssen, Erik N. "Dissent from Normalcy: Progressives in Congress, 1918-1925." Ph.D. dissertation, Duke University, 1970.

404. Rogers, Lindsay. "Short Session of Congress." *American Political Science Review* 13 (May 1919): 251-263.

405. Rogers, Lindsay. "American Government and Politics: The Special Session of Congress (1919)." *American Political Science Review* 14 (Feb. 1920): 74-92.

406. Rogers, Lindsay. "American Government and Politics: The Second Session of the Sixty-Sixth Congress." *American Political Science Review* 14 (Nov. 1920): 659-671.

407. Rogers, Lindsay. "American Government and Politics: The Third Session of the Sixty-Sixth Congress, December 6, 1920–March 4, 1921." *American Political Science Review* 15 (Aug. 1921): 366-379.

408. Scott, Anne F. "A Progressive Wind from the South, 1906–1913." *Journal of Southern History* 29 (Feb. 1963): 53-70.

409. Scott, S. C. T. "Congress and Anarchy: A Suggestion." *North American Review* 173 (Oct. 1901): 433-436.

410. Smith, Edwina C. "Southerners on Empire: Southern Senators and Imperialism, 1898-1899." *Mississippi Quarterly* 31 (Winter 1978): 89-107.

411. Snapp, Meredith A. "Defeat the Democrats: The Congressional Union for Woman Suffrage in Arizona, 1914 and 1916." *Journal of the West* 14 (Oct. 1975): 131-139.

412. Sutton, Walter A. "Texas Congressmen and the Mexican Revolution of 1910." *Journal of the West* 13 (Oct. 1974): 90-107.

413. Watson, Richard L. "A Testing Time for Southern Congressional Leadership: The War Crisis of 1917-1918." *Journal of Southern History* 44 (Feb. 1978): 3-40.

1921–1933   Republican Years

414. Beckman, Everett G. "The Changing Conceptions of the Role of Religion with Reference to Social Justice as Reflected in the Congressional Record, 1930-1960." Ph.D. dissertation, University of Pittsburgh, 1965.

415. Dollar, Charles M. "The Senate Progressive Movement, 1921–1933: A Roll Call Analysis." Ph.D. dissertation, University of Kentucky, 1966.

416. Grant, Philip A. "Iowa Congressional Leaders, 1921-32." *Annals of Iowa* 42 (Fall 1974): 430-442.

417. Grant, Philip A. "Southern Congressmen and Agriculture, 1921–1932." *Agricultural History* 53 (Jan. 1979): 338-351.

418. Herring, Edward P. "Seventy-Second Congress, First Session, December 7, 1931 to July 16, 1932." *American Political Science Review* 26 (Oct. 1932): 846-874.

419. Herring, Edward P. "Seventy-Second Congress, Second Session, December 5, 1932 to March 4, 1933." *American Political Science Review* 27 (June 1933): 404-422.

420. Macmahon, Arthur W. "American Government and Politics: First Session of the Sixty-Ninth Congress." *American Political Science Review* 20 (Aug. 1926): 604-622.

421. Macmahon, Arthur W. "American Government and Politics: Second Session of the Sixty-Ninth Congress." *American Political Science Review* 21 (May 1927): 217-317.

422. Macmahon, Arthur W. "American Government and Politics: First Session of the Seventieth Congress." *American Political Science Review* 22 (Aug. 1928): 650-683.

423. Macmahon, Arthur W. "American Government and Politics: Second Session of the Seventieth Congress." *American Political Science Review* 23 (May 1929): 364-383.

424. Macmahon, Arthur W. "American Government and Politics: First Session of the Seventy-First Congress." *American Political Science Review* 24 (Feb. 1930): 38-59.

425. Macmahon, Arthur W. "American Government and Politics: Second Session of the Seventy-First Congress, December 2, 1929 to July 3, 1930; Special Session of the Senate, July 7-21." *American Political Science Review* 24 (Nov. 1930): 913-946.

426. Macmahon, Arthur W. "American Government and Politics: Seventy-First Congress, Third Session, December 1, 1930 to March 4, 1931." *American Political Science Review* 25 (Nov. 1931): 932-955.

427. Rogers, George A. "President Hoover and the Seventy-Second Congress." Master's thesis, University of Illinois, 1947.

428. Rogers, Lindsay. "American Government and Politics: The First Special Session of the Sixty-Seventh Congress, April 11, 1921-November 28, 1921." *American Political Science Review* 16 (Feb. 1922): 41-52.

429. Rogers, Lindsay. "American Government and Politics: 67th Congress, 2d. 3d. and 4th Sessions." *American Political Science Review* 18 (Feb. 1924): 79-95.

430. Rogers, Lindsay. "American Government and Politics: First and Second Sessions of the Sixty-Eighth Congress." *American Political Science Review* 19 (Nov. 1925): 761-772.

431. Savage, Hugh J. "Political Independents of the Hoover Era: The Progressive Insurgents of the Senate." Ph.D. dissertation, University of Illinois at Urbana-Champaign, 1961.

432. Schwarz, Jordan A. *The Interregnum of Despair: Hoover, Congress, and the Depression.* Urbana: University of Illinois Press, 1970.

1933–1945 New Deal and Democrats

433. Altman, O. R. "Second Session of the Seventy-Fourth Congress, (Jan 3, 1936 to June 20, 1936)." *American Political Science Review* 30 (Dec. 1936): 1086-1107.

434. Altman, O. R. "First Session of the Seventy-Fifth Congress: January 5, 1937 to Aug. 21, 1937." *American Political Science Review* 31 (Dec. 1937): 1071-1093.

435. Altman, O. R. "Second and Third Sessions of the Seventy-Fifth Congress 1937-38." *American Political Science Review* 32 (Dec. 1938): 1099-1123.

436. Bulman, John S. "Congress: Death Throes or Renascence." *Georgetown Law Journal* 31 (May 1943): 435-449.

437. Coode, Thomas H. "Georgia Congressmen and the First Hundred Days of the New Deal." *Georgia Historical Quarterly* 53 (June 1969): 129-146.

438. Coode, Thomas H. "Georgia Congressmen and the New Deal, 1933-1938." Ph.D. dissertation, University of Georgia, 1966.

439. Donovan, John C. "Congressional Isolationists and the Roosevelt Foreign Policy." *World Politics* 3 (April 1951): 299-317.

440. Drury, Allen. *A Senate Journal, 1943-1945.* New York: McGraw-Hill, 1963.

441. Hall, Alvin L. "Politics and Patronage: Virginia's Senators and the Roosevelt Purges of 1938." *Virginia Magazine of History and Biography* 82 (July 1974): 331-350.

442. Hanlon, Edward F. "Urban-Rural Cooperation and Conflict in the Congress: The Breakdown of the New Deal Coalition, 1933–1938." Ed.D. dissertation, Georgetown University, 1967.

443. Herring, Edward P. "Seventy-Third Congress, First Session, March 9, 1933 to June 16, 1933." *American Political Science Review* 28 (Feb. 1934): 65-83.

444. Herring, Edward P. "Second Session of the Seventy-Third Congress, January 3, 1934 to June 18, 1934." *American Political Science Review* 28 (Oct. 1934): 852-866.

445. Herring, Edward P. "First Session of the Seventy-Fourth Congress, January 3, 1935 to August 26, 1935." *American Political Science Review* 29 (Dec. 1935): 985-1005.

446. Higgins, George A. "Strengthening the Congress, 1941-1946." Ph.D. dissertation, Fordham University, 1949.

447. Imler, Joseph A. "The First One Hundred Days of the New Deal: The View from Capitol Hill." Ph.D. dissertation, Indiana University, 1975.

448. Lee, R. Alton. "The Turnip Session of the Do-Nothing Congress: Presidential Campaign Strategy." *Social Science Quarterly* 44 (Dec. 1963): 256-267.

449. Mihelich, Dennis N. "The Congressional Mavericks, 1935-1939." Ph.D. dissertation, Case Western Reserve University, 1972.

450. Mulder, Ronald A. "Progressive Insurgents in the United States Senate, 1935-1936: Was There a Second New Deal." *Mid-America* 57 (April 1957): 106-125.

451. O'Connor, John J. "Principal Legislation of the Seventy-Fourth Congress." *U.S. Law Review* 69 (Sept. 1935): 466-473.

452. "One Hundred and Fiftieth Anniversary of First Meeting of Congress." *American Bar Association Journal* 25 (April 1939): 283-290.

453. Patterson, James. T. *Congressional Conservatism and the New Deal.* Lexington: University Press of Kentucky, 1968.

454. Porter, David L. *Congress and the Waning of the New Deal.* Port Washington, N.Y.: Kennikat Press, 1979.

455. Porter, David L. *The Seventy-Sixth Congress and World War II, 1939-1940.* Columbia: University of Missouri Press, 1979.

456. Riddick, Floyd M. "Congress Versus the President in 1944." *South Atlantic Quarterly* 44 (July 1945): 308-315.

457. Riddick, Floyd M. "House Versus the Senate in the Third Session of the Seventy-Sixth Congress." *South Atlantic Quarterly* 40 (April 1941): 169-184.

458. Riddick, Floyd M. "American Government and Politics: First Session of the Seventy-Sixth Congress, January 3 to August 5, 1939." *American Political Science Review* 33 (Dec. 1939): 1022-1043.

459. Riddick, Floyd M. "American Government and Politics: Third Session of the Seventy-Sixth Congress, January 3, 1940 to January 3, 1941." *American Political Science Review* 35 (April 1941): 284-303.

460. Riddick, Floyd M. "American Government and Politics: First Session of the Seventy-Seventh Congress, January 3, 1941 to January 2, 1942." *American Political Science Review* 36 (April 1942): 290-302.

461. Riddick, Floyd M. "American Government and Politics: Second Session of the Seventy-Seventh Congress, January 6 to December 16, 1942." *American Political Science Review* 37 (April 1943): 290-305.

462. Riddick, Floyd M. "American Government and Politics: The First Session of the Seventy-Eighth Congress." *American Political Science Review* 38 (April 1944): 301-317.

463. Riddick, Floyd M. "American Government and Politics: The Second Session of the Seventy-Eighth Congress." *American Political Science Review* 39 (April 1945): 317-336.

464. Schapsmeier, Edward L. and Schapsmeier, Frederick H. "Farm Policy from FDR to Eisenhower: Southern Democrats and the Politics of Agriculture." *Agricultural History* 53 (Jan. 1979): 352-376.

465. Schnurer, Herman. "Counter Attack in Congress." *Antioch Review* 3 (Spring 1943): 32-53.

466. Young, Roland A. *Congressional Politics in the Second World War.* New York: Columbia University Press, 1956.

1945–1969   Postwar Era

467. Bernstein, Barton J. "Truman, the Eightieth Congress, and the Transformation of Political Culture." *Capitol Studies* 2 (Spring 1973): 64-75.

468. Grant, Philip A. "A Composite Profile of Virginia's Political Leaders, 1945-1960." *Virginia Social Science Journal* 14 (April 1979): 53-58.

469. Johnson, Arthur T. "Congress and Professional Sports: 1951-1978." *American Academy of Political and Social Science, The Annals* 445 (Sept. 1979): 102-115.

470. Jones, E. Terrence. "The House of Representatives and Keynesian Economics, 1945-1964." Ph.D. dissertation, Georgetown University, 1967.

471. Knight, K. W. "President Johnson and the Eighty-Ninth Congress." *World Review* 5 (July 1966): 39-46.

472. Koenig, Louis W. "Kennedy and the 87th Congress." In *American Government Annual, 1962-63,* ed. Ivan Hinderaker, pp. 71-86. New York: Holt, Rinehart, and Winston, 1962.

473. Kolodziej, Edward A. *The Uncommon Defense and Congress, 1945-1963.* Columbus: Ohio State University Press, 1966.

474. Neustadt, Richard E. "Congress and the Fair Deal: A Legislative Balance Sheet." *Public Policy* 5 (1954): 349-381.

475. Picque, Nicholas D. "Lyndon Johnson and the 89th Congress." *Christianity and Crisis* 25 (Sept. 1965): 184-187.

476. "President Eisenhower and Congress: Peace and Prosperity Under Strain." *World Today* 13 (March 1957): 103-109.

477. Reichard, Gary W. *The Reaffirmation of Republicanism: Eisenhower and the Eighty-Third Congress.* Knoxville: University of Tennessee Press, 1975.

478. Riddick, Floyd M. "American Government and Politics: The First Session of the Seventy-Ninth Congress." *American Political Science Review* 40 (April 1946): 256-271.

479. Riddick, Floyd M. "American Government and Politics: The Second Session of the Seventy-Ninth Congress." *American Political Science Review* 41 (Feb. 1947): 12-27.

480. Riddick, Floyd M. "American Government and Politics: The First Session of the Eightieth Congress." *American Political Science Review* 42 (Aug. 1948): 677-693.

481. Riddick, Floyd M. "American Government and Politics: Second Session of the Eightieth Congress." *American Political Science Review* 43 (June 1949): 483-492.

482. Riddick, Floyd M. "American Government and Politics: The Eighty-First Congress: First and Second Sessions." *Western Political Quarterly* 4 (Mar. 1951): 48-66.

483. Riddick, Floyd M. "American Government and Politics: The Eighty-Second Congress, First Session." *Western Political Quarterly* 5 (Mar. 1952): 94-108.

484. Riddick, Floyd M. "American Government and Politics: The Eighty-Second Congress, Second Session." *Western Political Quarterly* 5 (Dec. 1952): 619-634.

485. Riddick, Floyd M. "American Government and Politics: The Eighty-Third Congress, First Session." *Western Political Quarterly* 6 (Dec. 1953): 776-794.

486. Riddick, Floyd M. "American Government and Politics: The Eighty-Third Congress, Second Session." *Western Political Quarterly* 7 (Dec. 1954): 636-655.

487. Riddick, Floyd M. "Eighty-Fourth Congress: First-Second Sessions." *Western Political Quarterly* 8 and 10 (Dec. 1955 and Mar. 1957): 612-629 and 63-79.

488. Riddick, Floyd M. "American Government and Politics: Eighty-Fifth Congress, First-Second Sessions." *Western Political Quarterly* 11 and 12 (Mar. 1958 and Mar. 1959): 86-103 and 177-192.

489. Riddick, Floyd M. "American Government and Politics: Eighty-Sixth Congress, First Session." *Western Political Quarterly* 13 (Mar. 1960): 113-130.

490. Riddick, Floyd M. "American Government and Politics: Eighty-Sixth Congress, Second Session." *Western Political Quarterly* 14 (June 1961): 415-431.

491. Riddick, Floyd M. "American Government and Politics: Eighty-Seventh Congress, First Session." *Western Political Quarterly* 15 (June 1962): 254-273.

492. Riddick, Floyd M. "American Government and Politics: Eighty-Seventh Congress, Second Session." *Western Political Quarterly* 16 (Mar. 1963): 133-148.

493. Riddick, Floyd M. and Zweben, Murry. "American Government and Politics: Eighty-Eighth Congress, First Session." *Western Political Quarterly* 17 (June 1964): 235-255.

494. Riddick, Floyd M. and Zweben, Murry. "American Government and Politics: Eighty-Eighth Congress, Second Session." *Western Political Quarterly* 18 (June 1965): 344-349.

495. Riddick, Floyd M. and Zweben, Murry. "American Government and Politics: Eighty-Ninth Congress, First Session." *Western Political Quarterly* 19 (June 1966): 354-374.

496. Riddick, Floyd M. and Zweben, Murry. "American Government and Politics: Eighty-Ninth Congress, Second Session." *Western Political Quarterly* 20 (Mar. 1967): 173-190.

497. Riddick, Floyd M. and Dove, Robert B. "American Government and Politics: Ninetieth Congress, First Session." *Western Political Quarterly* 21 (June 1968): 206-226.

498. Ripley, Randall B. *Kennedy and the Congress.* Morristown, N.J.: General Learning Press, 1972.

499. Shannon, William V. "Liberal Hopes and Congress Realities." *Commentary* 27 (May 1959): 409-412.

500. Thompson, Francis H. *The Frustration of Politics: Truman, Congress, and the Loyalty Issue, 1945-1953.* Rutherford, N.J.: Fairleigh Dickinson University Press, 1979.

501. White, Larry. "Southern Congressional Politics: Change and Continuity Since the 1965 Voting Rights Act." Ph.D. dissertation, Yale University, 1978.

502. Williams, Robert and Kershaw, David. "Kennedy and Congress: The Struggle for the New Frontier." *Political Studies* 27 (Sept. 1979): 390-404.

1969–1980   Reform Years

503. Cohen, Richard E. "The Last Year of the 95th: Reading Congress's Crystal Ball." *National Journal* 10 (Jan. 7, 1978): 4-9.

504. Cohen, Richard E. "The Making of Congress, 1980: There's a New National Wrinkle This Year." *National Journal* 12 (Jan. 5, 1980): 20-24.

505. Cohen, Richard E. "The 96th Congress: Who'll Be Calling the Shots?" *National Journal* 10 (Nov. 11, 1978): 1804-1817.

506. Cohen, Richard E. "A Report Card for Congress: An 'F' for Frustration." *National Journal* 11 (Aug. 11 1979):1326-1330.

507. Cohen, Richard E. "Republicans in the 96th Congress: Still the 'Loyal' Opposition." *National Journal* 10 (Dec. 30, 1978): 2053-2055.

508. "A History of Nixon's Relations with Congress, 1969-73." *Congressional Quarterly Weekly Report* 31 (Sept. 15, 1973): 2428-2429.

509. Lanouette, William J. "Congress Takes a Peek into Its Crystal Balls." *National Journal* 10 (July 1, 1978): 1050-1051.

II. The Congressional Process

Congressional Procedures

510. Blydenburgh, John C. "The Closed Rule and the Paradox of Voting." *Journal of Politics* 33 (Feb. 1971): 57-71.

511. Brown, Everett S. "Time of Meetings of Congress." *American Political Science Review* 25 (Nov. 1931): 955-960.

512. Burns, James MacGregor. *Congress on Trial: Legislative Process and the Administrative State.* New York: Harper and Row, 1949.

513. Carmack, Paul A. "Evolution in Parliamentary Procedure." *Speech Teacher* 11 (Jan. 1962): 26-39.

514. Case, Clifford P. "Changing Role of Congress: The Growing Concern with the Legislative Process." *George Washington Law Review* 32 (June 1964): 929-931.

515. Drew, Elizabeth B. "A Tendency to Legislate." *The New Yorker* 54, 26 June 1978, pp. 80-89.

516. Frantzich, Stephen E. "Who Makes Our Laws? The Legislative Effectiveness of Members of the U. S. Congress." *Legislative Studies Quarterly* 4 (Aug. 1979): 409-428.

517. Gibson, Rankin M. "Congressional Concurrent Resolutions: An Aid (to) Statutory Interpretation?" *American Bar Association Journal* 37 (Jan. 1951): 421-424, 479-483.

518. Gooch, R. K. "The Legal Nature of Legislative Rules of Procedure." *Virginia Law Review* 12 (May 1926): 529-545.

519. Harbeson, John F. "The National Legislative Chambers." *Journal of the American Institute of Architects* 17 (Dec. 1952): 259-262.

520. Hoar, George F. "The Conduct of Business in Congress." *North American Review* 128 (Feb. 1879): 111-134.

521. Isralsky, Jeffrey. "Legislative Primer." *NLADA Briefcase* 35 (June 1978): 76-79, 92-93.

522. Lawson, James. F. *The General Welfare Clause: A Study of the Power of Congress Under the Constitution of the United States.* Washington: J. F. Lawson, 1934.

523. Lesnick, Howard. "The Federal Rule-Making Process: Time for Re-examination." *American Bar Association Journal* 61 (May 1975): 579-584.

524. Luce, Robert. "Petty Business in Congress." *American Political Science Review* 26 (Oct. 1932): 815-827.

525. MacCallum, Gerald C. "Legislative Intent." *Yale Law Journal* 75 (April 1966): 754-787.

526. Moore, James W. and Bendix, Helen I. "Congress, Evidence and Rulemaking." *Yale Law Journal* 84 (Nov. 1974): 9-38.

527. Mussman, M. A. "Changing the Date for Congressional Sessions." *American Political Science Review* 18 (Feb. 1924): 108-113.

528. Myers, Denys P. "Joint Resolutions Are Laws." *American Bar Association Journal* 28 (Jan. 1942): 33-37.

529. Orloski, R. J. "Enforcement Clauses of the Civil War Amendments: A Repository of Legislative Power." *St. John's Law Review* 49 (Spring 1975): 493-510.

530. Orth, Samuel P. "Special Legislation." *Atlantic Montly* 97 (Jan. 1906): 69-76.

531. "Private Bills in Congress." *Harvard Law Review* 79 (June 1966): 1684-1706.

532. Riddick, Floyd M. "Political Procedure in the First Session of the Seventy-Sixth Congress." *South Atlantic Quarterly* 39 (Jan. 1940): 1-17.

533. Reinsch, Paul S. *American Legislatures and Legislative Methods.* New York: Century, 1907.

534. "Results of CQ Poll on Congressional Practice." *Congressional Quarterly Weekly Report* 16 (April 25, 1958): 497-499.

535. "Rules Fights Due in Both House and Senate." *Congressional Quarterly Weekly Report* 21 (Jan. 4, 1963): 9-12.

536. "Scheduling Changes Sought to Speed Legislation." *Congressional Quarterly Weekly Report* 21 (June 7, 1963): 892-894.

537. Schuman, F. L. " 'Bill of Attainder' in the Seventy-Eighth Congress." *American Political Science Review* 37 (Oct. 1943): 819-829.

538. Thompson, J. D. "Analysis of Present Methods of Congressional Legislation." *American Political Science Review* 8 (Feb. 1914): 168-175.

539. Ward, Paul E. "A History of the Special Sessions of Congress: Threats of War, War, and Its Effects." Ph.D. dissertation, St. John's University, 1959.

540. Zweig, Franklin M., ed. *Evaluation in Legislation.* Beverly Hills, Calif.: Sage Publications, 1979.

House of Representatives

General Studies

541. Bogue, Allan G., Clubb, Jerome M., McKibbin, Carroll R., and Traugott, Santa A. "Members of the House of Representatives and the Processes of Modernization, 1789-1960." *Journal of American History* 63 (Sept. 1976): 275-302.

542. Bolling, Richard. *House Out of Order.* New York: Dutton, 1965.

543. Bolling, Richard. *Power in the House: A History of the Leadership of the House of Representatives.* New York: Capricorn Books, 1974.

544. Brenner, Philip J. "An Examination of Conflict in the U.S. House of Representatives." Ph.D. dissertation, Johns Hopkins University, 1975.

545. Davidson, Roger H. and Oleszek, Walter J. "Adaption and Consolidation: Structural Innovation in the U.s. House of Representatives." *Legislative Studies Quarterly* 1 (Feb. 1976): 37-65.

546. Dodd, Lawrence C. and Oppenheimer, Bruce I. "The House in Transition." In their *Congress Reconsidered*, pp. 21-53. New York: Praeger, 1977.

547. Fenno, Richard F. "The Internal Distribution of Influence: The House." In *The Congress and America's Future*, ed. David B. Truman, pp. 52-76. Englewood Cliffs, N.J.: Prentice-Hall, 1965.

548. Fiorina, Morris P., Rohde, David W., and Wissell, Peter. "Historical Change in House Turnover." In *Congress in Change: Evolution and Reform*, ed. Norman J. Ornstein, pp. 24-57. New York: Praeger, 1975.

549. Fraser, Donald M. and Nathanson, Iric. "Rebuilding the House of Representatives." In *Congress in Change: Evolution and Reform,* ed. Norman J. Ornstein, pp. 288-294. New York: Praeger, 1975.

550. Friedman, Yoram. "Sources of Division in the United States House of Representatives (1947-1968): An Informational-Theoretic Approach." Ph.D. dissertation, University of Chicago, 1972.

551. Furlong, Patrick J. "The Evolution of Political Organization in the House of Representatives, 1789-1801." Ph.D. dissertation, Northwestern University, 1966.

552. Galloway, George B. and Wise, Sidney. *History of the House of Representatives.* 2d rev. ed. New York: Crowell, 1976.

553. Grant, Lawrence V. "Decision-Making in the United States House of Representatives: A Computer Simulation." Ph.D. dissertation, University of Illinois at Urbana-Champaign, 1970.

554. Holcombe, Arthur N. "Majority Rule in the House of Representatives." In his *Our More Perfect Union,* pp. 149-190. Cambridge, Mass.: Harvard University Press, 1950.

555. King, Larry L. "Inside Capitol Hill: How the House Really Works." *Harper's Magazine* 237 (Oct. 1968): 58-71.

556. Korey, John L. "Constituency and the Analysis of Legislative Politics: A Study of the United States House of Representatives in the Eighty-Eighth Congress." Ph.D. dissertation, University of Florida, 1971.

557. Mabie, Jan E. "A Political-Economic Theory of Decision Making in the U.S. House of Representatives." Ph.D. dissertation, Washington University, 1975.

558. MacNeil, Neil. *Forge of Democracy: The House of Representatives.* New York: McKay, 1963.

559. Marwell, Gerald. "Party, Region and the Dimensions of Conflict in the House of Representatives, 1949-1954." *American Political science Review* 61 (June 1967): 380-399.

560. Norris, Parthenia E. "The Revolt in the House of Representatives, 1909-1911." Master's thesis, Indiana University, 1939.

561. Peabody, Robert L., ed. *New Perspectives on the House of Representatives.* 3rd ed. Chicago: Rand McNally College Publishing Company, 1977.

562. Polsby, Nelson W. "Institutionalization of the U.S. House of Representatives." *American Political Science Review* 62 (March 1968): 144-168.

563. Riemer, Neal, ed. *The Representative: Trustee? Delegate? Partisan? Politico?* Boston: D. C. Heath, 1967.

564. Roessner, John D. "The House as a Political System: Congressional Control of NIH, 1959-1964." Ph.D. dissertation, Case Western Reserve University, 1970.

565. Sinclair, Barbara Deckard. "Party Realignment and the Transformation of the Political Agenda: The House of Representatives, 1925-1938." *American Political Science Review* 71 (Sept. 1977): 940-953.

566. Stathis, Stephen W. and Sheridan, Peter B. *A Compendium of Records and Firsts of the United States House of Representatives.* Washington: Congressional Research Service, 1975.

567. Stone, Walter J. "Representation in the United States House of Representatives: 1956-1974." Ph.D. dissertation, University of Michigan, 1975.

568. Struble, Robert. "House Turnover and the Principle of Rotation." *Political Science Quarterly* 94 (Winter 1979-80): 649-667.

569. White, William S. *Home plate: The Story of the U.S. House of Representatives.* Boston: Houghton Mifflin, 1965.

Rules and Practices

570. Alexander, DeAlva S. *History and Procedure of the House of Representatives.* Boston: Houghton Mifflin, 1916.

571. Bach, Stanley I. *House Consideration of Nongermane Senate Amendments.* Washington: Congressional Research Service, 1976.

572. Bach, Stanley I. *Voting in the House of Representatives When Resolved into Committee of the Whole.* Washington: Congressional Research Service, 1976.

573. Bensel, Richard F. "Reciprocal Behavior and the Rules of the House of Representatives." Ph.D. dissertation, Cornell University, 1978.

574. Bowsher, Prentice. "The Speaker's Man: Lewis Deschler, House Parliamentarian." *Washington Monthly* 2 (April 1970): 22-27.

575. Briscoe, Cynthia A. *Cosponsorship of Bills and Resolutions in the House of Representatives.* Washington: Congressional Research Service, 1976.

576. Cooper, Ann. "House Use of Suspensions Grows Drastically." *Congressional Quarterly Weekly Report* 36 (Sept. 30, 1978): 2693-2695.

577. Damon, Richard E. "The Standing Rules of the United States House of Representatives." Ph.D. dissertation, Columbia University, 1971.

578. Downey, Marvin. "The Rules and Procedure of the United States House of Representatives, 1789 to 1949." Ph.D. dissertation, University of Chicago, 1957.

579. Gross, Bertram M. *Toward a House of Worse Repute or How to Be a Rubber Stamp with Honor.* Working Papers on House Committee Organization and Operation. Presented to House Select Committee on Committees. Washington: GPO, 1973.

580. House, Albert V. "The Contributions of Samuel J. Randall to the Rules of the National House of Representatives." *American Political Science Review* 29 (Oct. 1935): 837-841.

581. Johnson, Allen. "Organization and Procedure of the House of Representatives." In his *Readings in American Constitutional History, 1776-1876.* Boston: Houghton Mifflin, 1912.

582. Kogan, Richard. *Limitations on Time for Debate Under the Rules and Precedents of the House of Representatives.* Washington: Congressional Research Service, 1976.

583. Lehman, Mildred L. *The Discharge Petition in the House of Representatives: Background and Statistics.* Washington: Congressional Research Service, 1976.

584. Ludlum, Robert P. "The Antislavery 'Gag-Rule': History and Argument." *Journal Of Negro History* 26 (April 1941): 203-243.

585. Marsel, Louis. "Process and Policy in the House of Representatives: The Case of Housing Policy, 1961-1968." Ph.D. dissertation, Columbia University, 1971.

586. Rable, George C. "Slavery, Politics, and the South: The Gag Rule as a Case Study." *Capitol Studies* 3 (Fall 1975): 69-87.

587. Rhodes, John J. "Floor Procedures in the House of Representatives." In his *We Propose: A Modern Congress,* pp. 201-213. New York: McGraw-Hill, 1966.

588. Riddick, Floyd M. "Political and Parliamentary Procedure in the House of Representatives." Ph.D. dissertation, Duke University, 1935.

589. Riddick, Floyd M. "Procedure in the House of Representatives and Its Relation to the Quality of Legislation." *South Atlantic Quarterly* 37 (Oct. 1938): 367-376.

590. Rowland, Buford. "Recordkeeping Practices of the House of Representatives." *National Archives Accessions* 53 (Jan. 1957): 1-19.

591. Schotland, Roy A. *The First Weeks: From Victory, Through Confusion to Effectiveness: A New Member's Manual of Introduction to the United States House of Representatives.* 3rd ed. Washington: Georgetown University Law Center, 1978.

592. Tienken, Robert L. *Precedents of the House of Representatives Relating to Exclusion, Expulsion, and Censure.* Washington: Congressional Research Service, 1973.

593. U.s. Congress. House. House Administration Committee. *Studies Dealing with Budgetry, Staffing, and Administrative Activities of the U.S. House of Representatives, 1946-1978.* Washington: GPO, 1978.

594. U.S. Congress. House. Rules Committee. *Hearings on Congressional Procedures. April 26-July 31, 1978.* Washington: GPO, 1979.

595. Weiner, Gordon M. "Pennsylvania Congressmen and the 1836 Gag Rule: A Quantitative Note." *Pennsylvania History* 36 (July 1969): 335-340.

596. Wilson, Woodrow S. and Simpson, R. M. "House Rules: Democratic Discipline." *Georgetown Law Journal* 30 (June 1942): 763-767.

597. Yacker, Marc. *A Functional Analysis of the Office Operations in the House of Representatives.* Washington: Congressional Research Service, 1977.

Senate

General Studies

598. Andrews, William G. "Democracy and Representation in the Senate." *South Atlantic Quarterly* 59 (Fall 1960): 461-468.

599. Baker, Richard A. "Managing Congressional Papers: A View of the Senate." *The American Archivist* 41 (July 1978): 291-296.

600. Baker, Ross K. *Friend and Foe in the U.S. Senate.* New York: Free Press, 1980.

601. Bradley, Samuel R. "A Descriptive Study of United States Senate Staff Speech Writing, 90th Congress, 1st Session, 1967." Master's thesis, University of Maryland, 1968.

602. Cannon, Charles A. "The Politics of Interest and Ideology: The Senate Air-Power Hearings of 1956." *Armed Forces and Society* 3 (Summer 1977): 595-608.

603. Carter, Douglas. "Contentious Lords of the Senate." *Reporter* 27, 16 Aug. 1962, pp. 27-28, 29.

604. Clark, Joseph S., et al. *The Senate Establishment.* New York: Hill and Wang, 1963.

605. Clem, Alan L. "Popular Representation and Senate Vacancies." *Midwest Journal of Political Science* 10 (Feb. 1966): 52-77.

606. Davis, E. "Our Unemployed Matadors of the Senate Bull Ring." *Our World* 4 (Mar. 1921): 17-22.

607. Elliott, Rodney D. "United States Senators: A Sociological and Historical Study of a Political Elite." Ph.D. dissertation, University of Colorado, 1958.

608. Everett, William. "The United States Senate." *Atlantic Monthly* 97 (Feb. 1906): 157-166.

609. Fisher, Louis. "Relationship Between the Senate and the Executive Branch." In *Committees and Senate Procedures: A Compilation of Papers Prepared for the Commission on the Operation of the Senate.* 94th Cong., 2nd sess. pp. 115-130. Washington: GPO, 1977.

610. Freed, Bruce F. "Study of Senate Poses Challenge to Panel." *Congressional Quarterly Weekly Report* 33 (Dec. 13, 1975): 2715-2721.

611. Freidin, Seymour. *A Sense of the Senate.* New York: Dodd, Mead, 1972.

612. Gammon, Gary E. "The Role of the United States Senate: Its Conception and Its Performance." Ph.D. dissertation, Claremont Graduate School, 1978.

613. Hacker, Andrew. "The Elected and the Anointed:Two American Elites (Senators and Corporation Presidents)." *American Political Science Review* 55 (Sept. 1961): 539-539.

614. Haines, Lynn. *The Senate from 1907 to 1912*. Bethesda, Md.: The Author, 1912.

615. Harold, Francis. "The Upper House in Jeffersonian Political Theory." *Virginia Magazine of History and Biography* 77 (July 1970): 281-294.

616. Harris, Joseph P. "The Courtesy of the Senate." *Political Science Quarterly* 67 (Mar. 1952): 36-63.

617. Hatch, Louis. *A History of the Vice-Presidency of the United States*. Rev. and edited by Earl C. Shoup. New York: Greenwood Press, 1970.

618. Haynes, George H. *The Senate of the United States,* 2 vols. Boston: Houghton Mifflin, 1938.

619. Hirsch, Eleanor G. "Grandma Felton and the U.S. Senate." *Mankind* 4 (1974): 53-57.

620. Huitt, Ralph K. "The Internal Distribution of Influence: The Senate." In *The Congress and America's Future*, ed. David B. Truman, pp. 77-101. Englewood Cliffs, N.J.: Prentice-Hall, 1965.

621. Hurst, Louis, as told to Frances Spatz Leighton. *The Sweetest Little Club in the World: The U.S. Senate*. Englewood Cliffs, N.J.: Prentice-Hall, 1980.

622. Jeffers, Harry P. *How the U.S. Senate Works: The ABM Debate*. New York: McGraw-Hill, 1970.

623. Kent, F. R. "General Dawes and the Senate." *Spectator* 135, 15 August 1925, pp. 260-261.

624. Kernell, Samuel. "Is the Senate More Liberal than the House?" *Journal of Politics* 35 (May 1973): 332-366.

625. Kerr, Clara H. "The Origin and Development of the United States Senate." Ph.D. dissertation, Cornell University, 1895.

626. Kirkpatrick, Samuel A. and Pettit, Lawrence K. *Sources of Organizational and Personal Power in the U.S. Senate: A Test of Alternative Models*. Norman, Okla.: Bureau of Government Research, University of Oklahoma, 1973.

627. Kunz, Frank A. "The Senate and Contemporary Politics, 1925-1961: A Reappraisal." Ph.D. dissertation, McGill University, 1963.

628. Lodge, Henry C. *The Senate of the United States and Other Essays*. New York: Charles Scribner's Sons, 1921.

629. Lucas, Lydia. "Managing Congressional Papers: A Repository View." *The American Archivist* 41 (July 1978): 275-280.

630. McCall, Samuel W. "The Power of the Senate." *Atlantic Monthly* 92 (Oct. 1903): 433-442.

631. Mansfield, Michael J. "The Meaning of the Term 'Advice and Consent'." *American Academy of Political and Social Science, Annals* 289 (Sept. 1953): 127-133.

632. Marriott, John A. R. "The American Senate." In his *Second Chambers: An Inductive Study in Political Science*, pp. 89-113. Oxford: Clarendon Press, 1910.

633. Marriott, John A. R. *Second Chambers: An Inductive Study in Political Science*. Oxford: Clarendon Press, 1910.

634. Matthews, Donald R. "United States Senators: A Study of the Recruitment of Political Leaders." Ph.D. dissertation, Princeton University, 1953.

635. Matthews, Donald R. "United States Senators and the Class Structure." *Public Opinion Quarterly* 18 (Spring 1954): 5-22.

636. Mital, P. N. "Institutional Prestige of the United States Senate." *Journal of Political Studies* 1 (Sept. 1968): 29-37.

637. Morse, Wayne L. "The Senate as Envisioned by the Framers of the Constitution." In *The Senate Institution*, ed. Nathaniel S. Preston, pp. 7-17. New York: Van Nostrand Reinhold, 1969.

638. Myers, Henry L. *The United States Senate: What Kind of a Body?* Philadelphia: Dorrance and Co., 1939.

639. Nelson, Albert J. "A Test of Burns' Four-Party Thesis in the U.S. Senate: 1969-1973." *Georgia Political Science Association Journal* 6 (Spring 1978): 55-76.

640. Ornstein, Norman J., Peabody, Robert L., and Rohde, David W. "The Changing Senate: From the 1950s to the 1970s." In *Congress Reconsidered*, eds. Lawrence C. Dodd and Bruce I. Oppenheimer, pp. 3-20. New York: Praeger Publishers, 1977.

641. Peabody, Robert L., et al. "United States Senate as a Presidential Incubator: Many Are Called But Few Are Chosen." *Political Science Quarterly* 91 (Summer 1976): 237-258.

642. Peffer, William A. "The U.S. Senate: Its Origins, Personnel, and Organization." *The North American Review* 167 (July 1898): 48-63.

643. Pettit, Lawrence K. "Influence Potential in the United States Senate." In *The Legislative Process in the U.S. Senate*, eds. Lawrence Pettit and Edward Keynes, pp. 227-244. Chicago: Rand McNally, 1969.

644. Phayre, Ignatius. "When the President and Senate Disagree: A Survey of 'Differences' from Washington's Day to Mr. Hoover's." *Landmark* 14 (1932): 75-78.

645. Preston, Nathaniel S., ed. *The Senate Institution.* New York: Van Nostrand Reinhold, 1969.

646. Riker, William H. "The Senate and American Federalism." *American Political Science Review* 49 (June 1955): 452-469.

647. Ripley, Randall B. "Power in the Post-World War II Senate." *Journal of Politics* 31 (May 1969): 465-492.

648. Ripley, Randall B. *Power in the Senate.* New York: St. Martin's, 1969.

649. Rogers, Lindsay. *The American Senate.* New York: A. A. Knopf, 1926.

650. Rosenthal, Alan. *Toward Majority Rule in the U.S. Senate.* New York: McGraw-Hill, 1962.

651. Rothman, David J. *Politics and Power: The United States Senate, 1869-1901.* Cambridge, Mass.: Harvard University Press, 1966.

652. Schulz, George J. *Monography Relating to the Creation of the Senate of the United States.* S. Doc. 45, 75th Cong., 1st sess. Washington: GPO, 1937.

653. *Senate Communications with the Public: A Compilation of Papers Prepared for the Commission on the Operation of the Senate.* 94th Cong., 2nd sess. Washington: GPO, 1977.

654. Stidham, Clara H. "Origin and Development of the United States Senate." Ph.D. dissertation, Cornell University, 1895.

655. Swanstrom, Roy. *The United States Senate, 1787-1801: A Dissertation on the First Fourteen Years of the Upper Legislative Body.* S. Doc. 64, 87th Cong., 1st sess. Washington: GPO, 1962.

656. Swanstrom, Roy. "The United States Senate, 1787-1801." Ph.D. dissertation, University of California, Berkeley, 1959.

657. Temperly, Harold W. V. *Senates and Upper Chambers, Their Use and Function in the Modern State.* London: Chapman and Hall, 1910.

658. Tucker, Ray T. and Barkley, Frederick R. *Sons of the Wild Jackass.* Boston: L. C. Page, 1932.

659. Uhlman, Thomas M. and Kritzer, Herbert M. "The Presidential Ambition of Democratic Senators: Its Timing and Impact." *Presidential Studies Quarterly* 9 (Summer 1979): 316-328.

660. U.S. Congress. Senate. *Creation of the Senate.* S. Doc. 75-45, 75th Cong., 1st sess. Washington: GPO, 1937.

661. U.S. Congress. Senate. *History of the Senate Seals: A History of the Seals Used by the Senate of the United States, 1804-1952.* S. Doc. 82-164, 82nd Cong., 2nd sess. Washington: GPO, 1953.

662. Von Holst, H. "Shall the Senate Rule the Republic?" *Forum* 16 (Nov. 1893): 263-271.

663. White, William S. *Citadel: The Story of the U.S. Senate.* New York: Harper and Row, 1956.

664. Wigmore, John H. "The Federal Senate as a Fifth Wheel." *Illinois Law Review* 24 (May 1929): 89-96.

665. Wigmore, John H. "Senate Pool of Power." *Illinois Law Review* 22 (Jan. 1928): 529-532.

666. Witmer, T. Richard. "The Aging of the Senate." *Political Science Quarterly* 79 (Dec. 1964): 526-541.

Rules and Practices

667. Abrams, Albert J. "Printing Management in the U.S. Senate." In *Senate Administration: A Compilation of Papers Prepared for the Commission on the Operation of the Senate,* pp. 89-97. 94th Cong., 2nd sess. Washington: GPO, 1976.

668. Abrams, Albert J. "Strategies for Management Improvements in the U.S. Senate." In *Senate Administration: A Compilation of Papers Prepared for the Commission on the Operation of the Senate,* pp. 3-16. 94th Cong., 2nd sess. Washington: GPO, 1976.

669. Axler, Bernard and Leiman, Eugene A. "Power of the Senate to Punish for Contempt." *Air Law Review* 6 (April 1935): 180-183.

670. Breslin, Janet. "Orientation and Training." In *Senators: Offices, Ethics and Pressures: A Compilation of Papers,* pp. 47-60. 94th Cong., 2nd sess. Washington: GPO, 1976.

671. Brigham, Maija. "Present Administrative Functions of the Secretary of the Senate, Sergeant at Arms, Architect of the Capitol, and the Rules Committee." In *Senate Administration: A Compilation of Papers Prepared for the Commission on the Operation of the Senate,* pp. 17-28. 94th Cong., 2nd sess. Washington: GPO, 1976.

672. Chlan, Frank. "Observations on Accounting and Fiscal Management in the Senate." In *Senate Administration: A Compilation of Papers Prepared for the Commission on the Operation of the Senate,* pp. 58-67. 94th Cong., 2nd sess. Washington: GPO, 1976.

673. Clem, Alan L. "Pair Voting Association in the 1966 United States Senate." *Rocky Mountain Social Science Journal* 6 (Oct. 1969): 91-107.

674. *Committees and Senate Procedures: A Compilation of Papers Prepared for the Commission on the Operation of the Senate.* 94th Cong., 2nd sess. Washington: GPO, 1977.

675. Dodd, William E. "The Principle of Instructing United States Senators." *South Atlantic Quarterly* 1 (Jan. 1902): 326-332.

676. Eaton, Clement. "Southern Senators and the Right of Instruction, 1789-1860." *Journal of Southern History* 18 (Aug. 1952): 303-319.

677. Eaton, Dorman B. *Secret Sessions of the Senate: Their Origin, Their Motive, Their Object, Their Effect.* New York: H. Bessey, 1886.

678. Fisher, Louis. "The Senate's Legislative Power." In *Techniques and Procedures for Analysis and Evaluation: A Compilation of Papers Prepared for the Commission on the Operation of the Senate,* pp. 3-13. 94th Cong., 2nd sess. Washington: GPO, 1977.

679. Frost, Stanley. "The Senate's Right to Meddle." *Outlook* 137, 7 May 1924, pp. 15-17.

680. Gammon, Gary E. "The Role of the United States Senate: Its Conception and Its Performance." Ph.D. dissertation, Claremont Graduate School, 1978.

681. Grotta, Gerald L. "Philip Freneau's Crusade for Open Sessions of the U.S. Senate." *Journalism Quarterly* 48 (Winter 1971): 667-671.

682. Holcombe, Arthur N. "The Role of the Senate in the Legislative Process." In his *Our More Perfect Union,* pp. 191-235. Cambridge, Mass.: Harvard University Press, 1950.

683. Jasper, Herbert N. "Scheduling of Senate Business." In *Committees and Senate Procedures: A Compilation of Papers Prepared for the Commission on the Operation of the Senate,* pp. 131-139. 94th Cong., 2nd sess. Washington: GPO, 1977.

684. Johnson, Allen. "Senate as an Executive Council." In his *Readings in American Constitutional History, 1776-1876,* pp. 160-167. Boston: Houghton Mifflin, 1912.

685. Keith, Robert. "The Use of Unanimous Consent in the Senate." In *Committees and Senate Procedures: A Compilation of Papers Prepared for the Commission on the Operation of the Senate,* pp. 140-168. 94th Cong., 2nd sess. Washington: GPO, 1977.

686. Keynes, Edward. "The Dirksen Amendment: A Study of Legislative Strategy, Tactics, and Public Policy." Ph.D. dissertation, University of Wisconsin, 1967.

687. Keynes, Edward. "The Senate Rules and the Dirksen Amendment: A Study in Legislative Strategy and Tactics." In *The Legislative Process in the U.S. Senate,* eds. Lawrence Pettit and Edward Keynes, pp. 107-149. Chicago: Rand McNally, 1969.

688. Lancaster, Lane W. "The Initiative of the United States Senate in Legislation, 1789-1809." *South Western Political and Social Science Quarterly* 9 (June 1928): 67-75.

689. Learned, Henry B. "Casting Votes of the Vice-Presidents, 1789-1915." *American Historical Review* 20 (April 1915): 571-576.

691. Lehman, Herbert H. "Reforms in Senatorial Procedures." *American Bar Association Journal* 37 (Oct. 1951): 774-776.

692. Leuchtenburg, William E. "The Disposition of Senators' Papers." *Prologue* 11 (Winter 1979): 251-255.

693. Low, A. Maurice. "Usurped Powers of the Senate." *American Political Science Review* 1 (Nov. 1906): 1-16.

694. McClendon, Robert E. "Violations of Secrecy *In Re* Senate Executive Sessions, 1789-1929." *American Historical Review* 51 (Oct. 1945): 35-54.

695. Peffer, William A. "The United States Senate: Its Privileges, Power and Functions, Its Rules and Methods of Doing Business." *North American Review* 167 (Aug. 1898): 176-190.

696. Pettit, Lawrence K. and Keynes, Edward, eds. *The Legislative Process in the U.S. Senate.* Chicago: Rand McNally, 1969.

697. Roberts, Dorothy. "Partisanship and the Advice and Consent Powers, 1945-1955." Ph.D. dissertation, University of Chicago, 1957.

698. Rogers, Lindsay. "The Most Remarkable of All Inventions of Modern Politics." *Parliamentary Affairs* 3 (Winter 1949): 104-113.

699. *Senate Administration: A Compilation of Papers Prepared for the Commission on the Operation of the Senate.* 94th Cong., 2nd sess. Washington: GPO, 1976.

700. Southwick, Thomas P. "Panel Urges Overhaul of Senate Operations." *Congressional Quarterly Weekly Report* 34 (Dec. 18, 1976): 3319-3320.

701. U.S. Congress. Senate. *Senate Legislative Procedural Flow (and Related House Action).* Washington: GPO, 1978.

702. U.S. Congress. Senate. *Senate Procedure,* compiled by Floyd M. Riddick. 93rd Cong., 1st sess. Washington: GPO, 1974.

703. U.S. Congress. Senate. *Statement of the Rules and Practice of the Senate of the United States in the Appointment of Committees from March 4, 1789 to March 14, 1863.* S. Doc. 1122, 62nd Cong., 3rd sess. Washington: GPO, 1913.

704. U.S. Congress. Senate. Commission on the Operation of the Senate. *Senators: Offices, Ethics and Pressures: A Compilation of Papers.* 94th Cong., 2nd sess. Washington: GPO, 1976.

705. U.S. Congress. Senate. Commission on the Operation of the Senate. *Toward a Modern Senate. Final Report of the Commission on the Operation of the Senate.* 94th Cong., 1st sess. Washington: GPO, 1976.

706. U.S. Congress. Senate. Parliamentarian. *Enactment of a Law: Procedural Steps in the Legislative Process.* S. Doc. 94-152, 94th Cong., 2nd sess. Washington: GPO, 1977.

707. U.S. Congress. Senate. Parliamentarian. *Senate Procedures: Presidents and Practices.* S. Doc. 21, 93rd Cong., 2nd sess. Washington: GPO, 1973.

708. U.S. Congress. Senate. Republican Policy Committee. *Senate Rules and the Senate as a Continuing Body.* S. Doc. 4, 83rd Cong., 1st sess. Washington: GPO, 1953.

709. U.S. Congress. Senate. Rules and Administration Committee. *Recommendations for Improving Program Review by Senate Committees.* Washington: GPO, 1978.

710. U.S. Congress. Senate. Subcommittee on Privileges and Elections. Senate Election, Expulsion and Censure Cases from 1793 to 1972. S. Doc. 92-7, 92nd Cong., 1st sess. Washington: GPO, 1972.

711. Valentine, C. Braxton. "The Office of the Senate Legislative Counsel." In *Committees and Senate Procedures: A Compilation of Papers Prepared for the Commission on the Operation of the Senate,* pp. 191-201. 94th Cong., 2nd sess. Washington: GPO, 1977.

712. Walker, Jack L. "Setting the Agenda in the U.S. Senate." In *Policymaking Role of Leadership in the Senate: A Compilation of Papers,* pp. 96-120. Washington: GPO, 1976.

713. Walker, Jack L. "Setting the Agenda in the U.S. Senate: A Theory of Problem Selection." *British Journal of Political science* 7 (Oct. 1977): 423-445.

714. Walsh, Samuel L. "Personnel Practices and Policies of the Sergeant of Arms, Secretary of the Senate and Architect of the Capitol." In *Senate Administration: A Compilation of Papers Prepared for the Commission on the Operation of the Senate,* pp. 68-88. 94th Cong., 2nd sess. Washington: GPO, 1976.

715. Wigmore, John H. "The President, Senate, Constitution and the Executive Order of May 8, 1926." *Illinois Law Review* 21 (June 1926): 142-146.

Debate

716. Bachrach, Peter. "Senate Debate on the Right to Jury Trial Versus the Right to Vote Controversy: A Case Study in Liberal Thought." *Ethics* 68 (April 1958): 210-216.

717. Bradley, Craig M. "Speech or Debate Clause: Bastion of Congressional Independence or Haven for Corruption?" *North Carolina Law Review* 57 (Feb. 1979): 197-230.

718. Bryan, J. W. "Constitutional Aspects of the Senatorial Debate upon the Rate Bill." *American Law Review* 41 (Nov. 1907): 801-844.

719. Cain, Earl R. "An Analysis of Debates on Neutrality Legislation in the United States Senate, 1935-1941." Ph.D. dissertation, Northwestern University, 1951.

720. Camp, Leon R. "The Senate Debates on the Treaty of Paris of 1898." Ph.D. dissertation, Pennsylvania State University, 1969.

721. Cella, Alexander J. "Doctrine of Legislative Privilege of Speech or Debate: The New Interpretation as a Threat to Legislative Coequality." *Suffolk University Law Review* 8 (Summer 1974): 1019-1095.

722. Dedmon, Donald N. "The Functions of Discourse in the Hawaiian Statehood Debates." *Speech Monographs* 33 (Mar. 1966): 30-39.

723. Edwards, Richard C. "Economic Sophistication in Nineteenth Century Congressional Tariff Debates." *Journal of Economic History* 30 (Dec. 1970): 802-838.

724. Engdahl, Lynn H. "A Study of Debate in the United States Senate as Revealed by the 1957 Debate over Civil Rights." Ph.D. dissertation, University of Iowa, 1969.

725. Fisher, Walter R. "An Analysis of the Arguments in the Senate Debate on the Crittenden Compromise Resolutions, 1860-1861." Ph.D. dissertation, University of Iowa, 1960.

726. Godfrey, Donald G. "A Rhetorical Analysis of the Congressional Debates on Broadcast Regulation in the United States, 1927." Ph.D. dissertation, University of Washington, 1975.

727. Hopkins, Bruce R. "The Decline of the Congressional Art." *American Bar Association Journal* 53 (May 1967): 480-484.

728. Kane, Peter E. "Extended Debate and the Rules of the United States Senate." *Quarterly Journal of Speech* 57 (Feb. 1971): 43-49.

729. Kane, Peter E. "The Senate Debate on the 1964 Civil Rights Act." Ph.D. dissertation, Purdue University, 1967.

730. Kutner, Luis. "Due Process of Debate: A Senator's Dilemma." *Baylor Law Review* 26 (Summer 1974): 287-330.

731. Lehnen, Robert G. "Behavior on the Senate Floor: An Analysis of Debate in the U.S. Senate." *Midwest Journal of Political Science* 11 (Nov. 1967): 505-521.

732. McCoy, Pressley C. "An Analysis of the Debates on Recognition of the Union of Soviet Socialist Republics, in the United States Senate, 1917-1934." Ph.D. dissertation, Northwestern University, 1954.

733. McPherson, Elizabeth G. "The Southern States and the Reporting of Senate Debates, 1789-1802." *Journal of Southern History* 12 (May 1946): 223-246.

734. Moore, Carl M. "The Issues, Strategies, and Structure of the Senate Debate over the Full Employment Bill of 1945." Ph.D. dissertation, Wayne State University, 1972.

735. Murphy, John M. "A Vote for Common Sense: The United States Senate and the SST." Ph.D. dissertation, New School for Social Research, 1974.

736. Peeples, Dale H. "The Senate Debate on the Philippine Legislation of 1902." Ph.D. dissertation, University of Georgia, 1964.

737. Quadro, David F. "An Analysis of the Arguments Used in the United States Senate Debates on Negro Suffrage, 1864-1869." Ph.D. dissertation, University of California at Los Angeles, 1972.

738. Rhine, Robly D. "The Debate on the Foote Resolution, United States Senate, 1829-1830." Ph.D. dissertation, University of Wisconsin, 1967.

739. Yaremchuk, William A. "A Rhetorical Study of Congressional Speaking During the Movement to Establish the National Cancer Institute 1927-1937." Ph.D. dissertation, New York University, 1976.

Filibuster and Cloture

740. Beeman, Richard R. "Unlimited Debate in the Senate: The First Phase." *Political Science Quarterly* 83 (Sept. 1968): 419-434.

741. Bookbinder, Hyman H. "Dethroning King Filibuster." *American Federationist* 65 (Nov. 1958): 16-17.

742. Bormann, Ernest. "The Southern Senator's Filibuster on Civil Rights." *Southern Speech Communication Journal* 27 (Spring 1962): 183-194.

743. Burdette, Franklin L. *Filibustering in the Senate*. Princeton, N.J.: Princeton University Press, 1940.

744. Carlisle, Margo. "Changing the Rules of the Game in the U.S. Senate." *Policy Review* 7 (Winter 1979): 79-92.

745. Cooper, Ann. "The Senate and the Filibuster: War of Nerves—and Hardball." *Congressional Quarterly Weekly Report* 36 (Sept. 2, 1978): 2307-2310.

746. Donnelly, Thomas C. "Freedom of Speech in the Senate: A Restatement of the Case in the Light of Contemporary Events." *Social Science* 7 (July 1932): 225-236.

747. Drew, Elizabeth B. "Politics of Cloture." *Reporter* 31, 16 July 1964, pp. 19-23.

748. "Election to Strengthen Senate Anti-Filibuster Forces." *Congressional Quarterly Weekly Report* 16 (Oct. 17, 1958): 1316-1319.

749. "History, Techniques of Senate Filibusters." *Congressional Quarterly Weekly Report* 15 (April 19, 1957): 489-491.

750. "History, Techniques of Senate Filibusters." *Congressional Quarterly Weekly Report* 18 (Mar. 4, 1960): 337-339.

751. "History, Techniques of Senate Filibusters." *Congressional Quarterly Weekly Report* 20 (April 27, 1962): 661-662.

752. Javits, Jacob K. "Again the Senate Debates Unlimited Debate." *New York Times Magazine*, 3 August 1958, pp. 11, 41-42.

753. Malbin, Michael J. "Congress Report 'Compromise by Senate Eases Anti-Filibuster Rule.'" *National Journal* 7 (March 15, 1975): 397-400.

754. Myers, Francis J. "Limitation of Debate in the United States Senate: Discussion of the Issues and Results of the Fateful 1949 Senate Filibuster over Filibustering." *Temple Law Quarterly* 23 (July 1949): 1-12.

755. Pepper, George W. "A Fifty-One Percent Cloture." *The Forum* 74 (Oct. 1925): 586-588.

756. Pepper, George W. "Senate Cloture." *University of Pennsylvania Law Review* 74 (Dec. 1925): 131-138.

757. Potterf, Rex M. "Limitation of Debate in the United States Senate: A Phase of the Law-Making Power." *Indiana Law Journal* 1 (Marc. 1926): 139-148.

758. "Reformers Consider Filibuster Compromise." *Congressional Quarterly Weekly Report* 33 (Mar. 1, 1975): 448-462.

759. Rogers, Lindsay and Javits, Jacob K. "The Filibuster Debate." *The Reporter* 20, 8 Jan. 1959, pp. 21-25.

760. Rundquist, Paul S. *Recent Filibuster Trends*. Washington: Congressional Research Service, 1976.

761. "Senate Close to Accord on Filibuster Change." *Congressional Quarterly Weekly Report* 33 (Mar. 8, 1975): 502-505.

762. "Senate Limits Post-Cloture Filibusters." *Congressional Quarterly Weekly Report* 37 (Feb. 24, 1979): 319-320.

763. "Senators Propose to Limit Debate, Cut Out Filibuster." *Congressional Quarterly Weekly Report* 14 (Nov. 30, 1956): 1391-1393.

764. Shuman, Howard E. "Senate Rules and the Civil Rights Bills." *American Political Science Review* 51 (Dec. 1957): 955-975.

765. "26 Senators Hold Cloture Balance of Power." *Congressional Quarterly Weekly Report* 15 (July 26, 1957): 881-884.

766. U.S. Congress. Senate. Committee on Rules and Administration. *Senate Cloture Rule: Limitation of Debates in the Congress of the United States, and Legislative History of Paragraphs 2 and 3 of Rule XXII of the Standing Rules of the U.S. Senate.* Washington: GPO, 1975.

767. Wheildon, L. B. "Majority Cloture for the Senate." *Educational Research Reports* 1 (Mar. 1947): 119-218.

768. "Will the Senate Change Rule 22?" *Congressional Quarterly Weekly Report* 17 (Jan. 2, 1959): 13-20.

769. Wolfinger, Raymond E. "Filibusters: Majority Rule, Presidential Leadership and Senate Norms." In *Readings on Congress,* ed. Raymond E. Wolfinger, pp. 286-305. Englewood Cliffs, N.J.: Prentice-Hall, 1971.

Congressional Veto

770. Abourezk, James. "The Congressional Veto: A Contemporary Response to Executive Encroachment on Legislative Prerogative." *Indiana Law Journal* 52 (Winter 1977): 323-343.

771. Bolton, John R. "The Legislative Veto: Unseparating the Powers. Washington: American Enterprise Institute for Public Policy Research, 1977.

772. Bruff, Harold H. and Gellhorn, Ernest. "Congressional Control of Administrative Regulation: A Study of Legislative Vetoes." *Harvard Law Review* 90 (May 1977): 1369-1440.

773. Cohen, Richard E. "Junior Members Seek Approval for Wider Use of the Legislative Veto." *National Journal* 9 (Aug. 6, 1977): 1228-1232.

774. "Congressional Veto: Constitutionality Challenged." *Congressional Quarterly Weekly Report* 34 (July 31, 1976): 2029-2030.

775. Cooper, Joseph. "The Legislative Veto and the Constitution." *George Washington Law Review* 30 (Mar. 1962): 467-516.

776. Cooper, Joseph. "The Legislative Veto: Its Promise and Its Perils." *Public Policy* 7 (1956): 128-174.

777. Dixon, Robert G. "The Congressional Veto and Separation of Powers: The Executive on a Leash." *North Carolina Law Review* 56 (April 1978): 423-494.

778. Fisher, Louis. "A Political Context for Legislative Vetoes." *Political Science Quarterly* 93 (Summer 1978): 241-254.

779. Javits, Jacob K. and Klein, Gary J. "Congressional Oversight and Legislative Veto: A Constitutional Analysis." *New York University Law Review* 52 (June 1977): 455-497.

780. "Legislative Veto in the Arms Export Control Act of 1976." *Law and Policy in International Business* 9 (1977): 1029-1044.

781. Mansfield, Harvey C. "Legislative Veto and the Deportation of Aliens." *Public Administration Review* 1 (Spring 1941): 281-286.

782. Melsheimer, John T. *Congressional Veto of Executive Actions.* Washington: Congressional Research Service, 1976.

783. Miller, Arthur S. and Knapp, George M. "Congressional Veto: Preserving the Constitutional Framework." *Indiana Law Journal* 52 (Winter 1977): 367-395.

784. Millett, John D. and Rogers, Lindsay. "The Legislative Veto and the Reorganization Act of 1939." *Public Administration Review* 1 (Winter 1941): 176-189.

785. Nicola, Thomas J., Norton, Clark F., and Melsheimer, John T. *Congressional Veto of Executive Actions.* Washington: Congressional Research Service, 1979.

786. Norton, Clark F. *Congressional Review, Defferal and Disapproval of Executive Actions: A Summary and an Inventory of Statutory Authority.* Washington: Congressional Research Service, 1976.

787. Riggs, Richard A. "Separation of Powers: Congressional Riders and the Veto Power." *University of Michigan Journal of Law Reform* 6 (Spring 1973): 735-759.

788. Schauffler, Peter. "The Legislative Veto Revisited." *Public Policy* 8 (1958): 296-327.

789. Stewart, Geoffrey. S. "Constitutionality of the Legislative Veto." *Harvard Journal on Legislation* 13 (June 1976): 593-619.

790. U.S. Congress. House. Rules Committee. *Studies on the Legislative Veto.* 96th Cong., 2nd sess. Washington: GPO, 1980.

Seniority

791. Abram, Michael and Cooper, Joseph. "The Rise of Seniority in the House of Representatives." *Polity* 1 (Fall 1968): 52-84.

792. Balch, Stephen H. "Getting That Extra Edge: Seniority and Early Appointments to the United States Senate." *Polity* 11 (Fall 1978): 138-146.

793. Berg, John C. "The Effects of Seniority Reform on Three House Committees in the 94th Congress." In *Legislative Reform: The Policy Impact,* ed. Leroy N. Riselbach, pp. 49-59. Lexington, Mass.: Lexington Books, 1978.

794. Berg, John C. "Reforming Seniority in the House of Representatives: Did It Make Any Difference." *Policy Studies Journal* 5 (Summer 1977): 437-443.

795. Brooks, Richard S. "The Sectional and Seniority Bases of the Standing Committee Chairmanships of the United States House of Representatives, 1889-1954." Ph.D. dissertation, University of Oklahoma, 1956.

796. Butler, Robert N. "Fighting Seniority with Bigotry." *Washington Monthly* 3 (June 1971): 37-42.

797. Celler, Emmanuel. "Seniority Rule in Congress." *Western Political Quarterly* 14 (Mar. 1961): 160-167.

798. "Challenges of Seniority System by Both Parties." *Congressional Quarterly Weekly Report* 29 (Jan. 15, 1971): 134-140.

799. Clem, Alan L. "Do Representatives Increase in Conservatism as They Increase in Seniority." *Journal of Politics* 39 (Feb. 1977): 193-200.

800. Cohen, David. "The Continuing Challenge of Congressional Reform." *Democratic Review* 1 (Feb.-Mar. 1975): 21-24.

801. "Congressional Seniority: A Crusty Tradition." *Congressional Quarterly Weekly Report* 31 (Jan. 6, 1973): 21-26.

802. Democratic Study Group. *The Seniority System in the U.S. House of Representatives.* Washington: Democratic Study Group, 1970.

803. Farnsworth, David N. and Stanga John E. "Seniority, Reform and Democratic Committee Assignments in the House of Representatives." *Policy Studies Journal* 5 (Summer 1977): 431-436.

804. Goldstein, Dan and Scamell, Richard. "Congressional Seniority and Unequal Representation: A Proposal for Reform." *Texas Law Review* 51 (April 1973): 722-742.

805. Goodwin, George. " Seniority System in Congress." *American Political Science Review* 53 (June 1959): 412-436.

806. Hawley, Jonathan P. "Seniority and Committee Leadership: The Emergence of Choice." In *To Be a Congressman: The Promise and the Power*, eds. Sven Groenning and Jonathan P. Hawley, pp. 121-150. Washington: Acropolis Books, 1973.

807. Hays, Janet. *Organizations That Rate Members of Congress on Their Voting Records.* Washington: Congressional Research Service, 1978.

808. Hinckley, Barbara. "Seniority in the Committee Leadership Selection of Congress." *American Journal of Political Science* 13 (Nov. 1969): 613-630.

809. Hinckley, Barbara. "Seniority 1975: Old Theories Confront New Facts." *British Journal of Political Science* 6 (Oct. 1976): 383-399.

810. Hinckley, Barbara. *The Seniority System in Congress.* Bloomington: Indiana University Press, 1971.

811. "Industry Has Strong Friends on Finance Committee." *Congressional Quarterly Weekly Report* 27 (Sept. 26, 1969): 1787-1795.

812. Krock, Arthur. "The Lords Proprietors of Congress." *New York Times Magazine*, 22 Jan. 1967, pp. 28-29, 74-77.

813. Lindsay, John V. "The Seniority System." In *We Propose: A Modern Congress*, ed. Mary McInnis, pp. 23-33. New York: McGraw-Hill, 1966.

814. Malbin, Michael J. "Congress Report 'House Democrats Oust Senior Members from Power'." *National Journal* 7 (Jan. 25, 1975): 129-134.

815. Neuberger, Richard L. "A Senator's Case Against Seniority." *New York Times Magazine,* 7 April 1957, pp. 15, 38, 42, 44, 47.

816. "New Setbacks for House Seniority System." *Congressional Quarterly Weekly Report* 37 (Feb. 3, 1979): 183-187.

817. Ornstein, Norman J. and Rohde, David W. "Seniority and Future Power in Congress." In *Congress in Change: Evolution and Reform*, ed. Norman J. Ornstein, pp. 72-87. New York: Praeger, 1975.

818. Packwood, Robert W. "The Senate Seniority System." In *Congress in Change: Evolution and Reform*, ed. Norman J. Ornstein, pp. 60-71. New York: Praeger, 1975.

819. Pollock, James K. "The Seniority Rule in Congress." *North American Review* 222 (Dec. 1925): 235-245.

820. Polsby, Nelson W., Gallaher, Miriam, and Rundquist, Barry S. "Growth of the Seniority System in the U.S. House of Representatives." *American Political Science Review* 63 (Sept. 1969): 787-807.

821. Ritt, Leonard G. "Committee Position, Seniority, and the Distribution of Government Expenditures." *Public Policy* 24 (Fall 1976): 463-489.

822. "Seniority Rule: Change in Procedure, Not In Practice." *Congressional Quarterly Weekly Report* 31 (Jan. 27, 1973): 137-138.

823. Stanga, John E. and Farnsworth, David N. "Seniority and Democratic Reforms in the House of Representatives: Committees and Subcommittees." In *Legislative Reform: The Policy Impact.* ed. Leroy N. Rieselbach, pp. 35-47. Lexington, Mass.: Lexington Books, 1978.

824. Udall, Stewart L. "A Defense of the Seniority System." *New York Times Magazine*, 13 Jan. 1957, pp. 17, 64, 67.

825. Vogler, David J. "Flexibility in the Congressional Seniority System: Conference Representation." *Polity* 2 (Summer 1970): 494-506.

826. Wallenfang, John M. "Attitudes of Democratic Representatives Toward Seniority Reform in the Ninety-Third Congress." Ph.D. dissertation, Purdue University, 1974.

827. Walsh, John. "Reform in the House: Amending the Seniority Rule." *Science* 179 (Mar. 1973): 877-881.

828. Wolanin, Thomas R. "Committee Seniority and the Choice of House Subcommittee Chairmen: 80th-91st Congresses." *Journal of Politics* 36 (Aug. 1974): 687-702.

829. Wolfinger, Raymond E. and Heifetz, Joan. "Safe Seats, Seniority, and Power in Congress." *American Political Science Review* 59 (June 1965): 337-349.

III. Congressional Reform

Reform of Congress

General Studies

830. Abrams, Paul F. "Legislative Reform: A Question of Reality." *Publius* 4 (Spring 1974): 123-131.

831. Adler, Madeleine W. "Congressional Reform: An Exploratory Case." Ph.D. dissertation, University of Wisconsin, 1969.

832. American Political Science Association. Committee on Political Parties. *Toward a More Responsible Two-Party System. A Report of the Committee on Political Parties.* New York: Rinehart, 1950.

833. Anderson, Bruce L. "Legislative Reform and the Political System: A Survey of British and American Proposals." *South Carolina Journal of Political Science* 4 (1972): 88-111.

834. Auster, R. D. "Some Economic Determinants of the Characteristics of Public Workers." In *Economics of Public Choice,* eds. Robert D. Leiter and Gerald Sirkin, pp. 185-198. New York: City College and the City University of New York, 1975.

835. Bailey, Stephen K. "Is Congress Obsolete." In *Critical Issues and Decisions,* ed. Jerold N. Willmore, pp. 105-121. Washington: U.S. Department of Agriculture, 1962.

836. Barnett, James D. "One House of Congress as Two." *American Political Science Review* 19 (Feb. 1925): 82-83.

837. Bazelon, David T. "Non-Legislative Arts." *Commentary* 38 (Dec. 1964): 82-85.

838. Beard, M. K. and Burch, V. "Conform or Reform." *Engage/Social Action* 1 (Jan. 1973): 22-28.

839. Bendiner, Robert. "Just How Bad Is Congress: A Balance Sheet, as of 1952." *Commentary* 13 (Feb. 1952): 135-141.

840. Bernick, E. Lee and Wiggins, Charles W. "Legislative Reform and Legislative Turnover." In *Legislative Reform: The Policy Impact,* ed. Leroy N. Rieselbach, pp. 23-34. Lexington, Mass.: Lexington Books, 1978.

841. Bezold, Clement. "Strategic Policy Assessment and Congressional Reform: The Future in Committee." Ph.D. dissertation, University of Florida, 1976.

842. Borchardt, Kurt. "Legislative Supremacy and Congressional Reorganization." *Georgetown Law Journal* 34 (Mar. 1946): 310-322.

843. Brenner, Philip J. "Congressional Reform: Analyzing the Analysts." *Harvard Journal on Legislation* 14 (April 1977): 651-681.

844. Broughton, Philip S. *For a Stronger Congress.* New York: Public Affairs Committee, 1946.

845. Bullock, Charles S. "Congress in the Sunshine." In *Legislative Reform: The Policy Impact,* ed. Leroy N. Riselbach, pp. 209-221. Lexington, Mass.: Lexington Books, 1978.

846. Burnham, Walter D. "Has Congress a Future?" *The Nation,* 29 June 1963, pp. 546-548, 556.

847. Case, Clifford P. "Toward Responsible Government: Revitalizing Congress." *Social Action* 30 (Mar. 1964): 9-13.

848. Chamberlin, Lawrence H. "Congress: Diagnosis and Prescription." *Political Science Quarterly* 60 (Sept. 1945): 437-445.

849. Childs, Richard S. "What's the Matter with Congress?" *National Municipal Review* 13 (Nov. 1924): 621-626.

850. Clark, Joseph S. "The Case for Congressional Reform." In *The Senate Institution,* ed. Nathaniel S. Preston, pp. 175-191. New York: Van Nostrand Reinhold, 1969.

851. Clark, Joseph S., ed. *Congressional Reform: Problems and Prospects.* New York: Thomas Y. Crowell, 1965.

852. Clark, Joseph S. "Making Congress Work." In *The Crossroad Papers: A Look into the American Future,* ed. Hans J. Morganthau, pp. 205-221. New York: W. W. Norton, 1965.

853. Clark, Joseph S. "The Hesitant Senate." *Atlantic Monthly* 209 (Mar. 1962): 55-60.

854. Clark, Joseph S. "Toward a Modern Congress: The Crisis in Confidence and Plan for Reform." *American Association of University Women Journal* 61 (May 1968): 175-178.

855. Clubb, Jerome M. "Congressional Opponents of Reform 1901–1913." Ph.D. dissertation, University of Washington, 1963.

856. Cohen, Richard E. "The 96th Congress Is In for an Overhaul." *National Journal* 10 (Nov. 25, 1978): 1908-1911.

857. Committee for Economic Development. *Making Congress More Effective: A Statement on National Policy.* New York: CED, 1970.

858. "Congress Long the Object of Change and Reform." *Congressional Quarterly Weekly Report* 21 (June 7, 1963): 859-868.

859. Congressional Quarterly. *Congressional Reform: An Examination of the Structure, Operation, Rules and Customs of Congress, and Proposals for Revision.* Rev. ed. Washington: Congressional Quarterly, 1964.

860. Cooper, Joseph. "Strengthening the Congress: An Organizational Analysis." *Harvard Journal on Legislation* 12 (April 1975): 307-368.

861. Cowan, Wayne H. "Reform in Congress." *Christianity and Crisis* 23 (April 1963): 55-56.

862. Coyle, David C. "Reorganizing Congress." *Virginia Quarterly Review* 24 (Winter 1948): 13-26.

863. Davidson, Roger H. "Our Changing Congress: The Inside (and Outside) Story." In *The Presidency and the Congress: A Shifting Balance of Power?* eds. William S. Livingston, Lawrence C. Dodd and Richard L. Schott, pp. 341-362. Austin: Lyndon B. Johnson School of Public Affairs, University of Texas, 1979.

864. Davidson, Roger H., Kovenock, David M., and O'Leary, Michael K. *Congress in Crisis: Politics and Congressional Reform.* Belmont, Calif.: Wadsworth, 1966.

865. Davis, Eric L. "Legislative Reform and the Decline of Presidential Influence on Capitol Hill." *British Journal of Political Science* 9 (Oct. 1979): 465-479.

866. De Grazia, Alfred. "Toward a New Model of Congress." In *Twelve Studies of the Organization of Congress,* ed. Alfred de Grazia, pp. 1-22. Washington: American Enterprise Institute for Public Policy Research, 1966.

867. De Grazia, Alfred. *Toward a New Model of Congress: A First Report on "Project Politist."* Washington: American Enterprise Institute for Public Policy Research, 1965.

868. Demkovich, Linda E. "Congress's New Consumer Faces Say It's Time for Some Tinkering." *National Journal* 9 (April 23, 1977): 634-637.

869. Esch, Marvin L. "The Need for Reform." In *Republican Papers*, ed. Melvin R. Laird, pp. 489-500. New York: Praeger, 1968.

870. Eubanks, Cecil L. "A Structural-Functional Analysis of Congressional Reform in the Twentieth Century." Ph.D. dissertation, University of Michigan, 1970.

871. Fenno, Richard F. "If, as Ralph Nader Says, Congress Is 'The Broken Branch,' How Come We Love Our Congressmen So Much." In *Congress in Change: Evolution and Reform,* ed. Norman J. Ornstein, pp. 277-287. New York: Praeger, 1975.

872. Fenno, Richard F. "Strengthening a Congressional Strength." In *Congress Reconsidered,* eds. Lawrence C. Dodd and Bruce I. Oppenheimer, pp. 261-268. New York: Praeger, 1977.

873. Galloway, George B. "Congress: Problem, Diagnosis, Proposals." *American Political Science Review* 36 (Dec. 1942): 1091-1092.

874. Galloway, George B. *Congressional Reorganization Revisited.* College Park, Md.: Bureau of Governmental Research, College of Business and Public Administration, University of Maryland, 1956.

875. Galloway, George B. "Congressional Reorganization: Unfinished Business." In *The Philosophy and Policies of Woodrow Wilson,* ed. Earl Latham, pp. 214-227. Chicago: University of Chicago Press, 1958.

876. Galloway, George B. "A Legislative Timetable for Congress." *American Bar Association Journal* 34 (Dec. 1948): 1114-1115.

877. Galloway, George B. *Next Steps in Congressional Reform.* Urbana: University of Illinois Press, 1952.

878. Galloway, George B. "On Reforming Congress." *Free World* 7 (June 1944): 518-523.

879. Haines, Wilder H. "Congressional Caucus of Today." *American Political Science Review* 9 (Nov. 1915): 696-706.

880. Heller, Robert. *Strengthening the Congress.* Washington: National Planning Association, 1945.

881. Heller, Robert. *Strengthening the Congress: A Progress Report.* Washington: National Planning Association, 1947.

882. Hodgkin, Douglas I. "Congress and the President, 1968 Style." *Polity* 1 (Winter 1968): 271-276.

883. Hopkins, Bruce R. "Congressional Reform Advances in the Ninety-Third Congress." *American Bar Association Journal* 60 (Jan. 1974): 47-51.

884. Hopkins, Bruce R. "Congressional Reform and the Ninety-Second Congress." *American Bar Association Journal* 59 (Jan. 1973): 33-37.

885. Hopkins, Bruce R. "Congressional Reform: Toward a Modern Congress." *Notre Dame Lawyer* 47 (Feb. 1972): 442-513.

886. Hopkins, Bruce R. "The Ninety-Fourth: A Congress in Transition." *American Bar Association Journal* 61 (Jan. 1976): 65-71.

887. Hopkins, Bruce R. "The Ninety-Third: An Authentic Reform Congress." *American Bar Association Journal* 61 (Jan. 1975): 37-41.

888. Hopkins, Bruce R. "The Ninety-Fourth Congress: Congressional Reform Progresses." *American Bar Association Journal* 63 (Feb. 1977): 211-215.

889. Hopkins, Bruce R. and Oleszek, Walter J. "Ninety-Fifth Congress: Legislative Reform in 1977." *American Bar Association Journal* 64 (Mar. 1978): 341-347.

890. Humphrey, Hubert H. "Modernizing Congress." *American Federationist* 70 (April 1963): 1-4.

891. Johannes, John R. "Statutory Reporting Requirements: Information and Influence for Congress." In *Comparative Legislative Reforms and Innovations,* eds. Abdo I. Baaklini and James J. Heaphey, pp. 33-60. Albany, N.Y.: Comparative Development Studies Center, Graduate School of Public Affairs, State University of New York, 1977.

892. "Joint Committee Proposes Congressional Reform." *Congressional Quarterly Weekly Report* 24 (July 29, 1966): 1627-1629.

893. Jones, Charles O. "How Reform Changes Congress." In *Legislative Reform and Public Policy,* eds. Susan Welch and John G. Peters, pp. 11-29. New York: Praeger, 1977.

894. Jones, Charles O. "Will Reform Change Congress." In *Congress Reconsidered,* eds. Lawrence C. Dodd and Bruce I. Oppenheimer, pp. 247-260. New York: Praeger, 1977.

895. Kefauver, Estes. "What's to Be Done About Congress." *New York Times Magazine,* 11 Sept. 1949, pp. 9, 32-34,

896. Kefauver, Estes. "The Challenge to Congress." *Federal Bar Association Journal* 6 (April 1945): 325-332.

897. Kefauver, Estes. "The Need for Better Executive Legislative Teamwork in the National Government." *American Political Science Review* 38 (April 1944): 317-324.

898. LaFollette, Robert M. "Systematizing Congressional Control." *American Political Science Review* 41 (Feb. 1947): 58-68.

899. Lees, John D. "Reorganization and Reform in Congress: Legislative Responses to Political and Social Change." *Government and Opposition* 8 (Spring 1973): 195-216.

900. "Legislative Reform: Will It Be Real or Imaginary." *Congressional Quarterly Weekly Report* 28 (Dec. 25, 1970): 3061-3064.

901. Leventhal, Paul L. "Congressional Report 'Political Reaction Overshadows Reform Aim of Massive Nader Congress Study'." *National Journal* 4 (Sept. 23, 1972): 1483-1495.

902. Lippmann, Walter. "A Critique of Congress." *Newsweek,* 20 Jan. 1964, pp. 18-19.

903. Lowe, David E. "The Bolling Committee and the Politics of Reorganization." *Capitol Studies* 6 (Spring 1978): 39-61.

904. Lowe, David E. "The 'Impossible Task': Organizational Innovation, Congressional Reform, and the Bolling Committee." Ph.D. dissertation, Johns Hopkins University, 1976.

905. Maass, Arthur A. "Congress Has Been Maligned." *Social Action* 30 (Mar. 1964): 23-28.

906. McClellan, James. "State of the American Congress." *Modern Age* 21 (Summer 1977): 227-239.

907. Malbin, Michael J. "Congress Report 'Senate, House to Vote on Legislative Procedure Changes.'" *National Journal* 7 (Jan. 11, 1975): 62-66.

908. Malbin, Michael J. "New Democrats Don't See Eye to Eye with Their Senior Comrades." *National Journal* 9 (July 9, 1977): 1080-1082.

909. Malbin, Michael J. "The Obey Commission Report: The House Braces for More Reform." *National Journal* 9 (Sept. 3, 1977): 1368-1371.

910. Mezey, Michael L. "Legislative Policy-Making Through the Imposition of Constraints." *Policy Studies Journal* 5 (Summer 1977): 402-407.

911. Monroney, A. S. Mike. "Modernizing the Congress: A Must." *Tax Review* 26 (Mar. 1965): 9-12.

912. Monroney, A. S. Mike and Kuchel, Thomas H. "Reform of Congress: The Congress and America's Future—A Discussion." *Political Science Quarterly* 80 (Dec. 1965): 606-620.

913. Nelson, Dalmas H. and Price, Eugene C. "Realignment, Readjustment, Reform: The Impact of the Ombudsman on American Constitutional and Political Institutions." *American Academy of Political and Social Sciences, Annals* 377 (May 1968): 128-137.

914. O'Leary, Michael K., ed. *Congressional Reorganization: Problems and Prospects: A Conference Report.* Hanover, N.H.: Public Affairs Center, Dartmouth College, 1964.

915. Oleszek, Walter J. "A Perspective on Congressional Reform." In *Legislative Reform and Public Policy,* eds. Susan Welch and John G. Peters, pp. 3-10, New York: Praeger, 1977.

916. Ornstein, Norman J. and Rohde, David W. "Political Parties and Congressional Reform." In *Parties and Elections in an Anti-Party Age: American Politics and the Crisis of Confidence,* ed. Jeff Fishel, pp. 280-294. Bloomington: Indiana University Press, 1978.

917. Outland, George E. "Congress Still Needs Reorganization." *Western Political Quarterly* 1 (June 1948): 154-164.

918. Patterson, Samuel C. "Legislative Research and Legislative Reform: Evaluating Regime Policy." *Publius* 4 (Spring 1974): 109-115.

919. Pennock, J. Roland. "Responsiveness, Responsibility and Majority Rule." *American Political Science Review* 46 (Sept. 1962): 790-807.

920. Perkins, John. "Congressional Self-Improvement." *American Political Science Review* 38 (June 1944): 499-511.

921. Price, David E. "The Ambivalence of Congressional Reform." *Public Administration Review* 34 (Nov./Dec. 1974): 601-608.

922. Reilly, John F. "Is Congress Outmoded?: A Study of Proposals for Reorganization." *Goergetown Law Journal* 34 (Jan. 1946): 201-219.

923. Renfro, William L. "The Future and Congressional Reform." *American Bar Association Journal* 64 (April 1978): 561-563.

924. "Republicans Seek Vote on Democrats Reforms." *Congressional Quarterly Weekly Report* 34 (July 24, 1976): 1957-1961.

925. Reuss, Henry S. "Barriers to Democratic Rule." *Social Action* 30 (Mar. 1964): 18-23.

926. Reuss, Henry S. "An 'Ombudsman' for America." *New York Times Magazine,* 13 Sept. 1964, pp. 30, 134, 135.

927. Rhodes, John J. *The Futile System: How to Unchain Congress and Make the System Work Again.* Garden City, N.Y.: Doubleday, 1976.

928. Rieselbach, Leroy N. *Congressional Reform in the Seventies.* Morristown, N.J.: General Learning Press, 1977.

929. Rieselbach, Leroy N. "Congressional Reform: Some Policy Implications." *Policy Studies Journal* 4 (Winter 1975): 180-188.

930. Rieselbach, Leroy N. "In the Wake of Watergate: Congressional Reform?" *Review of Politics* 36 (July 1974): 371-393.

931. Rieselbach, Leroy N., ed. *Legislative Reform: The Policy Impact.* Lexington, Mass.: Lexington Books, 1978.

932. Rieselbach, Leroy N. "Reform, Change, and Legislative Policy Making." In his *Legislative Reform: The Policy Impact*, pp. 1-7. Lexington, Mass.: Lexington Books, 1978.

933. Rohde, David W. and Shepsle, Kenneth A. "Membership Turnover and Congressional Reform: The More Things Change, The More They May or May Not Stay the Same." *Policy Studies Journal* 5 (Summer 1977): 469-476.

934. Rohde, David W. and Shepsle, Kenneth A. "Thinking About Legislative Reform." In *Legislative Reform: The Policy Impact*, ed. Leroy N. Rieselbach, pp. 9-21. Lexington, Mass.: Lexington Books, 1978.

935. Schattschneider, Elmer E. "Congress in Conflict." *Yale Review* 41 (Winter 1952): 181-193.

936. Schwartz, Bernard. "A Congressional Ombudsman Is Feasible." *American Bar Association Journal* 56 (Jan. 1970): 57-59.

937. Scoble, Harry M. "Political Money: A Study of Contributors to the National Committee for an Effective Congress." *Midwest Journal of Political Science* 7 (Aug. 1963): 229-253.

938. Shaw, L. Earl. "A Prolegomenon to Responsive Legislative Reform." *Policy Studies Journal* 5 (Summer 1977): 395-401.

939. Shinn, Roger L. "Urgency of Congressional Reform." *Christianity and Crisis* 24 (Dec. 1964): 257-258.

940. Silbert, Edward M. "Support for Reform Among Congressional Democrats, 1897-1913." Ph.D. dissertation, University of Florida, 1966.

941. Sittig, Robert F. "United States Congress and Internal Reform." *Vanderbilt Law Review* 20 (Dec. 1966): 61-78.

942. Smith, George H. and Davis, Richard P. "Do the Voters Want the Parties Changes?" *Public Opinion Quarterly* 11 (Summer 1947): 236-243.

943. Sparkman, John J. "Let Us Preserve Safeguards." *Social Action* 30 (Mar. 1964): 14-18.

944. Steel, Ronald. "Is Congress Obsolete." *Commentary* 38 (Sept. 1964): 59-64.

945. Szulc, Tad. "Is Congress Obsolete?" *Saturday Review*, 3 March, 1979, pp. 20-23.

946. Tarr, David R. "Congressional Reorganization Bill Provokes Controversy in House." *National Journal* 2 (Jan. 24, 1970): 197-199.

947. Tatalovich, Raymond. "Legislative Quality and Legislative Policy Making: Some Implications for Reform." In *Legislative Reform: The Policy Impact*, ed. Leroy N. Rieselbach, pp. 223-231. Lexington, Mass.: Lexington Books, 1978.

948. Truman, David B. "The Prospects for Change." In *The Congress and America's Future*, ed. David B. Truman, pp. 176-183. Englewood Cliffs, N.J.: Prentice-Hall, 1965.

949. United States. Commission on Federal Paperwork. *The Role of Congress: A Report of the Commission on Federal Paperwork.* Washington: The Commission, 1977.

950. U.S. Congress. Joint Commmittee on the Organization of the Congress of the United States. *Organization of Congress: Hearings Before the Joint Committee, Part I and II.* 89th Cong., 1st sess. Washington: GPO, 1965.

951. Vandenbosch, Amry. "Need for Some Constitutional Changes." *Kentucky Law Journal* 37 (May 1949): 343-357.

952. Voorhis, Jerry. "Congress and the Future: Proposals for Reorganization and for Strengthening the Position of Our National Legislative Body." *Review of Politics* 7 (April 1945): 131-141.

953. Ways, Max. "Congress Should Be Stronger Partner in National Policy." *Fortune* 87 (Jan. 1973): 63-67, 170-172.

954. Weaver, Warren. *Both Your Houses: The Truth About Congress.* New York: Praeger, 1972.

955. Wehr, Elizabeth. "Federal Paperwork: Congress Is the Culprit." *Congressional Quarterly Weekly Report* 35 (July 30, 1977): 1608-1609.

956. Weindenbaum, Murry L. *Ten Suggestions for Congressional Reform.* Working Papers on House Committee Organization and Operation. Presented to House Select Committee on Committees. Washington: GPO, 1973.

957. Welch, Susan and Peters, John, eds. *Legislative Reform and Public Policy.* New York: Praeger, 1977.

958. "What's Wrong with Congress: 118 Members Answer." *U.S. News and World Report* 12 Sept. 1960, pp. 56-77.

959. Whitesel, Russell G. "Congress: Old Powers, New Techniques." In *Aspects of Liberty: Essays Presented to Robert E. Cushman,* eds. Milton R. Konvitz and Clinton Rossiter, pp. 323-346. Ithaca, N.Y.: Cornell University Press, 1958.

960. Wicker, Tom. "Winds of Change in the Senate." *New York Times Magazine,* 12 Sept. 1965, pp. 52-53.

961. Yacker, Marc D. *Congressional Reform: 93rd and 94th Congresses.* Washington: Congressional Research Service, 1976.

962. Zagorca, Sam. "To Make It a 'Do Something' Congress." *New York Times Magazine,* 8 Sept. 1963, pp. 26, 115-116.

963. Zink, Harold. "Reorganiztion Efforts in Congress." *Parliamentary Affairs* 3 (Winter 1949): 94-103.

Reform of the House

964. Bach, Stanley I. *Congressional Reform —House of Representatives (95th Congress).* Washington: Congressional Research Service, 1978.

965. Bazelon, David T. "Non-Rule in America." *Commentary* 36 (Dec. 1963): 438-445.

966. "Bolling Committee: Members Reforming House System." *Congressional Quarterly Weekly Report* 31 (Nov. 24, 1973): 3083-3088.

967. Cooper, Ann. "House Faces Votes on Controversial Reforms." *Congressional Quarterly Weekly Report* 35 (Sept. 17, 1977): 1973-1975.

968. "Democratic Study Group: A Winner on House Reforms." *Congressional Quarterly Weekly Report* 31 (June 2, 1973): 1366-1373.

969. Dodd, Lawrence C. "The House of Representatives and Institutional Change: An Analysis of Internal Organizational Reform." In *Forging America's Future: Strategies for National Growth and Development,* ed. National Commission on Supplies and Shortages, Appendix, Vol. II. Washington: GPO, 1977.

970. Donnelly, Harrison, H. "Obey Commission Studies House Support System." *Congressional Quarterly Weekly Report* 35 (Aug. 6, 1977): 1665-1666.

971. Gardner, John W. "Restructuring the House of Representatives." *American Academy of Political and Social Science, Annals* 411 (Jan. 1974): 169-176.

972. Glass, Andrew J. "Legislative Reform Effort Builds New Alliances Among House Members." *National Journal* 2 (July 25, 1970): 1607-1614.

973. Green, Michael. "Obstacles to Reform: Nobody Covers the House." *Washington Monthly* 2 (June 1970): 67-73.

974. "House Democratic Caucus Rejects Reform Proposals." *Congressional Quarterly Weekly Report* 31 (Feb. 10, 1973): 277-278.

975. "House Reform: Easy to Advocate, Hard to Define." *Congressional Quarterly Weekly Report* 31 (Jan. 20, 1973): 69-72.

976. "House Reforms: More Moves Toward Modernization." *Congressional Quarterly Weekly Report* 31 (Feb. 24, 1973): 419.

977. Keeffe, Arthur J. and Copeland, Gary W. "Facelifting Time at the House of Representatives." *American Bar Association Journal* 60 (Nov. 1974): 1444-1447.

978. Malbin, Michael J. "House Reforms: The Emphasis Is on Productivity, Not Power." *National Journal* 8 (Dec. 4, 1976): 1731-1737.

979. Mullen, Patrick R. "Congressional Reform: Minority Staffing in the House of Representatives." *GAO Review* 10 (Summer 1975): 32-40.

980. Oppenheimer, Bruce I. "Policy Effects of U.S. House Reform: Decentralization and the Capacity to Resolve Energy Issues." *Legislative Studies Quarterly* 5 (Feb. 1980): 5-30.

981. Ornstein, Norman J. "The Democrats Reform Power in the House of Representatives, 1969-1975." In *America in the Seventies: Problems, Policies, and Politics,* ed. Allan P. Sindler, pp. 2-48. Boston: Little, Brown, 1977.

982. Parkins, Ivan W. "Let's Disassemble the House: A Proposal for Reform of Congress." *South Atlantic Quarterly* 59 (Spring 1960): 226-238.

983. Reed, Thomas B. "Reforms Needed in the House." *North American Review* 150 (May, 1890): 537-546.

984. Smith, Herbert C. "The Political and Organizational Dynamics of Reform in the United States House of Representatives." Ph.D. dissertation, Johns Hopkins University, 1977.

985. Treen, David C. "Call the House to Order." In his *Can You Afford This House?* pp. 3-12. Ottawa, Ill.: Green Hill Publishers, 1978.

986. Treen, David C., ed. *Can You Afford This House?* Ottawa, Ill.: Green Hill Publishers, 1978.

987. U.S. Congress. House. Commission on Administrative Review. *Administrative Reorganization and Legislative Management.* Washington: GPO, 1977.

988. Workshop on Congressional Oversight and Investigation, Washington, D.C., 1978. *Proceedings of the Three-Day Workshop on Congressional Oversight and Investigations, December 1, 6, and 7, 1978.* H. Doc. 96-217, 96th Cong., 1st sess. Washington: GPO, 1979.

Reform of the Senate

989. Bach, Stanley I. *Congressional Reform —Senate (95th Cong.).* Washington: Congressional Research Service, 1978.

990. Bonham, Milledge L. "Chaos of Congress." *Southern Atlantic Quarterly* 24 (July 1925): 269-277.

991. Davidson, Roger H. "Senate Reorganization Study Calls on Political Scientists." *PS* 9 (Summer 1976): 288-289.

992. Ervin, Sam J. "The Case Against Reform: A Nobler Purpose Than Political Efficiency." In *The Senate Institution,* ed. Nathaniel S. Preston, pp. 192-202. New York: Van Nostrand Reinhold, 1969.

993. Glass, Andrew J. "Congressional Report 'Mansfield Reforms Spark Quiet Revolution in Senate'." *National Journal* 3 (Mar. 6, 1971): 499-512.

994. Hoar, George F. "Has the Senate Degenerated." *Forum* 23 (April 1897): 129-144.

995. Humphrey, Hubert H. "The Senate on Trial." *American Political Science Review* 44 (Sept. 1950): 650-660.

996. Lawrence, David. "Shall the Senate Destroy Itself." *U.S. News and World Report* 37 (Oct. 1954): 138-144.

997. Miller, Charles R. "Has the Senate Degenerated? A Reply to Senator Hoar." *Forum* 23 (May 1897): 271-281.

Legislative Reorganization

998. Broughton, Philip S. "Congress Is Far from Reorganized." *New York Times Magazine,* 18 May 1947, pp. 7, 64-66, 70.

999. Brown, James R. "The Implementation of the Legislative Reorganization Act of 1946 by the 80th and 81st Congresses." Ph.D. dissertation, Fordham University, 1954.

1000. Ford, Aaron I. "The Legislative Reorganization Act of 1946." *American Bar Association Journal* 32 (Nov. 1946): 741-744.

1001. Galloway, George B. "Brownlow on the Legislative Reorganization Act." *American Political Science Review* 58 (June 1964): 398-400.

1002. Galloway, George B. "The Operation of the Legislative Reorganization Act of 1946." *American Political Science Review* 45 (Mar. 1951): 41-68.

1003. Harris, Joseph P. "The Reorganization of Congress." *Public Administration Review* 6 (Summer 1946): 267-282.

1004. Heady, Ferrel. "The Reorganization Act of 1949." *Public Administration Review* 9 (Summer 1949): 165-174.

1005. Hoffmann, Malcolm A. "Congress Streamlined." *Federal Bar Association Journal* 7 (July 1946): 378-383.

1006. Hopkins, Bruce R. "Congressional Reform: A Little, But Possible, Bit." *American Bar Association Journal* 57 (Jan. 1971): 62-65.

1007. Hopkins, Bruce R. "Congressional Reform: The Clash with Tradition." *American Bar Association Journal* 54 (Jan. 1968): 80-83.

1008. Kefauver, Estes. "Congressional Reorganization: Better Teamwork Between the Legislative and Executive Branches of Government Is Essential." *Journal of Politics* 9 (Feb. 1947): 96-107.

1009. Kefauver, Estes. "Did We Modernize Congress? Progress Made by 1946 Act and Job Still to Be Done." *National Municipal Review* 36 (Nov. 1947): 552-557.

1010. Kravitz, Walter. *The Legislative Reorganization Act of 1970: Summary and Analysis of Provisions Affecting Committees and Committee Staff of the House of Representatives.* Washington: Congressional Research Service, 1975.

1011. LaFollette, Robert M. "Congress Wins a Victory over Congress: Legislative Reorganization Act of 1946," *New York Times Magazine,* 4 Aug. 1946, pp. 11, 45-46.

1012. "Legislative Reorganization Act: First Year's Record." *Congressional Quarterly Weekly Report* 30 (Mar. 4, 1972): 485-491.

1013. Monroney, A. S. Mike. "The Legislative Reorganization Act of 1946: A First Appraisal." In his *The Strengthening of American Political Institutions,* pp. 1-31. Ithaca, N.Y.: Cornell University Press, 1949.

1014. St. Sure, Phyllis C. "An Analysis and Description of the Legislative Reform Act of 1946." Master's thesis, George Washington University, 1964.

1015. Shull, Charles W. "The Legislative Reorganization Act of 1946." *Temple Law Quarterly* 20 (Jan. 1947): 375-395.

1016. Thomas, Elbert D. "How Congress Functions Under Its Reorganization Act." *American Political Science Review* 43 (Dec. 1949): 1179-1189.

1017. Thomas, Elbert D. "The Senate During and Since the War." *Parliamentary Affairs* 3 (Winter 1949): 114-126.

1018. Thompson, L. Fred. "The Legislative Reorganization Act of 1970." *GAO Review* (Winter 1971): 24-31.

1019. U.S. Congress. Special Committee on the Organization of the Congress. *Amendments Made to the Legislative Reorganization Act of 1946 by S. 355, A Bill to Improve the Operation of the Legislative Branch of the Federal Government, and for Other Purposes.* Washington: GPO, 1967.

1020. U.S. Congress. Joint Committee on the Organization of Congress. *The Organization of Congress, Hearings, March 13--June 29, Parts 1--4.* 79th Cong. 1st sess. Washington: GPO, 1945.

1021. U.S. Congress. Joint Committee on the Organization of the Congress. *Organization of Congress, Hearings, May 10--September 9, 1965, Parts 1--12.* 89th Cong., 1st sess. Washington: GPO, 1965.

1022. U.S. Congress. Senate. Special Committee on the Organization of the Congress. *Organization of Congress, Hearings, August 21 and September 8, 1966.* 89th Cong., 2nd sess. Washington: GPO, 1966.

1023. U.S. Congress. Joint Committee on the Organization of the Congress. *The Organization of Congress: Symposium on Congress.* 79th Cong., 1st sess. Washington: GPO, 1945.

Terms of Office

1024. Barnstead, William A. "The Case for Limited Terms." *Ripon Forum* 13 (June 1977): 3-5.

1025. Behn, Dick. "A Sunset for Congress." *Ripon Forum* 13 (April 1977): 1-3.

1026. Burnham, Walter D. "Four-Year Terms?" *Commonweal* 84 (April 1966): 79-81.

1027. Cooper, Ann. "Congressional Term Limits Get More Public Support, But Still Unpopular on Hill." *Congressional Quarterly Weekly Report* 36 (Feb. 25, 1978): 533-534.

1028. Gallup, George H. "Editors for Congress: Single Term Proposed to Attract Outstanding Citizens." *National Municipal Review* 47 (May 1958): 210-215.

1029. Polsby, Nelson W. "A Note on the President's Modest Proposal." *Public Administration Review* 26 (Sept. 1966): 156-159.

1030. Shannon, William V. "Reforming the House: A Four-Year Term?" *New York Times Magazine,* 10 Jan. 1965, pp. 22-24, 67-68.

1031. Shelton, Willard. "Reforming the House." *American Federationist* 72 (May 1965): 6-7.

1032. U.S. Congress. Senate. Judiciary Committee. *Four-Year U.S. House of Representatives terms.* 96th Cong., 1st sess. Washington: GPO, 1979.

1033. U.S. Congress. Senate. Judiciary Committee. *Congressional Tenure.* 95th Cong., 2nd sess. Washington: GPO, 1978.

Broadcasting

1034. Allen, Len. "Television from the Senate Floor." In *Senate Communications with the Public: A Compilation of Papers Prepared for the Commission on the Operation of the Senate,* pp. 87-108. Washington: GPO, 1977.

1035. "Committee Studies Broadcasting Sessions of Congress." *Congressional Quarterly Weekly Report* 32 (Mar. 2, 1974): 563-564.

1036. "Congress on T.V.: Who Will Control the Camera?" *Congressional Quarterly Weekly Report* 33 (April 26, 1975): 866-870.

1037. "Curtain Rising on House TV Amid Aid-to-Incumbent Fears." *Congressional Quarterly Weekly Report* 37 (Feb. 10, 1979): 252-257.

1038. Ellsworth, Robert F. "The Case for Television and Radio Coverage." In *We Propose: A Modern Congress,* ed. Mary McInnis, pp. 265-268. New York: McGraw-Hill, 1966.

1039. Garay, Ronald. "Implementing Televised Coverage of Sessions of the U.S. Congress." *Journalism Quarterly* 55 (Autumn 1978): 527-539.

1040. Garay, Ronald. "Television and the 1951 Senate Crime Committee Hearings." *Journal of Broadcasting* 22 (Fall 1978): 469-490.

1041. Goldman, Ralph M. "Congress on the Air (A Proposal)." *Public Opinion Quarterly* 14 (1950); 744-752.

1042. Gossett, William T. "Justice and TV: Some Thoughts on Congressional Investigations." *American Bar Association Journal* 38 (Jan. 1952): 15-18, 84.

1043. "House Gets Set to Televise Sessions with Its Own Hand on the Cameras." *Congressional Quarterly Weekly Report* 35 (Dec. 17, 1977): 2605-2608.

1044. Jones, Harry W. "Congress and Television: A Dissenting Opinion." *American Bar Association Journal* 37 (May 1951): 392-393.

1045. Long, Gillis. "Television in the House of Representatives: A New Epoch on the Hill." *Capitol Studies* 6 (Spring 1978): 5-12.

1046. MacCann, Richard D. "Televising Congress." *American Scholar* 44 (Summer 1975): 466-472.

1047. Merrick, Patricia A. "The Telecasting of Congressional Hearings." Master's thesis, American University, 1960.

1048. Paletz, David L. "Television Drama: The Appeals of the Senate Watergate Hearings." *Midwest Quarterly* 18 (Oct. 1976): 103-109.

1049. Partain, Eugene G. "The Use of Broadcast Media in the Congressional, Legislative and Quasi-Judicial Proceedings." *Journal of Broadcasting* 4 (Spring 1960): 123-139.

1050. Peirce, Neal R. and Hagstrom, Jerry. "Congress Report 'And Now from Washington: It's the Congress Show.'" *National Journal* 9 (Mar. 19, 1977): 430-432.

1051. Robinson, Michael J. "Impact of the Televised Watergate Hearings." *Journal of Communication* 24 (Spring 1974): 17-30.

1052. Robinson, Michael J. "A Twentieth-Century Medium in a Nineteenth-Century Legislature: The Effects of Television on the American Congress." In *Congress in Change: Evolution and Reform,* ed. Norman J. Ornstein, pp. 240-261. New York: Praeger, 1975.

1053. Shaffer, Helen B. "Televising Congress." *Editorial Research Reports* (April 1953): 279-296.

1054. Snee, Joseph M. "One for the Money, Two for the Show: The Case Against Televising Congressional Hearings." *Georgetown Law Journal* 41 (Nov. 1953): 1-43.

1055. Summers, Robert E. "The Role of Congressional Broadcasting in a Democratic Society." Ph.D. dissertation, Ohio State University, 1955.

1056. Tannenbaum, Percy H. "What Effect When TV Covers a Congressional Hearing." *Journalism Quarterly* 32 (Fall 1955): 434-440.

1057. Twentieth Century Fund. Task Force on Broadcasting and the Legislature. *Openly Arrived At: Report of the Twentieth Century Task Force on Broadcasting and the Legislature.* New York: Twentieth Century Fund, 1974.

1058. U.S. Congress. Joint Committee on Congressional Operations. *Broadcasting House and Senate proceedings, Interim Report, October 10, 1974.* Washington: GPO, 1974.

1059. Wiebe, G. D. "Merchandising Commodities and Citizenship on Television." *Public Opinion Quarterly* 15 (Winter 1951): 679-691.

1060. Wiebe, G. D. "Responses to the Televised Kefauver Hearings: Some Social Psychological Implications." *Public Opinion Quarterly* 16 (Summer 1952): 179-200.

IV. Powers of Congress

General Studies

1061. Baldwin, Gordon B. "Congressional Power to Demand Disclosure of Foreign Intelligence Agreements." *Brooklyn Journal of International Law* 3 (Fall 1976): 1-30.

1062. Barnett, James D. "Delegation of the Legislative Power by Congress to the States." *American Political Science Review* 2 (May 1908): 347-377.

1063. Brooke, Francis C. "Legislation Impairing the Rights Obtained by Contract with the Federal Government." *Georgetown Law Journal* 15 (Jan. 1927): 184-186.

1064. Cohen, William. "Congressional Power to Interpret Due Process and Equal Protection." *Stanford Law Review* 27 (Feb. 1975): 603-620.

1065. Cohn, Morris M. "Concerning the Power of the United States in War Time as to Taking Property." *American Law Review* 53 (Jan.-Feb. 1919): 87-98.

1066. Curreri, Anthony. "Power of Congress to Nullify Contractual Obligations." *St. John's Law Review* 9 (May 1935): 362-369.

1067. Darrow, Clarence S. "Power of Congress Re Volstead Act." *Lawyer and Banker* 22 (May-June 1929): 167-168.

1068. Donahoe, Bernard and Smelser, Marshall. "Congressional Power to Raise Armies: The Constitutional and Ratifying Conventions, 1787-1788." *Review of Politics* 33 (April 1971): 202-211.

1069. Eaton, James S. "The Power of Congress to Limit the Jurisdiction of District Courts." *Mississippi Law Journal* 7 (April 1935): 405-411.

1070. Emerson, J. Terry. "Congress' Power to Enhance the Civil War Amendments." *Notre Dame Laywer* 49 (Feb. 1974): 544-567.

1071. Nichol, Gene R. "Examination of Congressional Powers Under Section 5 of the 14th Amendment." *Notre Dame Lawyer* 52 (Dec. 1976): 175-189.

1072. Farrand, Max. "The Legislation of Congress for the Government of the Organized Territories of the United States." Ph.D. dissertation, Princeton University, 1896.

1073. Farrell, Norman. "Congressional Power to Restrict Scope of Charges of Federal Judges." *American Bar Association Journal* 11 (Oct. 1925): 661-662.

1074. Faust, George. "Congressional Control of U.S. Supreme Court Jurisdiction." *Cleveland-Marshall Law Review* 7 (Sept. 1958): 513-523.

1075. Flowers, J. N. "The State vs. the Congressman." *Alabama Lawyer* 6 (Jan. 1945): 60-72.

1076. Frankfurter, Felix and Greene, Nathaniel. "Congressional Power over the Labor Injunction." *Columbia Law Review* 31 (Mar. 1931): 385-412.

1077. Frankham, Markley. "An Analysis of the Delegations of Power in Some of the Recent Congressional Enactments." *Brooklyn Law Review* 3 (Oct. 1933); 38-56.

1078. Frantz, Laurent B. "Congressional Power to Enforce the Fourteenth Amendment Against Private Acts." *Yale Law Journal* 73 (July 1964): 1353-1384.

1079. Garrison, Lloyd K. "The Power of Congress over Corporate Reorganizations." *Virginia Law Review* 19 (Feb. 1933): 343-350.

1080. Gellhorn, Walter and Lauer, Louis. "Congressional Settlement of Tort Claims Against the United States." *Columbia Law Review* 55 (Jan. 1955): 1-36.

1081. Givens, Richard A. "Power to Define the Constitutional Rights of Defendants: Congress and the Federal Courts." *Fordham Law Review* 46 (Dec. 1977): 383-412.

1082. Gross, Bertram M. "Role of Congress in Contract Termination." *Law and Contemporary Problems* 10 (Winter 1944): 540-558.

1083. Gurski, Walter. "The Right of Congress to Regulate the Navigation of the Air." *Bi-monthly Law Review* 14 (Sept.-Oct. 1930): 1-7.

1084. Hannah, Paul F. "The Power of Congress Retroactively to Reduce Interest Rates on Judgements and Refunds Against the Federal Government." *George Washington Law Review* 1 (Mar. 1933): 366-371.

1085. Hart, Henry M. "The Power of Congress to Limit the Jurisdiction of Federal Courts: An Exercise in Dialectic." *Harvard Law Review* 66 (June 1953): 1362-1402.

1086. Hurst, Harold E. "Can Congress Take Away Citizenship?" *Rocky Mountain Law Review* 29 (Dec. 1956): 62-81.

1087. Johnson, William F. "Power of Congress over Labor Relations." Ph.D. dissertation, New York University, 1941.

1088. Kinzler, David. "State's Power to Enable Congress to Enact Laws for the State." *Air Law Review* 5 (April 1934): 171-187.

1089. Kohansky, Donna L. "Coverage of Appointees of State and Local Elected Officials Under the Equal Employment Opportunity Act of 1972 and Congressional Power to Enforce the Fourteenth Amendment." *Goergetown Law Journal* 65 (Feb. 1977): 809-836.

1090. Kuykendall, E. D. "Power of Congress to Diminish the Retired Salaries of Federal Judges." *North Carolina Law Review* 12 (June 1934): 367-369.

1091. LaPorte, Alphonse A. and Leuschner, Frederick D. "Extending State Jurisdiction by Act of Congress." *American Bar Association Journal* 15 (April 1929): 199-201.

1092. Latimer, J. Austin. "The Power of Congress to Subpoena Members and Documents from the Executive Branch." *South Carolina Law Quarterly* 7 (Spring 1955): 379-393.

1093. Lewis, Frederick P. "Civil Rights, Federalism and Pluralism: The Dilemma of Congressional Power to Enforce the Fourteenth Amendment." Ph.D. dissertation, Tufts University, 1972.

1094. Luedde, Henry W. "New Limitations on the Power of Congress: the A.A.A. Decision." *St. Louis Law Review* 21 (Feb. 1936): 149-160.

1095. Mannenbach, Stephen F. "How Broad Discretion?: Congressional Delegation of Authority to the Standing Committee of Correspondents." *Administrative Law Review* 31 (Summer 1979): 367-384.

1096. Meyers, Trienah A. "False Claims Act: Potential Application to Members of Congress." *University of Dayton Law Review* 4 (Winter 1979): 155-175.

1097. Moomaw, Wilmer E. "The Power of Congress to Enforce the Fourteenth Amendment." Ph.D. dissertation, University of Virginia, 1970.

1098. Nisen, Charles M. "Admiralty—Power of Congress to Extend Jurisdiction—Constitutional Limitations." *Michigan Law Review* 33 (May 1935): 1051-1059.

1099. Nowak, John E. "The Scope of Congressional Power to Create Causes of Action Against State Governments and the History of the 11th and 14th Amendments." *Columbia Law Review* 75 (Dec. 1975): 1413-1469.

1100. Nygh, P. E. "Federal and Territorial Aspects of Federal Legislative Power over the Territories: A Comparative Study." *Australian Law Journal* 37 (July 1963): 72-81.

1101. "On the Disregard of the Constitutional Role of the House of Representatives in the Disposition of Property of the United States." *Inter-American Economic Affairs* 33 (Summer 1979): 91-94.

1102. Post, Russell L. and Willard, Charles H. "The Power of Congress to Nullify Gold Clauses." *Harvard Law Review* 46 (June 1933): 1225-1257.

1103. Redish, Martin H. and Woods, Curtis E. "Congressional Power to Control the Jurisdiction of Lower Federal Courts: A Critical Review and a New Synthesis." *University of Pennsylvania Law Review* 124 (Nov. 1975): 45-109.

1104. Revercomb, Edmund P. G. "Power of Congress to Limit the Prescription of Intoxicating Liquor." *Virginia Law Review* 13 (Feb. 1927): 311-316.

1105. Rogers, Lindsay. "The Postal Power of Congress: A Study in Constitutional Expansion." Ph.D. dissertation, Johns Hopkins University, 1915.

1106. "Tenth Amendment as a Limitation on the Powers of Congress." *Harvard Law Review* 52 (June 1939): 1342-1348.

1107. Tuttle, Alonzo H. and Bennett, Dale E. "Extent of Power of Congress over Aviation." *University of Cincinnati Law Review* 5 (May 1931): 261-292.

1108. U.S. Congress. House. Merchant Marine and Fisheries Committee. *Power of Congress to Dispose of U.S. Property.* 95th Cong., 2nd sess. Washington: GPO, 1978.

1109. Van Alstyne, William N. "Role of Congress in Determining Incidental Powers of the President and of Federal Courts: A Comment on the Horizontal Effect of the Sweeping Clause." *Ohio State Law Journal* 36 (1975): 788-825.

1110. Voorhies, MacIlburne Van. "Judicial Functions and Powers of Congress." *Virginia Law Review* 13 (June 1927): 632-641.

1111. Warren, Charles. "Spies, and the Power of Congress to Subject Certain Classes of Civilians to Trial by Military Tribunal." *American Law Review* 53 (Mar. 1919): 195-228.

1112. Weinfeld, Abraham C. "Power of Congress over State Ratifying Conventions." *Harvard Law Review* 51 (Jan. 1938): 473-506.

1113. Whitesel, Russel G. "The Powers of Congress to Remove Federal Officers." Ph.D. dissertation, Cornell University, 1948.

1114. Yablon, Jeffrey L. "Congressional Power Under Section Five of the Fourteenth Amendment." *Stanford Law Review* 25 (June 1973): 885-904.

Budgeting

General Studies

1115. Aderman, Gary. "Turning Off the Federal Faucet: Congress Finds It's No Easy Task." *National Journal* 11 (Sept. 22, 1979): 1571-1573.

1116. *Advance Budgeting: A Report to the Congress: A Compilation of Technical Background Papers.* Washington: Congressional Budget Office, 1977.

1117. Banfield, Edward C. "Congress and the Budget: A Planner's Criticism." *American Political Science Review* 43 (Dec. 1949): 1217-1228.

1118. Bow, Frank T. "The Federal Budget." In *Republican Papers,* ed. Melvin R. Laird, pp. 419-427. New York: Praeger, 1968.

1119. "Budget Control: Making Haste Carefully." *Congressional Quarterly Weekly Report* 33 (Mar. 22, 1975): 589-594.

1120. *Budgeting in the United States Senate: A Compilation of Papers Prepared for the Commission on the Operation of the Senate.* 94th Cong., 2nd sess. Washington: GPO, 1977.

1121. Cameron, Juan. "Noble Experiment in Congressional Budget Discipline." *Fortune* 93 (May 1976): 206-210, 214, 218.

1122. Clark, Timothy B. "It's Back to the Drawing Board for Congressional Budget Cutters." *National Journal* 11 (Dec. 22, 1979): 2148-2151.

1123. Clark, Timothy B. and Cohen, Richard E. "Balancing the Budget a Test for Congress: Can It Resist the Pressures to Spend?" *National Journal* 12 (April 12, 1980); 588-594.

1124. Cohen, Richard E. "Is Congress's Budget Worth the Fuss?" *National Journal* 11 (Sept. 29, 1979): 1593-1632.

1125. "Congress and the Budget: Better Days Ahead." *Congressional Quarterly Weekly Report* 31 (April 28, 1973): 1013-1018.

1126. Finley, James J. "Congressional Budgetmaking—'74." *Federal Accountant* 23 (June 1974): 22-34.

1127. Fisher, Louis. *Budget Concepts and Terminology: The Appropriations Phase.* Washington: Congressional Research Service, 1974.

1128. Fisher, Louis. "Congress, The Executive and the Budget." *American Academy of Political and Social Science, Annals* 411 (Jan. 1974): 102-113.

1129. Gulick, Clarence S. "The United States Congress and the Timing of Fiscal Decisions." Ph.D. dissertation, Harvard University, 1948.

1130. Havemann, Joel. *Congress and the Budget.* Bloomington: Indiana University Press, 1978.

1131. Havemann, Joel. "Congress Is Preparing a Budget Larger Than Ford's—and Very Different." *National Journal* 8 (Mar. 27, 1976): 408-412.

1132. Havemann, Joel. "The Congressional Budget Is in Step with Carter's." *National Journal* 9 (Sept. 24, 1977): 1476-1485.

1133. Hirsch, Werner Z. "Congress and Program Budgeting: Problems and Potentials." In *Information Support, Program Budgeting and the Congress,* eds. Robert L. Chartrand, Kenneth Janda and Michael Hugo, pp. 195-206. New York: Spartan Books, 1968.

1134. Hrebenar, Ronald J. "The Utility of Role in Budgetary Decision-Making." *Western Political Quarterly* 29 (Dec. 1976): 575-588.

1135. Hunter, Kenneth W. *Statement (on Congressional Budgetary Control). Working Papers on House Committee Organization and Operation. Presented to House Select Committee on Committees. 93rd Cong.* Washington: GPO, 1973.

1136. LeLoup, Lance T. *Budgetary Politics: Dollars, Deficits, Decisions.* Brunswick, Ohio: King's Court Communications, 1977.

1137. Lieberman, Charles J. "Fiscal Policy Formation in Congress: The Legislative Budgetary Process." Ph.D. dissertation, University of California—Santa Barbara, 1976.

1138. McAllister, Eugene J. *Congress and the Budget: Evaluating the Process.* Washington: Heritage Foundation, 1979.

1139. Ott, David J. and Ott, Altiat F. *Federal Budget Policy.* 3rd ed. Washington: Brookings Institution, 1977.

1140. Rapoport, Daniel. "How F. Edward Herbert Shaved $46 Billion from the Defense Budget." *Washington Monthly* 8 (Nov. 1976): 20-23.

1141. Saloma, John S. *The Responsible Use of Power: A Critical Analysis of the Congressional Budget Process.* Washington: American Enterprise Institute for Public Policy Research, 1964.

1142. Schick, Allen. *Congress Versus the Budget. Working Papers on House Committee Organization and Operation. Presented to House Select Committee on Committees, 93rd Cong.* Washington: GPO, 1973.

1143. Shull, Steven A. "Budgetary Policy-Making: Congress and the President Compared." *Presidential Studies Quarterly* 9 (Spring 1979): 180-191.

1144. Silverman, Eli B. "Public Budgeting and Public Administration: Enter the Legislature." *Public Finance Quarterly* 2 (Oct. 1974): 472-484.

1145. Tax Foundation. *Congress and the Federal Budget.* New York: Tax Foundation, 1973.

1146. U.S. Congress. Senate. Budget Committee. *Can Congress Control the Power of the Purse?* Washington: GPO, 1978.

1147. U.S. Congress. Senate. Committee on Rules and Administration. *Federal Budget Control by Congress, Hearings, January 15, 1974.* Washington: GPO, 1974.

1148. Wallace, Robert A. "Congressional Control of the Budget." *Midwest Journal of Political Science* 3 (May 1959): 151-167.

1149. Weidenbaum, Murray L. "On the Effectiveness of Congressional Control of the Public Purse." *National Tax Journal* 17 (Dec. 1965): 370-374.

1150. Wildavsky, Aaron B. *The Politics of the Budgetary Process.* 3rd ed. Boston: Little, Brown, 1979.

Legislative–Executive Relations

1151. "Budget Bureau vs. Congress." *Congressional Quarterly Weekly Report 16 (June 13, 1958): 743-749.*

1152. De Rubertis, William A. "Congress, the Executive, and the Politics of Defense Budgeting: A Comparative Analysis of Fiscal 1950 and Fiscal 1963." Ph.D. dissertation, Claremont Graduate School, 1972.

1153. Fisher, Louis. "Reprogramming of Funds by the Defense Department." *Journal of Politics* 36 (Feb. 1974): 77-102.

1154. Jones, Roger W. "The Role of the Bureau of the Budget in the Federal Legislative Process." *American Bar Association Journal* 40 (Nov. 1954): 995-998.

1155. Kolodziej, Edward A. "Congressional Responsibility for the Common Defense: The Money Problem." *Western Political Quarterly* 16 (Mar. 1963): 149-160.

1156. Kolodziej, Edward A. "Rational Consent and Defense Budgets: The Role of Congress, 1945-1962." *Orbis* 7 (Winter 1964): 748-777.

1157. Lawton, Frederick J. "Legislative–Executive Relationships in Budgeting as Viewed by the Executive." *Public Administration Review* 13 (Summer 1953): 169-176.

1158. LeLoup, Lance T. and Moreland, William B. "Agency Strategies and Executive Review: The Hidden Politics of Budgeting." *Public Administration Review* 38 (May/June 1978): 232-239.

1159. Mansfield, Edwin. "Congressional Alternation of the Executive Budget." *Southern Economic Journal* 20 (Jan. 1954): 252-257.

1160. Meier, Kenneth J. and Van Lohuizen, J. R. "Bureaus, Clients, and Congress: The Impact of Interest Group Support on Budgeting." *Administration and Society* 9 (Feb. 1978): 447-466.

1161. Mettler, John C. "Proposals for Improving Congressional Consideration of the President's Budget." Ph.D. dissertation, Clark University, 1959.

1162. Moyer, Burton B. "DOD and the New Congressional Budget Process." *Defense Management Journal* 11 (Jan. 1975): 25-30.

1163. Moyer, Burton B. "The Department of Defense and the New Budget Process." *National Defense* 60 (July/August 1975): 50-52.

1164. Penner, Rudolph G. *The 1978 Budget in Transition: From Ford to Carter to Congress.* Washington: American Enterprise Institute For Public Policy Research, 1977.

1165. Rivlin, Alice M. "Sharing Fiscal Information: A Legislative Branch View." *Bulletin of the American Society for Information Science* 5 (Dec. 1978): 25-26.

1166. Schick, Allen. "Whose Budget? It All Depends on Whether the President or Congress Is Doing the Counting." In *The Presidency and the Congress: A Shifting Balance of Power?*, eds. William S. Livingston, Lawrence C. Dodd and Richard L. Schott, pp. 97-123. Austin: Lyndon B. Johnson School of Public Affairs, University of Texas, 1979.

1167. Smith, Harold D. "The Budget as an Instrument of Legislative Control and Eecutive Management." *Public Administration Review* 4 (Summer 1944): 181-188.

1168. U.S. Congress. Senate. Budget Committee. *Legislative Approaches to Limiting Federal Spending.* 96th Cong., 2nd sess. Washington: GPO, 1980.

1169. Wanat, John. "Personnel Measures of Budgetary Interaction." *Western Political Quarterly* 29 (June 1976): 295-297.

Budget Reform

1170. Adams, Brock. "New Tools of the Trade: Congress's Budget Machinery." *Bulletin of the American Society for Information Science* 1 (April 1975): 14-15.

1171. "Budget Reform: Action Likely Before 1974." *Congressional Quarterly Weekly Report* 31 (Sept. 15, 1973): 2448-2451.

1172. Burkhead, Jessee V. and Knerr, Charles. "Congressional Budget Reform: New Decision Structures." In *Fiscal Responsibility in Constitutional Democracy,* eds. James M. Buchanan and Richard E. Wagner, pp. 119-155. Boston: Leiden, 1978.

1173. Burkhead, Jesse V. "Federal Budgetary Developments: 1947–1948." *Public Administration Review* 8 (Autumn 1948): 267-274.

1174. Casper, Gerhard. "Disclosure of Intelligence Budgets." *University of Chicago Law School Record* 23 (Fall 1977): 19-22.

1175. "Conferees Approve Budget Procedures Reform." *Congressional Quarterly Weekly Report* 32 (June 15, 1974): 1590-1594.

1176. "Congressional Budget Reform: Will It Work?" *Congressional Quarterly Weekly Report* 32 (Sept. 7, 1974): 2415-2418.

1177. "Congressional Budget: Toughest Test Ahead." *Congressional Quarterly Weekly Report* 33 (Sept. 6, 1975): 1921-1928.

1178. Ellwood, John W. and Thurber, James A. "The New Congressional Budget Process: Its Causes, Consequences, and Possible Success." In *Legislative Reform and Public Policy,* eds. Susan Welch and John G. Peters, pp. 82-97. New York: Praeger, 1977.

1179. Ellwood, John W. and Thurber, James A. "The New Congressional Budget Process: The Hows and Whys of House-Senate Differences." In *Congress Reconsidered*, eds. Lawrence C. Dodd and Bruce I. Oppenheimer, pp. 163-192. New York: Praeger, 1977.

1180. Fielder, Clinton. "Reform of the Congressional Legislative Budget." *National Tax Journal* 4 (Mar. 1951): 65-76.

1181. Finley, James J. "The 1974 Congressional Initiative in Budget Making." *Public Administration Review* 35 (May/June 1975): 270-278.

1182. Fischer, C. William. "The New Congressional Budget Establishment and Federal Spending: Choices for the Future." *National Tax Journal* 29 (Mar. 1976): 9-14.

1183. Fisher, Louis. "Congressional Budget Reform: The First Two Years." *Harvard Journal on Legislation* 14 (April 1977): 413-457.

1184. Hale, Russell D. and Jordan, Leland G. "New Congressional Budgeting Procedures: An Initial Analysis of Effects on the Department of Defense." In *The Changing World of the American Military*, ed. Franklin D. Margiotta, pp. 119-128. Boulder, Colo.: Westview Press, 1978.

1185. Harris, Joseph P. "Needed Reforms in the Federal Budget System (Congress Poorly Organized to Review and Pass on the Federal Budget)." *Public Administration Review* 12 (1952): 242-250.

1186. Hartman, Robert W. "Next Steps in Budget Reform: Zero-Base Review and the Budgetary Process." *Policy Analysis* 3 (Summer 1977): 387-394.

1187. Havemann, Joel. "Budget Panels to Propose Economic Goals for Fiscal 1976." *National Journal* 7 (Mar. 15, 1975): 390-395.

1188. Havemann, Joel. "Budget Process Nearly Ambushed by Carter and by Congress." *National Journal* 9 (May 21, 1977): 785-789.

1189. Havemann, Joel. "Conferees Approve Changes in Budgeting Procedures." *National Journal* 6 (June 15, 1974): 894-898.

1190. Havemann, Joel. "Congress Must Move at Frenzied Pace to Meet Its Budget Deadlines." *National Journal* 8 (Mar. 6, 1976): 296-297.

1191. Havemann, Joel. "Congress Nears Approval of Second Budget Resolution." *National Journal* 7 (Dec. 13, 1975): 1697-1700.

1192. Havemann, Joel. "The Congressional Budget: On Time and a Long Time Coming." *National Journal* 8 (Sept. 18, 1976): 1306-1317.

1193. Havemann, Joel. "House Votes for a Budget—And for a Budget Process." *National Journal* 8 (May 8, 1976): 634-635.

1194. "House Votes to Reform Federal Oversight." *Congressional Quarterly Weekly Review* 31 (Dec. 8, 1973): 3174-3176.

1195. Korb, Lawrence J. "Analysis of the Congressional Budget Act of 1974." *Naval War College Review* 29 (Summer 1977): 40-52.

1196. Kotler, Neil G. "The Politics of the New Congressional Budget Process: Or, Can Reformers Use It to Undo the System of Privilege." In *The Federal Budget and Social Reconstruction: The People and the State*, prepared by The Study Group on the Federal Budget, Institute for Policy Studies, pp. 3-30. New Brunswick, N.J.: Transaction Books, 1978.

1197. Lee, L. Douglas. "Political Confrontation over Fiscal Processes: The Impact of the U.S. Congressional Budget Act." *Journal of Policy Modeling* 1 (May 1979): 235-249.

1198. Levy, Michael E. "New Congressional Budget Process in Action." *Conference Board Record* 13 (Aug. 1976): 26-31.

1199. Levy, Michael E. and Smith, Delos R. "Congressional Budget Process Again Reformed." *Conference Board Record* 12 (Mar. 1975): 12-17.

1200. Licata, Anthony R. "Zero-Base Sunset Review." *Harvard Journal on Legislation* 14 (April 1977): 505-541.

1201. McClory, Robert. "Reforming the Budgetary and Fiscal Machinery of Congress." In *We Propose: A Modern Congress,* ed. Mary McInnis, pp. 105-131. New York: McGraw-Hill, 1966.

1202. McGuire, O. R. "Legislative or Executive Control over Accounting for Federal Funds." *Illinois Law Review* 20 (Jan. 1926): 455-474.

1203. Moyer, B. B. "The First Use of the New Congressional Budget Process Has Been a Success." *Armed Forces Comptroller* 21 (April 1976): 14-15.

1204. Picciano, Joseph. "Effects of the New Congressional Budget Act on State and Local Grantees." *Governmental Finance* 4 (Aug. 1975): 23-25.

1205. Rivlin, Alice M. "A Guide to the Congressional Budget Process." *Challenge* 18 (July-Aug. 1975): 26-31.

1206. Rivlin, Alice M. *Improving the Congressional Budget Process. Working Papers on House Committee Organization and Operation. Presented to House Select Committee on Committees.* 93rd Cong., Washington: GPO, 1973.

1207. Schick, Allen. "Budget Reform Legislation: Reorganizing Congressional Centers of Fiscal Power." *Harvard Journal on Legislation* 11 (Feb. 1974): 303-350.

1208. Schick, Allen. *The Congressional Budget Act of 1974: Legislative History and Analysis.* Washington: Congressional Research Service, 1976.

1209. Schick, Allen. *The First Years of the Congressional Budget Process.* Washington: Congressional Research Service, 1976.

1210. Shillingburg, John D. *Budget Information for the New Congressional Budget Process: A Case Study of Two Problems.* Austin: Lyndon B. Johnson School of Public Affairs, University of Texas, 1976.

1211. Skillington, James. E. "Proposed Modifications in Congressional Participation in the Budgetary Process, 1946-1950." Ph.D. dissertation, American University, 1951.

1212. Smith, Donald. "New Budget System Survives First Year Intact." *Congressional Quarterly Weekly Report* 33 (Dec. 27, 1975): 2863-2869.

1213. Smith, Linda L. "The Congressional Budget Process: Why It Worked This Time." *Bureaucrat* 6 (Spring 1977): 88-111.

1214. Staats, Elmer B. "The Nation's Stake in Congressional Budget Reform." *National Public Accountant* 20 (Dec. 1975): 10-15.

1215. Steinman, Michael. "Congressional Budget Reform: Prospects." In *Legislative Reform and Public Policy,* eds. Susan Welch and John G. Peters, pp. 73-81. New York: Praeger, 1977.

1216. Thurber, James A. "Congressional Budget Reform and New Demands for Policy Analysis." *Policy Analysis* 2 (Spring 1976): 197-214.

1217. Thurber, James A. "New Powers of the Purse: An Assessment of Congressional Budget Reform." In *Legislative Reform: The Policy Impact,* ed. Leroy N. Rieselbach, pp. 159-172. Lexington, Mass.: Lexington Books, 1978.

1218. U.S. Congress. House. Committee on the Budget. *Congressional Budget Reform.* 93rd Cong., 2nd sess. Washington: GPO, 1975.

1219. Weidenbaum, Murry L. "The Need for Budgetary Reform." In *Republican Papers,* ed. Melvin R. Laird, pp. 405-418. New York: Praeger, 1968.

1220. Wildavsky, Aaron B. "Political Implications of Budgetary Reform." *Public Administration Review* 21 (Autumn 1961): 183-190.

1221. Wildavsky, Aaron B. "Toward a Radical Incrementalism: A Proposal to Aid Congress in Reform of the Budgetary Process." In *Twelve Studies of the Organization of Congress*, pp. 115-165. Washington: American Enterprise Institute for Public Policy Research, 1966.

1222. Williams, Walter. *Congress, Budget-making, and Policy Analysis: A Critique After the Fiscal Year 1976 Budget Trial Run.* Seattle: University of Washington, Institute of Governmental Research, 1976.

Taxes and Spending

1223. Burstein, Paul. "Party Balance, Replacement of Legislators, and Federal Government Expenditures, 1941-1976." *Western Political Quarterly* 32 (June 1979): 203-208.

1224. Campbell, Colin and Reese, Thomas. "The Energy Crisis and Tax Policy in Canada and the United States: Federal–Provincial Diplomacy v. Congressional Lawmaking." *The Social Science Journal* 14 (Jan. 1977): 17-33.

1225. Cohen, Richard E. "Sophomore Democrats Are Restless on Taxes, House Procedures." *National Journal* 10 (July 29, 1978): 1203-1205.

1226. Committee for Economic Development. *Controlling Federal Government Expenditures: The Roles of Congress and the Administration.* New York: Committee for Economic Development, 1973.

1227. Conable, Barber B. "Aspects of Legislative Persuasion: Congress." *National Tax Journal* 32 (Sept. 1979): 307-312.

1228. "Congress' Diminished Control of the Purse Debated." *Congressional Quarterly Weekly Report* 19 (May 19, 1961): 849-851.

1229. Corwin, Edward S. "The Spending Power of Congress: Apropos the Maternity Act." *Harvard Law Review* 36 (Mar. 1923): 548-582.

1230. Davenport, Charles. "Impact of the Congressional Budget Process on Tax Legislation." *National Tax Journal* 32 (Sept. 1979): 262-269.

1231. Davis, Gerald W. "Congressional Power to Require Defense Expenditures." *Fordham Law Review* 33 (Oct. 1964): 39-60.

1232. Doughton, Robert L. "The Congressional Viewpoint on Conflicting Taxation." *Tax Magazine* 13 (June 1935): 319-320.

1233. Evans, Medford. "At the Public Trough: Congress Itself Is the Issue." *American Opinion* 19 (July 1976): 39-52.

1234. "Federal Tax Policy and the Tax Legislative Process." *National Tax Journal* 32 (Sept. 1979): 221-428.

1235. Findley, William. *Review of the Revenue System Adopted by the First Congress.* Philadelphia: T. Dobson, 1794.

1236. Fisher, Louis. *Congressional Control of Budget Execution. Working Papers on House Committee Organization and Operation. Presented to House Select Committee on Committees.* 93rd Cong. Washington: GPO, 1973.

1237. Fisk, John D. *Legislation to Limit Federal Expenditures: Past and Present.* Washington: Congressional Research Service, 1979.

1238. Gardner, Judy. "Budget Panel Probes Spending 'Shortfall'." *Congressional Quarterly Weekly Report* 33 (Nov. 27, 1976): 3232-3233.

1239. Havemann, Joel. "Budget Report 'Committees Seek Stimulus But Call for Spending Curbs.'" *National Journal* 7 (April 5, 1975): 495-501.

1240. Havemann, Joel. "Budget Report: 'New Senate, House Panels Making Mark on Spending Bills.'" *National Journal* 7 (Nov. 1, 1975): 1499-1507.

1241. Kim, Sun Kil. "Congressional Authorization of Public Debt Transactions as a Means of Backdoor Financing." Ph.D. dissertation, American University, 1962.

1242. Kim, Sun Kil. "Politics of a Congressional Budgetary Process: Backdoor Spending." *Western Political Quarterly* 21 (Dec. 1968): 606-623.

1243. Korb, Lawrence J. "Congressional Impact on Defense Spending, 1962-1973: The Programmatic and Fiscal Hypotheses." *Naval War College Review* 26 (Nov.-Dec. 1973): 49-62.

1244. Lee, R. Alton. "The Truman–80th Congress Struggle over Tax Policy." *Historian* 33 (Nov. 1970): 68-82.

1245. LeLoup, Lance T. "The Impact of Domestic Spending Patterns on Senate Support: An Examination of Three Policy Areas." *American Politics Quarterly* 5 (April 1977): 219-236.

1246. Lowenhaupt, Abraham. "The Power of Congress to Impose Excise Taxes Retroactively." *St. Louis Law Review* 21 (Feb. 1936): 109-120.

1247. Madeo, Silvia A. "The Accumulated Earning Tax: An Empirical Analysis of the Tax Court's Implementation of Congressional Intent." Ph.D. dissertation, North Texas State University, 1977.

1248. Marrs, Aubrey R. "Constitutional Power of Congress over the Administration of Federal Taxation." *Taxes* 31 (July 1953): 503-515.

1249. Matsunaga, Spark M. "Recent Tax Trends in Congress." *Taxes* 50 (Nov. 1972): 683-689.

1250. Morrison, Edward F. "Energy Tax Legislation: The Failure of the 93rd Congress." *Harvard Journal on Legislation* 12 (April 1975): 369-414.

1251. Mulock, Bruce K. *Economic and Inflation Impact Statements: Their Use by the Legislative and Executive Branches*. Washington: Congressional Research Service, 1978.

1252. Parker, Lovell H. "Congressional Study of Conflicting Taxation." *Tax Magazine* 13 (May 1935): 263-264, 300.

1253. Perkins, E. M. "Power of Congress to Levy Taxes for Distribution to the States." *North Carolina Law Review* 12 (June 1934): 326-349.

1254. Portney, P. R. "Congressional Delays in U.S. Fiscal Policy-making: Simulating the Effects." *Journal of Public Economics* 5 (April-May 1976): 237-247.

1255. Power, John R. "Current Congressional Proposals to Reduce the Income Tax Avoidance Use of Real Estate Tax Shelters." *Harvard Journal on Legislation* 13 (April 1976): 578-592.

1256. Proxmire, William, et al. *Can Congress Control Spending?* Washington: American Enterprise Institute for Public Policy Research, 1973.

1257. Ray, Bruce A. "Congressional Influence and the Geographical Distribution of Federal Spending." Ph.D. dissertation, Washington University, 1977.

1258. "Regionalism in Congress: Formulas Debated." *Congressional Quarterly Weekly Report* 35 (Aug. 20, 1977): 1747-1752.

1259. Schroeher, Kathy. *Gimme Shelters: A Common Cause Study of the Review of Tax Expenditures by the Congressional Tax Committees*. Washington: Common Cause, 1978.

1260. Schulman, Walter H. "The Constitutionality of Section 611 (Revenue Act of 1928) In the Light of Its Remedial Purpose." *National Income Tax Magazine* 8 (Feb.-Mar. 1930): 52-56, 76-78, 96-101.

1261. Steeg, Moise S. "Limitations on the Congressional Power to Spend." *Tulane Law Review* 10 (April 1936): 446-461.

1262. Steeg, Moise S. "Limitation on the Congressional Power to Spend—II." *Tulane Review* 11 (April 1937): 451-468.

1263. Steeg, Moise S. "Limitation on the Congressional Power to Spend—III." *Tulane Law Review* 12 (Dec. 1937): 138-154.

1264. Stern, David J. "Congress, Politics, And Taxes: A Case Study of the Revenue Act of 1962." Ph.D. dissertation, Claremont Graduate School, 1965.

1265. Surrey, Stanley W. *Tax Expenditures in Relation to Congressional Control Over Budgetary Outlay and Receipt Totals. Working Papers on House Committee Organization and Operation. Presented to House Select Committee on Committees.* 93rd Cong. Washington: GPO, 1973.

1266. Tax Foundation. *Congressional Control of Federal Expenditures.* New York: Tax Foundation, 1965.

1267. Tax Foundation. *Congressional Expenditure Limitations: An Evaluation.* New York: Tax Foundation, 1969.

1268. Wallace, Robert A. *Congressional Control of Federal Spending.* Detroit, Mich.: Wayne State University Press, 1960.

1269. Wildavsky, Aaron B. "The Annual Expenditure Increment: Or, How Congress Can Regain Control of the Budget." *Public Interest* 33 (Fall 1973): 84-108.

1270. Wildavsky, Aaron B. *The Annual Expenditure Increment. Working Papers on House Committee Organization and Operation. Presented to House Select Committee on Committees.* 93rd Cong. Washington: GPO, 1973.

1271. Wilmerding, Lucius. *The Spending Power*: A History of the Efforts of Congress to Control Expenditures. New Haven, Conn.: Yale University Press, 1943.

1272. Wittkopf, Eugene R. "Incrementalism and Change in the Distribution of U.S. Foreign Policy Expenditures." *International Interactions* 2 (May 1976): 93-100.

1273. Young, Roland A. "Congressional Controls on Federal Finance." PH.D. dissertation, Harvard University, 1940.

Appropriations

1274. Bozik, Edward E. "National Defense and Congressional Behavior: Congressional Action on Authorizing and Appropriating Legislation for Military Budgets and Military Construction, 1951-1966." Ph.D. dissertation, Georgetown University, 1968.

1275. Cameron, Juan. "Those Frayed Congressional Purse Strings." *Fortune* 87 (Feb. 1973): 98-110.

1276. Cole, Babalola. "Appropriation, Politics and Black Schools: Howard University in the U.S. Congress, 1879-1928." *Journal of Negro Education* 46 (Winter 1977): 7-23.

1277. "Congress' Fiscal Role is Object of Growing Concern." *Congressional Quarterly Weekly Report* 21 (June 7, 1963): 886-891.

1278. Cronin, Richard P. *An Analysis of Congressional Reductions in the Defense Budget: Fiscal Years 1971-1976.* Washington: Congressional Research Service, 1976.

1279. Cunnea, Patricia E. "Water Resources Policy Formation in the Appropriations Process: Congress and the Bureau of Reclamation." Ph.D. dissertation, University of Chicago, 1963.

1280. Danco, A. G. "Effects of Congressional Funding Limitations on Development of Major Defense Systems." *Armed Forces Comptroller* 21 (Oct. 1976): 24-27.

1281. Davis, Otto A., Dempster, M. A. H., and Wildavsky, Aaron B. "Towards a Predictive Theory of Government Expenditures: U.S. Domestic Appropriations." *British Journal of Political Science* 4 (Oct. 1974): 419-452.

1282. Dine, Thomas A. "Politics of the Purse." In *Congress and Arms Control,* eds. Alan Platt and Lawrence D. Weiler, pp. 59-96. Boulder, Colo.: Westview Press, 1978.

1283. Fairlie, Henry. "Defense Spending: The Dodos and Platypuses." *Washington Monthly* 7 (Feb. 1976): 36-41.

1284. Fenno, Richard F. "The Impact of PPBs on the Congressional Appropriations Process." In *Information Support, Program Budgeting and the Congress,* eds. Robert L. Chartrand, Kenneth Janda and Michael Hugo, pp. 175-194. New York: Spartan Books, 1968.

1285. Fox, Douglas M. "Congress and U.S. Military Service Budgets in the Post-War Period: A Research Note." *Midwest Journal of Political Science* 15 (May 1971): 382-393.

1286. Fuller, Jon W. "Congress and the Defense Budget: A Study of the McNamara Years." Ph.D. dissertation, Princeton University, 1972.

1287. Gist, John R. "Appropriations Politics and Expenditure Control." *Journal of Politics* 40 (Feb. 1978): 163-178.

1288. Gist, John R. "'Increment' and 'Base' in the Congressional Appropriations Process." *American Journal of Political Science* 21 (May 1977): 341-352.

1289. Gordon, Bernard K. "Military Budget: Congressional Phase." *Journal of Politics* 23 (Nov. 1961): 689-710.

1290. Habacivch, William. "Congressional Preferences for Expenditure Proposals: Some Theoretical and Empirical Considerations." Ph.D. dissertation, University of Illinois at Urbana-Champaign, 1967.

1291. Huzar, Elias. "Congress and the Army: Appropriations." *American Political Science Review* 37 (Aug. 1943): 661-676.

1292. Huzar, Elias. *The Purse and the Sword: Control of the Army by Congress Through Military Appropriations, 1933-1950.* Ithaca, N.Y.: Cornell University Press, 1950.

1293. Julian, William B. "The United States Senate and Military Spending: An Exploration of the Relationship Between Issues and Coalitions." Ph.D. dissertation, University of Wisconsin, 1975.

1294. Kanter, Arnold. "Congress and the Defense Budget: 1960-1970." *American Political Science Review* 66 (Mar. 1972): 129-143.

1295. Kirby, James C. "The House-Senate Appropriations Dispute in the 87th Congress." *American Bar Association Journal* 48 (Dec. 1962): 1167-1169.

1296. Kirst, Michael. *Government Without Passing Laws: Congress' Nonstatutory Techniques for Appropriations Control.* Chapel Hill: University of North Carolina Press, 1969.

1297. Knapp, David C. "Congressional Control of Agricultural Conservation Policy: A Case Study of the Appropriations Process." *Political Science Quarterly* 71 (June 1956): 257-281.

1298. Kolodziej, Edward A. "Congress' Use of Its Appropriations Power to Determine Force Levels and Weapon Systems, 1946–1958." Ph.D. dissertation, University of Chicago, 1962.

1299. Leiserson, Avery. "Coordination of the Federal Budgetary and Appropriations Procedures Under the Legislative Reorganization Act of 1946." *National Tax Journal* 1 (June 1948): 118-126.

1300. Marvick, L. Dwaine. "Congressional Appropriation Politics: A Study of Institutional Conditions for Expressing Supply Intent." Ph.D. dissertation, Columbia University, 1952.

1301. Meier, Kenneth J. and Van Lohuizen, J. R. "Interest Groups in the Appropriations Process: The Wasted Profession Revisited." *Social Science Quarterly* 59 (Dec. 1978): 482-495.

1302. Murray, Alan P. "Congressional Control over Fiscal Affairs." *Financial Executive* 44 (May 1976): 42-47.

1303. Nelson, Dalmas H. "The Omnibus Appropriations Act of 1950." *Journal of Politics* 15 (May 1953): 274-288.

1304. Pressman, Jeffry L. *House vs. Senate: Conflict in the Appropriations Process.* New Haven, Conn.: Yale University Press, 1966.

1305. "Procedures Used by Congress to Appropriate Money." *Congressional Quarterly Weekly Report* 15 (May 3, 1957): 533-534.

1306. Reagan, Michael D. "Congress Meets Science: The Appropriations Process." *Science* 164 (May 1969): 926-931.

1307. Roback, Herbert. "Congress and the Science Budget: Adaptation of Address, December 28, 1967." *Science* 160 (May 1968): 964-971.

1308. Sargent, Noel. "Bills for Raising Revenue Under the Federal and State Constitutions." *Minnesota Law Review* 4 (April 1920): 330-352.

1309. Sharkansky, Ira. "Four Agencies and an Appropriations Subcommittee: A Comparative Study of Budget Strategies." *Midwest Journal of Political Science* 9 (Aug. 1965): 254-281.

1310. Sievers, Michael A. "Funding the California Indian Superintendency: A Case Study of Congressional Appropriations." *Southern California Quarterly* 59 (Spring 1977): 49-73.

1311. Sims, William P. "Role of Congress in Shaping Fiscal Policy: The Legislative Budget." *Goergetown Law Journal* 36 (Nov. 1947): 34-47.

1312. Terry, Joseph G. "A Methodology for Analyzing Congressional Behavior Toward Department of Defense Budget Requests." Master's thesis, Naval Postgraduate School, 1973.

1313. Thomas, Morgan. "Appropriations Control and the Atomic Energy Program." *Western Political Quarterly* 9 (Sept. 1956): 713-725.

1314. Thomas, Robert D. and Handberg, Roger B. "Congressional Budgeting for Eight Agencies, 1947-1972." *American Journal of Political Science* 18 (Feb. 1974): 179-185.

1315. U.S. Congress. Senate. Committee on Government Operations. *The Authority of the Senate to Originate Appropriation Bills.* 88th Cong., 1st sess. Washington: GPO, 1963.

1316. U.S. General Accounting Office. *Reimbursements to Appropriations: Legislative Suggestions for Improved Congressional Control* Washington: GPO, 1976.

1317. Walsh, John. "Appropriations: The Critics of Congress Often Slight an Inner Redoubt of the System." *Science* 143 (Feb. 1964): 548-551.

1318. Warren, Charles. *Congress as Santa Claus: Or, National Donations and the General Welfare Clause of the Constitution.* Charlottesville, Va.: The Michie Co., 1932.

1319. Whelan, John W. "Purse Strings, Payments and Procurement." *Public Law* 1964 (Winter 1964): 322-366.

Impoundment

1320. Abascal, R. S. and Kramer, J. R. "Presidential Impoundment—Historical Genesis and Constitutional Framework: Judicial and Legislative Responses." *Georgetown Law Journal* 62 (July 1974): 1549-1618; 63 (Oct. 1974): 149-189.

1321. Bendes, Barry J. "The President and the Congress: Impoundment of Domestic Funds." *New York University Review of Law and Social Change* 3 (Spring 1973): 93-118.

1322. Betts, Ernest C. and Miller, Richard E. "More About the Impact of the Congressional Budget and Impoundment Control Act." *Bureaucrat* 6 (Spring 1977): 112-120.

1323. Boggs, Hale. "Executive Impoundment of Congressionally Appropriated Funds." *University of Florida Law Review* 24 (Winter 1972): 221-229.

1324. Easterling, James T. "The Amended Rural Electrification Act: Congressional Response to Administrative Impoundment." *Harvard Journal on Legislation* 11 (Feb. 1974): 205-231.

1325. Fisher, Louis. "Funds Impounded by the President: The Constitutional Issue." *George Washington Law Review* 38 (Oct. 1969): 124-137.

1326. Fisher, Louis. "The Politics of Impounded Funds." *Administrative Science Quarterly* 15 (Sept. 1970): 361-377.

1327. Gordon, Seymour. "Initial Implementation and the Congressional Budget and Impoundment Control Act in the Context of the Continuing Redistribution of Budget Power Within the Congress and Between the Congress and the President." Ph.D. dissertation, George Washington University, 1977.

1328. Miles, Jerome A. "The Congressional Budget and Impoundment Control Act: A Departmental Budget Officer's View." *Bureaucrat* 5 (Jan. 1977): 391-404.

1329. Munselle, William G. "Congressional Reform: The Case of Impoundment." *Policy Studies Journal* 5 (Summer 1977): 480-485.

1330. Munselle, William G. "Presidential Impoundment and Congressional Reform." In *Legislative Reform: The Policy Impact*, ed. Leroy N. Rieselbach, pp. 173-181. Lexington, Mass.: Lexington Books, 1978.

1331. Pfiffner, James P. *The President, the Budget and Congress: Impoundment and the 1974 Budget Act.* Boulder, Colo.: Westview Press, 1979.

1332. Pfiffner, James P. "Presidential Impoundment of Funds and Congressional Control of the Budget." Ph.D. dissertation, University of Wisconsin, 1975.

1333. "Protecting the Fisc: Executive Impoundment and Congressional Power." *Yale Law Journal* 82 (July 1973): 1636-1658.

1334. Schick, Allen. *The Congressional Budget and Impoundment Act (P.L. 93-344): A Summary of Its Provisions.* Washington: Congressional Research Service, 1976.

1335. Schick, Allen. *The Impoundment Control Act of 1974: Legislative History and Implementation.* Washington: Congressional Research Service, 1976.

1336. "Separation of Power—Impoundent of Funds—Congress Attempts to Curtail the President's Power to Impound Appropriated Funds." *Indiana Law Review* 6 (Mar. 1973): 523-530.

1337. Vale, Vivian. "The Obligation to Spend: Presidential Impoundment of Congressional Appropriations." *Political Studies* 25 (Dec. 1977): 508-522.

Oversight Function

1338. Aberbach, Joel D. "Changes in Congressional Oversight." *American Behavioral Scientist* 22 (May-June 1979): 493-515.

1339. Aberbach, Joel D. "The Development of Oversight in the United States Congress: Concepts and Analysis." In *Techniques and Procedures for Analysis and Evaluation: A Compilation of Papers Prepared for the Commission on the Operation of the Senate,* pp. 53-69. 94th Cong., 2d sess. Washington: GPO, 1977.

1340. Adams, Bruce. "Sunset: A Proposal for Accountable Government." *Administrative Law Review* 28 (Summer 1976): 511-542.

1341. Association of the Bar of the City of New York. Committee on Civil Rights. *The Central Intelligence Agency: Oversight and Accountability by the Committee on Civil Rights and the Committee on International Human Rights.* New York: The Association, 1975.

1342. Behn, Robert D. "The False Dawn of the Sunset Laws." *Public Interest* 49 (Fall 1977): 103-118.

1343. Bibby, John F. "Committee Characteristics and Legislative Oversight of Administration." *Midwest Journal of Political Science* 10 (Feb. 1966): 78-98.

1344. Bibby, John F. "Congress' Neglected Function." In *Republican Papers*, ed. Melvin R. Laird, pp. 477–488. New York: Praeger, 1968.

1345. Bibby, John F. "Legislative Oversight of Administration: A Case Study of a Congressional Committee." Ph.D. dissertation, University of Wisconsin, 1963.

1346. Bibby, John F. and Huckshorn, Robert J. *Current Politics: The Way Things Work in Washington.* Minneapolis, Minn.: Winston Press, 1973.

1347. Blackstock, Paul W. "Congressional Watchdogs and Current Misconceptions." In his *The Strategy of Subversion: Manipulating the Politics of Other Nations,* pp. 273-286. Chicago: Quadrangle Books, 1964.

1348. Brademas, John, Pierce, Neil R., Richardson, Elliot, Ostrom, Vincent, and Weinberger, Casper W. "Organizational Rationality, Congressional Oversight, and Decentralization: An Exchange." *Publius* 8 (Spring 1978): 111-120.

1349. Brown, MacAlister. "The Demise of State Department Public Opinion Polls: A Study in Legislative Oversight." *Midwest Journal of Political Science* 5 (Feb. 1961): 1-17.

1350. Christian, Betty J. " 'Sunset' Laws: A New Approach to Congressional Oversight." *ICC Practitioners' Journal* 44 (Jan.-Feb. 1977): 186-192.

1351. "The CIA: Congress Seeks Better Oversight." *Congressional Quarterly Weekly Report* 32 (Dec. 7, 1974): 3277-3279.

1352. Cohen, Richard E. "Sunset Proposals in Congress: Sinking Below the Horizon." *National Journal* 11 (Nov. 24, 1979): 1965-2008.

1353. Cohen, Richard E. "Will the 96th Congress Become the 'Oversight' Congress." *National Journal* 11 (Jan. 13, 1979): 44-49.

1354. Collier, Ellen C. "Monitoring Reports to Congress Required by Law." In *Legislative Oversight and Program Evaluation: A Seminar Sponsored by the Congressional Research Service,* 94th Cong., 2d sess., pp. 94-104. Washington: GPO, 1976.

1355. Cotter, Cornelius P. "Legislative Oversight." In *Twelve Studies of the Organization of Congress,* ed. Alfred de Grazia, pp. 25-81. Washington: American Enterprise Institute for Public Policy Research, 1966.

1356. Cotter, Cornelius P. and Smith, Malcolm J. "Administrative Accountability: Reporting to Congress." *Western Political Quarterly* 10 (June 1957): 405-415.

1357. Cotter, Cornelius P. and Smith, Malcolm J. "Congress: The Concurrent Resolution." *Western Political Quarterly* 9 (Dec. 1956): 955-966.

1358. Cotter, Cornelius P. and Smith, Malcolm J. "Administrative Responsibility: Congressional Prescription of Interagency Relationship." *Western Political Quarterly* 10 (Dec. 1957): 765-782.

1359. Crystal, E. Susan. "Congressional Authorization and Oversight of International Fishery Agreements Under the Fishery Conservation and Management Act of 1976." *Washington Law Review* 52 (July 1977): 495-511.

1360. Dawson, Raymond H. "Congressional Innovation and Intervention in Defense Policy: Legislative Authorization of Weapons Systems." *American Political Science Review* 56 (Mar. 1962): 42-57.

1361. Dimock, Marshall E. "Forms of Control over Administrative Action." In *Essays on the Law and Practice of Governmental Administration,* ed. Charles G. Haines and Marshall E. Dimock, pp. 287-321. Baltimore: Johns Hopkins University Press, 1935.

1362. Falkenberg, Robert H. "The Rule of Congress in Military Aid: Increasing or Decreasing Legislative Oversight? A Case Study of the Military Assistance Program in Latin America, 1952-1970." Ph.D. dissertation, American University, 1973.

1363. Fisher, Louis. "Presidential Spending Discretion and Congressional Controls." *Law and Contemporary Problems* 37 (Winter 1972): 135-172.

1364. Fitzgerald, John L. "Congressional Oversight or Congressional Foresight: Guidelines from Founding Fathers." *Administrative Law Review* 28 (Summer 1976): 429-445.

1365. Freed, Bruce F. "Congress May Step Up Oversight of Programs." *Congressional Quarterly Weekly Report* 33 (Mar. 22, 1975): 595-600.

1366. Hammond, Susan W., Fox, Harrison W., Moraski, Richard, and Nicholson, Jeanne B. "Senate Oversight Activities." In *Techniques and Procedures for Analysis and Evaluation: A Compilation of Papers Presented for the Commission on the Operation of the Senate,* 94th Cong., 2nd sess., pp. 70-105. Washington: GPO, 1977.

1367. Hardin, Charles M. "The Problem of Bureaucracy." In his *Presidential Power and Accountability: Toward a New Constitution,* pp. 66-75. Chicago: University of Chicago Press, 1974.

1368. Harris, Oren. "Improving the Regulatory Process." *Public Utilities Fortnightly* 64 (July 1959): 19-26.

1369. Hyneman, Charles S. "Direction and Control by Congress." In his *Bureaucracy in a Democracy,* pp. 75-203. New York: Harper and Brothers, 1950.

1370. Johannes, John R. "Casework as a Technique of U.S. Congressional Oversight of the Executive." *Legislative Studies Quarterly* 4 (Aug. 1979): 325-351.

1371. Jones, Harry W. " 'Oversight' Function of Congressional Standing Committees." *American Bar Association Journal* 34 (Nov. 1948): 1018-1019.

1372. Jones, Harry W. " 'Watchdog Committees in the 80th Congress." *American Bar Association Journal* 34 (Aug. 1948): 726-727.

1373. Kaiser, Frederick M. *Congressional Oversight of Intelligence: Status and Recommendations.* Washington: Congressional Research Sercice, 1976.

1374. Kerr, James R. "Congress and Space: Overview or Oversight?" *Public Administration Review* 25 (Sept. 1965): 185-192.

1375. Kerr, James R. "Congressmen as Overseers: Surveillance of the Space Program." Ph.D. dissertation, Stanford University, 1963.

1376. Knezo, Genevieve and Oleszek, Walter J. "Legislative Oversight and Program Evaluation." *Bureaucrat* 5 (April 1976): 37-51.

1377. Krasnow, Erwin G. and Shooshan, Harry M. "Congressional Oversight: The Ninety-Second Congress and the Federal Communications Commission." *Harvard Journal on Legislation 10 (Feb. 1973): 297-329.*

1378. Lea, Doug. "Senate's Antitrust Watchdog Moves into Environment, Consumer Areas." *National Journal* 2 (Aug. 22 1970): 1824-1832.

1379. Lee, Mordecai, K. "Congressional Oversight of Federal Public Relations." Ph.D. dissertation, Syracuse University, 1975.

1380. Lees, John D. "Legislative Oversight and Review: The Dynamics of Congressional Responsibility and Administrative Accountability." *Journal of American Studies* 5 (Aug. 1971): 201-206.

1381. Lees, John D. "Legislative Review and Bureaucratic Responsibility: The Impact of Fiscal Oversight by Congress on the American Federal Administration." *Public Administration* 45 (Winter 1967): 369-386.

1382. Lees, John D. "Legislatures and Oversight: A Review Article on a Neglected Area of Research." *Legislative Studies Quarterly* 2 (May 1977): 193-208.

1383. Levy, Arthur B. "Formal Techniques of Oversight: The Case of the House Agriculture Committee, 1964-1965." Ph.D. dissertation, Harvard University, 1971.

1384. Levy, Beryl H. "Congressional Oversight of Administrative Agencies." *American Bar Association Journal* 36 (Mar. 1950): 236-237.

1385. Little, Dennis L. "Ask the Right Questions." In *Legislative Oversight and Program Evaluation: A Seminar Sponsored by the Congressional Research Service,* 94th Cong., 2d sess., pp. 63-70. Washington: GPO, 1976.

1386. Macmahon, Arthur W. "Congressional Oversight of Administration: The Power of the Purse." *Political Science Quarterly* 58 (June-Sept. 1943): 161-190, 380-414.

1387. McMurty, Virginia. *Sunset Laws: Establishing Systematic Oversight Procedure.* Washington: Congressional Research Service, 1979.

1388. Maurer, George J. "Congressional Oversight of Defense Production." *George Washington Law Review* 21 (Oct. 1952): 26-36.

1389. Maxfield, David M. "Congress Considers CIA Oversight Plans." *Congressional Quarterly Weekly Report* 34 (Feb. 7, 1976): 285-290.

1390. Maxfield, David M. "Congress Weighs Proposals to Control CIA." *Congressional Quarterly Weekly Report* 33 (July 19, 1975): 1544-1551.

1391. Moore, John M. "Military Strategy and Legislative Oversight." Ph.D. dissertation, University of Georgia, 1970.

1392. Morrow, William L. "Legislative Control of Administrative Discretion: The Case of Congress and Foreign Aid." *Journal of Politics* 30 (Nov. 1968): 985-1011.

1393. Ogden, Gregory L. "Reducing Administrative Delay: Timeliness Standards, Judicial Review of Agency Procedures, Procedural Reform, and Legislative Oversight." *University of Dayton Law Review* 4 (Winter 1979): 71-137.

1394. Ogul, Morris S. *Congress Oversees the Bureaucracy: Studies in Legislative Supervision.* Pittsburgh, Pa.: University of Pittsburgh Press, 1976.

1395. Ogul, Morris S. "Congressional Oversight: Structures and Incentives." In *Congress Reconsidered,* eds. Lawrence C. Dodd and Bruce I. Oppenheimer, pp. 207-221. New York: Praeger, 1977.

1396. Ogul, Morris S. *Legislative Oversight of Bureaucracy. Working Papers on House Committee Organization and Operation. Presented to House Select Committee and Committees.* 93rd Cong. Washington: GPO, 1973.

1397. Oleszek, Walter J. *Congressional Oversight: Methods and Reform Proposals. Working Papers on House Committee Organization and Operation. Presented to House Select Committee on Committees.* 93rd Cong. Washington: GPO, 1973.

1398. Oleszek, Walter J. "Congressional Oversight: A Review of Recent Legislative Service." In *Legislative Oversight and Program Evaluation: A Seminar Sponsored by the Congressional Research Service,* 94th Cong., 2nd sess., pp. 44-54. Washington: GPO, 1976.

1399. Paldy, Lester G., ed. "Congressional Review of NSF Implementation Programs: Politics and Polemics." *Journal of College Science Teaching* 5 (Mar. 1976): 246-251.

1400. Pearson, James B. "Oversight: A Vital Yet Neglected Congressional Function." *Kansas Law Review* 23 (Winter 1975): 277-288.

1401. Piliawsky, Monte E. "Legislative Oversight: The Politics of Investigation." Ph.D. dissertation, Tulane University, 1971.

1402. Porter, Laurellen. "Congress and Agricultural Policy." *Policy Studies Journal* 6 (Summer 1978): 427-479.

1403. "Regulatory Agencies: Congress Taking a Fresh Look." *Congressional Quarterly Weekly Report* 31 (Dec. 29, 1973): 3347–3452.

1404. Ribicoff, Abraham A. "Congressional Oversight and Regulatory Reform." *Administrative Law Review* 28 (Summer 1976): 415-427.

1405. Roberts, Steven M. "Congressional Oversight of Monetary Policy." *Journal of Monetary Economics* 4 (Aug. 1978): 543-556.

1406. Sanford, Jonathan and Goodman, Margaret. "Congressional Oversight and the Multilateral Development Banks." *International Organization* 29 (Autumn 1975): 1055-1064.

1407. Scher, Seymour. "Conditions for Legislative Control." *Journal of Politics* 25 (Aug. 1963): 526-551.

1408. Schick, Allen. "Congress and the 'Details' of Administration." *Public Administration Review* 36 (Sept. 1976): 516-528.

1409. Schnurer, Eric. "A Slight Oversight: Congress Space Probe." *Washington Monthly* 11 (Sept. 1979): 23-27.

1410. Schwartzman, Robin B. "Fiscal Oversight of the Central Intelligence Agency: Can Accountability and Confidentiality Coexist." *New York University Journal of International Law and Politics* 7 (Winter 1974): 493-544.

1411. Shipley, George C. "Congress and the Agencies: An Analysis of Legislative Oversight in the United States House of Representatives." Ph.D. dissertation, University of Texas at Austin, 1977.

1412. Smith, Malcolm J. and Cotter, Cornelius P. "Administrative Accountability: Reporting to Congress." *Western Political Quarterly* 10 (June 1957): 405-415.

1413. Stewart, Richard B. "Lawyers and the Legislative Process." *Harvard Journal on Legislation* 10 (Feb. 1973): 151-174.

1414. Sullivan, John H. "Foreign Affairs Oversight: Role of Staff Survey Mission." In *Legislative Oversight and Program Evaluation: A Seminar Sponsored by the Congressional Research Service*, 94th Cong., 2nd sess., pp. 173-187. Washington: GPO, 1976.

1415. Thurber, James A. "Legislative--Administrative Relations." *Policy Studies Journal* 5 (Autumn 1976): 56-65.

1416. Tunney, John V. "Federal Legislative Process: Misinformation, Reaction and Excessive Delegation." *Environmental Law* 7 (Spring 1977): 499-508.

1417. U.S. Congress. House. Committee on Government Operations. *Oversight Plans of the Committees of the U.S. House of Representatives*. 94th Cong., 1st sess. Washington: GPO 1975.

1418. U.S. Congress. House. Judiciary Committee. *Congressional Review of Administrative Rule Making, Hearing*. Washington: GPO, 1975.

1419. U.S. Congress. House. Rules Committee. *Recommendations on Establishment of Procedures for Congressional Review of Agency Rules*. 96th Cong., 2nd sess. Washington: GPO, 1980.

1420. U.S. Congress. House. Rules Committee. *Regulatory Reform and Congressional Review of Agency Rules*. 96th Cong., 1st sess. Washington: GPO, 1979.

1421. U.S. Congress. Senate. Governmental Affairs Committee. *Congressional Review of Federal Agencies' Rules and Regulations.* 96th Cong., 1st sess. Washington: GPO, 1979.

1422. U.S. Congress. Senate. Government Operations Committee. *Improving Congressional Oversight of Federal Regulatory Agencies.* Washington: GPO, 1976.

1423. U.S. Congress. Senate. Governmental Affairs Committee. *Public Attitude Toward Congressional Review of Programs.* 95th Cong., 2nd sess. Washington: GPO, 1978.

1424. U.S. General Accounting Office. *Finding Out How Programs Are Working: Suggestions for Congressional Oversight.* Washington: GPO, 1977.

1425. Vinyard, Dale. "Congressional Checking on Executive Agencies." *Business and Government Review* 11 (Sept.-Oct. 1970): 14-18.

1426. Walsh, John. "Congress: Legislative Oversight Problem Acquires New Dimensions as Great Society Bills are Passed." *Science* 148 (April 1965): 474-482.

1427. White, Roger S. and Smale, Pauline. *Oversight and Legislative Activities of the 95th Congress Relating to the Monetary Policy Functions of the Federal Reserve System.* Washington: Congressional Research Service, 1979.

1428. White, Roger S., Smale, Pauline, and Wells, F. Jean. *Federal Reserve System: Summary of Congressional Oversight and Structural Reform Proposals in the 94th Congress.* Washington: Congressional Research Service, 1976.

1429. Wolff, Hugh W. *Intelligence Community: Congressional Oversight.* Washington: Congressional Research Service, 1978.

Confirmations

1430. Adams, Bruce. *The Senate Rubberstamp Machine: A Common Cause Study of the U.S. Senate's Confirmation Process.* Washington: Common Cause, 1977.

1431. Berger, Harriet F. "Appointment and Confirmation to the National Labor Relations Board: Democratic Constraints on Presidential Power?" *Presidential Studies Quarterly* 8 (Fall 1978): 403-416.

1432. Black, Charles L. "A Note on Senatorial Consideration of Supreme Court Nominees." *Yale Law Journal* 79 (Mar. 1970): 657-664.

1433. Black, Forrest R. "Role of the United States Senate in Passing on the Nominations to Membership in the Supreme Court of the United States." *Kentucky Law Journal* 19 (Mar. 1931): 226-238.

1434. Black, Forrest R. "Should the Senate Pass on the Social and Economic Views of Nominees to the Supreme Court of the United States." *St. John's Law Review* 6 (May 1932): 257-271.

1435. Bloch, Charles J. "Does the Senate Neglect Its Duty? *Georgia Bar Journal* 12 (May 1950: 431-438.

1436. Cole, Kenneth C. "Mr. Justice Black and Senatorial Courtesy." *American Political Science Review* 31 (Dec. 1937): 1113-1115.

1437. Cole, Kenneth C. "Role of the Senate in the Confirmation of Judicial Nominations." *American Political Science Review* 28 (Oct. 1934): 875-894.

1438. Crouch, Barry A. "Dennis Chavez and Roosevelt's 'Court-Packing' Plan." *New Mexico Historical Review* 42 (Oct. 1967): 261-280.

1439. Curl, Donald W. "The Long Memory of the United States Senate." *Ohio History* 76 (Summer 1967): 103-113.

1440. Dinnerstein, Leonard. "The Senate's Rejection of Aubrey Williams as Rural Electrification Administrator." *Alabama Review* 21 (April 1968): 133-143.

1441. Dynia, Philip A. "Senate Rejection of Supreme Court Nominees: Factors Affecting Rejection, 1795-1972." Ph.D. dissertation, Georgetown University, 1973.

1442. Ferling, John. "The Senate and Federal Judges: The Intent of the Founding Fathers." *Capitol Studies* 11 (Winter 1974): 57-70.

1443. Fowler, Dorothy G. "Congressional Dictation of Local Appointments: A Historical Survey." *Journal of Politics* 7 (Feb. 1945): 25-57.

1444. Frank, John P. "The Appointment of Supreme Court Justices: Prestige, Principles, and Politics." *Wisconsin Law Review* (Mar.-May-July 1941): 170-210, 343-379, 461-512.

1445. Grachek, Arthur F. "United States Senate Debates on Supreme Court Nominations Between 1925 and 1970." Ph.D. dissertation, Wayne State University, 1970.

1446. Griffin, Robert P. and Hart, Philip A. "The Fortas Controversy: The Senate's Role of Advice and Consent to Judicial Nominations." *Prospects* 2 (April 1969): 283-310.

1447. Grossman, Joel B. and Wasby, Stephen L. "The Senate and Supreme Court Nominations: Some Reflections." *Duke Law Journal* 1972 (Aug. 1972): 557-591.

1448. Hahn, Harlan. "President Taft and the Discipline of Patronage." *Journal of Politics* 28 (May 1966): 368-390.

1449. Harris, Josph P. *The Advice and Consent of the Senate: A Study of the Confirmation of Appointments by the United States Senate.* Berkeley: University of California Press, 1953.

1450. Harris, Joseph P. "The Senatorial Rejection of Leland Olds: A Case Study." *American Political Science Review* 45 (Sept. 1951): 674-692.

1451. James, Louis C. "Senatorial Rejections of Presidential Nominations to the Cabinet: A Study in Constitutional Custom." *Arizona Law Review* 3 (Winter 1961): 232-261.

1452. Keeffe, Arthur J. "The New Is Always Old." *American Bar Association Journal* 59 (May 1973): 536-538.

1453. Key, Valdimer O. "Congressional Nominations." In his *Politics, Parties, and Pressure Groups,* 5th ed., pp. 434-455. New York: Thomas Y. Crowell Co., 1964.

1454. Kripke, Homer. "Constitutional Law: Conclusiveness of Consent of Senate to Presidential Appointment." *Michigan Law Review* 31 (Nov. 1932): 77-85.

1455. Kurland, Philip B. "The Appointment and Disappointment of Supreme Court Justices." *Arizona State Law Journal* (1972): 183-223.

1456. McConnell, A. Mitchell. "Haynsworth and Carswell: A New Senate Standard of Excellence." *Kentucky Law Journal* 59 (Fall 1970): 7-34.

1457. McGuire, O. R. "Power of the Senate to Unseat an Officer Whose Appointment It Has Confirmed and Notified the President Thereof." *University of Pennsylvania Law Review* 79 (April 1931): 769-773.

1458. MacKenzie, G. Calvin. "Senate Confirmation Procedures." In *Committees and Senate Procedures: A Compilation of Papers Prepared for the Commission on the Operation of the Senate,* 94th Cong., 2nd sess., pp. 100-114. Washington: GPO, 1977.

1459. McMahon, Arthur W. "Senatorial Confirmation." *Public Administration Review* 3 (Autumn 1943): 281-296.

1460. MacVeagh, Rogers. "The St. Paul Railway Reorganization." *Oregon Law Review* 7 (June 1928): 280-300.

1461. Marszalek, John F. "Grover Cleveland and the Tenure of Office Act." Duquesne Review 15 (Spring 1970): 206-219.

1462. Massaro, John. "Advice and Dissent: Factors in the Senate's Refusal to Confirm Supreme Court Nominees, with Special Emphasis on the Cases of Abe Fortas, Clement Haynsworth." Ph.D. dissertation, Southern Illinois University, 1973.

1463. Mendelsohn, Rona H. "Senate Confirmation of Supreme Court Appointments: The Nomination and Rejection of John J. Parker." *Howard Law Journal 14 (Winter 1968): 105-148.*

1464. Moe, Ronald C. "Senate Confirmation of Executive Appointments: The Nixon Era." *Academy of Political Science Proceedings* 32 (1975): 141-152.

1465. Neustadt, Richard E. "On Patronage, Power, and Politics." Review of *The Advice and Consent of the Senate: A Study of the Confirmation of Appointments by the United States Senate,* by J. P. Harris. *Public Administration Review* 15 (Spring 1955): 108-114.

1466. Nigro, Felix A. "Lilienthal Case." *Southwestern Social Science Quarterly* 40 (Sept. 1959): 147-158.

1467. Nigro, Felix A. "Pauley Case." *Southwestern Social Science Quarterly* 40 (Mar. 1960): 341-349.

1468. Nigro, Felix A. "Senate Confirmation." *Georgetwon Law Journal* 42 (Jan. 1954): 241-260.

1469. Nigro, Felix A. "Senate Confirmation." Ph.D. dissertation, University of Wisconsin, 1948.

1470. Nigro, Felix A. "Senate Confirmation and Foreign Policy." *Journal of Politics* 14 (May 1952): 281-299.

1471. Nigro, Felix A. "Van Buren Confirmation Before the Senate." *Western Political Quarterly* 14 (Mar. 1961): 148-159.

1472. Nigro, Felix A. "The Warren Case." *Western Political Quarterly* 11 (Dec. 1958): 835-856.

1473. Overmeyer, Philip H. "Attorney General Williams and the Chief Justiceship." *Pacific Northwest Quarterly* 28 (July 1937): 251-262.

1474. Pierce, Carl A. "A Vacancy on the Supreme Court: The Politics of Judicial Appointment, 1893-94." *Tennessee Law Review* 39 (Summer 1972): 555-612.

1475. Ressequie, Harry E. "Federal Conflict of Interest: The A.T. Stewart Case." *New York History* 47 (July 1966): 271-301.

1476. Schiffman, Irving. "Senatorial Discourtesy: The Nomination of Francis X. Morrissey." In *Public Choice and Public Policy: Seven Cases in American Government,* ed. Robert S. Ross, pp. 29-52. Chicago: Markham Publishing, 1971.

1477. Schmidhauser, John R. "The Senate's Role in Appellate Judicial Selection." In his *Judges and Justices: The Federal Appellate Judiciary,* pp. 18-28. Boston: Little, Brown, 1979.

1478. Scott, Ernest. "Constitutional Function of the Senate in Respect to Appointments." *University of Pennsylvania Law Review* 81 (Nov. 1932): 43-57.

1479. "Senate Rule XXXVIII: The Nomination of George Otis Smith." *U.S. Law Review* 65 (Mar. 1931): 121-126.

1480. Shogun, Robert. *A Question of Judgment: The Fortas Case and the Struggle for the Supreme Court.* Indianapolis: Bobbs-Merrill, 1972.

1481. Songer, Donald R. "The Relevance of Policy Values for the Confirmation of Supreme Court Nominees." *Law and Society Review* 13 (Summer 1979): 927-948.

1482. Swindler, William F. "The Politics of 'Advice and Consent': The Senate's Role in Selection of Supreme Court Justices." *American Bar Association Journal* 56 (June 1970): 533-542.

1483. Tannenbaum, Donald G. "The Senate Rejects a Cabinet-Level Appointee: The Case of Lewis L. Strauss." Ph.D. dissertation, New York University, 1970.

1484. Thorpe, James A. "The Appearance of Supreme Court Nominees Before the Senate Judiciary Committee." *Journal of Public Law* 18 (1969): 371-402.

1485. U.S. Congress. Senate. Committee on Foreign Relations. *The Senate Role in Foreign Affairs Appointments.* 92nd Cong., 1st sess. Washington: GPO, 1971.

1486. Vatz, Richard E. and Windt, Theodore G. "The Defeats of Judges Haynsworth and Carswell: Rejection of Supreme Court Nominees." *Quarterly Journal of Speech* 60 (Dec. 1974): 477-488.

1487. Watson, Richard L. "The Defeat of Judge Parker: A Study in Pressure Groups and Politics." *Mississippi Valley Historical Review* 50 (Sept. 1963): 213-234.

1488. Wigmore, John H. "To Abolish the Federal Senate's Confirming Power over the Executive's Appointments." *Illinois Law Review* 25 (Mar. 1931): 801-803.

1489. Williams, Cleveland A. "Senate Confirmation: The Eisenhower Years." Ph.D. dissertation, Southern Illinois University, 1962.

1490. Wukasch, Barry C. "Abe Fortas Controversy: A Research Note on the Senate's Role in Judicial Selection." *Western Political Quarterly* 24 (Mar. 1971): 24-27.

Regulating Commerce

1491. Albertsworth, Edwin F. "Congressional Assent to State Taxation Otherwise Unconstitutional." *American Bar Association Journal* 17 (Dec. 1931): 821-826.

1492. Anderson, T. J. "Currency Powers of Congress." *Bankers Monthly* 130 (Jan. 1935): 21-35.

1493. Anderson, T. J. "Powers of Congress over Banking." *Bankers Monthly* 130 (Feb. 1935): 153-166.

1494. Armstrong, J. Sinclair. "Congress and the Securities and Exchange Commission." *Virginia Law Review* 45 (Oct. 1959): 795-816.

1495. Bilke, Henry W. "Silence of Congress." *Harvard Law Review* 41 (Dec. 1927): 200-224.

1496. Black, Forrest R. "Has Congress Circumvented the Ashton Decision?" *American Bar Association Journal* 23 (Sept. 1937): 683-684, 692.

1497. Burns, Joseph W. "Congress Studies Effects of Business Size." *Social Science* 31 (Oct. 1956): 199-205.

1498. Celler, Emmanuel. "Congress, Compacts, and Interstate Authorities." *Law and Contemporary Problems* 26 (Autumn 1961): 682-702.

1499. Cohen, Richard E. "Regulatory Reform: 535 Different Meanings for Members of Congress." *National Journal* 8 (April 10, 1976): 476-481.

1500. "Congress and the Port of New York Authority: Federal Supervision of Interstate Compacts." *Yale Law Journal* 70 (April 1961): 812-820.

1501. "Congressional Supervision of Interstate Commerce." *Yale Law Journal* 75 (July 1966): 1416-1433.

1502. Cooke, Frederick H. "The Exclusiveness of the Power of Congress to Regulate Commerce." *American Law Review* 43 (Nov. 1909): 813-820.

1503. Cooke, Frederick H. "Power of Congress and the States Respectively to Regulate the Conduct and Liability of Carriers." *Columbia Law Review* 10 (Jan. 1910): 35-40.

1504. Corwin, Edward S. "Congress's Power to Prohibit Commerce: A Crucial Constitutional Issue." *Cornell Law Quarterly* 18 (June 1933): 477-506.

1505. Dunham, Allison. "Congress, the States and Commerce." *Journal of Public Law* 8 (1959): 47-65.

1506. Esch, John J. "The Interstate Commerce Commission and Congress: Its Influence on Legislation." *George Washington Law Review* 5 (Mar. 1937): 462-502.

1507. Gilbert, Gary G. "Foreign Banking in the United States: The Congressional Debate." *Magazine of Bank Administration* 52 (Oct. 1976): 40-42.

1508. Goodnow, Frank J. "The Power of Congress to Regulate Commerce." *Political Science Quarterly* 25 (June 1910): 220-256.

1509. Grant, J. A. C. "Commerce, Production, and the Fiscal Power of Congress." *Yale Law Journal* 45 (Mar. 1936): 751-778, 991-1021.

1510. Hartman, Paul J. and Sanders, Paul H. "Power of Congress to Prohibit Discrimination in the Assessment of Property of Interstate Carriers for State Ad Valorem Taxes." *ICC Practitioners' Journal* 33 (May 1966): 654-700.

1511. Hartwig, Lawrence E. "Federal Control over Crime: Scope of Power of Congress to Regulate Crime Under the Commerce Clause." *Michigan Law Review* 32 (Jan. 1934): 378-387.

1512. Haycroft, Everett F. "The Attempt of Congress to Promote and Protect Free Competition in Commerce." *National University Law Review* 8 (Jan. 1928): 39-60.

1513. Himbert, Arthur R. and Stone, Ferdinand F. "Congressional Assistance to the States Under the Commerce Clause." *Rocky Mountain Law Review* 9 (Feb. 1937): 101-117.

1514. Huitt, Ralph K. "Congressional Organization and Operations in the Field of Money and Credit." In *Fiscal and Debt Management Policies,* ed. Commission on Money and Credit, pp. 399-495. Englewood Cliffs, N.J.: Prentice-Hall, 1963.

1515. Keasbey, Edward Q. "Powers of Corporations Created by Act of Congress." *Harvard Law Review* 32 (April 1919): 689-708.

1516. Liddy, Sylvester J. "Has Congress the Constitutional Power to Legislate on the Substantive Law of Trademarks?" *Fordham Law Review* 6 (Nov. 1937): 408-415.

1517. Maggs, Douglas B. "Congressional Power to Control Cotton and Tobacco Production." *Law and Contemporary Problems* 1 (June 1934): 376-389.

1518. Malbin, Michael J. "New House and Senate Favor More Business Regulation." *National Journal* 6 (Nov. 16, 1974): 1724-1736.

1519. Miller, Richard B. "Congress and the Banks." *The Bankers Magazine* 159 (Autumn 1976): 28-32.

1520. Morrow, William L. "Congress and ICA: A Study in Legislative Control of Administrative Discretion, 1955-1960." Ph.D. dissertation, University of Iowa, 1961.

1521. Mueller, Charles E. "Antitrust and Congressional Trustbusting: They Wouldn't Dare!" *Antitrust Law and Economics Review* 9 (1977): 55-72.

1522. Norton, Hugh S. "Congress and Transportation Policy." *ICC Practitioners' Journal* 33 (Jan. 1966): 353-357.

1523. Oliver, Dale H. and Snyder, Stephen J. "Antitrust, Bargaining, and Cooperatives: ABC's of the National Agricultural Marketing and Bargaining Act of 1971." *Harvard Journal on Legislation* 9 (Mar. 1972): 498-542.

1524. "Power of Congress to Provide for Compulsory Retirement and Pension System for Carriers." *Minnesota Law Review* 20 (Dec. 1935): 49-56.

1525. Rush, Kenneth. "Expansion of Federal Supervision of Securities Through the Inquisitional and Census Powers of Congress: A Suggestion." *Michigan Law Review* 36 (Jan. 1938): 409-433.

1526. Shields, Geoffrey B. "Congressional Authority to Regulate State Taxation of State Banks: Federal Reserve's Recommendations for an Alternative to PL-156." *Banking Law Journal* 89 (April 1972): 330-344.

1527. Smith, Russell A. "Power to Enact Federal Securities Act of 1933." *Michigan Law Review* 32 (April 1934): 811-831.

1528. Sneeden, Emory M. "Illinois Brick: Do We Look to the Courts or Congress?" *The Antitrust Bulletin* 24 (Summer 1979): 205-231.

1529. Sunseri, J. M. "Statutes of Limitations on 10B-5 Actions: Proposal for Congressional Legislation." *Syracuse Law Review* 24 (1973): 1154-1172.

1530. Torvestad, John N. "The Growth and Development of a National Police Power as Implied in the Constitutional Grant to Congress to Regulate Commerce Among the Several States." D.C.L., American University, 1921.

1531. Woods, H. Jack. "If Congress Has Its Way." *State Government* 49 (Winter 1976): 27-30.

1532. Young, Mark D. "A Test of Federal Sunset: Congressional Reauthorization of the Commodity Futures Trading Commission." *Emory Law Journal* 27 (Fall 1978): 853-907.

1533. Zecher, Richard. "Money and Congress: A Review of Congressional Activity Relating to Monetary Policy." *Journal of Money, Credit and Banking* 3 (Aug. 1971): 680-692.

Impeachment

1534. "Anatomy of a Committee: Impeachment Inquiry Begins." *Congressional Quarterly Weekly Report* 32 (Jan. 26, 1974): 127-130, 155-156.

1535. Bates, William. "Vagueness in the Constitution: The Impeacment Power." *Stanford Law Review* 25 (June 1973): 908-926.

1536. Beloff, Max. "Impeachment." *The Parliamentarian* 55 (April 1974): 69-71.

1537. Benedict, Michael L. *The Impeachment of Andrew Johnson.* New York: Norton, 1973.

1538. Berger, Raoul. *Impeachment: The Constitutional Problems.* Cambridge, Mass.: Harvard University Press, 1974.

1539. Berger, Raoul. "The President, Congress, and the Courts." *Yale Law Journal* 83 (May 1974): 1111-1155.

1540. Black, Charles L. *Impeachment.* New Haven, Conn.: Yale University Press, 1974.

1541. Brant, Irving. *Impeachment: Trials and Errors.* New York: A. A. Knopf, 1972.

1542. Congressional Quarterly. *Impeachment and the U.S. Congress,* ed. Robert A. Diamond. Washington: Congressional Quarterly, 1974.

1543. Eilberg, Joshua. "Investigation by the Committee on the Judiciary of the House of Representatives into the Charges of Impeachable Conduct Against Richard M. Nixon." *Temple Law Quarterly* 48 (Winter 1975): 209-240.

1544. Fenton, Paul S. "The Scope of the Impeachment Power." *Northwestern University Law Review* 65 (Nov./Dec. 1970: 715-758.

1545. Futterman, Stanley N. "Rules of Impeachment." *Kansas Law Review* 24 (Fall 1975): 105-142.

1546. Greene, Richard S. "Balance of Power, the Impeachment Powers and the Supreme Power of Congress." *Federal Bar Journal* 34 (Winter 1975): 42-53.

1547. Havens, Murray C. and McNeil, D. M. "Presidents, Impeachment, and Political Accountability." *Presidential Studies Quarterly* 8 (Winter 1978): 5-18.

1548. Howard, Brett. "The Plot to Impeach Johnson." *Mankind* 1 (Oct. 1968): 10-19.

1549. "Impeachment Inquiry Staff: Large, Young and Busy." *Congressional Quarterly Weekly Report* 32 (Mar. 2, 1974): 540-543.

1550. Israel, Richard E. *Grounds for Impeachment: Summaries of the Reports of the Department of Justice, House Judiciary Committee Staff, and White House Staff on the Grounds for the Impeachment of the President.* Washington: Congressional Research Service, 1974.

1551. Kurland, Philip B. *Watergate and the Constitution.* Chicago: University of Chicago Press, 1978.

1552. Labovitz, John R. *Presidential Impeachment.* New Haven, Conn.: Yale University Press, 1978.

1553. Lewis, H. H. Walker. "The Impeachment of Andrew Johnson: A Political Tragedy." *American Bar Association Journal* 40 (Jan. 1954): 15-18, 80-87.

1554. Maness, Lonnie E. and Chesterton, Richard D. "The First Attempt at Presidential Impeachment: Partisan Politics and Intra-Party Conflict at Loose." *Presidential Studies Quarterly* 10 (Winter 1980): 51-62.

1555. Reuss, Henry S. "Introduction to the Vote of No Confidence." *George Washington Law Review* 43 (Jan. 1975): 333-335.

1556. Swindler, William F. "High Court of Congress: Impeachment Trials, 1797-1936." *American Bar Association Journal* 60 (April 1974): 420-428.

1557. Trefousse, Hans L. *Impeachment of a President: Andrew Johnson, The Blacks, and Reconstruction.* Knoxville: University of Tennessee Press, 1975.

1558. Van Alstyne, William W. "Third Impeachment Article: Congressional Bootstrapping." *American Bar Association Journal* 60 (Oct. 1974): 1199-1202.

1559. Wainer, Howard. "Predicting the Outcome of the Senate Trial of Richard M. Nixon." *Behavioral Science* 19 (Nov. 1974): 404-406.

Electing the President

1560. Baker, !ewton D. "Some Constitutional Problems." *American Bar Association Journal* 11 (Aug. 1925): 539-546.

1561. Bookbinder, Martin E. "Electoral College Reform: A Case Study in Congressional Politics, 1966-1970." Ph.D. dissertation, University of Maryland, 1972.

1562. Brams, Steven J. and Lake, Mark. "Power and Satisfaction in a Representative Democracy." In *Game Theory and Political Science,* ed. Peter C. Ordeshook, pp. 529–562. New York: New York University Press, 1978.

1563. Dargo, George. "American Politics' Coming of Age." *King's Crown Essays* 4 (Winter 1956): 5-20, 47-48.

1564. Doyle, Vincent A. and Tienken, Robert L. *Contingent Election of the President by the House of Representatives: Newly Elected or "Lame Duck" House?* Washington: Legislative Reference Service, 1968.

1565. Eshelman, Edwin D. "Congress and Electoral Reform: An Analysis of Proposals for Changing Our Method of Selecting a President." *Christian Century,* 5 Feb. 1969, pp. 178-181.

1566. MacDonald, William. "When Congress Elects the President." *Current History* 21 (Oct. 1924): 41-46.

1567. Morgan, William G. "The Congressional Nominating Caucus of 1816: The Struggle Against the Virginia Dynasty." *Virginia Magazine of History and Biography* 80 (Oct. 1972): 461-475.

1568. Morgan, William G. "The Decline of the Congressional Nominating Caucus." *Tennessee Historical Quarterly* 24 (Fall 1965): 245-255.

1569. Morgan, William G. "The Origin and Development of the Congressional Nominating Caucus." *Proceedings of the American Philosophical Society* 113 (April 1969): 184-196.

1570. "New Interest Shown in Reform of Electoral College." *Congressional Quarterly Weekly Report* 19 (Feb. 17, 1961): 279-288.

1571. Ostrogorskii, Moisei I. "The Rise and Fall of the Nominating Caucus, Legislative and Congressional." *American Historical Review* 5 (Dec. 1899): 253-283.

1572. Rosenthal, Albert J. "The Constitution, Congress, and Presidential Elections." *Michigan Law Review* 67 (Nov. 1968): 1-38.

1573. "Strong Sentiments Voiced for Electoral College Reform." *Congressional Quarterly Weekly Report* 19 (Aug. 11, 1961): 1402-1408.

1574. Tansill, Charles C. "Congressional Control of the Electoral System." *Yale Law Journal* 34 (Mar. 1925): 511-525.

1575. Thompson, Charles S. *An Essay on the Rise and Fall of the Congressional Caucus as a Machine for Nominating Candidates for the Presidency.* New Haven, Conn.: Yale University Press, 1902.

District of Columbia

1576. Arnold, Linda M. "Congressional Government of the District of Columbia, 1800-1846." Ph.D. dissertation, Georgetown University, 1974.

1577. Cress, Lawrence D. "Whither Columbia? Congressional Residence and the Politics of the New Nation, 1776-1787." *William and Mary Quarterly* 32 (Oct. 1975): 581-600.

1578. "D.C. Home Rule: Fight Moves to House Floor." *Congressional Quarterly Weekly Report* 31 (Sept. 29, 1973): 2595-2599.

1579. Ellenberger, Jack S. "Marriage of Inconvenience: Congress and the District of Columbia." *Law Library Journal* 59 (Nov. 1966): 456-483.

1580. Gerard, Jules B. "On Treating the District of Columbia as Though It Were a State." *Policy Review* 7 (Winter 1979): 69-78.

1581. Gordon, Martin K. "Congress and the District of Columbia: The Military Impact on Federal Control." *Capitol Studies* 6 (Fall, 1978): 39-53.

1582. Harman, Bryan D. "Congress and Urban Renewal in the District of Columbia." Master's thesis, American University, 1964.

1583. Mathias, Charles M. "Managing the District of Columbia." In *We Propose: A Modern Congress,* ed. Mary McInnis, pp. 271-278. New York: McGraw-Hill, 1966.

1584. Moore, Charles. "The Government of the City of Washington by Congress." *Daughters of the American Revolution Magazine* 58 (April 1924): 197-209.

1585. O'Keefe, Dennis J. "Decision Making in the House Committee on the District of Columbia." Ph.D. dissertation, University of Maryland, 1969.

1586. Raven-Hansen, Peter. "Congressional Representation for the District of Columbia: A Constitutional Analysis." *Harvard Journal on Legislation* 12 (Feb. 1975): 167-192.

1587. Schmeckebier, Laurence F. *The District of Columbia: Its Government and Administration.* Baltimore: Johns Hopkins University Press, 1928.

1588. U.S. Congress. Senate. Committee on the Judiciary. *Congressional Representation for the District of Columbia, Hearings.* Washington: GPO, 1978.

1589. Vose, Clement E. "When District of Columbia Representation Collides with the Constitutional Amendment Institution." *Publius* 9 (Winter 1979): 105-125.

V. Congressional Investigations

General Studies

1590. Barth, Alan. *Government by Investigation.* New York: Viking Press, 1955.

1591. Basil, Thomas T. "Constitutional Limitations on the Legislative Power of Investigations." *Buffalo Law Review* 7 (Winter 1958): 267-278.

1592. Baskir, Lawrence M. "Reflections on the Senate Investigation of Army Surveillance." *Indiana Law Journal* 49 (Summer 1974): 618-653.

1593. Berger, Raoul. "Congressional Subpoenas to Executive Officials." *Columbia Law Review* 75 (June 1975): 865-896.

1594. Boudin, Louis B. "Congressional and Agency Investigations: Their Uses and Abuses." *Virginia Law Review* 35 (Feb. 1949): 143-213.

1595. Brice, Bill E. "Constitutional Aspects of Congressional Investigations into Subversive Activities." *Southwestern Law Journal* 8 (Spring 1954): 212-224.

1596. Carr, Robert K. "Congressional Investigating Committees and the Control of Subversive Activities." *Confluence* 3 (Sept. 1954): 330-341.

1597. Carr, Robert K. *The Constitution and Congressional Investigating Committees: Individual Liberty and Congressional Power.* New York: Carrie Chapman Catt Memorial Fund, 1954.

1598. Carr, Robert K. "Constitutional and Statutory Limitations on Congressional Investigations." *Capitol Studies* 5 (Fall 1977): 11-39.

1599. Chase, Harold W. "Improving Congressional Investigations: A No-Progress Report." *Temple Law Quarterly* 30 (Winter 1957): 126-155.

1600. Chester, Edward. "The Impact of the Covode Congressional Investigation." *Western Pennsylvania Historical Magazine* 42 (Dec. 1959): 343-350.

1601. Cohen, Nachman S. "Legislative Investigations—Due Process—John T. Watkins v. United States." *Boston University Law Review* 37 (Fall 1957): 515-518.

1602. "Congressional Informants in Trouble with Pentagon." *Congressional Quarterly Weekly Report* 27 (Jan. 17, 1969): 133-137.

1603. Cousens, Theodore W. "The Purpose and Scope of Investigation Under Legislative Authority." *Georgetown Law Journal* 26 (May 1938): 905-929.

1604. Davidson, Roger H. "The Political Dimensions of Congressional Investigations." *Capitol Studies* 5 (Fall 1977): 41-63.

1605. Dillard, Irving. "Congressional Investigations: The Role of the Press." *University of Chicago Law Review* 18 (Spring 1951): 585-590.

1606. Dimock, Marshall E. *Congressional Investigating Committees.* Baltimore: Johns Hopkins University Press, 1929.

1607. Donlan, Joseph F. and Gillian, Thomas A. "The Investigating Power of Congress: Its Scope and Limitations (1792-1954)." *Dicta* 31 (Aug. 1954): 285-319.

1608. Eberling, Ernest J. *Congressional Investigations: A Study of the Origin and Development of the Power of Congress to Investigate and Punish for Contempt.* New York: Columbia University Press, 1928.

1609. Fay, George M. "A Prosecutor's Views of Congressional Investigations." *Pennsylvania Bar Association Quarterly* 19 (April 1948): 258-260.

1610. Fleischmann, Hartly. "Watkins v. U.S. and Congressional Power of Investigation." *Hastings Law Journal* 9 (Feb. 1978): 145-166.

1611. Forrester, Ray. "History and Function of Congressional Investigations." *Arkansas Review* 8 (Spring 1954): 352-359.

1612. Frazier, Linda B. "Power of the Courts to Offer Equitable Relief from a Congressional Subpoena." *Houston Law Review* 11 (Mar. 1974): 746-753.

1613. Fulbright, J. William. "Congressional Investigations: Significance for Legislative Process." *University of Chicago Law Review* 18 (Spring 1951): 440-448.

1614. Galloway, George B. "Congressional Investigation: Proposed Reforms." *University of Chicago Law Review* 18 (Spring 1951): 478-502.

1615. Galloway, George B. "Investigative Function of Congress." *American Political Science Review* 21 (Feb. 1927): 47-70.

1616. Gilligan, John W. "Congressional Investigations." *Illinois Law Review* 45 (Nov.-Dec. 1950): 633-652.

1617. Glassie, Henry H. and Cooley, Thomas M. "Congressional Investigations: Salvation in Self Regulation." *Georgetown Law Journal* 38 (Mar. 1950): 343-367.

1618. Gose, Jack. "The Limits of Congressional Investigations." *Washington Law Review* 10 (April 1935): 61-77, 138-154.

1619. Gossett, William T. "Are We Neglecting Constitutional Liberty? A Call to Leadership." *American Bar Association Journal* 38 (Oct. 1952): 817-820, 866.

1620. Grove, J. W. "Un-American Activities and the Congressional Investigating Power." *Parliamentary Affairs* 7 (Spring 1954): 205-212.

1621. Hailsham, Viscount. "Parliamentary Inquiry and Congressional Investigation Compared." *American Bar Association Journal* 40 (Sept. 1954): 787-789.

1622. Hamilton, Bryce L. "Inquisitoral Power of Congress." *American Bar Association Journal* 23 (July 1937): 511-516, 561-563.

1623. Hamilton, James. *The Power to Probe: A Study of Congressional Investigations.* New York: Random House, 1976.

1624. Harrison, Joseph H. and McCoy, Robert F. "Congressional Investigations: Limitations on the Implied Power of Inquiry." *Notre Dame Lawyer* 28 (Spring 1953): 373-388.

1625. Hays, Frank E. "Senate Blackball." *Georgetown Law Journal* 29 (Nov. 1940): 215-240.

1626. Heubel, Edward J. "Congressional Resistance to Reform: The House Adopts a Code for Investigating Committees." *Midwest Journal of Political Science* 1 (Nov. 1957): 313-329.

1627. Hicks, F. H. "Congressional Investigations." *Notre Dame Lawyer* 23 (Mar. 1948): 353-357.

1628. Hoffmann, Walter F. "The Legitimate Functions of a Congressional Investigation." *Rutgers Law Review* 9 (Spring 1955): 528-543.

1629. Horack, Frank. "Congressional Investigations: A Plan for Legislative Review." *American Bar Association Journal* 40 (Mar. 1954): 191-194.

1630. "How Congressional Committees Staff Investigations." *Congressional Quarterly Weekly Report* 29 (April 23, 1971): 939-941.

1631. Johnsen, Julia E., ed. *The Investigating Powers of Congress.* New York: Wilson, 1951.

1632. Junz, Alfred. "Congressional Investigating Committees." *Social Research* 21 (Winter 1954): 379-396.

1633. Keating, Kenneth B. "The Investigating Powers of Congress." *Federal Bar Journal* 14 (April-June 1954): 171-181.

1634. Keele, Harold M. "Note on Congressional Investigations." *American Bar Association Journal* 40 (Feb. 1954): 154-156.

1635. "Key House Committee: FBI Agents for Investigators." *Congressional Quarterly Weekly Report* 29 (April 23, 1971): 937-939.

1636. Kline, Howard M. "Some Practices of Congressional Investigating Committees." Ph.D. dissertation, Syracuse University, 1938.

1637. Landis, James M. "Constitutional Limitations on the Congressional Power of Investigation." *Harvard Law Review* 40 (Dec. 1926): 153-221.

1638. Lashley, Miriam. "The Investigating Power of Congress: Its Scope and Limitations." *American Bar Association Journal* 40 (Sept. 1954): 763-766, 808-815.

1639. "The Lattimore Case: Congressional Investigations and Constitution." *Northwestern University Law Review* 49 (Mar.-April 1954): 77-86.

1640. Lord, B. Thorn. "Legislative Investigation." *Law Notes* 34 (Jan. 1931): 186-188.

1641. Loring, Charles. "Powers of Congressional Investigation Committees." *Minnesota Law Review* 8 (June 1924): 595-603.

1642. McClory, Robert. "Congressional Investigations: The Proper Approach." *Capitol Studies* 5 (Fall 1977): 5-10.

1643. McDonnell, James L. "Congressional Investigating Committees: Past, Present and to Come." *British Journal of Administrative Law* 1 (May 1954): 20-29.

1644. McGeary, Martin N. "Congressional Investigations: Historical Development." *University of Chicago Law Review* 18 (Spring 1951): 425-439.

1645. McGeary, Martin N. "Congressional Power of Investigation." *Nebraska Law Review* 28 (May 1949): 516-529.

1646. McGeary, Martin N. The Developments of Congressional Investigative Power. New York: Columbia University Press, 1940.

1647. Maslow, Will. "Fair Procedure in Congressional Investigations: A Proposed Code." *Columbia Law Review* 54 (June 1954): 839-892.

1648. Mavrinac, A. A. "Congressional Investigations." *Confluence* 3 (Dec. 1954): 463-479.

1649. Meader, George. "Limitations on Congressional Investigations." *Michigan Law Review* 47 (April 1949): 775-786.

1650. Merry, Henry J. "The Investigating Power of Congress: Its Scope and Limitations." *American Bar Association Journal* 40 (Dec. 1954): 1073-1076, 1097-1101.

1651. Meyers, Abram F. "The Power of Congress to Investigate the Executive." *Georgetown Law Journal* 12 (Nov. 1923): 1-18.

1652. Millikan, Kent B. "Congressional Investigations: Imbroglio in the Court." *William and Mary Law Review* 8 (Spring 1967): 400-420.

1653. "Money for Probes." *Congressional Quarterly Weekly Report* 12 (Sept. 24, 1954): 1189-1194.

1654. Morgan, G. D. "Congressional Investigations and Judicial Review: Kilbourn v. Thompson Revisited." *California Law Review* 37 (Dec. 1949): 556-574.

1655. Mundt, Karl E. "The Role of Committee Investigations." In *The Senate Institution,* ed. Nathaniel S. Preston, pp. 132-144. New York: Van Nostrand Reinhold, 1969.

1656. Nellis, Joseph L. "Scope and Limitations on Congressional Committee Action." *Federal Bar Journal* 14 (Jan.-Mar. 1954): 35-58.

1657. "90th Congress Investigations Cost $22 Million." *Congressional Quarterly Weekly Report* 27 (July 4, 1969): 1196-1198.

1658. Nutting, Charles B. "Congressional Investigations: A Turn in the Road?" *American Bar Association Journal* 45 (Aug. 1959): 843, 850.

1659. O'Reilly, Kenneth. "The Stamler Challenge: Congressional Investigative Power and the First Amendment." *Congressional Studies* 7 (Spring 1979): 57-72.

1660. Perkins, James A. "Congressional Investigations of Matters of International Import." *American Political Science Review* 34 (April 1940): 284-294.

1661. "The Power of Congressional Investigating Committees to Issue Subpoena *Duces Tecum.*" *Yale Law Journal* 45 (June 1936): 1503-1509.

1662. Richardson, James R. "Investigating Power of Congress: Its Scope and Limitations." *Kentucky Law Journal* 44 (Winter 1956): 318-332.

1663. Schwartz, Bernard. "Legislative Powers of Investigation." *Dickenson Law Review* 57 (Oct. 1952): 31-45.

1664. Shils, Edward A. "Congressional Investigations: The Legislator and His Environment." *University of Chicago Law Review* 18 (Spring 1951): 571-584.

1665. Shull, Charles W. "Ten Years of Congressional Inquiry: Contempt for a Decade." *Temple University Law Quarterly* 13 (April 1939): 322-333.

1666. Stebbins, Albert K. "Limitations of the Powers of Congressional Investigating Committees." *American Bar Association Journal* 16 (July 1930): 425-430.

1667. "Supreme Court Upholds Congressional Investigation of Communism in Education: Major Portions of This Decision." *Current History* 37 (Aug. 1959): 105-116.

1668. Taylor, Telford. *Grand Inquest: The Story of Congressional Investigations.* New York: Simon and Schuster, 1955.

1669. U.S. Congress. House. Armed Services Committee. *Committee Rules and Rules for Investigative Hearings Conducted by Subcommittees.* 95th Cong. Washington: GPO, 1977.

1670. Voorhis, Jerry. "Congressional Investigations: Inner Workings." *University of Chicago Law Review* 18 (Spring 1951): 455-463.

1671. Wigmore, John H. "Legislative Power to Compel Testimonial Disclosure." *Illinois Law Review* 19 (Feb. 1925): 452-454.

1672. Wigmore, John H. "Scopotropismic Senators Stalled by a Sturdy Scot." *Illinois Law Review* 22 April 1928): 883-887.

1673. Worth, Stephen W. "The Congressional Investigating Committee as an Instrument of Subversive Control: An Analysis of the Nature of the Committee, Its Procedures, and Its Scope of Inquiry." Ph.D. dissertation, University of Washington, 1957.

Contempt Power

1674. Barlow, Homer J. M. "Legislative Power to Punish Contempt." *George Washington Law Review* 3 (May 1935): 468-482.

1675. Barlow, Robert A. "Congressional Committee—Contempt: Application of Immunity Statute to Testimony Consisting of Statement of Refusal to Testify Before Committee." *Nebraska Law Review* 27 (Mar. 1948): 465-467.

1676. Bronaugh, Minor. "Power of Congress to Punish for Contempt." *Law Notes* 30 (Feb. 1927): 207-210.

1677. "Congressional Contempt Power in Investigations into the Area of Civil Liberties." *University of Chicago Law Review* 14 (Fall 1947): 256-269.

1678. Gilligan, John W. "Congressional Investigations." *Journal of Criminal Law* 41 (Jan.-Feb. 1951): 618-638.

1679. Goldfarb, Ronald L. *The Contempt Power.* New York: Columbia University Press, 1963.

1680. Hitz, William. "Criminal Prosecution for Contempt of Congress." *Federal Bar Journal* 14 (April-June 1954): 139-170.

1681. Kalven, Harry. "Congressional Testing of Linus Pauling." *Bulletin of the Atomic Scientists* 16 (Dec. 1960): 383-390.

1682. Kalven, Harry. "Congressional Testing of Linus Pauling. Part II: Sourwine in an Old Bottle." *Bulletin of the Atomic Scientists* 17 (Jan. 1961): 12-19.

1683. Linenthal, Eleanor T. "Freedom of Speech and the Power of Courts and Congress to Punish for Contempt." Ph.D. dissertation, Cornell University, 1956.

1684. Potts, Charles S. "Power of Legislative Bodies to Punish for Contempt." *University of Pennsylvania Law Review* 74 (May 1926): 691-725, 780-829.

1685. Rashid, Baddia J. "Problem of Willful Default Before a Congressional Committee." *Georgetown Law Journal* 35 (May 1947): 527-537.

1686. "Revival of Arrest Power Considered in Contempt Cases." *Congressional Quarterly Weekly Report* 20 (Aug. 17, 1962): 1378-1379.

1687. Shull, Charles W. "Congressional Investigations and Contempt." *United States Law Review* 63 (July 1929): 326-327.

1688. Shull, Charles W. "Contempt of Congress." Ph.D. dissertation, Ohio State University, 1929.

1689. Shull, Charles W. "Legislative Contempt: An Auxiliary Power of Congress." *Temple Law Quarterly* 8 (Jan. 1934): 198-217.

1690. Siddons, F. L. "Constitutional Aspect of the Tillman-McLaurin Controversy." *Yale Law Journal* 12 (Nov. 1902): 21-25.

1691. Stamps, Norman L. "The Power of Congress to Inquire and Punish for Contempt." *Baylor Law Review* 4 (Fall 1951): 29-54.

1692. "What Is Contempt of Congress?" *Congressional Quarterly Weekly Report* 13 (Oct. 14, 1955): 1125-1127.

1693. Young, G. C. "Senate's Punishing Power for Contempt Is Upheld by Court." *Oklahoma State Bar Journal* 5 (Mar. 1935): 247-249.

Rights of Witnesses

1694. Bioff, Allan L. "*Watkins v. United States* as a Limitation on Power of Congressional Investigating Committees." *Michigan Law Review* 56 (Dec. 1957): 272-284.

1695. Cappello, Henry J. "Congressional Investigations and Individual Rights." *Catholic University Law Review* 2 (Jan. 1952): 34-41.

1696. Clark, William N. "Congressional Investigations: Their Effect on a Witness' Right to a Fair Trial." *Alabama Law Review* 22 (Summer 1970): 554-590.

1697. Coker, Francis W. "Academic Freedom and the Congressional Investigations: Free Speech and the Silent Professor." *Journal of Politics* 16 (Aug. 1954): 491-508.

1698. Coudert, Frederic R. "Congressional Inquisition vs. Individual Liberty." *Virginia Law Review* 15 (April 1929): 537-552.

1699. Coward, Raymond. "The Fifth Amendment: Its Use in Congressional Investigations." *American Bar Association Journal* 44 (May 1958): 433-436, 490-493.

1700. Fay, George M. "Legislative Investigations: Safeguards for Witnesses: Judicial Protection Against Abusive Practices: Trends in Judicial Relief for Legislative Witnesses." *Notre Dame Lawyer* 29 (winter 1954): 225-242.

1701. Flynn, John T. "Senate Inquisitors and Private Rights." *Harper's Magazine* 161 (Aug. 1930: 357-364.

1702. Fortas, Abe. "Legislative Investigations: Safeguards for Witnesses: Abusive Practices of Investigating Committees—Methods of Committee Investigating Subversion: A Critique." *Notre Dame Lawyer* 29 (Winter 1954): 192-212.

1703. Garrison, Lloyd K. "Congressional Investigations: Are They a Threat to Civil Liberties?" *American Bar Association Journal* 40 (Feb. 1954): 125-128.

1704. Glenn, Frank W. "Power of Congress to Compel Attendance of Witnesses Before Committees." *Georgetown Law Journal* 15 (Mar. 1927): 344-346.

1705. Gossett, William T. "Legislative Investigations: Safeguards for Witnesses—Introductory Statement." *Notre Dame Lawyer* 29 (Winter 1954): 159-163.

1706. Griswold, E. N. "The Fifth Amendment: The Privilege Against Self-Incrimination." *Australian Quarterly* 26 (Sept. 1954): 25-42.

1707. Gross, Avrum M. "Congressional Investigation of Political Activity: Watkins vs. United States Reexamined." *Michigan Law Review* 58 (Jan. 1960): 406-428.

1708. Hoffmann, Julius J. "Whom Are We Protecting? Some Thoughts on the Fifth Amendment." *American Bar Association Journal* 40 (July 1954): 582-585.

1709. Inman, Leslie L. "Congressional Investigations: Rights of Witnesses." *Tulane Law Review* 26 (April 1952): 381-388.

1710. Joyner, Thomas E. "Self-Incrimination and the Duty to Testify: Changing Concepts." *Journal of Politics* 16 (Aug. 1954): 509-538.

1711. Keating, Kenneth B. "Legislative Investigations: Safeguards for Witnesses: Proposed Remedial Legislation—Protection for Witnesses in Congressional Investigations." *Notre Dame Lawyer* 29 (Winter 1954): 212-224.

1712. Kornstein, Daniel J. "Defendant's Right to Inspect Pretrial Congressional Testimony of Government Witnesses." *Yale Law Journal* 80 (June 1971): 1388-1417.

1713. Kullman, Frederick S. "Congressional Investigations: First Amendment Rights." *Tulane Law Review* 34 (Dec. 1959): 192-197.

1714. "Legislative Investigations: Safeguards for Witnesses—A Symposium at Notre Dame." *Notre Dame Lawyer* 29 (Winter 1954): 157-285.

1715. Maloney, Joseph. "Judicial Interpretation of the Constitutional Rights of Private Witnesses Before Congressional Committees." Ph.D. dissertation, Fordham University, 1955.

1716. Massey, M. Minnette. "Congressional Investigations and Individual Liberties." *University of Cincinnati Law Review* 25 (Summer 1956): 323-341.

1717. Moreland, Allen B. "Congressional Investigations and Private Persons." *Southern California Law Review* 40 (Winter 1967): 189-273.

1718. Mott, W. C. "Testifying Before a Congressional Committee: The Attorney and His Witness." *American Bar Association Journal* 47 (June 1961): 641-643.

1719. Nutting, Charles B. "Congressional Investigating Committees: The Coming Dawn?" *American Bar Association Journal* 46 (Dec. 1960): 1353-1354.

1720. Nutting, Charles B. "The *Watkins* Case: A Critique." *American Bar Association Journal* 43 (Nov. 1957): 1029-1030.

1721. O'Meara, Joseph. "Legislative Investigations: Safeguards for Witnesses—Foreword." *Notre Dame Lawyer* 29 (Winter 1954): 157-159.

1722. Pollitt, Daniel H. "Pleading the Fifth Amendment Before a Congressional Committee: A Study and Explanation." *Notre Dame Lawyer* 32 (Dec. 1956): 43-84.

1723. Shull, Charles W. "Answer That Question: The Congressional Witness and His Quandary." *Temple Law Quarterly* 23 (Oct. 1949): 117-121.

1724. Shull, Charles W. "Congress and Its Witnesses." *Temple Law Quarterly* 5 (April 1931): 425-441.

1725. Shull, Charles W. "Rights of Congressional Witnesses." *United States Law Review* 66 (Feb. 1932): 86-89.

1726. Slotnick, Michael C. "The Congressional Investigating Power: Ramifications of the Watkins-Barenblatt Enigma." *University of Miami Law Review* 14 (Spring 1960): 381-411.

1727. Smelser, Marshall. "Legislative Investigations: Safeguards for Witnesses: The Problem in Historical Perspective—The Grand Inquest of the Nation 1792-1948." *Notre Dame Lawyer* 29 (Winter 1954): 164-192.

1728. Smith, Geoffrey S. "The Power of the Senate to Compel Attendance of Witnesses." *University of Pennsylvania Law Review* 73 (Nov. 1924): 60-65.

1729. Taylor, Harold. "The Dismissal of Fifth Amendment Professors." *American Academy of Political and Social Science, Annals* 300 (July 1955): 79-86.

1730. Taylor, Telford. "The Constitutional Privilege Against Self-Incrimination." *American Academy of Political and Social Science, Annals* 300 (July 1955): 114-122.

1731. Taylor, Telford. "Legislative Investigations: Safeguards for Witnesses: Judicial Protection Against Abusive Practices—Judicial Review of Legislative Investigations." *Notre Dame Lawyer* 29 (Winter 1954): 242-285.

1732. Trimble, E. G. "Self-Incrimination and Congressional Investigations." *Kentucky Law Journal* 44 (Winter 1956): 333-342.

1733. Van Der Slik, Jack R. and Stenger, Thomas C. "Citizen Witnesses Before Congressional Committees." *Political Science Quarterly* 92 (Fall 1977): 465-485.

1734. West, Blake. "Scope of Legislative Investigations: Refusal to Testify Before the House Committee on Un-American Activities." *Tulane Law Review* 24 (Dec. 1949): 237-240.

1735. Wiles, Walter E. "Congressional Investigations: A Reexamination of the Basic Problem." *American Bar Association Journal* 41 (June 1955): 538-540.

Executive Privilege

1736. Berger, Raoul. *Executive Privilege: A Constitutional Myth.* Cambridge, Mass.: Harvard University Press, 1974.

1737. Berger, Raoul. "Executive Privilege vs. Congressional Investigation." *UCLA Law Review* 12 (1965): 1043-1120, 1287-1364.

1738. Brown, Peter C. "Executive Papers: The President and the Congress." *New York State Bar Association Bulletin* 20 (July 1948): 166-176.

1739. Collins, Phillip R. "The Power of Congressional Committees of Investigation to Obtain Information from the Executive Branch." *Georgetown Law Review* 39 (May 1951): 563-598.

1740. Collins, Philip R. "A Problem in American Constitutional Law: The Power of Congressional Investigating Committees to Require Information from the Executive." Ph.D. dissertation, Georgetown University, 1950.

1741. Cox, Arthur M. "Congress and Executive Secrecy." In his *The Myths of National Security: The Peril of Secret Government,* pp. 150-180. Boston: Beacon Press, 1975.

1742. Dixon, Robert G. "Congress Shared Administration, and the Executive Privilege." In *Congress Against the President,* ed. H. C. Mansfield, pp. 125-140. New York: Praeger, 1975.

1743. Dorsen, Norman and Shattuck, John F. "Executive Privilege, the Congress and the Courts." *Ohio State Law Journal* 35 (1974): 1-40.

1744. Ehlke, Richard C. *Congressional Access to Information and Executive Privilege.* Washington: Congressional Research Service, 1976.

1745. Ehlke, Richard C. *The Proposed Congressional Right to Information Act and Executive Privilege: A Constitutional Analysis.* Washington: Congressional Research Service, 1974.

1746. Ervin, Sam J. "Controlling 'Executive Privilege.'" *Loyola Law Review* 20 (1973-1974): 11-31.

1747. Evans, Thomas E. "Executive Privilege and the Congress: Perspectives and Recommendations." *DePaul Law Review* 23 (Winter 1974): 692-736.

1748. "Executive Privilege Issue Splits House Committee." *Congressional Quarterly Weekly Report* 32 (April 20, 1974): 998-999.

1749. Goodsell, Charles T. "Congressional Access to Executive Information: A Problem of Legislative–Executive Relations in American National Government." Ph.D. dissertation, Howard University, 1961.

1750. Keighton, Robert L. "The Executive Privilege and the Congressional Right to Know: A Study of the Investigating Power of Congressional Committees." Ph.D. dissertation, University of Pennsylvania, 1961.

1751. Luscombe, Mark A. "Congressional Control of Agency Privilege." *University of Michigan Journal of Law Reform* 9 (Winter 1976): 348-374.

1752. Mathias, Charles M. "Executive Privilege and the Congress." In *Secrecy and Foreign Policy,* eds. Thomas M. Franck and Edward Weisband, pp. 69-86. New York: Oxford Univesity Press, 1974.

1753. Milloy, Richard P. "The Power of the Executive to Withhold Information from Congressional Investigating Committees." *Georgetown Law Journal* 43 (June 1956): 643-660.

1754. Ramsey, Mary L. *Executive Privilege: Withholding Information from the Congress— Selected Issues and Judicial Decisions.* Washington: Congressional Research Service, 1975.

1755. Randolph, Robert C. and Smith, Daniel C. "Executive Privilege and the Congressional Right of Inquiry." *Harvard Journal on Legislation* 10 (June 1973): 621-671.

1756. Rogers, William P. "Constitutional Law: The Papers of the Executive Branch." *American Bar Association Journal* 44 (Oct. 1958): 941-944, 1007-1014.

1757. Rosenthal, Paul C. and Grossman, Robert S. "Congressional Access to Confidential Information Collected by Federal Agencies." *Harvard Journal on Legislation* 15 (Dec. 1977): 74-118.

1758. Rourke, Francis E. "Administrative Secrecy: A Congressional Dilemma." *American Political Science Review* 54 (Sept. 1960): 684-694.

1759. Schwartz, Bernard. "ExecutiVe Privilege and Congressional Investigatory Power." *California Law Review* 47 (Mar. 1959): 3-50.

1760. "Secrecy: Review of Policies by Executive, Congress." *Congressional Quarterly Weekly Report* 29 (Aug. 21, 1971): 1785-1788.

1761. U.S. Congress. Senate. Judiciary Committee. *Refusals by the Executive Branch to Provide Information to the Congress 1964-1973.* 93rd Cong., 2nd sess. Washington: GPO, 1974.

1762. Younger, Irving. "Congressional Investigations and Executive Secrecy: A Study in the Separation of Powers." *University of Pittsburgh Law Review* 20 (June 1959): 755-784.

Congressional Immunity

1763. Betts, James T. "The Scope of Immunity for Legislators and Their Employees." *Yale Law Journal* 77 (Dec. 1967): 366-389.

1764. Bolton, John R., Vanderstar, John, and Baldwin, Gordon B. "Legislators Shield: Speech of Debate Clause Protection Against State Interrogation." *Marquette Law Review* 62 (Spring 1979): 351-374.

1765. Bradley, Craig M. "The Speech or Debate Clause: Bastion of Congressional Independence or Haven for Corruption?" *North Carolina Law Review* 57 (Feb. 1979): 197-230.

1766. Brewer, F. M. "Congressional Immunity." *Editorial Research Reports,* 25 April 1952, pp. 313-330.

1767. Brownell, Herbert. "Immunity from Prosecution Vs. Privilege Against Self-Incrimination." *Federal Bar Journal* 14 (April-June 1954): 91-112.

1768. Brunetti, Louis L. "The Speech or Debate Clause and Immunity for Congressional Aides." *Duquesne Law Review* 11 (Summer 1973): 677-686.

1769. Busfield, Roger M. "The Hermitage Walking Stick: First Challenge to Congressional Immunity." *Tennessee Historical Quarterly* 21 (June 1962): 122-130.

1770. Channing, Charles E. "Congress' Cloak." *Georgetown Law Journal* 30 (Feb. 1942): 381-385.

1771. Charney, Leon H. and Selvers, Jerome M. "Executive Encroachment on Congressional Immunity." *St. John's Law Review* 50 (Fall 1975): 38-50.

1772. Cleveland, James C. "Legislative Immunity and the Role of the Representative." *New Hampshire Bar Journal* 14 (Spring 1973): 139-155.

1773. "Congressional Immunity: Does It Extend to Bribery?" *Congressional Quarterly Weekly Report* 29 (ct. 9, 1971): 2074-2077.

1774. "Constitutional Law—Congressional Immunity—Speech of Debate Clause Held No Bar to Declaratory Judgment and Injunction Against Publication of Congressional Committee Report by Public Printer." *New York Law Forum* 16 (Feb. 1970): 934-941.

1775. Fisher, Wheeler Y. "Congressional Exemption from Suit and Responsibility and the Long Case." *George Washington Law Review* 3 (Jan. 1935): 231-239.

1776. Foster, Martin C. "The Elected Officials' Limited Right to Financial Privacy." *New England Law Review* 15 (Winter 1980): 192-217.

1777. Fuess, Claude M. "Congressional Immunity and Privilege." *Proceedings of the Massachusetts Historical Society* 70 (1957): 148-157.

1778. Fuhr, William. "Congressional Immunity from Libel and Slander." *Nebraska Law Review* 30 (Nov. 1950): 107-111.

1779. Niebler, John H. "Congressional Immunity and Conflict of Interest." *Wisconsin Law Review* 1965 (Summer 1965): 702-710.

1780. Oppenheim, Edward E. "Congressional Free Speech." *Loyola Law Review* 8 (1955-1956): 1-34.

1781. Redfield, Emanuel. "Immunities of Congress from Process." *George Washington Law Review* 10 (Mar. 1942): 513-527.

1782. Sharp, Freeman W. *The Constitutional Privileges from Arrest and of Speech or Debate of Members of Congress: United States Constitution, Article I, Section 6—Historical Aspects and Legal Precedents.* Washington: Congressional Research Service, 1972.

1783. Simmons, Robert G. "Freedom of Speech in Congress: The History of a Constitutional Clause." *American Bar Association Journal* 38 (Aug. 1952): 649-652, 707-711.

1784. Simon, Bert. "Legislative Immunity: Congressional Investigators Immune from Charges of Invasion of Privacy." *University of Florida Law Review* 28 (Spring 1976): 843-850.

1785. Sohier, Walter D. "Congressional Immunity: Conflicting Policies and a Possible Remedy." *American Bar Association Journal* 36 (Dec. 1950): 1035-1036.

1786. "Speech or Debate Clause: Alleged Criminal Conduct of Congressmen Not Within Scope of Legislative Immunity." *Vanderbilt Law Review* 26 (Mar. 1973): 327-339.

1787. Suarez, X. L. "Congressional Immunity: A Criticism of Existing Distinctions and a Proposal for a New Definitional Approach." *Villanova Law Review* 20 (Nov. 1974): 97-146.

1788. Thomas, Robert M. "Freedom of Debate: Protector of the People or Haven for the Criminals?" *Harvard Review* 3 (Fall 1965): 75-88.

1789. "Unenforced Congressional Subpoenas: Judicial Action and Congressional Immunity." *Iowa Law Review* 59 (Feb. 1974): 581-595.

1790. Williams, Nathan B. "Congressional Immunity and the Citizen." *Journal of the Bar Association of the District of Columbia* 17 (Dec. 1950): 602-606.

1791. Witt, Elder. "Court Affirms Broad Congressional Immunity." *Congressional Quarterly Weekly Report* 33 (May 31, 1975): 1129-1131.

1792. Yankwick, Leon R. "The Immunity of Congressional Speech: Its Origins, Meaning and Scope." *University of Pennsylvania Law Review* 49 (1950-1951): 960-977.

1793. Young, G. C. "Congressional Privilege in Respect to Subpoena." *Oklahoma Bar Association Journal* 13 (Jan. 1942): 4-7.

Specific Investigatory Committees

1794. Aldous, E. Ralph and Johnson, William G. "Interpersonal Trust and Reactions to the Senate Watergate Committee." *Personality and Social Psychology Bulletin* 1 (1974): 166-167.

1795. Beck, Carl. *Contempt of Congress: A Study of the Prosecutions Initiated by the Committee on Un-American Activities, 1945-1957.* New Orleans, La.: Hauser Press, 1959.

1796. Benson, Thomas W. "Congressional Debates on the Dies Committee, 1937-1944." Ph.D. dissertation, Cornell University, 1967.

1797. Black, Hugo L. "Inside a Senate Investigation." *Harper's Magazine* 172 (Feb. 1936): 275-286.

1798. Blanchard, Robert O. "The Moss Committee and a Federal Public Records Law, 1955–1965." Ph.D. dissertation, Syracuse University, 1966.

1799. Braden, Anne. *House Un-American Activities Committee: Bulwark of Segregation.* Los Angeles: National Bureau to Abolish the House Un-American Activities Committee, 1964.

1800. Buckley, William F. *The Committee and Its Critics: A Calm Review of the House Committee on Un-American Activities.* New York: Putnam, 1962.

1801. Cantelon, Philip L. "In Defense of America: Congressional Investigations of Communism in the United States, 1919-1935." Ph.D. dissertation, Indiana University, 1971.

1802. Carr, Robert K. *The House Committee on Un-American Activities, 1945-1950.* Ithaca, N.Y.: Cornell University Press, 1952.

1803. Civil Rights Congress. *America's 'Thought Police': A Record of the Un-American Activities Committee.* New York: Civil Rights Congress, 1947.

1804. Coker, William L. "The United States Senate Investigation of the Mississippi Election of 1875." *Journal of Mississippi History* 37 (May 1975): 143-163.

1805. Cook, Donald C. "Investigations in Operations: Senate Preparedness Subcommittee." *University of Chicago Law Review* 18 (Spring 1951): 634-646.

1806. Costello, John A. "Congress and Internal Security: The Overman Committee, 1918-1919." Master's thesis, American University, 1966.

1807. "Crime Up to States and Cities: Kefauver Committee Suggestions for Action Against Politico-Criminal Alliances." *National Municipal Review* 40 (July 1951): 354-359.

1808. Cushman, Robert E. "The Purge of Federal Employees Accused of Disloyalty." *Public Administration Review* 3 (Autumn 1943): 297-316.

1809. Dash, Samuel. *Chief Counsel: Inside the Ervin Committee—The Untold Story.* New York: Random House, 1976.

1810. Donner, Frank J. "Congressional Pillory." *Nation* 192, 18 Feb. 1961, pp. 143-146.

1811. Donner, Frank J. *The Un-Americans.* New York: Ballantine, 1961.

1812. Fey, Harold E. "Burying HUAC." *Christian Century* 92, 26 Feb. 1975, pp. 189-191.

1813. Fey, Harold E. "Why the H.U.A.C. Should Go." *Christian Century* 80, 9 Jan. 1963, pp. 42-47.

1814. Fisher, Louis. "Grover Cleveland Against the Senate." *Congressional Studies* 7 (Spring 1979): 11-26.

1815. Fonseca, Roger W. "Blacklisting Through the Official Publication of Congressional Reports." *Yale Law Journal* 81 (Dec. 1971): 188-230.

1816. Freeman, J. Leiper. "Investigating the Executive Intelligence: The Fate of the Pike Committee." *Capitol Studies* 5 (Fall 1977): 103-118.

1817. Furlong, Patrick J. "The Investigation of General Arthur St. Clair, 1792-1793." *Capitol Studies* 5 (Fall 1977): 65-86.

1818. Gellhorn, Walter. "Report on a Report of the House Committee on Un-American Activities." *Harvard Law Review* 60 (Oct. 1947): 1193-1234.

1819. Goodman, Walter. *The Committee: The Extraordinary Career of the House Committee on Un-American Activities.* New York: Farrar, Strauss, and the Giroux, 1968.

1820. Hacker, Andrew. "Dialogue on Un-American Activities." *Yale Review* 52 (Oct. 1962): 25-38.

1821. Heubel, Edward J. "Reorganization and Reform of Congressional Investigations, 1945-1955." Ph.D. dissertation, University of Minnesota, 1955.

1822. "House Communist Hunters Change Name and Tactics." *Congressional Quarterly Weekly Report* 18 (April 24, 1970): 1130-1133.

1823. Huck, Susan L. M. "The Operation: To Destroy America's Internal Security." *American Opinion* 18 (May 1975): 23-32.

1824. Kahn, Albert E. *Treason in Congress: The Record of the House Un-American Activities Committee.* New York: Progressive Citizens of New York, 1948.

1825. Kaplan, Lewis A. "House Un-American Activities Committee and Its Opponents: A Study in Congressional Dissonance." *Journal of Politics* 30 (Aug. 1968): 647-671.

1826. Kefauver, Estes. *Crime in America.* Garden City, N.Y.: Doubleday, 1951.

1827. Kelly, Beverly M. "The Impact of John Dean's Credibility Before the Senate Select Committee on Presidential Practices." Ph.D. dissertation, University of California at Los Angeles, 1977.

1828. Kennedy, Robert F. *The Enemy Within.* New York: Harper, 1960.

1829. Kirk, Russell. "Conformity and Legislative Committees." *Confluence* 3 (Sept. 1954): 342-353.

1830. Kraines, Oscar. "The Cockrell Committee, 1887-1889: First Comprehensive Congressional Investigation into Administration." *Western Political Quarterly* 4 (Dec. 1951): 583-609.

1831. Kraines, Oscar. *Congress and the Challenge of Big Business.* New York: Bockman Associates, 1958.

1832. Lapin, Adam. *The Un-American Dies Committee.* New York: Workers Library Publishers, 1939.

1833. Livingston, Ellis N. "Senate Investigating Committees, 1900-1938." Ph.D. dissertation, University of Minnesota, 1953.

1834. McClellan, John L. *Crime Without Punishment.* New York: Duell, Sloan and Pierce, 1962.

1835. McGeary, Martin N. "Congressional Investigations During Franklin D. Roosevelt's First Term." *American Political Science Review* 31 (Aug. 1937): 680-694.

1836. Maher, M. Patrick E. "The Role of the Chairman of a Congressional Investigating Committee: A Case Study of the Special Committee of the Senate to Investigate the National Defense Program, 1941-1948." Ph.D. dissertation, St. Louis University, 1962.

1837. Markoe, Arnold. "The Black Committee: A Study of the Senate Investigation of the Public Utility Holding Company Lobby." Ph.D. dissertation, New York University, 1972.

1838. Moore, William H. *The Kefauver Committee and the Politics of Crime, 1950-1952.* Columbia: University of Missouri Press, 1974.

1839. Morgan, Daniel C. and Allison, Samuel E. "The Kefauver Drug Hearings in Perspective." *Southwestern Social Science Quarterly* 45 (June 1964): 59-68.

1840. Mowery, Edward J. *HUAC and FBI: Targets for Abolition.* New York: Bookmaker, 1961.

1841. Nelson, C. D. "Future of the Un-American Activities Committee." *Social Action* 27 (Sept. 1960): 17-24.

1842. Nelson, Harold L. *Libel in News of Congressional Investigating Committees.* Minneapolis: University of Minnesota Press, 1961.

1843. Nelson, Harold L. "Qualified Privilege in Press Reports of Congressional Investigating Committees, with Special Reference to the House Committee on Un-American Activities." Ph.D. dissertation, University of Minnesota, 1956.

1844. Ogden, August R. "The Dies Committee," Ph.D. dissertation, Catholic University of America, 1944.

1845. Oxnam, Garfield B. *I Protest.* New York: Harper, 1954.

1846. Perkins, James A. "Congress Investigates Our Foreign Relations." Ph.D. dissertation, Princeton University, 1937.

1847. Polenberg, Richard. "Franklin Roosevelt and Civil Liberties: The Case of the Dies Committee." *Historian* 30 (Feb. 1968): 165-178.

1848. Raiford, William N. *To Create a Senate Select Committee on Intelligence: A Legislative History of Senate Resolution 400.* Washington: Congressional Research Service, 1976.

1849. Randel, William P. *The Ku Klux Klan: A Century of Infamy.* Philadelphia: Chilton Books, 1965.

1850. Relyea, Harold C. "The Permanent Investigatory Committee in the Legislative Process: The House Committee on Un-American Activities and the Organizational Conspiracies Act of 1966." Master's thesis, American University, 1968.

1851. Riddle, Donald H. *The Truman Committee: A Study in Congressional Responsibility.* New Brunswick, N.J.: Rutgers University Press, 1964.

1852. Ritchie, Donald A. "The Legislative Impact of the Pecora Investigation." *Capitol Studies* 5 (Fall 1977): 87-101.

1853. Rushford, Gregory G. "Making Enemies: The Pike Committee's Struggle to Get the Facts." *Washington Monthly* 8 (July-Aug. 1976): 42-52.

1854. Sanford, Delacy W. "Congressional Investigation of Black Communism 1919-1967." Ph.D. dissertation, State University of New York at Stony Brook, 1973.

1855. Schlesinger, Arthur M. and Burns, Roger. *Congress Investigates: A Documented History 1792-1974.* New York: Chelsea House Publishers, 1975. 5v.

1856. Schneier, Edward V. "The Politics of Anti-Communism: A Study of the House Committee on Un-American Activities and Its Role in the Political Process." Ph.D. dissertation, Claremont Graduate School, 1964.

1857. Sheerin, John B. "The Un-American Activities Committee." *Catholic World* 204 (Oct. 1966): 7-10.

1858. Simmons, Jerold L. "Operation Abolition: The Campaign to Abolish the House Un-American Activities Committee, 1938–1965." Ph.D. dissertation, University of Minnesota, 1971.

1859. Smith, Fred L. "The Selling of the First Amendment: An Analysis of Congressional Investigations of Four CBS Television Documentary Projects." Ph.D. dissertation, Florida State University, 1972.

1860. Soller, Charles M. "Validity of the House Committee on Un-American Activities Committee Inquiries into Professional and Political Affiliations." *Michigan Law Review* 46 (Feb. 1948): 521-532.

1861. Stanley, Timothy W. "Congressional Investigations and National Security: A Study of Legislative–Executive Relations in the Area of Foreign and Military Policies, 1947-1957." Ph.D. dissertation, Harvard University, 1959.

1862. Stroud, Virgil C. "Congressional Investigations of the Conduct of War." Ph.D. dissertation, New York University, 1955.

1863. Sullivan, Thomas P., Kamin, Chester T., and Sussman, Arthur M. "The Case Against HUAC: The *Stamler* Litigation." *Harvard Civil Rights-Civil Liberties Law Review* 11 (Spring 1976): 243-262.

1864. Sutherland, Keith A. "Senate Investigates Harper's Ferry." *Prologue* 8 (Winter 1976): 193-207.

1865. Syme, Samuel A. "Congressional Investigation of Subversion in Education, 1952-1955." Ed.D. dissertation, Duke University, 1962.

1866. Thompson, Fred D. *At That Point in Time: The Inside Story of the Senate Watergate Committee.* New York: Quadrangle, 1975.

1867. Toulmin, Harry A. *Diary of Democracy: The Senate War Investigating Committee.* New York: R. R. Smith, 1947.

1868. Trefousse, Hans L. "Joint Committee on Conduct of War: A Reassessment." *Civil War History* 10 (Mar. 1964): 5-19.

1869. Vaughan, Robert F. "A Historical Study of the Influence of the House Committee on Un-American Activities on the American Theatre, 1938-1958." Ph.D. dissertation, University of Southern California, 1971.

1870. Veenstra, Charles. "House Un-American Activities Committee's Restriction of Free Speech." *Today's Speech* 22 (Winter 1974): 15-22.

1871. Waters, Bertram G. "The Politics of Hunger: Forming a Senate Select Committee." In *To Be a Congressman: The Promise and the Power,* eds. Sven Groennings and Jonathan P. Hawley, pp. 151-167. Washington: Acropolis Books, 1973.

1872. Welch, Joseph N. *Senate Hearings.* Iowa City: State University of Iowa, 1954.

1873. Wilkinson, Frank. "From HUAC to S.1." *Center Magazine* 8 (Sept. 1975): 35-43.

1874. Willson, Roger E. "The Truman Committee." Ph.D. dissertation, Howard University, 1966.

1875. Wilson, O. W. "Local Responsibility in the Suppression of Organized Crime." *Public Management* 33 (Aug. 1951): 170-174.

1876. Wiltz, John E. *In Search of Peace: The Senate Munitions Inquiry, 1934-1936.* Baton Rouge: Louisiana State University Press, 1963.

1877. Yang, Matthew Y. "The Truman Committee." Ph.D. dissertation, Harvard University, 1948.

1878. Young, William W. "Congressional Investigations of the Federal Administration." Ph.D. dissertation, University of California at Berkeley, 1956.

1879. Zeisel, Hans and Stamler, Rose. "The Evidence: A Content Analysis of the HUAC Record." *Harvard Civil Rights-Civil Liberties Law Review* 11 (Spring 1976): 263-298.

VI. Foreign Affairs

General Studies

1880. Abrams, Richard M. "United States Intervention Abroad: The First Quarter Century." *American Historical Review* 79 (Feb. 1974): 72-102.

1881. Abshire, David M. *Foreign Policy Makers: President vs. Congress.* Beverly Hills, Calif.: Sage Publications, 1979.

1882. Adler, E. "Executive Command and Control in Foreign Policy: The CIA's Covert Activities." *Orbis* 23 (Fall 1979): 671-696.

1883. Avery, William P. and Forsythe, David P. "Human Rights, National Security, and the U.S. Senate: Who Votes for What, and Why." *International Studies Quarterly* 23 (June 1979): 303-320.

1884. Baldwin, David A. "Congressional Initiative in Foreign Policy." *Journal of Politics* 28 (Nov. 1966): 754-773.

1885. Bax, Frans R. "The Legislative–Executive Relationship in Foreign Policy: New Partnership or New Competition?" *Orbis* 20 (Winter 1977): 881-904.

1886. Bennet, Douglas J. "Congress in Foreign Policy: Who Needs It?" *Foreign Affairs* 57 (Fall 1978): 40-50.

1887. Bennet, Douglas J. "Congress: Its Role in Foreign Policy-Making." *Department of State Bulletin* 78 (June 1978): 35-36.

1888. Buckwalter, Doyle W. "The Congressional Concurrent Resolution: A Search for Foreign Policy Influence." *Midwest Journal of Political Science* 14 (Aug. 1970): 434-458.

1889. Burdette, Franklin L. "Influence of Noncongressional Pressures on Foreign Policy." *American Academy of Political and Social Science, Annals* 289 (Sept. 1953): 92-99.

1890. Butner, John C. "Congressmen-Diplomats: Legislative–Executive Collaboration in the Conduct of American Foreign Relations." Ph.D. dissertation, University of Maryland, 1977.

1891. Carroll, Holbert N. *The House of Representatives and Foreign Affairs.* rev. ed. Boston: Little, Brown, 1966.

1892. Chace, James. "Is a Foreign Policy Consensus Possible?" *Foreign Affairs* 57 (Fall 1978): 1-16.

1893. Church, Frank. "Has the U.S. Executive Usurped Foreign Policy Prerogatives of the Congress." *American Association of University Women Journal* 64 (Nov. 1970): 31-33.

1894. Cimbala, Stephen J. "Senate Voting and Foreign Policy: Symbols and Issues." Ph.D. dissertation, University of Wisconsin, 1969.

1895. Cohen, Benjamin V. "Evolving Role of Congress in Foreign Affairs." *American Philosophical Society, Proceedings* 92 (1948): 211-216.

1896. Colegrove, Kenneth S. *The American Senate and World Peace.* New York: Vanguard Press, 1944.

1897. Colegrove, Kenneth S. "The Role of Congress and Public Opinion in Formulating Foreign Policy." *American Political Science Review* 38 (Oct. 1944): 956-969.

1898. Conable, Barber B. "Our Limits are Real." *Foreign Policy* 11 (Summer 1973): 73-80.

1899. "Congressional Foreign Policy at Its Worst." *Inter-American Economic Affairs* 29 (1975): 95-96.

1900. "Congressional Influence on Foreign Policy." *Congressional Quarterly Weekly Report* 17 (Oct. 30, 1959): 1442-1445.

1901. Crabb, Cecil V. *Bipartisan Foreign Policy: Myth or Reality?* Evanston, Ill.: Row, Peterson and Co., 1957.

1902. Crabb, Cecil V. "The Role of Congress in Foreign Relations." In *Congress and the President: Allies and Adversaries,* ed. Ronald C. Moe, pp. 210-224. Pacific Palisades, Calif.: Goodyear, 1971.

1903. Crabb, Cecil V. and Holt, Pat M. *Invitation to Struggle: Congress, the Presidency and Foreign Policy.* Washington: Congressional Quarterly, 1980.

1904. Dahl, Robert A. *Congress and Foreign Policy.* New York: Harcourt, Brace and World, 1950.

1905. DeForest, John H. "The Social Sciences and Foreign Policy-Making in Congress." Ph.D. dissertation, Georgetown University, 1970.

1906. Divine, Robert A. "Congress and the President: The Struggle over Foreign Policy." In *The Presidency and Congress: A Shifting Balance of Power?* eds. William S. Livingston, Lawrence C. Dodd, and Richard L. Schott, pp. 166-181. Austin: Lyndon B. Johnson School of Public Affairs, University of Texas, 1979.

1907. Fascell, Dante B. "Congress and Foreign Policy." *Congressional Studies* 7 (Winter 1980): 5-10.

1908. "Foreign Policy: How Much Partisanship?" *Congressional Quarterly Weekly Report* 33 (Mar. 8, 1975): 480-482.

1909. Frye, Alton. "Congress: The Virtue of Its Vices." *Foreign Policy* 3 (Summer 1971): 108-125.

1910. Fulbright, J. William. "Congress and Foreign Policy." In *Congress and the President: Allies and Adversaries,* ed. Ronald C. Moe, pp. 197-209. Pacific Palisades, Calif.: Goodyear, 1971.

1911. Fulbright, J. William. "The Legislator as Educator." *Foreign Affairs* 57 (Spring 1979): 19-32.

1912. Gallagher, Hugh G. *Advise and Consent: The Role of the United States Senate in Foreign Policy Decisions.* New York: Delacorte Press, 1969.

1913. Garn, Jake. "Toward a Positive Attitude in American Foreign Policy." *Journal of Social and Political Affairs* 1 (April 1976): 99-112.

1914. Gelb, Leslie H. and Lake, Anthony. "Congress: Politics and Bad Policy." *Foreign Policy* 20 (Fall 1975): 232-238.

1915. Gibbons, William C. "Political Action Analysis as an Approach to the Study of Congress and Foreign Policy." Ph.D. dissertation, Princeton University, 1961.

1916. Gillette, Guy M. "The Senate in Foreign Relations." *American Academy of Political and Social Science, Annals* 289 (Sept. 1953): 49-57.

1917. Grassmuck, George L. *Sectional Biases in Congress on Foreign Policy.* Baltimore: Johns Hopkins University Press, 1951.

1918. Griffith, Ernest S. "The Place of Congress in Foreign Relations." *American Academy of Political and Social Science, Annals* 289 (Sept. 1953): 11-21.

1919. Griffith, William E. "Congress Is Wrecking Our Foreign Policy." *Readers' Digest* 108 (Feb. 1976): 71-76.

1920. Hagen, Christopher G. "Responses in the U.S. Senate to Issues of International Significance: The Confluence of International and Domestic Considerations in Decision-Making." Ph.D. dissertation, Brown University, 1974.

1921. Hauptman, Laurence M. "To the Good Neighbor: A Study of the Senate's Role in American Foreign Policy." Ph.D. dissertation, New York University, 1972.

1922. Hebert, F. Edward. "The Last of the Titans." *Strategic Review* 5 (Winter 1977): 14-20.

1923. Herter, Christian A. "Relationship of the United States to International Problems." *American Society of International Law, Proceedings* 42 (1948): 91-96.

1924. Huck, Susan L. M. "Council on Foreign Relations and the Senate." *American Opinion* 22 (Nov. 1979): 13-18.

1925. Humphrey, Hubert H. "The Senate in Foreign Policy." *Foreign Affairs* 37 (July 1959): 525-536.

1926. Ingersoll, Robert S. "Executive and the Congress in Foreign Policy: Conflict or Cooperation?" *Department of State Bulletin* 74 (Feb. 9, 1976): 147-152.

1927. Javits, Jacob K. "The Congressional Presence in Foreign Relations." *Foreign Affairs* 48 (Jan. 1970): 221-234.

1928. Jewell, Malcolm E. *Senatorial Politics and Foreign Policy.* Lexington: University Press of Kentucky, 1962.

1929. Jones, Harry L. "Congressional Affairs." *International Lawyer* 8 (1974): 637-649.

1930. Jones, Harry W. "The President, Congress, and Foreign Relations." *California Law Review* 29 (July 1941): 565-585.

1931. Jones, Harry W. "The Role of Congress in the Development of Foreign Policy." *American Bar Association Journal* 34 (Sept. 1948): 813-814.

1932. Kalijarvi, Thorsten V. "The Future of Congress in Foreign Relations." *American Academy of Political and Social Science, Annals* 289 (Sept. 1953): 172-177.

1933. Katzenbach, Nicholas D. "Comparative Roles of the President and the Congress in Foreign Affairs: Statement, August 17, 1967." *Department of State Bulletin* 57 (Sept. 11, 1967): 333-336.

1934. Kendrick, Joseph T. "The Consultative Process: The Legislative–Executive Relationship in the Formulation of Foreign Policy." Ph.D. dissertation, George Washington University, 1979.

1935. Kesselman, Mark. "Presidential Leadership in Congress and Foreign Policy: A Reapplication of a Hypothesis." *Midwest Journal of Political Science* 9 (Nov. 1965): 401-406.

1936. Kesselman,, Mark. "Presidential Leadership in Congress on Foreign Policy." *Midwest Journal of Political Science* 5 (Aug. 1961): 284-289.

1937. Kessler, Frank. "Presidential–Congressional Battles: Toward a Truce on the Foreign Policy Front." *Presidential Studies Quarterly* 8 (Spring 1978): 115-126.

1938. Kling, Merle. "The Tenability of Isolationism and Internationalism as Designations of the Foreign Policy of the United States: A Case Study of Senator Arthur H. Vanderberg and Representative Vito Marcantonio." Ph.D. dissertation, Washington University, 1949.

1939. Kolodziej, Edward A. "Congress and Foreign Policy Through the Looking Glass." *Virginia Quarterly Review* 42 (Winter 1966): 12-27,

1940. Kuklick, Bruce. "Congress and Foreign Policy." In *Encyclopedia of American Foreign Policy,* ed. Alexander DeConde, pp. 141-150. New York: Charles Scribner's Sons, 1978.

1941. Langer, William L. "Mechanism of American Foreign Policy." *International Affairs* 24 (July 1948): 319-328.

1942. Legette, Caroline M. "Income Redistribution and Foreign Policy: Presidential Influence and Congressional Response." Ph.D. dissertation, State University of New York at Buffalo, 1977.

1943. Lehman, John F. "Functional Analysis of Congress and the Executive in Foreign Policy." Ph.D. dissertation, University of Pennsylvania, 1974.

1944. Levitan, David M. "Constitutional Developments in the Control of Foreign Affairs: A Quest for Democratic Control." *Journal of Politics* 7 (Feb. 1945): 58-92.

1945. McCloskey, Robert J. "Congress and Foreign Policy." *Department of State Bulletin* 75 (July 26, 1976): 139-143.

1946. Manley, John F. "The Rise of Congress in Foreign Policy-Making." *American Academy of Political and Social Science, Annals* 397 (Sept. 1971): 60-70.

1947. Manning, Bayless. "The Congress, Executive and Intermestic Affairs: Three Proposals." *Foreign Affairs* 55 (Jan. 1977): 306-324.

1948. Marcy, Carl. "The Impact of Secrecy on Congressional Ability to Participate in Foreign Policy Decision Making." *Towson State Journal of International Affairs* 10 (1975): 13-18.

1949. Martin, Charles E. "Executive Determination of Legal Questions." *American Society of International Law, Proceedings* 42 (1948): 53-82.

1950. Mathews, John M. "Joint Resolution Method." *American Journal of International Law* 32 (April 1938): 349-352.

1951. Meyers, Denys P. "Legislatures and Foreign Relations." *American Political Science Review* 11 (Nov. 1917): 643-684.

1952. Murphy, John. "Knowledge Is Power: Foreign Policy and Information Interchange Among Congress, the Executive Branch and the Public." *Tulane Law Review* 49 (Mar. 1975): 505-554.

1953. Nobleman, Eli E. "Financial Aspects of Congressional Participation in Foreign Relations." *American Academy of Political and Social Science, Annals* 289 (Sept. 1953): 145-164.

1954. Ogul, Morris S. "Reforming Executive–Legislative Relations in the Conduct of American Foreign Policy: The Executive-Legislative Council as a Proposed Solution." Ph.D. dissertation, University of Michigan, 1958.

1955. Oliver, Covey T. "United States and the World." *American Academy of Political and Social Science, Annals* 426 (July 1976): 166-212.

1956. Olson, William C. "The American Congress and Foreign Policy: A Functional Adaptation of the Constitution." *Jahrbuch des Öffentlichen Rechts der Gegenwart* 21 (1972): 591-601.

1957. Olson, William C. "Congressional Competence in Foreign Affairs: The Measure of Information and Analysis." *Round Table* 250 (April 1973): 247-258.

1958. Olson, William C. "President, Congress and American Foreign Policy: Confrontation or Collaboration?" *International Affairs* 52 (Oct. 1976): 565-581.

1959. Olson, William C. "The Role of Congress in Making the Foreign Policy of the United States." *The Parliamentarian* 56 (July 1975): 151-158.

1960. Reid, Ogden R. "Congress and Foreign Policy." In *We Propose: A Modern Congress*, ed. Mary McInnis, pp. 85-101. New York: McGraw-Hill, 1966.

1961. Richards, James P. "The House of Representatives in Foreign Affairs." *American Academy of Political and Social Science, Annals* 289 (Sept. 1953): 66-72.

1962. Rieselbach, Leroy N. "Congressional Ideology, the Vote on Foreign Policy, and the Prospects for Party Realignment." *Public Policy* 14 (1965): 49-70.

1963. Rieselbach, Leroy N. *The Roots of Isolationism: Congressional Voting and Presidential Leadership in Foreign Policy*. Indianapolis, Ind.: Bobbs-Merrill, 1966.

1964. Robinson, James A. "Congress and Foreign Policy-Making. rev. ed. Homewood, Ill.: Dorsey Press, 1967.

1965. Rosenau, James N. "The Senate and Dean Acheson: A Case Study in Legislative Attitudes." Ph.D. dissertation, Princeton University, 1957.

1966. Rosenfeld, Stephen S. "Pluralism and Policy." *Foreign Affairs* 52 (Jan. 1974): 263-272.

1967. Rourke, John T. "The Future Is History: Congress and Foreign Policy." *Presidential Studies Quarterly* 9 (Summer 1979): 275-282.

1968. Schlesinger, Arthur M. "Congress and the Making of American Foreign Policy." *Foreign Affairs* 51 (Oct. 1972): 78-113.

1969. Searcy, Hubert. "The Use of the Congressional Joint Resolution in Matters Relating to Foreign Affairs." Ph.D. dissertation, Duke University, 1937.

1970. Sparkman, John J. "Congress and the Conduct of Foreign Policy." *American Society of International Law, Proceedings* 46 (1952): 204-208.

1971. Sparkman, John J. "The Role of the Senate in Determining Foreign Policy." In *The Senate Institution*, ed. Nathaniel S. Preston, pp. 31-39. New York: Van Nostrand, 1969.

1972. Stennis, John Cornelius and Fulbright, J. William. *The Role of Congress in Foreign Policy*. Washington: American Enterprise Institute for Public Policy Research, 1971.

1973. Strum, Philippa. "Unbalance Power: The President, Congress, and Foreign Policy." In his *Presidential Power and American Democracy*, pp. 41-76. Santa Monica, Calif.: Goodyear, 1979.

1974. Taylor, Stan A. "Congressional Resurgence." In *Problems of American Foreign Policy*, 2d ed., ed. Martin B. Hickman, pp. 106-118. Beverly Hills, Calif.: Glencoe Press, 1975.

1975. United Nations Association. *Congressional Survey Report: A Report on the Foreign Policy Attitudes of the Members of the United States House of Representatives*. Washington: United Nations Association, 1975.

1976. U.S. Congress. House. Committee on International Relations. Special Subcommittee on Investigations. *Congress and Foreign Policy: Report of the Special Subcommittee on Investigations of the Committee on International Relations, House of Representatives*. 94th Cong., 2nd sess. Washington: GPO, 1976.

1977. U.S. Congress. Senate. Foreign Relations Committee. *Congress, Information and Foreign Affairs*. 95th Cong., 2nd sess. Washington: GPO, 1978.

1978. Vorys, John M. "Party Responsibility for Foreign Policy." *American Academy of Political and Social Science, Annals* 289 (Sept. 1953): 165-171.

1979. Wigmore, John H. "Government by Secret Diplomacy." *Illinois Law Review* 23 (Mar. 1929): 689-694.

1980. Wilcox, John C. Congress, The Executive and Foreign Policy. New York: Harper and Row, 1971.

1981. Willis, David K. "Dealing with Congress." *American Academy of Political and Social Science, Annals* 380 (Nov. 1968): 112-117.

1982. Womeldorph, Stuart E. "The Conduct of American Foreign Relations, with Special Emphasis on the Participation of Congress." D.C.L., American University, 1928.

1983. Wright, Quincy. "The Control of Foreign Relations." *American Political Science Review* 15 (Feb. 1921): 1-26.

Historical Studies

Before 1917

1984. Allen, Howard W. "Republican Reformers and Foreign Policy, 1913-1917." *Mid-American* 44 (Oct. 1962): 222-229.

1985. Carter, Purvis M. "Congressional and Public Reaction to Wilson's Caribbean Policy, 1913-1917." Ph.D. dissertation, University of Chicago, 1970.

1986. Champagne, Raymond W. "The House of Representatives and American Foreign Policy During the Washington Administration, 1789-1797." Ph.D. dissertation, Loyola University, 1973.

1987. Geary, James W. "A Lesson in Trial and Error: The United States Congress and the Civil War Draft, 1862-1865." Ph.D. dissertation, Kent State University, 1976.

1988. Goebel, Dorothy B. "Congress and Foreign Relations Before 1900." *American Academy of Political and Social Science, Annals* 289 (Sept. 1953): 22-39.

1989. Johnson, Leland R. "The Suspense Was Hell: The Senate Vote for War in 1812." *Indiana Magazine of History* 65 (Dec. 1969): 247-269.

1990. McDonald, Timothy G. "Southern Democratic Congressmen and the First World War, August 1914-April 1917: The Public Record of Their Support for or Opposition to Wilson's Policies." Ph.D. dissertation, University of Washington, 1962.

1991. Nichols, Jeannette P. "United States Congress and Imperialism, 1861-1897." *Journal of Economic History* 21 (Dec. 1961): 526-538.

1992. Pohl, James W. "The Congress and the Secretary of War, 1915: An Instance of Political Pressure." *New Jersey History* 89 (Fall 1971): 163-170.

1993. Schroeder, John H. "Dilemmas of Dissent: Congress and Opposition to the Mexican War." *Capitol Studies* 3 (Fall 1975): 15-30.

1994. Snyder, Louis L. "Bismarck and the Lasker Resolution, 1884." *Review of Politics* 29 (Jan. 1967): 41-64.

1995. Sutton, Walter A. "The Command of Gold: Progressive Republican Senators and Foreign Policy, 1912-1917." Ph.D. dissertation, University of Texas at Austin, 1964.

1996. Sutton, Walter A. "Republican Progressive Senators and Preparedness, 1915-1916." *Mid-America* 52 (July 1970): 155-176.

1997. Vahle, Cornelius W. "Congress, the President, and Overseas Expansion, 1897-1901." Ph.D. dissertation, Georgetown University, 1967.

1917–1932   World War I and Isolationism

1998. Bradshaw, Mary E. "Congress and Foreign Policy Since 1900." *American Academy of Political and Social Science, Annals* 289 (Sept. 1953): 40-48.

1999. Bryson, Thomas A. "Woodrow Wilson, the Senate, Public Opinion and the Armenian Mandate, 1919-1920." Ph.D. dissertation, University of Georgia, 1965.

2000. Clark, John H. *American and World Peace.* New York: H. Holt, 1925.

2001. Garcia, Rogelio. "Opposition Within the Senate to the American Military Intervention in Nicaragua, 1926-1933." Ph.D. dissertation, Columbia University, 1973.

2002. Girard, Jolyon P. "Congress and Presidential Military Policy: The Occupation of Germany, 1919-1923." *Mid-America* 56 (Oct. 1974): 211-220.

2003. Guinsburg, Thomas N. "Senatorial Isolationism in America, 1919-1941." Ph.D. dissertation, Columbia University, 1969.

2004. Horner, Richard K. "The House at War: The House of Representatives During WWI, 1917-1919." Ph.D. dissertation, Louisiana State University and Agricultural and Mechanical College, 1977.

2005. Merz, Charles. "Congress and the War." *Yale Review* 6 (July 1917): 684-698.

2006. Mickey, David H. "Senatorial Participation in Shaping Certain United States Foreign Policies, 1921-1941 (Being Largely a Study of the Congressional Record)." Ph.D. dissertation, University of Nebraska, 1954.

2007. Vinson, John C. *The Parchment Peace: The United States Senate and the Washington Conference, 1921-1922.* Athens: University of Georgia Press, 1955.

2008. Wickersham, George W. "Senate and Our Foreign Relations." *Foreign Affairs* 2 (Dec. 1923): 177-192.

1932-1945—Good Neighbor Policy and World War II

2009. Cleary, Charles R. "Congress, the Executive, and Neutrality: 1935 to 1940." Ph.D. dissertation, Fordham University, 1953.

2010. Doenecke, Justus D. "Non-Intervention of the Left: The Keep American Out of the War Congress, 1938-41." *Journal of Contemporary History* 12 (April 1977): 221-236.

2011. Donovan, John C. "Congress and the Making of Neutrality Legislation, 1935-1939." Ph.D. dissertation, Harvard University, 1949.

2012. Donovan, John C. "Congressional Isolationists and the Roosevelt Foreign Policy." *World Politics* 3 (April 1951): 299-316.

2013. Howards, Irving. "The Influence of Southern Senators on American Foreign Policy from 1939 to 1950." Ph.D. dissertation, University of Wisconsin, 1955.

2014. Libby, Justin H. "The Irresolute Years: American Congressional Opinion Towards Japan, 1937-1941." Ph.D. dissertation, Michigan State University, 1971.

2015. Munkres, Robert L. "The Use of the Congressional Resolution as an Instrument of Influence over Foreign Policy, 1925-1950." Ph.D. dissertation, University of Nebraska, 1956.

2016. O'Sullivan, John J. "From Voluntarism to Conscription: Congress and Selective Service, 1940-1945." Ph.D. dissertation, Columbia University, 1971.

2017. Patterson, James T. "Eating Humble Pie: A Note on Roosevelt, Congress, and Neutrality Revision in 1939." *Historian* 31 (May 1969): 407-414.

2018. Perez-Reilly, Mario. "Southern Senators and Isolationism: A Longitudinal Study." Ph.D. dissertation, University of Tennessee, 1974.

2019. Poole, DeWitt C. "Structural Improvements in the Administration of Foreign Affairs." *American Philosophical Society Proceedings* 72 (1933): 77-86.

2020. Porter, David L. "Congress and the Coming of the War, 1939–1940." Ph.D. dissertation, Pennsylvania State University, 1970.

2021. Rieselbach, Leroy N. "Congressional Isolationist Behavior, 1939-1958." Ph.D. dissertation, Yale University, 1964.

2022. Wilcox, Francis O. "The Neutrality Fight in Congress: 1939." American Political Science Review 33 (Oct. 1939): 811-825.

1945–1964—Cold War

2023. Bryniarski, Joan L. "Against the Tide: Senate Opposition to the Internationalist Foreign Policy of Presidents Franklin D. Roosevelt and Harry S Truman, 1943-1949." Ph.D. dissertation, University of Maryland, 1972.

2024. Crabb, Cecil V. "The President, Congress, and American Foreign Relations, 1942-1952: The Quest for a Bipartisan Foreign Policy." Ph.D. dissertation, Johns Hopkins University, 1953.

2025. Craft, James P. "The Role of Congress in the Determination of Naval Strategy in Support of United States Foreign Policy 1956-1966." Ph.D. dissertation, University of Pennsylvania, 1969.

2026. Duane, Edward A. "Congress and Inter-American Relations 1961-1965." Ph.D. dissertation, University of Pennsylvania, 1969.

2027. Fuchs, Lawrence H. "The World Federation Resolution: A Case Study in Congressional Decision-Making." *Midwest Journal of Political Science* 1 (Aug. 1957): 151-162.

2028. Grimmett, Richard F. "The Politics of Containment: The President, the Senate, and American Foreign Policy, 1947–1956." Ph.D. dissertation, Kent State University, 1973.

2029. Grimmett, Richard F. "Who Were the Senate Isolationists." *Pacific Historical Review* 42 (Nov. 1973): 479-498.

2030. Hedlund, Richard P. "Congress and the British Loan, 1945–1946: A Congressional Study." Ph.D. dissertation, University of Kentucky, 1976.

2031. Jewell, Malcolm E. "The Role of Political Parties in the Formation of Foreign Policy in the Senate, 1947-1956." Ph.D. dissertation, Pennsylvania State University, 1958.

2032. Lofgren, Charles A. "Congress and the Korean Conflict." Ph.D. dissertation, Stanford University, 1966.

2033. Morgenthau, Hans J. "Conduct of American Foreign Policy." *Parliamentary Affairs* 3 (Winter 1949): 147-161.

2034. Paterson, Thomas G. "Presidential Foreign Policy, Public Opinion, and Congress: The Truman Years." *Diplomatic History* 3 (Winter 1979): 1-18.

2035. Reichard, Gary W. "Divisions and Dissent: Democrats and Foreign Policy, 1952-1956." *Political Science Quarterly* 93 (Spring 1978): 51-72.

2036. Riggs, James R. "Congress and the Conflict of the Korean War." Ph.D. dissertation, Purdue University, 1972.

2037. Robinson, James A. *The Monroney Resolution: Congressional Initiative in Foreign Policy Making.* New York: Holt, 1959.

2038. Rossiter, Clinton L. "Constitutional Dictatorship in the Atomic Age." *Review of Politics* 11 (Oct. 1949): 395-418.

2039. Rossiter, Clinton L. "What of Congress in Atomic War." *Western Political Quarterly* 3 (Dec. 1960): 602-606.

1964–1975—Vietnam War

2040. Berg, John C. "Why the Congressional Doves Failed to End United States Participation in the Vietnam War." Ph.D. dissertation, Harvard University, 1975.

2041. "Congress: Views on Reaching the End of the Tunnel." *Congressional Quarterly Weekly Report* 31 (Jan. 27, 1973): 166-170.

2042. Fagen, Patricia W. "U.S. Foreign Policy and Human Rights: The Role of Congress." In *Parliamentary Control over Foreign Policy: Legal Essays,* ed. Antonio Cassese, pp. 111-136. Germantown, Md.: Sijthoff and Noordhoff, 1980.

2043. Goldberg, Ronald A. "The Senate and Vietnam: A Study in Acquiescence." Ph.D. dissertation, University of Georgia, 1972.

2044. Hamre, John J. "Congressional Dissent and American Foreign Policy: Constitution War-Making in the Vietnam Years." Ph.D. dissertation, Johns Hopkins University, 1978.

2045. Kolodziej, Edward A. "Congress and Foreign Policy: The Nixon Years." *The Academy of Political Science, Proceedings* 32 (1975): 167-179.

2046. Lehman, John F. *The Executive, Congress, and Foreign Policy: Studies of the Nixon Administration.* New York: Praeger, 1976.

2047. Manske, Robert G. "The Fulbright Foreign Policy Thought, 1964–1971: A Co-Organic Critique." Ph.D. dissertation, American University, 1973.

2048. Moore, J. N. "Contemporary Issues in an Ongoing Debate: The Roles of Congress and the President in Foreign Affairs." *International Lawyer* 7 (Oct. 1973): 733-745.

2049. Rosenburg, Michael P. "Congress and the Vietnam War: A Study of the Critics of the War in 1967 and 1968." Ph.D. dissertation, New School for Social Research, 1973.

2050. Sherill, Robert G. "Wedge of Dissent: Democratic Rebels in Congress." *Nation* 203, 19 Oct. 1966, pp. 341-346.

2051. Welch, Edwin H. "An Ethical Analysis of Decision-Making: The Response of the United States Senate to the Nonproliferation Treaty." Ph.D. dissertation, Boston University, 1971.

2052. Wilcox, Francis O. "President Nixon, the Congress, and Foreign Policy." *Michigan Quarterly Review* 9 (Winter 1970): 37-43.

2053. Zelman, Walter A. "Senate Dissent and the Vietnam War, 1964-1968." Ph.D. dissertation, University of California at Los Angeles, 1971.

1975–1980—Contemporary Foreign Policy

2054. Barberis, Mary A. "The Arab-Israeli Battle on Capitol Hill." *Virginia Quarterly Review* 52 (Spring 1976): 203-223.

2055. Fraser, Donald M. "Human Rights and the United States Foreign Policy: The Congressional Perspective." In *Human Rights and U.S. Foreign Policy,* eds. Barry M. Rubin and Elizabeth P. Spiro, pp. 95-105. Boulder, Colo.: Westview Press, 1979.

2056. Gardner, Judy. "Congress More Cautious in Post-Vietnam Era." *Congressional Quarterly Weekly Report* 33 (June 28, 1975): 1347-1351.

2057. Gelb, Leslie H. and Lake, Anthony. "Washington Dateline: A Tale of Two Compromises." *Foreign Policy* 22 (Spring 1976): 224-237.

2058. Goldstein, Martin E. "Congressional Participation in Foreign Policy Before and After Watergate." *Political Science* 27 (July/Dec. 1975): 111-116.

2059. Lanouette, William J. "Who's Setting Foreign Policy: Carter or Congress?" *National Journal* 10 (July 15, 1978): 1116-1123.

2060. Maxfield, David M. and Towell, Pat. "Foreign Policy: Congress Retains Active Role." *Congressional Quarterly Weekly Report* 34 (Sept. 4, 1976): 2387-2391.

2061. Olson, William C. "Re-Assertion and Diplomacy: Recent Congressional Actions in the Field of American Foreign Policy." *Jahrbuch des Öffentlichen Rechts der Gegenwart* 25 (1976): 403-416.

2062. Olson, William C. "The World from Both Ends of Pennsylvania Avenue: President Carter's Foreign Policy Problems." *Round Table* 272 (Oct. 1978): 333-339.

2063. U.S. Congress. House. Foreign Affairs Committee. *Congress and Foreign Policy,* 1978. 96th Cong., 1st sess. Washington: GPO, 1979.

Treaty-Making Power

2064. Adkins, Hartwell S. "The Treaty-Making Power in Relation to the Power of Congress and the Power of the States." Ph.D. dissertation, George Washington University, 1922.

2065. Anderson, Chandler P. "The Senate and Obligatory Arbitration Treaties." *American Journal of International Law* 26 (April 1932): 328-333.

2066. Anderson, Chandler P. "Treaties as Domestic Law." *American Journal of International Law* 29 (July 1935): 472-476.

2067. Black, Forrest R. "The Role of the President and the Senate in the Treaty Making Power." *St. Louis Law Review* 11 (1926): 203-222.

2068. Black, Forrest R. "The United States Senate and the Treaty Power." *Rocky Mountain Law Review* 4 (Nov. 1931): 1-19.

2069. Borchard, Edwin. "Proposed Constitutional Amendment on Treaty-Making." *American Journal of International Law* 29 (July 1945): 537-541.

2070. Bronaugh, Minor. "Treaties Versus the Constitution and Congress." *Law Notes* 27 (Dec. 1923): 168-170.

2071. Collier, Ellen C. *The Meaning of "Advice and Consent of the Senate" in the Treaty-Making Process.* Washington: Legislative Reeference Service, 1969.

2072. Dangerfield, Royden J. and Wright, Quincy. *In Defense of the Senate: A Study in Treaty Making.* Norman: University of Oklahoma Press, 1933.

2073. Daniel, Price. "Congress and International Law: The Treaty-Making Power and the Continental Shelf." *American Society of International Law, Proceedings* 47 (1953): 171-179.

2074. Dean, Arthur H. "The Bricker Amendment and Authority over Foreign Affairs." *Foreign Affairs* 32 (Oct. 1953): 1-19.

2075. Dewhurst, William W. "Does the Constitution Make the President Sole Negotiator of Treaties?" *Yale Law Journal* 34 (Mar. 1921): 478-487.

2076. Dobie, Edith. "Attitude of the United States Senate upon General Arbitration Treaties." *Southwestern Political and Social Science Quarterly* 8 (Mar. 1928): 413-424.

2077. Evans, Alona E. "Some Aspects of the Problem of Self-Executing Treaties." *American Society of International Law, Proceedings* 45 (1951): 66-75.

2078. Fleming, Denna F. "The Advice of the Senate in Treaty-Making." *Current History* 32 (Sept. 1930): 1090-1094.

2079. Fleming, Denna F. "Role of the Senate in Treaty-Making: A Survey of Four Decades." *American Political Science Review* 28 (Aug. 1934): 583-598.

2080. Fleming, Denna F. *The Treaty Veto of the American Senate.* New York: G. P. Putnam's Sons, 1930.

2081. Foster, John W. "The Treaty-Making Power Under the Constitution." *Yale Law Journal* 11 (Dec. 1901): 69-79.

2082. Garner, James W. "Acts and Joint Resolutions of Congress as Substitutes for Treaties." *American Journal of International Law* 29 (July 1935): 482-488.

2083. Goldwater, Barry M. "Treaty Termination Is a Shared Power." *Policy Review* 8 (Spring 1979): 115-124.

2084. Gower, Holly J. "Democratic Control of United States Foreign Policy: The Treaty-Making Power and the Senate." Ph.D. dissertation, University of Chicago, 1969.

2085. Guinsburg, Thomas N. "Victory in Defeat: The Senatorial Isolationists and the Four-Power Treaty." *Capitol Studies* 2 (Spring 1973): 23-36.

2086. Gulick, Mary S. "Legal Effect of an Act of Congress upon a Prior Treaty." *George Washington Law Review* 2 (Nov. 1933): 74-76.

2087. Hayden, Joseph R. *The Senate and Treaties, 1789-1817: The Development of the Treaty Making Functions of the United States Senate During Their Formative Period.* New York: Macmillan, 1920.

2088. Henkin, Louis. "Treaty Makers and the Law Makers: The Law of the Land and Foreign Relations." *University of Pennsylvania Law Review* 107 (May 1959): 903-936.

2089. Herter, Christian A. "Relation of the House of Representatives to the Making and Implementation of Treaties (with Discussion)." *American Society of International Law, Proceedings* 45 (1951): 55-65.

2090. Hindman, E. James. "General Arbitration Treaties of William Howard Taft.'.' *Historian* 36 (Nov. 1973): 52-65.

2091. Holt, William S. *Treaties Defeated by the Senate: A Study of the Struggle Between President and Senate over the Conduct of Foreign Relations.* Baltimore: Johns Hopkins University Press, 1933.

2092. Huddle, Franklin P. "The Limited Nuclear Test Ban Treaty and the United States Senate." Ph.D. dissertation, American University, 1965.

2093. Johnson, Allen. "The Part of the House in Treaty-Making: Debate in the House of Representatives on the Jay Treaty." In his *Readings in American Constitutional History 1776-1876,* pp. 197-205. Boston: Houghton Mifflin, 1912.

2094. Jones, J. Mervyn. *Full Powers and Ratification: A Study in the Development of Treaty-Making Procedure.* Cambridge: At the University Press, 1946.

2095. Kefauver, Estes. "The House of Representatives Should Participate in Treaty Making." *Tennessee Law Review* 19 (Dec. 1945): 44-51.

2096. Korey, William. "Human Rights Treaties: Why Is the U.S. Stalling?" *Foreign Affairs* 45 (Apr. 1967): 414-424.

2097. McClendon, Robert E. "I. Origin of the Two-Thirds Rule in Senate Action upon Treaties; II. The Two-Thirds Rule in Senate Action upon Treaties, 1789-1901." Ph.D. dissertation, University of Wisconsin, 1929.

2098. McClendon, Robert E. "Two-Thirds Rule in Senate Action upon Treaties, 1789-1901." *American Journal of International Law* 26 (Jan. 1932): 37-56.

2099. MacMaster, Donald. "United States Senate and the Treaty-Making Powers." *Journal of Comparative Legislation* 3d S., 2 (1920): 189-195.

2100. Marcy, Carl. "A Note on Treaty Ratification." *American Political Science Review* 47 (Dec. 1953): 1130-1133.

2101. Mikell, William E. "Extent of the Treaty-Making Power of the President and the Senate of the United States." *University of Pennsylvania Law Review* 57 (April 1909): 435-458, 528-562.

2102. Oliver, Covey T. "Treaties, the Senate, and the Constitution: Some Current Questions." *American Journal of International Law* 51 (July 1957): 606-611.

2103. Potter, D. Roland. "Development of Treaty Procedure in the United States Senate." *Federal Bar Association Journal* 2 (Oct. 1936): 325-330.

2104. Reisenfeld, Stefan A. "The Power of Congress and the President in International Relations: Three Recent Supreme Court Decisions." *California Law Review* 25 (Sept. 1937): 643-675.

2105. Roots, John M. "The Treaty of Versailles in the United States Senate." Honors thesis, Harvard University, 1925.

2106. Sargent, Noel. "Congress and Treaties." *Central Law Journal* 89 (Nov. 1919): 370-380.

2107. Stone, Ivan M. "The House of Representatives and the Treaty-Making Power." *Kentucky Law Journal* 17 (Mar. 1929): 216-257.

2108. Tansill, Charles C. "The Treaty-Making Powers of the Senate." *American Journal of International Law* 18 (July 1924): 459-482.

2109. Thomas, Charles S. "Power of Congress to Establish Peace." *American Law Review* 55 (Jan. 1921): 86-104.

2110. "Transfer of the Panama Canal by Treaty Without House Approval: *Edwards v. Carter* (580 F 2d 1055)." *Harvard Law Review* 92 (Dec. 1978): 524-535.

2111. U.S. Congress. Senate. Foreign Relations Committee. *The Role of the Senate in Treaty Ratification.* Washington: GPO, 1977.

2112. Washburn, Albert H. "Legislative Compacts with Foreign Nations." *American Law Review* 55 (Jan.-Feb. 1921): 68-85.

2113. Webb, Richard E. "Treaty-Making and the President's Obligation to Seek the Advice and Consent of the Senate with Special Reference to the Vietnam Peace Negotiations." *Ohio State Law Journal* 31 (Summer 1970): 490-519.

2114. Wigmore, John H. "The Federal Senate's Neglect of the Nation's International Interests." *Illinois Law Review* 26 (Mar. 1932): 794-796.

2115. Wise, Jennings C. "The Unconstitutionality of 'Foreign Legislative Contracts'." *Virginia Law Review* 18 (June 1932): 875-885.

2116. Wright, Herbert. "Two-Thirds Vote of the Senate in Treaty-Making." *American Journal of International Law* 38 (Oct. 1944): 643-650.

2117. Wright, Quincy. "Congress and the Treaty-Making Power." *American Society of International Law, Proceedings* 46 (1952): 43-58.

Executive Agreements

2118. Borchard, Edwin. "Shall the Executive Agreement Replace the Treaty?" *American Journal of International Law* 38 (Oct. 1944): 637-643.

2119. Borchard, Edwin. "Treaties and Executive Agreements: A Reply." *Yale Law Journal* 54 (June 1945): 615-664.

2120. Bricker, John W. "Making Treaties and Other International Agreements." *American Academy of Political and Social Science, Annals* 289 (Sept. 1953): 134-144.

2121. Browne, Marjorie A. *Executive Agreements and the Congress.* Washington: Congressional Research Service, 1978.

2122. "Executive Agreements: Any Role for Congress?" *Congressional Quarterly Weekly Report* 30 (May 6, 1972): 1007-1008.

2123. Gardner, Judy. "Members Seek Veto over Executive Agreements." *Congressional Quarterly Weekly Report* 33 (Aug. 2, 1975): 1712-1717.

2124. Johnson, Lock and McCormick, James M. "The Making of International Agreements: A Reappraisal of Congressional Involvement." *Journal of Politics* 40 (May 1978): 468-478.

2125. Kitler, John W. "Non-Self-Executing Treaties and Congressional Action in the United States." Ph.D. dissertation, George Washington University, 1957.

2126. McDougal, Myres S. and Lans, Asher. "Treaties and Congressional–Executive or Presidential Agreements: Interchangeable Instruments of National Policy I, II." *Yale Law Journal* 54 (Mar. 1945): 181-351, 534-615.

2127. Nelson, Randall H. "Legislative Participation in the Treaty and Agreement Making Process." *Western Political Quarterly* 13 (Mar. 1960): 154-171.

2128. Ohly, D. Christopher. "Advice and Consent: International Executive Claims Settlement Agreements." *California Western International Law Journal* 5 (Spring 1975): 271-296.

2129. Slonim, Solomon. "Congressional–Executive Agreements." *Columbia Journal of Transnational Law* 14 (1975): 434-450.

2130. Stevens, Charles J. "The Use and Control of Executive Agreements: Recent Congressional Initiatives." *Orbis* 20 (Winter 1977): 905-931.

2131. U.S. Congress. Senate. Judiciary Committee. *Congressional Oversight of Executive Agreements, Hearings.* Washington: GPO, 1975.

2132. U.S. Congress. House. International Relations Committee. *Congressional Review of International Agreements, Hearings.* Washington: GPO, 1976.

2133. Wigmore, John H. "May Federal Senate Hamstring Executive's Power to Confer with Other Nations?" *Illinois Law Review* 20 (Mar. 1926): 688-690.

2134. Witman, Shepherd L. "International Agreements Concluded by the President Without Submission to the Senate." Ph.D. dissertation, Yale University, 1937.

2135. Woolsey, L. H. "Executive Agreements Relating to Panama." *American Journal of International Law* 37 (July 1943): 482-489.

2136. Wright, Quincy. "United States and International Agreements: Treaties and Executive Agreements." *American Journal of International Law* 38 (July 1944): 341-355.

War Powers

2137. Allison, Graham T. "Making War: The President and Congress." *Law and Contemporary Problems* 40 (Summer 1976): 86-105.

2138. Angst, Gerald L. "1973 War Powers Legislation: Congress Reasserts Its Warmaking Power." *Loyola University Law Journal* (Chicago) 5 (Winter 1974): 83-106.

2139. Berger, Raoul. "Tug-of-War Between Congress and the Presidency: Foreign Policy and Power to Make War." *Washburn Law Journal* 16 (Fall 1976): 1-11.

2140. Bickel, Alexander M. "Congress, Presidents and War: A Review of Foreign Affairs and the Constitution." In *Perspectives on the Presidency*, ed. A. Wildavsky, pp. 484-486. Boston: Little, Brown, 1975.

2141. Bickel, Alexander M. "Congress, the President and the Power to Wage War." *Chicago-Kent Law Review* 48 (Fall-Winter 1971): 131-147.

2142. Black, Forrest R. "The Power of Congress to Declare Peace." *Kentucky Law Journal* 19 (May 1931): 327-335.

2143. Black, Forrest R. "Theory of the War Power Under the Constitution." *American Law Review* 60 (Jan. 1926): 31-66.

2144. "Bombing and War Powers: Congress Prepares to Act." *Congressional Quarterly Weekly Report* 31 (April 21, 1973): 923-927.

2145. Bresler, Robert J. "War Powers: The Illusory Reform." *Inquiry Magazine* 1 (June 1978): 11-15.

2146. "Congress, the President, and the Power to Commit Forces to Combat." *Harvard Law Review* 81 (June 1968): 1771-1805.

2147. Corwin, Edward S. "The War and the Constitution: President and Congress." *American Political Science Review* 37 (Feb. 1943): 18-25.

2148. Dorsey, Barry M. "The Struggle Between the President and Congress over the War-Making Power." Master's thesis, American University, 1969.

2149. Eagleton, Thomas F. "August 15 Compromise and the War Powers of Congress." *St. Louis University Law Journal* 18 (Fall 1973): 1-11.

2150. Eagleton, Thomas F. "Congress and the War Powers." *Missouri Law Review* 37 (Winter 1972): 1-32.

2151. Eagleton, Thomas F. *War and Presidential Power: A Chronicle of Congressional Surrender.* New York: Liveright, 1974.

2152. Emerson, J. Terry. "War Powers: An Invasion of Presidential Prerogative." *American Bar Association Journal* 58 (Aug. 1972): 809-814.

2153. Franck, Thomas M. "After the Fall: The New Procedural Framework for Congressional Control over War Power." *American Journal of International Law* 71 (Oct. 1977): 605-641.

2154. Fulbright, J. William. "Congress, the President and the War Power." *Arkansas Law Review* 25 (Spring 1971): 71-84.

2155. Glennon, Michael J. "Strengthening the War Powers Resolution: The Case for Purse-Strings Restrictions." *Minnesota Law Review* 60 (Nov. 1975): 1-43.

2156. Harrison, Stanley L. "President and Congress: The War Powers Wrangle." *Military Review* 54 (July 1974): 404-409.

2157. Holt, Pat M. *The War Powers Resolution: The Role of Congress in Armed Intervention.* Washington: American Enterprise Institute for Public Policy Research, 1978.

2158. Javits, Jacob K. and Kellerman, Don. *Who Makes War: the President Versus Congress.* New York: William Morrow and Co., 1973.

2159. Jenkins, Gerald L. "The War Powers Resolution: Statutory Limitation on the Commander-in-Chief." *Harvard Journal on Legislation* 11 (Feb. 1974): 181-204.

2160. King, Donald E. and Leavens, Arthur B. "Curbing the Dog of War: The War Powers Resolution." *Harvard International Law Journal* 18 (Winter 1977): 55-96.

2161. Latzer, Barry. "The Constitutional Authority of the President to Commence Hostilities Without a Congressional Declaration of War." Ph.D. dissertation, University of Massachusetts, 1977.

2162. Lofgren, Charles A. "War-Making Under the Constitution: The Original Understanding." *Yale Law Journal* 81 (Mar. 1972): 672-702.

2163. MacIver, Kenneth F., Wolff, Beverly M., and Locke, Leonard B. "The Supreme Court as Arbitrator in the Conflict Between Presidential and Congressional War-Making Powers." *Boston University Law Review* 50 (Spring 1970): 78-116.

2164. Maffre, John. "Senate Attempts to Limit President's Power to Make War." *National Journal* 4 (Mar. 11, 1972): 443-450.

2165. Nanes, Allen S. "Congress and Military Commitments: An Overview." *Current History* 57 (Aug. 1969): 105-111, 116.

2166. Ratner, Leonard G. "The Coordinated Warmaking Power: Legislative, Executive, and Judicial Roles." *Southern California Law Review* 44 (Winter 1971): 461-489.

2167. Reed, Randal P. "Foreign Policy and the Initiation of War: The Congress and the Presidency in the Dispute over War Powers." *Potomac Review* 6 (Winter 1973): 1-29.

2168. Reveley, W. Taylor. "Constitutional Allocation of the War Powers Between the President and Congress, 1787-1788." *Virginia Journal of International Law* 15 (Fall 1974): 73-147.

2169. Reveley, W. Taylor. "Presidential War-Making: Constitutional Prerogative or Usurpation." *Virginia Law Review* 55 (Nov. 1969): 1243-1305.

2170. Rogers, William P. "Congress, the President and the War Powers." *California Law Review* 59 (Sept. 1971): 1194-1214.

2171. Schlesinger, Arthur M. "Who Makes War and How." *American Bar Association Journal* 63 (Jan. 1977): 78-79.

2172. Scribner, Jeffrey L. "The President Versus Congress on War-Making Authority." *Military Review* 52 (April 1972): 87-96.

2173. Sims, Henry U. "Power of the Federal Government to Extend the Recent War Acts of Congress into Times of Peace." *Virginia Law Review* 6 (Nov. 1919): 87-97.

2174. Sofaer, Abraham D. *War, Foreign Affairs and Constitution Power: The Origins.* Cambridge, Mass.: Ballinger, 1976.

2175. Spong, William B. "Can Balance Be Restored in the Constitutional War Powers of the President and Congress?" *University of Richmond Law Review* 6 (Fall 1971): 1-31.

2176. Thomson, Harry C. "The War Powers Resolution of 1973: Can Congress Make It Stick?" *World Affairs* 139 (Summer 1976): 3-9.

2177. U.S. Congress. House. Committee on Foreign Affairs. *Congress, the President and the War Powers, Hearings.* Washington: GPO, 1970.

2178. Van Alstyne, William W. "Congress, the President, and the Power to Declare War: A Requiem for Vietnam." *University of Pennsylvania Law Review* 121 (Nov. 1972): 1-28.

National Defense

2179. Aspin, Les. "Defense Budget and Foreign Policy: The Role of Congress." *Daedalus* 104 (Summer 1975): 155-174.

2180. Aspin, Les. "Parliamentary Control of Defense: The American Example." *Survival* 15 (July 1973): 166-170.

2181. Atwell, Mary K. W. "Congressional Opponents of Early Cold War Legislation." Ph.D. dissertation, St. Louis University, 1973.

2182. Berger, Henry W. "A Conservative Critique of Containment: Senator Taft on the Early Cold War Program." In *Containment and Revolution,* ed. David Horowitz, pp. 125-139. Boston: Beacon Press, 1967.

2183. Briggs, Philip J. "Executive–Congressional Relations in the Formulation of American Post World War II Collective Security Agreements." Ph.D. dissertation, Syracuse University, 1969.

2184. Briggs, Philip J. "Congress and Collective Security: The Resolutions of 1943." *World Affairs* 132 (Mar. 1970): 332-344.

2185. Cahn, Anne H. *Congress, Military Affairs, and (a Bit of) Information.* Beverly Hills, Calif.: Sage Publications, 1974.

2186. Caraley, Demetrios. *The Politics of Military Unification.* New York: Columbia University Press, 1966.

2187. Cobb, Stephen A. "Defense Spending and Foreign Policy in the House of Representatives." *Journal of Conflict Resolution* 13 (Sept. 1969): 358-369.

2188. Donnelly, Warren H. "Congress and Nonproliferation, 1945–1977." In *Congress and Arms Control,* eds. Alan Platt and Lawrence D. Weiler, pp. 135-155. Boulder, Colo.: Westview Press, 1978.

2189. Dorley, Albert J. "The Role of Congress in the Establishment of Bases in Spain." Ph.D. dissertation, St. John's University, 1969.

2190. Driggs, Don W. "Executive–Legislative Relationships and the Control of American Foreign Policy with Respect to Collective Security, 1921-1933." Ph.D. dissertation, Harvard University, 1956.

2191. Emmerich, Herbert. "It Won't Work." *Public Administration Review* 18 (Summer 1958): 237-238.

2192. Frye, Alton. *Congress Evolves: The Changing Politics of American Defense.* Washington: Woodrow Wilson International Center for Scholars, 1971.

2193. Goss, Carol F. "Congress and Defense Policy: Strategies and Patterns of Committee Influence." Ph.D. dissertation, University of Arizona, 1971.

2194. Harrison, Stanley L. "Congress and Foreign Military Sales." *Military Review* 51 (Oct. 1971): 79-87.

2195. Harrison, Stanley L. "Congress in Conflict: Enlarging Its Role in Defense and Foreign Policy." *Military Review* 52 (July 1972): 73-84.

2196. Kampelman, Max M. "Decision-Making in Defense: The Role of Organization—Congressional Control vs. Executive Flexibility." *Public Administration Review* 18 (Summer 1958): 185-188.

2197. Kastner, Lawrence D. "Doves, Hawks, and Domestic Legislation in the United States Senate, 1967-1968." Ph.D. dissertation, University of California at Irvine, 1972.

2198. Kessler, Bruce L. "The Senate and Defense: A Correlational Analysis." Ph.D. dissertation, University of California at Irvine, 1972.

2199. Laurance, Edward J. "The Changing Role of Congress in Defense Policy-Making." *Journal of Conflict Resolution* 20 (June 1976): 213-253.

2200. Levantrosser, William F. *Congress and the Citizen-Soldier: Legislative Policy-Making for the Federal Armed Forces Reserve.* Columbus: Ohio State University Press, 1967.

2201. Liske, Craig. "Defense Policy and Congression–Executive Politics: The Common Defense Revisited." Ph.D. dissertation, University of North Carolina at Chapel Hill, 1972.

2202. Long, Clarence D. "Nuclear Proliferation: Can Congress Act in Time?" *International Security* 1 (Spring 1977): 52-76.

2203. *Major U.S. Foreign and Defense Issues: A Compilation of Papers Prepared for the Commission on the Operation of the Senate by the Congressional Research Service.* Washington: GPO, 1977.

2204. Radway, Laurence I. "Uniforms and Mufti: What Place in Policy?" *Public Administration Review* 18 (Summer 1958): 180-185.

2205. Rapoport, Daniel. "House's About-Face on Defense: A Sign of the Times or the Members?" *National Journal* 8 (May 8, 1976): 629.

2206. Rogers, Lindsay. "Legislature and Executive in Wartime." *Foreign Affairs* 19 (July 1941): 715-726.

2207. Rothchild, John. "Cooing Down the War: The Senate's Lame Doves." *Washington Monthly* 3 (Aug. 1971): 6-19.

2208. Russell, Robert W. "The United States Congress and the Power to Use Military Force Abroad." Ph.D. dissertation, Tufts University, 1967.

2209. Sarros, Panayiotis P. "Congress and the New Diplomacy: The Formulation of Mutual Security Policy: 1953-1960." Ph.D. dissertation, Princeton University, 1964.

2210. Shill, Harold B. "Senate Activism and Security Commitments: The Troops-to-Europe and National Commitments Resolutions." Ph.D. dissertation, University of North Carolina at Chapel Hill, 1973.

2211. Wright, Quincy. "Constitutional Procedure in the United States for Carrying Out Obligations for Military Sanctions." *American Journal of International Law* 38 (Oct. 1944): 678-684.

National Security

2212. Boylan, Robert W. "The United States House of Representatives and the Military: A Study of Congressional Behavior in National Security Matters." Master's thesis, Western Michigan University, 1972.

2213. Carroll, Holbert N. "The Congress and National Security Policy." In *The Congress and America's Future,* ed. David B. Truman, pp. 150-175. Englewood Cliffs, N.J.: Prentice-Hall, 1965.

2214. Committee for Economic Development. *Congressional Decision Making for National Security: A Statement on National Policy.* New York: The Committee, 1974.

2215. Dickinson, William L. "Congress and National Security." *Air University Review* 26 (Mar.-April 1975): 2-15.

2216. Franklin, Dan. "Congress and National Security Policy in the 1970's." Master's thesis, University of Texas at Austin, 1979.

2217. Frye, Alton. *A Responsible Congress: The Politics of National Security.* New York: McGraw-Hill, 1975.

2218. Goldstein, Walter. "Skepticism on Capitol Hill: The Congress Revives Its Role as a Critic of National Security Policy." *Virginia Quarterly Review* 46 (Summer 1970): 390-410.

2219. Gordon, Bernard K. "The Senate in Its National Security Role." In *Policy Analysis on Major Issues: A Compilation of Papers Prepared for the Commission on the Operation of the Senate,* 94th Cong., 2nd sess., pp. 148-167. Washington: GPO, 1977.

2220. Havens, Murray C. "Metropolitan Areas and Congress: Foreign Policy and National Security." *Journal of Politics* 26 (Nov. 1964): 758-774.

2221. Heighberger, Neil R. "Representatives' Constituency and National Security." *Western Political Quarterly* 26 (June 1973): 224-235.

2222. Pitsvada, Bernard T. "The Role of the Senate in Formulation of National Security Policy 1961-1968." Ph.D. dissertation, American University, 1972.

2223. Rourke, John T. "Congress and the Cold War." *World Affairs* 139 (Spring 1977): 259-277.

2224. Rourke, John T. "Congress and the Cold War: Congressional Influence on the Foreign Policy Process." Ph.D. dissertation, University of Connecticut, 1975.

2225. Westerfield, H. Bradford. "Congress and Closed Politics in National Security Affairs." *Orbis* 10 (Fall 1966): 737-753.

Arms Policy

2226. Aspin, Les. "The Power of Procedure." In *Congress and Arms Control,* eds. Alan Platt and Lawrence D. Weiler, pp. 43-57. Boulder, Colo.: Westview Press, 1978.

2227. Berdes, George. "Congress' New Leverage." *Center Magazine* 9 (July 1976): 76-80.

2228. Butterworth, Robert L. "Bureaucratic Politics and Congress' Role in Weapons Development: The Arms Control Impact Statement—A Programmatic Assessment." *Policy Studies Journal* 8 (Autumn 1979): 76-84.

2229. Clark, Joseph S. "The Influence of Congress in the Formulation of Disarmament Policy." *American Academy of Political and Social Science, Annals* 342 (July 1962): 147-153.

2230. Coode, Thomas H. "Southern Congressmen and the American Naval Revolution, 1880-1898." *Alabama Historical Quarterly* 30 (Fall-Winter 1968): 89-110.

2231. Cranston, Alan. "How Congress Can Shape Arms Control." In *Congress and Arms Control,* eds. Alan Platt and Lawrence D. Weiler, pp. 205-213. Boulder, Colo.: Westview Press, 1978.

2232. Dancy, Albert G. "Effects of Congressional Limitations on Research and Development for Major Defense Systems." D.B.A. dissertation, George Washington University, 1975.

2233. Dexter, Lewis A. "Congressmen and the Making of Military Policy." In *Readings on Congress,* ed. Raymond D. Wolfinger, pp. 371-387. Englewood Cliffs, N.J.: Prentice-Hall, 1971.

2234. Dobson, John M. "The Forty-Seventh Congress and the Birth of the New American Navy." *Capitol Studies* 2 (Spring 1973): 5-22.

2235. Erhart, Robert C. "The Politics of Military Rearmament, 1935-1940: The President, the Congress, and the United States Army." Ph.D. dissertation, University of Texas at Austin, 1975.

2236. Farley, Philip J. "The Control of United States Arms Sales." In *Congress and Arms Control,* eds. Alan Platt and Lawrence D. Weiler, pp. 111-113. Boulder, Colo.: Westview Press, 1978.

2237. Flanagan, Stephen J. "Congress, the White House and SALT." *Bulletin of the Atomic Scientists* 34 (Nov. 1978): 34-40.

2238. Hart, Gary. "The U.S. Senate and the Future of the Navy." *International Security* 2 (Spring 1978): 175-184.

2239. Kemp, Jack F. "Congressional Expectations of SALT II." *Strategic Review* 7 (Winter 1979): 16-25.

2240. Krell, Gert. "Military Industrial Complex, Armaments Policy and the National Priorities Debate in the 92nd U.S. Senate, 1971-72." *Instant Research on Peace and Violence* 5 (1975): 98-107.

2241. Lauk, Kurt J. "A European Perspective." In *Congress and Arms Control,* eds. Alan Platt and Lawrence D. Weiler, pp. 185-204. Boulder, Colo.: Westview Press, 1978.

2242. Liske, Craig and Rundquist, Barry S. *The Politics of Weapons Procurement: The Role of Congress.* Denver: University of Colorado, 1974.

2243. Medalia, Jonathan E. "Congress and the Political Guidance of Weapons Procurement." Naval War College Review 28 (Fall 1975): 12-31.

2244. Medalia, Jonathan E. "The U.S. Senate and Strategic Arms Limitation Policymaking 1963-1972." Ph.D. dissertation, Stanford University, 1975.

2245. Platt, Alan. "Congress and Arms Control: A Historical Perspective 1969-1976." In *Congress and Arms Control,* eds. Alan Platt and Lawrence D. Weiler, pp. 1-18. Boulder, Colo.: Westview Press, 1978.

2246. Platt, Alan. *The U.S. Senate and Strategic Arms Policy, 1969–1977.* Boulder, Colo.: Westview Press, 1978.

2247. Platt, Alan and Weiler, Lawrence D., eds. *Congress and Arms Control.* Boulder, Colo.: Westviee Press, 1978.

2248. Rich, Michael D. *Competition in the Acquisition of Major Weapon Systems: Legislative Perspectives.* Santa Monica, Calif.: Rand, 1976.

2249. Rotherham, James A. "The Role of Congress in the Development of American Strategic Air Power, 1933-1941." Ph.D. dissertation, Tufts University, 1970.

2250. Runquist, Barry S. "Congressional Influences on the Distribution of Prime Military Contracts." Ph.D. dissertation, Stanford University, 1973.

2251. Sexton, Donal J. "Forging the Sword: Congress and the American Naval Renaissance, 1880-1890." Ph.D. dissertation, University of Tennessee, 1976.

2252. Sutton, Walter A. "Progressive Republican Senators and the Submarine Crisis, 1915-1916." *Mid-America* 47 (April 1965): 75-88.

2253. Watson, Richard L. "Congressional Attitudes Toward Military Preparedness, 1829-1835." *Mississippi Valley Historical Review* 34 (Mar. 1948): 611-636.

2254. Weiler, Lawrence D. *The Arms Race, Secret Negotiations and the Congress.* Muscatine, Iowa: Stanley Foundation, 1976.

2255. Weiler, Lawrence D. "Secrecy in Arms Control Negotiations." In *Congress and Arms Control,* eds. Alan Platt and Lawrence D. Weiler, pp. 157-183. Boulder, Colo.: Westview Press, 1978.

Trade Policy

2256. Barrie, Robert W. *Congress and the Executive: The Making of U.S. Foreign Trade Policy.* Ph.D. dissertation, University of Minnesota, 1968.

2257. Bauer, Raymond A., Pool, Ithiel de Sola, and Dexter, Lewis A. *American Business and Public Policy: The Politics of Foreign Trade.* New York: Atherton Press, 1963.

2258. Belcher, Jack B. "Economic Initiatives to American Foreign Policy: A Quantitative Analysis of Congress, 1886-1896." Ph.D. dissertation, Georgetown University, 1976.

2259. Fletcher, Duncan U. "What Congress Has Done to Build Up an American Mercantile Marine." *The Academy of Political Science, Proceedings* 6 (Oct. 1915): 1-27.

2260. Geib, Peter J. "The Congressional Role in the Formulation of Commercial Legislation Toward Communist Countries." Ph.D. dissertation, University of Michigan, 1971.

2261. Gerber, David J. "United States Sugar Quota Program: A Study in the Direct Congressional Control of Imports." *Journal of Law and Economics* 19 (April 1976): 103-147.

2262. Gleeck, L. E. "96 Congressmen Make Up Their Minds: Study of Factors Determining Votes of Congressmen on Repeal of the Embargo Provisions of the Neutrality Act." *Public Opinion Quarterly* 4 (Mar. 1940): 3-24.

2263. Hardin, Charles M. "Congressional Farm Politics and Economic Foreign Policy." *American Academy of Political and Social Science, Annals* 331 (Sept. 1960): 98-102.

2264. Havens, Murry C. "Congress and the Tariff, 1945-1946." Ph.D. dissertation, Johns Hopkins University, 1958.

2265. Howell, Leon. "Senate and Multinationals." *Christianity and Crisis* 35 (Oct. 1975): 237-240.

2266. Hughes, Kent H. *International Economic Decision Making in Congress: Trade, Taxes, and Transnationals.* New York: Praeger, 1979.

2267. Keeffe, Arthur J. "Of Soft Drinks and Human Rights." *American Bar Association Journal* 60 (Jan. 1974): 111-113.

2268. Lillich, Richard B. "The Gravel Amendment to the Trade Reform Act of 1974: Congress Checkmates a Presidential Lump Sum Agreement." *American Journal of International Law* 69 (Oct. 1975): 837-847.

2269. Pastor, Robert A. "Legislative–Executive Relations and the Politics of United States Foreign Economic Policy: 1929–1976." Ph.D. dissertation, Harvard University, 1977.

2270. "Presidential Emergency Powers Related to International Economic Transactions: Congressional Recognition of Customary Authority." *Vanderbilt Journal of Transnational Law* 11 (Summer 1978): 515-534.

2271. Rehm, John B. "A New Legislative Approach to International Trade Negotiations." *Columbia Journal of Transnational Law* 11 (Fall 1972): 380-401.

2272. Stetson, Nancy H. "Congress and Foreign Policy: The 1972 U.S.-USSR Trade Agreement and Trade Reform Act." Ph.D. dissertation, Columbia University, 1979.

2273. Theroux, Eugene A. "Congress and the Question of Most Favored Nation Status for the People's Republic of China." *Catholic University Law Review* 23 (Fall 1973): 28-60.

2274. Travis, Paul D. "Gore, Bristow and Taft: Reflections on Canadian Reciprocity, 1911." *Chronicles of Oklahoma* 53 (Summer 1975): 212-224.

Foreign Aid

2275. Bardes, Barbara A. "Senatorial Realignment on Foreign Aid, 1953-1972: A Discriminant Analysis of Inter-Party Factions." Ph.D. dissertation, University of Cincinnati, 1975.

2276. "Congress, Executive Share Foreign Aid Powers." *Congressional Quarterly Weekly Report* 21 (Oct. 18, 1963): 1815-1817.

2277. Cozort, William T. "House Opposition to Foreign Aid Legislation." *Southwestern Social Science Quarterly* 42 (Sept. 1961): 159-161.

2278. Gawthrop, Louis C. "Congress and Foreign Aid: A Study of Congressional Control over the Administration of Foreign Aid Policy." Ph.D. dissertation, Johns Hopkins University, 1963.

2279. Gonzalez, Heliodoro. "Domestic Political Effects of Foreign Aid Case: The Failure in Bolivia." *Inter-American Economic Affairs* 15 (Fall 1961): 77-88.

2280. Gustafson, Milton O. "Congress and Foreign Aid: The First Phase, UNRRA, 1943-1947." Ph.D. dissertation, University of Nebraska, 1966.

2281. Harrison, Gale A. "Congress and Foreign Aid: A Study of the Role of Congress in Foreign Policymaking, 1961-1975." Ph.D. dissertation, Vanderbilt University, 1976.

2282. Haviland, H Field. "Foreign Aid and the Policy Process: 1957." *American Political Science Review* 52 (Sept. 1958): 689-724.

2283. Herman, Margaret G. "Some Personal Characteristics Related to Foreign Aid Voting of Congressmen." Master's thesis, Northwestern University, 1963.

2284. Hitchens, Harold L. Congress and the Adoption of the Marshall Plan." Ph.D. dissertation, University of Chicago, 1960.

2285. Hitchens, Harold L. "Influences on the Congressional Decision to Pass the Marshall Plan." *Western Political Quarterly* 21 (Mar. 1968): 51-68.

2286. Lev, Christopher A. "Congress and the Role of Private Enterprise in the United States Foreign Assistance Programs." Ph.D. dissertation, University of California at Los Angeles, 1973.

2287. Maheshivari, Bhanwarlal L. "Foreign Aid and the Policy Process: A Study of the Struggle over Foreign Aid in Congress, 1961-1965." Ph.D. dissertation, University of Pennsylvania, 1966.

2288. Mangan, Mary. "The Congressional Image of Aid to the Underdeveloped Countries (1949-1959): as Revealed in the Congressional Hearings and Debates." Ph.D. dissertation, Yale University, 1964.

2289. Moore, Heyward. "Congressional Committees and the Formulation of Foreign Aid Policy. ' Ph.D. dissertation, University of North Carolina at Chapel Hill, 1965.

2290. Patton, James M. "Congressional Influence on Foreign Policy Exercised Through Restraint of the United States Military Assistance Program." Ph.D. dissertation, Tufts University, 1972.

2291. Ripley, Randall B. "The Politics of Focus: The Roles and Relations of Congress, the Executive, the Universities and the Foundations in American Aid to India, 1950-1962." Ph.D. dissertation, Harvard University, 1963.

2292. Rousseau, Rudolph R. "Factors Affecting Decisions of the United States Senate on Bilateral and Multilateral Foreign Assistance Legislation 1965 to 1974." Ph.D. dissertation, Tufts University, 1976.

2293. Schiller, Herbert I. "The United States Congress and the American Financial Contribution to the United Nations Relief and Rehabilitation Administration." Ph.D. dissertation, New York University, 1960.

2294. Scowcroft, Brent. "Congress and Foreign Policy: An Examination of Congressional Attitudes Toward the Foreign Aid Programs to Spain and Yugoslavia." Ph.D. dissertation, Columbia University, 1967.

2295. Spier, Edwin G. "Congress and Foreign Economic Policy: The Role of Key Congressional Committees in the Formulation of Development Assistance Legislation During the 1960's." Ph.D. dissertation, University of Denver, 1965.

2296. Sturner, William F. "Aid to Yugoslavia: A Case Study of the Influence of Congress on the Foreign Policy Implementation." Ph.D. dissertation, Fordham University, 1966.

2297. Wilford, Walton T. "The Congressional Mandate on U.S. Foreign Aid: Can It Break the Vicious Circle of Poverty." *Journal of Social and Political Studies* 4 (Fall 1979): 261-268.

International Organizations

2298. Barth, Frank. *The Lost Peace; A Chronology: The League of Nations and the U.S. Senate, 1918-1921.* New York: Woodrow Wilson Foundation, 1945.

2299. Binder, Norman E. "The United Nations as a Learning Experience for United States Congressional Delegates." Ph.D. dissertation, University of Arizona, 1974.

2300. Briggs, Herbert W. "The UNRRA Agreement and Congress." *American Journal of International Law* 38 (Oct. 1944): 650-658.

2301. Corbett, Percy E. "Congress and Proposals for International Government." *International Organization* 4 (Aug. 1950): 383-399.

2302. Fox, Annette B. "NATO and Congress." *Political Science Quarterly* 80 (Sept. 1965): 395-414.

2303. Gareau, Frederick H. "Congressional Representatives to the U.N. General Assembly: Corruption by Foreign Gentry." *Orbis* 21 (Fall 1977): 701-724.

2304. Grantham, Dewey W. "The Southern Senators and the League of Nations, 1918-1920." *North Carolina Historical Review* 26 (April 1949): 187-205.

2305. Heindel, Richard H., Kalijarri, Thorsten V., and Wilcox, Francis O. "North Atlantic Treaty in the United States Senate." *American Journal of International Law* 43 (Oct. 1949): 633-665.

2306. Hudson, Manley O. "The United States Senate and the Permanent Court of International Justice." *American Journal of International Law* 20 (April 1926): 330-335.

2307. Hudson, Manley O. "United States Senate and the World Court." *American Journal of International Law* 29 (April 1935): 301-307.

2308. Karns, David A. "Effect of Interparliamentary Meetings on the Foreign Policy Attitudes of United States Congressmen.' *International Organization* 31 (Summer 1977): 497-513.

2309. Kellor, Frances A. and Hatvany, Antonia. *The United States Senate and the International Court.* New York: T. Seltzer, 1925.

2310. Kendrick, Jack E. "The League of Nations and the Republican Senate, 1918-1921." Ph.D. dissertation, University of North Carolina at Chapel Hill, 1953.

2311. Lien, Arnold J. "The Senate Reservations in Geneva." *St. Louis Law Review* 12 (1927): 47-53.

2312. Lodge, Henry C. *The Senate and the League of Nations.* New York: Scribner's, 1925.

2313. Logan, Rayford W. *The Senate and the Versailles Mandate System.* Washington: The Minorities Publishers, 1945.

2314. McCrone, Bruce M. "The United States Congress and the International Court of Justice: A Study of American Attitudes Toward Compulsory Jurisdiction." Ph.D. dissertation, Ball State University, 1975.

2315. Marcy, Carl and Hansen, Morella. "Note on American Participation in Interparliamentary Meetings." *International Organization* 13 (Summer 1959): 433-438.

2316. Margulies, Herbert F. "The Senate and the World Court." *Capitol Studies* 4 (Fall 1976): 37-51.

2317. Mervin, David. "The Senate Opposition to the League of Nations: A Study in Legislative Conflict." Ph.D. dissertation, Cornell University, 1968.

2318. Michalak, Stanley J. "The Senate and the United Nations: A Study of Changing Perceptions About the Utilities and Limitations of the United Nations as an Instrument of Peace and Security and Its Role in American National Security Policy." Ph.D. dissertation, Princeton University, 1967.

2319. Miller, David H. "The Senate Reservations and the Advisory Opinions of the Permanent Court of International Justice." *Columbia Law Review* 26 (June 1926): 654-669.

2320. Phillips, Claude S. "Questions of International Law in the Consideration of Selected Issues by the United States Congress, 1937-1941." Ph.D. dissertation, Duke University, 1954.

2321. Preuss, Lawrence. "International Court of Justice, the Senate,,and Matters of Domestic Jurisdiction." *American Journal of International Law* 40 (Oct. 1946): 720-736.

2322. Reid, Stewart M. "Congressional Power to Abrogate the Domestic Effect of a United Nations Treaty Commitment: Diggs v. Shultz (D.C. Cir. 1972)." *Columbia Journal of Transnational Law* 13 (1974): 155-172.

2323. Riggs, Robert E. "More on 'Corruption' by Foreign Gentry." *Orbis* 22 (Fall 1978): 737-746.

2324. Riggs, Robert E. "One Small Step for Functionalism: U.N. Participation and Congressional Attitude Change." *International Organization* 31 (Summer 1977): 515-539.

2325. Riggs, Robert E. and Mykleton, I. Jostein. "Congressional Attitudes Toward the U.N." In their *Beyond Functionalism: Attitudes Toward International Organization in Norway and the United States,* pp. 110-144. Minneapolis: University of Minnesota Press, 1979.

2326. Schmidt, John F. "International Organization and the Senate." *Tennessee Law Review* 19 (Dec. 1945): 29-39.

2327. Snyder, Charles K. "The Department of State and the Congress: A Study of the Effect of Foreign Policies of Positive Internationalism and Membership in the United Nations on Organization and Procedure." Ph.D. dissertation, Cornell University, 1953.

2328. Wickersham, George W. "The World Court and the Senate Reservations." *George Washington Law Review* 1 (Nov. 1932): 3-17.

2329. Wriston, Henry M. "American Participation in International Conferences." *American Journal of International Law* 20 (Jan. 1926): 33-45.

Relations with Specific Countries

2330. Ashton, Charles H. "Congressional Decision-Making in the Foreign Policy-Making Process: The Case of the Bokaro Steel Mill Project in Indo-American Relations." Ph.D. dissertation, University of Pennsylvania, 1972.

2331. Babcock, Fenton. "Issues of China Policy Before Congress, Sepptember 1945 to September 1949." Ph.D. dissertation, Yale University, 1956.

2332. Bachrack, Stanley D. "The Committee of One Million and United States China Policy, 1953-1963: Access and Foreign Policy." Ph.D. dissertation, University of California at Los Angeles, 1973.

2333. Berger, Raoul. "Must the House Consent to Cession of the Panama Canal?" *Cornell Law Review* 64 (Jan. 1979): 275-318.

2334. Berry, Lee Roy. "The United States Congress and Cuba: Four Case Studies of Congressional Influence on American Foreign Policy." Ph.D. dissertation, University of Notre Dame, 1976.

2335. Bishara, Ghassan. "The Middle East Arms Package: A Survey of the Congressional Debates." *Journal of Palestine Studies* 7 (Summer 1978): 67-78.

2336. Brownback, Annadrue H. "Congressional and Insular Opposition to Puerto Rican Autonomy." Ph.D. dissertation, University of Alabama, 1966.

2337. Chapman, Charles E. "The Cuban Constitution and Congress." *California Law Review* 14 (Nov. 1925): 22-35.

2338. Chern, Kenneth S. "A Prelude to Cold War: The United States Senate and the Abortive China Debate, 1945." Ph.D. dissertation, University of Chicago, 1974.

2339. Cohen, Ira S. "Congressional Attitudes Towards the Soviet Union, 1917-1941." Ph.D. dissertation, University of Chicago, 1955.

2340. Copson, Raymond W. *African Policy: Congressional Restrictions on Presidential Authority.* Washington: Congressional Research Service, 1979.

2341. Cromwell, William C. "The Marshall Non-Plan, Congress and the Soviet Union." *Western Political Quarterly* 32 (Dec. 1979): 422-443.

2342. Dobell, Peter C. "Influence on the United States Congress on Canadian-American Relations." *International Organization* 28 (Autumn 1974): 903-929.

2343. Fetzer, James A. "Congress and China, 1941-1950." Ph.D. dissertation, Michigan State University, 1969.

2344. Feverwerger, Marvin C. *Congress and Israel: Foreign Aid Decision-Making in the House of Representatives, 1969–1976.* Westport, Conn.: Greenwood Press, 1979.

2345. Feverwerger, Marvin C. "Congress and the Middle East." *Middle East Review* 10 (Winter 1977-1978): 43-46.

2346. Garnham, David. "Factors Influencing Congressional Support for Israel During the 93rd Congress." *Jerusalem Journal of International Relations* 2 (Spring 1977): 23-45.

2347. Gibert, Stephen P. "Selected Studies in Congressional Attitudes with Respect to Soviet Russia and American-Soviet Relations." Ph.D. dissertation, Johns Hopkins University, 1958.

2348. Goldstein, Walter. "Vietnam and the Congressional Record—A Symposium: The Military Options." *Michigan Quarterly Review* 7 (Summer 1968): 153-155.

2349. Gonzalez, Heliodoro. "Congressional Foreign Policy at Its Worst." *Inter-American Economic Affairs* 29 (Winter 1975): 95-96.

2350. Gonzalez, Heliodoro. "On the Congressional Effort to Influence U.S. Relations with Latin America." *Inter-American Economic Affairs* 29 (Summer 1975): 93-95.

2351. Grundy, Kenneth. "The Congressional Image of Africa." *Africa Today* 14 (Dec. 1966): 8-13.

2352. Hickey, J. "Role of the Congress in Foreign Policy: The Cuban Disaster." *Inter-American Economic Affairs* 14 (Spring 1961): 67-89.

2353. Hosack, Robert E. "Shantung Question and the Senate." *South Atlantic Quarterly* 43 (April 1944): 181-193.

2354. Kemp, Virginia. "Congress and China, 1945-1959." Ph.D. dissertation, University of Pittsburgh, 1966.

2355. Kent George, "Congress and American Middle East Policy." In *The Middle East: Quest for an American Policy*, ed. Willard A. Beling, pp. 286-305. Albany: State University of New York Press, 1973.

2356. Klingaman, William K. "Congress and American Foreign Policy for the Middle East, 1956-1958." Ph.D. dissertation, University of Virginia, 1978.

2357. "Law of Treaty Terminations as Applied to the United States De-Recognition of the Republic of China." *Harvard International Law Journal* 19 (Fall 1978): 931-1009.

2358. Li, Tien-Lu. *Congressional Policy of Chinese Immigration.* New York: Arno Press, 1978, c. 1916.

2359. Livingstone, Neil C. and Von Nordheim, Manfred. "The United States Congress and the Angola Crisis." *Strategic Review* 5 (Spring 1977): 34-44.

2360. Meisler, Stanley. "The U.S. Congress and Africa." *Africa Report* 9 (Aug. 1964): 3-7.

2361. Murphey, Rhoads. "Vietnam and the Congressional RecordP4A Symposium: Political Settlement and the Future." *Michigan Quarterly Review* 7 (Summer 1968): 156-158.

2362. Pastor, Robert A. "On the Congressional Effort to Influence U.S. Relations with Latin America: Congressional Foreign Policy at Its Best." *Inter-American Economic Affairs* 29 (Winter 1975): 85-94.

2363. Pramod, Vyas. "The United States Congress and India: A Study in the Congressional Attitudes Towards India." Ph.D. dissertation, American University, 1961.

2364. Sellen, Albert R. "Congressional Opinion of Soviet-American RelationS, 1945-1950." Ph.D. dissertation, University of Chicago, 1955.

2365. Trice, Robert H. "Congress and the Arab-Israeli Conflict: Support for Israel in the U.S. Senate, 1970-1973." *Political Science Quarterly* 92 (Fall 1977): 443-463.

2366. Wagner, J. Richard. "Congress and Canadian-American Relations: The Norman Case." *Rocky Mountain Social Science Journal* 10 (Oct. 1973): 85-92.

2367. Williams, Daniel R. "Is Congress Empowered to Alienate Sovereignty of the United States?" *Virginia Law Review* 12 (Nov. 1925): 1-33.

VII. Committee Structure and Work

Committees

General Studies

2368. Abbasi, Susan R. *Congressional Energy Jurisdiction.* Washington: Congressional Research Service, 1975.

2369. "Ad Hoc Committees: A Way to Pressure Congress." *Congressional Quarterly Weekly Report* 29 (Aug. 18, 1971): 1864-1865.

2370. Aghassi, Marjorie E. "Little Legislatures: Four Committees and the Foreign Aid Program, 1947-1964." Ph.D. dissertation, Columbia University, 1967.

2371. Asher, Herbert B. "Committees and the Norm of Specialization." *American Academy of Political and Social Science, Annals* 411 (Jan. 1974): 63-74.

2372. Bagley, Walton M. "Congressional Committee Representation and the Distribution of Defense Spending by States." Ph.D. dissertation, Texas Tech University, 1973.

2373. Bax, Frans R. "The Committee–Party Nexus: Committee Cues in the House of Representatives." Ph.D. dissertation, Harvard University, 1977.

2374. Bezold, Clement. "Citizen Participation in Congressional Foresight." *The Futurist* 12 (April 1978): 117-121.

2375. Bezold, Clement, Anderson, R. Lee, Chasen, Nancy, Mills, John L., and Haggard, Lenore. "Congressional Committees and National Growth Policy." In *Forging America's Future: Strategies for National Growth and Development,* Appendix, Vol. II. Washington: National Commission on Supplies and Shortages, 1976.

2376. Brenner, Philip J. "Committee Conflict in the Congressional Arena." *American Academy of Political and Social Science, Annals* 411 (Jan. 1974): 87-101.

2377. Broden, Thomas F. "Congressional Committee Reports: Their Role and History." *Notre Dame Lawyer* 33 (Mar. 1958): 209-238.

2378. Cardozo, Michael H. "Committees Touching Foreign Relations Indirectly." *American Academy of Political and Social Science, Annals* 289 (Sept. 1953): 84-91.

2379. Casper, Gerhard. "The Committee System of the United States Congress." *American Journal of Comparative Law* 26 (supp.) (1978): 359-375.

2380. Casstevens, Thomas W. "The Committee Function: An Influence Equation." *American Political Science Review* 66 (Mar. 1972): 160-162.

2381. Casstevens, Thomas W. "Mathematical Models of Congressional Committee in the United States and Cabinet Government in Parliamentary System." *Indian Political Science Review* 13 (July 1979): 168-178.

2382. Christenson, Phyllis R. *Congressional Committee Calendars: A Comparative Summary.* Washington: Library of Congress, Law Library, 1977.

2383. "Committees Dominated by Seniority System." *Congressional Quarterly Weekly Report* 21 (June 7, 1963): 875-885.

2384. "Committees Look at Executive Secrecy." *Congressional Quarterly Weekly Report* 17 (April 17, 1959): 535.

2385. Cooper, Joseph. "Congress and Its Committees: A Historical and Theoretical Approach to the Proper Role of Committees in the Legislative Process." Ph.D. dissertation, Harvard University, 1961.

2386. Cooper, Joseph. "The Study of Congressional Committees: Current Research and Future Trends." *Polity* 4 (Autumn 1971): 123-133.

2387. Davidson, Roger H. "Representation and Congressional Committees." *American Academy of Political and Social Science, Annals* 411 (Jan. 1974): 48-62.

2388. Dodd, Lawrence D. and Pierce, John C. "Roll Call Measurement of Committee Integration: The Impact of Alternative Methods." *Polity* 7 (Spring 1975): 386-401.

2389. Feig, Douglas G. "A Formal Model of Congressional Committee Activity." Ph.D. dissertation, University of Minnesota, 1975.

2390. Fenno, Richard F. *Congressmen in Committees.* Boston: Little, Brown, 1973.

2391. Fiorina, Morris P. and Plott, Charles R. "Committee Decisions Under Majority Rule: An Experimental Study." *American Political Science Review* 72 (June 1978): 575-598.

2392. Goodwin, George. *The Little Legislatures: Committees of Congress.* Amherst: University of Massachusetts Press, 1971.

2393. Griffin, Robert P. "Rules and Procedure of the Standing Committees." In *We Propose: A Modern Congress,* ed. Mary McInnis, pp. 37-53. New York: mcGraw-Hill, 1966.

2394. Hall, Mary Jo S. "The 'Little Legislatures' and Urban Affairs: A Study of Congressional Jurisdictions." Master's thesis, University of Oregon, 1968.

2395. Jacobson, Gary C. *The 95th Congress and Its Committees.* Washington, Conn.: Center for Information on America, 1977.

2396. Jahnige, Thomas P. "Congressional Committee System and the Oversight Process: Congress and NASA." *Western Political Quarterly* 21 (June 1968): 227-239.

2397. Jones, Charles O. "Between Party Battalions and Committee Suzerainty." *American Academy of Political and Social Science, Annals* 411 (Jan. 1974): 158-168.

2398. Jones, Charles O. *Congressional Committees and the Two Party System. Working Papers on House Committee Organization and Operation.* Presented to House Select Committee on Committees. 93rd Cong. Washington: GPO, 1973.

2399. Jones, Charles O. "The Relationship of Congressional Committee Action to a Theory of Representation." Ph.D. dissertation, University of Wisconsin, 1960.

2400. Lakoff, Sanford A. "Congress and National Science Policy." *Political Science Quarterly* 89 (Fall 1974): 589-611.

2401. Lees, John D. "Committees of Congress: A Comparative Evaluation." *Capitol Studies* 3 (Fall 1975): 5-12.

2402. Lees, John D. *The Committee System of the United States Congress.* New York: Humanities Press, 1967.

2403. Lees, John D. "Committees in the United States Congress." In *Committees in Legislatures: A Comparative Analysis,* eds. John D. Lees and Malcolm Shaw, pp. 11-60. Durham, N.C.: Duke University Press, 1979.

2404. Lees, John D. "Opposition in Congressional Committees: The Rights of the Minority Party." *Journal of American Studies* 3 (July 1969): 17-32.

2405. Leibowitz, Arleen and Tollison, Robert D. "A Theory of Legislative Organization: Making the Most of Your Majority." *Quarterly Journal of Economics* 94 (Mar. 1980): 261-278.

2406. Lutzker, Paul. "The Behavior of Congressmen in a Committee Setting: A Research Report." *Journal of Politics* 31 (Feb. 1969): 140-166.

2407. McConachie, Lauros. *Congressional Committees.* New York: Crowell, 1898.

2408. Morrow, William L. *Congressional Committees.* New York: Scribner, 1969.

2409. Murphy, Thomas P. *The Politics of Congressional Committees: The Power of Seniority.* Woodbury, N.Y.: Barron's, 1978.

2410. Nelson, Garrison. "Assessing the Congressional Committee System: Contributions from a Comparative Perspective." *American Academy of Political and Social Science, Annals* 411 (Jan. 1974): 120-132.

2411. Nevins, Allan. "The Development of the Committee System in the American Congress." *Parliamentary Affairs* 3 (Winter 1949): 136-146.

2412. Payne, James L. "Show Horses and Work Horses in the United States House of Representatives." *Polity* 12 (Spring 1980): 428-456.

2413. Perkins, Lynette P. "Influence of Members' Goals on Their Committee Behavior: The U.S. House Judiciary Committee." *Legislative Studies Quarterly* 5 (Aug. 1980): 373-392.

2414. Price, David E. "Policy Making in Congressional Committees: The Impact of 'Environmental' Factors." *American Political Science Review* 72 (June 1978): 548-574.

2415. Price, Hugh D. "Careers and Committees in the American Congress: The Problem of Structural Change." In *The History of Parliamentary Behavior,* ed. William O. Aydelotte, pp. 28-62. Princeton, N.J.: Princeton University Press, 1977.

2416. "Proxy Voting in Committees Provokes Controversy." *Congressional Quarterly Weekly Report* 21 (Aug. 23, 1963): 1491.

2417. Rhode, William E. *Committee Clearance of Administrative Decisions.* East Lansing: Bureau of Social and Political Research, Michigan State University, 1959.

2418. Rhode, William E. "Congressional Review of Administrative Decision-Making by Committee Clearance and Resolutions." Ph.D. dissertation, Michigan State University, 1958.

2419. Richardson, James R. "Legislative Committees: Power and Limitations." *Tennessee Law Review* 21 (April 1951): 748-760.

2420. Ripley, Randall B. "Congressional Government and Committee Management." *Public Policy* 14 (1965): 28-48.

2421. Rundquist, Barry S. and Griffith, David E. "An Interrupted Time-Series Test of the Distributive Theory of Military Policy-Making." *Western Political Quarterly* 29 (Dec. 1976): 620-626.

2422. Russell, Mary. "The Press and the Committee System." *American Academy of Political and Social Science, Annals* 411 (Jan. 1974): 114-119.

2423. Scher, Seymour. "Congressional Committee Members as Independent Agency Overseers: A Case Study." *American Political Science Review* 54 (Dec. 1960): 911-920.

2424. Shaman, Jeffrey M. "Use of Congressional Committee Reports in the Administrative Process." *Indiana Law Review* 6 (Mar. 1973): 481-489.

2425. Shapley, L. S. and Shubik, Martin. "A Method for Evaluating the Distribution of Power in a Committee System." *American Political Science Review* 48 (Sept. 1954): 787-792.

2426. Small, N. *The Committee Veto: Its Current Use and Appraisals of Its Validity.* Washington: Library of Congress Reference Service, 1967.

2427. Tape, Gerald F. *The Structure and Function of Congressional Committees. Working Papers on House Committee Organization and Operation. Presented to House Select Committee on Committees.* 93rd Cong. Washington: GPO, 1973.

2428. Townsend, Alair A. "Congressional Committee Case Studies: Studies in Public Welfare." In *Legislative Oversight and Program Evaluation: A Seminar Sponsored by the Congressional Research Service,* 94th Cong., 2nd sess., pp. 206-223. Washington: GPO, 1976.

2429. Unekis, Joseph K. "Congressional Reform and Committee Decision-Making." *Congressional Studies* 7 (Winter 1980): 53-62.

2430. U.S. Congress. Joint Committee on Congressional Operations. *Rules Adopted by the Committees of Congress.* Washington: GPO, 1975.

2431. U.S. Congress. Senate. Committee on Expenditures in the Executive Departments. *Some Problems of Committee Jurisdiction.* 82nd Cong., 1st sess. Washington: GPO, 1951.

2432. Wolkinson, Herman. "Demands of Congressional Committees for Executive Papers." *Federal Bar Journal* 10 (April-Oct. 1949): 103-150, 223-259, 319-350.

House Committees

2433. Bolling, Richard. "Committees in the House." *American Academy of Political and Social Science, Annals* 411 (Jan. 1974): 1-14.

2434. Bullock, Charles S. "Committee Transfers in the United States House of Representatives." *Journal of Politics* 35 (Feb. 1973): 85-120.

2435. Cooper, Joseph. "Jeffersonian Attitudes Toward Executive Leadership and Committee Development in the House of Representatives, 1789-1829." *Western Political Quarterly* 18 (Mar. 1965): 45-63.

2436. Cooper, Joseph. *Origins of the Standing Committees and Development of the Modern House.* Houston, Texas: Rice University, 1971.

2437. Cooper, Joseph and Brady, David W. *The House and Its Committees: Some Organizational Perspectives. Working Papers on House Committee Organization and Operation. Presented to House Select Committee on Committees.* 93rd Cong. Washington: GPO, 1973.

2438. Donahue, Maurice A. *Statement (on Committee System). Working Papers on House Committee Organization and Operation. Presented to House Select Committee on Committees.* 93rd Cong. Washington: GPO, 1973.

2439. Galloway, George B. "Development of the Committee System in the House of Representatives." *American Historical Review* 65 (Oct. 1959): 17-30.

2440. Goodwin, George. *The Little Legislatures Revisited. Working Papers on House Committee Organization and Operation. Presented to House Select Committee on Committees.* 93rd Cong. Washington: GPO, 1973.

2441. Lewis, Anne L. "Congressional Committees and Their Effectiveness: An Exploratory Study of the House of Representatives." Ph.D. dissertation, University of North Carolina at Chapel Hill, 1974.

2442. Lewis, Anne L. "Floor Success as a Measure of Committee Performance in the House." *Journal of Politics* 40 (May 1978): 460-467.

2443. Miller, Arthur H. "The Impact of Committees on the Structure of Issues and Voting Coalitions: The United States House of Representatives 1955-1962." Ph.D. dissertation, University of Michigan, 1971.

2444. Ornstein, Norman J. and Rohde, David W. "Shifting Forces, Changing Rules, and Political Outcomes: The Impact of Congressional Change on Four House Committees." In *New Perspectives on the House of Representatives,* 3rd ed., eds. Robert L. Peabody and Nelson W. Polsby, pp. 186-269. Chicago: Rand McNally, 1977.

2445. Parker, Glenn R. and Parker, Suzanne L. "Factions in Committees: The U.S. House of Representatives." *American Political Science Review* 73 (Mar. 1979): 85-102.

2446. "Politics of House Committees: The Path to Power." *Congressional Quarterly Weekly Report* 31 (Feb. 10, 1973): 279-283.

2447. Schneier, Edward V. *Legislative Intelligence and the Committee System. Working Papers on House Committee Organization and Operation. Presented to House Select Committee on Committees.* 93rd Cong. Washington: GPO, 1973.

2448. Scott, Hugh D. and King, Rufus. "Rules for Congressional Committees: An Analysis of House Resolution 447." *Virginia Law Review* 40 (April 1954): 249-272.

2449. Seamans, Robert C. *Statement (on Committee System). Working Papers on House Committee Organization and Operation. Presented to House Select Committee on Committees.* 93rd Cong., Washington: GPO, 1973.

2450. Seidman, Harold. *Congressional Committees and Executive Organization. Working Papers on House Committee Organization and Operation. Presented to House Select Commitee on Committees.* 93rd Cong. Washington: GPO, 1973.

2451. U.S. Congress. House. Select Committee on Committees. *Committee Organization in the House, Hearings.* 93rd Cong., 1st sess. Washington: GPO, 1973.

2452. U.S. Congress. House. Select Committee on Committees. *Committee Structure and Procedures of the House of Representatives, Working Draft of Report of the Select Committee on Committees.* 93rd Cong., 1st sess. Washington: GPO, 1973.

2453. U.S. Congress. House. Select Committee on Committees. *Monographs on the Committees of the House of Representatives.* Washington: GPO, 1974.

2454. Vardys, Vytas S. "Select Committees of the House of Representatives." *Midwest Journal of Political Science* 6 (Aug. 1962): 247-265.

Senate Committees

2455. Bezold, Clement. "Senate Committee Foresight." In *Techniques and Procedures for Analysis and Evaluation: A Compilation of Papers Prepared for the Commission on the Operation of Senate.* 94th Cong., 2nd sess. Washington: GPO, 1977.

2456. Bone, Hugh A. "Introduction to the Senate Policy Committees." *American Political Science Review* 50 (June 1956): 339-359.

2457. Brock, Bill. "Committees in the Senate." *American Academy of Political and Social Science, Annals* 411 (Jan. 1974): 15-26.

2458. Diehl, Philip. "Patterns of Congressional Committee Surveillance in the U.S. Senate, 1947-70." Master's thesis, University of Texas at Austin, 1976.

2459. Dodd, Lawrence C. "Committee Integration in the Senate: A Comparative Analysis." *Journal of Politics* 34 (Nov. 1972): 1135-1171.

2460. Kravitz, Walter. "Evolution of the Senate's Committee System." *American Academy of Political and Social Science, Annals* 411 (Jan. 1974): 27-38.

2461. Muskie, Edmund S. "Committees and Subcommittees in the Senate." In *The Senate Institution,* ed. Nathaniel S. Preston, pp. 121-131. New York: Van Nostrand Reinhold, 1969.

2462. Oleszek, Walter J. "Overview of the Senate Committee System." In *Committees and Senate Procedures: A Compilation of Papers Prepared for the Commission on the Operation of the Senate,* 94th Cong., 2nd sess., pp. 5-22. Washington: GPO, 1977.

2463. Price, David E. *Who Makes the Laws? Creativity and Power in Senate Committees.* Cambridge, Mass.: Schenkman Publishing Co., 1972.

2464. Redburn, Thomas. "Wedding Presents, Cigars, and Deference." *Washington Monthly* 7 (June 1975): 4-10.

2465. Robinson, George L. "The Development of the Senate Committee system." Ph.D. dissertation, New York University, 1955.

2466. Samuelson, Betsy. "An Overview of Senate Committee Procedures." In *Committees and Senate Procedures: A Compilation of Papers Presented for the Conmission on the Operation of the Senate,* 94th Cong., 2nd sess., pp. 23-40. Washington: GPO, 1977.

2467. Samuelson, Betsy. "Senate Committee Operations." In *Committees and Senate Procedures: A Compilation of Papers Prepared for the Commission on the Operation of the Senate,* 94th Cong., 2nd sess., pp. 41-61. Washington: GPO, 1977.

2468. Tansill, Charles C. "The Smith-Vare Case and Its Relation to Senate Procedure." *National University Law Review* 8 (May 1928): 3-42.

2469. U.S. Congress. Senate. Committee on Rules and Administration. *Expenditure Authorizations for Senate Committees.* Washington: GPO, 1978.

Committee Assignments

2470. Bullock, Charles S. "Apprenticeship and Committee Assignments in the House of Representatives." *Journal of Politics* 32 (Aug. 1970): 717-720.

2471. Bullock, Charles S. "House Committee Assignments." In *The Congressional System: Notes and Readings,* 2d ed., ed. Leroy N. Rieselbach, pp. 58-86. North Scituate, Mass.: Duxbury Press, 1979.

2472. Bullock, Charles S. and Sprague, John. "Research Note on the Committee Reassignments of Southern Democratic Congressmen." *Journal of Politics* 31 (May 1969): 493-512.

2473. Campbell, Colin. "The Interplay of Institutionalization and the Assignment of Tasks in Parliamentary and Congressional Systems: The House of Commons and the House of Representatives." *International Journal of Comparative Sociology* 18 (Mar.-June 1977): 127-153.

2474. Cohen, Richard E. "The Mysterious Ways Congress Makes Committee Assignments." *National Journal* 11 (Feb. 3, 1979): 183-188.

2475. Cooper, Ann. "Political Fashions of 1979." *Congressional Quarterly Weekly Report* 37 (Jan. 27, 1979): 155-164.

2476. Degnan, Francis P. "Assignment with the House Appropriations Committee: Is It Right for You?" *GAO Review* 12 (Spring 1977): 52-57.

2477. Fowler, Linda L., Douglass, Scott R., and Clark, Wesley D. "The Electoral Effects of House Committee Assignments." *Journal of Politics* 42 (Feb. 1980): 307-319.

2478. Gawthrop, Louis C. "Changing Membership Patterns in House Committees." *American Political Science Review* 60 (June 1966) 366-373.

2479. Gertzog, Irwin N. "Routinization of Committee Assignments in the U.S. House of Representatives." *American Journal of Political Science* 20 (Nov. 1976): 693-712.

2480. Healy, Robert. "Committees and the Politics of Assignments." In *To Be a Congressman: The Promise and the Power*, pp. 99-120. Washington: Acropolis Books, 1973.

2481. Hinckley, Barbara. "Policy Content, Committee Membership and Behavior." *American Journal of Political Science* 19 (Aug. 1975): 543-557.

2482. Huitt, Ralph K. "Morse Committee Assignment Controversy: A Study in Senate Norms." *American Political Science Review* 51 (June 1957): 313-329.

2483. Jewell, Malcolm E. and Chui, Chi-Hung. "Membership Movement and Committee Attractiveness in the U.S. House of Representatives, 1963-1971." *American Journal of Political Science* 18 (May 1974): 433-441.

2484. Malbin, Michael J. "Committee Assignments Reflect House, Senate Turnover." *National Journal* 7 (Feb. 1, 1975): 166-174.

2485. Masters, Nicholas A. "Committee Assignments in the House of Representatives." *American Political Science Review* 55 (June 1961): 345-357.

2486. Mezey, Michael L. "A Multi-Variate Analysis of Committee Assignments in the House of Representatives 1949-1967." Ph.D. dissertation, Syracuse University, 1969.

2487. Rohde, David W. and Shepsle, Kenneth A. "Democratic Committee Assignments in the House of Representatives: Strategic Aspects of a Social Choice Process." *American Political Science Review* 67 (Sept. 1973): 889-905.

2488. Shepsle, Kenneth A. "Congressional Committee Assignments: An Optimization Model with Institutional Constraints." *Public Choice* 22 (Summer 1975): 56-78.

2489. Shepsle, Kenneth A. *The Giant Jigsaw Puzzle: Democratic Committee Assignments in the Modern House.* Chicago: University of Chicago Press, 1978.

2490. Swanson, Wayne R. "Committee Assignments and the Nonconformist Legislator: Democrats in the U.S. Senate." *American Journal of Political Science* 13 (Feb. 1969): 84-94.

2491. U.S. Congress. Senate. *Rules and Practice of the Senate of the United States in the Appointment of Committees from March 4, 1789 to March 14, 1863.* 62nd Cong., 3rd sess. Washington: GPO, 1913.

2492. Uslaner, Eric M. *Congressional Committee Assignments: Alternative Models for Behavior.* Beverly Hills, Calif.: Sage Publications, 1974.

Committee Leadership

2493. Bolling, Richard. "What the New Congress Needs Most: Concerning Choice of Chairmanships." *Harper's Magazine* 234 (Jan. 1967): 79-81.

2494. Evans, Medford. "Chairmen: Our Powerful Feudal Chieftains." *American Opinion* 17 (July-Aug. 1974): 73-88.

2495. Fritchey, Clayton. "Who Belongs to the Senate's Inner Club." *Harper's Magazine* 234 (May 1967): 104-110.

2496. Gregory, Neal. "House Democrats Seek to Limit Powers of Chairmen, Senior Members." *National Journal* 3 (Jan. 2, 1971): 16-24.

2497. Hardy, J. D. "A Study of the Chairmanship of the Judiciary Committee of the U.S. House of Representatives from 1955 to 1972." Master's thesis, Pennsylvania State University, 1971.

2498. Jones, Harry W. "Congressional Committee Chairmen: Status, Influence, and Selection." *American Bar Association Journal* 35 (Dec. 1949): 1034-1035.

2499. Kravitz, Walter and Schaibley, John R. *Senate Rules and Practices on Committee, Subcommittee, and Chairmanship Assignment Limitations, as of April 15, 1978.* Washington: Congressional Research Service, 1978.

2500. Low, A. Maurice. "The Oligarch of the Senate." *North American Review* 174 (Feb. 1902): 231-244.

2501. Leventhal, Paul L. "Outlook '73' 'Turnover in Key Committee Chairmanships Foreshadows Policy Changes in 93rd Congress.'" *National Journal* 4 (Nov. 11, 1972): 1750-1761.

2502. Malbin, Michael J. "Major Shifts Coming in Leadership of Committees." *National Journal* 6 (July 27, 1974): 1115-1123.

2503. Parker, Glenn R. "The Selection of Committee Leaders in the House of Representatives." *American Politics Quarterly* 7 (Jan. 1979): 71-93.

2504. Peabody, Robert L. "Committees from the Leadership Perspective." *American Academy of Political and Social Science, Annals* 411 (Jan. 1974): 133-146.

2505. Ripley, Randall B. "Congressional Party Leaders and Standing Committees." *Review of Politics* 36 (July 1974): 394-409.

2506. Ripley, Randall B. *Party Leaders and Standing Committees in the House of Representatives. Working Papers on House Committee Organization and Operation. Presented to House Select Committee on Committees.* 93rd Cong. washington: GPO, 1973.

Committee Hearings

2507. Cohen, Julius. "Hearing on a Bill: Legislative Folklore?" *Minnesota Law Review* 37 (Dec. 1952): 34-45.

2508. Del Sesto, Steven L. "Nuclear Reactor Safety and the Role of the Congressman: A Content Analysis of Congressional Hearings." *Journal of Politics* 42 (Feb. 1980): 227-241.

2509. Fraser, Donald M. "Congress and the Psychologist." *American Psychologist* 25 (April 1970): 323-327.

2510. Isbell, Florence B. "Congressional Hearings as Theater." *Civil Liberties Review* 5 (July/Aug. 1978): 33-36.

2511. Jones, Harry W. "Congressional Committee Hearings." *American Bar Association Journal* 35 (Mar. 1949): 220-221.

2512. Miller, Susan H. "Congressional Committee Hearings and the Media: Rules of the Game." *Journalism Quarterly* 55 (Winter 1978): 657-663.

2513. Smeltzer, David A. "The Problem of Alternatives in Congressional Decision-Making: The Role of Committee Hearings." Ph.D. dissertation, University of Michigan, 1964.

Committee Secrecy

2514. "Closed Congressional Hearings Maintain High Mark." *Congressional Quarterly Weekly Report* 19 (Dec. 22, 1961): 1961-1962.

2515. Closed Committee Hearings Total 31.9%." *Congressional Quarterly Weekly Report* 14 (April 20, 1956): 441-442.

2516. "Committees Opened 93% of 1975 Meetings." *Congressional Quarterly Weekly Report* 34 (Jan. 24, 1976): 152-155.

2517. "Committee Secrecy: Still Fact of Life in Congress." *Congressional Quarterly Weekly Report* 30 (Nov. 11, 1972): 2974-2976.

2518. "Committee Secrecy: House Opens Up Its Sessions in 1973." *Congressional Quarterly Weekly Report* 32 (Feb. 16, 1974): 369-372.

2519. "Committee Secrecy: Minor Impact of Reform Act." *Congressional Quarterly Weekly Report* 30 (Feb. 12, 1972): 301-303.

2520. "Committee Secrecy: Reformers Thwarted in Senate." *Congressional Quarterly Weekly Report* 31 (Mar. 10, 1973): 501-504.

2521. "Congress Approaches Decision on Secrecy Statute." *Congressional Quarterly Weekly Report* 16 (Jan. 21, 1958): 131.

2522. "Congress Closed 30% of Committee Meetings." *Congressional Quarterly Weekly Report* 17 (Oct. 16, 1959): 1420-1421.

2523. "Congress Closes 34% of Committee Meetings." *Congressional Quarterly Weekly Report* 16 (Jan. 17, 1958): 57-58.

2524. "Congress Closes 34% of Committee Meetings." *Congressional Quarterly Weekly Report* 15 (July 12, 1957): 835-836.

2525. "Congress Closes 36% of Committee Meetings." *Congressional Quarterly Weekly Report* 14 (Sept. 7, 1956): 1097-1098.

2526. "Congress Closes 33% of Committee Meetings." *Congressional Quarterly Weekly Report* 16 (April 18, 1958): 473-474.

2527. "Congressional, Executive Secrecy Still at Issue." *Congressional Quarterly Weekly Report* 19 (April 21, 1961): 669-672.

2528. "Congressional Secrecy Down in First Quarter of 1964." *Congressional Quarterly Weekly Report* 22 (May 15, 1964): 966-968.

2529. "Congressional Secrecy Increases in 1960." *Congressional Quarterly Weekly Report* 18 (Dec. 16, 1960): 1957-1958.

2530. "Congressional Secrecy Up in First Quarter of 1965." *Congressional Quarterly Weekly Report* 23 (April 23, 1965): 756-757.

2531. Eckhardt, Bob. "The Presumption of Committee Openness Under House Rules." *Harvard Journal of Legislation* 11 (Feb. 1974): 279-302.

2532. "45% of Committee Meetings Closed in First Quarter." *Congressional Quarterly Weekly Report* 25 (April 21, 1967): 642-644.

2533. "41 Percent of Committee Sessions Held in Secret." *Congressional Quarterly Weekly Report* 12 (Nov. 26, 1954): 1393.

2534. "42% of Committee Meetings Closed in First Quarter." *Congressional Quarterly Weekly Report* 26 (April 12, 1968): 830-832.

2535. Gore, Albert. "Legislative Secrecy." In *None of Your Business: Government Secrecy in America,* eds. Norman Dorsen and Stephen Gillers, pp. 137-150. New York: Viking Press, 1974.

2536. "More Closed Committee Meetings Conducted in 1970." *Congressional Quarterly Weekly Report* 29 (Feb. 12, 1971): 387-389.

2537. "New Record Set for Closed Committee Meetings—43%." *Congressional Quarterly Weekly Report* 26 (Nov. 8, 1968): 3103-3105.

2538. "Open Committee Trend in House and Senate." *Congressional Quarterly Weekly Report* 33 (Jan. 11, 1975): 81-82.

2539. Schmidt, Benno C. "Does Congress Have a Legal Case Against Schorr?" *Columbia Journalism Review* 15 (May 1976): 24-25.

2540. "Secret Committee Meetings Decline Slightly." *Congressional Quarterly Weekly Report* 13 (Sept. 9, 1955): 1046.

2541. "Secret Hearings." *Congressional Quarterly Weekly Report* 13 (April 29, 1955): 463-464.

2542. Stern, Laurence. "Daniel Schorr Affair." *Columbia Journalism Review* 15 (May 1976): 20-25.

2543. "Third of Committee Meetings Closed So Far This Year." *Congressional Quarterly Weekly Report* 20 (April 13, 1962): 589-591.

2544. "30% of Congressional Committee Meetings Secret." *Congressional Quarterly Weekly Report* 15 (April 22, 1960): 670-671.

2545. "35% of Committee Sessions Closed in 1966 Quarter." *Congressional Quarterly Weekly Report* 24 (May 20, 1966): 1020-1022.

2546. "34 Percent of Committee Meetings Closed in 1965." *Congressional Quarterly Weekly Report* 24 (Feb. 11, 1966): 372-373.

2547. "39% of 1967 Committee Hearings Held in Closed Session." *Congressional Quarterly Weekly Report* 26 (Jan. 26, 1978): 128-130.

2548. "37% of Committee Meetings Closed in First Quarter." *Congressional Quarterly Weekly Report* 27 (April 25, 1969): 604-605.

2549. "Upward Trend Indicated in Congressional Secrecy." *Congressional Quarterly Weekly Report* 21 (April 19, 1963): 638-641.

2550. Vaden, Ted. "Senate Votes 'Sunshine' Rules for Committees." *Congressional Quarterly Weekly Report* 33 (Nov. 8, 1975): 2413-2414.

Committee Staff

2551. Cochrane, James D. "Partisan Aspects of Congressional Committee Staffing." *Western Political Quarterly* 17 (June 1964): 338-348.

2552. Eidenberg, Eugene. "The Congressional Bureaucracy." Ph.D. dissertation, Northwestern University, 1966.

2553. Kammerer, Gladys M. *Congressional Committee Staffing Since 1946.* Lexington, Ky.: Bureau of Governmental Research, 1951.

2554. Kammerer, Gladys M. "The Record of Congress in Committee Staffing." *American Political Science Review* 45 (Dec. 1951): 1126-1136.

2555. Kammerer, Gladys M. *The Staffing of the Committees of Congress.* Lexington: University Press of Kentucky, 1949.

2556. Kayali, Khaled M. "Patterns of Congressional Staffing: The House Committee on Appropriations." In *Comparative Legislative Reforms and Innovations,* eds. Abdo I. Baaklini and James J. Heaphey, pp. 61-90. Albany: Comparative Development Studies Center, Graduate School of Public Affairs, State University of New York, 1977.

2557. Kofmehl, Kenneth. *Three Major Aspects of House Committee Staffing. Working Papers on House Committee Organization and Operation. Presented to House Select Committee on Committees.* 93rd Cong. Washington: GPO, 1973.

2558. Kravitz, Walter. *Improving Some Skills of Committee Staff. Working Papers on House Organization and Operation. Presented to House Select Committee on Committees.* 93rd Cong. Washington: GPO, 1973.

2559. Malbin, Michael J. "Congressional Committee Staffs: Who's in Charge Here?" *Public Interest* 47 (Spring 1977): 16-40.

2560. Malbin, Michael J. "Senate Preparing for Study of Committee Staffing Problems." *National Journal* 7 (May 5, 1975): 647-651.

2561. Patterson, Samuel C. "The Professional Staffs of Congressional Committees." *Administrative Science Quarterly* 15 (Mar. 1970): 22-37.

2562. Patterson, Samuel C. *Staffing House Committees. Working Papers on House Committee Organization and Operation. Presented to House Select Committee on Committees.* 93rd Cong. Washington: GPO, 1973.

2563. Price, David E. "Professionals and Entrepreneurs: Staff Orientations and Policy Making on Three Senate Committees." *Journal of Politics* 33 (May 1971): 316-336.

2564. "Republicans Seek More Policy Help from Staff Committees." *Congressional Quarterly Weekly Report* 20 (May 4, 1962): 764-766.

2565. Robinson, James A. *Committee Staffing. Working Papers on House Committee Organization and Operation. Presented to House Select Committee on Committees.* 93rd Cong. Washington: GPO, 1973.

2566. Shampansky, Jay R. *Compilation of Federal Statutes and Rules Related to Senate Committee Staffs.* Washington: Congressional Research Service, 1976.

2567. Shapiro, Bernard. "Congressional Committees, Congressional Staff and Related Aspects." *National Tax Journal* 32 (Sept. 1979): 241-247.

2568. Stenger, Thomas C. "Congressional Committee Staff Members: Policy Advocates or Process Administrators?" Ph.D. dissertation, Southern Illinois University, 1978.

2569. Trescavage, Bernard J. "Journey Through the Corridors of Power: Assignment to a Congressional Committee." *GAO Review* 11 (Winter 1976): 49-51.

2570. U.S. Congress. Senate. Rules and Administration Committee. *Committee-Related Senate Employees, Hearings.* Washington: GPO, 1975.

2571. U.S. Congress. Senate. *Senate Committee Staffing.* S. Doc. 16, 88th Cong., 1st sess. Washington: GPO, 1963.

2572. Walsh, Samuel L. "Senate Committee Personal Practices." In *Committees and Senate Procedures: A Compilation of Papers Prepared for the Commission on the Operation of the Senate,* 94th Cong., 2nd sess., pp. 62-73. Washington: GPO, 1977.

Committee Reform

2573. Bibby, John F. *Reforming the Committees While Retaining the Unique Role of the House. Working Papers on House Committee Organization and Operation. Presented to House Select Committee on Committees.* 93rd Cong. Washington: GPO, 1973.

2574. "Committee Spending, Staffing Come Under House Scrutiny." *Congressional Quarterly Weekly Report* 21 (Mar. 1, 1963): 239-240.

2575. Cottin, Jonathan. "House Gets Proposals for Procedural, Committee Reform." *National Journal* 6 (Mar. 23, 1974): 419-430.

2576. Davidson, Roger H. "Breaking Up Those Cozy Triangles: An Impossible Dream?" In *Legislative Reform and Public Policy,* eds. Susan Welch and John G. Peters, pp. 30-53. New York: Praeger, 1977.

2577. Davidson, Roger H. "Two Roads of Change: House and Senate Committee Reorganization." *Congressional Studies* 7 (Winter 1980): 11-32.

2578. Eulau, Heinz. "The Committees in a Revitalized Congress." In *Twelve Studies of the Organization of Congress,* pp. 213-256. Washington: American Enterprise Institute for Public Policy Research, 1966.

2579. "House Democrats Split on Committee Reorganization." *Congressional Quarterly Weekly Report* 32 (May 4, 1974): 1146-1147.

2580. "House Reorganization: Smaller Committee Proposed." *Congressional Quarterly Weekly Report* 31 (Dec. 15, 1973): 3314.

2581. Humphrey, Hubert H. "To Move Congress Out of Its Ruts." *New York Times Magazine,* 7 April 1963, pp. 39, 129-130, 132.

2582. "Jurisdiction Overhaul: Recommended for House." *Congressional Quarterly Weekly Report* 31 (Dec. 22, 1973): 3358-3366.

2583. Lees, John D. "Committee Reform in the U.S. Congress: A Progress Report." *Journal of Parliamentary Information* 20 (1974): 553-560.

2584. Malbin, Michael J. "House Committee Reforms Will Change 94th Congress." *National Journal* 6 (Oct. 26, 1974): 1614-1619.

2585. Malbin, Michael J. "You Can Please Some of the Senators Some of the Time." *National Journal* 9 (Jan. 15, 1977): 106-111.

2586. Nathanson, Iric. "Rationalizing the Committees." *Nation,* 11 Dec. 1976, pp. 613-615.

2587. Oleszek, Walter J. "Toward a Stronger Legislative Branch: Congress Proposes Committee and Oversight Reforms." *Bureaucrat* 3 (Jan. 1975): 444-461.

2588. Olmsted, H. M. "Congress Takes Steps to Modernize Procedure." *National Municipal Review* 34 (Mar. 1945): 130-131.

2589. Oppenheimer, Bruce I. "Policy Implications of Rules Committee Reforms." In *Legislative Reform: The Policy Impact,* ed. Leroy N. Riselbach, pp. 91-104. Lexington, Mass.: Lexington Books, 1978.

2590. Ornstein, Norman J. "Towards Restructuring the Congressional Committee System." *American Academy of Political and Social Science, Annals* 441 (Jan. 1974): 147-157.

2591. Parris, Judith H. "The Senate Reorganizes Its Committees, 1977." *Political Science Quarterly* 94 (Summer 1979): 319-337.

2592. "Reform for Congress: Overweening Power of Committees." *Round Table* 53 (Dec. 1962): 40-45.

2593. "Restructuring of Committees Stalled in House." *Congressional Quarterly Weekly Report* 32 (Oct. 5, 1974): 2655-2657.

2594. Rhodes, Jack A. "Congressional Committee Reorganization in 1946." *Southwestern Social Science Quarterly* 28 (June 1947): 36-52.

2595. Rudder, Catherine E. "Committee Reform and the Revenue Process." In *Congress Reconsidered,* eds. Lawrence C. Dodd and Bruce I. Oppenheimer, pp. 117-139. New York: Praeger, 1977.

2596. "Rules, Traditions to Govern Committee Changes." *Congressional Quarterly Weekly Report* 19 (Jan. 6, 1961): 10-11.

2597. Rundquist, Paul S. *Senate Committee System Reform.* Washington: Congressional Research Service, 1978.

2598. "Should Un-American Activities Committee Be Reformed." *Congressional Quarterly Weekly Report* 16 (July 4, 1958): 847-848.

2599. "Showdown Nears on House Committee Reorganization." *Congressional Quarterly Weekly Report* 32 (April 27, 1974): 1026-1028.

2600. Southwick, Thomas P. "Senate Approves Committee Changes." *Congressional Quarterly Weekly Report* 35 (Feb. 12, 1977): 279-284.

2601. Southwick, Thomas P. "Senate Committee Changes: Major Impact." *Congressional Quarterly Weekly Report* 35 (Feb. 19, 1977): 330-333.

2602. "Studies of Senate Committee System Sought." *Congressional Quarterly Weekly Report* 33 (Mar. 15, 1975): 541-543.

2603. U.S. Congress. House. Select Committee on Committees. *Committee Reform Amendments of 1974, Part I, Hearings, February 4, 6, 7, 20-23, 25, 27, 28, 1974.* 93rd Cong., 2nd sess. Washington: GPO, 1974.

2604. U.S. Congress. House. Select Committee on Committees. *Committee Reform Amendments of 1974, Part II, Hearings, March 1, 4-8, 13, 1974.* 93rd Cong., 2nd sess. Washington: GPO, 1974.

2605. U.S. Congress. House. Select Committee on Committees. *Committee Reform Amendments of 1974, Staff Report.* 93rd Cong., 2nd sess. Washington: GPO, 1974.

2606. U.S. Congress. House. Select Committee on Committees. *A Summary of H. Res. 988 Committee Reform Amendments of 1974.* 93rd Cong., 2nd sess. Washington: GPO, 1974.

2607. U.S. Congress. Senate. Temporary Select Committee to Study the Senate Committee System. *The Senate Committee System: Jurisdictions, Referrals, Numbers and Sizes, and Limitations of Assignments. First Staff Report.* Washington: GPO, 1976.

2608. U.S. Congress. Senate. Temporary Select Committee to Study the Senate Committee System. *Structure of the Senate Committee System: Jurisdictions, Numbers and Sizes, and Limitations on Memberships and Chairmanships, Referral Procedures, and Scheduling; First Report Together with Additional Views.* Washington: GPO, 1976.

Standing Committees

Agriculture

2609. "House Agriculture: New Faces, New Issues." *Congressional Quarterly Weekly Report* 33 (Feb. 22, 1975): 379-384.

2610. Jones, Charles O. "Representation in Congress: The Case of the House Agriculture Committee." *American Political Science Review* 55 (June 1961): 358-367.

2611. Ralph Nader Congress Project. *The Environment Committees: A Study of the House and Senate Interior, Agriculture, and Science Committees.* New York: Grossman Publishers, 1975.

2612. U.S. Congress. Senate. Committee on Agriculture and Forestry. *A Brief History of the Committee on Agriculture and Forestry, United States Senate, and Landmark Agricultural Legislation, 1825-1970.* 91st Cong., 2nd sess. Washington: GPO, 1970.

2613. U.S. Congress. Senate. Committee on Interior and Insular Affairs. *Committee's History, Jurisdiction, and Summary and Its Accomplishments During the 87th, 88th, 89th, 90th and 91st Congresses.* 92nd Cong., 1st sess. Washington: GPO, 1971:

Appropriations

2614. Brown, Robert E. "Politics and the Appropriations Committees of Congress." Ph.D. dissertation, George Washington University, 1977.

2615. Clark, Timothy B. "Appropriations Committees: Losing Their Grip on Spending." *National Journal* 10 (July 22, 1978): 1169-1174.

2616. Esbrandt, Philip S. "The Effects of Congressional Appropriations Committees upon Educational Research Policy." Ed.D. dissertation, Temple University, 1974.

2617. "FBI Agents: Use by House Appropriations Committee." *Congressional Quarterly Weekly Report* 29 (July 23, 1971): 1565-1569.

2618. Fenno, Richard F. "House Appropriations Committee as a Political System: The Problem of Integration." *American Political Science Review* 56 (June 1962): 310-324.

2619. Fenno, Richard F. *The Power of the Purse: Appropriation Politics in Congress.* Boston: Little, Brown, 1973.

2620. Friedman, Robert S. "Policy Formation in the Appropriation Process, with Special Emphasis on the House Appropriations Committee." Ph.D. dissertation, University of Illinois at Urbana-Champaign, 1953.

2621. Horn, Stephen. *Unused Power: The Work of the Senate Committee on Appropriations.* Washington: Brookings Institution, 1970.

2622. Jernberg, James E. "Information Change and Congressional Behavior: A Caveat for PPB Reformers." *Journal of Politics* 31 (Aug. 1969): 722-740.

2623. Meier, Kenneth J. "Interest Groups in the Appropriations Process: The Wasted Profession Revisited." *Social Science Quarterly* 59 (Dec. 1978): 482-495.

2624. Menge, Edward. "Congress and Agency Appropriations: An Explanation of House Appropriations Committee Actions for Federal Agencies." Ph.D. dissertation, Ohio State University, 1973.

2625. Sharkansky, Ira. "Appropriations Subcommittee and Its Client Agencies: A Comparative Study of Supervision and Control." *American Political Science Review* 59 (Sept. 1965): 622-628.

2626. Sullivan, Terry. "Voter's Paradox and Logrolling: An Initial Framework for Committee Behavior on Appropriations and Ways and Means." *Public Choice* 25 (Spring 1976): 31-44.

2627. Taylor, Edward T. *History of the Committee on Appropriations.* Washington: GPO, 1941.

2628. U.S. Congress. Senate. *Committee on Appropriations, United States Senate, 100th Anniversary, 1867-1967.* S. Doc. 21, 90th Cong., 1st sess. Washington: GPO, 1967.

2629. Ward, Shirley. "Assignment on Capitol Hill." *GAO Review* 10 (Fall 1975): 23-27.

Armed Services

2630. "Armed Services Committees: Advocates or Overseers?" *Congressional Quarterly Weekly Report* 30 (Mar. 25, 1972): 673-677.

2631. "A Change of Style on House Armed Services." *Congressional Quarterly Weekly Report* 33 (Feb. 15, 1975): 336-341.

2632. Entin, Kenneth. "The House Armed Services Committee: Political Communication and Defense Policy-Making." Ph.D. dissertation, New York University, 1971.

2633. Entin, Kenneth. "The House Armed Services Committee: Patterns of Decision-Making During the McNamara Years." *Journal of Political and Military Sociology* 2 (Spring 1974): 73-87.

2634. Entin, Kenneth. "Information Exchange in Congress: The Case of the House Armed Services Committee." *Western Political Quarterly* 26 (Sept. 1973): 427-439.

2635. Fleer, Jack D. "Congressional Committees and the Making of Military Policy: Authorizations and Appropriations for Major Weapons Systems in the Legislative Process." Ph.D. dissertation, University of North Carolina at Chapel Hill, 1965.

2636. Futterman, Stanley N. "Toward Legislative Control of the C.I.A." *New York University Journal of International Law and Politics* 4 (Winter 1971): 431-458.

2637. Goss, Carol F. "Military Committee Membership and Defense Related Benefits in the House of Representatives." *Western Political Quarterly* 25 (June 1972): 215-233.

2638. Hersh, Seymour M. "The Military Committees." *Washington Monthly* 1 (April 1969): 84-92.

2639. Norris, John G. "The House Armed Services Committee Has Key Role in Shaping Defense Posture." *Navy* 10 (June 1967): 7-11.

2640. Shaw, Samuel E. "The House Armed Services Committee: Defense Procurement and Research Authorization 1961-1968." Ph.D. dissertation, City University of New York, 1971.

2641. Stephens, Herbert W. "Role of the Legislative Committees in the Appropriations Process: A Study Focused on the Armed Services Committees." *Western Political Quarterly* 24 (Mar. 1971): 146-162.

2642. Stephens, Herbert W. "The Role of a Legislative Committee in the Appropriations Process: A Study Focused on the House Armed Services Committee." Ph.D. dissertation, Florida State University, 1967.

2643. Whelan, John T. "Some Conditions Affecting Continuity and Change in Congressional Committee Involvement in Defense Policy: The Case of the House Committee on Armed Services." Ph.D. dissertation, University of Pittsburgh, 1972.

Banking

2644. Carter H. Golembe Associates. *The Economic Power of Commercial Banks: An Examination of the Report of the Subcommittee on Domestic Finance Dealing with Banking Concentration and Trust Accounts of Commercial Banks.* New York: American Bankers Association, 1970.

2645. Fisher, R. M. "Senate Committee on Banking and Currency: Functions and Operations of 50-Year-Old Standing Committee." *Banking* 55 (June 1963): 53-54.

2646. Huitt, Ralph K. "Congressional Committee: A Case Study." *American Political Science Review* 48 (June 1954): 340-365.

2647. Norton, Bruce D. F. "The Committee on Banking and Currency as a Legislative Subsystem of the House of Representatives." Ph.D. dissertation, University of Syracuse, 1970.

2648. Pecora, Ferdinand. *Wall Street Under Oath: The Story of Our Modern Money Changers.* New York: Simon and Schuster, 1939.

2649. Ralph Nader Congress Project. *The Money Committees: A Study of the House Banking and Currency Committee and Senate Banking Committee.* New York: Grossman Publishers, 1975.

2650. U.S. Congress. Senate. Committee on Banking and Currency. *Committee on Banking and Currency, United States Senate, 50th Anniversary, 1913-1963.* S. Doc. 15, 88th Cong. 1st sess. Washington: GPO, 1963.

Budget

2651. Havemann, Joel. "The Congressional Budget Committees: High Marks After the First Years." *National Journal* 8 (Sept. 25, 1976): 1346-1352.

2652. Havemann, Joel. "New Budget Committees Already Have Ambitious Plans." *National Journal* 6 (Sept. 28, 1974): 1445-1453.

2653. Jasper, Herbert N. "A Congressional Budget: Will It Work This Time?" *Bureaucrat* 3 (Jan. 1975): 429-443.

2654. LeLoup, Lance T. "Process Versus Policy: The U.S. House Budget Committee." *Legislative Studies Quarterly* 4 (May 1979): 227-254.

Commerce

2655. Ornstein, Norman J. and Rohde, David W. "Revolt from Within: Congressional Change, Legislative Policy, and the House Commerce Committee." In *Legislative Reform and Public Policy,* eds. Susan Welch and John G. Peters, pp. 54-72. New York: Praeger, 1977.

2656. Price, David E. "The Impact of Reform: The House Commerce Subcommittee on Oversight and Investigations." In *Legislative Reform: The Policy Impact,* ed. Leroy N. Rieselbach, pp. 133-157. Lexington, Mass.: Lexington Books, 1978.

2657. Ralph Nader Congress Project. *The Commerce Committees: A Study of the House and Senate Commerce Committees.* New York: Grossman Publishers, 1975.

2658. Schwartz, Bernard. *The Professor and the Commissions.* New York: Knopf, 1959.

2659. U.S. Congress. House. Committee on Interstate and Foreign Commerce. *180 Years of Service: A Brief History of the Committee on Interstate and Foreign Commerce.* 94th Cong., 1st sess. Washington: GPO, 1975.

2660. U.S. Congress. Senate. Committee on Commerce. *History, Membership and Jurisdiction of the Senate Committee on Commerce from 1816-1966.* 89th Cong., 2nd sess. Washington: GPO, 1966.

Education and Labor

2661. Auerbach, Jerold S. *Labor and Liberty: The LaFollette Committee and the New Deal.* Indianapolis, Ind.: Bobbs-Merrill, 1966.

2662. Auerbach, Jerold S. "The LaFollette Committee and the C.I.O." *Wisconsin Magazine of History* 48 (Autumn 1964): 3-20.

2663. Auerbach, Jerold S. "The LaFollette Committee: Labor and Civil Liberties in the New Deal." Ph.D. dissertation, Columbia University, 1965.

2664. Auerbach, Jerold S. "The LaFollette Committee: Labor and Civil Liberties in the New Deal." *Journal of American History* 51 (Dec. 1964): 435-459.

2665. Cohen, Matthew C. "Decision Making in a Committee Context: The House Education and Labor Committee Deliberations of the Elementary and Secondary Education Act Extension of 1974." Ph.D. dissertation, Carnegie-Mellon University, 1978.

2666. Murray, Michael A. "The House Education Labor Committee and the 1967 Poverty Controversy: A Study of Congressional Avoidance." Ph.D. dissertation, University of Illinois at Urbana-Champaign, 1969.

2667. Ostrom, Donald I. "The House Education and Labor Committee: An Alternative Strategy." Ph.D. dissertation, Washington University, 1972.

Finance

2668. Arrandale, Tom. "Ways and Means in 1975: No Longer Pre-Eminent." *Congressional Quarterly Weekly Report* 34 (Jan. 10, 1976): 40-44.

2669. Balz, Daniel J. "Initial Hearings Illustrate Ways and Means Changes." *National Journal* 7 (Feb. 1, 1975): 175.

2670. Balz, Daniel J. "Ways and Means Seeks to Maintain Power and Prestige." *National Journal* 6 (June 22, 1974): 913-920.

2671. Balz, Daniel J. "Why the Bright New Congressmen Couldn't Deliver on Tax Reform." *Washington Monthly* 8 (July-Aug. 1976): 25-28.

2672. Bond, J. R. "Oiling the Tax Committees in Congress, 1900–1974: Sub-Government Theory, the Overrepresentation Hypothesis, and the Oil Depletion Allowance." *American Journal of Political Science* 23 (Nov. 1979): 651-664.

2673. Cameron, Juan. "And They Call It the Most Important Committee in Congress." *Fortune* 93 (Mar. 1976): 140-148.

2674. Cataldo, Everett F. "The House Committee on Ways and Means." Ph.D. dissertation, Ohio State University, 1965.

2675. Curtis, Thomas B. "House Committee on Ways and Means: Congress Seen Through a Key Committee." *Wisconsin Law Review* 1966 (Winter 1966): 121-147.

2676. Fowkes, Frank V. and Lenhart, Harry. "Two Money Committees Wield Power Differently." *National Journal* 3 (April 10, 1971): 779-807.

2677. Furlong, Patrick J. "Origins of the House Committee of Ways and Means." *William and Mary Quarterly* 25 (Oct. 1968): 587-604.

2678. Lammers, Bernard J. "The Role of Congressional Tax Committees in Internal Revenue Legislation, 1953-1964." Ph.D. dissertation, Columbia University, 1967.

2679. Manley, John F. "The House Committee on Ways and Means: Conflict Management in a Congressional Committee." *American Political Science Review* 59 (Dec. 1965): 927-939.

2680. Manley, John F. *The Politics of Finance: The House Committee on Ways and Means.* Boston: Little, Brown, 1970.

2681. Pincus, Walter. "New Ways, Better Means?" *New Republic* 172, 8 Feb. 1975, pp. 7-9.

2682. Ralph Nader Congress Project. *The Revenue Committees: A Study of the House Ways and Means and Senate Finance Committees and House and Senate Appropriations Committees.* New York: Grossman Publishers, 1975.

2683. Rudder, Catherine E. "The Policy Impact of Reform of the Committee on Ways and Means." In *Legislative Reform: The Policy Impact,* ed. Leroy N. Rieselbach, pp. 72-89. Lexington, Mass.: Lexington Books, 1978.

2684. U.S. Congress. House. Ways and Means Committee. *95th Congress Legislative Record of the Committee on Ways and Means, U.S. House of Representatives Along with Brief Historical and Other Pertinent Information Concerning the Committee.* 95th Cong., 2nd sess. Washington: GPO, 1979.

2685. U.S. Congress. Senate. Committee on Finance. *History of the Committee on Finance, United States Senate.* 3rd ed. 95th Cong., 1st sess. Washington: GPO, 1977.

2686. "Ways and Means Committee is Key to Major Proposals." *Congressional Quarterly Weekly Report* 25 (Feb. 24, 1967): 273-275.

Foreign Affairs

2687. Andrew, Jean D. "The Effect of Senate Foreign Relations Committee Membership in Terms of Support of Foreign Policy, 1946-1966." Ph.D. dissertation, University of Connecticut, 1968.

2688. Burnette, Ollen L. "The Senate Foreign Relations Committee and the Diplomacy of Garfield, Arthur, and Cleveland." Ph.D. dissertation, University of Virginia, 1952.

2689. Chiperfield, Robert B. "The Committee on Foreign Affairs." *American Academy of Political and Social Science, Annals* 289 (Sept. 1953): 73-83.

2690. Clark, Dick. "The Foreign Relations Committee and the Future of Arms Control." In *Congress and Arms Control,* eds. Alan Platt and Lawrence D. Weiler, pp. 97-110. Boulder, Colo.: Westview Press, 1978.

2691. Collier, Ellen C. *Postwar Presidents and the Senate Foreign Relations Committee.* Washington: Legislative Reference Service, 1969.

2692. Dangerfield, Royden J. "The Senatorial Diplomats." *American Mercury* 37 (Mar. 1936): 359-362.

2693. Daughan, George C. "From Lodge to Fulbright: The Chairman of the Senate Foreign Relations Committee." Ph.D. dissertation, Harvard University, 1968.

2694. Dennison, Eleanor E. *The Senate Foreign Relations Committee.* Stanford, Calif.: Stanford University press, 1942.

2695. Farnsworth, David N. "Comparison of the Senate and Its Foreign Relations Committee on Selected Roll-Call Votes." *Western Political Quarterly* 14 (Mar. 1961): 168-175.

2696. Farnsworth, David N. *The Senate Committee on Foreign Relations: A Study of the Decision-Making Process.* Urbana: University of Illinois Press, 1961.

2697. Gambrill, Leonard L. "The Influence of the Senate Foreign Relations Committee Chairman in the Making of United States Foreign Policy: A Case Analysis." Ph.D. dissertation, University of Virginia, 1971.

2698. Gould, James W. "Origins of the Senate Committee on Foreign Relations, 1789-1816." *Western Political Quarterly* 12 (Sept. 1959): 670-682.

2699. Halperin, Morton. "Is the Senate's Foreign Relations Research Worthwhile?" *American Behavioral Scientist* 4 (Sept. 1960): 21-24.

2700. Hayden, Ralston. "The Origin of the United States Senate Committee on Foreign Relations." *American Journal of International Law* 11 (Jan. 1917): 113-130.

2701. Housel, Jerry W. "The Committee on Foreign Relations of the United States Senate." Ph.D. dissertation, American University, 1941.

2702. Johnson, Victor C. "Congress and Foreign Policy: The House Foreign Affairs and Senate Foreign Relations Committees." Ph.D. dissertation, University of Wisconsin at Madison, 1975.

2703. Kaiser, Frederick M. "Congressional Change and Foreign Policy: the House Committee on International Relations." In *Legislative Reform: The Policy Impact,* ed. Leroy N. Rieselbach, pp. 61-71. Lexington, Mass.: Lexington Books, 1978.

2704. Kaiser, Frederick M. "Oversight of Foreign Policy: The U.S. House Committee on International Relations." *Legislative Studies Quarterly* 2 (Aug. 1977): 255-279.

2705. Kaiser, Frederick M. "Structural and Policy Change: The House Committee on International Relations." *Policy Studies Journal* 5 (Summer 1977): 443-450.

2706. Lanouette, William J. "A New Kind of Bipartisanship for the Foreign Relations Committee." *National Journal* 11 (Mar. 31, 1979): 525-528.

2707. Linthicum, J. Charles. "Committee on Foreign Affairs of the House of Representatives and the Treaty-Making Power." *American Society of International Law, Proceedings* (1932): 249-256.

2708. McGinnis, Kathleen. "The Foreign Policy Committees and the Congressional Research Service." Ph.D. dissertation, University of Virginia, 1978.

2709. Maffre, John. "New Leaders, Staff Changes Stimulate House Foreign Affairs Committee." *National Journal* 3 (June 19, 1971): 1314-1322.

2710. Marcy, Carl. "The Research Program of the Senate Committee on Foreign Relations." *PROD* 2 (Nov. 1958): 28-30.

2711. Olson, Magne B. "The Evolution of a Senate Institution: The Committee on Foreign Relations to 1861." Ph.D. dissertation, University of Minnesota, 1971.

2712. Poole, Frederick. "Congress v. Kissinger: The New Equalizers." *Washington Monthly* 7 (May 1975): 23-30.

2713. Raith, Charles Adolphe. "The Anti-U.N. Coalition Before the Senate Foreign Relations and the House Foreign Affairs Committees During the Years 1945-1955." Ph.D. dissertation, University of Pennsylvania, 1962.

2714. Robinson, James A. "Another Look at Senate Research on Foreign Policy." *American Behavioral Scientist* 4 (Nov. 1960): 12-15.

2715. "Senate, House Committees Differ on Foreign Affairs." *Congressional Quarterly Weekly Report* 28 (Nov. 20, 1970): 2825-2828.

2716. Strikwerda, Charles E. "The House Foreign Affairs Committee and Changing Executive–Legislative Relations in Foreign Policy." Ph.D. dissertation, University of Kentucky, 1977.

2717. Turesky, Stanley F. "A Time to Talk and a Time to Listen: A Study of the Relationship Between the Chairman of the Senate Foreign Relations Committee and the President of the United States." Ph.D. dissertation, Brown University, 1973.

2718. U.S. Congress. Senate. *Committee on Foreign Relations: 160th Anniversary 1816-1976.* 94th Cong., 2nd sess. Washington: GPO, 1976.

2719. Vardys, Vytas S. "Select Committees of Congress in Foreign Relations: A Case Study in Legislative Process." Ph.D. dissertation, University of Wisconsin, 1958.

2720. Westphal, Albert C. F. *The House Committee on Foreign Affairs.* New York: Columbia University Press, 1942.

2721. Wiley, Alexander. "The Committee on Foreign Relations." *American Academy of Political and Social Science, Annals* 289 (Sept. 1953): 58-65.

Government Affairs

2722. Henderson, Thomas A. *Congressional Oversight of Executive Agencies: A Study of the House Committee on Government Operations.* Gainesville: University of Florida Press, 1970.

2723. Malbin, Michael J. "Senate Governmental Affairs: The Committee with a Consensus." *National Journal* 9 (Aug. 27, 1977): 1344-1377.

2724. Michel, Robert H. "Reorganization of the Committee on Government Operations and Minority Control of Investigation." In *We Propose: A Modern Congress,* ed. Mary McInnis, pp. 163-176. New York: McGraw-Hill, 1966.

Judiciary

2725. Devitt, Edward J. "House Committee on the Judiciary: An Historic Committee and Its Broadened Duties." *American Bar Association Journal* 33 (May 1947): 458-460.

2726. Farrelly, David G. "Operational Aspects of the Senate Judiciary Committee: A Study of Committee Procedure 1923-1947, with Special Reference to the Congressional Reorganization Act of 1946." Ph.D. dissertation, Princeton University, 1949.

2727. Farrelly, David G. "The Senate Judiciary Committee: Qualifications of Members." *American Political Science Review* 37 (June 1943): 469-475.

2728. Fields, Howard. *High Crimes and Misdemeanors: The Untold Dramatic Story of the Rodino Committee.* New York: W. W. Norton, 1978.

2729. Jameson, Guilford S. "Judiciary Committee of the House of Representatives." *American Bar Association Journal* 12 (Jan. 1926): 53-54.

2730. Mizell, Winton R. "The United States Senate Committee on the Judiciary and Presidential Nominations of the Supreme Court, 1965-1971." Ph.D. dissertation, University of Oklahoma, 1974.

2731. Perkins, Lynette P. "Member Goals and Committee Behavior: The House Judiciary Committee." Ph.D. dissertation, University of Pittsburgh, 1977.

2732. Ralph Nader Congress Project. *The Judiciary Committees: A Study of the House and Senate Judiciary Committees.* New York: Grossman Publishers, 1975.

2733. Salmond, J. A. "Great Southern Commie Hunt: Aubrey Williams, the South Conference Education Fund, and the International Security Subcommittee." *South Atlantic Quarterly* 77 (Autumn 1978): 433-452.

2734. U.S. Congress. House. Committee on the Judiciary. History of the Committee on the Judiciary of the House of Representatives. 92nd Cong., 2nd sess. Washington: GPO, 1973.

2735. U.S. Congress. Senate. Committee on the Judiciary. *History of the Committee on the Judiciary, 1816-1976.* 94th Cong., 2nd sess. Washington: GPO, 1976.

2736. Van Nuys, Frederick. "The Work of the Senate Judiciary Committee." *Federal Bar Association Journal* 4 (Dec. 1942): 338, 356-357.

Public Works and Welfare

2737. Ferejohn, John A. *Pork Barrel Politics: Rivers and Harbors Legislation, 1947-1968.* Stanford, Calif.: Stanford University Press, 1974.

2738. Murphy, James T. "Congressional Pork and Project Discounting: A Comment on Ferejohn's *Pork Barrel Politics.*" *Harvard Journal on Legislation* 12 (April 1975): 495-510.

2739. Murphy, James T. "The House Public Works Committee: Determinants and Consequences of Committee Behavior." Ph.D. dissertation, University of Rochester, 1970.

2740. Murphy, James T. "Political Parties and the Porkbarrel: Party Conflict and Cooperation in House Public Works Committee Decision Making." *American Political Science Review* 68 (Mar. 1974): 169-185.

2741. Sevitch, Benjamin. "Stonewalling the Senate: Elbert H. Gary's Testimony on the Open Shop." *Communication Quarterly* 24 (Spring 1976): 20-27.

2742. Strom, Gerald S. "Congressional Policy Making: A Test of a Theory." *Journal of Politics* 37 (Aug. 1975): 711-735.

2743. U.S. Congress. Senate. *Committee on Labor and Public Welfare: 100th Anniversary 1869-1969.* 90th Cong., 2nd sess. Washington: GPO, 1970.

Rules

2744. Allen, James B. "The Rules and Administration Committee of the United States Senate." Ph.D. dissertation, University of Alabama, 1979.

2745. American Enterprise Institute for Public Policy Research. *History and Powers of the House Committee on Rules.* Washington: GPO, 1963.

2746. Cummings, Milton C. and Peabody, Robert L. "The Decision to Enlarge the Committee on Rules: An Analysis of the 1961 Vote." In *New Perspectives on the House of Representatives,* eds. Nelson W. Polsby and Robert L. Peabody, pp. 253-281. Chicago: Rand McNally, 1969.

2747. Fox, Douglas M. and Clapp, Charles H. "House Rules Committees' Agenda-Setting Function, 1961-1968." *Journal of Politics* 32 (May 1970): 440-443.

2748. Fox, Douglas M. and Clapp, Charles H. "The House Rules Committee and the Programs of the Kennedy and Johnson Administration." *Midwest Journal of Political Science* 14 (Nov. 1970): 667-672.

2749. "House Rules Committee Regains Image Independence." *Congressional Quarterly Weekly Report* 32 (Mar. 30, 1974): 804-810.

2750. Kravitz, Walter. "The Influence of the House Rules Committee on Legislation in the 87th Congress." In *Congressional Reform: Problems and Prospects,* ed. Joseph S. Clark, pp. 127-137. New York: Thomas Y. Crowell, 1965.

2751. Kravitz, Walter, rev. by Walter J. Oleszek. *A Short History of the Development of the House Committee on Rules.* Washington: Congressional Research Service, 1975.

2752. Lewis, Eleanor G. "The House Committee on Rules and the Legislative Program of the Kennedy and Johnson Administrations." *Capitol Studies* 6 (Fall 1978): 27-39.

2753. MacKaye, William R. *A New Coalition Takes Control: The House Rules Committee Fight of 1961.* New York: McGraw-Hill, 1963.

2754. Matsunaga, Spark M. and Chen, Ping. *Rulemakers of the House.* Urbana: University of Illinois Press, 1976.

2755. O'Brien, John. "The 81st Congress and the House Committee on Rules." *American Bar Association Journal* 35 (May 1949): 431-432.

2756. Oppenheimer, Bruce I. "The Rules Committee: New Arm of Leadership in a Decentralized House." In *Congress Reconsidered,* eds. Lawrence C. Dodd and Bruce I. Oppenheimer, pp. 96-116. New York: Praeger, 1977.

2757. Parshall, G. "Czar Cannon." *American History Illustrated* 11 (June 1976): 34-41.

2758. Peabody, Robert L. "The Enlarged Rules Committee." In *New Perspectives on the House of Representatives,* eds. Robert L. Peabody and Nelson W. Polsby, pp. 129-164. Chicago: Rand McNally, 1963.

2759. Price, Hugh D. "Race, Religion and the Rules Committee: The Kennedy Aid-to-Education Bills." In *The Use of Power,* ed. Alan F. Westin, pp. 1-72. New York: Harcourt, Brace, 1962.

2760. Robinson, James A. "Decision Making in the House Rules Committee." *Administrative Science Quarterly* 3 (June 1958): 73-86.

2761. Robinson, James A. *The House Rules Committee.* Indianapolis, Ind.: Bobbs-Merrill, 1963.

2762. Robinson, James A. "Organizational and Constituency Backgrounds of the House Rules Committee." In *The American Political Arena,* ed. Joseph R. Fiszman, pp. 211-218. Boston: Little, Brown, 1962.

2763. Robinson, James A. "Role of the Rules Committee in Arranging the Program of the U.S. House of Representatives." *Western Political Quarterly* 12 (Sept. 1959): 653-669.

2764. Robinson, James A. "The Role of the Rules Committee in Regulating Debate in the U.S. House of Representatives." *Midwest Journal of Political Science* 5 (Feb. 1961): 59-69.

2765. "Rules Committee No Longer Impenetrable Barrier." *Congressional Quarterly Weekly Report* 23 (Nov. 12, 1965): 2323-2325.

2766. Sachs, Nancy. "Who Rules the House?" *Environmental Action,* 11 (Oct. 1975), pp. 4-8.

2767. Siff, Ted and Weil, Alan, eds. *Ruling Congress: A Study on How the House and Senate Rules Govern the Legislative Process.* New York: Grossman, 1975.

2768. Van Hollen, Christopher. "The House Rules Committee (1933–1951): Agent to Party and Agent of Opposition." Ph.D. dissertation, Johns Hopkins University, 1951.

Other Committees

2769. Cadieux, Marcel. "The Senate Special Committee on Science Policy." *External Affairs* 21 (July 1969): 278-283.

2770. Church, Frank and Fong, Hiram L. "U.S. Senate Special Committee on Aging: Victim of Ageism?" *Gerontologist* 16 (Dec. 1976): 489-490.

2771. Elliff, John T. "Congress and the Intelligence Committee." In *Congress Reconsidered,* eds. Lawrence C. Dodd and Bruce I. Oppenheimer, pp. 193-206. New York: Praeger, 1977.

2772. Haak, Harold H. "Congress and the Politics of Personnel." Ph.D. dissertation, Princeton University, 1963.

2773. Harader, William H. "The Committee on Veterans' Affairs: A Study of the Legislative Process and Milieu as They Pertain to Veterans Legislation." Ph.D. dissertation, Johns Hopkins University, 1968.

2774. U.S. Congress. House of Representatives. *Toward the Endless Frontier: History of the Committee on Science and Technology, 1959-79.* Washington: GPO, 1980.

2775. U.S. Congress. Senate. Committee on Aeronautical and Space Sciences. *Committee on Aeronautical and Space Sciences, United States Senate: Tenth Anniversary, 1958-1968.* 90th Cong., 2nd sess. Washington: GPO, 1968.

2776. U.S. Congress. Senate. Select Committee on Indian Affairs. *History, Jurisdiction, and a Summary of Legislative Activities.* 96th Cong., 2nd sess. Washington: GPO, 1980.

2777. Vinyard, Dale. "Congressional Committees on Small Business." Ph.D. dissertation, University of Wisconsin, 1964.

2778. Vinyard, Dale. "Congressional Committees on Small Business." *Midwest Journal of Political Science* 10 (Aug. 1966): 364-377.

2779. Vinyard, Dale. "Congressional Committees on Small Business." *Michigan Business Review* 19 (Jan. 1967): 5-9.

2780. Vinyard, Dale. "Congressional Committees on Small Business: Pattern of Legislative Committee-Executive Agency Relations." *Western Political Quarterly* 21 (Sept. 1968): 391-399.

2781. Vinyard, Dale. "The Senate Committee on the Aging and the Development of a Policy System." *Michigan Academician* 5 (Winter 1973): 281-299.

Conference Committees

2782. "Closed Conferences Often Wield Legislative Power." *Congressional Quarterly Weekly Report* 27 (Dec. 12, 1969): 2573-2576.

2783. Ferejohn, John A. "Who Wins in Conference Committee?" *Journal of Politics* 37 (Nov. 1975): 1033-1046.

2784. Gore, Albert. "The Conference Committee: Congress' Final Filter." *Washington Monthly* 3 (June 1971): 43-48.

2785. McGown, Ada C. *The Congressional Conference Committee.* New York: Columbia University Press, 1927.

2786. Oleszek, Walter J. "House–Senate Relationships: Comity and Conflict." *American Academy of Political and Social Science, Annals* 411 (Jan. 1974): 75-86.

2787. Paletz, David L. "Influence in Congress: An Analysis of the Nature and Effects of Conference Committees on Utilizing Case Studies of Poverty, Traffic Safety, and Congressional Redistricting Legislation." Ph.D. dissertation, University of California at Los Angeles, 1970.

2788. "Reform Penetrates Conference Committees." *Congressional Quarterly Weekly Report* 33 (Feb. 8, 1975): 290-294.

2789. Rogers, Lindsay. "Conference Committee Legislation." *North American Review* 215 (Mar. 1922): 300-307.

2790. Steiner, Gilbert Y. *The Congressional Conference Committee: Seventieth to Eightieth Congresses.* Urbana: University of Illinois Press, 1951.

2791. Strom, Gerald S. and Rundquist, Barry S. "A Revised Theory of Winning in House–Senate Conferences." *American Political Science Review* 71 (June 1977): 448-453.

2792. Vogler, David J. "Patterns of One House Dominance in Congressional Conference Committees." *Midwest Journal of Political Science* 14 (May 1970): 303-320.

2793. Vogler, David J. *The Third House: Conference Committees in the United States Congress.* Evanston, Ill.: Northwestern University Press, 1971.

2794. Zinn, Charles J. "Conference Procedure in Congress." *American Bar Association Journal* 38 (Oct. 1952): 864-866.

Joint Committees

2795. Anderson, Clinton P. and Raney, James T. "Congress and Research: Experience in Atomic Research and Development." *American Academy of Political and Social Science, Annals* 327 (Jan. 1960): 85-94.

2796. Common Cause. *Stacking the Deck: A Case Study of Procedural Abuses by the Joint Committee on Atomic Energy.* Washington: Common Cause, 1976.

2797. Cook, Kenneth F. "Joint Committee on Atomic Energy and Atomic Energy Policy." Ph.D. dissertation, Washington University, 1976.

2798. Green, Harold P. *Government of the Atom: The Integration of Powers.* New York: Atherton Press, 1963.

2799. Green, Harold P. "The Joint Committee on Atomic Energy: A Model for Legislative Reform?" *George Washington Law Review* 32 (June 1964): 932-946.

2800. Jones, Harry W. "The Joint Committee on the Economic Report." *American Bar Association Journal* 35 (April 1949): 343-344.

2801. Killeen, Denis. "Joint Economic Committee: The Politics of Cultivation." Ph.D. dissertation, Columbia University, 1969.

2802. Kirschten, J. Dicken. "Is Doomsday at Hand for the Joint Atomic Energy Committee?" *National Journal* 8 (Nov. 20, 1976): 1658-1665.

2803. Macesich, G. "Joint Economic Committee's Study of Inflation." *Social Research* 29 (Autumn 1962): 357-379.

2804. Manley, John F. "Congressional Staff and Public Policy-Making: The Joint Committee on Internal Revenue Taxation." *Journal of Politics* 30 (Nov. 1968): 1046-1067.

2805. Milne, R. S. "American Council on Economic Advisors and Joint Committee on the Economic Report." *Political Studies* 3 (June 1955): 123-142.

2806. Rosen, Gerald R. "Congress' Controversial Think Tank." *Dun's Review* 99 (Mar. 1972): 51-53, 84-86.

Subcommittees

2807. "Defense Subcommittees: Profiles of Two Key Groups." *Congressional Quarterly Weekly Report* 30 (May 20, 1972): 1140-1144.

2808. Freed, Bruce F. "House Reforms Enhance Subcommittees' Power." *Congressional Quarterly Weekly Report* 33 (Nov. 8, 1975): 2407-2412.

2809. French, Burton L. "Sub-committees of Congress." *American Political Science Review* 9 (Feb. 1915): 68-92.

2810. Goodwin, George. "Subcommittees: The Miniature Legislatures of Congress." *American Political Science Review* 56 (Sept. 1962): 596-604.

2811. Haeberle, Steven H. "The Institutionalization of the Subcommittee in the United States House of Representatives." *Journal of Politics* 40 (Nov. 1978): 1054-1065.

2812. Jones, Charles O. "The Role of the Congressional Subcommittee." *Midwest Journal of Political Science* 6 (Nov. 1962): 327-344.

2813. Ornstein, Norman J. "Causes and Consequences of Congressional Change: Subcommittee Reforms in the House of Representatives, 1970-1973." In *Congress in Change: Evolution and Reform,* ed. Norman J. Ornstein, pp. 88-116. New York: Praeger, 1975.

2814. Rohde, David W. "Committee Reform in the House of Representatives and the Subcommittee Bill of Rights." *American Academy of Political and Social Science, Annals* 411 (Jan. 1974): 39-47.

2815. "Study of Senate Subcommittees Released." *Congressional Quarterly Weekly Report* 34 (April 10, 1976): 837-840.

2816. "Subcommittee Roles, Staff Use Questioned." *Congressional Quarterly Weekly Report* 33 (Mar. 8, 1975): 496-497.

VIII. Legislative Analysis

Decision Making

2817. Bach, Stanley I. "A Game Theoretical Approach to the Legislative Process." *Polity* 4 (Summer 1972): 479-490.

2818. Berman, Daniel M. "The Legislative Process in the U.S. Congress." *Journal of Constitutional and Parliamentary Studies* 2 (April-June 1968): 34-46.

2819. Clausen, Aage R. *How Congressmen Decide: A Policy Focus.* New York: St. Martin's Press, 1973.

2820. Curtis, Thomas B. *Decision Making in the U.S. Congress.* Los Angeles: Institute of Government and Public Affairs, University of California, 1969.

2821. Entin, Kenneth. *Bureaucratic Politics and Congressional Decision-Making: A Case Study.* Providence, R.I.: Brown University, 1977.

2822. Froman, Lewis A. *The Congressional Process: Strategies, Rules and Procedures.* Boston: Little, Brown, 1967.

2823. Galloway, George B. "Congress in Action." *Nebraska Law Review* 28 (May 1949): 493-505.

2824. Galloway, George B. *The Legislative Process in Congress.* New York: Crowell, 1953.

2825. Haines, Lynn. *Law Making in America.* Bethesda, Md.: Lynn Haines, 1912.

2826. Hart, Philip A. "The Future of the Government Process." *American Academy of Political and Social Science, Annals* 408 (July 1973): 94-102.

2827. Kammerer, Gladys M. "The Administration of Congress." *Public Administration Review* 9 (Summer 1949): 175-181.

2828. Kernochan, John M. "Congressional Processes: Critical Points and Individual Pressure." *American Bar Association Journal* 37 (Nov. 1951): 848-849.

2829. Luce, Robert. Legislative Principles: The History and Theory of Law-Making by Representative Government. Boston: Houghton Mifflin, 1930.

2830. Luce, Robert. *Legislative Procedure: Parliamentary Practices and the Curse of Business in the Framing of Statutes.* Boston: Houghton Mifflin, 1922.

2831. Mitchell, Joyce C. "Congress and National Security: An Exploration of Legislative Decision-Making." Ph.D. dissertation, University of California, 1964.

2832. Moe, Ronald C. and Teel, Steven C. "Congress as Policy-Maker: A Necessary Reappraisal." *Political Science Quarterly* 85 (Sept. 1970): 443-470.

2833. Mollan, Robert W. "Congressional Policy-Making During the Eisenhower Administration Regarding Internal Security: A Description and Evaluation." Ph.D. dissertation, University of Minnesota, 1967.

2834. Mosher, Charles A. "Needs and Trends in Congressional Decision-Making." *Science* 178, 13 Oct. 1972, pp. 134-138.

2835. Nutting, Charles B. "Congress at Work." *American Bar Association Journal* 39 (April 1953): 326-327.

2836. Oleszek, Walter J. *Congressional Procedures and the Policy Process.* Washington: Congressional Quarterly, 1978.

2837. Patterson, Samuel C. "The Semi-Sovereign Congress." In *The New American Political System,* ed. Anthony King, pp. 125-177. Washington: American Enterprise Institute for Public Policy Research, 1978.

2838. Robinson, James A. "Decision Making in Congress." In *Twelve Studies of the Organization of Congress,* ed. Alfred de Grazia, pp. 259-294. Washington: American Enterprise Institute for Public Policy Research, 1966.

2839. Rogers, Lindsay. "Notes on Congressional Procedure." *American Political Science Review* 15 (Feb. 1921): 71-81.

2840. Silverman, Corinne. "The Legislators' View of the Legislative Process." *Public Opinion Quarterly* 18 (Summer 1954): 180-190.

2841. Stimson, James A. "Five Propositions About Congressional Decision-Making." *Political Methodology* 2 (Aug. 1975): 415-436.

2842. Ulmer, S. Sidney, ed. *Political Decision-Making.* New York: Van Nostrand Reinhold, 1970.

2843. Walker, Harvey. *The Legislative Process: Law Making in the United States.* New York: Ronald Press, 1948.

2844. Washington Monitor. *A Reference Manual to Accompany Understanding Congress: A Seminar on the Legislative Process.* Washington: Washington Monitor, 1978.

2845. Zinn, Charles J. *American Congressional Procedure.* St. Paul, Minn.: West Publishing Co., 1957.

Legislative Behavior

2846. Asher, Herbert B. "Learning of Legislative Norms." *American Political Science Review* 67 (June 1973): 499-513.

2847. Bartlett, Robert V. "The Marginality Hypothesis: Electoral Insecurity, Self-Interest, and Voting Behavior." *American Politics Quarterly* 7 (Oct. 1979): 498-508.

2848. Belknap, George. "A Method for Analyzing Legislative Behavior." *Midwest Journal of Political Science* 2 (Nov. 1958): 377-402.

2849. Bezold, Clement. *Voting on the House Floor: Information Seeking and Congressional Decision-Making.* Center for Governmental Responsibility, University of Florida, 1974.

2850. Born, Richard J. "Cue-Taking Within State Party Delegations in the U.S. House of Representatives." *Journal of Politics* 38 (Feb. 1976): 71-94.

2851. Clausen, Aage R. "State Party Influence on Congressional Policy Decision." *Midwest Journal of Politics* 16 (Feb. 1972): 77-102.

2852. Clausen, Aage R. and Van Horn, Carl E. "Congressional Response to a Decade of Change: 1963-1972." *Journal of Politics* 39 (Aug. 1977): 624-666.

2853. Cnudde, Charles F. and McCrone, Donald J. "The Linkage Between Constituency Attitudes and Congressional Voting Behavior: A Causal Model." *American Political Science Review* 60 (Mar. 1966): 66-72.

2854. Currie, Hector. "Motive or Purpose and Acts of Congress." *Mississippi Law Journal* 44 (Sept. 1973): 619-636.

2855. Erikson, Robert S. "Constituency Opinion and Congressional Behavior: A Reexamination of the Miller-Stokes Representation Data." *American Journal of Political Science* 22 (Aug. 1978): 511-535.

2856. Ferejohn, John A. and Fiorina, Morris P. "Optimizing Models of Public Decision Making: Purposive Models of Legislative Behavior." *American Economic Review* 65 (May 1975): 407-414.

2857. Fiellin, Alan. "Recruitment and Legislative Role Conception: A Conceptual Scheme and a Case Study." *Western Political Quarterly* 20 (June 1967): 271-287.

2858. Froman, Lewis A. "Inter-Party Constituency Differences and Congressional Voting Behavior." *American Political Science Review* 57 (Mar. 1963): 57-61.

2859. Frost, Murray. "Senatorial Ambition and Legislative Behavior." Ph.D. dissertation, Michigan State University, 1972.

2860. Gilbert, Charles E. *Problems of a Senator: A Study of Legislative Behavior.* Evanston, Ill.: Gilbert, 1956.

2861. Grant, Lawrence V. "Specialization as a Strategy in Legislative Decision-Making." *American Journal of Political Science* 17 (Feb. 1973): 123-147.

2862. Gross, Donald A. "Representative Styles and Legislative Behavior." *Western Political Quarterly* 31 (Sept. 1978): 359-371.

2863. Herbert, F. Ted and McLemore, Lelan E. "Character and Structure of Legislative Norms: Operationalizing the Norm Concept in the Legislative Setting." *American Journal of Political Science* 17 (Aug. 1973): 506-527.

2864. Hinckley, Barbara. "'Stylized' Opposition in the U.S. House of Representatives: The Effects of Coalition Behavior." *Legislative Studies Quarterly* 2 (Feb. 1977): 5-28.

2865. Huitt, Ralph K. "The Outsider in the Senate: An Alternative Role." *American Political Science Review* 55 (Sept. 1961): 566-575.

2866. Hurley, Patricia A. "Assessing the Potential for Significant Legislative Output in the House of Representatives." *Western Political Quarterly* 32 (Mar. 1979): 45-58.

2867. Hurley, Patricia A. "The Electoral Basis of Congressional Performance." Ph.D. dissertation, Rice University, 1976.

2868. Hurley, Patricia A., Brady, David W., and Cooper, Joseph. "Measuring Legislative Potential for Policy Change." *Legislative Studies Quarterly* 2 (Nov. 1977): 385-398.

2869. Johnston, Robert E. "Constituency Characteristics and Congressional Voting Behavior on Aid-for-Education Legislation." Ph.D. dissertation, University of California at Berkeley, 1971.

2870. Karns, David A. "Congressional Transnational Activity and Legislative Behavior." Ph.D. dissertation, University of Michigan, 1973.

2871. Kirkpatrick, Samuel A. and Pettit, Lawrence K. *Legislative Role Structures, Power Bases, and Behavior Patterns: An Empirical Examination of the U.S. Senate.* Norman: Bureau of Government Research, University of Oklahoma, 1973.

2872. Kovenock, David M. "Influence in the U.S. House of Representatives: A Statistical Analysis of Communications." *American Politics Quarterly* 1 (Oct. 1973): 407-464.

2783. Landis, Mark L. "Personality and Style in the United States Congress." Ph.D. dissertation, Columbia University, 1973.

2874. Lehnen, Robert G. *Floor Behavior and the Legislative Process: The Case of the United States Senate.* Iowa City: Laboratory for Political Research, University of Iowa, 1967.

2875. McCrone, Donald J. and Kuklinski, James H. "The Delegate Theory of Representation." *American Journal of Political Science* 23 (May 1979): 278-300.

2876. March, James G. "Party Legislative Representation as a Function of Election Results." *Public Opinion Quarterly* 21 (Winter 1957-1958): 521-542.

2877. Matthews, Donald R. "The Folkways of the United States Senate: Conformity to Group Norms and Legislative Effectiveness." *American Political Science Review* 53 (Dec. 1959): 1064-1089.

2878. Matthews, Donald R. and Stimson, James A. "Cue-Taking by Congressmen: A Model and Computer Simulation." In *The History of Parliamentary History,* ed. William O. Aydellotte, pp. 247-273. Princeton, N.J.: Princeton University Press, 1977.

2879. Meller, Norman. "Legislative Behavior Research." *Western Political Quarterly* 13 (Mar. 1960): 131-153.

2880. Meller, Norman. " 'Legislative Behavior Research' Revisited: A Review of Five Years' Publications." *Western Political Quarterly* 18 (Dec. 1965): 776-793.

2881. Olson, David M. "District Party Organization and Legislative Performance in Congress." *Journal of Politics* 36 (May 1974): 483-486.

2882. Olson, David M. "U.S. Congressmen and Their Diverse Congressional District Parties." *Legislative Studies Quarterly* 3 (May 1978): 239-264.

2883. Olson, David M. and Nonidez, Cynthia T. "Measures of Legislative Performance in the U.S. House of Representatives." *American Journal of Political Science* 16 (May 1972): 269-277.

2884. Patterson, Samuel C. *American Legislative Behavior: A Reader.* Princeton, N.J.: Van Nostrand, 1968.

2885. Patterson, Samuel C. "Inter-Generational Occupational Mobility and Legislative Voting." *Social Forces* 43 (Oct. 1964): 90-92.

2886. Patterson, Samuel C. *Toward a Theory of Legislative Behavior.* Stillwater: Oklahoma State University, 1967.

2887. Peterson, David J. "Longitudinal Analysis of Senate Behavior: A Methodological Inquiry." Ph.D. dissertation, Michigan State University, 1970.

2888. Polsby, Nelson W., ed. *Congressional Behavior.* New York: Random House, 1971.

2889. Price, Hugh D. "Congress and the Evolution of Legislative 'Professionalism.' " In *Congress in Change: Evolution and Reform,* ed. Norman J. Ornstein, pp. 2-23. New York: Praeger, 1975.

2890. Rice, Stuart A. "The Behavior of Legislative Groups: A Method of Measurement." *Political Science Quarterly* 40 (Mar. 1925): 60-72.

2891. Rosenau, James N. "Private Preferences and Political Responsibilities: The Relative Potency of Individual and Role Variables in the Behavior of U.S. Senators." In *Quantitative International Politics: Insights and Evidence,* ed. Joel D. Singer, pp. 17-50. New York: Free Press, 1968.

2892. Schwarz, John E. and Fenmore, Barton. "Presidential Election Results and Congressional Roll Call Behavior: The Cases of 1964, 1968, and 1972." *Legislative Studies Quarterly* 2 (Nov. 1977): 409-422.

2893. Shields, Johanna N. "The Making of American Congressional Mavericks: A Contrasting of the Cultural Attitudes of Mavericks and Conformists in the United States House of Representatives, 1836-1860." Ph.D. dissertation, University of Alabama, 1973.

2894. Silberman, Jonathan I. and Durden, Garey C. "Determining Legislative Preferences on the Minimum Wage: An Economic Approach." *Journal of Political Economy* 84 (April 1976): 317-329.

2895. Stimson, James A. "The Diffusion of Evaluations: Patterns of Cue-Taking in the United States House of Representatives.' Ph.D. dissertation, University of North Carolina at Chapel Hill, 1970.

2896. Sullivan, John L. and Uslaner, Eric M. "Congressional Behavior and Electoral Marginality." *American Journal of Political Science* 22 (Aug. 1978): 536-553.

2897. Uslaner, Eric M. "Policy Entrepreneurs and Amateur Democrats in the House of Representatives: Toward a More Party-Oriented Congress." In *Legislative Reform: The Policy Impact,* ed. Leroy N. Rieselbach, pp. 105-116. Lexington, Mass.: Lexington Books, 1978.

2898. Wahlke, John C. and Eulau, Heinz. *Legislative Behavior: A Reader in Theory and Research.* New York: Free Press, 1959.

2899. Yarwood, Dean L. "Norm Observance and Legislative Integration: The U.S. Senate in 1850 and 1860." *Social Science Quarterly* 51 (June 1970): 57-69.

2900. Zemsky, Robert M. "American Legislative Behavior." *American Behavioral Scientist* 16 (May 1973): 675-694.

Policy Analysis

2901. Bach, Stanley I. "Policy Making in the House of Representatives: The Prospects for a More Integrative and Comprehensive Approach." In *Forging America's Future: Strategies for National Growth and Development,* appendix, vol. II. Washington: National Commission on Supplies and Shortages, 1976.

2902. Beckman, Norman. "Policy Analysis for Congress." *Public Administration Review* 37 (May-June 1977): 237-244.

2903. Borchardt, Kurt. "Congressional Use of Administrative Organization and Procedure for Policy-Making Purposes: Six Case Studies and Some Conclusions." *George Washington Law Review* 30 (Mar. 1962): 429-466.

2904. Carroll, James D. "Policy Analysis for Congress: A Review of the Congressional Research Service." In *Congressional Support Agencies: A Compilation of Papers Prepared for the Commission on the Operation of the Senate,* pp. 4-30. Washington: GPO, 1976.

2905. Carron, Andrew S. "Congress and Energy: A Need for Policy Analysis and More." *Policy Analysis* 2 (Spring 1976): 283-297.

2906. Chartrand, Robert L. "The Quest for Certainty: PPBS and the Congress." In *Planning - Programming - Budgeting Systems,* pp. 4-12. Chicago: American Society of Planning Officials, 1969.

2907. Coleman, James S. "Policy Research in the Social Sciences." In *Policy Analysis on Major Issues: A Compilation of Papers Prepared for the Commission on the Operation of the Senate,* 94th Cong., 2nd sess., pp. 25-58. Washington: GPO, 1977.

2908. Daddario, Emilio Q. "Congress and the Social Sciences." *American Journal of Orthopsychiatry* 40 (Jan. 1970): 14-21.

2909. Davidson, Roger H. "Congressional Committees: The Toughest Customers." *Policy Analysis* 2 (Spring 1976): 299-323.

2910. Davis, Ross P. "Federal Programs and Urban Policies in Metropolitan America." In *Policy Analysis on Major Issues: A Compilation of Papers Prepared for the Commission on the Operation of the Senate,* 94th Cong., 2nd sess., pp. 99-113. Washington: GPO, 1977.

2911. Dienstfrey, Harry. "Fabianism in Washington." *Commentary* 30 (July 1960): 22-28.

2912. Dine, Thomas A. "Military R & D: Congress' Next Area of Policy Penetration." *Bulletin of the Atomic Scientists* 34 (Feb. 1978): 32-37.

2913. Dreyfus, Daniel A. "The Limitations of Policy Research in Congressional Decision-Making." *Policy Studies Journal* 4 (Spring 1976): 269-274.

2914. "Energy, Environment, and Economics: A Seminar Conducted by the Congressional Research Service." In *Policy Analysis on Major Issues: A Compilation of papers prepared for the Commission on the Operation of the Senate,* 94th Cong., 2nd sess., pp. 114-133. Washington: GPO, 1977.

2915. "Examples of Policy Integration in the U.S. Senate from the Income Security Field: A Seminar Conducted by the Congressional Research Service." In *Committees and Senate Procedures: A Compilation of Papers Prepared for the Commission on the Operation of the Senate,* 94th Cong., 2nd sess., pp. 94-99. Washington: GPO, 1977.

2916. Foskett, William H. "Practical Application of Evaluation in Legislative Processes." In *Legislative Oversight and Program Evaluation: A Seminar Sponsored by the Congressional Research Science,* 94th Cong., 2nd Sess., pp. 288-302. Washington: GPO, 1976.

2917. Foskett, William H. and Fox, Harrison W. "Program Evaluation: A Manual for Legislators and Legislative Staffs." In *Legislative Oversight and Program Evaluation: A Seminar Sponsored by the Congressional Research Service,* 94th Cong., 2nd sess., pp. 464-498. Washington: GPO, 1976.

2918. Frye, Alton. "Congressional Politics and Policy Analysis: Bridging the Gap." *Policy Analysis* 2 (Spring 1976): 265-281.

2919. Giltmier, James W. "Policy Formation Through Program Evaluation and Systems Analysis: A Congressional View." In *Legislative Oversight and Program Evaluation: A Seminar Sponsored by the Congressional Research Service,* 94th Cong., 2nd sess., pp. 224-244. Washington: GPO, 1976.

2920. Haveman, Robert H. "Policy Analysis and the Congress: An Economist's View." *Policy Analysis* 2 (Spring 1976): 235-250.

2921. Hayes, Frederick. "The Uses for Policy Analysis in the United States Senate." In *Policymaking Role of Leadership in the Senate: A Compilation of Papers,* pp. 58-71. Washington: GPO, 1976.

2922. Hedlund, Ronald D. and Hamm, Keith E. "Institutional Innovation and Performance Effectiveness in Public Policy Making." In *Legislative Reform: The Policy Impact,* ed. Leroy N. Rieselbach, pp. 117-132. Lexington, Mass.: Lexington Books, 1978.

2923. Johannes, John R. *Policy Innovation in Congress.* Morristown, N.J.: General Learning Press, 1972.

2924. Jones, Charles O. "The Senate Minority and Policy Analysis." In *Policymaking Role of Leadership in the Senate: A Compilation of Papers,* pp. 34-39. Washington: GPO, 1976.

2925. Jones, Charles O. "Why Congress Can't Do Policy Analysis (or Words to That Effect)." *Policy Analysis* 2 (Spring 1976): 251-264.

2926. Jones, E. Terrence. "Congressmen and Social Scientists: The Communication Gap." *Midwest Quarterly* 9 (Jan. 1968): 185-194.

2927. Knezo, Genevieve. "Program Evaluation Concepts." In *Legislative Oversight and Program Evaluation: Seminar Sponsored by the Congressional Research Service,* 94th Cong., 2nd sess., pp. 55-62. Washington: GPO, 1976.

2928. Knezo, Genevieve. *Program Evaluation: Emerging Issues of Possible Legislative Concern to the Conduct and Use of Evaluation in the Congress and the Executive Branch.* Washington: Congressional Research Service, 1974.

2929. Kornbluh, Marvin, Little, Dennis L., and Renfro, William L. "The Tools of Futures Research: Some Questions and Answers." In *Techniques and Procedures for Analysis and Evaluation: A Compilation of Papers Prepared for the Commission on the Operation of the Senate,* 94th Cong., 2nd sess., pp. 14-20. Washington: GPO, 1977.

2930. Long, Richard W. "Applying Computers to Analyze Decision Intelligence Information." In *Techniques and Procedures for Analysis and Evaluation: A Compilation of Papers Prepared for the Commission on the Operation of Senate,* 94th Cong., 2nd sess., pp. 121-128. Washington: GPO, 1977.

2931. Lyden, Fremont J. "Congressional Decision Making and PPB." *Public Administration Review* 30 (Mar.-April 1970): 167-168.

2932. Lynn, Laurence E. "Policy Relevant Social Research: What Does It Look Like?" In *Policy Analysis on Major Issues: A Compilation of Papers Prepared for the Commission on the Operation of the Senate,* 94th Cong., 2nd sess., pp. 59-71. Washington: GPO, 1977.

2933. MacKenzie, G. Calvin. "Committee Coordination and Policy Integration in the Senate." In *Committees and Senate Procedures: A Compilation of Papers Prepared for the Commission on the Operation of the Senate,* 94th Cong., 2nd sess., pp. 74-93. Washington: GPO, 1977.

2934. Morrison, Peter A. *How Demographers Can Help Members of Congress.* Santa Monica, Calif.: Rand, 1978.

2935. Murphy, Thomas P. "Congress, PPBS, and Reality." *Polity* 1 (Summer 1969): 460-478.

2936. Nichols, Rodney W. "R and D Outlook: Selected Issues on National Policies for Science and Technology." In *Policy Analysis on Major Issues: A Compilation of Papers Prepared for the Commission on the Operation of the Senate,* 94th Cong., 2nd sess., pp. 72-98. Washington: GPO, 1977.

2937. Oppenheimer, Bruce I. "Capacities for Integrative Policy Analysis in the House of Representatives: Problems and Prescriptions." In *Forging America's Future: Strategies for National Growth and Development,* Appendix, Vol. II. Washington: National Commission on Supplies and Shortages, 1976.

2938. *Policy Analysis on Major Issues: A Compilation of Papers Prepared for the Commission on the Operation of the Senate,* 94th Cong., 2nd sess. Washington: GPO, 1977.

2939. Polsby, Nelson W. "Policy Analysis and Congress." *Public Policy* 18 (Fall 1969): 61-74.

2940. Polsby, Nelson W. "Strengthening Congress in National Policy-Making." *Yale Review* 59 (June 1970): 481-497.

2941. Renfro, William L. "Foresight in the Senate." In *Techniques and Procedures for Analysis and Evaluation: A Compilation of Papers Prepared for the Commission on the Operation of Senate,* 94th Cong., 2nd sess., pp. 47-52. Washington: GPO, 1977.

2942. Royce, Richard. "Considerations of Policy Analysis and Formulation in the Senate." In *Policymaking Role of Leadership in the Senate: A Compilation of Papers,* pp. 86-95. Washington: GPO, 1976.

2943. Schick, Allen. "Complex Policymaking in the United States Senate." In *Policy Analysis on Major Issues: A Compilation of Papers Prepared for the Commission on the Operation of the Senate,* 94th Cong., 2nd sess., pp. 4-24. Washington: GPO, 1977.

2944. Schick, Allen. "Evaluating Evaluation: A Congressional Perspective." In *Legislative Oversight and Program Evaluation: A Seminar Sponsored by the Congressional Research Service,* 94th Cong. 2nd sess., pp. 341-353. Washington: GPO, 1976.

2945. Stassen, Glen H. "Individual Preference Versus Role-Constraint in Policy-Making: Senatorial Response to Secretaries Acheson and Dulles." *World Politics* 25 (Oct. 1972): 96-119.

2946. Susman, Ralph M. "Drug Abuse, Congress and the Fact-Finding Process." *American Academy of Political and Social Science, Annals* 417 (Jan. 1975): 16-26.

2947. *Techniques and Procedures for Analysis and Evaluation: A Compilation of Papers Prepared for the Commission on the Operation of Senate,* 94th Cong., 2nd sess. Washington: GPO, 1977.

2948. Thurber, James A. "Policy Analysis on Capitol Hill: Issues Facing the Four Analytic Support Agencies of Congress." *Policy Studies Journal* 6 (Autumn 1977): 101-111.

2949. U.S. Congress. Senate. Committee on Government Operations. *Legislative Oversight and Program Evaluation: Seminar Sponsored by the Congressional Research Service,* 94th Cong., 2nd sess. Washington: GPO, 1976.

2950. Wolanin, Thomas R. "Congress, Information, and Policy Making for Postsecondary Education: Don't Trouble Me with the Facts." *Policy Studies Journal* 4 (Summer 1976): 382-394.

Voting Studies

General Studies

2951. Achen, Christopher H. "Measuring Representation." *American Journal of Political Science* 22 (Aug. 1978): 475-510.

2952. Achen, Christopher H. "Measuring Representation: Perils of the Correlation Coefficient." *American Journal of Political Science* 21 (Nov. 1977): 805-815.

2953. "Analysis of the 'Conservative Coalition'." *Congressional Quarterly Weekly Report* 17 (Feb. 13, 1959): 271-276.

2954. "Analysis of Positions in Liberal-Conservative Split." *Congressional Quarterly Weekly Report* 16 (Dec. 26, 1958): 1547-1548.

2955. Anderson, Lee F., Watts, Meredith W., and Wilcox, Allen R. *Legislative Roll-Call Analysis.* Evanston, Ill.: Northwestern University Press, 1966.

2956. Bach, Stanley I. *Pairing in Congressional Voting: Current Practices and Historical Development.* Washington: Congressional Research Service, 1978.

2957. "Basic Democratic Division Examined." *Congressional Quarterly Weekly Report* 16 (Dec. 12, 1958): 1515-1520.

2958. Beyle, Herman C. *Identification and Analysis of Attribute-Cluster Blocs.* Chicago: University of Chicago Press, 1931.

2959. Bookman, John T. "A Note on the Explanation of Congressional Role Call Voting Behavior." *Rocky Mountain Social Science Journal* 9 (Jan. 1972): 101-104.

2960. Born, Richard J. and Nevison, Christopher. "A Probabilistic Analysis of Roll Call Cohesion Measures." *Political Methodology* 2 (1975): 131-149.

2961. Casstevens, Thomas W. "Linear Algebra and Legislative Voting Behavior: Rice's Indices." *Journal of Politics* 32 (Nov. 1970): 769-783.

2962. Castel, Albert E. and Gibson, Scott L. *The Yeas and Nays: Key Congressional Decisions, 1774-1945.* Kalamazoo, Mich.: New Issues Press, 1975.

2963. Clausen, Aage R. "Measurement Identity in the Longitudinal Analysis of Legislative Voting." *American Political Science Review* 61 (Dec. 1967): 1020-1035.

2964. Cohen, Jozef Bertram. "Note on Carlson and Harrell's 'Factor Analysis of Voting Among Congressmen.'" *Journal of Social Psychology* 20 (Nov. 1944): 313-314.

2965. Colburn, Kenneth S. *Congressional Votes on Important Issues for Blacks.* Washington: Joint Center for Political Studies, 1974.

2966. "Democrats to Study Changes in Recorded Teller Voting." *Congressional Quarterly Weekly Report* 30 (Jan. 22, 1972): 151-153.

2967. "Disagreeing Senators." *Congressional Quarterly Weekly Report* 12 (Sept. 17, 1954): 1169-1172.

2968. "Disagreeing Senators." *Congressional Quarterly Weekly Report* 13 (Oct. 7, 1955): 1103-1104.

2969. Enelow, James M. "Noncooperative Counter-Threats to Vote Trading." *American Journal of Political Science* 23 (Feb. 1979): 121-138.

2970. Enelow, James M. and Koehler, David H. "Vote Trading in a Legislative Context: An Analysis of Cooperative and Noncooperative Strategic Voting." *Public Choice* 34 (1979): 157-175.

2971. "Extent of North–South Democratic Split Analyzed." *Congressional Quarterly Weekly Report* 22 (April 24, 1964): 777-781.

2972. "Extent of North–South Democratic Split Analyzed." *Congressional Quarterly Weekly Report* 17 (Nov. 20, 1959): 1491-1496.

2973. "Extent of North–South Democratic Split Analyzed." *Congressional Quarterly Weekly Report* 19 (Nov. 3, 1961): 1806-1810.

2974. "Extent of North–South Democratic Split Analyzed." *Congressional Quarterly Weekly Report* 18 (Dec. 2, 1960): 1929-1933.

2975. "Extent of North–South Democratic Split Analyzed." *Congressional Quarterly Weekly Report* 20 (Nov. 30, 1962): 2213-2217.

2976. Fenton, John H. "Liberal–Conservative Divisions by Sections of the United States." *American Academy of Political and Social Science, Annals* 344 (Nov. 1962): 122-127.

2977. Fiorina, Morris P. "Majority Rule Models and Legislative Elections." *Journal of Politics* 41 (Nov. 1979): 1081-1104.

2978. Green, Justin J., Schmidhauser, John R., Berg, Larry L., and Brady, David W. "Lawyers in Congress: A New Look at Some Old Assumptions." *Western Political Quarterly* 26 (Sept. 1973): 440-452.

2979. Greenstein, Fred I. and Jackson, Alton F. "A Second Look at the Validity of Roll Call Analysis." *Midwest Journal of Political Science* 7 (May 1963): 156-166.

2980. Hall, Durward G. "Electric Voting in the House." In *We Propose: A Modern Congress,* ed. Mary McInnis, pp. 217-221. New York: McGraw-Hill, 1966.

2981. Hardin, Russell. "Hollow Victory: The Minimum Winning Coalition." *American Political Science Review* 70 (Dec. 1976): 1202-1214.

2982. Hayes, Samuel P. "A Note on MacDonald's Brain Weight and Legislative Ability in Congress." *Journal of Social Psychology* 8 (May 1937): 269-282.

2983. Henderson, H. James. "Quantitative Approaches to Party Formation in the United States Congress: A Comment." *William and Mary Quarterly* 30 (April 1973): 307-324.

2984. Historical Records Survey. *A Description of the Atlas of Congress Roll Calls: An Analysis of Yea-Nay Votes.* Newark, N.J.: Historical Records Survey, 1941.

2985. Hoar, William P. "How They Vote: Our Congressional Scoreboard." *American Opinion* 19 (July 1976): 53-66.

2986. "House Group Seeks More Roll Calls to Record Votes." *Congressional Quarterly Weekly Report* 28 (June 26, 1970): 1650-1652.

2987. "House Voting: The Roll Call Goes Electronic." *Congressional Quarterly Weekly Report* 30 (Dec. 16, 1972): 3155-3156.

2988. "How Big Is the North–South Democratic Split." *Congressional Quarterly Weekly Report* 15 (Nov. 1, 1957): 1217-1221.

2989. Kau, James B. and Rubin, Paul H. "Self-Interest, Ideology, and Logrolling in Congressional Voting." *Journal of Law and Economics* 22 (Oct. 1979): 365-384.

2990. Kingdon, John W. *Congressmen's Voting Decisions.* New York: Harper and Row, 1973.

2991. Kingdon, John W. "Models of Legislative Voting." *Journal of Politics* 39 (Aug. 1977): 563-595.

2992. Kuklinski, James H. and McCrone, Donald J. "Policy Salience and the Causal Structure of Representation." *American Politics Quarterly* 8 (April 1980): 139-164.

2993. McMurray, Carl D. and Hagan, Charles B. "A Rank Order Comparison of Scale Patterns Produced by Factor-Scale and Guttman Scale Procedures in a Roll-Call Analysis." *Research Reports in Social Science* (Florida State University) 7 (Aug. 1964): 1-13.

2994. MacRae, Duncan. "Cluster Analysis of Congressional Votes with the BCTRY System." *Western Political Quarterly* 19 (Dec. 1966): 631-638.

2995. MacRae, Duncan. "Roll Call Votes and Leadership." *Public Opinion Quarterly* 20 (Fall 1956): 543-558.

2996. MacRae, Duncan. "Some Underlying Variables in Legislative Roll Call Votes." *Public Opinion Quarterly* 18 (Summer 1954): 191-196.

2997. MacRae, Duncan and Schwarz, Susan B. "Identifying Congressional Issues by Multidimensional Models." *Midwest Journal of Political Science* 12 (May 1968): 181-201.

2998. Malbin, Michael J. "Times Change, But Congressmen Still Vote the Way They Used To." *National Journal* 8 (Mar. 20, 1976): 370-374.

2999. Ornstein, Norman J. "What Makes Congress Run?" *Washington Monthly* 5 (Dec. 1973): 47-49.

3000. Panning, William H. "Probabilistic Politics: A Model of Congressional Vote Trading." Ph.D. dissertation. University of Pennsylvania, 1974.

3001. Rice, Stuart A. *Quantitative Methods in Politics.* New York: Alfred A. Knopf, 1928.

3002. Riker, William H. "Paradox of Voting and Congressional Rules for Voting on Amendments." *American Political Science Review* 52 (June 1958): 349-366.

3003. "Same-State Senators Disagreed Fourth of the Time." *Congressional Quarterly Weekly Report* 20 (Dec. 28, 1962): 2296-2297.

3004. "Same-State Senators Disagreed on 25 Percent of Votes." *Congressional Quarterly Weekly Report* 23 (Dec. 10, 1965): 2447-2448.

3005. "Same-State Senators Disagreed on 26% of Roll Calls." *Congressional Quarterly Weekly Report* 19 (Dec. 22, 1961): 1964-1965.

3006. "Same-State Senators Disagreed 22% of the Time." *Congressional Quarterly Weekly Report* 23 (Feb. 12, 1965): 247-248.

3007. "Senate Delegations Voted Alike 77% of the Time in 1959." *Congressional Quarterly Weekly Report* 17 (Oct. 30, 1959): 1435-1437.

3008. Senate Republican Policy Committee. *U.S. Senate Record Votes: The Twenty-One Year Trend, 1952-1972: Republican Report.* Washington: GPO, 1973.

3009. Stimson, James A. "Teller Voting in the House of Representatives: The Conservative Screening Hypothesis." *Polity* 8 (Winter 1976): 317-325.

3010. "Turning Screws: Winning Votes in Congress." *Congressional Quarterly Weekly Report* 34 (April 24, 1976): 947-954.

3011. U.S. Congress. House. Committee on House Administration. *The Electronic Voting System for the United States House of Representatives.* Washington: GPO, 1979.

3012. "Voting Records." *Congressional Quarterly Weekly Report* 13 (Sept. 9, 1955): 1039-1042.

3013. Warwick, Paul. "A Re-Evaluation of Alternative Methodologies in Legislative Voting Analysis." *Social Science Research* 4 (Sept. 1975): 241-267.

3014. Weisberg, Herbert F. "Evaluating Theories of Congressional Roll-Call Voting." *American Journal of Political Science* 22 (Aug. 1978): 554-577.

3015. Weisberg, Herbert F. "Scaling Models for Legislative Roll Call Analysis." *American Political Science Review* 66 (Dec. 1972): 1306-1315.

3016. Wheeler, Tim. "The 95th Congress: A Record of Betrayal." *Political Affairs* 57 (Dec. 1978): 18-23.

Party Voting

3017. Anderson, Lee F. "The Volume and Stability of Intraparty Consensus in the House of Representatives During Four Recent Congresses." Ph.D. dissertation, University of Illinois at Urbana-Champaign, 1961.

3018. Baker, Jean H. "A Loyal Opposition: Northern Democrats in the Thirty-Seventh Congress." *Civil War History* 25 (June 1979): 139-155.

3019. Bell, Rudolph M. *Party and Faction in American Politics: The House of Representatives, 1789-1801.* Westport, Conn.: Greenwood Press, 1974.

3020. "Bipartisan Congress Group Seeks to Influence Policy." *Congressional Quarterly Weekly Report* 28 (July 31, 1970): 1952-1956.

3021. "Bipartisan Foreign Policy." *Congressional Quarterly Weekly Report* 12 (Oct. 29, 1954): 1307-1315.

3022. "Bipartisanship Shared by Both Parties." *Congressional Quarterly Weekly Report* 16 (Nov. 28, 1958): 1485-1488.

3023. "Bipartisan Voting Declined in 1977." *Congressional Quarterly Weekly Report* 36 (Jan. 14, 1978): 84-88.

3024. "Bipartisan Voting Increased During 1976." *Congressional Quarterly Weekly Report* 34 (Nov. 13, 1976): 3178-3182.

3025. "Bipartisan Voting: 1974 Percentage Climbs to 63." *Congressional Quarterly Weekly Report* 33(Jan.25, 1975): 204-208.

3026. "Bipartisan Voting: Percentage Drops to 59 from 67." *Congressional Quarterly Weekly Report* 32 (Feb. 2, 1974): 204-208.

3027. "Bipartisan Voting Sets Record in 1970 Session." *Congressional Quarterly Weekly Report* 29 (Jan. 29, 1971): 248-252.

3028. "Bipartisan Voting: Sharp Drop in 1971 Session." *Congressional Quarterly Weekly Report* 30 (Jan. 15, 1972): 92-96.

3029. "Bipartisan Voting Showed Decline in 1975." *Congressional Quarterly Weekly Report* 34 (Jan. 24, 1976): 184-188.

3030. "Bipartisan Voting Slips in 1970 Session of Congress." *Congressional Quarterly Weekly Report* 29 (Jan. 29, 1971): 237-241.

3031. "Bipartisanship." *Congressional Quarterly Weekly Report* 13 (July 29, 1955): 897-900.

3032. "Bipartisanship Again Appeared on 54% of Roll Calls." *Congressional Quarterly Weekly Report* 24 (Dec. 16, 1966): 3019-3023.

3033. "Bipartisanship Appeared on 65 Percent of Roll Calls." *Congressional Quarterly Weekly Report* 25 (Dec. 29, 1967): 2643-2647.

3034. "Bipartisanship Appeared on 67 Percent of Roll Calls." *Congressional Quarterly Weekly Report* 26 (Oct. 25, 1968): 2938-2942.

3035. "Bipartisan Voting Up Slightly in 1978." *Congressional Quarterly Weekly Report* 36 (Dec. 23, 1978): 3483-3487.

3036. Brady, David W. "Congressional Leadership and Party Voting in the McKinley Era: A Comparison to the Modern House." *American Journal of Political Sciences* 16 (Aug. 1972): 439-459.

3037. Brady, David W. *Congressional Voting in a Partisan Era: A Study of the McKinley Houses and a Comparison to the Modern House of Representatives.* Lawrence: University of Kansas Press, 1973.

3038. Brady, David W. "A Research Note on the Impact of Interparty Competition on Congressional Voting in a Competitive Era." *American Political Science Review* 67 (Mar. 1973): 153-156.

3039. Brady, David W. and Althoff, Phillip. "Party Voting in the U.S. House of Representatives, 1890-1910: Elements of a Responsible Party System." *Journal of Politics* 36 (Aug. 1974): 753-775.

3040. Brady David W., Cooper, Joseph, and Hurley, Patricia A. "The Decline of Party in the U.S. House of Representatives, 1887-1968." *Legislative Studies Quarterly* 4 (Aug. 1979): 381-407.

3041. "Caucus Votes: Freshmen United, South Split." *Congressional Quarterly Weekly Report* 33 (April 5, 1975): 693-694.

3042. Clubb, Jerome M. and Traugott, Santa A. "Partisan Cleavage and Cohesion in the House of Representatives, 1861-1974." *Journal of Interdisciplinary History* 7 (Winter 1977): 375-401.

3043. " 'Conservative Coalition' Appeared in 22% of Roll Calls." *Congressional Quarterly Weekly Report* 18 (Sept. 30, 1960): 1625-1633.

3044. "Conservative Coalition Appeared in 15% of Roll Calls." *Congressional Quarterly Weekly Report* 22 (Nov. 27, 1964): 2741-2750.

3045. " 'Conservative Coalition' Appeared on 14% of Roll Calls." *Congressional Quarterly Weekly Report* 20 (Nov. 2, 1962): 2065-2074.

3046. " 'Conservative Coalition' Appeared on 17% of Roll Calls." *Congressional Quarterly Weekly Report* 22 (April 17, 1964): 737-746.

3047. " 'Conservative Coalition' Appeared on 28% of Roll Calls." *Congressional Quarterly Weekly Report* 19 (Nov. 3, 1961): 1796-1805.

3048. "Conservative Coalition Remains Potent in Congress." *Congressional Quarterly Weekly Report* 28 (Jan. 16, 1970): 158-165.

3049. "Conservatives' Voting Strength Rises." *Congressional Quarterly Weekly Report* 36 (Jan. 7, 1978): 3-8.

3050. Cooper, Joseph, Brady, David W., and Hurley, Patricia A. "The Electoral Basis of Party Voting: Patterns and Trends in the House of Representatives, 1887-1969." In *The Impact of the Electoral Process,* eds. Louis Maisel and Joseph Cooper, pp. 133-165. Beverly Hills, Calif.: Sage Publications, 1977.

3051. Crane, Wilder, "A Caveat on Roll-Call Studies of Party Voting." *Midwest Journal of Political Science* 4 (Aug. 1960): 237-249.

3052. "Democratic Split: Highest Percentage Since 1960." *Congressional Quarterly Weekly Report* 30 (Jan. 15, 1972): 97-100.

3053. "Democrats from North and South Split on 24% of Votes." *Congressional Quarterly Weekly Report* 22 (Dec. 25, 1964): 2835-2840.

3054. "Democrats in Congress Divided on 29 Percent of Votes." *Congressional Quarterly Weekly Report* 25 (Feb. 3, 1967): 176-179.

3055. "Democrats in Congress Split on 34 Percent of Votes." *Congressional Quarterly Weekly Report* 26 (Nov. 1, 1968): 2991-2994.

3056. Dempsey, Paul. "Liberalism–Conservatism and Party Loyalty in the U.S. Senate." *Journal of Social Psychology* 56 (April 1962): 159-170.

3057. Donnelly, Harrison H. "Democrats' Regional Split Decline Continues." *Congressional Quarterly Weekly Report* 36 (Dec. 23, 1978): 3479-3482.

3058. Dunlap, Riley E. and Allen, Michael P. "Partisan Differences on Environmental Issues: A Congressional Roll-Call Analysis." *Western Political Quarterly* 29 (Sept. 1976): 384-397.

3059. Goudinoff, Peter A. "Party, Constituency, and Issue Salience in Congressional Voting." Ph.D. dissertation, Ohio State University, 1969.

3060. Hickey, Donald R. "Federalist Party Unity and the War of 1812." *Journal of American Studies* 12 (April 1978): 23-39.

3061. "House Members' Votes Show Conservative Trend." *Congressional Quarterly Weekly Report* 36 (April 15, 1978): 911-929.

3062. "How Members Supported Party Majorities in 1961." *Congressional Quarterly Weekly Report* 19 (Dec. 8, 1961): 1928-1932.

3063. "How Members Supported Party Majorities in 1963." *Congressional Quarterly Weekly Report* 22 (April 3, 1964): 649-653.

3064. Huntington, Samuel P. "A Revised Theory of American Party Politics." *American Political Science Review* 44 (Sept. 1950): 669-677.

3065. Johnson, John B. "The Extent and Consistency of Party Voting in the United States Senate." Ph.D. dissertation, University of Chicago, 1943.

3066. Lenchner, Paul. "Partisan Conflict in the Senate and the Realignment Process," *Journal of Politics* 41 (May 1979): 680-686.

3067. Livernash, Bob. "Party Unity Down in the House, Up in Senate." *Congressional Quarterly Weekly Report* 36 (Dec. 16, 1978): 3447-3451.

3068. "Parties Agree on 53% of 1957 Roll Calls." *Congressional Quarterly Weekly Report* 15 (Oct. 18, 1957): 1183-1187.

3069. "Parties Opposed on 50 Percent of 1959 Roll Calls." *Congressional Quarterly Weekly Report* 17 (Oct. 16, 1959): 1393-1397.

3070. "Parties Opposed on 42 Percent of 1960 Roll Calls." *Congressional Quarterly Weekly Report* 18 (Oct. 21, 1960): 1723-1727.

3071. "Parties Opposed on 31 Percent of 1962 Roll Calls." *Congressional Quarterly Weekly Report* 20 (Nov. 2, 1962): 2075-2085.

3072. "Parties Opposed on 36 Percent of 1961 Roll Calls." *Congressional Quarterly Weekly Report* (Nov. 24, 1961): 1877-1884.

3073. "Parties in Opposition on 47% of Roll Calls." *Congressional Quarterly Weekly Report* 15 (Oct. 11, 1957): 1163-1168.

3074. "Parties in Opposition on 42 Percent of Roll Calls." *Congressional Quarterly Weekly Report* 16 (Oct. 24, 1958): 1343-1347.

3075. "Partisan Voting Score Lowest in 12 Years." *Congressional Quarterly Weekly Report* 25 (Dec. 29, 1967): 2662-2666.

3076. "Partisanship at Unusually High Level." *Congressional Quarterly Weekly Report* 15 (May 24, 1957): 631-634.

3077. "Party Majorities Agreed on 50% of Roll Calls in 1959." *Congressional Quarterly Weekly Report* 17 (Nov. 13, 1959): 1477-1480.

3078. "Party Majorities Agreed on 58% of Roll Calls in 1960." *Congressional Quarterly Weekly Report* 18 (Nov. 25, 1960): 1477-1480.

3079. "Party Majorities Agreed on 28% of 1961 Roll Calls." *Congressional Quarterly Weekly Report* 19 (Nov. 24, 1961): 1884-1892.

3080. "Party Majorities Agreed on 46% of 1962 Roll Calls." *Congressional Quarterly Weekly Report* 20 (Dec. 7, 1962): 2233-2237.

3081. "Party Majorities Agreed on 52% of 1963 Roll Calls." *Congressional Quarterly Weekly Report* 22 (April 24, 1964): 782-786.

3082. "Party Majorities Agreed on 49.6% of 1964 Roll Calls." *Congressional Quarterly Weekly Report* 22 (Dec. 11, 1964): 2797-2802.

3083. "Party Majorities Again Split on 'Great Society' Items." *Congressional Quarterly Weekly Report* 24 (Dec. 9, 1966): 2989-2993.

3084. "Party Majorities Agreed on More Than Half of Votes." *Congressional Quarterly Weekly Report* 23 (Nov. 12, 1965): 2313-2317.

3085. "Party Majorities Split on 40.9% of Roll Calls in 1964." *Congressional Quarterly Weekly Report* 22 (Oct. 30, 1964): 2589-2592.

3086. "Party Unity." *Congressional Quarterly Weekly Report* 13 (Sept. 23, 1955): 1067-1070.

3087. "Party Unity." *Congressional Quarterly Weekly Report* 13 (June 10, 1955): 657-659.

3088. "Party Unity: Highest Levels Since 1966." *Congressional Quarterly Weekly Report* 30 (Jan. 15, 1972): 86-91.

3089. "Party Unity Voting Rose in 1977." *Congressional Quarterly Weekly Report* 36 (Jan. 14, 1978): 79-83.

3090. "Party Unity Voting: Sharp Rise in 1973 Session." *Congressional Quarterly Weekly Report* 32 (Feb. 2, 1974): 209-213.

3091. Phillips, Harry A. "The Relationship Between Party Regularity on Legislative Roll Calls and Subsequent Re-Election Attempts: The Case of the United States House of Representatives, 1953-1962." Ph.D. dissertation, Indiana University, 1972.

3092. "Regional Divisions Among Democrats Declined in 1973." *Congressional Quarterly Weekly Report* 32 (Feb. 2, 1974): 214-217.

3093. "Senate, House Democrats Increase Party Vote Victories." *Congressional Quarterly Weekly Report* 28 (Jan. 16, 1970): 171-177.

3094. Silbey, Joel H. *The Shrine of Party: Congressional Voting Behavior, 1841-1852.* Pittsburgh: University of Pittsburgh Press, 1967.

3095. Sinclair, Barbara Deckard. "From Party Voting to Regional Fragmentation: The House of Representatives, 1933-1956." *American Politics Quarterly* 6 (April 1978): 125-146.

3096. Sinclair, Barbara Deckard. "The Policy Consequences of Party Realignment: Social Welfare Legislation in the House of Representatives, 1933-1954." *American Journal of Political Science* 22 (Feb. 1978): 83-105.

3097. "Southern Democrats—GOP Won 71% of Test Votes." *Congressional Quarterly Weekly Report* 17 (Dec. 4, 1959): 1519-1524.

3098. Stone, Clarence N. "Congressional Party Differences in Civil-Liberties and Criminal Procedure Issues." *Southwestern Social Science Quarterly* 47 (Sept. 1966): 161-171.

3099. Stone, Clarence N. "Issue Cleavage Between Democrats and Republicans in the U.S. House of Representatives." *Journal of Public Law* 14 (1965): 343-358.

3100. Uslaner, Eric M. "Conditions for Party Responsibility: Partisanship in the House of Representatives: 1947–1970." Ph.D. dissertation, Indiana University, 1973.

3101. "Vote Study Shows Parties Split on Federal Responsibility." *Congressional Quarterly Weekly Report* 18 (Oct. 28, 1960): 1761-1767.

3102. Westerfield, H. Bradford. *Foreign Policy and Party Politics.* New Haven, Conn.: Yale University Press, 1955.

3103. Wolff, Gerald W. "Party and Section: The Senate and the Kansas-Nebraska Bill." *Civil War History* 18 (Dec. 1972): 293-311.

Voting Participation

3104. "Attendance During Votes Improved in 1977." *Congressional Quarterly Weekly Report* 36 (Jan. 7, 1978): 16-20.

3105. "Average Congressman Voted on 87% of '65 Roll Calls." *Congressional Quarterly Weekly Report* 23 (Nov. 12, 1965): 2308-2312.

3106. "Average Member Maintains 90 Percent Voting Record." *Congressional Quarterly Weekly Report* 17 (July 3, 1959): 895-898.

3107. "Average Member Voted on 88% of 1961 Roll Calls." *Congressional Quarterly Weekly Report* 19 (Dec. 15, 1961): 1946-1950.

3108. "Average Member Voted on 82% of 1962 Roll Calls." *Congressional Quarterly Weekly Report* 20 (Nov. 2, 1962): 2086-2089.

3109. "Average Member Voted on 85% of 1967 Roll Calls." *Congressional Quarterly Weekly Report* 25 (Dec. 22, 1967): 2618-2622.

3110. "Average Member Voted on 80% of 1968 Roll Calls." *Congressional Quarterly Weekly Report* 26 (Oct. 25, 1968): 2943-2947.

3111. "Average Member Voted on 86% of 1969 Roll Calls." *Congressional Quarterly Weekly Report* 28 (Jan. 16, 1970): 141-142.

3112. "Average Member Voted on 79% of 1970 Roll Calls." *Congressional Quarterly Weekly Report* 29 (Jan. 29, 1971): 232-236.

3113. "Congress Maintains 88% Voting Record." *Congressional Quarterly Weekly Report* 16 (June 13, 1958): 731-735.

3114. "Congress Sets Records for Attendance, Votes." *Congressional Quarterly Weekly Report* 34 (Jan. 24, 1976): 164-168.

3115. "Congress Ties Record for Voting Participation." *Congressional Quarterly Weekly Report* 32 (Jan. 19, 1974): 107-111.

3116. "Congressmen Vote Almost 90% of the Time." *Congressional Quarterly Weekly Report* 14 (Sept. 21, 1956): 1123-1124.

3117. "Congressmen Vote on 88% of 1957 Roll Calls." *Congressional Quarterly Weekly Report* 15 (Sept. 20, 1957): 1105-1109.

3118. "Congressmen Voted on 87% of 1958 Roll Calls." *Congressional Quarterly Weekly Report* 16 (Oct. 17, 1958): 1311-1315.

3119. "Congressmen Voted on 89% of 1959 Roll Calls." *Congressional Quarterly Weekly Report* 17 (Oct. 23, 1959): 1423-1427.

3120. "Congressmen Voted on 87% of 1960 Roll Calls." *Congressional Quarterly Weekly Report* 18 (Oct. 14, 1960): 1685-1689.

3121. "Did Bipartisanship Mark 1955 Session?" *Congressional Quarterly Weekly Report* 13 (Oct. 7, 1955): 1110-1111.

3122. "Election Year Had Little Effect on Voting Participation." *Congressional Quarterly Weekly Report* 22 (Oct. 30, 1964): 2598-2601.

3123. "House Voting Participation on Major Issues Doubles." *Congressional Quarterly Weekly Report* 29 (Sept. 25, 1971): 1967-1970.

3124. "Members' Roll-Call Vote Record 79%, Lowest in Years." *Congressional Quarterly Weekly Report* 26 (Nov. 4, 1966): 2749-2753.

3125. "Members' Voting-Participation in 1971 Votes." *Congressional Quarterly Weekly Report* 30 (Jan. 15, 1972): 81-85.

3126. "Members' Voting Scores Remain High Despite Absenteeism." *Congressional Quarterly Weekly Report* 22 (Jan. 31, 1964): 218-222.

3127. "23% of Members Miss Monday, Friday Roll Call Votes." *Congressional Quarterly Weekly Report* 25 (Dec. 29, 1967): 2667-2671.

3128. "Voting Participation: Near-Record Levels in 1974." *Congressional Quarterly Weekly Report* 33 (Jan. 25, 1975): 184-188.

3129. "Voting Participation: 1973 Record Best Since 1959." *Congressional Quarterly Weekly Report* 31 (Sept. 22, 1973): 2509-2514.

3130. "Voting Participation." *Congressional Quarterly Weekly Report* 12 (Oct. 8, 1954): 1247-1254.

Roll Call Analysis

General Studies

3131. Abrams, Burton A. "Legislative Profits and the Economic Theory of Representative Voting: An Empirical Investigation." *Public Choice* 31 (Fall 1977): 111-119.

3132. Anderson, Lee F. "Individuality in Voting in Congress: A Research Note." *Midwest Journal of Political Science* 8 (Nov. 1964): 425-429.

3133. Ash, Philip. "The 'Liberalism' of Congressmen Voting for and Against the Taft-Hartley Act." *Journal of Applied Psychology* 32 (Dec. 1948): 636-640.

3134. Asher, Herbert B. and Weisberg, Herbert F. "Voting Change in Congress: Some Dynamic Perspectives on an Evolutionary Process." *American Journal of Political Science* 22 (May 1978): 391-425.

3135. Barrett, Archie D. "Legislative Decision Making: A Longitudinal Analysis Using Intercongressional Scaling." Ph.D. dissertation, Harvard University, 1971.

3136. Beer, Samuel H. "Adoption of General Revenue Sharing: A Case Study in Public Sector Politics." *Public Policy* 24 (Spring 1976): 127-195.

3137. Bell, Rudolph M. "Mr. Madison's War and Long-Term Congressional Voting Behavior." *William and Mary Quarterly* 36 (July 1979): 373-395.

3138. Berg, Larry L., Green, Justin J., and Schmidhauser, John R. "Judicial Regime Stability and the Voting Behavior of Lawyer-Legislators." *Notre Dame Lawyer* 49 (June 1974): 1012-1022.

3139. Black, Merle. "Regional and Partisan Bases of Congressional Support for the Changing Agenda of Civil Rights Legislation." *Journal of Politics* 41 (May 1979): 665-679.

3140. Brimhall, Dean R. and Otis, Arthur S. "Consistency of Voting by Our Congressmen." *Journal of Applied Psychology* 32 (Feb. 1948): 1-14.

3141. Carlson, Hilding B. and Harrell, Willard. "Voting Groups Among Leading Congressmen Obtained by Means of the Inverted Factor Technique." *Journal of Social Psychology* 16 (Aug. 1942): 51-61.

3142. Cherryholmes, Cleo H. and Shapiro, Michael J. *Representatives and Roll Calls: A Computer Simulation of Voting in the Eighty-Eighth Congress.* Indianapolis, Ind.: Bobbs-Merrill, 1969.

3143. Cimbala, Stephen J. "Foreign Policy as an Issue Area: A Roll Call Analysis," *American Political Science Review* 63 (Mar. 1969): 148-156.

3144. Clausen, Aage R. "Policy Dimensions in Congressional Roll Calls: A Longitudinal Analysis." Ph.D. dissertation, University of Michigan, 1964.

3145. Clausen, Aage R. "Subjectivity and Objectivity in Dimensional Analysis: Illustrations from Congressional Voting." *Mathematical Applications in Political Science* 4 (1974): 15-39.

3146. Clausen, Aage R. and Cheney, Richard B. "A Comparative Analysis of Senate-House Voting on Economic and Welfare Policy: 1953-1964." *American Political Science Review* 64 (Mar. 1970): 138-152.

3147. Danielsen, Albert L. and Rubin, Paul H. "An Empirical Investigation of Voting on Energy Issues." *Public Choice* 31 (Fall 1977): 121-128.

3148. Dennis, James R. "Roll-Call Votes and National Security: Focusing in on the Freshmen." *Orbis* 22 (Fall 1978): 713-736.

3149. Dodd, Lawrence C., Lopreato, Sally, and Smoller, Frederic. *Congressional Voting Patterns: The Question of Regionalism and Energy.* Austin: Center for Energy Studies, University of Texas, 1978.

3150. Dreier, John A. "The Politics of Isolationism: A Quantitative Study of Congressional Foreign Policy Voting, 1937-1941." Ph.D. dissertation, University of Kentucky, 1977.

3151. Eilenstein, Donald L., Farnsworth, David L., and Fleming, James S. "Trends and Cycles in the Legislative Productivity of the United States Congress, 1789-1976." *Quality and Quantity* 12 (Mar. 1978): 19-44.

3152. Erikson, Robert S. "Electoral Impact of Congressional Roll Call Voting." *American Political Science Review* 65 (Dec. 1971): 1018-1032.

3153. Farnsworth, David L. and Fleming, James S. "Quantitative Dimensions of Congressional Performance in the Twentieth Century." *Quality and Quantity* 9 (Sept. 1975): 265-275.

3154. Farris, Charles D. "A Scale Analysis of Ideological Factors in Congressional Voting." In *Legislative Behavior: A Reader in Theory and Research,* eds. John C. Wahlke and Heinz Eulau, pp. 399-413. New York: Free Press, 1959.

3155. Feagin, Joe R. "Civil Rights Voting by Southern Congressmen." *Journal of Politics* 34 (May 1972): 484-499.

3156. Flinn, Thomas A. and Wolman, Harold L. "Constituency and Roll Call Voting: The Case of Southern Democratic Congressmen." *Midwest Journal of Political Science* 10 (May 1966): 192-199.

3157. Fowler, Hubert R. *The Unsolid South: Voting Behavior of Southern Senators, 1947-1960.* University, Ala.: Bureau of Public Administration, University of Alabama, 1968.

3158. Froman, Lewis A. "The Importance of Individuality in Voting in Congress." *Journal of Politics* 25 (May 1963): 324-332.

3159. Froman, Lewis A. "Inter-Party Constituency Differences and Congressional Voting Behavior." *American Political Science Review* 57 (Mar. 1963): 57-61.

3160. Geib, Peter J. *East–West Trade and Congressional Party Voting, 1947-1970.* Emporia: Kansas State Teachers College, 1972.

3161. Gibson, George C. "Congressional Voting on Defense Policy: An Examination of Voting Dimensions, Determinants and Change." Ph.D. dissertation, Ohio State University, 1975.

3162. Gray, Charles H. "A Scale Analysis of the Voting Records of Senators Kennedy, Johnson, and Goldwater, 1957-60." *American Political Science Review* 59 (Sept. 1965): 615-621.

3163. Grum, John G. "A Factor Analysis of Legislative Behavior." *Midwest Journal of Political Science* 7 (Nov. 1963): 336-356.

3164. Hatzenbuehler, Ronald L. "Foreign Policy Voting in the United States Congress, 1808-1812." Ph.D. dissertation, Kent State University, 1972.

3165. Hood, Janice C, "Brotherly Hate: A Quantitative Study of Southern Reconstruction Congressmen, 1867-1877." Ph.D. dissertation, Washington State University, 1974.

3166. Jackson, John E. *Constituencies and Leaders in Congress: Their Effects on Senate Voting Behavior.* Cambridge, Mass.: Harvard University Press, 1974.

3167. Jones, Bryan D. "Path Models of Congressional Voting: The Case of the 1964 Freshmen Democratic Cohort." *Social Science Research* 3 (Dec. 1974): 343-360.

3168. Jones, E. Terrence. "Congressional Voting on Keynesian Legislation, 1945-1964." *Western Political Quarterly* 21 (June 1968): 240-251.

3169. Kolchin, Peter. "Scalawags, Carpet-baggers, and Reconstruction: A Quantitative Look at Southern Congressional Politics, 1868-1972." *Journal of Southern History* 45 (Feb. 1979): 63-76.

3170. Kuklinski, James H. and Elling, Richard C. "Representational Role, Constituency Opinion, and Legislative Roll-Call Behavior." *American Journal of Political Science* 21 (Feb. 1977): 135-147.

3171. Lerche, Charles O. "Southern Congressmen and the 'New Isolationism.'" *Political Science Quarterly* 75 (Sept. 1960): 321-337.

3172. Linden, Glenn M. *Politics or Principle: Congressional Voting on the Civil War Amendments and Pro-Negro Measures.* Seattle: University of Washington Press, 1976.

3173. McCrone, Donald J. "Identifying Voting Strategies from Roll Call Votes: A Method and an Application." *Legislative Studies Quarterly* 2 (May 1977): 177-191.

3174. McMurray, Carl D. "A Factor Method for Roll Call Vote Studies." *American Behavioral Scientist* 7 (April 1963): 26-27.

3175. MacRae, Duncan. *Dimensions of Congressional Voting.* Berkeley: University of California Press, 1958.

3176. MacRae, Duncan. "Occupations and the Congressional Vote, 1940-1950." *American Sociological Review* 20 (June 1955): 332-340.

3177. Markus, Gregory B. "Electoral Coalitions and Senate Roll Call Behavior: An Ecological Analysis." *American Journal of Political Science* 18 (Aug. 1974): 595-607.

3178. Martin, Jeanne L. "Presidential Elections and Administration Support Among Congressmen." *American Journal of Political Science* 20 (Aug. 1976): 483-489.

3179. Moyer, Henry W. "Congressional Voting on Defense in World War II and Viet Nam: Toward a General Ideological Explanation." Ph.D. dissertation, Yale University, 1977.

3180. Perloff, Evelyn and Perloff, Robert. "Demographic Variables Accounting for Congressmen's Votes for Arts Legislation." *Psychological Reports* 33 (Dec. 1973): 751-754.

3181. Rieselbach, Leroy N. "Congressmen as 'Small Town Boys': A Research Note." *Midwest Journal of Political Science* 14 (May 1970): 321-330.

3182. Riselbach, Leroy N. "The Demography of the Congressional Vote on Foreign Aid, 1939-1958." *American Political Science Review* 58 (Sept. 1964): 577-588.

3183. Roach, Hannah G. "Sectionalism in Congress (1870-1890)." *American Political Science Review* 19 (Aug. 1925): 500-526.

3184. Sabine, Gordon A. "The Voting Pattern of the United States Congress, 1946 and 1947." Ph.D. dissertation, University of Minnesota, 1949.

3185. Schneider, Jerrold E. *Ideological Coalitions in Congress.* Westport, Conn.: Greenwood Press, 1978.

3186. Shannon, W. Wayne. *Party, Constituency and Congressional Voting.* Baton Rouge: Louisiana State University Press, 1968.

3187. Shapiro, Michael J. "The House and the Federal Role: A Computer Simulation of Roll-Call Voting." Ph.D. dissertation, Northwestern University, 1966.

3188. Sharkansky, Ira. "Voting Behavior of Metropolitan Congressmen: Prospects for Changes with Reapportionment." *Journal of Politics* 28 (Nov. 1966): 774-793.

3189. Shelly, Mack C. "The Conservative Coalition in the United States Congress, 1933-1976: Time Series Analysis of a Policy Coalition." Ph.D. dissertation, University of Wisconsin, 1977.

3190. Swift, Donald P. "Midwestern Congressmen Vote on the Issues, 1869-1870." *Illinois Quarterly* 34 (Dec. 1971): 54.

3191. Turner, Julius and Schneier, Edward V. *Party and Constituency: Pressures on Congress.* rev. ed. Baltimore: Johns Hopkins University Press, 1970.

3192. Unekis, Joseph K. "From Committee to Floor: Consistency in Congressional Voting." *Journal of Politics* 40 (Aug. 1975): 761-769.

3193. Van der Slik, Jack R. "Constituency Characteristics and Roll Call Voting on Negro Rights in the 88th Congress." *Social Science Quarterly* 49 (Dec. 1968): 720-731.

3194. Watson, Richard A. "The Tariff Revolution: A Study of Shifting Party Attitudes." *Journal of Politics* 18 (Nov. 1956): 678-701.

3195. Weinbaum, Marvin G. and Judd, Dennis R. "In Search of a Mandated Congress." *Midwest Journal of Political Science* 14 (May 1970): 276-302.

3196. Weissberg, Robert. "Collective vs. Dyadic Representation in Congress." *American Political Science Review* 72 (June 1978): 535-547.

3197. Weiner, Don E. "Heterogeneity, Electoral Competitiveness and Congressional Voting Behavior." Master's thesis, Florida Atlantic University, 1972.

3198. Wolff, Gerald W. "The Kansas-Nebraska Bill and Congressional Voting Behavior in the Thirty-Third Congress." Ph.D. dissertation, University of Iowa, 1969.

House Voting

3199. Alexander, Thomas B. *Sectional Stress and Party Strength: A Study of Roll-Call Voting in the United States House of Representatives, 1830-1860.* Nashville, Tenn.: Vanderbilt University, 1967.

3200. Anderson, Lee F. "Variability in the Unidimensionality of Legislative Voting." *Journal of Politics* 26 (Aug. 1964): 568-585.

3201. Atkins, Burton M. and Baer, Michael A. "Effect of Recruitment upon Metropolitan Voting Cohesion in the House of Representatives: A Research Note." *Journal of Politics* 32 (Feb. 1970): 177-180.

3202. Born, Richard J. "The Influence of State Party Delegations on House Roll Call Voting in the United States House of Representatives." Ph.D. dissertation, Stanford University, 1973.

3203. Brady, David W., Schmidhauser, John R., and Berg, Larry L. "House Lawyers and Support for the Supreme Court." *Journal of Politics* 35 (Aug. 1973): 724-729.

3204. Cherryholmes, Cleo H. "The House of Representatives and Foreign Affairs: A Computer Simulation of Roll Call Voting." Ph.D. dissertation, Northwestern University, 1966.

3205. Cobb, Stephen A. "Defense Spending and Defense Voting in the House: An Empirical Study of an Aspect of the Military-Industrial Complex Thesis." *American Journal of Sociology* 82 (July 1976): 163-182.

3206. Deckard, Barbara Sinclair. "Electoral Marginality and Party Loyalty in House Roll Call Voting." *American Journal of Political Science* 20 (Aug. 1976): 469-481.

3207. Deckard, Barbara Sinclair. "Political Upheavel and Congressional Voting: The Effects of the 1960s on Voting Patterns in the House of Representatives." *Journal of Politics* 38 (May 1976): 326-345.

3208. Diffenbaugh, Donald L. "The Influence of Political and Socio-Economic Variables on Roll-Call Votes: A Study of Voting Behavior in the United States House of Representatives." Ph.D. dissertation, George Washington University, 1973.

3209. Dyson, James W. and Soule, John W. "Congressional Committee Behavior on Roll Call Votes: The U.S. House of Representatives, 1955-64." *Midwest Journal of Political Science* 14 (Nov. 1970): 626-647.

3210. Folmar, John K. "The Erosion of Republican Support for Congressional Reconstruction in the House of Representatives, 1871-1877: A Roll-Call Analysis." Ph.D. dissertation, University of Alabama, 1968.

3211. Harlow, Carolina W. "A Longitudinal Analysis of the Stability of Voting Blocs in the United States House of Representatives During the Eisenhower Years, 1955-1958." Ph.D. dissertation, University of Minnesota, 1969.

3212. Heighberger, Neil R. "Congress and Postwar National Security Policy: A Study of Roll-Call Voting in the House of Representatives." Ph.D. dissertation, University of Cincinnati, 1971.

3213. Koenig, David J. "Latent Ideological Components of Legislative Voting: A Guttman Scale Analysis of Roll Call Votes in the House of Representatives, 1955-1962." Ph.D. dissertation, University of North Carolina at Chapel Hill, 1973.

3214. Kram, Sanford E. "Correlates of Legislative Voting in the United States House of Representatives, 1967–1968." Ph.D. dissertation, University of California at Riverside, 1973.

3215. Kritzer, Herbert M. "Ideology and American Political Elites." *Public Opinion Quarterly* 42 (Winter 1978): 484-502.

3216. Lane, Ruth A. "A Computer Simulation of Voting in the U.S. House of Representatives." Ph.D. dissertation, Georgetown University, 1968.

3217. Linden, Glenn M. "Radicals and Economic Policies: The House of Representatives 1861-1873." *Civil War History* 13 (Mar. 1967): 51-65.

3218. McCarthy, John L. "Reconstruction Legislation and Voting Alignments in House of Representatives, 1863-1869." Ph.D. dissertation, Yale University, 1970.

3219. MacRae, Duncan. *Dimensions of Congressional Voting: A Statistical Study of the House of Representatives in the Eighty-First Congress.* Berkeley: University of California Press, 1958.

3220. MacRae, Duncan. "A Method for Identifying Issues and Factions from Legislative Votes." *American Political Science Review* 59 (Dec. 1965): 909-926.

3221. Marcus, Robert S. "Federal Spending and Congressional Voting: A Study of the House of Representatives." Ph.D. dissertation, State University of New York at Albany, 1975.

3222. Moyer, Wayne. "House Voting on Defense: An Ideological Explanation." In *Military Force and American Society,* eds. Bruce M. Russett and Alfred Stepan, pp. 106-141. New York: Harper and Row, 1973.

3223. Nunes, Ralph de Costa. "Patterns of Congressional Change: Critical Realignment, Policy Clusters, and Party Voting in the House of Representatives." Ph.D. dissertation, Columbia University, 1978.

3224. Randle, Roselyn K. "Coalition Behavior of Central City, Suburban, and Rural Members of the United States House of Representatives, 1963-1973." Ph.D. dissertation, University of Wisconsin at Milwaukee, 1977.

3225. Riker, William H. and Niemi, D. "Stability of Coalitions on Roll Calls in the House of Representatives." *American Political Science Review* 56 (Mar. 1962): 58-65.

3226. Ritt, Leonard G. and Ostheimer, John M. "Congressional Voting and Ecological Issues." *Environmental Affairs* 3 (1974): 459-472.

3227. Shannon, W. Wayne. "Electoral Margins and Voting Behavior in the House of Representatives: The Case of the Eighty-Sixth and Eighty-Seventh Congresses." *Journal of Politics* 30 (Nov. 1968): 1028-1045.

3228. Shapiro, Michael J. "House and the Federal Role: A Computer Simulation of Roll-Call Voting." *American Political Science Review* 62 (June 1969): 494-517.

3229. Sinclair, Barbara Deckard. "Who Wins in the House of Representatives: The Effect of Declining Party Cohesion on Policy Outputs, 1959-1970." *Social Science Quarterly* 58 (June 1977): 121-128.

3230. Smith, Bruce L. R. "Isolationist Voting in the U.S. House of Representatives." *Public Policy* 12 (1963): 337-370.

3231. Smith, Howard R. and Hart, John F. "American Tariff Map." *Geographical Review* 45 (July 1955): 327-346.

3232. Spafford, Duff. "A Note on the 'Equilibrium' Division of the Vote." *American Political Science Review* 65 (Mar. 1971): 180-183.

3233. Turner, Julius. "Voting Behavior in the House of Representatives: A Study of Representative Government and Political Pressure." Ph.D. dissertation, Johns Hopkins University, 1950.

3234. Unekis, Joseph K. "Illuminating Wilson's Dim Dungeons of Silence: An Analysis of House Committee Roll Call Voting Since Enactment of the Reorganization Act of 1970." Ph.D. dissertation, Indiana University, 1977.

3235. Van der Slik, Jack R. "Constituencies and Roll Call Voting: An Analysis of the House of Representatives for the 88th Congress." Ph.D. dissertation, Michigan State University, 1967.

Senate Voting

3236. Allen, Howard W. "Geography and Politics: Voting on Reform Issues in the United States Senate, 1911-1916." *Journal of Southern History* 27 (May 1961): 216-228.

3237. Andrain, Charles F. "A Scale Analysis of Senators' Attitudes Toward Civil Rights." *Western Political Quarterly* 17 (Sept. 1964): 488-503.

3238. Belknap, George M. "A Study of Senatorial Voting by Scale Analysis." Ph.D. dissertation, University of Chicago, 1951.

3239. Belknap, Loren C. "Demographic and Socioeconomic Structures of Liberal Voting in the United States Senate, 1950 and 1960." Ph.D. dissertation, State University of New York at Buffalo, 1968.

3240. Bernstein, Robert A. and Anthony, William W. "The ABM Issue in the Senate, 1968-1970: The Importance of Ideology." *American Political Science Review* 68 (Sept. 1974): 1198-1206.

3241. Bogue, Allan G. "The Radical Voting Dimension in the U.S. Senate During the Civil War." *Journal of Interdisciplinary History* 3 (Winter 1973): 449-474.

3242. Bozeman, Barry and James, Thomas E. "Toward a Comprehensive Model of Foreign Policy Voting in the U.S. Senate." *Western Political Quarterly* 28 (Sept. 1975): 477-495.

3243. Burstein, Paul. "A New Method for Measuring Legislative Content and Change: Senate Voting on Vietnam War Bills." *Sociological Methods and Research* 6 (Feb. 1978): 337-364.

3244. Burstein, Paul and Freudenburg, William. "Changing Public Policy: The Impact of Public Opinion, Antiwar Demonstrations, and War Costs on Senate Voting on Vietnam War Motions." *American Journal of Sociology* 84 (July 1978): 99-122.

3245. Burstein, Paul and Freudenburg, William. "Ending the Vietnam War: Components of Change in Senate Voting on Vietnam War Bills." *American Journal of Sociology* 82 (Mar. 1977): 991-1006.

3246. Chaples, Ernest A. "The Voting Behavior of United States Senators for Four Selected Issues, 1953-1964." Ph.D. dissertation, University of Kentucky, 1967.

3247. Clem, Alan L. "Variations in Voting Blocs Across Policy Fields: Pair Agreement Scores in the 1967 U.S. Senate." *Western Political Quarterly* 23 (Sept. 1970): 530-551.

3248. Clotfelter, James. "Senate Voting and Constituency Stake in Defense Spending." *Journal of Politics* 32 (Nov. 1970): 979-983.

3249. Cobb, Stephen A. "The Impact of Defense Spending on Senatorial Voting Behavior." *Sage International Yearbook of Foreign Policy Studies* 1 (1969): 135-159.

3250. Curry, Lawrence H. "Southern Senators and Their Roll-Call Votes in Congress, 1941-1944." Ph.D. dissertation, Duke University, 1971.

3251. Davis, Otto A. and Jackson, John E. "Senate Defeat of the Family Assistance Plan." *Public Policy* 22 (Summer 1974): 245-273.

3252. Demack, Gary C. "Demographic Determinants of Senators' Rollcall Voting Positions on Foreign Aid Legislation 1947-1974." Master's thesis, Florida Atlantic University, 1976.

3253. Dollar, Charles M. "South and the Fordney-McCumber Tariff of 1922: A Study in Regional Politics." *Journal of Southern History* 29 (Feb. 1973): 45-66.

3254. Eisele, Frederick R. "Age and Political Change: A Cohort Analysis of Voting Among Careerists in the United States Senate, 1947-1970." Ph.D. dissertation, New York University, 1972.

3255. Fitch, James D. "Predicting Votes of Senators of the 83rd Congress (1953-54): A Comparison of Similarity Analysis and Factor Analysis." Ph.D. dissertation, University of Illinois, 1959.

3256. Gage, N. L. and Shimberg, Ben. "Measuring Senatorial 'Progressivism.'" *Journal of Abnormal Social Psychology* 44 (Jan. 1949): 112-117.

3257. Gray, Charles H. and Gregory, Glenn W. "Military Spending and Senate Voting: A Correlational Study." *Journal of Peace Research* 5 (1968): 44-54.

3258. Harris, Chester W. "Factor Analysis of Selected Senate Roll Calls, 80th Congress." *Educational and Psychological Measurement* 8 (Winter 1948): 583-591.

3259. Hayes, Robert E. "Senatorial Voting Behavior with Regard to the 'Southern Interest.'" Ph.D. dissertation, University of Colorado, 1964.

3260. Hilty, James W. "Voting Alignments in the United States Senate 1933-1944." Ph.D. dissertation, University of Missouri at Columbia, 1973.

3261. Jackson, John E. "Statistical Models of Senate Roll Call Voting." *American Political Science Review* 65 (June 1971): 451-470.

3262. Jackson, John E. "A Statistical Model of United States Senators' Voting Behavior." Ph.D. dissertation, Harvard University, 1969.

3263. Jewell, Malcolm E. "Evaluating the Decline of Southern Internationalism Through Senatorial Roll Call Votes." *Journal of Politics* 21 (Nov. 1959): 624-646.

3264. Lenchner, Paul. "Senate Voting Patterns and American Politics, 1949-1965." Ph.D. dissertation, Cornell University, 1973.

3265. Linden, Glenn M. " 'Radical' Political and Economic Policies: The Senate, 1873-1877." *Civil War History* 14 (Sept. 1968): 240-249.

3266. Liske, Craig. "Changing Patterns of Partisanship in Senate Voting on Defense and Foreign Policy, 1946-1969." *Sage International Yearbook of Foreign Policy Studies* 3 (1975): 135-176.

3267. MacRae, Duncan and Price, Hugh D. "Scale Positions and 'Power' in the Senate." *Behavioral Science* 4 (July 1959): 212-218.

3268. Maggiotto, Michael A. "Senators, Constituencies and Roll Calls: Legislative Policy-Making in the 92nd Senate." Ph.D. dissertation, Indiana University, 1977.

3269. Martin, Jeanne L. "Exchange Theory and Legislative Behavior: A Computer Simulation of Roll-Call Voting in the United States Senate." Ph.D. dissertation, Michigan State University, 1971.

3270. Moffett, S. E. "Is the Senate Unfairly Constituted?" *Political Science Quarterly* 10 (June 1895): 248-256.

3271. Moonan, William J. "The Application of Dispersion Analysis to a Political Problem." *Journal of Experimental Education* 20 (Mar. 1952): 281-291.

3272. O'Brien, Patrick G. "A Study of Political and Sectional Voting Alignments in the United States Senate, 1921-1929." Ph.D. dissertation, Wayne State University, 1968.

3273. Pernacciaro, Samuel J. "A Dimensional Analysis of Roll Call Voting in the Senate off the 91st Congress." Ph.D. dissertation, Southern Illinois University, 1975.

3274. Price, Hugh D. "Are Southern Democrats Different?: An Application of Scale Analysis to Senate Voting Patterns." In *Politics and Social Life,* eds. Nelson W. Polsby, Robert A. Dentler, and Paul A. Smith, pp. 740-756. Boston: Houghton Mifflin, 1963.

3275. Price, Hugh D. "Scale Analysis of Senate Voting Patterns, 1949-1956." Ph.D. dissertation, Harvard University, 1958.

3276. Robinson, David A. and Henry, Alker. "Age, Seniority and Voting on Selected Issues in the United States Senate." *Cornell Journal of Social Relations* 5 (Spring 1970): 51-56.

3277. Ross, Robert S. "The Evolution of the United States Senate, 1945-1964: A Study of Roll Call Votes." Ph.D. dissertation, University of Colorado, 1968.

3278. Stegmaier, Mark J. "The U.S. Senate in the Sectional Crisis, 1846-1861: A Roll-Call Voting Analysis." Ph.D. dissertation, University of California at Santa Barbara, 1975.

3279. Tidmarch, Charles M. and Sabatt, Charles M. "Presidential Leadership Change and Foreign Policy Roll-Call Voting in the U.S. Senate." *Western Political Quarterly* 25 (Dec. 1972); 613-625.

3280. Van der Slik, Jack R. and Pernacciaro, Samuel J. "Office Ambitions and Voting Behavior in the U.S. Senate: A Longitudinal Study." *American Politics Quarterly* 7 (April 1979): 198-224.

3281. Wainer, Howard, Gruvaeus, Gunnar, and Zill, Nicholas. "Senatorial Decision Making: I. The Determination of Structure." *Behavioral Science* 18 (Jan. 1973): 7-19.

3282. Wainer, Howard, Gruvaeus, Gunnar, and Zill, Nicholas. "Senational Decision Making: II. Prediction." *Behavioral Science* 18 (Jan. 1973): 20-26.

3283. Wooddy, Carroll H. "Is the Senate Unrepresentative." *Political Science Quarterly* 41 (June 1926): 219-239.

IX. Legislative Case Studies

General Studies

3284. Bach. Stanley I. "Perceptions of Political Protest: Congressional Reactions to Dissent and Disorder." Ph.D. dissertation, Yale University, 1971.

3285. Bardach, Eugene. *The Implementation Game: What Happens After a Bill Becomes Law.* Cambridge, Mass.: M.I.T. Press, 1977.

3286. Bendiner, Robert. *Obstacle Course on Capitol Hill.* New York: McGraw-Hill, 1964.

3287. Benedict, Arthur H. "Federal Centralization Through Congressional Legislation, 1924-1939." Ph.D. dissertation, Ohio State University, 1948.

3288. Bessette, Joseph M. "Deliberation in Congress: A Preliminary Investigation." Ph.D. dissertation, University of Chicago, 1978.

3289. Buchanan, G. Sidney. "Quest for Freedom: A Legal History of the Thirteenth Amendment: The Thirteenth Amendment and Congressional Regulation of Associational Choice." *Houston Law Review* 13 (Oct. 1975): 63-83.

3290. Curry, Leonard P. *Blueprint for Modern America: Nonmilitary Legislation of the First Civil War Congress.* Nashville, Tenn.: Vanderbilt University Press, 1968.

3291. Eagle, Robert E. "A Comparison of Interest Representation by Congressmen and Administrators in Nation Water Resources Politics." Ph.D. dissertation, American University, 1967.

3292. Goldberg, Delphis C. "Intergovernmental Relations: From the Legislative Perspective." *American Academy of Political and Social Science, Annals* 416 (Nov. 1974): 52-66.

3293. Gross, Bertram M. *The Legislative Struggle: A Study in Social Combat.* New York: McGraw-Hill, 1953.

3294. Harader, William H. *Legisim: A Legislative Simulation.* Philadelphia, Pa.: Center for the Study of Federalism, Temple University, 1973.

3295. Hartley, Eugene L. and Weibe, Gerhart D., eds. *Casebook in Social Processes.* New York: Thomas Y. Crowell, 1960.

3296. Hendrickson, John P. "Legislative Record of Republicans in the Seventy-Third Congress in Relation to the Republican Platform of 1932 and the Campaign Speeches of Mr. Hoover." Ph.D. dissertation, University of Iowa, 1952.

3297. Huckshorn, Robert J. "Congressional Reaction to the Second Hoover Commission." Ph.D. dissertation, University of Iowa, 1957.

3298. Hudzik, John K. "Firearms Legislation: The 90th Congress." Ph.D. dissertation, Michigan State University, 1971.

3299. "Job of the 81st Congress." *Antioch Review* 8 (Dec. 1948): 387-416.

3300. Lankford, John E. *Congress and the Foundations in the Twentieth Century.* River Falls: Wisconsin State University, 1964.

3301. Levine, Milton. "Reorganization Plans Submitted by the President to the 83rd Congress." Ph.D. dissertation, American University, 1956.

3302. Levine, Richard O. "The Congressional Role in Formulating National Policy: Some Observations on the First Session of the Ninety-Third Congress." *Harvard Journal on Legislation* 11 (Feb. 1974): 161-180.

3303. Lewis, Sarah E. "Digest of Congressional Action on the Annexation of Texas, December, 1844 to March, 1845." *Southwestern Historical Quarterly* 50 (Oct. 1946): 251-268.

3304. Lorch, Robert S. "The Administrative Court Idea Before Congress." *Western Political Quarterly* 20 (Mar. 1967): 65-81.

3305. Nabors, Eugene. "Legislative History and Government Documents: Another Step in Legal Research." *Government Publications Review* 3 (Spring 1976): 15-41.

3306. Nathanson, Iric. "Getting a Bill Through Congress." *American Journal of Nursing* 75 (July 1975): 1179-1181.

3307. Nellis, Joseph L. "International Narcotic Control Efforts and Policies as Seen in Congress." *Contemporary Drug Problems* 6 (Winter 1977): 479-490.

3308. Olson, David M. *The Politics of Legislation: A Congressional Simulation.* New York: Praeger, 1976.

3309. Redman, Eric. *The Dance of Legislation.* New York: Simon and Schuster, 1973.

3310. Reisner, Ralph. "Selective Service Appeal Boards and the Conscientious Objector Claimant: Congressional Standards and Administrative Behavior." *Wisconsin Law Review* (1971): 521-546.

3311. Slevin, Joseph R. "Washington Desk: Achievements of the 88th Congress." *Dun's Review* 84 (Nov. 1964): 5-6.

3312. Smurr, John W. "Territorial Constitutions: A Legal History of Frontier Governments Erected by Congress in the American West, 1787-1900." Ph.D. dissertation, Indiana University, 1960.

3313. Sutherland, Keith A. "Congress and Crisis: A Study in the Legislative Process, 1860." Ph.D. dissertation, Cornell University, 1966.

3314. Waltzer, Herbert. "Federal Corrupt Practices Legislation: A History and Analysis of the Efforts of Congress to Curb Non-Financial Corrupt Practices." Ph.D. dissertation, New York University, 1959.

3315. Zemsky, Robert M., Westbrook, Nicholas, and Koons, William. "The Congressional Game: A Prospectus." *Social Science History* 1 (Fall 1976): 101-113.

3316. Zimmermann, Frederick L. and Wendell, Mitchell. "Congress: A Second Umpire of the Federal System." *Georgetown Law Journal* 40 (May 1952): 499-522.

Domestic Policy

3317. Bolner, James and Eubanks, Cecil L. "Poverty of Justice: Congress and the Case of Hunger." *Capital University Law Review* 8 (1978): 31-57.

3318. Donley, Robert T. "Veterans' Legislation and Limitations upon the Implied Powers of Congress." *West Virginia Law Quarterly* 39 (April 1933): 197-224.

3319. Edwards, Rhoda D. "The Seventy-Eighth Congress on the Home Front: Domestic Legislation, 1943-1944." Ph.D. dissertation, Rutgers University, 1967.

3320. Farganis, James. "Politics and Civil Liberties: A Study in Congressional Attitudes." Ph.D. dissertation, Cornell University, 1965.

3321. Foster, Granville J. "Southern Congressmen and Welfare Policy in the 1960s: A Case Study of Redistributive Politics." Ph.D. dissertation, University of Southern California, 1972.

3322. McPike, Timothy K. "Criminal Diversion in the Federal System: Congressional Examination." *Probation* 42 (Dec. 1978): 10-15.

3323. Marmor, Theodore R. "The Congress: Medicare Politics and Policy." In *American Political Institutions and Public Policy: Five Contemporary Studies,* ed. Allan P. Sindler, pp. 3-66. Boston: Little, Brown, 1969.

3324. Miller, Annie P. "Policy Sciences Examined: Congressional Health Policy in the Sixties." Ph.D. dissertation, Case Western Reserve University, 1975.

3325. Relyea, Harold C. "Faithful Execution of the FOI Act: A Legislative Branch Perspective." *Public Administration Review* 39 (July 1979): 328-332.

3326. Rogge, O. John. "Congress Shall Make No Law. . . . " *Michigan Law Review* 56 (Jan. 1958): 331-374; (Feb. 1958): 579-618.

3327. Silverstein, Arthur M. "Congressional Politics and Biomedical Science." *Federation Proceedings* 37 (Feb. 1978): 105-106.

3328. Stockman, David A. "The Social Pork Barrel." *Public Interest* 39 (Spring 1975): 3-30.

3329. Viorst, Milton. "The Political Good Fortune of Medical Research." *Science* 144 (April 1964): 267-270.

3330. Wald, Patricia M. "Justice in the Ninety-Fifth Congress: An Overview." *American Bar Association Journal* 64 (Dec. 1978): 1854-1859.

3331. Williams, Andrew K. "Congressional Hearing on Child Care: An Identification and Analysis of Selected Issues." Ed.D. dissertation, University of Massachusetts, 1973.

Economic Policy

3332. Burt, William C. and Kennedy, William F. "Congressional Review of Price Control." *University of Pennsylvania Law Review* 101 (Nov. 1952): 333-377.

3333. Friedrich, Carl J. and Sternberg, Evelyn. "Congress and the Control of Radiobroadcasting." *American Political Science Review* 37 (Oct.-Dec. 1943): 797-818, 1014-1026.

3334. Goolrick, Robert M. "The Role of Congress." In his *Public Policy Toward Corporate Growth: The ITT Merger Cases,* pp. 186-195. Port Washington, N.Y.: Kennikat Press, 1978.

3335. Haney, Lewis H. *A Congressional History of Railways.* Madison, Wisc.: Democratic Publishing Co., 1910.

3336. Hassenauer, Leo J. "Congressional Legislation Affecting Railroad Employees." *Notre Dame Lawyer* 8 (May 1933): 429-450.

3337. Holland, Michael L. "An Investigation of Federal Farm Income Taxation: Its Development with Attention to Congressional Intent and Its Effects on the Georgia Egg Industry." Ph.D. dissertation, University of Georgia, 1978.

3338. Krasnow, Erwin G. and Robb, Scott H. "Telecommunications and the 94th Congress: An Overview of Major Congressional Actions." *Federal Communications Bar Journal* 29 (1976): 117-171.

3339. Linden, Glenn M. "Congressmen, 'Radicalism' and Economic Issues, 1861-1873." Ph.D. dissertation, University of Washington, 1963.

3340. Linden, Glenn M. "Radicals and Economic Policies: The Senate, 1861-1873." *Journal of Southern History* 32 (May 1966): 189-199.

3341. McDaniel, Paul R. "Simplification Symposium—Federal Income Tax Simplification: The Political Process." *Tax Law Review* 34 (Fall 1978): 27-77.

3342. McDonald, Lee C. "Congress and FEPC: A Case Study in the Legislative Process." Ph.D. dissertation, Harvard University, 1952.

3343. McHugh, Donald P. "Labor Unions and the Seventy-Seventh Congress." *Georgetown Law Journal* 31 (Jan. 1943): 172-184.

3344. Madeo, Silvia A. "The Accumulated Earnings Tax: An Empirical Analysis of the Tax Court's Implementation of Congressional Intent." Ph.D. dissertation, North Texas State University, 1977.

3345. Mansfield, Harvey C. "The Congress and Economic Policy." In *The Congress and America's Future,* ed. David B. Truman, pp. 121-149. Englewood Cliffs, N.J.: Prentice-Hall, 1965.

3346. Paul, Eliza. "Conning Congress: The Wild Card Story." *Washington Monthly* 5 (Jan. 1974): 47-50.

3347. Redford, Emmette S. "Case Analysis of Congressional Activity: Civil Aviation, 1957-58." *Journal of Politics* 22 (May 1960): 228-258.

3348. Roberson, Jere W. "To Build a Pacific Railroad: Congress, Texas, and the Charleston Convention of 1854." *Southwestern Historical Quarterly* 78 (Oct. 1974): 117-139.

3349. Rumsey, D. Lake. "Truth-in-Lending: Congress Reacts to the Creditors' Dilemma." *Emory Law Journal* 24 (Spring 1975): 379-398.

3350. Sanborn, John B. "Congressional Grants of Land in Aid of Railways." Ph.D. dissertation, University of Wisconsin, 1899.

3351. Saxon, Sydney. "The Proposed Federal Legislation on Minimum Wages and Hours." *St. John's Law Review* 12 (April 1938): 292-304.

3352. Scanlan, Alfred L. "Administrative Abnegation in the Face of Congressional Coercion: The Interstate Natural Gas Company Affair." *Notre Dame Lawyer* 23 (Jan. 1948): 173-207.

3353. Witney, Fred. "Taft-Hartley and the Eighty-Third Congress." *Labor Law Journal* 5 (Jan. 1954): 3-6, 76-79.

Educational Policy

3354. Amrine, Michael. "The 1965 Congressional Inquiry into Testing." *American Psychology* 20 (Nov. 1965): 859-870.

3355. Bell, Alphonso. "Congressional Response to Busing." *Georgetown Law Journal* 61 (Mar. 1973): 963-990.

3356. Farmer, Randy L. "Higher Education and Its National Spokesmen: A Congressional Perspective." Ed.D. dissertation, Indiana University, 1975.

3357. Gladieux, Lawrence E. and Wolanin, Thomas R. *Congress and the Colleges: The National Politics of Higher Education.* Lexington, Mass.: Lexington Books, 1976.

3358. Guthrie, James W. "City Schools in a Federal Vise: The Political Dynamics of Federal Aid to Urban Schools." *Education and Urban Society* 2 (Feb. 1970): 199-218.

3359. Hawkinson, Robert E. "Presidential Program Formulation in Education: Lyndon Johnson and the 89th Congress." Ph.D. dissertation, University of Chicago, 1977.

3360. Kaagan, Stephen S. "Executive Initiative Yields to Congressional Dictate: A Study of Educational Renewal, 1971-1972." Ed.D. dissertation, Harvard University, 1973.

3361. Keesbury, Forrest E. "Radical Republicans and the Congressional Abandonment of the Mixed School Idea, 1870-1875." Ed.D. dissertation, Lehigh University, 1971.

3362. Kelly, Alfred H. "Congressional Controversy over School Segregation, 1867-1875." *American Historical Review* 64 (April 1959): 537-563.

3363. Krash, Otto. "Power-Group Strategy in the Development of a National Educational Policy: A Study of the Congressional Committee Hearings on Federal Aid to Education." Ph.D. dissertation, Columbia University, 1951.

3364. Mallue, Henry E. "A Study of the Role of Congressional Intent and the Protection Afforded Local School Districts Against a Reduction in State Aid Funds as a Consequence of Receiving Federal Revenue Sharing Funds." Ed.D. dissertation, Oklahoma State University, 1974.

3365. Monahan, A. C. "Sixty-Ninth Congress and Education." *American School Board Journal* 72 (Jan. 1926): 106, 108, 111.

3366. Munger, Frank J. and Fenno, Richard F. *National Politics and Federal Aid to Education.* Syracuse, N.Y.: Syracuse University Press, 1962.

3367. Orfield, Gary. "Congress, the President and Anti-Busing Legislation." *Journal of Law and Education* 4 (Jan. 1975): 81-139.

3368. Pettit, Lawrence K. "Constitutional Ambiguity and Legislative Decision Making: The Establishment Clause and Aid to Higher Education." In *The Legislative Process in the U.S. Senate,* eds. Lawrence K. Pettit and Edward Keynes, pp. 251-271. Chicago: Rand McNally, 1969.

3369. Pettit, Lawrence K. "The Policy Process in Congress: Passing the Higher Education Academic Facilities Act of 1963." Ph.D. dissertation, University of Wisconsin, 1965.

3370. Rainsford, George N. *Congress and Higher Education in the Nineteenth Century.* Knoxville: University of Tennessee Press, 1972.

3371. Rogers, Paul G. "Congressional Perspectives on Government and Quality of Medical Education." *Journal of Medical Education* 51 (Jan. 1976): 3-6.

3372. Smietana, Walter. "The 84th Congress and Federal Financial Support of Education: A Content Analysis of the Congressional Record, Second Session." Ed.D. dissertation, Boston University, 1965.

3373. Wicklund, Gail A. "Truth-in-Testing: Congressional Hearings." *Personnel Psychology* 33 (Spring 1980): 33-39.

3374. Wise, Michael. "Congress, Busing and Federal Law." *Civil Rights Digest* 5 (Summer 1973): 28-35.

Energy Policy

3375. Del Sesto, Steven L. "Conflicting Ideologies of Nuclear Power: Congressional Testimony on Nuclear Reactor Safety." *Public Policy* 28 (Winter 1980): 39-70.

3376. Drinan, Robert F. "Nuclear Power and the Role of Congress." *Environmental Affairs* 4 (Fall 1975): 595-627.

3377. McCormack, Mike. "U.S. Congressional Attitudes and Policies Affecting Nuclear Power Development in the World." *Atomic Energy Law Journal* 17 (Winter 1976): 289-321.

3378. Marks, Henry S. "Congress and the Atom." *Stanford Law Review* 1 (Nov. 1948): 23-42.

3379. Mitchell, E. J. "Basis of Congressional Energy Policy." *Texas Law Review* 57 (Mar. 1979): 591-613.

3380. Thomas, Morgan. *Atomic Energy and Congress.* Ann Arbor: University of Michigan Press, 1956.

3381. Wiener, Don E. "Congress and Natural Gas Policy." Ph.D. dissertation, University of Wisconsin, 1977.

3382. Wirth, Timothy E. "Congressional Policy Making and the Politics of Energy." *Journal of Energy and Development* 1 (Autumn 1975): 93-104.

3383. Witt, Elder and Arrandale, Tom. "Overestimating the Capability of Congress?" *Congressional Quarterly Weekly Report* 33 (June 28, 1975): 1343-1346.

Environmental Policy

3384. Cooley, Richard A. and Wandesforde-Smith, Geoffrey, ed. *Congress and the Environment*. Seattle: University of Washington Press, 1970.

3385. Eichert, Magdalen. "A Consideration of the Interests Which Lay Behind the Attitudes of Benton, Clay, Webster, and Calhoun in the Development of Public Land Policy, 1830-1841." Ph.D. dissertation, New York University, 1950.

3386. Ferejohn, John A. "Congressional Influences on Water Politics." Ph.D. dissertation, Stanford University, 1972.

3387. Grundy, Richard D. "Environmental Policies as Congressional Requirement for Efficacy." *Environmental Affairs* 2 (Spring 1973): 639-652.

3388. Jackson, Henry M. "Environmental Policy and the Congress." *Public Administration Review* 28 (July 1968): 303-305.

3389. Kolb, K. H. "Congress and the Ocean Policy Process." *Ocean Development and International Law* 3 (1976): 261-286.

3390. Kraft, Michael E. "Congressional Attitudes Toward the Environment: Attention and Issue-Oreintion in Ecological Politics." Ph.D. dissertation, Yale University, 1973.

3391. Maass, Arthur A. "Congress and Water Resources." *American Political Science Review* 44 (Sept. 1950): 576-593.

3392. Maass, Arthur A. *Muddy Waters*. Cambridge, Mass.: Harvard University Press, 1951.

3393. McBride, Ralph L. "Conservatism in the Mountain West: Western Senators and Conservative Influences in the Consideration of National Progressive Legislation 1906-1914." Ph.D. dissertation, Brigham Young University, 1976.

3394. Magnuson, Warren G. "U.S. Ocean Policy: The Congressional View." *Columbia Journal of World Business* 10 (Spring 1975): 20-28.

3395. Miller, Joseph A. "Congress and the Origins of Conservation: Natural Resource Policies, 1865-1900." Ph.D. dissertation, University of Minnesota, 1973.

3396. Oppenheimer, Jack C. and Miller, Leonard A. "Environmental Problems and Legislative Responses." *American Academy of Political and Social Science, Annals* 389 (May 1970): 77-86.

3397. Palmer, William D. "Endangered Species Protection: A History of Congressional Action." *Environmental Affairs* 4 (Spring 1975): 255-293.

3398. Ridgeway, Marian E. "The Missouri Basin's Pick-Sloan Plan: A Case Study in Congressional Policy Determination." Ph.D. dissertation, University of Illinois at Urbana-Champaign, 1952.

3399. Scheele, Paul E. "President Carter and the Water Projects: A Case Study in Presidential and Congressional Decision-Making." *Presidential Studies Quarterly* 8 (Fall 1978): 348-364.

3400. Strom, Gerald S. "Congressional Policy Making and the Federal Waste Treatment Construction Grant Program." Ph.D. dissertation, University of Illinois at Urbana-Champaign, 1973.

3401. Taylor, Randall L. "NEPA Pre-Emption Legislation: Decision-Making Alternative for Crucial Federal Projects." *Environmental Affairs* 6 (1978): 373-389.

Science Policy

3402. Anderson, John B. "Science Policy and Congress." In *We Propose,* ed. Mary McInnis, pp. 73-81. New York: McGraw-Hill, 1966.

3403. Baer, Walter S. *Communications Technology and the Congress.* Santa Monica, Calif.: Rand, 1974.

3404. Bozeman, Barry. "Reflections on the End of Carte Blanche: The Inevitability of Conflict Between Congress and the Scientific Community." *Policy Studies Journal* 5 (Winter 1976): 175-180.

3405. Daddario, Emilio Q. "Science, Technology, and the American Congress." *The Parliamentarian* 51 (Oct. 1970): 253-262.

3406. Dornan, Robert K. "Exporting American Technology: A National Security Perspective." *Journal of Social and Political Studies* 2 (Fall 1977): 131-142.

3407. Doty, Paul. "Science Advising and the ABM Debate." In *Controversies and Decisions: The Social Sciences and Public Policy,* ed. Charles Frankel, pp. 185-203. New York: Russell Sage Foundation, 1976.

3408. Green, Harold P. "Congress and Science." In *The Congress and America's Future,* ed. David B. Truman, pp. 13-16. George Washington University American Assembly Report, 1965.

3409. Greenberg, Daniel S. "Congress Looks at Science." *American Psychologist* 19 (Feb. 1964): 102-104.

3410. Hall, Harry S. "Congressional Attitudes Toward Science and Scientists: A Study of Legislative Reactions to Atomic Energy and Political Participation of Scientists." Ph.D. dissertation, University of Chicago, 1962.

3411. Kofmehl, Kenneth. "COSPUP: Congress and Scientific Advice." *Journal of Politics* 28 (Feb. 1966): 100-120.

3412. Lamson, Robert W. "Scientists and Congressmen." Ph.D. dissertation, University of Chicago, 1961.

3413. Miller, Nathan. "The Making of a Majority: The Senate and the ABM." *Washington Monthly* 1 (Oct. 1969): 60-72.

3414. Miller, Nathan. "The Making of a Majority: Safeguard and the Senate." In *Inside the System,* 2nd ed., eds. Charles Peters and John Roth Child, pp. 115-133. New York: Praeger, 1973,

3415. Muskie, Edmund S. "The Role of Congress in Promoting and Controlling Technological Advance." *George Washington Law Review* 36 (July 1968): 1138-1149.

3416. Poke, Carl F. "Congress and Outer Space." Ph.D. dissertation, University of Pittsburgh, 1968.

3417. Ratchford, J. Thomas. "How Scientists Advise the Congress." *Physics Today* 27 (June 1974): 38-41.

Urban Policy

3418. Ashley, Thomas L. "Congress and New Towns." *Public Administration Review* 35 (May-June 1975): 239-246.

3419. Beckman, Norman and Harding, Susan. "National Urban Growth Policy: 1974 Congressional and Executive Action." *Journal of the American Institute of Planners* 41 (July 1975): 234-249.

3420. Caraley, Demetrios. "The Carter Congress and Urban Problems: First Soundings." In *American Politics and Public Policy,* eds. Walter Dean Burnham and Martha Wagner Weinberg, pp. 188-221. Cambridge, Mass.: M.I.T. Press, 1978.

3421. Caraley, Demetrios. "Congressional Politics and Urban Aid." *Political Science Quarterly* 91 (Spring 1976): 19-45.

3422. Caraley, Demetrios. "Congressional Politics and Urban Aid: A 1978 Postscript." *Political Science Quarterly* 93 (Fall 1978): 411-420.

3423. Cleaveland, Frederic N. "Congress and Urban Problems: Legislating for Urban Areas." *Journal of Politics* 28 (May 1966): 289-307.

3424. Cleaveland, Frederic N. and Associates. *Congress and Urban Problems: A Casebook on the Legislative Process.* Washington: Brookings Institution, 1969.

3425. Feagin, Joe R. and Hahn, Harlan. *Ghetto Revolts: The Politics of Violence in American Cities.* New York: Macmillan, 1973.

3426. Green, Michael."The Congressional History of New Towns Legislation." Master's thesis, University of Texas at Austin, 1978.

3427. Hahn, Harlan and Feagin, Joe R. "Rank and File Versus Congressional Perceptions of Ghetto Riots." *Social Science Quarterly* 51 (Sept. 1970): 361-373.

3428. Hart, Henry C. "Legislative Abdication in Regional Development." *Journal of Politics* 13 (Aug. 1951): 393-417.

3429. Ingram, Helen. "Congress and Housing Policy." Ph.D. dissertation, Columbia University, 1967.

3430. Ingram, Helen. "A Question of Representation: The Impact of Urban Congressmen on Housing Legislation." *Journal of Urban Law* (Spring 1971): 84-111.

3431. Kushner, James A. and Werner, Frances E. "Revenue Sharing and Relocation: The Administrative Dilemma of Ostensibly Conflicting Congressional Directives." *Ecology Law Quarterly* 5 (1976): 433-460.

3432. Mields, Hugh. "Congress and Urban Growth Policy." *Bureaucrat* 2 (Spring 1973): 59-67.

3433. Myers, Will S. "A Legislative History of the Revenue Sharing." *American Academy of Political and Social Science, Annals* 419 (May 1975): 1-11.

3434. Picque, Nicholas D. "Congress and the Urban Crisis." *Christianity and Crisis* 28 (Mar. 1968): 28-31.

3435. Williams, J. Kerwin. "Municipal Problems Facing the 75th Congress." *National Municipal Review* 25 (Nov. 1936): 641-644.

3436. Wright, Deil S. "Perspectives on Federal Grants-in-Aid." In *Republican Papers,* ed. Melvin R. Laird, pp. 1-59. New York: Praeger, 1968.

Legislative Histories

3437. Alexander, Jim R. "Congress and the Nixon Welfare Reform Proposals: A Study in the Formation of Public Policy." Ph.D. dissertation, American University, 1974.

3438. Allen, George H. "A Content Analysis and Evaluation of Hearings Held by the Federal Congress Relative to Legislation Authorizing Institutional Grants and the Establishment of a National Science Foundation." Ed.D. dissertation, Boston University, 1971.

3439. Bailey, Stephen K. *Congress Makes a Law: The Story Behind the Employment Act of 1946.* New York: Columbia University Press, 1950.

3440. Balz, Daniel J. "Why Johnny Can't Eat: The Saga of the Farm Bill." *Washington Monthly* 7 (July-Aug. 1975): 37-48.

3441. Barfield, Claude E. "Our Share of the Booty: The Democratic Party, Cannonism, and the Payne-Aldrich Tariff." *Journal of American History* 57 (Sept. 1970): 308-323.

3442. Berman, Daniel M. *A Bill Becomes Law: The Civil Rights Act of 1960.* New York: Macmillan, 1962.

3443. Brezina, Dennis W. *Congress in Action: The Environmental Education Act.* New York: Free Press, 1974.

3444. Burnett, Donald L. "An Historical Analysis of the 1968 'Indian Civil Rights' Act." *Harvard Journal on Legislation* 9 (May 1972): 557-626.

3445. Burstein, Paul. "Public Opinion, Demonstrations, and the Passage of Antidiscrimination Legislation." *Public Opinion Quarterly* 43 (Summer 1979): 157-172.

3446. Cahalan, Joseph M. "Congress, Mass Communications and Public Policy: The Public Broadcasting Act of 1967." Ph.D. dissertation, New York University, 1971.

3447. Campbell, Harry J. "The Congressional Debate over the Seaman's Sickness and Disability Act of 1789: The Origins of the Continuing Debate on the Socialization of American Medicine." *Bulletin of the History of Medicine* 48 (Fall 1974): 423-426.

3448. Ciliberti, Barrie S. "The Legislative Process and the Making of Educational Policy: The General School Aid Bill in the 81st Congress." Ph.D. dissertation, Catholic University of America, 1976.

3449. Cox, Charles W. "The Congressional Struggle to Create a Separate Department of Education." Ed.D. dissertation, Ball State University, 1971.

3450. Dalrymple, Donald W. "Food Policy: Legislative Prospects for the 96th Congress." *Food Drug Cosmetic Law Journal* 34 (Feb. 1979): 81-86.

3451. Dierst, John R. "Pre-Legislative Decision Making: A Case Study of the Revision of Copyright Legislation 1955-1971." Ph.D. dissertation, University of Pittsburgh, 1972.

3452. Derby, E. Stephen. "Section 315: Analysis and Proposal." *Harvard Journal on Legislation* 3 (1965-1966): 257-321.

3453. DeZafra, Dorothea E. "A Management Model for the Implementation of Omnibus Legislation: A Case Study from the U.S. Public Health Service." *Public Administration Review* 38 (May/June 1978): 276-279.

3454. Dinnerstein, Leonard. "Anti-Semitism in the Eightieth Congress: The Displaced Person Act of 1948." *Capitol Studies* 6 (Fall 1978): 11-26.

3455. DiSprito, Donald D. "A Study of Congressional–Higher Education Relations and Communications in Relationship to the Educational Amendments of 1972." Ph.D. dissertation, University of Pittsburgh, 1974.

3456. Eidenberg, Eugene and Morey, Roy D. *An Act of Congress: The Legislative Process and the Making of Education Policy.* New York: W. W. Norton, 1969.

3457. Entin, Kenneth. "Energy Politics in the House of Representatives: The National Energy Plan." *Connecticut Law Review* 11 (Spring 1979): 403-429.

3458. Finn, Terrence T. "Conflict and Compromise: Congress Makes a Law; The Passage of the National Environmental Policy Act." Ph.D. dissertation, Georgetown University, 1972.

3459. Finn, Vaughan. "The Clean Air Amendments of 1970: Can Congress Compel State Cooperation in Achieving National Environmental Standards." *Harvard Civil Rights and Civil Liberties Law Review* 11 (Summer 1976): 701-732.

3460. Fjelstad, Ralph S. "Congress and Civil Service Legislation." Ph.D. dissertation, Northwestern University, 1948.

3461. Florer, John H. "Major Issues in the Congressional Debate of the Morrill Act of 1862." *History of Education Quarterly* 8 (Winter 1968): 459-478.

3462. Graev, Lawrence G. "S.1035—Congress in the Vanguard: The Establishment of Rights for Federal Employees." *George Washington Law Review* 37 (Oct. 1968): 101-131.

3463. Green, Ronald C. "Determining Legislative Intent: A Methodology Study of Public Housing Legislation." Ph.D. dissertation, State University of New York at Albany, 1971.

3464. Griepentrog, Daniel N. "An Analysis and Comparison of the Three Main Revenue Sharing Proposals Before the 92nd Congress, 1st Session." Master's thesis, California State University at Long Beach, 1972.

3465. Hagen, Sam. "The Acts and Proposals of Congress to Aid Education from 1857-1890." Ph.D. dissertation, University of North Dakota, 1934.

3466. Hardesty, David C. "A Case Study of Legislative Implementation: The Federal Coal Mine Health and Safety Act of 1969." *Harvard Journal on Legislation* 10 (Dec. 1972): 99-137.

3467. Hughes, Kent H. "International Economic Decision-Making in Congress: A Case Study of the Burke-Hartke Bill." Ph.D. dissertation, Washington University, 1976.

3468. Karis, Thomas G. "Congressional Behavior at Constitutional Frontiers from 1906, The Beveridge Child-Labor Bill, to 1938, The Fair Labor Standards Act." Ph.D. dissertation, Columbia University, 1951.

3469. Kimball, Warren F. " '1776': Lend-Lease Gets a Number." *New England Quarterly* 42 (June 1969): 260-267.

3470. Lachman, Seymour P. "Cardinal, the Congressmen, and the First Lady." *Journal of Church and State* 7 (Winter 1965): 35-66.

3471. Levine, Murray. "Congress (and Evaluators) Ought to Pay More Attention to History." *American Journal of Community Psychology* 7 (Feb. 1979): 1-18.

3472. Levine, Richard O. "The Federal Advisory Committee Act." *Harvard Journal on Legislation* 10 (Feb. 1973): 217-235.

3473. Long, James S. "Congress' Definition of Educational Administrative Roles for Agencies Participating in the General Extension Program Authorized in the Higher Education Act of 1965." Ph.D. dissertation, University of Wisconsin, 1966.

3474. McAuliffe, Mary S. "Liberals and the Communist Control Act of 1954." *Journal of American History* 63 (Sept. 1976): 351-367.

3475. McDowell, Timothy L. *The Wagner Housing Act: A Case Study.* Chicago: Loyola University Press, 1957.

3476. Manley, John F. "U.S. Civil Rights Act of 1964." *Contemporary Review* 206 (Jan. 1965): 10-13.

3477. Mann, Seymour Z. "Congressional Behavior and the National Labor Policy: Structural Determinants of the Taft-Hartley Act." Ph.D. dissertation, University of Chicago, 1952.

3478. Miller, Bryon S. "A Law is Passed: The Atomic Energy Act of 1946." *University of Chicago Law Review* 15 (Summer 1948): 799-821.

3479. Moe, Ronald C. "Telecommunications Policy: The Legislative History of the Communications Satellite Act of 1962." Ph.D. didsertation, Columbia University, 1968.

3480. Morse, Wayne L. "Congress and the Comprehensive Education Bill." *Journal of Higher Education* 34 (Mar. 1963): 121-128.

3481. Murphy, John P. "Congress and the Colleges a Century Ago: A Political History of the First Morrill Act, Other Congressional Support for Educational Purposes, and the Political Climate of the United States as It Involved Education Prior to 1862." Ed.D. dissertation, Indiana University, 1967.

3482. Nathan, Richard P. and Calkins, Susannah E. "The Story of Revenue Sharing." In *Cases in American Politics,* ed. Robert L. Peabody, pp. 11-43. New York: Praeger, 1976.

3483. Parkinson, Thomas I. "The New Tariff Act and Delegations of Legislative Power." *American Bar Association Journal* 9 (Mar. 1923): 177-178.

3484. Riggs, Fred W. "Pressures on Congress: A Study of the Repeal of Chinese Exclusion." Ph.D. dissertation, Columbia University, 1951.

3485. Rulon, Philip R. and Butchart, Ronald E. "Congress and the Morrill Act." *Illinois Quarterly* 35 (Feb. 1973): 52-63.

3486. Russell, Robert R. "Issues in the Congressional Struggle over the Kansas-Nebraska Bill, 1854." *Journal of Southern History* 29 (Feb. 1963): 187-210.

3487. Sargent, James E. "Roosevelt's Economy Act: Fiscal Conservatism and the Early New Deal." *Congressional Studies* 7 (Winter 1980): 33-52.

3488. Schober, Milton W. "Development of the Truth in Lending Act in Congress and the Courts." *Oklahoma City University Law Review* 3 (Spring 1979): 457-476.

3489. Senecal, Robert J. "Title I of the Higher Education Act of 1965: A Study of Program Compliance with Congressional Intent." Ph.D. dissertation, University of Iowa, 1969.

3490. Sherman, Dennis M. "The National Security Act, a Blueprint for the Congressional Role in Weapons Development: A Case Study of the B-70 Bomber." Ph.D. dissertation, University of Wisconsin, 1978.

3491. Shuman, Howard E. "Senate Rules and the Civil Rights Bill: A Case Study." *American Political Science Review* 51 (Dec. 1957): 955-975.

3492. Smith, George H. E. and Riddick, Floyd M. *Congress in Action: How a Bill Becomes a Law.* 2nd ed. Manassas, Va.: National Capitol Publishers, 1949.

3493. Stevens, John D. "Congressional History of the 1798 Sedition Law." *Journalism Quarterly* 43 (Summer 1966): 247-256.

3494. Strickland, D. A. "On Ambiguity in Political Rhetoric: Defeat of the Rat Control Bill in the House of Representatives, July 1967." *Canadian Journal of Political Science* 2 (Sept. 1969): 338-344.

3495. Strickland, Ronald G. "The Years of Congressional Review Under the Wilderness Act of 1964: Wilderness Classification Through 'Affirmative Action'." Ph.D. dissertation, Georgetown University, 1976.

3496. Tanner, William R. and Griffith, Robert. "Legislative Politics and McCarthyism: The Internal Security Act of 1950." In *The Specter: Original Essays on the Cold War and Origins of McCarthyism,* eds. Robert Griffith and Athan Theoharis, pp. 172-189. New York: New Viewpoints, 1974.

3497. Tyler, Gus. *A Legislative Campaign for a Federal Minimum Wage: 1955.* New York: Holt, 1959.

3498. Vaughn, William P. "Separate and Unequal: The Civil Rights Act of 1875 and Defeat of the School Integration Clause." *Southwestern Social Science Quarterly* 48 (Sept. 1967): 146-154.

3499. Westwood, Howard C. and Bennet, Alexander E. "Footnote to the Legislative History of the Civil Aeronautics Act of 1938 and Afterword." *Notre Dame Lawyer* 42 (Feb. 1967): 309-381.

3500. Willis, H. Parker. "The Tariff of 1913." *Journal of Political Economy* 22 (Jan. 1914): 1-42.

3501. Young, Allyn A. "The Sherman Act and New Anti-Trust Legislation." *Journal of Political Economy* 23 (April 1915): 305-326.

X. Leadership in Congress

Party Government

3502. Balch, Stephen H. "Party Government in the United States House of Representatives, 1911-1919." Ph.D. dissertation, University of California at Berkeley, 1972.

3503. Ball, Carolyn L. "State Party and Congressional Party." Ph.D. dissertation, University of North Carolina at Chapel Hill, 1973.

3504. Barfield, Claude E. "The Democratic Party in Congress, 1909-1913." Ph.D. dissertation, Northwestern University, 1965.

3505. Berdahl, Clarence A. "Some Notes on Party Membership in Congress." *American Political Science Review* 43 (April, June, Aug. 1949): 309-321, 492-509, 721-735.

3506. Bowers, Claude G. *The Party Battles of the Jackson Period.* Boston: Houghton Mifflin, 1922.

3507. Burns, James MacGregor. "Legislative Leadership: The Price of Consensus." In his *Leadership,* pp. 344-368. New York: Harper and Row, 1978.

3508. Clubb, Jerome M. and Allen, Howard W. "Party Loyalty in the Progressive Years: The Senate, 1909-1915." *Journal of Politics* 29 (Aug. 1967): 567-584.

3509. Conway, M. Margaret. "Participatory Democracy and the Democratic Party in the House of Representatives: Implications for Policy Making." *Policy Studies Journal* 5 (Summer 1977): 459-464.

3510. Dodd, Lawrence C. "The Emergence of Party Government in the House of Representatives." *DEA News* (American Political Science Association. Division of Educational Affairs) 10 (Summer 1976): 51-55.

3511. Evans, Rowland. "Whither the Republicans?" *Reporter,* 28 Feb. 1963, pp. 32-34.

3512. Freedman, Stanley R. "Party Government and the Salience of Congress Revisited—1970." In *Public Opinion and Public Policy,* rev. ed., ed. Norman R. Luttbeg, pp. 126-131. Homewood, Ill.: Dorsey Press, 1974.

3513. Fritz, Harry W. "The Collapse of Party: President, Congress, and the Decline of Party Action, 1807-1817." Ph.D. dissertation, Washington University, 1971.

3514. Glick, Edward M. "Propaganda Strategy and Tactics of the Party in Power During the 1958 Congressional Campaign." Ph.D. dissertation, Ohio State University, 1960.

3515. Goodman, William T. "How Much Political Party Centralization Do We Want." *Journal of Politics* 13 (Nov. 1951): 536-561.

3516. Gordon, Glen. "The Legislative Process in a Divided Government: A Case Study on the Role of the Majority Party in Congress." Ph.D. dissertation, University of Chicago, 1964.

3517. Grodzins, Morton. "American Political Parties and the American System." *Western Political Quarterly* 13 (Dec. 1960): 974-998.

3518. Harris, Carl V. "Right Fork or Left Fork? The Section-Party Alignments of Southern Democrats in Congress, 1873-1897." *Journal of Southern History* 42 (Nov. 1976): 471-506.

3519. Hasbrouck, Paul D. *Party Government in the House of Representatives.* New York: Macmillan, 1927.

3520. Hatzenbuehler, Ronald L. "Party Unity and the Decision for War in the House of Representatives, 1812." *William and Mary Quarterly* 29 (July 1972): 367-390.

3521. Holt, Laurence J. *Congressional Insurgents and the Party System, 1909-1916.* Cambridge, Mass.: Harvard University Press, 1967.

3522. Jeffrey, Harry P. "The Republican Party as a Minority Party in Congress in Wartime, 1943-1944." Ph.D. dissertation, Columbia University, 1974.

3523. Jones, Charles O. "Minority Party and Policy-Making in the House of Representatives." *American Political Science Review* 62 (June 1968): 481-493.

3524. Jones, Charles O. *The Minority Party in Congress.* Boston: Little, Brown, 1970.

3525. Key, Valdimer O. "Party Leadership in Legislation." In his *Politics, Parties, and Pressure Groups,* 5th ed., pp. 653-689. New York: Thomas Y. Crowell, 1964.

3526. Lenchner, Paul. "Congressional Party Unity and Executive–Legislative Relations." *Social Science Quarterly* 57 (Dec. 1976): 589-596.

3527. Lenchner, Paul. "Partisan Realignments and Congressional Behavior: Some Preliminary Snapshots." *American Politics Quarterly* 4 (April 1976): 223-236.

3528. Lincoln, C. H. "The Position of the American Representative in Congress." *American Academy of Political and Social Science, Annals* 6 (July 1895): 117-124.

3529. Lowell, A. Lawrence. "The Influence of Party upon Legislation in England and America." *Annual Report of the American Historical Association for 1901* 1 (1902): 321-544.

3530. Lowi, Theodore J. "Towards Functionalism in Political Science: The Case of Innovation in Party Systems." *American Political Science Review* 57 (Sept. 1963): 570-583.

3531. Luce, R. Duncan and Rogow, Arnold A. "A Game Theoretic Analysis of Congressional Power Distributions for a Stable Two-Party System." *Behavioral Science* 1 (April 1956): 83-95.

3532. Lynn, Alvin W. "Party Formation and Operation in the House of Representatives, 1824-1837." Ph.D. dissertation, Rutgers University, 1972.

3533. McCann, James C. "Differential Mortality and the Formation of Political Elites: The Case of the U.S. House of Representatives," *American Sociological Review* 37 (Dec. 1972): 689-700.

3534. McGinnis, Patrick E. "Republican Party Resurgence in Congress, 1936-1946." Ph.D. dissertation, Tulane University, 1967.

3535. Mansfield, Harvey C. "The Dispersion of Authority in Congress." *The Academy of Political Science, Proceedings* 32 (1975): 1-19.

3536. Mayhew, David R. *Party Loyalty Among Congressmen: The Difference Between Democrats and Republicans, 1947-1962.* Cambridge, Mass.: Harvard University Press, 1966.

3537. Mayer, George H. *The Republican Party, 1854-1964.* New York: Oxford University Press, 1964.

3538. Miller, Warren E. "Majority Rule and the Representative System of Government." In *Cleavages, Ideologies and Party Systems,* eds. E. Allardt and Y. Littonen, pp. 343-376. Helsinki: Transactions of the Westermarck Society, 1964.

3539. Nelson, Garrison. "Party Control Periods of the United States House of Representatives and the Recruitment of Its Leaders, 1789-1971." Ph.D. dissertation, University of Iowa, 1973.

3540. Nielsen, George R. "The Indispensable Institution: The Congressional Party During the Era of Good Feelings." Ph.D. dissertation, University of Iowa, 1968.

3541. Norpoth, Helmut. "Explaining Party Cohesion in Congress: The Case of Shared Policy Attitudes." *American Political Science Review* 70 (Dec. 1976): 1156-1171.

3542. Norpoth, Helmut. "Sources of Party Cohesion in the United States House of Representatives." Ph.D. dissertation, University of Michigan, 1974.

3543. Ranney, Austin. "Toward a More Responsible Two-Party System: A Commentary." *American Political Science Review* 45 (June 1951): 488-499.

3544. Riddick, Floyd M. "Party Government in a Session of the House of Representatives." *South Atlantic Quarterly* 36 (Oct. 1937): 361-375.

3545. Roady, Elston E. "Party Regularity in the Sixty-Third Congress." Ph.D. dissertation, University of Illinois at Urbana-Champaign, 1951.

3546. Ryan, Mary P. "Party Formation in the United States Congress, 1789 to 1796: A Quantitative Analysis." *William and Mary Quarterly* 28 (Oct. 1971): 523-542.

3547. Schattschneider, Elmer E. *Party Government.* New York: Holt, Rinehart, and Winston, 1942.

3548. Schwarz, Susan B. "Party and Structure in the Postwar United States House of Representatives: A New Index and Some Applications." Ph.D. dissertation, University of Chicago, 1972.

3549. Shade, William G., Hopper, Stanley D., Jacobson, David, and Moiles, Stephen E. "Partisanship in the United States Senate: 1869-1901." *Journal of Interdisciplinary History* 4 (Autumn 1973): 185-205.

3550. Shannon, W. Wayne. "Congressional Party Behavior: Data, Concept and Theory in and Search for Historical Reality." *Polity* 3 (Winter 1970): 280-284.

3551. Sinclair, Barbara Deckard. "Determinants of Aggregate Party Cohesion in the U.S. House of Representatives, 1901-1956." *Legislative Studies Quarterly* 2 (May 1977): 155-175.

3552. Smiley, Donald V. "A Comparative Study of Party Discipline in the Houses of Commons of the United Kingdom and Canada and in the Congress of the United States." Ph.D. dissertation, Northwestern University, 1954.

3553. Smith, Carl O. and Field, G. Lowell. "The Responsibility of Parties in Congress: Myth and Reality," *Southwestern Social Science Quarterly* 34 (June 1953): 23-39.

3554. Smith, Donald. "Democrats Worry About Minority Rule." *Congressional Quarterly Weekly Report* 33 (June 18, 1975): 1333-1342.

3555. Smith, Frank E. "The Democratic Idea and Southern Congressional Politics." *Mississippi Quarterly* 18 (Fall 1965): 223-230.

3556. "Solid South: Makings of a New Senate Majority?" *Congressional Quarterly Weekly Report* 30 (Oct. 28, 1972): 2779-2781.

3557. Stanley, Judith M. "The Congressional Democrats, 1918-1928." Ph.D. dissertation, University of California at Berkeley, 1969.

3558. Stokes, Donald E. and Miller, Warren E. "Party Government and the Saliency of Congress." *Public Opinion Quarterly* 26 (Winter 1962): 531-546.

3559. Truman, David B. *The Congressional Party: A Case Study.* New York: Wiley, 1959.

3560. Truman, David B. "The Presidency and Congressional Leadership: Some Notes on Our Changing Constitution." *The American Philosophical Society, Proceedings* 103 (Oct. 1959): 687-692.

3561. Turner, Julius, "Responsible Parties: A Dissent from the Floor." *American Political Science Review* 45 (Mar. 1951): 133-152.

3562. Uslaner, Eric M. "Partisanship and Coalition Formation in Congress." *Political Methodology* 2 (1975): 381-414.

3563. Ware, Alan. "Party Democracy and the Denver Democrats." In his *The Logic of Party Democracy,* pp. 93-129. New York: St. Martin's Press, 1979.

Party Leadership

General Studies

3564. "Congress Strives to Fill Leadership Vacuum." *Congressional Quarterly Weekly Report* 32 (Dec. 28, 1974): 3415-3441.

3565. Foley, Michael. *The New Senate: Liberal Influence on a Conservative Institution, 1959-1972.* New Haven, Conn.: Yale University Press, 1980.

3566. Grant, Philip A. "Congressional Leaders from the Great Plains 1921-1932." *North Dakota History* 46 (Winter 1979): 19-23.

3567. Hatzenbuehler, Ronald L. "War Hawks and the Question of Congressional Leadership in 1812." *Pacific Historical Review* 45 (Feb. 1976): 1-22.

3568. Hinckley, Barbara. "Congressional Leadership Selection and Support: A Comparative Analysis." *Journal of Politics* 32 (May 1970): 268-287.

3569. Jones, Charles O. "Somebody Must Be Trusted: An Essay on Leadership of the U.S. Congress." In *Congress in Change: Evolution and Reform,* ed. Norman J. Ornstein, pp. 265-276. New York: Praeger, 1975.

3570. Kravitz, Walter. "Relations Between the Senate and the House of Representatives: The Party Leadership." In *Policymaking Role of Leadership in the Senate: A Compilation of Papers,* pp. 121-138. Washington: GPO, 1976.

3571. Patterson, Samuel C. "Legislative Leadership and Political Ideology." *Public Opinion Quarterly* 27 (Fall 1963): 399-410.

3572. Peabody, Robert L. *Leadership in Congress: Stability, Succession, and Change.* Boston: Little, Brown, 1975.

3573. Rapoport, Daniel. "It's Not a Happy Time for House, Senate Leadership," *National Journal* 8 (Feb. 7, 1976): 169-175.

3574. Riker, William H. and Eldersveld, Samuel. "The Roles of Congressional Leaders: National Party vs. Constituency." *American Political Science Review* 46 (Dec. 1952): 1024-1032.

3575. Ripley, Randall B. *Minority Party Leadership in Congress.* Boston: Little, Brown, 1969.

3576. Roberts, Chalmers M. "Nine Men Who Control Congress." *Atlantic* 213 (April 1964): 63-68.

3577. Schlesinger, Joseph A. "Political Careers and Party Leadership." In *Political Leadership in Industrialized Societies: Studies in Comparative Analysis,* ed. Lewis J. Edinger, pp. 266-293. New York: Wiley, 1967.

3578. Sullivan, William E. "Criteria for Selecting Party Leadership in Congress: An Empirical Test." *American Politics Quarterly* 3 (Jan. 1975): 25-44.

House Leadership

3579. Balz, Daniel J. "The Majority Leader Race: The 'Silly Season' in the House." *National Journal* 8 (Nov. 11, 1978): 1704-1708.

3580. Branyan, Robert L. and Lee, R. Alton. "Lyndon B. Johnson and the Art of the Possible." *Southwestern Social Science Quarterly* 45 (Dec. 1964): 213-225.

3581. Dodd, Lawrence C. "The Expanded Roles of the House Democratic Whip System: The 93rd and 94th Congresses." *Congressional Studies* 7 (Spring 1979): 27-56.

3582. Froman, Lewis A. and Ripley, Randall B. "Conditions for Party Leadership: The Case of the House Democrats." *American Political Science Review* 59 (Mar. 1965): 52-63.

3583. Galloway, George B. "Leadership in the House of Representatives." *Western Political Quarterly* 12 (June 1959): 417-441.

3584. Glass, Andrew J. "Uncommitted Democrats Hold Key to Choice of New House Majority Leader." *National Journal* 3 (Jan. 9, 1971): 68-76.

3585. Goodman, Paul. "Social Status of Party Leadership: The House of Representatives, 1797-1804." *William and Mary Quarterly* 25 (July 1968): 465-474.

3586. Hard, William. "Leadership in the House." *Review of Reviews* 74 (Aug. 1926): 159-164.

3587. "House Democratic Whips: Counting, Coaxing, Cajoling." *Congressional Quarterly Weekly Report* 36 (May 27, 1978): 1301-1306.

3588. "House Leaders Face a Difficult Year." *Congressional Quarterly Weekly Report* 33 (Jan. 4, 1975): 3-5.

3589. Jones, Charles O. "Joseph G. Cannon and Howard W. Smith: An Essay on the Limits of Leadership in the House of Representatives." *Journal of Politics* 30 (Aug. 1968): 617-646.

3590. Lapham, Lewis J. "Party Leadership and the House Committee on Rules." Ph.D. dissertation, Harvard University, 1954.

3591. Malbin, Michael J. "House Democrats Are Playing with a Strong Leadership Lineup." *National Journal* 9 (June 18, 1977): 940-946.

3592. Nelson, Garrison. "Change and Continuity in the Recruitment of U.S. House Leaders, 1789-1975." In *Congress in Change: Evolution and Reform,* ed. Norman J. Ornstein, pp. 155-183. New York: Praeger, 1975.

3593. Nelson, Garrison. "Leadership Position: Holding in the United States House of Representatives." *Capitol Studies* 4 (Fall 1976): 11-36.

3594. Nelson, Garrison. "Partisan Patterns of House Leadership Change, 1789-1977." *American Political Science Review* 71 (Sept. 1977): 918-939.

3595. Oppenheimer, Bruce I. and Peabody, Robert L. "How the Race for Majority Leader Was Won—by One Vote." *Washington Monthly* 9 (Nov. 1977): 46-56.

3596. Peabody, Robert L. *House Leadership, Party Caucuses and the Committee Structure. Working Papers on House Committee Organization and Operation. Presented to House Select Committee on Committees.* 93rd Cong. Washington: GPO, 1973.

3597. Peabody, Robert L. "Party Leadership Change in the United States House of Representatives." *American Political Science Review* 61 (Sept. 1967): 675-693.

3598. Peabody, Robert L. "Political Parties: House Republican Leadership." In *American Political Institutions and Public Policy: Five Contemporary Studies,* ed. Allan P. Sindler, pp. 181-229. Boston: Little, Brown, 1969.

3599. Polsby, Nelson W. "Two Strategies of Influence: Choosing a Minority Leader, 1962." In *New Perspectives on the House of Representatives,* 3rd ed., eds. Robert L. Peabody and Nelson W. Polsby, pp. 324-354. Chicago: R and McNally, 1977.

3600. "Power in the House: Days of the Brokers Are Gone." *Congressional Quarterly Weekly Report* 31 (April 7, 1973): 767-771.

3601. Riddick, Floyd M. "Leadership in the House." *South Atlantic Quarterly* 36 (Jan. 1937): 1-13.

3602. Ripley, Randall B. *Party Leaders in the House of Representatives.* Washington: Brookings Institution, 1967.

3603. Ripley, Randall B. "Party Whip Organizations in the United States House of Representatives." *American Political Science Review* 58 (Sept. 1964): 561-576.

3604. Romans, Maureen R. "Party Leadership Fights in the House of Representatives: The Cause of Conflict, 1895-1955." Ph.D. dissertation, University of Massachusetts, 1976.

3605. U.S. Congress. House. *The History and Operation of the House Majority Whip Organization.* H. Doc. 94-162. Washington: GPO, 1975.

3606. Westerfield, Louis P. "Majority Party Leadership and the Committee System in the House of Representatives." *American Political Science Review* 68 (Dec. 1974): 1593-1604.

3607. Westerfield, Louis P. "Party Leaders and Followers in the House of Representatives." Ph.D. dissertation, Washington University, 1973.

3608. "Whips' Effectiveness Tested on Close 1961 House Votes." *Congressional Quarterly Weekly Report* 19 (June 16, 1961): 992-997.

Senate Leadership

3609. Alexander, Holmes M. *The Famous Five.* New York: The Bookmailer, 1958.

3610. Cronin, Jean T. "Minority Leadership in the United States Senate: The Role and Style of Everett Dirksen." Ph.D. dissertation, Johns Hopkins University, 1973.

3611. Donnelly, Thomas C. "Party Leadership in the United States Senate." Ph.D. dissertation, New York University, 1930.

3612. Drier, Thomas. *Heroes of Insurgency.* Boston: Human Life, 1910.

3613. Hamilton, Holman. "Democratic Senate Leadership in the Compromise of 1850." *Mississippi Valley Historical Review* 41 (Dec. 1954): 403-418.

3614. Hill, Thomas M. "The Senate Leadership and International Policy from Lodge and Vanderburg." Ph.D. dissertation, University of Washington, 1970.

3615. Huitt, Ralph K. "Democratic Party Leadership in the Senate." *American Political Science Review* 55 (June 1961): 333-344.

3616. Huitt, Ralph K. "Lyndon B. Johnson and Senate Leadership." In *The Presidency and the Congress: A Shifting Balance of Power?* eds. William S. Livingston, Lawrence C. Dodd and Richard L. Schott, pp. 253-264. Austin: Lyndon B. Johnson School of Public Affairs, University of Texas, 1979.

3617. Jones, Charles O. "Senate Party Leadership in Public Policy." In *Policymaking Role of Leadership in the Senate: A Compilation of Papers,* pp. 18-33. Washington: GPO, 1976.

3618. Kuchel, Thomas H. "The Role of the Senate Minority." In *The Senate Institution,* ed. Nathaniel S. Preston, pp. 75-82. New York: Van Nostrand, Reinhold, 1969.

3619. Malbin, Michael J. "The Senate Republican Leaders: Life Without a President." *National Journal* 9 (May 21, 1977): 776-780.

3620. Mansfield, Michael J. "The Senate and Its Leadership." In *The Senate Institution,* ed. Nathaniel S. Preston, pp. 59-74. New York: Van Nostrand Reinhold, 1969.

3621. Mervin, David. "United States Senate Norms and the Majority Whip Election of 1969." *Journal of American Studies* 9 (Dec. 1975): 321-333.

3622. Munk, Margaret R. "Origin and Development of the Party Floor Leadership in the United States Senate." Ph.D. dissertation, Harvard University, 1970.

3623. Munk, Margaret R. "Origin and Development of the Party Leadership in the United States Senate." *Capitol Studies* 2 (Winter 1974): 23-41.

3624. Oleszek, Walter J. *Majority and Minority Whips of the Senate: History and Development of the Party Whip System in the U.S. Senate.* Washington: GPO, 1979.

3625. Oleszek, Walter J. "Party Whips in the United States Senate." *Journal of Politics* 33 (Nov. 1971): 955-979.

3626. Ripley, Randall B. "Party Leaders, Policy Committees, and Policy Analysis in the United States Senate." In *Policymaking Role of Leadership in the Senate: A Compilation of Papers,* pp. 5-17. Washington: GPO, 1976.

3627. Ripley, Randall B. "Policy Leadership in United States Senate: Potential for Expanded Policy Committee Activity." *Policy Studies Journal* 5 (Summer 1977): 464-469.

3628. Robinson, Donald A. "If the Senate Democrats Want Leadership: An Analysis of the History and Prospects of the Majority Policy Committee." In *Policymaking Role of Leadership in the Senate: A Compilation of Papers,* pp. 40-57. Washington: GPO, 1976.

3629. Stewart, John G. "Independence and Control: The Challenge of Senatorial Party Leadership." Ph.D. dissertation, University of Chicago, 1968.

3630. Stogdill, Ralph M., Goode, Omar S., and Day, David R. "The Leader Behavior of United States Senators." *Journal of Psychology* 56 (July 1963): 3-8.

3631. U.S. Congress. Senate. *Majority and Minority Whips of the Senate: History and Development of the Party Whip System in the U.S. Senate.* S. Doc. 92-86, 92nd Cong., 2nd sess, Washington: GPO, 1972.

3632. U.S. Congress. Senate. *Majority and Minority Leaders of the Senate: History and Development of the Offices of Floor Leaders.* S.Doc. 94-66. Washington: GPO, 1975.

3633. U.S. Congress. Senate. Commission on the Operation of the Senate. *Policymaking Role of Leadership in the Senate: A Compilation of Papers.* Washington: GPO, 197&.

3634. White, William S. "Who Really Runs the Senate?" *Harpers'* 213 (Dec. 1956): 35-40.

Speaker of the House

3635. Atkinson, C. R. and Beard, C. A. "The Syndication of the Speakership." *Political Science Quarterly* 26 (Sept. 1911): 381-414.

3636. Baker, John D. "The Character of the Congressional Revolution of 1910." *Journal of American History* 60 (Dec. 1973): 679-691.

3637. Brown-Peterside, Gally. "Speaker of the Nigeria House of Representatives, Speaker of the United States House of Representatives: A Comparative Study." Master's thesis, American University, 1960.

3638. Bryce, James. "A Word as to the Speakership." *North American Review* 151 (Oct. 1890): 385-398.

3639. Cannon, Joseph G. "The Power of the Speakership.: Is He an Autocrat or a Servant." *Century* 78 (June 1909): 306-312.

3640. Carlisle, J. G. "The Limitations of the Speakership." *North American Review* 150 (Mar. 1890): 390-399.

3641. Chiu, Chang-Wei. *The Speaker of the House of Representatives Since 1896.* New York: Columbia University Press, 1928.

3642. Crenshaw, Ollinger. "Speakership Contest of 1859-60: John Sherman's Election a Cause of Disruption." *Mississippi Valley Historical Review* 29 (Dec. 1942): 323-338.

3643. Follet, Mary P. *The Speaker of the House of Representatives.* New York: Longmans, Green, 1896.

3644. Fuller, Hubert B. *The Speakers of the House.* Boston: Little, Brown, 1909.

3645. Hardeman, D. B. "Sam Rayburn and the House of Representatives." In *The Presidency and the Congress: A Shifting Balance of Power?*, eds. William S. Livingston, Lawrence C. Dodd and Richard L. Schott, pp. 226-252. Austin: Lyndon B. Johnson School of Public Affairs, University of Texas, 1979.

3646. Hart, Albert B. "The Speaker as Premier." In his *Practical Essays on American Government,* pp. 1-19. New York: Longmans, Green, 1893.

3647. Hinds, Asher C. "The Speaker and the House." *McClure's* 35 (June 1910): 195-202.

3648. Hinds, Asher C. "Speaker of the House of Representatives: Origin of the Office, Its Duties and Powers." *American Political Science Review* 3 (May 1909): 155-166.

3649. Hitchner, Dell G. "The Speaker of the House of Representatives." *Parliamentary Affairs* 13 (Spring 1960): 185-197.

3650. Hollcraft, T. R. and Morgan, E. B., eds. "A Congressman's Letters on the Speaker Election in the Thirty-Fourth Congress." *Mississippi Valley Historical Review* 43 (Dec. 1956): 444-458.

3651. House, Albert V. "Speakership Contest of 1875: Democratic Response to Power." *Journal of American History* 52 (Sept. 1965): 252-274.

3652. Lientz, Gerald R. "House Speaker Elections and Congressional Parties, 1789-1860." *Capitol Studies* 6 (Spring 1978): 63-89.

3653. Reed, Thomas B. "The Limitations of the Speakership." *North American Review* 150 (Mar. 1890: 382-390.

3654. Smith, William H. *Speakers of the House of Representatives of the United States.* Baltimore, Md.: S. J. Gaeng, 1928.

3655. "The Speaker of the House of Representatives." *Congressional Quarterly Weekly Report* 19 (Nov. 17, 1961): 1847-1854.

Formal and Informal Groups

3656. Barnett, Marguerite R. "The Congressional Caucus: Symbol, Myth, and Reality." *The Black Scholar* 8 (Jan.-Feb. 1977): 17-26.

3657. Beach, Walter E. "The Democratic Steering Committee in the House of Representatives, 1933-1960." Master's thesis, Georgetown University, 1961.

3658. "Black Caucus: 60 Recommendations for the President." *Congressional Quarterly Weekly Report* 29 (April 2, 1971): 783-785.

3659. "Black House Members Form 'Shadow Cabinet' on Rights." *Congressional Quarterly* 28 (Oct. 16, 1970): 2577.

3660. Bolling, Richard. *Defeating the Leadership Nominee in the House Democratic Caucus.* Indianapolis, Ind.: Bobbs-Merrill, 1965.

3661. Bone, Hugh A. "The Capitol Hill Committees." *Parliamentary Affairs* 9 (Autumn 1956): 388-397.

3662. Bone, Hugh A. *Party Committees and National Politics.* Seattle: University of Washington Press, 1958.

3663. Broom, William. "California Congressmen: How Big a Stick Does the Delegation Carry? Who the Heavyweights Are." *California Journal* 5 (Feb. 1974): 44-51.

3664. Buckler, Leslie H. "Legislative Responsibility Through the Party Caucus." *Virginia Law Review* 1 (Dec. 1913): 210-225.

3665. Bullock, Charles S. "The Influence of State Party Delegations on House Committee Assignments." *Midwest Journal of Political Science* 15 (Aug. 1971): 525-546.

3666. Carney, George O. "Oklahoma's House Delegation in the Sixty-First Congress: Progressive or Conservative?" *Chronicles of Oklahoma* 55 (Summer 1977): 190-210.

3667. Carney, George O. "Oklahoma's United States House Delegation and Progressivism, 1901-1917." Ph.D. dissertation, Oklahoma State University, 1972.

3668. "Changing Role of the Congressional Caucus." *Congressional Quarterly Weekly Report* 18 (Jan. 15, 1960): 99.

3669. "Committee of 15 Formed by House Republicans." *Congressional Quarterly Weekly Report* 16 (Aug. 15, 1958): 1084-1085.

3670. Deckard, Barbara Sinclair. "State Party Delegations in the House of Representatives." Ph.D. dissertation, University of Rochester, 1970.

3671. Deckard, Barbara Sinclair. "State Party Delegations in the United States House of Representatives: An Analysis of Group Action." *Polity* 5 (Spring 1973): 311-334.

3672. Deckard, Barbara Sinclair. "State Party Delegations in the U.S. House of Representatives: A Comparative Study of Group Cohesion." *Journal of Politics* 34 (Feb. 1972): 199-222.

3673. DeJanes, Robert B. "Informal Influences: Friendship Groups and the Ideology of Southern Senators." *Georgia Political Science Association Journal* 1 (Fall 1973): 17-32.

3674. "Democratic Study Group Shifts Role in 91st Congress." *Congressional Quarterly Weekly Report* 27 (Oct. 10, 1969): 1940-1945.

3675. Ehrenhalt, Alan. "Black Caucus: A Wary Carter Ally." *Congressional Quarterly Weekly Report* 35 (May 21, 1977): 967-972.

3676. Ehrenhalt, Alan. "The Right in Congress: Seeking a Strategy." *Congressional Quarterly Weekly Report* 36 (Aug. 5, 1978): 2022-2028.

3677. Elliott, John M. "Communication and Small Groups in Congress: The Case of Republicans in the House of Representatives." Ph.D. dissertation, Johns Hopkins University, 1974.

3678. Ellis, Lewis E. "A History of the Chicago Delegation in Congress, 1843-1925." Ph.D. dissertation, University of Chicago, 1927.

3679. Ferber, Mark F. "The Democratic Study Group: A Study of Intr-Party Organization in the House of Representatives." Ph.D. dissertation, University of California, Los Angeles, 1964.

3680. Ferber, Mark F. "The Formation of the Democratic Study Group." In *Congressional Behavior,* ed. Nelson W. Polsby, pp. 249-269. New York: Random House, 1971.

3681. Fiellin, Alan. "The Behavior of a 'Legislative Group' in the House of Representatives: A Case Study of New York Democrats." Ph.D. dissertation, New York University, 1961.

3682. Fiellin, Alan. "Functions of Informal Groups in Legislative Institutions: A Case Study." *Journal of Politics* 24 (Feb. 1962): 72-91.

3683. Fiellin, Alan. "Group Life of a State Delegation in the House of Representatives." *Western Political Quarterly* 23 (June 1970): 305-320.

3684. Freed, Bruce F. "House Democrats: Dispute over Caucus Role." *Congressional Quarterly Weekly Report* 33 (May 3, 1975): 911-915.

3685. Glass, Andrew J. "National Republican Congressional Committee." In *Political Brokers: Money, Organizations, Power and People,* ed. Judith G. Smith, pp. 167-199. New York: Liveright, 1972.

3686. Greenberg, Barbara. "New York Congressmen and Local Party Organization." Ph.D. dissertation, University of Michigan, 1973.

3687. Groennings, Sven. "The Clubs in Congress: The House Wednesday Group." In *To Be a Congressman: The Promise and the Power,* eds. Sven Groennings and Jonathan P. Hawley, pp. 73-98. Washington: Acropolis Books, 1973.

3688. Haney, Jan P. "A Study of Southern Insurgency Within the Texas Congressional Delegation, 1933-1938." Master's thesis, North Texas State University, 1976,

3689. Humbert, W. H. "The Democratic Joint Policy Committee." *American Political Science Review* 26 (June 1932): 552-554.

3690. Jewell, Malcolm E. "Senate Republican Policy Committee and Foreign Policy." *Western Political Quarterly* 12 (Dec. 1959): 966-980.

3691. Jewell, Malcolm E. *Trends in the Organization of State Legislative Committees. Working Papers on House Committee Organization and Operation. Presented to House Select Committee on Committees.* 93rd Cong. Washington: GPO, 1973.

3692. Jones, Charles O. *Party and Policy-Making: The House Republican Policy Committee.* New Brunswick, N.J.: Rutgers University Press, 1964.

3693. Kessel, John H. "The Washington Congressional Delegation." *Midwest Journal of Political Science* 8 (Feb. 1964): 1-12.

3694. Lightfoot, Billy B. "The State Delegations in the Congress of the United States, 1789-1801." Ph.D. dissertation, University of Texas at Austin, 1958.

3695. Malbin, Michael J. "Where There's a Cause There's a Caucus on Capitol Hill." *National Journal* 9 (Jan. 8, 1977): 56-58.

3696. Maxwell, Neal A. "Conference of Western Senators." *Western Political Quarterly* 10 (Dec. 1957): 902-910.

3697. Maxwell, Neal A. *Regionalism in the United States Senate: The West.* Salt Lake City: University of Utah, 1961.

3698. Patenaude, Lionel V. "The Texas Congressional Delegation." *Texana* 9 (1971): 3-16.

3699. Polsby, Nelson W. "Goodbye to the Inner Club." *Washington Monthly* 1 (Aug. 1969): 30-34.

3700. Republican Congressional Committee. Public Relations Division. *One Hundred Years: A History of the National Republican Congressional Committee.* Washington: Republican Congressional Committee, 1966.

3701. Rosenthal, Alan. *State Legislative Committees: A Review and Some Proposals for Congress. Working Papers on House Committee Organization and Operation. Presented to House Select Committee on Committees.* 93rd Cong. Washington: GPO, 1973.

3702. Rundquist, Paul S. *Formal and Informal Congressional Groups.* Washington: Congressional Research Service, 1978.

3703. Sheppard, Nat. "The Congressional Black Caucus in Search of a Role" *Race Relations Reporter* 4 (Mar. 1973): 18-21.

3704. Stevens, Arthur G. "Informal Groups and Decision-Making in the United States House of Representatives." Ph.D. dissertation, University of Michigan, 1970.

3705. Stevens, Arthur G., Miller, Arthur H., and Mann, Thomas E. "Mobilization of Liberal Strength in the House, 1955-1970: The Democratic Study Group." *American Political Science Review* 68 (June 1974): 667-681.

3706. Stewart, John G. "Central Policy Organs in Congress." *The Academy of Political Science, Proceedings* 32 (1975): 20-33.

3707. Truman, David B. "State Delegations and the Structure of Party Voting in the United States House of Representatives." *American Political Science Review* 50 (Dec. 1956): 1023-1045.

3708. Walker, Alexander J. "The Virginia Congressional Delegation Since 1965." *University of Virginia News Letter* 55 (Oct. 1978): 1-4.

3709. Warren, Sarah E. "The New Look of the Congressional Caucuses." *National Journal* 10 (April 29, 1978): 677-679.

3710. Watson, Richard L. "Principle, Party, and Constituency: The North Carolina Congressional Delegation, 1917-1919." *North Carolina Historical Review* 56 (July 1979): 298-323.

3711. Wright, Waymond. "Congressional Black Caucus Arouses New Political Awareness." *Negro Historical Bulletin* 35 (May 1972): 108-110.

Blocs and Coalitions

3712. Ashby, Darrel L. "Progressivism Against Itself: The Senate Western Bloc in the 1920's." *Mid-America* 50 (Oct. 1968): 291-304.

3713. Bernstein, Barton J. and Leib, Franklin A. "Progressive Republican Senators and American Imperialism, 1898-1916: A Reappraisal." *Mid-America* 50 (July 1968): 163-205.

3714. Bogue, Allan G. "Bloc and Party in the United States Senate, 1861-1863." *Civil War History* 13 (Sept. 1967): 221-241.

3715. Boylan, James R. "Reconversion in Politics: The New Deal Coalition and the Election of the Eightieth Congress." Ph.D. dissertation, Columbia University, 1971.

3716. Bradley, Phillip. "The Farm Bloc." *Journal of Social Forces* 3 (May 1925): 714-718.

3717. Bratter, Herbert M. "The Silver Episode, I, II." *Journal of Political Economy* 46 (Oct. 1938): 609-652, 802-837.

3718. Brennan, John A. *Silver and the First New Deal.* Reno: University of Nevada Press, 1969.

3719. Black, John D. "The McNary-Haugen Movement." *American Economic Review* 18 (Sept. 1928): 405-427.

3720. Carothers, Neil. *Silver: A Senate Racket.* Bethlehem, Pa.: Lehigh University, 1932.

3721. "Conservative Bloc in Congress Remains Potent." *Congressional Quarterly Weekly Report* 21 (June 7, 1963): 921-923.

3722. Cooley, Everett L. "Silver Politics in the United States, 1918-1946." Ph.D. dissertation, University of California at Berkeley, 1951.

3723. Deckard, Barbara Sinclair, and Stanley, John. "Party Decomposition and Region: The House of Representatives, 1945-1970." *Western Political Quarterly* 27 (June 1974): 249-264.

3724. Everest, Allan S. "Morgenthau, the New Deal and Silver." Ph.D. dissertation, Columbia University, 1950.

3725. Farris, Charles D. "Method of Determining Ideological Groupings in the Congress." *Journal of Politics* 20 (May 1958): 308-338.

3726. Feinman, Ronald L. "The Decline of the Western Progressive Republican Bloc in the Senate During the New Deal, 1933-1945." Ph.D. dissertation, City University of New York, 1975.

3727. Feinman, Ronald L. "Progressive Republican Senate Bloc and the Presidential Election of 1932." *Mid-America* 59 (April 1977): 73-91.

3728. Fink, Gary M. "North Great Plains' Senators in the New Deal Era." *Capitol Studies* 3 (Fall 1975): 129-151.

3729. Gould, Lewis L. "Western Range Senators and the Payne-Aldrich Tariff." *Pacific Northwest Quarterly* 64 (April 1973): 49-56.

3730. Gray, Charles H. "Coalition, Consensus, and Conflict in the United States Senate (1957-1960)." Ph.D. dissertation, University of Colorado, 1962.

3731. Grumm, John G. "Systematic Analysis of Blocs in the Study of Legislative Behavior." *Western Political Quarterly* 18 (June 1965): 350-362.

3732. Hinckley, Barbara. "Coalitions in Congress: Size and Ideological Distance." *Midwest Journal of Political Science* 16 (May 1972): 197-207.

3733. Kofmehl, Kenneth. "The Institutionalization of a Voting Bloc." *Western Political Quarterly* 17 (June 1964): 256-272.

3734. Levine, Martin D. "A Theory of Coalition Formation in Legislatures: Bargaining in the United States Senate." Ph.D. dissertation, Michigan State University, 1972.

3735. Lutz, Donald S. and Williams, James R. *Minimum Coalitions in Legislatures: A Review of the Evidence.* Beverly Hills, Calif.: Sage Publications, 1976.

3736. McCune, Wesley. *The Farm Bloc.* Garden City, N.Y.: Doubleday, 1943.

3737. Mahnken, Norbert R. "The Congressmen of the Grain Belt States and Tariff Legislation, 1865-1900." Ph.D. dissertation, University of Nebraska, 1942.

3738. Manley, John F. "The Conservative Coalition in Congress." *American Behavioral Scientist* 17 (Nov.-Dec. 1973): 223-247.

3739. Manley, John F. "The Conservative Coalition in Congress." In *Congress Reconsidered,* eds. Lawrence C. Dodd and Bruce I. Oppenheimer, pp. 75-95. New York: Praeger, 1977.

3740. Margolis, Joel P. "The Conservative Coalition in the United States Senate, 1933-1968." Ph.D. dissertation, University of Wisconsin, 1973.

3741. Moore, John R. "Conservative Coalition in the United States Senate, 1942-1945." *Journal of Southern History* 33 (Aug. 1967): 368-376.

3742. Moser, Charles A. *The Speaker and the House Coalitions and Power in the United States House of Representatives.* Washington: Free Congress Research and Education Fund, 1979.

3743. Mulder, Ronald A. *The Insurgent Progressives in the United States Senate and the New Deal, 1933-1939.* New York: Garland Publishing Co., 1979.

3744. Mulder, Ronald A. "Reluctant New Dealers: The Progressive Insurgents in the United States Senate, 1933-1934." *Capitol Studies* 2 (Winter 1974): 5-22.

3745. Nelson, Albert J. "Issue Categories, Coalition Formations, and Presidential Support in the U.S. Senate, 1969-1973." Ph.D. dissertation, University of Oregon, 1974.

3746. Nichols, Jeannette P. "The Politics and Personalities of Silver Repeal in the United States Senate." *American Historical Review* 41 (Oct. 1935): 26-53.

3747. Nichols, Jeannette P. "Silver Inflation and the Senate in 1933." *Social Studies* 25 (Jan. 1934): 12-18.

3748. O'Brien, Patrick G. "A Re-Examination of the Senate Farm Bloc 1921-1933." *Agricultural History* 47 (July 1973): 248-263.

3749. Patterson, James T. "Conservative Coalition Forms in Congress: 1933-1939." *Journal of American History* 52 (Mar. 1966): 757-772.

3750. Rakow, Michael G. "Southern Politics in the United States Senate: 1948-1972." Ph.D. dissertation, Arizona State University, 1973.

3751. Risjord, Norman K. "The Old Republicans: Southern Conservatives in Congress, 1806-1824." Ph.D, dissertation, University of Virginia, 1960.

3752. Shelley, Mack C. "The Conservative Coalition in the U.S. Congress, 1933-1976: Time Series Analysis of a Legislative Policy Coalition." Ph.D. dissertation, University of Wisconsin, 1977.

3753. Timberlake, Richard H. "Repeal of Silver Monetization in the Late Nineteenth Century." *Journal of Money, Credit, and Banking* 10 (Feb. 1978): 27-45.

3754. Uslaner, Eric M. "Contextual Model of Coalition Formation in Congress: The Dimensions of Party and Political Time." *American Behavioral Scientist* 18 (Mar. 1975): 513-529.

3755. Watson, Richard L. "Testing Time for Southern Congressional Leadership: The War Crisis of 1917-1918." *Journal of Southern History* 44 (Feb. 1978): 3-40.

3756. Weingast, Barry R. "A Rational Choice Perspective on Congressional Norms." *American Journal of Political Science* 23 (May 1979): 245-262.

3757. Wellborn, Fred W. "The Influence of the Silver-Republican Senators, 1889-1891." *Mississippi Valley Historical Review* 14 (Mar. 1928): 462-472.

3758. Wellborn, Fred W. "The Silver Republicans, 1890-1900." Ph.D. dissertation, University of Wisconsin, 1926.

XI. Pressures on Congress

Presidential Relations

General Studies

3759. Andrews, William G. "The Presidency, Congress and Constitutional Theory." In *The Presidency in Contemporary Context,* ed. N. C. Thomas, pp. 13-32. New York: Dodd, Mead, 1975.

3760. Balch, Stephen H. "Do Strong Presidents Really Want Strong Legislative Parties? The Case of Woodrow Wilson and the House Democrats." *Presidential Studies Quarterly* 7 (Fall 1977): 231-238.

3761. Balz, Daniel J. "Carter's Honeymoon on the Hill: How Long Can It Last?" *National Journal* 8 (Nov. 13, 1976): 1618-1623.

3762. Binkley, Wilfred E. *President and Congress.* 3rd ed. New York: Vintage, 1962.

3763. Binkley, Wilfred E. "President and Congress." *Journal of Politics* 11 (Feb. 1949): 65-79.

3764. Binkley, Wilfred E. "The Relation of the President to Congress." *Parliamentary Affairs* 3 (Winter 1949): 20-28.

3765. Black, Charles L. "Presidency and Congress." *Washington and Lee Law Review* 32 (Fall 1975): 841-854.

3766. Bonafede, Dom. "Carter and Congress: It Seems That 'If Something Can Go Wrong, It Will.'" *National Journal* 9 (Nov. 12, 1977): 1756-1761.

3767. Bonafede, Dom. "Carter's Relationship with Congress: Making a Mountain Out of a 'Moorehill.'" *National Journal* 9 (Mar. 26, 1977): 456-463.

3768. Bonafede, Dom and Glass, Andrew J. "Nixon Deals Cautiously with Hostile Congress." *National Journal* 2 (June 27, 1970): 1353-1366.

3769. Bonafede, Dom, Rapoport, Daniel, and Havemann, Joel. "The President Versus Congress: The Score Since Watergate." *National Journal* 8 (May 29, 1976): 730-748.

3770. Chamberlain, Lawrence H. "The President, Congress and Legislation." *Political Science Quarterly* 61 (Mar. 1946): 42-60.

3771. Chamberlain, Lawrence H. *The President, Congress and Legislation.* New York: Columbia University Press, 1947.

3772. Cohen, Benjamin V. "Presidential Responsibility and American Democracy." In *The Prospect for Presidential-Congressional Government,* ed. Albert Lepawsky, pp. 17-34. Berkeley: Institute of Governmental Studies, University of California, 1977.

3773. Cohen, Richard E. "The Carter–Congress Rift: Who's Really to Blame." *National Journal* 10 (April 22, 1978): 630-632.

3774. "Congressional Government: Can It Happen?" *Congressional Quarterly Weekly Report* 33 (June 28, 1975): 1331-1332.

3775. Cooper, Ann. "Changes on the Hill Worsen Usual End-of-Year Logjam." *Congressional Quarterly Weekly Report* 36 (Sept. 2, 1978): 2303-2306.

3776. Curran, George A. "Woodrow Wilson's Theory and Practice Regarding Relations of President and Congress." Ph.D. dissertation, Fordham University, 1949.

3777. Dameron, Kenneth. "President Kennedy and Congress. Process and Politics." Ph.D. dissertation, Harvard University, 1975.

3778. Davis, James W. and Ringquist, Delbert. *The President and Congress: Toward a New Balance.* Woodbury, N.Y.: Barron's Educational Series, 1975.

3779. Dewey, Donald O. "Senate Control of the Presidency." *Connecticut Historical Society Bulletin* 31 (Jan. 1966): 21-23.

3780. Dodd, Lawrence C. "The Presidency, Congress and the Cycles of Power." In *The Post-Imperial Presidency,* ed. Vincent Davis, pp. 71-100. New Brunswick, N.J.: Transaction Books, 1979.

3781. Donnelly, Thomas C. "The Relations of the Senate with the President." *Social Science* 6 (April 1931): 168-172.

3782. Dunn, Charles. "The Congress and the Presidency in Military Crisis: A Communications Model." Ph.D. dissertation, Florida State University, 1965.

3783. Eggers, Rowland A. and Harris, Joseph P. *The President and Congress.* New York: McGraw-Hill, 1963.

3784. Ellis, Ellen D. "Congress and the President." *Current History* 27 (Oct. 1954): 201-207.

3785. Fainsod, Merle. "Presidency and Congress." *Public Administration Review* 11 (1951): 119-124.

3786. Fisher, Louis. "Delegating Power to the President." *Journal of Public Law* 19 (1970): 251-282.

3787. Fisher, Louis. *President and Congress: Power and Policy.* New York: Free Press, 1972.

3788. Folts, David W. "The Role of the President and Congress in the Formulation of United States Economic Policy Towards the Soviet Union, 1947-1968." Ph.D. dissertation, University of Notre Dame, 1971.

3789. "Frustration in Washington: The President and Congress." *World Today* 13 (Sept. 1957): 416-422.

3790. Gallagher, Hugh G. "Presidents, Congress and the Legislative Function." In *The President Reappraised,* eds. R. G. Tugwell and Thomas E. Cronin, pp. 217-233. New York: Praeger, 1974.

3791. Gallagher, Hugh G. "The President, Congress, and Legislation." In *The Presidency Reappraised,* 2d ed. eds. R. G. Tugwell and Thomas E. Cronin, pp. 267-282. New York: Praeger, 1977.

3792. Hartmann, Susan M. *Truman and the 80th Congress.* Columbia: University of Missouri Press, 1971.

3793. Haynes, George H. "The President and the Senate." *Colonial Society of Massachusetts Publications* 24 (1920-1923): 180-182.

3794. Helms, E. Allen. "The President and Party Politics." *Journal of Politics* 11 (Feb. 1949): 42-64.

3795. Holcombe, Arthur N. "Presidents and Congresses." In his *Our More Perfect Union,* pp. 236-283. Cambridge, Mass.: Harvard University Press, 1950.

3796. Johannes, John R. "From White House to Capitol Hill: How Far Will the Pendulum Swing?" *Intellect* 10 (Mar. 1975): 356-360.

3797. Johannes, John R. "The President Proposes and Congress Disposes—But Not Always: Legislative Initiative on Capitol Hill." *Review of Politics* 36 (July 1974): 356-370.

3798. Johannes, John R. "Where Does the Buck Stop?: Congress, President and the Responsibility for Legislative Initiation." *Western Political Quarterly* 25 (Sept. 1972): 396-415.

3799. Johnson, Allen. "President and Congress." In his *Readings in American Constitutional History*, pp. 151-159. Boston: Houghton Mifflin, 1912.

3800. Kehoe, Loretta. "The Relations of Herbert Hoover to Congress, 1929-1933." Master's thesis, Loyola University, 1949.

3801. Kilpatrick, Carroll. "The Kennedy Style and Congress." *Virginia Quarterly Review* 39 (Winter 1963): 1-11.

3802. Koenig, Louis W. *Congress and the President: Official Makers of Public Policy.* Glenview, Ill.: Scott, Foresman, 1965.

3803. Kraines, Oscar. "The President Versus Congress: The Keep Commission, 1905-1909: First Conprehensive Presidential Inquiry into Administration." *Western Political Quarterly* 23 (Mar. 1970): 5-54.

3804. Kulka, Giora. "Congressional Opposition to President Truman." Ph.D. dissertation, Harvard University, 1972.

3805. Lane, Gary. *The President Versus Congress: Freedom of Information.* Jamaica, N.Y.: Lanco Press, 1971.

3806. Lepawsky, Albert, ed. *The Prospect for Presidential–Congressional Government.* Berkeley: Institute of Governmental Studies, University of California, 1977.

3807. Lester, Robert L. "Developments in Presidential–Congressional Relations: Franklin D. Roosevelt–John F. Kennedy." Ph.D. dissertation, University of Virginia, 1969.

3808. Levine, David D. "The Executive Order: A Form of Presidential Participation in the Legislative Process." Ph.D. dissertation, American University, 1955.

3809. Levitan, Sar A. "Congress vs. President: The Myth and the Pendulum." In *The Presidency and the Congress: A Shifting Balance of Power?, eds. William S. Livingston, Lawrence C. Dodd, and Richard L. Schott, pp. 182-196. Austin: Lyndon B. Johnson School of Public Affairs, University of Texas, 1979.*

3810. Lindley, Ernest K. "A Review of President Roosevelt and Congress." *The Literary Digest* 117 (June 2, 1934), 7, 42.

3811. Livingston, William S., Dodd, Lawrence C., and Schott, Richard L., eds. *The Presidency and the Congress: A Shifting Balance of Power?* Austin: Lyndon B. Johnson School of Public Affairs, University of Texas, 1979.

3812. MacLean, Joan Coyne. *President and Congress: The Conflict of Powers.* New York: H. W. Wilson, 1955.

3813. Manley, John F. "The Presidency, Congress and National Policy Making." In *Political Science Annual,* ed. C. Cotter, pp. 227-266. Indianapolis, Ind.: Bobbs-Merrill, 1974.

3814. Mansfield, Harvey C., ed. *Congress Against the President.* New York: Academy of Political Science, 1975.

3815. Moe, Ronald C., ed. *Congress and the President: Allies and Adversaries.* Pacific Palisades, Calif.: Goodyear, 1971.

3816. Parker, Glenn R. *Political Beliefs About the Structure of Government: Congress and the Presidency.* Beverly Hills, Calif.: Sage Publications, 1974.

3817. Parris, Judith H. "Congress and the American Presidential System." *Current History* 66 (June 1974): 259-263.

3818. Pepper, George W. *Family Quarrels: The President, the Senate, the House.* New York: Baker, Voorhis, 1931.

3819. Polsby, Nelson W. *Congress and the Presidency,* 3d ed. Englewood Cliffs, N.J.: Prentice-Hall, 1976.

3820. "President and Congress." *World Today* 9 (Feb. 1953): 99-106.

3821. Prestage, Jewel L. "The Status of the First Hoover Commission Report: An Analysis of the Roles of the President and Congress." Ph.D. dissertation, University of Iowa, 1954.

3822. "Progress Report: Congress and the President." *Congressional Quarterly Weekly Report* 31 (April 14, 1973): 821-833.

3823. Riddick, Floyd M. "House of Representatives and the President." *South Atlantic Quarterly* 34 (Jan. 1935): 79-90.

3824. Rowe, James. "Cooperation or Conflict: The President's Relationships with an Opposition Congress." *Georgetown Law Journal* 36 (Nov. 1947): 1-15.

3825. Schlesinger, Arthur M. and de Grazia, Alfred. *Congress and the Presidency: Their Role in Modern Times.* Washington: American Enterprise Institute for Public Policy Research, 1967.

3826. Smith, Stephanie. *Advisory Bodies Created by the President and by Congress, 1955 Through 1976.* Washington: Congressional Research Service, 1976.

3827. Sundquist, James L. "Congress and the President: Enemies or Partners?" In *Congress Reconsidered,* eds. Lawrence C. Dodd and Bruce I. Oppenheimer, pp. 222-243. New York: Praeger, 1977.

3828. Thomas, Norman C. "Presidential Accountability Since Watergate." *Presidential Studies Quarterly* 8 (Fall 1978): 417-433.

3829. Travis, Walter Earl, ed. *Congress and the President: Reading in Executive–Legislative Relations.* New York: Teachers College Press, Columbia University, 1967.

3830. Truman, David B. "Functional Interdependence: Electric Leaders, the White House, and the Congressional Party." In *The Presidency,* ed. A. Wildavsky, pp. 454-476. Boston: Little, Brown, 1969.

3831. Wayne, Stephen J., Cole, Richard L., and Hyde, James F. C. "Advising the President on Enrolled Legislation: Patterns of Executive Influence." *Political Science Quarterly* 94 (Summer 1979): 303-317.

3832. Wicker, Tom. "It Is the People Who Face the Test, They Will Determine Whether the New President Can Overcome Standpattism in Congress." *New York Times Magazine,* 8 Dec. 1963, pp. 19, 115-117.

3833. Zeidenstein, Harvey G. "The Reassertion of Congressional Power: New Curbs on the President." *Political Science Quarterly* 93 (Fall 1978): 393-410.

Presidential Leadership

3834. Armstrong, Walter P. "The President and the Congress: Unsolved Problems of Leadership and Powers. *American Bar Association Journal* 33 (May 1947): 417-420, 511.

3835. Bailey, Gil. "Congress or the White House? The Contest for Leadership in Energy Policy." *Cry California* 10 (Summer 1975): 13-17.

3836. Binkley, Winfred E. "The President as Chief Legislator." *American Academy of Political and Social Science, Annals* 307 (Sept. 1956): 92-105.

3837. Bond, Jon R. and Fleisher, Richard. "The Limits of Presidential Popularity as a Source of Influence in the U.S. House." *Legislative Studies Quarterly* 5 (Feb. 1980): 69-78.

3838. Burns, James MacGregor. "Excellence and Leadership in President and Congress." *Daedalus* 90 (Fall 1961): 734-749.

3839. Chandler, Henry P. "Presidential Government." *American Bar Association Journal* 7 (April 1921): 149-155.

3840. Christenson, Reo M. "Presidential Leadership of Congress: Ten Commandments Point the Way." *Presidential Studies Quarterly* 8 (Summer 1978): 257-267.

3841. Clark, Ramsey. "The Erosion of Congressional Power: How Can We Check the Autocratic Actions of the President and Restore Constitutional Balance Between the Executive and Legislative Branches of the Federal Government." *Lithopinion* 8 (Fall 1973): 21-23.

3842. Edwards, George C. "The President and Congress: The Inevitability of Conflict." *Presidential Studies Quarterly* 8 (Summer 1978): 245-256.

3843. Edwards, George C. *Presidential Influence in Congress.* San Francisco: W. H. Freeman, 1980.

3844. Edwards, George C. "Presidential Influence in the House: Presidential Prestige as a Source of Presidential Power." *American Political Science Review* 70 (Mar. 1976): 101-113.

3845. Edwards, George C. "Presidential Influence in the Senate: Presidential Prestige as a Source of Presidential Power." *American Politics Quarterly* 5 (Oct. 1977): 481-500.

3846. Edwards, George C. "Presidential Legislative Skills as a Source of Influence in Congress." *Presidential Studies Quarterly* 10 (Spring 1980): 211-223.

3847. Fleishman, Joel L. and Aufses, Arthur H. "Law and Orders: The Problem of Presidential Legislation." *Law and Contemporary Problems* 40 (Summer 1976): 1-45.

3848. Gilmour, Robert S. "Central Legislative Clearance: A Revised Perspective." *Public Administration Review* 31 (Mar./April 1971): 150-158.

3849. Goetchus, Vernon M. "Presidential Party Leadership Relations Between President Johnson and House Democrats in the 89th Congress." Ph.D. dissertation, University of Wisconsin, 1967.

3850. Herring, Edward P. *Presidential Leadership: The Political Relations of Congress and the Chief Executive.* New York: Farrar and Rinehart, 1940.

3851. Hughes, Emmet J. "The Presidency in the American Power Structure." In *The Prospect for Presidential–Congressional Government,* ed. Albert Lepawsky, pp. 35-48. Berkeley: Institute of Governmental Studies, University of California, 1977.

3852. Ink, Dwight A. "The President as Manager." *Public Administration Review* 36 (Sept./Oct. 1976): 508-515.

3853. Leavel, Willard H. "Congressional Variables and Presidential Leadership." Ph.D. dissertation, University of Washington, 1962.

3854. Leloup, Lance T. and Shull, Steven A. "Congress Versus the Executive: The 'Two Presidencies' Reconsidered." *Social Science Quarterly* 59 (Mar. 1979): 704-719.

3855. Lepawsky, Albert. "Reconstituted Presidency and Resurgent Congress." In his *The Prospect for Presidential-Congress Government,* pp. 65-103. Berkeley: Institute of Governmental Studies, University of California, 1977.

3856. MacMahon, Arthur W. "Woodrow Wilson as a Legislative Leader and Administrator." *American Political Science Review* 50 (Sept. 1956): 641-675.

3857. Neustadt, Richard E. "Presidency and Legislation: The Growth of Central Clearance." *American Political Science Review* 48 (Sept. 1954):641-671.

3858. Riker, William H. and Bast, W. "Presidential Action in Congressional Nominations." In *The Presidency,* ed. A. Wildavsky, pp. 250-267. Boston: Little, Brown, 1969.

3859. Ryley, Thomas W. *A Little Group of Willful Men: A Study of Congressional/Presidential Authority.* Port Washington, N.Y.: Kennikat Press, 1975.

3860. Sharp, James R. "Andrew Jackson and the Limits of Presidential Power." *Congressional Studies* 7 (Winter 1980): 63-80.

3861. Silver, Howard J. "Presidential Performance with Congress: 1954-1973." Ph.D. dissertation, Ohio State University, 1975.

3862. Snowiss, Sylvia. "Presidential Leadership of Congress: An Analysis of Roosevelt's First Hundred Days." *Publius* 1 (1971): 59-60.

3863. Truman, David B. "Presidency and Congressional Leadership: Some Notes on Our Changing Constitution." *The American Philosophical Society, Proceedings* 103 (Oct. 1959): 687-692.

3864. Vazzano, Frank P. "Hayes, Congress, and the Resurrection of Presidential Authority." Ph.D. dissertation, Kent State University, 1972.

3865. Vile, Maurice J. C. "Presidential and Parliamentary Systems." In *The Prospect for Presidential-Congressional Government,* ed. Albert Lepawsky, pp. 49-64. Berkeley: Institute for Governmental Studies, University of California, 1977.

3866. Wayne, Stephen J. *The Legislative Presidency.* New York: Harper and Row, 1978.

3867. Wegge, David G. "Presidential Effectiveness in Congress: A Partial Test of Neustadt's Model." Ph.D. dissertation, University of Wisconsin, 1978.

3869. Black, Charles L. "Some Thoughts on the Veto." *Law and Contemporary Problems* 40 (Spring 1976): 87-101.

3870. Condo, Joseph A. "The Veto of S.3418: More Congressional Power in the President's Pocket?" *Catholic University Law Review* 22 (Winter 1973): 385-402.

3871. Dumbrell, John W. and Lees, John D. "Presidential Pocket-Veto Power: A Constitutional Anachronism?" *Political Studies* 28 (Mar. 1980): 109-116.

3872. Johnson, Allen. "President and Congress: The Veto Power." In his *Readings in American Constitutional History, 1776-1876,* pp. 370-379. Boston: Houghton Mifflin, 1912.

3873. Kennedy, Edward M. "Congress, the President, and the Pocket Veto." *Virginia Law Review* 63 (April 1977): 355-382.

3874. Miller, Arthur S. "Congressional Power to Define the Presidential Pocket Veto Power." *Vanderbilt Law Review* 25 (April 1972): 557-572.

3875. Rogers, Lindsay. "The Power of the President to Sign Bills After Congress Has Adjourned." *Yale Law Journal* 30 (Nov. 1920): 1-22.

3876. Shumaker, W. A. "Pocket Veto at Close of First Session of Congress." *Law Notes* 31 (April 1927): 5-8.

3877. Taylor, Frederick E. "An Analysis of Factors Purported to Influence the Use of, and Congressional Responses to the Use of, the Presidential Veto." Ph.D. dissertation, Georgetown University, 1971.

3878. Vose, Clement E. "The Memorandum Pocket Veto." *Journal of Politics* 26 (May 1964): 397-405.

Veto Power

3868. Berdahl, Clarence A. "The President's Veto of Private Bills." *Political Science Quarterly* 52 (Dec. 1937): 505-531.

Congress and the Cabinet

3879. Belmont, Perry. "Cabinet Officers in Congress." *North American Review* 197 (Jan. 1913): 22-30.

3880. Belmont, Perry. "Executive Officers in Congress: The Affirmative Point of View." *Constitutional Review* 12 (July 1928): 133-147.

3881. Bradford, Gamaliel. "Congress and the Cabinet." *The American Academy of Political and Social Science, Annals* 2 (Nov. 1891): 289-299.

3882. Brown, Willard. "Shall Members of the Cabinet Sit in Congress?" *Atlantic Monthly* 50 (July 1882): 95-99.

3883. Dodge, Edmund A. "Cabinet Officers in Congress." *Sewanee Review* 11 (April 1903): 129-143.

3884. Elder, Shirley. "The Cabinet's Ambassadors to Capitol Hill." *National Journal* 10 (July 29, 1978): 1196-1200.

3885. Fisher, Sydney G. "Cabinet Officers in Congress." *Overland Monthly* 9 (Feb. 1887): 209-213.

3886. Godkin, E. L. "The Admission of Cabinet Officers to Seats in Congress." *Nation*, 17 Feb. 1881, pp. 107-109.

3887. Hinsdale, Mary L. "The Cabinet and Congress: An Historical Inquiry." *American Political Science Association, Proceedings* 2 (1906): 126-148.

3888. Horn, Stephen. *The Cabinet and Congress.* New York: Columbia University Press, 1960.

3889. Leupp, Francis E. "The Cabinet in Congress." *Atlantic Monthly* 120 (Dec. 1917): 769-779.

3890. Michener, John H. "The United States Cabinet: A Study of Proposed Modifications, with Especial Reference to Cabinet–Congressional Relations." Ph.D. dissertation, University of California at Berkeley, 1956.

3891. Reed, Thomas B. "Should the Cabinet Officers Have Seats in Congress?" *The Illustrated American* 22 (July 1897): 137-138.

3892. White, Horace. "Cabinet Officers in Congress." *Nation*, 10 April 1879, pp. 243-244.

3893. White, Howard. "Executive Officers in Congress: The Negative Point of View." *Constitutional Review* 12 (July 1928): 148-156.

3894. Wright, Herbert F. "Congress Seats for Cabinet Members." *Constitutional Review* 13 (Jan. 1929): 36-44.

Separation of Powers

3895. Arnold, Perie E. and Roose, L. John. "Toward a Theory of Congressional–Executive Relation." *Review of Politics* 36 (July 1974): 410-429.

3896. Cheadle, John B. "Delegation of Legislative Functions." *Yale Law Journal* 27 (May 1918): 892-923.

3897. Coffin, Tristram. "Congress: Its Last Sacred Powers." *Bulletin of the Atomic Scientists* 23 (Dec. 1967): 35-37.

3898. Cole, Kenneth C. "Government, Law and the Separation of Powers." *American Political Science Review* 33 (June 1939): 424-440.

3899. Dexter, Lewis A. " 'Check and Balance' Today: What Does It Mean for Congress and Congressmen?" In *Twelve Studies of the Organization of Congress*, ed. Alfred de Grazia, pp. 83-113. Washington: American Enterprise Institute for Public Policy Research, 1966.

3900. Ely, John H. "United States v. Lovett: Litigating the Separation of Powers." *Harvard Civil Rights Law Review* 10 (Winter 1975): 1-32.

3901. Fetter, Theodore J. "Waging war Under the Separation of Powers: Executive–Congressional Relations During World War II." Ph.D. dissertation, University of Wisconsin, 1974.

3902. Field, G. Lowell. "Administration by Statute: The Question of Special Laws." *Public Administration Review* 6 (Autumn 1946): 325-338.

3903. Fisher, Louis. *The Constitution Between Friends: Congress, the President and the Law.* New York: St. Martin's Press, 1978.

3904. Frohnmayer, David B. "The Separation of Powers: An Essay on the Vitality of a Constitutional Idea." *Oregon Law Review* 52 (Spring 1973): 211-235.

3905. Gewirtz, Paul. "Courts, Congress, and Executive Policy-Making: Notes on Three Doctrines." *Law and Contemporary Problems* 40 (Summer 1976): 46-85.

3906. Green, Frederick. "Separation of Governmental Powers." *Yale Law Journal* 29 (Feb. 1920): 369-393.

3907. Hagen, Charles B. "The Story of an Unbalanced Government." *World Affairs* 140 (Summer 1977): 67-77.

3908. Hamilton, Lee H. and Van Dusen, Michael H. "Making the Separation of Powers Work." *Foreign Affairs* 57 (Fall 1978): 17-39.

3909. Jaffe, Louis L. "Delegation of Legislative Power: An Essay." *Columbia Law Review* 47 (April-May 1947): 359-376, 561-593.

3910. McKinley, Charles. "Federal Administrative Pathology and the Separation of Powers." *Public Administration Review* 11 (Winter 1951): 17-25.

3911. Miller, Ben R. "The Presidency and Separation of Powers." *American Bar Association Journal* 60 (Feb. 1974): 195-197.

3912. Reinstein, Robert J. and Silvergate, Harvey A. "Legislative Privilege and the Separation of Powers." *Harvard Law Review* 86 (May 1973): 1113-1182.

3913. Riggs, Richard A. "Separation of Powers: Congressional Riders and the Veto Powers." *University of Michigan Journal of Law Reform* 6 (Spring 1973): 735-759.

3914. Rogow, Arnold A. and Temple, Janis Y. "Congressional Government: Legislative Power v. Democratic Processes." *George Washington Law Review* 32 (June 1964): 947-953.

3915. Sauer, Robert A. "Separation of Powers and Legislative Delegation in Our Federal Government." Ph.D. dissertation, New York University, 1940.

3916. Taft, William Howard. "The Boundaries Between the Executive, the Legislative and the Judicial Branches of the Government." *Yale Law Journal* 25 (June 1916): 599-616.

3917. Zurcher, Arnold J. "The Presidency, Congress and Separation of Powers: A Reappraisal." *Western Political Quarterly* 3 (Mar. 1950): 75-97.

Legislative–Executive Relations

General Studies

3918. Abel, Robert B. "The Politics of Executive–Legislative Relationships in a Multiple Committee–Single Bureau Situation." Ph.D. dissertation, American University, 1972.

3919. Acheson, Dean G. "Legislative–Executive Relations." *Yale Review* 45 (June 1956): 481-495.

3920. Almund, Curtis A. "Executive–Legislative Imbalance: Truman to Kennedy?" *Western Political Quarterly* 18 (Sept. 1965): 640-645.

3921. Arnold, R. Douglas. *Congress and the Bureaucracy: A Theory of Influence.* New Haven, Conn.: Yale University Press, 1979.

3922. Binkley, Wilfred E. "The Relation of the Federal Executive of the United States to the Congress of the United States." Ph.D. dissertation, Ohio State University, 1937.

3923. Black, Henry C. *The Relation of the Executive Power to Legislation.* Princeton, N.J.: Princeton University Press, 1919.

3924. Boegehold, Donald G. "Planning for Staff in the Federal Government: Congressional Interests and Agency Practices." *GAO Review* 13 (Fall 1978): 37-41.

3925. Burns, James MacGregor. *The Deadlock of Democracy.* Englewood Cliffs, N.J.: Prentice-Hall, 1963.

3926. Chauhan, D. S. "Politics of Executive–Legislative Relationship in American Democracy: Conflict and Consensus of Uneasy Partnership." *Journal of Constitutional and Parliamentary Studies* 8 (April-June 1974): 141-168.

3927. Collins, Ernest M. "Congress Is Losing Its Grip." *Social Studies* 57 (Mar. 1966): 104-108.

3928. Costen, Dean W. "Bureaucratic Reactions to Congressional Pressures." *Bureaucrat* 2 (Fall 1973): 269-277.

3929. Davidson, Roger H. "Congress and the Executive: The Race for Representation." In *Twelve Studies of the Organization of Congress,* ed. Alfred de Grazia, pp. 377-413. Washington: American Enterprise Institute for Public Policy Research, 1966.

3930. Davis, Kenneth C. "Administrative Rules: Interpretative, Legislative, and Retroactive." *Yale Law Journal* 57 (April 1948): 919-959.

3931. De Grazia, Alfred. *Republic in Crisis: Congress Against the Executive Force.* New York: Federal Legal Publication, 1965.

3932. Dodd, Lawrence C. "Cycles of Congressional Power." *Society* 16 (Nov.-Dec. 1978): 65-68.

3933. Drew, Elizabeth B. "Why Congress Won't Fight." In *Watergate: Its Effects on the American Political System,* ed. D. C. Saffell, pp. 37-47. Cambridge, Mass. Winthrop Publishers, 1974.

3934. Edwards, Nancy A. "Congress and Administrative Reorganization." Ph.D. dissertation, Columbia University, 1955.

3935. Fiorina, Morris P. and Noll, Roger G. "Voters, Legislators and Bureaucracy: Institutional Design and Public Sector." *American Economic Review, Papers and Proceedings* 68 (May 1978): 256-260.

3936. Freeman, J. Leiper. *The Political Process: Executive Bureau–Legislative Committee Relations.* rev. ed. New York: Random House, 1965.

3937. Garner, James W. "Executive Participation in Legislation as a Means of Increasing Legislative Efficiency." *American Political Science Review* 8 (Feb. 1914): 176-190.

3938. Hall, Hugh M. "Responsibility of President and Congress for Regulatory Policy Development." *Law and Contemporary Problems* 26 (Spring 1961): 261-282.

3939. Handerson, Harold. "The Congressional and Regulatory Scene." *Bureaucrat* 8 (Spring 1979): 58-60.

3940. Harris, Joseph P. "The Progress of Administrative Reorganization in the Seventy-Fifth Congress." *American Political Science Review* 31 (Oct. 1937): 862-870,

3941. Havemann, Joel. "Congress Tries to Break to Ground Zero in Evaluating Federal Programs." *National Journal* 8 (May 22, 1976): 706-713.

3942. Herring, Edward P. "Executive–Legislative Responsibilities." *American Political Science Review* 38 (Dec. 1944): 1153-1165.

3943. Hilsman, Roger. "Congressional–Executive Relations and the Foreign Policy Consensus." *American Political Science Review* 52 (Sept. 1958): 725-744.

3944. Hopkins, Bruce R. "Congressional Relations with Executive and Judicial." *American Bar Association Journal* 59 (Feb. 1973): 145-149.

3945. Hyman, Sydney. "Shall Senatorial Power Be Curbed?" *New York Times Magazine,* 21 Mar. 1954, pp. 7, 28, 30, 32, 34.

3946. Johannes, John R. "Congress and the Initiation of Legislation." *Public Policy* 20 (Spring 1972): 281-309.

3947. Johannes, John R. "Executive Reports to Congress." *Journal of Communication* 26 (Summer 1976): 53-61.

3948. Johannes, John R. "When Congress Leads: Cases and Patterns of Congressional Initiative of Legislation." Ph.D. dissertation, Harvard University, 1971.

3949. Jones, Harry W. "A Joint Legislative-Executive Council for the 81st Congress." *American Bar Association Journal* 35 (Jan. 1949): 67-68.

3950. Learned, Henry B. "Relations of the Legislative and the Executive." *Nation,* 11 Feb. 1915, pp. 166-167.

3951. Levine, Richard O. "The Congressional Role in Formulating National Policy: Some Observations on the First Session of the Ninety-Third Congress." *Harvard Journal on Legislation* 11 (Feb. 1974): 161-180.

3952. McGee, Gale W. "The Role of Executive Leadership." In *The Senate Institution,* ed. Nathaniel S. Preston, pp. 18-30. New York: Van Nostrand Reinhold, 1969.

3953. MacWilliam, Scott. "Executive Legislative Relationships and the Watergate Affair." *Western Australian Institute of Technology Gazette* 6 (Dec. 1973): 24-28.

3954. Neumann, Robert G. *Toward a More Effective Executive–Legislative Relationship in the Conduct of America's Foreign Affairs.* Washington: Center for Strategic and Internation Studies, Georgetown University, 1977.

3955. Neustadt, Richard E. "Politicians and Bureaucrats." In *The Congress and America's Future,* ed. David B. Truman, pp. 102-120. Englewood Cliffs, N.J.: Prentice-Hall, 1965.

3956. Pritchard, Anita C. "Presidential Congressional Relations: Presidential Influence on Congressional Voting Behavior." Ph.D. dissertation, Ohio State University,. 1978.

3957. .Ripley, Randall B. and Franklin, Grace A. *Congress, the Bureaucracy, and Public Policy.* Homewood, Ill.: Dorsey Press, 1976.

3958. Roback, Herbert. "The Congress and Super Departments." *Bureaucrat* 1 (Spring 1972); 31-41.

3959. Rosenthal, Paul C. and Grossman, Robert S. "Congressional Access to Confidential Information Collected by Federal Agencies." *Harvard Journal on Legislation* 15 (Dec. 1977): 74-118.

3960. Sanders, Barefoot. "Congressional–Executive Relations During the 1960s." In *The Presidency and the Congress: A Shifting Balance of Power?,* eds. William S. Livingston, Lawrence C. Dodd and Richard L. Schott, pp. 286-299. Austin: Lyndon B. Johnson School of Public Affairs, University of Texas, 1979.

3961. Sapp, Carl R, "Executive Assistance in the Legislative Process." *Public Administration Review* 6 (Winter 1946): 10-19.

3962. Shull, Steven A. "Presidential-Congressional Support for Agencies and for Each Other: A Comparative Look." *Journal of Politics* 40 (Aug. 1978): 753-760.

3963. Somers, Herman M. "The President, the Congress, and the Federal Government Service." In *The Federal Government Service,* 2d ed., ed. Wallace S. Sayre, pp. 70-113. Englewood Cliffs, N.J.: Prentice-Hall, 1965.

3964. Thurber, James A. "Legislative–Administrative Relations." *Policy Studies Journal* 5 (Autumn 1976): 56-64.

3965. White, Howard. "The Concurrent Resolution in Congress." *American Political Science Review* 35 (Oct. 1941): 886-889.

3966. White, Howard. "Executive Responsibility to Congress via Concurrent Resolution." *American Political Science Review* 36 (Oct. 1952): 895-900.

3967. Willoughby, William F. "Correlation of the Organization of Congress with That of the Executive." *American Political Science Review* 8 (Feb. 1913): 155-167.

Legislative Control

3968. Alms, David E. "Legislative Control over Administrative Action: The Laying System." *John Marshall Journal of Practice and Procedure* 10 (Spring 1977): 515-545.

3969. "Congressional Mood: A Time to Limit Executive Powers." *Congressional Quarterly Weekly Report* 31 (July 21, 1973): 1948-1950.

3970. "Congressional Standing to Challenge Executive Action." *University of Pennsylvania Law Review* 122 (May 1974): 1366-1382.

3971. Cousens, Theodore W. "Delegation of Federal Legislative Power to Executive Officials." *Michigan Law Review* 33 (Feb. 1935): 512-544.

3972. "The Delegation of Power by Congress." *Harvard Law Review* 48 (Mar. 1935): 798-806.

3973. Fairlie, John A. "Congress and the National Administration." *Michigan Law Review* 26 (Jan. 1928): 237-259.

3974. Fiorina, Morris P. "Control of the Bureaucracy: A Mismatch of Incentives and Capabilities." In *The Presidency and the Congress: A Shifting Balance of Power?*, eds. William S. Livingston, Lawrence C. Dodd and Richard L. Schott, pp. 124-142. Austin: Lyndon B. Johnson School of Public Affairs, University of Texas, 1979.

3975. Gelford, Richard L. "Judicial Limitation of Congressional Influence on Administrative Agencies." *Northwestern University Law Review* 73 (Dec. 1978): 931-956.

3976. Ginnane, Robert W. "The Control of Federal Administration by Congressional Resolutions and Committees." *Harvard Law Review* 66 (Feb. 1953): 569-611.

3977. Gray, Kenneth E. "Congressional Interference in Administration." In *Cooperation and Conflict: Readings in American Federalism,* ed. Daniel J. Elazar, et al., pp. 521-542. Itasca, Ill.: F. E. Peacock, 1969.

3978. Harrington, Michael. "Intelligence: The Test for Congress." *Nation,* 7 Feb. 1976, pp. 138-140.

3979. Harris, Joseph P. *Congressional Control of Administration.* Washington: Brookings Institution, 1964.

3980. Harris, Joseph P. "Legislative Control of . Administration: Some Comparisons of American and European Practice." *Western Political Quarterly* 10 (June 1957); 465-467.

3981. Hart, James. "The Bearing of Myers v. United States upon the Independence of Federal Administrative Tribunals." *American Political Science Review* 23 (Aug. 1929): 657-672.

3982. Heady, Ferrel and Linenthal, Eleanor T. "Congress and Administrative Regulation." *Law and Contemporary Problems* 26 (Spring 1961): 238-260.

3983. Huzar, Elias. "Legislative Control Over Administration: Congress and the WPA." *American Political Science Review* 36 (Feb. 1942): 51-67.

3984. Jenks, Leland H. "Control of Administration by Congress." *American Review* 2 (Nov. 1924): 595-602.

3985. Johannes, John R. "Study and Recommend: Statutory Reporting Requirements as a Technique of Legislative Initiative in Congress: A Research Note." *Western Political Quarterly* 29 (Dec. 1976): 589-596.

3986. Kampelman, Max. M. "Congressional Control vs. Executive Flexibility." *Public Administration Review* 18 (Summer 1958): 185-188.

3987. Key, Valdimer O. "Legislative Control." In *Elements of Public Administration,* 2nd ed., ed. Fritz M. Marx, pp. 312-333. Englewood Cliffs, N.J.: Prentice-Hall, 1959.

3988. Newman, Frank and Keaton, Harry J. "Congress and the Faithful Execution of Laws: Should Legislators Supervise Administrators?" *California Law Review* 41 (Winter 1953-1954): 565-595.

3989. Nutting, Charles B. "Legislative Control over Administrative Action." *American Bar Association Journal* 47 (Mar. 1961): 309-310.

3990. Ransom, Harry H. "Congress and Reform of the C.I.A." *Policy Studies Journal* 5 (Spring 1977): 476-480.

3991. Rodino, Peter W. "Congressional Review of Executive Action." *Seton Hall Law Review* 5 (Spring 1974): 489-525.

3992. Scher, Seymour. "The National Labor Relations Board and Congress: A Study of Legislative Control of Regulatory Activity." Ph.D. dissertation, University of Chicago, 1957.

3993. Spater, George A. "Delegation of Federal Legislative Power to Executive or Administrative Agencies." *Michigan Law Review* 31 (April 1933): 786-797.

3994. Watson, H. Lee. "Congress Steps Out: A Look at Congressional Control of the Executive." *California Law Review* 63 (July 1975): 983-1094.

3995. White, L. D. "Congressional Control of the Public Service." *American Political Science Review* 93 (Feb. 1945): 1-11.

Liaison Relations

3996. Crafts, Edward D. and Schrer, Susan R. "Congressional Liaison in the Forest Service." *Forest History* 16 (Oct. 1972): 12-17.

3997. Davis, Eric L. "Building Presidential Coalitions in Congress: Legislative Liaison in the Johnson White House." Ph.D. dissertation, Stanford University, 1978.

3998. Davis, Eric L. "Legislative Liaison in the Carter Administration." *Political Science Quarterly* 94 (Summer 1979): 287-301.

3999. DeGrazia, Edward. "Congressional Liaison: An Inquiry into Its Meaning for Congress." In *Twelve Studies of the Organization of Congress,* ed. Alfred de Grazia, pp. 297-335. Washington: American Enterprise Institute for Public Policy Research, 1966.

4000. Elliott, William Y. "The Secretary and Congress." In *The Secretary of State,* ed. Don K. Price, pp. 112-138. Englewood Cliffs, N.J.: Prentice-Hall, 1960.

4001. Fisher, Louis. *White House–Congress Relationships: Information Exchange and Lobbying.* Washington: Congressional Research Service, 1978.

4002. Holtzman, Abraham. *Legislative Liaison: Executive Leadership in Congress.* Chicago: Rand McNally, 1970.

4003. Huitt, Ralph K. "White House Channels to the Hills." *The Academy of Political Science, Proceedings* 32 (1975): 71-84.

4004. "Hundreds Engage in Executive–Legislative Liaison Work." *Congressional Quarterly Weekly Report* 20 (Mar. 16, 1962): 439-442.

4005. Kefauver, Estes. "Executive–Congressional Liaison." *American Academy of Political and Social Science, Annals* 289 (Sept. 1953): 108-113.

4006. Knight, Jonathan. "On the Secretary of State's Relations with Congress: Resources, Skills, and Issues." Ph.D. dissertation, Columbia University, 1969.

4007. Light, Larry. "White House Lobby Gets Its Act Together." *Congressional Quarterly Weekly Report* 37 (Feb. 3, 1979): 195-200.

4008. Malloy, Isabelle. *Congressional Liaison Offices of the Executive Departments and Selected Independent Agencies.* Washington: Congressional Research Service, 1978.

4009. Manley, John F. "Presidential Power and White House Lobbying." *Political Science Quarterly* 93 (Summer 1978): 255-275.

4010. Murphy, Thomas P. "Congressional Liaison: The NASA Case." *Western Political Quarterly* 25 (June 1972): 192-214.

4011. O'Brien, Larry. "Larry O'Brien Discusses White House Contacts with Capitol Hill." In *The Presidency,* ed. Aaron B. Wildavsky, pp. 477-485. Boston: Little, Brown, 1969.

4012. Pika, Joseph A. "The White House Office of Congressional Relations: Exploring Institutionalization." Ph.D. dissertation, University of Wisconsin, 1978.

4013. Pipe, G. Russell. "Congressional Liaison: The Executive Branch Consolidates Its Relations with Congress." *Public Administration Review* 26 (Mar. 1966): 14-24.

4014. Renka, Russell. "Presidential Lobbying of Congress: Coalition Building in the Kennedy-Johnson Years." Ph.D. dissertation, University of Texas at Austin, 1979.

4015. Signal, Leon V. "Official Secrecy and Informal Communication in Congressional-Bureaucrat Relations." *Political Science Quarterly* 90 (Spring 1975): 71-92.

4016. Strum, Philippa. "The Isolation of the Presidency: Staff, Cabinet, and Congress." In his *Presidential Power and American Democracy,* pp. 95-118. Santa Monica, Calif.: Goodyear, 1979.

4017. "White House 'Lobby' Operates on Capitol Hill." *Congressional Quarterly Weekly Report* 19 (June 10, 1961): 1181-1182.

Case Studies

4018. Anagnason, J. Theodore. "Bureaucrats and Their Congressional Coalitions: A Study of Executive Decision-Making About Federal Grants-in-Aid." Ph.D. dissertation, University of Rochester, 1977.

4019. Baird, Frank L. "Congress' Role in Regulation: Radio and Television Programming." Ph.D. dissertation, University of Texas at Austin, 1964.

4020. Brown, Ben H. "Congress and the Department of State." *American Academy of Political and Social Science, Annals* 289 (Sept. 1953): 100-107.

4021. "CIA: Congress in Dark About Activities, Spending.".*Congressional Quarterly Weekly Report* 29 (Aug. 28, 1971): 1840-1843.

4022. Cook, Curtis G. "The Relationship of the Department of Defense to Congress: Exchange and Influence." Ph.D. dissertation, Johns Hopkins University, 1975.

4023. Durham, James A. "Congressional Response to Administrative Regulation. The 1951 and 1952 Price Control Amendments." *Yale Law Journal* 62 (Dec. 1952): 1-53.

4024. Elliff, John T. "Congress and the Intelligence Community." In *Congress Reconsidered,* eds. Lawrence C. Dodd and Bruce I. Oppenheimer, pp. 193-206. New York: Praeger, 1977.

4025. Fowler, Dorothy G. *Unmailable: Congress and the Post Office.* Athens: University of Georgia Press, 1977.

4026. Galloway, George B. "Consequences of the Myers Decision." *American Law Review* 61 (July-Aug. 1927): 481-508.

4027. Greene, Sheldon L. "Public Agency Distortion of Congressional Will: Federal Policy Toward Non-Resident Alien Labor." *George Washington Law Review* 40 (Mar. 1972): 440-463.

4028. Gregory, Nathaniel. *The Role of Congress in the Department of Defense Reorganization Act of 1958.* Washington: Congressional Research Service, 1975.

4029. Hall, Chester G. "The United States Civil Service Commission: Arm of the President or of Congress?" Ph.D. dissertation, American University; 1965.

4030. Hy, Ronn. "Presidential-Congressional Decision-Making: The Dixon–Yates Controversy." *Bureaucrat* 3 (Jan. 1975): 489-508.

4031. Ickes, Harold L. "The Federal Senate and Indian Affairs." *Illinois Law Review* 24 (Jan. 1930): 570-578.

4032. "Intelligence Community Remains a Problem for Congress." *Congressional Quarterly Weekly Report* 21 (Nov. 15, 1963): 1985-1990.

4033. Jenkins, Harold. "Legislative–Executive Disagreement: Interpreting the 1972 Amendment to the Guaranteed Student Loan Program." *Harvard Journal on Legislation* 10 (April 1973): 467-485.

4034. Johnson, Allen. "Congress and the Treasury Department." In his *Readings in American Constitutional History, 1776-1876,* pp. 178-187. Boston: Houghton Mifflin, 1912.

4035. Kaiser, Frederick M. *The U.S. Customs Service: History, Reorganization, and Congressional Jurisdiction.* Washington: Congressional Research Service, 1978.

4036. Kane, Edward J. "New Congressional Restraints and Federal Reserve Independence." *Challenge* 18 (Nov./Dec. 1975): 37-44.

4037. Kirkman, James L. "A Study of Congressional Cutbacks on Seven Federal Programs." Ph.D. dissertation, George Washington University,, 1976.

4038. Kissinger, Henry A. "Congress and the U.S. Intelligence Community." *Department of State Bulletin* 74 (Mar. 1, 1976): 274-277.

4039. Krasnow, Erwin G. "Ninety-First Congress and the Federal Communications Commission." *Federal Communications Bar Journal* 24 (1970-1971): 97-176.

4040. Lilie, Joyce R. "The Politics of Education: A Case Study of Congressional–Executive Interest Group Relations." Ph.D. dissertation, Johns Hopkins University, 1970.

4041. Longley, Lawrence D. "The Politics of Broadcasting: Industry, Congress and the F.C.C." Ph.D. dissertation, Vanderbilt University, 1969.

4042. Martiny, John H. "A View from the Hill." *Civil Service Journal* 13 (Jan.-Mar. 1973): 33-36.

4043. Nieburg, H. L. "The Eisenhower AEC and Congress: A Study in Executive–Legislative Relations." *Midwest Journal of Political Science* 6 (May 1962): 115-148.

4044. Paper, Lewis J. "Congress and the CIA." *Progressive* 40 (May 1976): 8-9.

4045. Perlmutter, Oscar W. "Acheson vs. Congress." *Review of Politics* 22 (Jan. 1960): 5-44.

4046. Ransom, Harry H. "Congress and the Intelligence Agencies." *The Academy of Political Science, Proceedings* 32 (1975): 153-166.

4047. Ransom, Harry H. "Secret Intelligence Agencies and Congress." *Society* 12 (Mar./April 1975): 33-38.

4048. Robinson, James A. "Process Satisfaction and Policy Approval in State Department–Congressional Relations." *American Journal of Sociology* 67 (Nov. 1961): 278-283.

4049. Rubin, Ronald I. "The Controversies over the Objectives of the United States Information Agency According to Congress, the Executive Branch, and the Agency." Ph.D. dissertation, New York University, 1965.

4050. Rubin, Ronald I. "The Legislative–Executive Relations of the United States Information Agency." *Parliamentary Affairs* 20 (Spring 1967): 158-169.

4051. Scher, Seymour. "Politics of Agency Organization: The Taft-Hartley Congress and NLRB Bifurcation." *Western Political Quarterly* 15 (June 1962): 328-344.

4052. Stewart, Irvin. "Congress, the Foreign Service, and the Department of State." *American Political Science Review* 24 (May 1930): 355-366.

4053. Thomas, Norman C. "Bureaucratic-Congressional Interaction and the Politics of Education." *Journal of Comparative Administration* 2 (May 1970): 52-80.

4054. Welch, Dean D. "Secrecy, Democracy and Responsibility: The Central Intelligence Agency and Congress." Ph.D. dissertation, Vanderbilt University, 1976.

Congress and the Judiciary

General Studies

4055. Andrews, William G., ed. *Coordinate Magistrates: Constitutional Law by Congress and President.* New York: Van Nostrand Reinhold, 1969.

4056. "Congress v. the Courts: Limitations on Congressional Investigation." *University of Chicago Law Review* 24 (Summer 1957): 740-751.

4057. "Congressional Access to the Federal Courts." *Harvard Law Review* 90 (June 1977): 1632-1655.

4058. Crow, John C. "The Role of Congress and the Federal Judiciary in the Exclusion of Aliens." *Missouri Law Review* 23 (Nov. 1958): 491-502.

4059. Frankfurter, Felix and Landix, James M. "Power of Congress over Procedure in Criminal Contempts in 'Inferior' Federal Courts: A Study in Separation of Powers." *Harvard Law Review* 37 (June 1924): 1010-1113.

4060. Glosser, Jeffrey M. "Congressional Reference Case in the United States Court of Claims: A Historical and Current Perspective." *American University Law Review* 25 (Spring 1976): 595-630.

4061. Gonzalez, Raymond B. "Expatriation: Congress Versus the Court." *Southern Quarterly* 7 (July 1969): 443-469.

4062. Green, Frederick. "The Judicial Censorship of Legislation." *American Law Review* 47 (Jan.-Feb. 1913): 90-110.

4063. Hines, N. William. "Decade of Nondegradation Policy in Congress and the Courts: The Erratic Pursuit of Clear Air and Clean Water." *Iowa Law Review* 62 (Feb. 1977): 643-711.

4064. Larkin, John D. "The Trade Agreement Act in Court and in Congress." *American Political Science Review* 31 (June 1937): 498-507.

4065. McGowan, Carl. "Congress and the Courts." *American Bar Association Journal* 62 (Dec. 1976): 1588-1591.

4066. McGowan, Carl. "Congress, Court, and Control of Delegated Power." *Columbia Law Review* 77 (Dec. 1977): 1119-1174.

4067. Melone, Albert P. "System Support Politics and the Congressional Court of Appeals." *North Dakota Law Review* 51 (Spring 1975): 597-613.

4068. Rundquist, Paul S. "A Uniform Rule: The Congress and the Courts in American Naturalization, 1865-1952." Ph.D. dissertation, University of Chicago, 1975.

4069. Satorius, John A. "Congress and the Judiciary: Congressional Oversight and Judicial Policy-Making in Securities and Labor Regulation." Ph.D. dissertation, Harvard University, 1977.

4070. Strawn, S. H. "Congress and the Courts." *Indiana Law Journal* 11 (June 1936): 474-478.

4071. Tapia, Raul R., James, John P., and Levine, Richard O. "Congress vs. the Executive: The Role of the Courts." *Harvard Journal on Legislation* 11 (Feb. 1974): 352-403.

4072. Ulmer, S. Sidney. "Congressional Predictions of Judicial Behavior." *PROD* 3 (Mar. 1960): 15-17.

4073. Wald, Patricia M. "Justice in the Ninety-Fifth Congress: An Overview." *American Bar Association Journal* 64 (Dec. 1978): 1854-1859.

4074. Wigmore, John H. "The Federal Senate and the Federal Judges." *Illinois Law Review* 7 (Feb. 1913): 443-444.

Supreme Court

4075. Berg, Larry L. "The Supreme Court and Congress: Conflict and Interaction, 1947-1968." Ph.D. dissertation, University of California, 1972.

4076. Berger, Raoul. *Congress v. the Supreme Court.* Cambridge, Mass.: Harvard University Press, 1969.

4077. Bowman, Harold M. "Congress and the Supreme Court." *Political Science Quarterly* 25 (Mar. 1910): 20-34.

4078. Breckenridge, Adam C. *Congress Against the Court.* Lincoln: University of Nebraska Press, 1970.

4079. Chase, Harold W. "The Warren Court and Congress." *Minnesota Law Review* 44 (Mar. 1960): 595-637.

4080. Clark, James T. "The United States Court of Claims with Special Consideration of Congressional Reference Cases." Ph.D. dissertation, Georgetown University, 1935.

4081. "Congressional Reversal of Supreme Court Decisions, 1945-1957." *Harvard Law Review* 71 (May 1958): 1324-1337.

4082. Currie, David P. "Congress, the Court, and Water Pollution." In *The Supreme Court Review 1977,* eds. Philip B. Kurland and Gerhard Casper, pp. 39-62. Chicago: University of Chicago Press, 1978.

4083. Ginsberg, Benjamin *"Berman v. Parker*: Congress, the Court, and the Public Purpose." *Polity* 4 (Autumn 1971): 48-74.

4084. Green, Justin J., Schmidhauser, John R., and Berg, Larry L. "Variations in Congressional Responses to the Warren and Burger Courts." *Emory Law Journal* 23 (Summer 1974): 725-743.

4085. Gregg, Philip E. "The Supreme Court's Interpretation of the Taxing and Spending Power of Congress." *Rocky Mountain Law Review* 8 (Feb. 1936): 145-151.

4086. Hall, Kermit L. "The Taney Court in the Second Party System: The Congressional Response to Federal Judicial Reform." Ph.D. dissertation, University of Minnesota, 1972.

4087. Harrell, Kenneth E. "Southern Congressional Leaders and the Supreme Court Fight of 1937." Master's thesis, Louisiana State University, 1959.

4088. Inger, Sarah. "Congress vs. the Supreme Court in 1868 and 1957: A Re-Examination of 'Ex Parte McCardle.'" Ph.D. dissertation, University of Chicago, 1963.

4089. Konop, Thomas F. "Congress and the Supreme Court." *Notre Dame Laywer* 1 (Jan./Feb. 1926): 67-76, 115-121.

4090. Lippe, Emil. "Uneasy Partnership: The Balance of Power Between Congress and the Supreme Court in Interpretation of the Civil War Amendments." *Akron Law Review* 7 (Fall 1973): 49-68.

4091. McGovney, Dudley O. "Supreme Court Fiction: How Congress Has Been Dissuaded from Withdrawing the Jurisdiction That Is Based upon Fiction." *Harvard Law Review* 56 (July 1943): 1225-1260.

4092. McKay, Robert B. "Congressional Investigations and the Supreme Court." *California Law Review* 51 (May 1963): 267-295.

4093. Morgan, John A. "Judicial Freedom in Statutory Interpretation: The Use of the Concept of Congressional Intent in the United States Supreme Court Opinions During the 1958, 1959 and 1960 Terms." Ph.D. dissertation, Duke University, 1963.

4094. Murray, William H. *The Presidency, the Supreme Court and Seven Senators.* Boston: Meador Publishing Co., 1939.

4095. Newman, Frank C. "The Supreme Court, Congressional Investigations, and Influence Peddling." *New York University Law Review* 33 (June 1958): 796-810.

4096. Nichols, Egbert R. *Congress or the Supreme Court: Which Shall Rule America? Containing the Principal Arguments Both for and Against the Proposition: Resolved that Congress Shall Have the Power to Override, by a Two-Thirds Majority Vote, Decisions of the Supreme Court Declaring Laws Passed by Congress Unconstitutional.* New York: Noble and Noble, 1935.

4097. Norton, Thomas J. "The Supreme Court's Five to Four Decisions." *American Bar Association Journal* 9 (July 1923): 417-420.

4098. Powell, Thomas R. "Commerce, Congress and the Supreme Court, 1922-1925." *Columbia Law Review* 25 (April-May 1926): 396-431, 521-549.

4099. Pritchett, Charles H. *Congress Versus the Supreme Court 1957-1960.* Minneapolis: University of Minnesota Press, 1961.

4100. Prives, Daniel. *E.F.T. Policy and Competitive Equality: The Roles of Courts and Congress.* Cambridge, Mass.: Harvard University Program on Information Resources, 1977.

4101. Rohde, David W. "Policy Goals, Strategic Choice and Majority Opinion Assignments in the U.S. Supreme Court." *Midwest Journal of Political Science* 16 (Nov. 1972): 652-682.

4102. Schmidhauser, John R. and Berg, Larry L. *The Supreme Court and Congress: Conflict and Interaction, 1945-1968.* New York: Free Press, 1972.

4103. Steamer, Robert J. "Congress and the Supreme Court During the Marshall Era." *Review of Politics* 27 (July 1965): 364-385.

4104. Stumpf, Harry P. "Congressional Response to Supreme Court Rulings: The Interaction of Law and Politics." *Journal of Public Law* 14 (1965): 377-395.

4105. Swindler, William F. "Supreme Court, the President and Congress." *International and Comparative Law Quarterly* 19 (Oct. 1970): 671-692.

4106. Warren, Charles. *Congress, the Constitution and the Supreme Court.* Boston: Little, Brown, 1925.

4107. Wright, Lloyd. "The Advantages of a Report to Congress by the Chief Justice of the United States." *American Bar Association Journal* 41 (April 1955): 29-31.

Judicial Review

4108. Beard, Charles A. "The Supreme Court: Usurper or Grantee?" *Political Science Quarterly* 27 (Mar. 1912): 1-35.

4109. Bikle, Henry W. "Judicial Determination of Questions of Fact Affecting the Constitutional Validity of Legislative Action." *Harvard Law Review* 38 (Nov. 1924): 6-27.

4110. Brabner-Smith, John W. "Congress vs. Supreme Court: A Constitutional Amendment?" *Virginia Law Review* 22 (April 1936): 665-675.

4111. Brest, Paul. "Conscientious Legislator's Guide to Constitutional Interpretation." *Stanford Law Review* 27 (Feb. 1975): 585-601.

4112. Brown, Walter A. "The Character of the Cases in Which Acts of Congress Have Been Declared Unconstitutional by the Supreme Court of the United States." D.C.L., American University, 1925.

4113. Brown, William H. "Judicial Review of Congressional Investigative Powers with Special Reference to the Period 1945-1957." Ph.D. dissertation, American University, 1959.

4114. Bullitt, William M. "The Supreme Court and Unconstitutional Legislation." *American Bar Association Journal* 10 (June 1924): 419-425.

4115. Carey, Sarah C. "The Court Found that Congress Exceeded Its Power." *Nations' Cities* 14 (Sept. 1976): 19-24.

4116. Choper, Jesse H. "Supreme Court and the Political Branches: Democratic Theory and Practice." *University of Pennsylvania Law Review* 122 (April 1974): 810-858.

4117. Corwin, Edward S. "The Supreme Court and Unconstitutional Laws of Congress." *Michigan Law Review* 4 (June 1906): 616-630.

4118. Dietze, Gottfried. "America and Europe: Decline and Emergence of Judicial Review." *Virginia Law Review* 44 (Dec. 1958): 1233-1272.

4119. Edgerton, Henry W. "The Incidence of Judicial Control over Congress." *Cornell Law Quarterly* 22 (April 1937): 299-348.

4120. Field, Oliver P. "Unconstitutional Legislation by Congress." *American Political Science Review* 39 (Feb. 1945): 54-61.

4121. Grant, J. A. C. "Judicial Control of the Legislative Process: The Federal Rule." *Western Political Quarterly* 3 (Sept. 1950): 364-389.

4122. Haines, Charles G. "Judicial Review of Acts of Congress and the Need for Constitutional Reform." *Yale Law Journal* 45 (Mar. 1936): 816-856.

4123. Hallam, Oscar. "Judicial Power to Declare Legislative Acts Void." *American Law Review* 48 (Jan.-Feb.; March-April 1914): 85-114; 225-273.

4124. Harris, Robert J. "Congressional Authority and the Federal Judicial Power." Ph.D. dissertation, Princeton University, 1934.

4125. Hatcher, John H. "The Power of Federal Courts to Declare Acts of Congress Unconstitutional." *West Virginia Law Review* 42 (Feb. 1936): 96-109.

4126. Hochman, Charles B. "The Supreme Court and the Constitutionality of Retroactive Legislation." *Harvard Law Review* 73 (Feb. 1960): 692-708.

4127. Johnson, Allen. "Power of the Federal Judiciary to Declare Acts of Congress Void." In his *Readings in American Constitutional History, 1776-1876,* pp. 246-253. Boston: Houghton Mifflin, 1912.

4128. Kurland, Philip B. "Government by Judiciary." *Modern Age* 20 (Fall 1976): 358-371.

4129. Lanier, Alexander S. "Congress and the Judicial Power of the Supreme Court." *Central Law Journal* 96 (April 1923): 133-139.

4130. Levine, Jeffrey L. "Judicial Review of Classified Documents: Amendments to the Freedom of Information Act." *Harvard Journal on Legislation* 12 (April 1975): 415-446.

4131. MacCorkle, Stuart A. "Alas, Poor Jefferson! The Executive, Congress and the Courts." *Sewanee Review* 44 (April 1936): 135-144.

4132. Moschzisker, Robert von. *Judicial Review of Legislation: A Consideration of the Warrants for and Merits of Our American System of Judicially Reviewing Legislation to Ascertain Its Constitutional Validity.* Washington: National Association for Constitutional Government, 1923.

4133. Muir, Gerald A. "The Supreme Court and Congress." *Bi-Montly Law Review* 18 (Jan.-Feb. 1927): 153-157.

4134. Neudick, Philip. "Shall the Power of the United States Supreme Court to Pass on the Constitutionality of Acts of Congress Be Abridged?" *Bi-Monthly Law Review* 8 (Jan.-Feb. 1925): 89-97.

4135. Peake, James F. "Power of the Supreme Court to Nullify Acts of Congress." *Constitutional Review* 8 (April 1924): 83-97.

4136. Pittman, R. Carter. "The Supremacy of the Judiciary: A Study of Preconstitutional History." *American Bar Association Journal* 40 (May 1954): 389-395.

4137. Potter, William W. "Judicial Power in the United States." *Michigan Law Review* 27 (Nov.-Dec.-Jan. 1928-1929): 1-22, 167-190, 285-313.

4138. Pound, Roscoe. "Supreme Court or Supreme Congress?" *California State Bar Journal* 6 (Aug. 1931): 203-204, 206.

4139. Sky, Theodore. "Judicial Review of Congressional Investigations: Is There an Alternative to Contempt." *George Washington Law Review* 31 (Dec. 1962): 399-430.

4140. Toomey, Lawrence J. "The Rights of Congress and of the State Legislatures to Pass Enactments Repugnant to the Federal Constitution." *Bi-Montly Law Review* 9 (Nov.-Dec. 1925): 43-51.

4141. Trickett, William. "Judicial Nullification of Acts of Congress." *North American Review* 185 (Aug. 1907): 848-856.

4142. Ulmer, S. Sidney. "Judicial Review as Political Behavior: A Temporary Check on Congress." *Administrative Science Quarterly* 4 (Mar. 1960): 426-445.

4143. "Who May Question the Constitutionality of Acts of Congress? Seventy-Four Cases Holding Federal Legislation Invalid." *George Washington Law Review* 4 (May 1936): 508-519.

Congressional Power

4144. Brant, Irving. "Appellate Jurisdiction: Congressional Abuse of the Exceptions Clause." *Oregon Law Review* 53 (Fall 1973): 3-28.

4145. Brown, Douglas W. "The Proposal to Give Congress the Power to nullify the Constitution." *Virginia Law Register* 8 (Feb. 1923): 721-739.

4146. Brown, George S. "The Proposal to Make Congress Omnipotent is Unconstitutional Unless Every State Consents Thereto." *Virginia Law Review* 10 (Nov. 1923): 30-36.

4147. "Congressional Legislation to Curb Court." *Congressional Quarterly Weekly Report* 15 (July 5, 1957): 807-808.

4148. "Congressional Power over State and Federal Court Jurisdiction: The Hill-Burton and Trans-Alaska Pipeline Examples." *New York University Law Review* 49 (April 1974): 131-163.

4149. "Court of Claims: Judicial Power and Congressional Review." *Harvard Law Review* 46 (Feb. 1933): 677-687.

4150. Cox, Archibald. "The Role of Congress in Constitutional Determination." *University of Cincinnati Law Review* 40 (Summer 1971): 199-261.

4151. Eisenberg, Theodore. "Congressional Authority to Restrict Lower Federal Court Jurisdiction." *Yale Law Journal* 83 (Jan. 1974): 498-533.

4152. Elliott, Shelden D. "Court-Curbing Proposals in Congress." *Notre Dame Lawyer* 33 (Aug. 1958): 597-616.

4153. Ettrude, Dormin J., ed. *Power of Congress to Nullify Supreme Court Decisions.* New York: H. H. Wilson, 1924.

4154. Frank, Theodore D. *A Footnote to a Dialogue: Some Reflections on Congressional Power and the Supreme Court's Appellate Jurisdiction.* Cambridge, Mass.: Harvard Law School, 1969.

4155. Goldberg, Arthur J. "The Supreme Court, Congress and Rules of Evidence." *Seton Hall Law Review* 5 (Spring 1974): 667-687.

4156. Lenoir, James J. "Congressional Control over she Appellate Jurisdiction of the Supreme Court." *University of Kansas Law Review* 5 (Oct. 1956): 16-41.

4157. Lewinson, Joseph L. "Limiting Judicial Review by Act of Congress." *California Law Review* 23 (Sept. 1935): 591-601.

4158. Littleton, Martin W. "Mob Rule and the Canonized Minority." *Constitutional Review* 7 (April 1923): 86-91.

4159. Lockman, Stuart M. "Congressional Discretion in Dealing with the Federal Rules of Evidence." *University of Michigan Journal of Law Reform* 6 (Spring 1973): 798-817.

4160. Martig, Ralph R. "Congress and the Appellate Jursidiction of the Supreme Court." *Michigan Law Review* 34 (Mar. 1936): 650-670.

4161. Norris, William A. and Burke, Julian. "Congress and the Supreme Court's Appellate Jurisdiction." *Los Angeles Bar Bulletin* 35 (May 1960): 212-215, 229-231.

4162. Nutting, Charles B. "Congressional Control of Judicial Decisions." *American Bar Association Journal* 45 (July 1959): 749-750.

4163. Pozgay, Jon R. "Moratorium on School Busing for the Purpose of Achieving Racial Balance: A New Chapter in Congressional Court-Curbing." *Notre Dame Lawyer* 48 (Oct. 1972): 208-231.

4164. Ratner, Leonard G. "Congressional Power over the Appellate Jurisdiction of the Supreme Court." *University of Pennsylvania Law Review* 109 (Dec. 1960): 157-202.

4165. Severance, Cordenio A. "The Proposal to Make Congress Supreme." *American Bar Association Journal* 8 (Aug. 1922): 459-464.

4166. Stumpf, Harry P. "The Congressional Reversal of Supreme Court Decisions, 1957-1961." Ph.D. dissertation, Northwestern University, 1964.

4167. Thompson, F. and Pollitt, Daniel H. "Congressional Control of Judicial Remedies: President Nixon's Proposed Moratorium on 'Busing Orders'." *North Carolina Law Review* 50 (June 1972): 810-841.

4168. Tobler, John O. "The Constitutional Controls of Congress over the Federal Judiciary." Ph.D. dissertation, Johns Hopkins University, 1939.

4169. Tydings, Joseph D. "Congress and the Courts: Helping the Judiciary to Help Itself." *American Bar Association Journal* 52 (April 1966): 321-325.

4170. Tydings, Joseph D. "The Courts and Congress." *Public Administration Review* 31 (Mar./April 1971): 113-120.

4171. Van Alstyne, William W. "Role of Congress in Determining Incidental Powers of the President and of the Federal Courts: A Comment on the Horizontal Effect of the Sweeping Clause." *Law and Contemporary Problems* 40 (Spring 1976): 102-134.

4172. Wilson, Lyle K. "Congressional Preemption of the Federal Rules of Evidence." *Washington Law Review* 49 April 1974): 1184-1197.

4173. Wolff, Irving M. "Congressional Consideration of the Supreme Court Quorum." *Georgetown Law Journal* 32 (Mar. 1944): 293-307.

Constituency Relations

4174. Alpert, Eugene J. "A Reconceptualization of Representational Role Theory." *Legislative Studies Quarterly* 4 (Nov. 1979): 587-605.

4175. Anderson, John B. *Between Two Worlds: A Congressman's Choice.* Grand Rapids, Mich.: Zondervan Publishing House, 1970.

4176. Arnold, R. Douglas. "Congressmen, Bureaucrats, and Constituency Benefits: The Politics of Geographical Allocation." Ph.D. dissertation, Yale University, 1977.

4177. Boehlert, Sherwood L. "Telling the Congressman's Story." In *The Voice of the Government,* eds. Ray E. Hiebert and Carlton E. Spitzer, pp. 127-140. New York: Wiley, 1968.

4178. Bosley, Charles E. "Senate Communication with the Public." In *Senate Communications with the Public: A Compilation of Papers Prepared for the Commission on the Operation of the Senate,* pp. 3-23. Washington: GPO, 1977.

4179. Boynton, George R. "Southern Conservatism: Constituency Opinion and Congressional Voting." *Public Opinion Quarterly* 29 (Summer 1965): 259-269.

4180. Boynton, George R., Patterson, Samuel C., and Hedlund, Ronald D. "The Missing Links in Legislative Politics: Attentive Constituents." *Journal of Politics* 31 (Aug. 1969): 700-721.

4181. Breslin, Janet. "Constituent Service." In *Senators: Offices, Ethics and Pressures: A Compilation of Papers,* pp. 19-36. Washington: GPO, 1976.

4182. Chall, Joseph G. "Constituency, Party, and Ideology in the House of Representatives: A Study of Coalition Behavior on School Aid in the Eighty-Fourth Congress." Ph.D. dissertation, Columbia University, 1966.

4183. Cover, Albert D. "Contacting Congressional Constituents: Some Patterns of Perquisite Use." *American Journal of Political Science* 24 (Feb. 1980): 125-135.

4184. Cronheim, Dorothy H. "Congressmen and Their Communication Practices." Ph.D. dissertation, Ohio State University, 1957.

4185. Dexter, Lewis A. "Congressmen and the People They Listen To." Ph.D. dissertation, Columbia University, 1960.

4186. Dexter, Lewis A. "The Representative and His District." *Human Organization* 16 (Spring 1957): 2-13.

4187. Eulau, Heinz and Karps, Paul D. "The Puzzle of Representation: Specifying Components of Responsiveness." *Legislative Studies Quarterly* 2 (Aug. 1977): 233-254.

4188. Feldstein, Mark. "Mail Fraud on Capitol Hill." *Washington Monthly* 11 (Oct. 1979): 41-48.

4189. Fenno, Richard F. *Home Style: House Members in Their Districts.* Boston: Little, Brown, 1978.

4190. Fenno, Richard F. "U.S. House Members in Their Constituencies: An Exploration." *American Political Science Review* 71 (Sept. 1977): 883-917.

4191. Fiorina, Morris P. "Constituency Influence." *Political Methodology* 2 (May 1975): 249-266.

4192. Fiorina, Morris P. *Representatives, Roll Calls and Constituencies.* Lexington, Mass.: Lexington Books, 1974.

4193. Froman, Lewis A. *The Congressmen and Their Constituencies.* Chicago: Rand McNally, 1963.

4194. "House Survey: Wide Gap Between Leaders, Voters." *Congressional Quarterly Weekly Report* 29 (Aug. 28, 1971): 1862-1863.

4195. Ingram, Helen. "Impact of Constituency on the Process of Legislating." *Western Political Quarterly* 22 (June 1969): 265-279.

4196. Jackson, John E. "Some Indirect Evidences of Constituency Pressure on the Senate." *Public Policy* 16 (1967): 253-270.

4197. Jones, Harry W. "The Modern Congressman: Legislator or Constituent Care-Taker?" *American Bar Association Journal* 34 (Oct. 1948): 912-913.

4198. Kanervo, David W. "Competition, Constituency, and Welfare Programs in Congress." Ph.D. dissertation, University of Wisconsin at Madison, 1976.

4199. Miller, Warren E. and Stokes, Donald E. "Constituency Influence in Congress." *American Political Science Review* 57 (Mar. 1963): 45-56.

4200. Olson, Kenneth G. "The Service Function of the United States Congress." In *Twelve Studies of the Organization of Congress,* ed. Alfred de Grazia, pp. 332-374. Washington: American Enterprise Institute for Public Policy Research, 1966.

4201. Parker, Glenn R. "Sources of Change in Congressional District Attentiveness." *American Journal of Political Science* 24 (Feb. 1980): 115-124.

4202. Parker, Glenn R. and Davidson, Roger H. "Why Do Americans Love Their Congressman So Much More than Their Congress." *Legislative Studies Quarterly* 4 (Feb. 1979): 53-61.

4203. Pennock, J. Roland. "Party and Constituency in Postwar Agricultural Price-Support Legislation." *Journal of Politics* 18 (May 1956): 167-210.

4204. Polk, Leslie D., Eddy, John, and Andre, Ann. "Uses of Congressional Publicity in Wisconsin District." *Journalism Quarterly* 52 (Autumn 1975): 543-546.

4205. Scott, Hugh D. "The Relationship of a Senator to His Constituency." In *The Senate Institute,* ed. Nathaniel S. Preston, pp. 50-56. New York: Van Bostrand Reinhold, 1969.

4206. Segal, David R. and Smith, Thomas S. "Congressional Responsibility and the Organization of Constituency Attitudes." *Social Science Quarterly* 51 (Dec. 1970): 743-749.

4207. Segal, David R. and Smith, Thomas S. "Congressional Responsibility and the Organization of Constituency Attitudes." In *Political Attitudes and Public Opinion,* eds. Dan D. Nimmo and Charles M. Bonjeans, pp. 562-568. New York: Wiley, 1966.

4208. Social Science Research Council's Inter-University Summer Seminar on Political Behavior. (University of Chicago, Summer 1951). "The Roles of Congressional Leaders: National Party vs. Constituency." *American Political Science Review* 46 (Dec. 1952): 1024-1032.

4209. Stokes, Donald E. "Compound Paths in Political Analysis." *Mathematical Applications in Political Science* 5 (1971): 70-92.

4210. Stone, Walter J. "Measuring Constituency-Representative Linkages: Problems and Prospects." *Legislative Studies Quarterly* 4 (Nov. 1979): 623-639.

4211. Sussman, Leila. "Mass Political Letter Writing in America: The Growth of an Institution." *Public Opinion Quarterly* 23 (Summer 1959): 203-212.

4212. U.S. Congress. Senate. Ad Hoc Committee on Legislative Immunity. *Communication with Constituents: The Senator's Duty to Inform the People: Report of the Ad Hoc Committee on Legislative Immunity.* 95th Cong., 1st sess. Washington: GPO, 1977.

4213. Wagner, Stanley P. "A Report on the Accessibility of United States Senators." *Social Science* 39 (Jan. 1964): 34-37.

4214. Weissberg, Robert. "Assessing Legislator-Constituency Policy Agreement." *Legislative Studies Quarterly* 4 (Nov. 1979): 605-622.

4215. Westen, T. Edward. "The Constituent Needs Help: Casework in the House of Representatives." In *To Be a Congressman: The Promise and the Power,* eds. Sven Groennings and Jonathan P. Hawley, pp. 53-72. Washington: Acropolis Books, 1973.

4216. Wood, Frederick B. *The Potential for Congressional Use of Emergent Telecommunications: An Exploratory Assessment.* Washington: Program of Policy Studies in Science and Technology, George Washington University, 1974.

4217. Wood, Frederick B. "Telecommunications Technology for Congress: An Exploratory Assessment of Its Potential for Congressional–Constituent Communication." D.B.A. dissertation, George Washington University, 1974.

4218. Wood, Frederick B., Coates, Vary T., Chartrand, Robert L., and Ericson, Richard F. "Videoconferencing via Satellite: Opening Government to the People." *Futurist* 12 (Oct. 1978): 321-326.

4219. Wright, Gerald C. "Constituency Response to Congressional Behavior: The Impact of the House Judiciary Committee Impeachment Votes." *Western Political Quarterly* 30 (Sept. 1977): 401-410.

4220. Wyant, Rowena. "Voting via the Senate Mailbag (Part I)." *Public Opinion Quarterly* 5 (Fall 1941): 359-382.

4221. Wyant, Rowena and Herzog, Herta. "Voting via the Senate Mailbag (Part II)." *Public Opinion Quarterly* 5 (Winter 1941): 590-624.

4222. Yarnell, Warren P. "Policy Representation in the Congress: A Constituent Perspective." Ph.D. dissertation, Ohio State University, 1976.

Lobbying

4223. Aberbach, Joel D. and Rockman, Bert A. "Bureaucrats and Clientele Groups: A View from Capitol Hill." *American Journal of Political Science* 22 (Nov. 1978): 818-832.

4224. Ablard, Charles D. "The Washington Lawyer-Lobbyist." *George Washington Law Review* 38 (May 1970): 641-650.

4225. "The AFL-CIO: How Much Clout in Congress?" *Congressional Quarterly Weekly Report* 33 (July 19, 1975): 1531-1539.

4226. Alderson, George. *How You Can Influence Congress: The Complete Handbook for the Citizen Lobbyist.* New York: Dutton, 1979.

4227. American Enterprise Institute for Public Policy Research. *Proposals to Revise the Lobbying Law: 1980.* Washington: The Institute, 1980.

4228. Andringa, Robert C. "Congressional Staff and Higher Education Policy." *Current Issues in Higher Education* 28 (1973): 13-20.

4229. Bacheller, John M. "Lobbyists and the Legislative Process: The Impact of Environmental Constraints." *American Political Science Review* 71 (Mar. 1977): 253-263.

4230. Bacon, Donald C. *Congress and You: A Primer for Participation in the Legislative Process.* Washington: American Association of University Women, 1969.

4231. Baldwin, Percy M. "Agriculture and Politics: Their Interrelations as Exemplified in the Legislative Activities of the Farm Bloc in the 67th Congress." Ph.D. dissertation, University of California at Berkeley, 1924.

4232. Barberis, Mary A. "The Arab-Israeli Battle on Capitol Hill." *Virginia Quarterly Review* 52 (Spring 1976): 203-223.

4233. Barr, Carl. "When Judges Lobby: Congress and Court Administration." Ph.D. dissertation, University of Chicago, 1970.

4234. Benson, Robert S. "The Military on Capitol Hill: Prospects in the Quest for Funds." *American Academy of Political and Social Science, Annals* 406 (Mar. 1973): 48-58.

4235. Bilmes, Linda. "Congress Doesn't Live Here Anymore." *Harvard Political Review* 7 (Spring 1979): 26-32.

4236. Brock, William A. Equilibrium in Political Markets on Pork-Barrel Issues: The Case of the Tariff. Austin: Graduate School of Business, University of Texas, 1977.

4237. Chaplin, Mortimer M. and Timbie, Richard E. "Legislative Activities of Public Charities." *Law and Contemporary Problems* 29 (Autumn 1975): 183-210.

4238. Casper, Barry M. "Scientists on the Hill." *Bulletin of the Atomic Scientists* 33 (Nov. 1977): 8-15.

4239. Celler, Emmanuel. "Pressure Groups in Congress." *American Academy of Political and Social Science, Annals* 319 (Sept. 1958): 1-10.

4240. Cherington, Paul W. and Gillen, Ralph L. "Lobbying Activities on Capitol Hill." In their *The Business Representative in Washington,* pp. 45-70. Washington: Brookings Institution, 1962.

4241. Chlopek, Anthony J. "The Plight of Injured Longshoremen Calls for Action of Congress." *American Labor Legislation Review* 17 (Mar. 1927): 16-19.

4242. Congressional Quarterly. *The Washington Lobby.* 3rd ed. Washington: Congressional Quarterly, 1979.

4243. *The Corporate Lobbies: Political Profiles of the Business Roundtable and the Chamber of Commerce.* Washington: Public Citizen, 1980.

4244. "Cost of Influencing Congress." *Congressional Quarterly Weekly Report* 17 (May 22, 1959): 713-716.

4245. Deakin, James. *The Lobbyists.* Washington: Public Affairs Press, 1966.

4246. Dexter, Lewis A. "Pros and Cons of Professional Lobbying in Washington." *Capitol Studies* 1 (Spring 1972): 3-10.

4247. Entin, Kenneth. "Interest Group Communication with a Congressional Committee." *Policy Studies Journal* 3 (Winter 1974): 147-150.

4248. Felicetti, Daniel A. *Mental Health and Retardation Politics: The Mind Lobbies in Congress.* New York: Praeger, 1975.

4249. Field, Barry C. "Congressional Bargaining in Agriculture: Cotton." *American Journal of Agricultural Economics* 50 (Feb. 1968): 1-12.

4250. Findley, Paul. "Lobbying." In *We Propose: A Modern Congress,* ed. Mary McInnis, pp. 135-140. New York: McGraw-Hill, 1966.

4251. Freeman, Dale C. "The Poor and the Political Process: Equal Access to Lobbying." *Harvard Journal on Legislation* 6 (Mar. 1969): 369-392.

4252. Gregory, Neal. "The National Committee for an Effective Congress." In *Political Brokers: Money, Organizations, Power and People,* ed. Judith G. Smith, pp. 145-165. New York: Liveright, 1972.

4253. Gruberg, Martin. "Senatorial Investigation of Natural Gas Lobbying: A Study in Legislative Politics." Ph.D. dissertation, Columbia University, 1963.

4254. Hagan, Charles B. and McMurray, Carl D. *Illinois Congressional Representatives and Agriculture Legislation.* Urbana: University of Illinois, Institute of Government and Public Affairs, 1961.

4255. Haider, Donald H. "Group Competition and Warfare in the Congress." In his *When Governments Come to Washington: Governors, Mayors, and Intergovernmental Lobbying,* pp. 182-211. New York: Free Press, 1974.

4256. Hall, Donald R. *Cooperative Lobbying - The Power of Pressure.* Tucson: University of Arizona Press, 1969.

4257. Hall, Donald R. "Intergroup and Cooperative Lobbying." *Capitol Studies* 1 (Spring 1972): 11-28.

4258. Hayes, Michael T. "Interest Groups and Congress: Toward a Transaction Theory." In *The Congressional System: Notes and Readings*, 2d ed., ed. Leroy N. Rieselbach, pp. 252-273. North Scituate, Mass.: Duxbury Press, 1979.

4259. Hayes, Michael T. "Semi-Sovereign Pressure Groups: A Critique of Current Theory and an Alternative Typology." *Journal of Politics* 40 (Feb. 1978): 134-161.

4260. Herring, Edward P. "Group Representation Before Congress." Ph.D. dissertation, Johns Hopkins University, 1929.

4261. Holbert, Robert L. "The Politics of Lobbying Regulation: The Roles of Congress, Supreme Court, and Internal Revenue Service." Ph.D. dissertation, University of Arizona, 1970.

4262. "How Much Congressional Influence Do Banks Have." *Congressional Quarterly Weekly Report* 27 (Aug. 8, 1969): 1441-1446.

4263. Hunt, Margaret A. "Congressional Perception of Organized Interest Group Activity." Ph.D. dissertation, University of North Carolina at Chapel Hill, 1963.

4264. Johnson, Dorothy E. "Organized Women as Lobbyists in the 1920s." *Capitol Studies* 1 (Spring 1972): 41-58.

4265. Jones, Harry W. "The Proposed Congressional Lobbying Investigation." *American Bar Association Journal* 35 (July 1949): 590-591.

4266. Kampelman, Max M. "The Washington Lawyer: Some Musings." *George Washington Law Review* 38 (May 1970): 589-606.

4267. Kennedy, John F. "Congressional Lobbies: A Chronic Problem Re-Examined." *Georgetown Law Journal* 45 (Summer 1957): 535-567.

4268. Key, Valdimer O. "The Veterans and the House of Representatives: A Study of Pressure Groups and Electoral Mortality." *Journal of Politics* 5 (Feb. 1943): 27-40.

4269. Klonoff, Robert. "The Congressman as Mediator Between Citizens and Government Agencies: Problems and Prospects." *Harvard Journal on Legislation* 16 (Summer 1979: 701-734.

4270. "The Labor Lobbyists: Powerful Friends in Congress." *Congressional Quarterly Weekly Report* 29 (Oct. 16, 1972): 2121-2124.

4271. Lane, Edgar. "Lessons from Past Congressional Investigations of Lobbying." *Public Opinion Quarterly* 14 (Spring 1950): 14-32.

4272. Lawrence, Joseph S. *Wall Street and Washington.* Princeton, N.J.: Princeton University Press, 1929.

4273. Light, Alfred R. "The Carter Administration's National Energy Plan: Pressure Groups and Organizational Politics in the Congress." *Policy Studies Journal* 7 (Autumn 1978): 68-76.

4274. Lohuizen, Jan van. "The Impact of Interest Groups on the Congressional Appropriation Process in Congress." Ph.D. dissertation, Rice University, 1979.

4275. Lyon, Carl V. and Stanhagen, William H. "Lobbying, Liberty, and the Legislative Process: An Appraisal of the Proposed Legislative Activities Disclosure Act." *George Washington Law Review* 26 (Mar. 1958): 391-417.

4276. Malick, Clay P. "These New Citizen Lobbies." *Western Humanities Review* 13 (Autumn 1959): 415-424.

4277. Mastro, Julius J. "The Pharmaceutical Manufacturers Association, The Ethical Drug Industry and the 1962 Drug Amendments: A Case Study of Congressional Action and Interest Group Reaction." Ph.D. dissertation, New York University, 1965.

4278. Mikinka, Ted. *The U.S. Declares War on Congress.* San Antonio, Texas: Other Side Pub. Co., 1978.

4279. Mikva, Abner J. "Interest Representation in Congress: The Social Responsibilities of the Washington Lawyer." *George Washington Law Review* 38 (May 1970): 651-674.

4280. Milbrath, Lester W. "Lobbying as a Communication Process." *Public Opinion Quarterly* 24 (Spring 1960): 32-53.

4281. Milbrath, Lester W. *The Washington Lobbyists.* Chicago: Rand McNally, 1970.

4282. "The 'Military Lobby': Its Impact on Congress, Nation." *Congressional Quarterly Weekly Report* 22 (Feb. 7, 1964): 271-278.

4283. Miller, Robert W. and Johnson, Jimmy D. "His Role with Congress." In their *Corporate Ambassadors to Washington,* pp. 49-63. Washington: Center for the Study of Private Enterprise, American University, 1970.

4284. Moore, John L. "Washington Pressures 'Business Forms Economic Study Unit to Support Bipartisan New England Caucus.'" *National Journal* 5 (Feb. 17, 1973): 226-233.

4285. Mulhollan, Daniel P. "An Overview of Lobbying by Organizations." In *Senators: Offices, Ethics and Pressures: A Compilation of Papers,* pp. 157-192. Washington: GPO, 1976.

4286. Muller, Helen M., ed. *Lobbying in Congress.* New York: H. W. Wilson Co., 1931.

4287. Murphy, Thomas P. *Pressures upon Congress, Legislation by Lobby.* Woodbury, N.Y.: Barron's Educational Series, 1973.

4288. "Nader's 'Congress Watch' to Lobby for Consumers." *Congressional Quarterly Weekly Report* 31 (July 21, 1973): 1957-1958.

4289. Nelson, Ancher. "Lobbying by the Administration." In *We Propose: A Modern Congress,* ed. Mary McInnis, pp. 143-159. New York: McGraw-Hill, 1966.

4290. Nelson, Michael. "How to Break the Ties that Bind Congress to the Lobbies and Agencies." *Washington Monthly* 8 (Dec. 1976): 36-38.

4291. "New Nader Project: 800-Person Study of Congress." *Congressional Quarterly Weekly Report* 30 (June 17, 1972): 1474-1477.

4292. Oppenheimer, Bruce I. "The Effects of Policy Variation on Interest Group Behavior in the Congressional Process: The Oil Industry in Two Domestic Issues." Ph.D. dissertation, University of Wisconsin at Madison, 1973.

4293. Oppenheimer, Bruce I. *Oil and the Congressional Process: The Limits of Symbolic Politics.* Lexington, Mass.: Lexington Books, 1974.

4294. Ornstein, Norman J. and Elder, Shirley. *Interest Groups, Lobbying and Policymaking.* Washington: Congressional Quarterly, 1978.

4295. Pennock, J. Roland. "The 'Pork Barrel' and Majority Rule: A Note." *Journal of Politics* 32 (Aug. 1970): 709-716.

4296. Pomper, Gerald. "Labor and Congress: The Repeal of Taft-Hartley." *Labor History* 2 (Fall 1961): 323-343.

4297. Ransdell, Joseph E. "The High Cost of the Pork Barrel." *American Academy of Political and Social Science, Annals* 64 (Mar. 1916): 43-55.

4298. Riddick, Floyd M. "Administration, Lobbyists, and Congress." *South Atlantic Quarterly* 41 (April 1942): 182-191.

4299. Ross, Robert L. "Dimensions and Patterns of Relations Among Interest Groups at the Congressional Level of Government." Ph.D. dissertation, Michigan State University, 1967.

4300. Rothberg, Diana S. "The Politics of Farm Support: A Study of Group Action in Congress." Ph.D. dissertation, Radcliffe College, 1960.

4301. Schattschneider, Elmer E. *Politics, Pressure, and the Tariff: A Study of Free Private Enterprise in Pressure Politics as Shown in the 1929-1930 Revision of the Tariff.* Englewood Cliffs, N.J.: Prentice-Hall, 1935.

4302. Schriftgiesser, Karl. *The Lobbyists: The Art and Business of Influencing Lawmakers.* Boston: Little, Brown, 1931.

4303. Scott, Andrew M. and Hunt, Margaret A. *Congress and Lobbies: Image and Reality.* Chapel Hill: University of North Carolina Press, 1966.

4304. Seybold, Leo. "Lobbyists and Lobbying." *Capitol Studies* 1 (Spring 1972): 29-39.

4305. Soelberg, Earl J. "Lobbying from a Legal Standpoint." *National University Law Review* 8 (Jan. 1928): 76-84.

4306. Surrey, Stanley S. "The Congress and the Tax Lobbyist: How Special Tax Provisions Get Enacted." *Harvard Law Review* 70 (May 1957): 1145-1182.

4307. Tomkins, Dorothy L. C. *Congressional Investigation of Lobbying: A Selected Bibliography.* Berkeley: University of California Press, 1956.

4308. Torgerson, Randall E. *Producer Power at the Bargaining Table: A Case Study of the Legislative Life of S.109.* Columbia: University of Missouri Press, 1970.

4309. Truman, David B. *Governmental Process: Political Interests and Public Opinion.* New York: Alfred A. Knopf, 1958.

4310. "What Do Congressmen Think of Lobbyists." *Congressional Quarterly Weekly Report* 15 (Aug. 9, 1957): 953.

4311. Williams, John A. "The Bituminous Coal Lobby and the Wilson Gorman Tariff of 1894." *Maryland Historical Magazine* 68 (Fall 1973): 273-287.

4312. Wolman, Harold L. and Thomas, Norman C. "Black Interests, Black Groups, and Black Influence in the Federal Policy Process: The Case of Housing and Education." *Journal of Politics* 32 (Nov. 1970): 875-897.

4313. Wright, Frank. "The Dairy Lobby Buys the Cream of the Congress." *The Washington Monthly* 3 (May 1971): 17-21.

4314. Zeller, Belle. "The Federal Regulation of Lobbying Act." *American Political Science Review* 42 (April 1948): 239-271.

Media Relations

4315. Allen, Len. "Makeup of the Senate Press." In *Senate Communications with the Public: A Compilation of Papers Prepared for the Commission on the Operation of the Senate,* pp. 24-40. Washington: GPO, 1977.

4316. Bagdikian, Ben H. "Congress and the Media: Partners in Propaganda: Why We Don't Know More About What Our Congressmen Are Doing." *Columbia Journalism Review* 12 (Jan.-Feb. 1974): 3-10.

4317. Balutis, Alan P. "Congress, the President and the Press." *Journalism Quarterly* 53 (Autumn 1976): 509-515.

4318. Beason, Martin S. "Public Relations in Congress." Master's thesis, American University, 1961.

4319. Becker, Lee B. "Two Tests of Media Gratifications: Watergate and the 1974 Election." *Journalism Quarterly* 53 (Spring 1976): 28-33, 87.

4320. Blanchard, Robert O., ed. *Congress and the News Media.* New York: Hastings House, 1974.

4321. Blanchard, Robert O. "Congress and the Press: An Historical Sketch." *Journal of Communication* 24 (Summer 1974): 78-81.

4322. Blanchard, Robert O. "A Profile of Congressional Correspondents." *Capitol Studies* 3 (Fall 1975): 53-68.

4323. Bosley, Charles E. "Senate Media Galleries." In *Senate Communications with the Public: A Compilation of Papers Prepared for the Commission on the Operation of the Senate,* pp. 77-86. Washington: GPO, 1977.

4324. Brenner, Saul. "Civil Liberties, Prestige Newspaper Response, and Congressional Reaction." Ph.D. dissertation, New York University, 1970.

4325. Cohen, Henry. *Journalists' Privilege to Withhold Information in Judicial and Legislative Proceedings.* Washington: Congressional Research Service, 1978.

4326. Dunn, Delmer D. "Symbiosis: Congress and the Press." In *To Be a Congressman: The Promise and the Power,* eds. Sven Groennings and Jonathan P. Hawley, pp. 37-51. Washington: Acropolis Books, 1973.

4327. Endres, Kathleen L. "Capitol Hill Newswoman: A Descriptive Study." *Journalism Quarterly* 53 (Spring 1976): 132-135.

4328. Ervin, Sam J. "In Pursuit of a Press Privilege." *Harvard Journal on Legislation* 11 (Feb. 1974): 233-278.

4329. Essary, J. Frederick. "President, Congress, and the Press Correspondents." *American Political Science Review* 22 (Nov. 1928): 902-909.

4330. Green, Barbara and Hurwitz, Leon. "Press Views of Executive vs. Senatorial Powers." *Journalism Quarterly* 55 (Winter 1978): 775-778.

4331. Gruenstein, Peter. "Press Release Politics: How Congressmen Manage the News." *The Progressive* 38 (Jan. 1974): 37-40.

4332. Howard, Vincent W. "The Two Congresses: A Study of the Changing Roles and Relationships of the National Legislature and Washington Reporters, as Revealed Particularly in the Press Accounts of Legislative Activity, 1860-1913." Ph.D. dissertation, University of Chicago, 1976.

4333. Johnson, Ralph H. and Altman, Michael. "Communists in the Press: A Senate Witchhunt of the 1950's Revisited." *Journalism Quarterly* 55 (Autumn 1978): 487-493.

4334. Kampelman, Max M. "Congress, the Media and the President." *The Academy of Political Science, Proceedings* 32 (1975): 85-97.

4335. Kreisman, Leonard. "Published Opinion in American Periodicals, and Senatorial Opinion." Ph.D. dissertation, New York University, 1955.

4336. Lambeth, Edmund B. and Byrne, John A. "Pipelines from Washington." *Columbia Journalism Review* 17 (May 1978): 52-55.

4337. Marbut, Frederick B. "Congress and the Standing Committee of Correspondents." *Journalism Quarterly* 38 (Winter 1961): 52-58.

4338. Miller, Susan H. "Congress and the News Media: Coverage, Collaboration, and Agenda Setting." Ph.D. dissertation, Stanford University, 1976.

4339. Miller, Susan H. "News Coverage of Congress: The Search for the Ultimate Spokesman." *Journalism Quarterly* 54 (Autumn 1977): 459-465.

4340. Puntigam, Clark A. "Television and the Congress: Preserving the Balance." *Federal Communications Bar Journal* 26 (1973): 209-241.

4341. Robinson, Michael J. and Appel, Kevin R. "Network News Coverage of Congress." *Political Science Quarterly* 94 (Fall 1979): 407-418.

4342. Rosenberg, John S. "Imperiled Experiment: Capitol Hill News Service." *Columbia Journalism Review* 16 (Sept. 1977): 59-60, 62, 64.

4343. Shaffer, Samuel. *On and Off the Floor: Thirty Years as a Correspondent on Capitol Hill.* New York: Newsweek Books, 1980.

4344. Shanor, Donald R. "Can a Congressman Sue a Columnist?" *Columbia Journalism Review* 6 (Spring 1967): 20-22.

4345. Stealey, Orlando O. *Twenty Years in the Press Gallery*. New York: Publishers Printing Company, 1906.

4346. U.S. Congress. Joint Committee on Congressional Operations. *Congress and Mass Communications: An Institutional Perspective*. 93rd Cong., 2d sess. Washington: GPO, 1974.

4347. U.S. Congress. Joint Committee on Congressional Operations. *Congress and Mass Communications, Hearings, February 20, 21, March 7, 20, April 9, 10*. 93rd Cong., 2d sess. Washington: GPO, 1974.

4348. U.S. Congress. House. Administrative Review Commission. *Congressional, Media, and People Who Work the Hill Panels, Business Meeting, Hearings, November 30 and December 1, 1976*. 94th Cong., 2d sess. Washington: GPO, 1977.

4349. Weaver, David H. and Wilhoit, G. Cleveland. "News Magazine Visibility of Senators." *Journalism Quarterly* 51 (Spring 1974): 67-72.

4350. Weaver, David H., Wilhoit, G., Cleveland, Dunwoody, Sharon, and Hagner, Paul. "Senatorial News Coverage: Agenda-Setting for Mass and Elite Media in the United States." In *Senate Communications with the Public: A Compilation of Papers Presented for the Commission on the Operation of the Senate*, pp. 41-62. Washington: GPO, 1977.

4351. Whelan, John T. "Legislative Process Textbooks and the News Media: A Neglected Link." *Teaching Political Science* 6 (Oct. 1978): 89-110.

4352. Wilhoit, G. Cleveland and Sherrill, Kenneth S. "Wire Service Visibility of U.S. Senators." *Journalism Quarterly* 45 (Spring 1968): 42-48.

Public Opinion

4353. Alpert, Harry, Hawver, Carl, Cantvell, Frank V., DeVany, Philip M., and Kriesberg, Martin. "Congressional Use of Polls." *Public Opinion Quarterly* 18 (Summer 1954): 121-141.

4354. Backstrom, Charles H. "Congress and the Public: How Representative Is One of the Other?" *American Politics Quarterly* 5 (Oct. 1977): 411-435.

4355. Brody, Richard A. and Tufte, Edward R. "Constituent–Congressional Communication on Fallout Shelters: The Congressional Polls." *Journal of Communication* 14 (Mar. 1964): 34-49.

4356. "Bumper Mail Crop Keeps Congressional Staffs Busy." *Congressional Quarterly Weekly Report* 27 (Nov. 14, 1969): 2282-2284.

4357. Cantwell, Frank V. "The Congressional Poll: Six Years' Experience." *Public Opinion Quarterly* 18 (Summer 1954): 130-135.

4358. Cantwell, Frank V. "Public Opinion and the Legislative Process." *American Political Science Review* 40 (Oct. 1946): 924-935.

4359. "Congressional Image with Public Slips to New Low." *Congressional Quarterly Weekly Report* 28 (April 3, 1970): 932.

4360. "Congressional Unpopularity: 5 Views from the Inside." *Congressional Quarterly Weekly Report* 32 (Mar. 9, 1974): 600-603.

4361. Declercq, Eugene. "Use of Polling in Congressional Campaigns." *Public Opinion Quarterly* 42 (Summer 1978): 247-258.

4362. DeVany, Philip M. "The 'Town Meeting' Poll in South Dakota." *Public Opinion Quarterly* 18 (Summer 1954): 135-140.

4363. Dexter, Lewis A. "What Do Congressmen Hear: The Mail." *Public Opinion Quarterly* 20 (Spring 1956): 16-27.

4364. Edwards, George C. "Congressional Responsiveness to Public Opinion: A Policy Perspective." *Policy Studies Journal* 5 (Summer 1977): 485-491.

4365. Harris, Louis. "Polls and Politics in the United States." *Public Opinion Quarterly* 27 (Spring 1963): 3-8.

4366. Hawver, Carl F. "The Congressman and His Public Opinion Poll." *Public Opinion Quarterly* 18 (Summer 1954): 123-129.

4367. Hawver, Carl F. "The Congressman's Conception of His Role: A Study of the Use of Public Opinion Polls by Members of the United States House of Representatives." Ph.D. dissertation, American University, 1963.

4368. Hedlund, Ronald D. and Friesema, H. Paul. "Representatives' Perceptions of Constituency Opinion." *Journal of Politics* 34 (Aug. 1972): 730-752.

4369. Jreisat, Jamil E. *Images and Policies in Senate Debates on Middle Eastern Issues.* Hyattsville, Md.: Institute of Middle Eastern and African Affairs, 1976.

4370. Kreisberg, Martin. "Toward the Improvement of Congressional Polls." *Public Opinion Quarterly* 18 (Summer 1954): 140-142.

4371. Kreisberg, Martin. "What Congressmen and Administrators Think About the Polls." *Public Opinion Quarterly* 9 (Fall 1945): 333-337.

4372. Lehnen, Robert G. "The Congress and Public Opinion." In his *American Institutions, Political Opinion and Public Policy,* pp. 153-175. Hinsdale, Ill.: Dryden Press, 1976.

4373. Lewis, George F. "Congressmen Look at the Public Opinion Polls." *Public Opinion Quarterly* 4 (June 1940): 229-231.

4374. Mannon, Virginia M. "What Kind of Congressmen Do We Need in Wartime." *National Municipal Review* 31 (July 1942): 376-378, 389.

4375. Marascuilo, Leonard and Amster, Harriett. "Survey of Congressional Polls." *Public Opinion Quarterly* 28 (Fall 1964): 497-506.

4376. Nedzi, Lucien N. "Public Opinion Polls: Will Legislation Help?" *Public Opinion Quarterly* 35 (Fall 1971): 336-341.

4377. Parker, Glenn R. "Some Themes in Congressional Unpopularity." *American Journal of Political Science* 21 (Feb. 1977): 93-109.

4378. Plog, Stanley C. "Flanders vs. McCarthy: A Study in the Technique and Theory of Analyzing Congressional Mail." Ph.D. dissertation, Harvard University, 1961.

4379. Sekulow, Eugene A. "Congressmen Ask the People: A Study of Congressionally Conducted Public Opinion Polls." Ph.D. dissertation, Johns Hopkins University, 1961.

4380. Tedin, Kent L. "Public Awareness of Congressional Representatives: Recall Versus Recognition." *American Politics Quarterly* 7 (Oct. 1979): 509-517.

4381. Topkis, Jay H. "How Bad Is Congress?" *Political Science Quarterly* 62 (Dec. 1947): 531-551.

4382. Zeidenstein, Harvey G. "Presidential Popularity and Presidential Support in Congress: Eisenhower to Carter." *Presidential Studies Quarterly* 10 (Spring 1980): 224-233.

Ratings of Congressmen

4383. "ADA Awards to Congressmen Stir Dispute in House." *Congressional Quarterly Weekly Report* 21 (May 31, 1963): 847-849.

4384. Berger, James R. and Cook, Rhodes. "Group Ratings: A Year of Dissatisfaction." *Congressional Quarterly Weekly Report* 35 (Feb. 5, 1977): 215-217.

4385. Bethell, Tom. "The Changing Fashions of Liberalism." *Public Opinion Quarterly* 2 (Jan.-Feb. 1979): 41-46.

4386. Carlson, Hilding B. and Harrell, Willard. "An Analysis of *Life's* 'Ablest Congressmen' Poll." *Journal of Social Psychology* 15 (Feb. 1942): 153-158.

4387. "Group Ratings: Trend to Liberalization Seen." *Congressional Quarterly Weekly Report* 33 (Feb. 22, 1975): 387-402.

4388. "Non-Party Groups Rate Each Senator, Representative." *Congressional Quarterly Weekly Report* 20 (Oct. 26, 1962): 2019-2028.

4389. "Non-Party Groups Rate Each Senator, Representative." *Congressional Quarterly Weekly Report* 24 (Nov. 4, 1966): 2754-2768.

4390. "Nonparty Groups Rate Each Senator, Representative." *Congressional Quarterly Weekly Report* 26 (April 26, 1968): 915-928.

4391. "Nonparty Groups Rate Each Senator, Representative." *Congressional Quarterly Weekly Report* 26 (Nov. 15, 1968): 3149-3159.

4392. "Pressure Groups Rate Each Senator, Representative." *Congressional Quarterly Weekly Report* 29 (April 16, 1971): 863-875.

4393. "Pressure Group Ratings of All Members of Congress." *Congressional Quarterly Weekly Report* 32 (Mar. 20, 1974): 813-828.

4394. "The 'Rating Game': Some Members Object." *Congressional Quarterly Weekly Report* 32 (July 6, 1974): 1748-1754.

4395. "Two Liberal, Three Conservative Groups Rate Congress." *Congressional Quarterly Weekly Report* 24 (Feb. 25, 1966): 467-474.

XII. Congress and the Electorate

Voting Regulations

4396. Banzhaf, John F. "Multi-Member Electoral Districts: Do They Violate the 'One Man, One Vote' Principle?" *Yale Law Journal* 75 (July 1966): 1309-1338.

4397. Burke, Albie. "Federal Regulation of Congressional Elections in Northern Cities." *American Journal of Legal History* 14 (Jan. 1970): 17-34.

4398. Burke, Albie. "Federal Regulation of Congressional Elections in Northern Cities, 1871-1894." Ph.D. dissertation, University of Chicago, 1968.

4399. Claude, Richard P. "Nationalization of the Electoral Process." *Harvard Journal on Legislation* 6 (Jan. 1969): 139-168.

4400. Garrison, George P. "History of Federal Control of Congressional Elections." Ph.D. dissertation, University of Chicago, 1896.

4401. Hamilton, James A. "Negro Suffrage and Congressional Representation." Ph.D. dissertation, New York University, 1909.

4402. Horn, Robert A. "National Control of Congressional Elections." Ph.D. dissertation, Princeton University, 1942.

4403. Koslowe, Neil H. "Expatriation Legislation." *Harvard Journal on Legislation* 6 (Jan. 1969): 95-111.

4404. Kozusko, Donald D. and Lambert, Paul J. "The Uncertain Impact of *Williams v. Rhodes* on Qualifying Minority Parties for the Ballot." *Harvard Journal on Legislation* 6 (Jan. 1969): 236-253.

4405. Linden, Glenn M. "Note on Negro Suffrage and Republican Politics." *Journal of Southern History* 36 (Aug. 1970): 411-420.

4406. Maurer, Robert A. "Congressional and State Control of Elections Under the Constitution." *Goergetown Law Journal* 16 (April 1928): 314-340.

4407. Minor, Raleigh C. "May Congress Constitutionally Prohibit Alien Enemies to Vote at Federal Elections." *Virginia Law Review* 5 (Mar. 1918): 412-418.

4408. Paper, Lewis J. "Legislative History of Title III of the Voting Rights Act of 1970." *Harvard Journal on Legislation* 8 (Nov. 1970): 123-157.

4409. Ritz, Wilfred J. "Free Elections and the Power of Congress over Voter Qualifications." *American Bar Association Journal* 49 (Oct. 1963): 949-954.

Campaigning

4410. Balz, Daniel J. "One Primary Day in Iowa: Traveling the Long Road to Congress." *National Journal* 8 (Sept. 11, 1976): 1280-1283.

4411. Bassett, Edward P. "Political News, Newspapermen and Politicians: The Roles Newspapers Played in Iowa's 1964 First District Congressional Campaign." Ph.D. dissertation, University of Iowa, 1967.

4412. Bell, Lillian S. "The Role and Performance of Black and Metro Newspapers in Relation to Political Campaigns in Selected Racially-Mixed Congressional Elections, 1960-1970." Ph.D. dissertation, Northwestern University, 1973.

4413. Belmont, Perry. *Return to Secret Party Funds: The Value of Reed Committee.* New York: Putnam, 1927.

4414. Berry, Jeffrey M. and Goldman, Jerry. "Congress and Public Policy: A Study of the Federal Election Campaign Act of 1971." *Harvard Journal on Legislation* 10 (Feb. 1973): 331-365.

4415. Bird, Agnes T. "Rsources Used in Tennessee Senatorial Campaigns, 1948-1964." Ph.D. dissertation, University of Tennessee, 1967.

4416. Bishop, Robert L. and Brown, Robert L. "Michigan Newspaper Bias in the 1966 Campaign." *Journalism Quarterly* 45 (Summer 1968): 337-338.

4417. Bone, Hugh A. *Party Committees and National Politics.* Seattle: University of Washington Press, 1958.

4418. Bone, Hugh A. "Some Notes on the Congressional Campaign Committees." *Western Political Quarterly* 9 (Mar. 1956): 116-137.

4419. Bowers, Thomas A. "An Analysis of Information Content in Newspaper Political Advertising in Selected Senatorial, Gubernatorial, and Congressional Campaigns of 1970." Ph.D. dissertation, Indiana University, 1971.

4420. Boyd, James. "The Ritual of Wiggle: From Ruin to Reelection." *Washington Monthly* 2 (Sept. 1970): 28-44.

4421. Carey, John. "How the Media Shape Campaigns." *Journal of Communication* 26 (Spring 1976): 50-57.

4422. Clark, Peter and Fredin, Eric. "Newspaper, Television, and Political Reasoning." *Public Opinion Quarterly* 42 (Summer 1978): 143-160.

4423. Clem, Alan L. "Analysis of the 1958 Congressional Campaign in the Third District of Nebraska." Ph.D. dissertation, American University, 1960.

4424. Clem, Alan L. *The Making of Congressmen: Seven Campaigns of 1974.* North Scituate, Mass.: Duxbury Press, 1976.

4425. Clem, Alan L. "Seven Campaigns for Congress: A Comparative Perspective." In his *The Making of Congressmen: Seven Campaigns of 1974,* pp. 235-254. North Scituate, Mass.: Duxbury Press, 1976.

4426. Cohen, Richard E. "Running Scared in Congress: The Parties Go Head-to-Head over Money." *National Journal* 10 (April 8, 1978): 557-561.

4427. Colldeweih, Jack H. "The Effects of Mass Media Consumption on Accuracy of Beliefs About the Candidates in a Local Congressional Election." Ph.D. dissertation, University of Illinois at Urbana-Champaign, 1968.

4428. Common Cause. "Operation Open Up the System: A Common Cause Manual for the 1972 Congressional Elections." *Common Cause Report from Washington* 2 (Oct. 1972): 1-36.

4429. Davidson, Roger H. "Choosing Congressmen." *Current History* 67 (Aug. 1974): 60-63, 86-88.

4430. Dawson, Paul A. and Zinser, James E. "Broadcast Expenditures and Electoral Outcomes in the 1970 Congressional Elections." *Public Opinion Quarterly* 35 (Fall 1971): 398-402.

4431. Dexter, Lewis A. "Candidates Make the Issues and Give Them Meaning." *Public Opinion Quarterly* 19 (Winter 1955-1956): 408-414.

4432. Dunlevy, James A. and Yeager, James H. "Legislators as Taxicabs: A Reconsideration." *Economic Inquiry* 17 (April 1979): 303-306.

4433. Fair Campaign Practices Committee. *The Arbitration of Politics.* Washington: The Committee, 1969.

4434. Finney, Robert G. "Television News Messages and Their Perceived Effects in a Congressional Election Campaign." Ph.D. dissertation, Ohio State University, 1971.

4435. Fiori, Patricia. *Congressional Employees and Campaign Activities: Participation by House Staff Employees in Member's Campaign Committee.* Washington: Congressional Research Service, 1976.

4436. Fisher, Joel M. "The Campaign." In *To Be a Congressman: The Promise and the Power,* eds. Sven Groennings and Jonathan P. Hawley, pp. 1-21. Washington: Acropolis Books, 1973.

4437. Fox, William L. "Running for Congress in Clarion County, 1894." *Pennsylvania Magazine of History and Biography* 91 (July 1967): 245-265.

4438. Glass, Andrew J. "Low Cost TV and Radio Facilities Prove Popular in Election Year." *National Journal* 2 (July 11, 1970): 1482-1487.

4439. Harlan, Douglas S. "Party and Campaign in a Congressional Election: A Case Study of Reciprocal Dependency." Ph.D. dissertation, University of Texas at Austin, 1968.

4440. Harris, D. Allan. "Campaigning in the Bloody Seventh: The Election of 1894 in the Seventh Congressional District." *Alabama Review* 27 (April 1974): 127-138.

4441. Hathorn, Guy B. "Congressional and Senatorial Campaign Committees in the Mid-Term Election Year 1954." *Southwestern Social Science Quarterly* 37 (Dec. 1956): 207-221.

4442. Himmelfarb, Milton. "Fertility, Social Action, Socialism." *Commentary* 32 (Sept. 1961): 235-238.

4443. Hoeh, David C. "The Biography of a Campaign: Strategy, Management Result—McCarthy in New Hampshire 1968." Ph.D. dissertation, University of Massachusetts, 1978.

4444. Huckshorn, Robert J. and Spencer, Robert C. *The Politics of Defeat: Campaigning for Congress.* Amherst: University of Massachusetts Press, 1971.

4445. Javits, Jacob K. "How I Used a Poll in Campaigning for Congress." *Public Opinion Quarterly* 11 (Summer 1947): 222-232.

4446. Jones, Charles O. "The Role of the Campaign in Congressional Politics." In *Essays on the Electoral Process,* eds. Harmon Zeigler and Kent Jennings, pp. 21-41. Englewood Cliffs, N.J.: Prentice-Hall, 1965.

4447. Jones, Charles O. "A Suggested Scheme for Classifying Congressional Campaigns." *Public Opinion Quarterly* 26 (Spring 1962): 126-132.

4448. Jordan, Daniel P., ed. "Congressional Electioneering in Early Western Virginia: A Mini-War in Broadsides." *West Virginia History* 33 (Oct. 1971): 61-78.

4449. Joyner, Conrad F. "Running a Congressional Campaign." In *Practical Politics in the United States,* ed. Cornelius P. Cotter, pp. 143-171. Boston: Allyn and Bacon, 1969.

4450. Kelly, Joseph P. "A Study of the 1960 Primary and General Election Campaigns for United States House of Representatives in Montana's Second Congressional District." Ph.D. dissertation, Washington University, 1963.

4451. Kirwan, Michael. *How to Succeed in Politics.* New York: MacFadden, 1964.

4452. Lawrence, Gary C. "Media Effects in Congressional Election Canpaigns." Ph.D. dissertation, Stanford University, 1972.

4453. Leuthold, David A. *Electioneering in a Democracy: Campaigns for Congress.* New York: Wiley, 1968.

4454. Loomis, Burdett A. "Resources into Results? Congressional Campaigns in Marginal Districts." Ph.D. dissertation, University of Wisconsin, 1974.

4455. Lowe, Francis E. "The Measurement of the Influence of Formal and Informal Leaders of Public Opinion During the 1950 Senatorial Election Campaign in Madison, Wisconsin." Ph.D. dissertation, University of Wisconsin, 1953.

4456. Lupfer, Michael and Price, David E. "On the Merits of Face-to-Face Campaigning." *Social Science Quarterly* 53 (Dec. 1972): 534-543.

4457. Manheim, Jarol B. "The Effect of Campaign Techniques on Voting Patterns in a Congressional Election." Ph.D. dissertation, Northwestern University, 1971.

4458. Manheim, Jarol B. "Urbanization and Differential Press Coverage of the Congressional Campaign." *Journalism Quarterly* 51 (Winter 1974): 649-669.

4459. Margolis, Michael S. "The Impact of Political Environment, Campaign Activity, and Party Organization on the Outcomes of Congressional Elections." Ph.D. dissertation, University of Michigan, 1968.

4460. Maskell, Jack. *Campaign Activities by Congressionnal Employees.* Washington: Congressional Research Service, 1976.

4461. Minow, Newton N. and Mitchell, Lee M. "Incumbent Television: A Case of Indecent Exposure." *American Academy of Political and Social Science, Annals* 425 (May 1976): 74-87.

4462. Morton, Thurston B. "Senatorial Campaigning." In *The Senate Institution,* ed. Nathaniel S. Preston, pp. 43-49. New York: Van Nostrand Reinhold, 1969.

4463. Mullen, James J. "How Candidates for the Senate Use Newspaper Advertising." *Journalism Quarterly* 40 (Autumn 1963): 532-538.

4464. Paletz, David L. "The Neglected Context of Congressional Campaigns." *Polity* 4 (Winter 1971): 195-216.

4465. Patton, James W. "Pastoral Politician: Theology and Strategy for a Congressional Campaign for the Seventh Congressional District of Alabama." D. Min., Louisville Presbyterian Theological Seminary, 1975.

4466. Peabody, Robert L., et al. *To Enact a Law: Congress and Campaign Financing.* New York: Praeger, 1972.

4467. Pittman, Russell. "The Effects of Industry Concentration and Regulation on Contributions in Three 1972 Senate Campaigns." *Public Choice* 27 (Fall 1976): 71-80.

4468. Roshwalb, Irving and Resnicoff, Leonard. "The Impact of Endorsements and Published Polls on the 1970 New York Senatorial Election." *Public Opinion Quarterly* 35 (Fall 1971): 410-414.

4469. Schoenberger, Robert A. "Campaign Strategy and Party Loyalty: The Electoral Relevance of Candidate Decision-Making in the 1964 Congressional Elections." *American Political Science Review* 63 (June 1969): 515-520.

4470. Shadegg, Stephen C. *How to Win an Election: The Art of Political Victory.* New York: Taplinger Publishing Co., 1964.

4471. Sharp, Philip R. "Challenger Campaigns for the United States House of Representatives: A Study of Indiana Democrats in 1972." Ph.D. dissertation, Georgetown University, 1973.

4472. Spragens, William C. "Press Coverage of Congressional Campaigns: A Content Analysis of the 1960 Campaign in Michigan and Tennessee." Ph.D. dissertation, Michigan State University, 1966.

4473. Stein, Buddy and Wellman, David. "The Scheer Campaign." *Studies on the Left* 7 (Jan.-Feb. 1967): 62-77.

4474. Sullivan, John L. and Minns, Daniel R. "Ideological Distance Between Candidates: An Empirical Examination." *American Journal of Political Science* 20 (Aug. 1976): 439-468.

4475. Wasby, Stephen L. "National Party Contributions to Nonincumbent Congressional Candidates: The Democrats in 1964." *Southwestern Social Science Quarterly* 48 (Mar. 1968): 573-585.

4476. Wolfe, Alan P. "The Senatorial Campaign." Ph.D. dissertation, University of Pennsylvania, 1967.

4477. Yarnell, Steven M. "Explaining Congressional Campaign Behavior: An Information Processing Perspective." Ph.D. dissertation, Ohio State University, 1978.

Campaign Finances

4478. American Enterprise Institute for Public Policy Research. *Public Financing of Congressional Campaigns.* Washington: American Enterprise Institute for Public Policy Research, Legislative and/or Special Analysis, 1978.

4479. Brock, Bill. "Adding Insult to Incumbency: Taxpayer Financing of Congressional Campaigns." *Commonsense: A Republican Journal of Thought and Opinion* 2 (Winter 1979): 11-22.

4480. Buchanan, William and Bird, Agnes T. *Money as a Campaign Resource: Tennessee Democratic Senatorial Primaries, 1948-1964.* Princeton, N.J.: Citizens' Research Foundation, 1966.

4481. Burton, Laurence J. "The Cost of Getting There and Length of Stay." In *We Propose: A Modern Congress,* ed. Mary McInnis, pp. 237-250. New York: McGraw-Hill, 1966.

4482. "Candidates' Campaign Costs for Congressional Contests Have Gone Up at a Fast Pace." *Congressional Quarterly Weekly Report* 37 (Sept. 29, 1979): 2151-2164.

4483. Cole, Roland J. "Campaign Spending in the United States Senate Elections." Ph.D. dissertation, Harvard University, 1975.

4484. Common Cause. *How Money Talks in Congress: A Common Cause Study of the Impact of Money on Congressional Decision-Making.* Washington: Common Cause, 1978.

4485. Copeland, Gary W. and Patterson, Samuel C. "Money in Congressional Elections." In *Legislative Reform: The Policy Impact,* ed. Leroy N. Rieselbach, pp. 195-208. Lexington, Mass.: Lexington Books, 1978.

4486. Copeland, Gary W. and Patterson, Samuel C. "Reform of Congressional Campaign Spending." *Policy Studies Journal* 5 (Summer 1977): 424-431.

4487. Court, H. Leonard and Harris, Charles E. "Campaign Spending Regulation: Failure of the First Step." *Harvard Journal on Legislation* 8 (1970-1971): 640-674.

4488. Crain, W. Mark and Tollison, Robert D. "Campaign Expenditures and Political Competition." *Journal of Law and Economics* 19 (April 1976): 177-188.

4489. Crain, W. Mark, Deaton, Thomas, and Tollison, Robert D. "Toenote to a Footnote." *Economic Inquiry* 17 (April 1979): 307-309.

4490. Dawson, Paul A. and Zinser, James E. "Political Finance and Participation in Congressional Elections." *American Academy of Political and Social Science, Annals* 425 (May 1976): 59-73.

4491. Dean, E. Joseph. "Undisclosed Earmarking: Violation of the Federal Elections Campaign Act of 1971." *Harvard Journal on Legislation* 10 (Feb. 1973): 175-197.

4492. Freed, Bruce F. Campaign Finance: Congress Weighing New Law." *Congressional Quarterly Weekly Report* 34 (Feb. 7, 1976): 267-274.

4493. Friedman, Richard D. "A New Approach to the Dilemma of Campaign Finance Reform." *American Bar Association Journal* 62 (Jan. 1976): 72-75.

4494. Giertz, J. Fred and Sullivan, Dennis H. "Campaign Expenditures and Election Outcomes: A Critical Note." *Public Choice* 31 (Fall 1977): 157-162.

4495. Jacobson, Gary C. "Effects of Campaign Spending in Congressional Elections." *American Political Science Review* 72 (June 1978): 469-491.

4496. Jacobson, Gary C. *Money in Congressional Elections.* New Haven, Conn.: Yale University Press, 1980.

4497. Jacobson, Gary C. "Practical Consequences of Campaign Finance Reform: An Incumbent Protection Act." *Public Policy* 24 (Winter 1976): 1-32.

4498. Jacobson, Gary C. "Public Funds for Congressional Campaigns: Who Benefits?" In *Political Finance*, ed. Herbert Alexander, pp. 99-128. Beverly Hills, Calif.: Sage Publications, 1979.

4499. Levine, Arthur. "Getting to Know Your Congressman: The $500 Understanding." *Washington Monthly* 6 (Feb. 1975): 47-59.

4500. McCarthy, Richard D. *Elections for Sale.* Boston: Houghton Mifflin, 1972.

4501. McDevitt, Ronald D. "The Changing Dynamics of Fund Raising in House Campaigns." In *Political Finance*, ed. Herbert Alexander, pp. 129-158. Beverly Hills, Calif.: Sage Publications, 1979.

4502. McDevitt, Roland D. "The Consequences of Regulating Congressional Campaign Funds." Ph.D. dissertation, University of California, Santa Barbara, 1978.

4503. McKeough, Kevin L. *Financing Campaigns for Congress: Contribution Patterns of National-Level Party and Non-Party Committees, 1964.* Princeton, N.J.: Citizens' Research Foundation, 1970.

4504. Mikan, Frank G. "An Evaluation of the Campaign Recommendations of the Senate Watergate Committee." Master's thesis, Duquesne University, 1975.

4505. Murray, Dennis J. "Campaign Finance and a Theory of Democracy: A Study of Congressional Elections." Ph.D. dissertation, University of Southern California, 1976.

4506. Napolitan, Joseph. "Media Costs and Effects in Political Campaigns." *American Academy of Political and Social Science, Annals* 427 (Sept. 1976): 114-124.

4507. Polk, James R. "Congressional Campaign Contributions: Harder to Conceal." *New Republic* 166 (April 1972): 16-18.

4508. Rosenthal, Albert J. "Campaign Financing and the Constitution." *Harvard Journal on Legislation* 9 (Mar. 1972): 359-423.

4509. Twentieth Century Fund. Task Force on Financing Congressional Elections." *Electing Congress: The Financial Dilemma.* New York: The Fund, 1970.

4510. U.S. Congress. House. House Administration Committee. *Public Financing of Congressional Elections. March 15-27, 1979.* 96th Cong., 1st sess. Washington: GPO, 1979.

4511. Wright, James C. "Clean Money for Congress." *Harpers Magazine* 234 (April 1967): 98-102, 105-106.

4512. Zeidenstein, Harvey G. "Correlates of Congressional Campaign Spending." *International Review* 12 (May 1975): 1-38.

Primaries

4513. Bernstein, Robert A. "Divisive Primaries: U.S. Senate Races, 1956-1962." *American Political Science Review* 71 (June 1977): 540-545.

4514. Everett, Robert B. "The 1948 Senatorial Primary in Tennessee: A History and an Analysis." Master's thesis, Memphis State University, 1962.

4515. Foster, Julian F. S. "Congressional Primaries." Ph.D. dissertation, University of California at Los Angeles, 1963.

4516. Hein, Clarence J. "The Operation of the Direct Primary in Minnesota: Nominations for State-Wide and Congressional Offices." Ph.D. dissertation, University of Minnesota, 1956.

4517. Moody, Eric N. "The Democratic Senatorial Primary, 1944: Vail Pittman." *Nevada Historical Society Quarterly* 15 (Summer 1972): 3-24.

4518. Owens, John R. *Money and Politics in California: Democratic Senatorial Primary, 1964.* Princeton, N.J.: Citizens' Research Foundation, 1966.

4519. Paul, Justus F. "Isolationism Versus Internationalism? The Republican Senatorial Primary in Nebraska, 1946." *Nebraska History* 56 (Spring 1975): 145-156.

4520. Schantz, Harvey L. "Nominations for the United States House of Representatives: Primary Elections for the United States House, 1956-1974." Ph.D. dissertation, Johns Hopkins University, 1978.

4521. Schmal, Stephen M. "An Analysis of Certain Factors Relating to the Presence or Absence of Contests in Congressional Primary Elections." Master's thesis, American University, 1966.

Election

General Studies

4522. Ackerman, Donald H. "Significance of Congressional Races with Identical Candidates in Successive District Selections." *Midwest Journal of Political Sciwnce* 1 (Aug. 1957): 173-180.

4523. Alpert, Eugene J. "Risk and Uncertainty in Political Choice: Candidates' Policy Positions in Congressional Elections." Ph.D. dissertation, Michigan State University, 1977.

4524. Angle, Charles H. "Safe Urban Congressional Districts, 1950-1966." Ph.D. dissertation, University of Kansas, 1969.

4525. Arcelus, Francisco J. and Meltzer, Allan H. "The Effect of Aggregate Economic Variables on Congressional Elections." *American Political Science Review* 69 (Dec. 1975): 1232-1239.

4526. Arcelus, Francisco J. "Effects of Aggregate Economic Variables on Congressional Elections." Ph.D. dissertation, Carnegie-Mellon University, 1976.

4527. Baxter, Sylvester. "Representative Inequality of Senators." *North American Review* 177 (Dec. 1903): 897-903.

4528. Brady, David W. "Critical Elections, Congressional Parties and Clusters of Policy Changes." *British Journal of Political Science* 8 (Jan. 1978): 79-99.

4529. Brady, David W. and Lynn, Naomi B. "Switched-Seat Congressional Districts: Their Effect on Party Voting and Public Policy." *American Journal of Political Science* 17 (Aug. 1973): 528-543.

4530. Bullock, Charles S. "Explaining Congressional Elections: Differences in Perceptions of Opposing Candidates." *Legislative Studies Quarterly* 2 (Aug. 1977): 295-308.

4531. Burnham, Walter D. "Insulation and Responsiveness in Congressional Elections." *Political Science Quarterly* 90 (Fall 1975): 411-435.

4532. Burstein, Paul. "Electoral Competition and Changes in the Party Balance in the U.S. Congress, 1789-1977." *Social Science Research* 8 (June 1979): 105-119.

4533. Carleton, William G. "Our Congressional Elections: In Defense of the Traditional System." *Political Science Quarterly* 70 (Sept. 1955): 341-357.

4534. Clem, Alan L. "Election and Representation." In his *The Making of Congressmen: Seven Campaigns of 1974*, pp. 1-23. North Scituate, Mass.: Duxbury Press, 1976.

4535. Coffey, Wayne R. *How We Choose a Congress.* New York: St. Martin's Press, 1980.

4536. Congressional Quarterly, Inc. *Electing Congress: Timely Reports to Keep Journalists, Scholars, and the Public Abreast of Developing Issues, Events, and Trends.* Washington: Congressional Quarterly, 1978.

4537. Cosman, Bernard. "Republicans in the South: Goldwater's Impact Upon Voting Alignments in Congressional, Gubernatorial, and Senatorial Races." *Southwestern Social Science Quarterly* 48 (June 1967): 13-23.

4538. Cover, Albert D. and Mayhew, David R. "Congressional Dynamics and the Decline of Competitive Elections." In *Congress Reconsidered,* eds. Lawrence C. Dodd and Bruce I. Oppenheimer, pp. 54-72. New York: Praeger, 1977.

4539. Cox, Edward F. "The Measurement of Party Strength." *Western Political Quarterly* 13 (Dec. 1960): 1022-1042.

4540. Crain, W. Mark, Deaton, Thomas, and Tollison, Robert D. "Legislators as Taxicabs: On the Value of Seats in the United States House of Representatives." *Economy Inquiry* 15 (April 1977): 298-302.

4541. Cummings, Milton C. *Congressmen and the Electorate: Elections for the U.S. House and President, 1920-1964.* New York: Free Press, 1966.

4542. Cummings, Milton C. "Nominations and Elections for the House of Representatives." In *The National Election of 1964,* ed. Milton C. Cummings, pp. 222-225. Washington: Brookings Institution, 1966.

4543. Deber, Raisa B. "Who Runs: Congressmen and Realignment Sequences." Ph.D. dissertation, M.I.T., 1977.

4544. Erikson, Robert S. "Is There Such a Thing as a Safe Seat." *Polity* 8 (Summer 1976): 623-632.

4545. Erikson, Robert S. "A Multivariate Analysis of Congressional Elections." Ph.D. dissertation, University of Illinois at Urbana-Champaign, 1969.

4546. Falco, Maria J. *"Bigotry!": Ethnic, Machine and Sexual Politics in a Senatorial Election.* Westport, Conn.: Greenwood Press, 1980.

4547. Ferejohn, John A. "On the Decline of Competition in Congressional Elections." *American Political Science Review* 71 (Mar. 1977): 166-176.

4548. Fiorina, Morris P. "Case of the Vanishing Marginals: The Bureaucracy Did It." *American Political Science Review* 71 (Mar. 1977): 177-181.

4549. Fiorina, Morris P. "Electoral Margins, Constituency Influence and Policy Moderation: A Critical Assessment." *American Politics Quarterly* 1 (Oct. 1973): 479-498.

4550. Fishel, Jeff. "Ambition and the Political Vocation: Congressional Challengers in American Politics." *Journal of Politics* 33 (Feb. 1971): 25-56.

4551. Fishel, Jeff. *Party and Opposition: Congressional Challengers in American Politics.* New York: McKay, 1973.

4552. Fishel, Jeff. "Party, Ideology, and the Congressional Challenger." *American Political Science Review* 63 (Dec. 1969): 1213-1332.

4553. Fishel, Jeff. *Representation and Responsiveness in Congress: The "Class of Eighty-Nine," 1965-1970.* Beverly Hills, Calif.: Sage Publications, 1973.

4554. Flavin, Michael. "Measuring Gains and Losses of Democrats and Republicans in Congressional Elections." Ph.D. dissertation, University of Arizona, 1977.

4555. Fowler, Linda L. "The Cycle of Defeat: Recruitment of Congressional Challengers." Ph.D. dissertation, University of Rochester, 1977.

4556. Harmon, Kathryn N. and Brauen, Marsha L. "Joint Electoral Outcomes as Cues for Congressional Support of U.S. Presidents." *Legislative Studies Quarterly* 4 (May 1979): 281-299.

4557. Hill, Kim Q. and Hurley, Patricia A. "Mass Participation, Electoral Competitiveness, and Issue-Attitude Agreement Between Congressmen and Their Constituents." *British Journal of Political Science* 9 (Oct. 1979): 507–511.

4558. Hinckley, Barbara. "Issues, Information Costs, and Congressional Elections." *American Politics Quarterly* 4 (April 1976): 131-152.

4559. Hinckley, Barbara, Hofstetter, Richard, and Kessel, John H. "Information and the Vote: A Comparative Election Study." *American Politics Quarterly* 2 (April 1974): 131-158.

4560. Historical Research Foundation, Washington D.C. *A Study of Voters' Inconsistencies in Selected Congressional Districts.* Washington: Historical Research Foundation, 1978.

4561. Israel, Michael L. "The Lost Cause Candidate: The Myth of Competition in Uncompetitive American Congressional Elections." Ph.D. dissertation, Rutgers University, 1974.

4562. Jones, Charles O. *Every Second Year: Congressional Behavior and the Two-Year Term.* Washington: Brookings Institution, 1967.

4563. Jones, Charles O. "Inter-Party Competition for Congressional Seats." *Western Political Quarterly* 17 (Sept. 1964): 461-476.

4564. Kabaker, Harvey M. "Estimating the Normal Vote in Congressional Elections." *Midwest Journal of Political Science* 13 (Feb. 1969): 58-83.

4565. Kazee, Thomas A. "The Decision to Run for the U.S. Congress: Challenger Attitudes in the 1970s." *Legislative Studies Quarterly* 5 (Feb. 1980): 79-100.

4566. Kenski, Henry C. "The Impact of Unemployment on Congressional Elections 1958-1974: A Cross-Sectional Analysis." *American Politics Quarterly* 7 (April 1979): 147-154.

4567. Key, Valdimer O. "Congressional Elections." In his *Politics, Parties, and Pressure Groups,* 5th ed. pp. 545-574. New York: Thomas Y. Crowell, 1964.

4568. Kinder, Donald R. and Kiewiet, D. Roderick. "Economic Discontent and Political Behavior: The Role of Personal Grievances and Collective Economic Judgements in Congressional Voting." *American Journal of Political Science* 23 (Aug. 1979): 495-527.

4569. King, Michael R. and Seligman, Lester G. "Critical Elections, Congressional Recruitment and Public Policy." In *Elite Recruitment in Democratic Politics: Comparative Studies Across Nations,* eds. Heinz Eulau and Moshe M. Czudnowski, pp. 263-299. New York: Halsted Press, 1976.

4570. Kirkpatrick, Samuel A., Morgan, David R., and Edwards, Larry G. *Oklahoma Voting Patterns: Congressional Elections.* Norman: Bureau of Government Research, University of Oklahoma, 1970.

4571. Kostroski, Warren L. "Elections and Legislative Reform: External and Internal Influences on Legislative Behavior." *Policy Studies Journal* 5 (Summer 1977): 414-418.

4572. Kostroski, Warren L. "Elections and Senatorial Accountability: 1920-1970." Ph.D. dissertation, Washington University, 1976.

4573. Kuklinski, James H. "Legislative Accountability: Election Margins, District Homogeneity, and the Responsiveness of Legislators." In *Accountability in Urban Society: Public Agencies Under Fire,* eds. Scott Greer, Ronald D. Hedlund, and James L. Gibson, pp. 197-216. Beverly Hills, Calif.: Sage Publications, 1978.

4574. Kurtz, Karl T. "Elections and the House of Representatives, 1882-1968." Ph.D. dissertation, Washington University, 1972.

4575. Leeds, Patricia L. "The Conditions for Issue Voting: A Comparison of Presidential and Congressional Elections." Ph.D. dissertation, University of Wisconsin, 1977.

4576. Leiserson, Avery. "National Party Organization and Congressional Districts." *Western Political Quarterly* 16 (Sept. 1963): 633-649.

4577. Lewis, Stuart. "Corrupt Practices in British Parliamentary and American Congressional Elections." Ph.D. dissertation, American University, 1923.

4578. Li, Richard P. Y. "A Dynamic Comparative Analysis of Presidential and House Elections." *American Journal of Political Science* 20 (Nov. 1976): 671-692.

4579. McNitt, Andrew D. "An Examination of Intra-Party Competition: Gubernatorial and Senatorial Nominations in the United States." Ph.D. dissertation, Michigan State University, 1978.

4580. McPhee, William N. and Glaser, William A., eds. *Public Opinion and Congressional Elections.* New York: Free Press, 1962.

4581. Mann, Thomas E. "Candidate Saliency and Congressional Elections." Ph.D. dissertation, University of Michigan, 1978.

4582. Mann, Thomas E. *Unsafe at Any Margin: Interpreting Congressional Elections.* Washington: American Enterprise Institute, For Public Policy Research, 1978.

4583. Mayhew, David R. *Congress: The Electoral Connection.* New Haven: Yale University Press, 1974.

4584. Mayhew, David R. "Congressional Elections: The Case of Vanishing Marginals." *Polity* 6 (Spring 1974): 295-317.

4585. Mervin, David. "Parochialism and Professionalism in a Congressional Election." *Political Studies* 20 (Sept. 1972): 277-286.

4586. Miller, Warren E. and Stokes, Donald E. *Representation in Congress.* Englewood Cliffs, N.J. Prentice-Hall, 1966.

4587. Nexon, David. "Elections, Parties and Representation: The U.S. House of Representatives, 1952-1970." In *The Impact of the Electoral Process*, eds. Louis Maisel and Joseph Cooper, pp. 167-206. Beverly Hills, Calif.: Sage Publications, 1977.

4588. Oshel, Robert E. "Success in Congress: The Relationship Between Margin of Electoral Victory and Legislative Success in the U.S. House of Representatives." Ph.D. dissertation, American University, 1974.

4589. Penniman, Howard R. 'The State of the Two-Party System." *Wilson Quarterly* 2 (Winter 1978): 83-89.

4590. Pomper, Gerald. "Future Southern Congressional Politics." *Southwestern Social Science Quarterly* 44 (June 1963): 14-24.

4591. Ponsford, Pearl O. "A History of Congressional Elections and Their Effect upon the Political Complex of Congress." Ph.D. dissertation, University of Southern California, 1936.

4592. Price, Hugh D. "The Electoral Arena.' In *The Congress and America's Future,* ed. David B. Truman, pp. 32-52. Englewood Cliffs, N.J.: Prentice-Hall, 1965.

4593. Roberts, Churchill. "Voting Intentions and Attitude Change in a Congressional Election." *Speech Magazine* 40 (Mar. 1973): 49-55.

4594. Selke, Albert G. "Special Elections to the United States House of Representatives, 1920-1941." Ph.D. dissertation, University of Michigan, 1944.

4595. Silberman, Jonathan I. and Durden, Garey C. "The Rational Behavior Theory of Voter Participation: The Evidence from Congressional Elections." *Public Choice* 23 (Fall 1975): 101-108.

4596. Somit, Albert and Tanenhaus, Joseph. "Veteran in the Electoral Process: The House of Representatives." *Journal of Politics* 19 (May 1957): 184-201.

4597. Stephen, Daryl S. "Voting Behavior in Congressional Gubernatorial and Presidential Elections: A Comparative Analysis." Ph.D. dissertation, Ohio State University, 1978.

4598. Strong, Mary K. "Foreign Affairs and Congressional Elections." *Current History* 10 (April 1946): 342-347.

4599. Tidmarch, Charles M. and Carpenter, Douglas. "Congressmen and the Electorate, 1968 and 1972." *Journal of Politics* 40 (May 1978): 479-487.

4600. Uhlmann, Michael M. "Congress and the Welfare State: The Electoral Connection." *Commonsense: A Republican Journal of Thought and Opinion* 1 (Fall 1978): 15-26.

4601. Uslaner, Eric M. "Party Reform and Electoral Disaggregation: A Paradox in Congress?" *Policy Studies Journal* 5 (Summer 1977): 454-459.

4602. Welch, Susan and Brown, Buster J. "Correlates of Southern Republican Success at the Congressional District Level." *Social Science Quarterly* 59 (Mar. 1979): 732-742.

4603. Weston, Warren. "A Comparison of the Methods of Filling Vacancies in the United States Senate and the United States House of Representatives, 1912-1954." Ph.D. dissertation, University of Minnesota, 1959.

4604. Wright, Gerald C. "Candidates' Policy Positions and Voting in U.S. Congressional Elections." *Legislative Studies Quarterly* 3 (Aug. 1978): 445-464.

4605. Zimmer, Troy A. "Urbanization, Social Diversity, Voter Turnout, and Political Competition in U. S. Elections: Analysis of Congressional Districts for 1972." *Social Science Quarterly* 56 (Mar. 1976): 689-697.

Midterm Elections

4606. Abramowitz, Alan I. "An Assessment of Party and Incumbent Accountability in Midterm Congressional Elections." Ph.D. dissertation, Stanford University, 1976.

4607. Balfour, Nancy. "Issues at the U.S. Congressional Elections: President Kennedy at Mid-Term." *World Today* 18 (Oct. 1962): 438-444.

4608. Bean, Louis. *The Midterm Battle.* Washington: Cantillon Book Co., 1950.

4609. Franklin, Mark N. "A 'Non-Election' in America ? Predicting the Results of the 1970 Mid-Term Election for the U.S. House of Representatives." *British Journal of Political Science* 1 (Oct. 1971): 508-513.

4610. Gertzog, Irwin N. "The Role of the President in the Midterm Congressional Election." Ph.D. dissertation, University of North Carolina at Chapel Hill, 1965.

4611. Hinckley, Barbara. "Interpreting House Midterm Elections: Toward a Measurement of the In-Party's Expected Loss of Seats." *American Political Science Review* 61 (Sept. 1967): 694-700.

4612. Kernell, Samuel. "Presidential Popularity and Negative Voting: An Alternative Explanation of the Midterm Congressional Decline of the President's Party." *American Political Science Review* 71 (Mar. 1977): 44-66.

4613. Lees, John D. "Campaigns and Parties: The 1970 American Mid-Term Elections and Beyond." *Parliamentary Affairs* 24 (Autumn 1971): 312-320.

4614. McKay, David H. and Wilson, Graham K. "The U.S. Mid-Term Elections." *Parliamentary Affairs* 28 (Spring 1975): 216-224.

4615. McLeod, Jack M. Brown, Jane D., and Becker, Lee B. "Watergate and the 1974 Congressional Elections." *Public Opinion Quarterly* 41 (Summer 1977): 181-195.

4616. Piereson, James E. "Presidential Popularity and Midterm Voting at Different Electoral Levels." *American Journal of Political Science* 19 (Nov. 1975): 683-694.

4617. Ponsford, Pearl O. *Evil Results of Mid-Term Congressional Elections and a Suggested Remedy.* Los Angeles: University of Southern California Press, 1937.

4618. Press, Charles. "The Prediction of Midterm Elections." *Western Political Quarterly* 9 (Sept. 1956): 691-698.

4619. Tufte, Edward R. "Determinants of the Outcomes of Midterm Congressional Elections." *American Political Science Review* 69 (Sept. 1975): 812-826.

4620. Ware, Alan. "The 1978 U.S. Mid-Term Elections in Historical Perspective." *Parliamentary Affairs* 32 (Spring 1979): 207-221.

4621. Warren, Sidney. "Mid-Term Elections." *Current History* 27 (Oct. 1954): 208-213.

4622. Zeidenstein, Harvey G. "Measuring Congressional Seat Losses in Mid-Term Elections." *Journal of Politics* 34 (Feb. 1972): 272-276.

Elections of Senators

4623. Barkworth, T. E. "Should United States Senators Be Elected by the People?" *Michigan Political Science Association* 1 (May 1893): 78-97.

4624. Burgess, John W. "The Elections of United States Senators by Popular Vote." *Political Science Quarterly* 17 (Dec. 1902): 650-663.

4625. Dayne, Byron W. "The Impact of the Direct Election of Senators on the Political System." Ph.D. dissertation, University of Chicago, 1972.

4626. Farrand, Max. "Popular Election of Senators." *Yale Review* 2 (Jan. 1913): 234-241.

4627. Haynes, George H. *The Election of Senators.* New York: Holt and Co., 1906.

4628. Haynes, George H. "Popular Control of Senatorial Elections." *Political Science Quarterly* 20 (Dec. 1905): 577-593.

4629. Haynes, John. *Popular Elections of United States Senators.* Baltimore: Johns Hopkins University Studies, 1893.

4630. Mitchell, John H. "Election of Senators by Popular Vote." *Forum* 21 (June 1896): 385-397.

4631. Perrin, John W. "Popular Election of United States Senators." *North American Review* 192 (Dec. 1910): 799-804.

4632. Thatcher, George A. "The Initiative, Referendum and Popular Election of Senators in Oregon." *American Political Science Review* 2 (Nov. 1908): 601-605.

4633. Winchester, Boyd. "The House and the Election of Senators." *Arena* 24 (July 1900): 14-20.

Contested Elections

4634. Barnett, V. M. "Contested Congressional Elections in Recent Years." *Political Science Ouarterly* 54 (June 1939): 187-215.

4635. McEwen, Robert C. "Contested Elections to the House of Representatives." In *We Propose: A Modern Congress,* ed. Mary McInnis, pp. 225-234. New York: McGraw-Hill, 1966.

4636. Rammelkamp, C. H. "Contested Congressional Elections." *Political Science Quarterly* 20 (Sept. 1905): 421-442.

4637. Shartess, Melvin H. and Douglas, Charles G. "State Courts and Federal Elections." *American Bar Association Journal* 62 (April 1976): 451-455.

4638. Watkins, Albert. "Contested Elections of Delegates to Congress from Nebraska." *Nebraska State Historical Society Publications* 19 (1919): 197-328.

Specific Elections

4639. Adler, Selig. "Congressional Election of 1918." *South Atlantic Quarterly* 36 (Oct. 1937): 447-465.

4640. Argersinger, Peter H. "The Most Picturesque Drama: The Kansas Senatorial Election of 1891." *Kansas Historical Quarterly* 38 (Spring 1972): 43-64.

4641. Bland, Gaye K. "Populism in the First Congressional District of Kentucky." *Filson Club Historical Quarterly* 51 (Jan. 1977): 31-43.

4642. Bromberg, Alan B. "The Virginia Congressional Elections of 1865: A Test of Southern Loyalty." *Virginia Magazine of History and Biography* 84 (Jan. 1976): 75-98.

4643. Burnham, Walter D. "The Alabama Senatorial Election of 1962: Return of Inter-Party Competition." *Journal of Politics* 26 (Nov. 1964): 798-829.

4644. Campbell, Angus and Cooper, Homer C. *Group Differences in Attitudes and Votes: A Study of the 1954 Congressional Election.* Ann Arbor: Survey Research Center, Institute for Social Research, University of Michigan, 1956.

4645. Cantril, Hadley and Harding, John. "The 1942 Elections: A Case Study in Political Psychology." *Public Opinion Quarterly* 7 (Summer 1943): 222-241.

4646. Casey, Carol. *Congressional Elections, 1978.* Washington: Congressional Research Service, 19779.

4647. Clark, Dan E. "The Election of the First United States Senators from Iowa." *Mississippi Valley Historical Association, Proceedings* 2 (1910): 190-195.

4648. Cohen, Richard E. "Open Seats: Where the Action is in This Year's Congressional Races." *National Journal* 10 (Oct. 7, 1978): 1588-1593.

4649. Conway, M. Margaret and Wyckoff, Mikel L. "Voter Choice in the 1974 Congressional Elections." *American Politics Quarterly* 8 (Jan. 1980): 3-14.

4650. Cox, Edward F. "Congressional District Party Strengths and the 1960 Election." *Journal of Politics* 24 (May 1962): 277-302.

4651. Ehrenhalt, Alan. "Political Numbers: No Watergate Landslide." *Washington Monthly* 5 (Feb. 1974): 43-47.

4652. Ewing, Cortez A. M. *Congressional Elections, 1896-1944: The Sectional Basis of Political Democracy in the House of Representatives.* Norman: University of Oklahoma Press, 1947.

4653. Finch, Glenn. "The Election of United States Senators in Kentucky: The Barkley Period." *Filson Club Historical Quarterly* 45 (July 1971): 286-304.

4654. Finch, Glenn. "The Election of United States Senators in Kentucky: The Beckham Period." *Filson Club Historical Quarterly* 44 (Jan. 1970): 38-50.

4655. Finch, Glenn. "The Election of United States Senators in Kentucky: The Cooper Period." *Filson Club Historical Ouarterly* 46 (April 1972): 161-178.

4656. Flynt, Wayne. "A Vignette in Southern Labor Politics: The 1936 Mississippi Senatorial Primary." *Mississippi Quarterly* 26 (Winter 1972–1973): 89-99.

4657. Flynt, Wayne and Roger, William W. "Reform Oratory in Alabama, 1890-1896." *Southern Speech Journal* 29 (Winter 1963): 94-106.

4658. Fry, Joseph A. "The 'Redemption of the Fighting Ninth': The Congressional Election of 1922 in Virginia's Ninth District." *Virginia Cavalcade* 21 (Spring 1972): 5-11.

4659. Grant, Philip A. "The Antimasons Retain Control of the Green Mountain State." *Vermont History* 34 (July 1966): 169-187.

4660. Grow, Stewart L. "Utah's Senatorial Election of 1889: The Election That Failed." *Utah Historical Quarterly* 39 (Winter 1971): 30-39.

4661. Hallett, George H. "Is Congress Representative?" *National Municipal Review* 22 (June 1933): 284-285, 288-289.

4662. Harding, John. "The 1942 Congressional Elections." *American Political Science Review* 38 (Feb. 1944): 41-58.

4663. Jennings, M. Kent and Zeigler, L. Harmon. "A Moderate's Victory in a Southern Congressional District." *Public Opinion Quarterly* 28 (Winter 1964): 595-603.

4664. Livermore, Seward W. "Sectional Issue in the 1913 Congressional Elections, as To Government Policy on Wheat and Cotton Prices." *Mississippi Valley Historical Review* 35 (June 1948): 29-60.

4665. McLemore, Frances W. "The Role of the Negroes in Chicago in the Senatorial Election, 1930." Master's thesis, University of Chicago, 1931.

4666. Malbin, Michael J. "The '76 Senate Races: Running Against Washington." *National Journal* 8 (Oct. 16, 1976): 1466-1473.

4667. Mantel, Martin E. "The Election of 1968: The Response to Congressional Reconstruction." Ph.D. dissertation, Columbia University, 1969.

4668. Meerse, David E. "The Northern Democratic Party and the Congressional Elections of 1858." *Civil War History* 19 (June 1973): 119-137.

4669. Miller, William. "First Fruits of Republican Organization: Political Aspects of the Congressional Election of 1794." *Pennsylvania Magazine of History and Biography* 63 (April 1939): 118-143.

4670. Murphy, William T. "Youth and Politics: A Study of Student Involvement in the 1970 Congressional Elections." Ph.D. dissertation, Princeton University, 1974.

4671. Murphy, William T. and Bienn, Henry. "Youthlash and the 1970 Congressional Elections." *American Politics Quarterly* 1 (Jan. 1973): 73-92.

4672. Partin, James W. "The Texas Senatorial Election of 1941." Master's thesis, Texas Tech University, 1941.

4673. Paul, Justus F. "Nebraska's Record in the Senate: Nine Senators in Three Years." *Nebraska History* 47 (Dec. 1966): 399-407.

4674. Paullin, Charles O. "The First Elections Under the Constitution." *Iowa Journal of History* 2 (Jan. 1904): 3-33.

4675. Plesur, Milton. "Republican Congressional Comeback of 1938." *Review of Politics* 24 (Oct. 1962): 525-562.

4676. Ramage, Thomas W. "The Bloody Tenth Congressional Election of 1892." *Richmond County History* 7 (Summer 1975): 65-74.

4677. Ranney, Austin. "The 1978 Congressional Elections: A Renaissance for Republicans?" *Public Opinion* 1 (Mar.-April 1978): 17-20.

4678. Roca, P. M. "West Virginia Senatorial Contest Case." *George Washington Law Review* 10 (Jan. 1942): 332-345.

4679. Rogers, William W., ed. "Georgia Elects a Senator: Political Conflict in 1840." *Georgia Historical Quarterly* 47 (Sept. 1963): 332-336.

4680. Schmidt, Louis B. "History of Congressional Elections in Iowa." *Iowa Journal of History* 10 (Oct. 1912): 463-502.

4681. Schmidt, Louis B. "History of Congressional Elections in Iowa." *Iowa Journal of History* 11 (Jan. 1913): 38-67.

4682. Seligmann, Gustav L. "The Purge That Failed: The 1934 Senatorial Election in New Mexico: Yet Another View." *New Mexico Historical Review* 47 (Oct. 1972): 361-381.

4683. Shumate, Roger V. "Minnesota's Congressional Election at Large." *American Political Science Review* 27 (Feb. 1933): 58-63.

4684. Singletary, Otis A. "The Election of 1878 in Louisiana." *Louisiana Historical Quarterly* 40 (Jan. 1957): 46-53.

4685. Strong, Mary K. "The 1910 Congressional Elections." *Current History* 10 (June 1946): 528-534.

4686. Strong, Mary K. "Post-War Congressional Elections." *Current History* 10 (May 1946): 435-441.

4687. Sullivan, John L. and O'Connor, R. E. "Electoral Choice and Popular Control of Public Policy: The Case of the 1966 House Elections." *American Political Science Review* 66 (Dec. 1972): 1256-1268.

4688. Tingley, Ronald R. "The Crowded Field: Eight Men for the Senate." *South Dakota History* 9 (Fall 1979): 316-336.

4689. Walker, David B. "The Age Factor in the 1958 Congressional Elections." *Midwest Journal of Political Science* 4 (Feb. 1960): 1-26.

4690. Walton, Brian G. "A Matter of Timing: Elections to the United States Senate in Tennessee Before the Civil War." *Tennessee Historical Quarterly* 31 (Summer 1972): 129-148.

4691. Walton, Brian G. "The Elections for the Thirtieth Congress and the Presidential Candidacy of Zachary Taylor." *Journal of Southern History* 35 (May 1969): 186-202.

4692. Walton, Brian G. "Elections to the United States Senate in Alabama Before the Civil War." *Alabama Review* 27 (Jan. 1974): 3-38.

4693. Walton; Brian G. "Elections to the United States Senate in North Carolina; 1835-1861." *North Carolina Historical Review* 53 (April 1976): 168-192.

4694. Wehtje, Myron F. "The Congressional Elections of 1799 in Virginia." *West Virginia History* 29 (July 1968): 251-274.

4695. Welch, June R. "The Texas Senatorial Election of 1948." Master's thesis, Texas Tech University, 1953.

4696. Zanger, Martin. "Upton Sinclair as California's Socialist Candidate for Congress, 1920." *Southern California Quarterly* 56 (Winter 1974): 359-373.

Coattails

4697. Baker, Kendall L. and Walter, Kendall. "Voter Rationality: A Comparison of Presidential and Congressional Voting in Wyoming." *Western Political Quarterly* 28 (June 1975): 316-329.

4698. Buck, J. Vincent. "Presidential Coattails and Congressional Loyalty." *Midwest Journal of Political Science* 16 (Aug. 1972): 460-472.

4699. Burns, James MacGregor. "Congressional Contests and the Presidential Elections." American Academy of Political and Social Science, *Annals* 283 (Sept. 1952): 115-122.

4700. Cummings, Milton "Congressmen and the Electorate: A Study of House Elections in Presidential Years, 1920–1956." Ph.D. dissertation, Harvard University, 1960.

4701. Edwards, George C. "The Impact of Presidential Coattails on Outcomes of Congressional Elections." *American Politics Quarterly* 7 (Jan. 1979): 94-108.

4702. Jacobson, Gary C. "Presidential Coattails in 1972." *Public Opinion Quarterly* 40 (Summer 1976): 194-200.

4703. Kritzer, Herbert M. and Eubank, Robert B. "Presidential Coattails Revisited: Partisanship and Incumbency Effects." *American Journal of Political Science* 23 (Aug. 1979): 615-626.

4704. Meulemans, William C. "The Presidential Majority: Presidential Campaigning in Congressional Elections." Ph.D. dissertation, University of Idaho, 1970.

4705. Miller, Warren E. "Political Coattails: A Study in Political Myth and Methodology." *Public Opinion Quarterly* 19 (Winter 1955-1956): 352-368.

4706. Moos, Malcolm. *Politics, Presidents, and Coattails.* Baltimore, Md.: Johns Hopkins University Press, 1952.

4707. Moreland, William B. "Angels, Pinpoints, and Voters: The Pattern for a Coattail." *American Journal of Political Science* 17 (Feb. 1973): 170-176.

4708. Press, Charles. "Presidential Coattails and Party Cohesion." *Midwest Journal of Political Science* 7 (Nov. 1963): 230-335.

4709. Waldman, Loren K. "Liberalism of Congressmen and the Presidential Vote in Their Districts." *Midwest Journal of Political Science* 11 (Feb. 1967): 73-85.

Incumbency

4710. Abramowitz, Alan I. "Name Familiarity, Reputation, and the Incumbency Effect in a Congressional Election." *Western Political Quarterly* 28 (Dec. 1975): 668-684.

4711. Born, Richard J. "Generational Replacement and the Growth of Incumbent Reelection Margins in the U. S. House." *American Political Science Review* 73 (Sept. 1979): 811-817.

4712. Born, Richard J. "House Incumbents and Inter-Election Vote Change." *Journal of Politics* 39 (Nov. 1977): 1008-1034.

4713. Cohen, Richard E. "Incumbents in Congress: Are the Cards Stacked in Their Favor? *National Journal* 10 (Sept. 23, 1978): 1509-1513.

4714. 'Computers and Direct Mail Are Being Married on the Hill to Keep Incumbents in Office." *Congressional Quarterly Weekly Report* 37 (July 21, 1979): 1445-1453.

4715. Cook, Timothy E. "Legislature vs. Legislator: A Note on the Paradox of Congressional Support." *Legislative Studies Quarterly* 4 (Feb. 1979): 43-52.

4716. Cover, Albert D. "The Advantage of Incumbency in Congressional Elections." Ph.D. dissertation, Yale University, 1977.

4717. Cover, Albert D. 'One Good Term Deserves Another; The Advantage of Incumbency in Congressional Elections." *American Journal of Political Science* 21 (Aug. 1977): 523-541.

4718. Erikson, Robert S. "The Advantage of Incumbency in Congressional Elections." *Polity* 3 (Spring 1971): 395-404.

4719. Fatemi, Fariborz S. "Can the Incumbent Be Defeated?" In *To Be A Congressman: The Promise and the Power*, eds. Sven Groennings and Jonathan P. Hawley, pp. 225-254. Washington: Acropolis Books, 1973.

4720. Fiorina, Morris P. and Noll, Roger G. *A Theory of the Congressional Incumbency Advantage.* Pasadena: California Institute of Technology, 1977 (Social Science Working Paper No. 158).

4721. Hinckley, Barbara. "Incumbency and the Presidential Vote in Senate Elections: Defining Parameters of Subpresidential Voting." *American Political Science Review* 64 (Sept. 1970): 836-842.

4722. Hutcheson, Richard G. "Inertial Effect of Incumbency and Two-Party Politics: Elections to the House of Representatives from the South, 1952-1974." *American Political Science Review* 69 (D&c. 1975): 1399-1401.

4723. Kostroski, Warren L. "The Effect of the Number of Terms on the Re-Election of Senators 1920-1970." *Journal of Politics* 40 (May 1978): 488-497.

4724. Kostroski, Warren L. "Elections, Parties, Incumbency: Democratic Linkage in U.S. Senate Elections, 1920-1970." Ph.D. dissertation, Washington University, 1976.

4725. Kostroski, Warren L. "Party and Incumbency in Post-War Senate Elections: Trends, Patterns and Models." *American Political Science Review* 67 (Dec. 1973): 1213-1234.

4726. McClendon, Robert E. "Reelection of United States Senators." *American Political Science Review* 28 (Aug. 1934): 636-642.

4727. Nelson, Candice J. "The Effect of Incumbency on Voting in Congressional Elections, 1964-1974." *Political Science Quarterly* 93 (Winter 1978): 665-678.

4728. Pohlmann, Marcus D. "The Electoral Impact of Partisanship and Incumbency Reconsidered: An Extension to Low Salience Elections." *Urban Affairs Quarterly* 13 (June 1978): 495-503.

4729. Powell, Lawrence N. "Rejected Republican Incumbents in the 1866 Congressional Nominating Conventions: A Study in Reconstruction Politics." *Civil War History* 19 (Sept. 1973): 219-237.

4730. "The Power of Incumbency: Money Flows to the Winners." *Congressional Quarterly Weekly Report* 31 (Sept. 22, 1973): 2515-2517.

4731. Tidmarch, Charles M. "A Comment on Erikson's Analysis of the Advantage of Incumbency in Congressional Elections." *Polity* 4 (Summer 1972): 523-526.

Reapportionment and Redistricting

Methods

4732. Adams, Bruce. *Toward A System of "Fair and Effective Representation.".: A Common Cause Report on State and Congressional Reapportionment.* Washington: Common Cause, 1977.

4733. American Political Science Association. Committee on Reapportionment of Congress. "The Reapportionment of Congress." *American Political Science Review* 45 (Mar. 1951): 153-157.

4734. "Apportionment of the House of Representatives." *Yale Law Journal* 58 (July 1949): 1360-1386.

4735. Baker, Gordon E. *The Reapportionment Revolution: Representation, Political Power, and the Supreme Court.* New York: Random House, 1966.

4736. Bowman, Harold M. "Congressional Redistricting and the Constitution." *Michigan Law Review* 31 (Dec. 1932): 149-179.

4737. Carpeneti, Walter L. "Legislative Apportionment: Multimember Districts and Fair Representation." *University of Pennsylvania Law Review* 120 (April 1972): 666-700.

4738. Celler, Emmanuel. "Congressional Apportionment: Past, Present, and Future." *Law and Contemporary Problems* 17 (1952): 268-275.

4739. Chafee, Zechariah. "Congressionsl Reapportionment." *Harvard Law Review* 42 (June 1929): 1015-1047.

4740. "Congressional Districting Issue to Confront High Court." *Congressional Quarterly Weekly Report* 21 (June 7, 1963): 938-942.

4741. Dixon, Robert G. "Congress and Reapportionment: Issues and Opportunities." In *The Congress and America's Future,* ed. David B. Truman, pp. 6-12. George Washington University, American Assembly Report, 1965.

4742. Dixon, Robert G. "Reapportionment in the Supreme Court and Congress: The Constitutional Struggle for Fair Representation." *Michigan Law Review* 63 (Dec. 1964): 209-242.

4743. Erikson, Ann M. *Congressional Redistricting.* Columbus, Ohio: Legislative Service Commission, 1965.

4744. Farrelly, David G. and Hinderaker, Ivan. "Congressional Reapportionment and National Political Power." *Law and Contemporary Problems* 17 (Spring 1952): 338-363.

4745. Gilbert, E. J. and Schutz, J. A. "Ill-Conceived Proposal for Apportionment of U.S. House of Representatives." *Operations Research* 12 (Sept. 1964): 768-773.

4746. Hacker, Andrew. *Congressional Districting: The Issue of Equal Representation.* Washington: Brookings Institution, 1963.

4747. Hamilton, Howard D. "Congressional Districting: A Landmark Decision of the Supreme Court." *Special Education* 29 (Jan. 1965): 23-26.

4748. Hatheway, Gordon W. "Congress in the Thicket: The Congressional Redistricting Bill of 1967." *George Washington Law Review* 36 (Oct. 1967): 224-234.

4749. Huntington, Edward V. "Mathematic Theory of the Apportionment of Representatives." *National Academy of Science, Proceedings* 7 (April 1921): 123-127.

4750. Huntington, Edward V. "Methods of Apportionment in Congress." *American Political Science Review* 25 (Nov. 1931): 961-965.

4751. Huntington, Edward V. "New Method of Apportionment of Representatives." *American Statistical Association Journal* 17 (Sept. 1921): 859-870.

4752. "Independent Power of State Legislatures to Create Congressional Election Districts." *Harvard Law Review* 45 (Dec. 1931): 355-364.

4753. Kaiser, Henry F. "An Objective Method for Establishing Legislative Districts." *Midwest Journal of Political Science* 10 (May 1966): 200-213.

4754. Killian, John H. *Congressional Districting: The Constitutional Standards in the Decade of the Seventies.* Washington: CongreSsional Research Service, 1971.

4755. Owens, F. W. "On the Apportionment of Representatives." *American Statistical Association Journal* 17 (Dec. 1921): 958-968.

4756. Reock, Ernest C. "Measuring Compactness as a Requirement of Legislative Apportionment." *Midwest Journal of Political Science* 5 (Feb. 1961): 70-74.

4757. "Report upon the Apportionment of Representatives." *American Statistical Association Journal* 17 (Dec. 1921): 1004-1013.

4758. Schar, Stephen L. "Constitutional Law—Congressional Districting: 'One ManOne Vote' Demands Near Mathematical Precision." *DePaul Law Review* 19 (Autumn 1969): 152-171.

4759. Schmeckebier, Laurence F. *Congressional Apportionment.* Washington: Brookings Institution, 1941.

4760. Schubert, Glendon and Press, Charles. "Measuring Malapportionment." *American Political Science Review* 58 (June 1964): 302-327.

4761. Searcy, Hubert. "Problems of Congressional Reapportionment." *Southwestern Social Science Quarterly* 16 (June 1935): 58-68.

4762. Shull, Charles W. "Legislative Apportionment and the Law." *Temple Law Quarterly* 18 (June 1944): 388-403.

4763. Sickels, Robert J. "Dragons, Bacon Strips and Dumbbells: Who's Afraid of Reapportionment." *Yale Law Journal* 75 (July 1966): 1300-1308.

4764. Tufte, Edward R. "Relationship Between Seats and Votes in Two-Party Systems." *American Poliitical Science Review* 67 (June 1973): 540-554.

4765. Ullman, Morris B. "Apportionment of Representatives in Congress on the Basis of Special Populations." *American Statistical Association Journal* 40 (Dec. 1945): 484-492.

4766. U.S. Congress. House. Committee on the Judiciary. *Congressional Districting, Hearings.* Washington: GPO, 1971.

4767. Willcox, Walter F. "Apportionment Problem and the Size of the House; A Return to Webster." *Cornell Law Review* 35 (Winter 1950): 367-389.

4768. Willcox, Walter F. "Last Words on the Apportionment Problem." *Law and Contemporary Problems* 17 (Spring 1952): 290-301.

4769. Willcox, Walter F. "Methods of Apportioning Seats in the House of Representatives." *Journal American Statistical Association* 49 (Dec. 1954): 685-695.

Case Studies

4770. Alexander, Ruth. "Congressional Redistricting in Tennessee from 1796-1936." Master's thesis, Duke University, 1937.

4771. "Analysis of 263 Congressional Districts." *Congressional Quarterly Weekly Report* 15 (Feb. 15, 1957): 201-203.

4772. Bartholomew, Paul C. *The Indiana Third Congressional District: A Political History* Notre Dame, Ind.: University of Notre Dame Press, 1970.

4773. Black, Merle. "Racial Composition of Congressional Districts and Support for Federal Voting Rights in the American South." *Social Sciece Quarterly* 59 (Dec. 1978): 435-450.

4774. Bullock, Charles S. "Redistricting and Congressional Stability, 1962-1972." *Journal of Politics* 37 (May 1975): 569-575.

4775. Burdette, Franklin L. "The Illinois Congressional Redistricting Case (Reapportionment)." *American Political Science Review* 40 (Oct. 1946): 958-962.

4776. "Census Figures Show Five New California House Seats." *Congressional Quarterly Weekly Report* 28 (Sept. 4, 1970): 2193-2196.

4777. Chafee, Zechariah. "Congressional Reapportionment Under the Census of 1950." *Proceeding of the Massachusetts Historical Society.* 70 (1957): 237-239.

4778. Chafee, Zechariah. "Reapportionment of the House of Representatives Under the 1950 Census." *Cornell Law Quarterly* 36 (Summer 1951): 643-665.

4779. "Congressional District Populations Still Vary Greatly." *Congressional Quarterly Weekly Report* 20 (June 8, 1962): 972-976.

4780. Congressional Quarterly. *Congressional Districts in the 1970s.* 2d ed. Washington: Congressional Quarterly, 1974.

4781. "Congressional Reapportionment: A Case Study." *Social Education* 29 (Dec. 1965): 541-552.

4782. "Congressional Redistricting." *Congressional Quarterly Weekly Report* 20 (Sept. 28, 1962): 1601-1689.

4783. "Congressional Redistricting in the 1960s: Unprecedented Wave of Redistricting Action Follows 1960 Census Reapportionment and Supreme Court Requirement of Equally Populated Districts." *Congressional Quarterly Weekly Report* 24 (Sept. 16, 1966): 2005-2139.

4784. Corbitt, D. L. "Congressional Districts of North Carolina, 1789-1934." *North Carolina Historical Review* 12 (April 1935): 173-188.

4785. Davis, Claude J. *Congressional Redistricting in West Virginia for the Sixties.* Morgantown: Bureau for Government Research, West Virginia University, 1960.

4786. Erikson, Robert S. "Malapportionment, Gerrymandering, and Party Fortunes in Congressional Elections." *American Political Science Review* 66 (Dec. 1972): 1234-1245.

4787. Eshleman, Kenneth L. "Racial Gerrymandering of Congressional Districts." Ph.D. dissertation, University of Virginia, 1975.

4788. Ewald, Peter K. "Congressional Apportionment and New York State." Ph.D. dissertation, New York University, 1955.

4789. Farrelly, David G. "Congressional Reapportionment and the West." *Western Political Quarterly* 12 (Supplement 1962): 41-42.

4790. Fryer, Benjamin A. *Congressional History of Berks (Pa.) District, 1789-1939.* Reading, Pa.: The Author, 1939.

4791. Goldman, Ralph M. "Some Dimensions of Rural and Urban Representation in Congress." Master's thesis, University of Chicago, 1948.

4792. "House Districts: Changes for at Least 41 States.' *Congressional Quarterly Weekly Report* 29 (Mar. 26, 1971): 643-646.

4793. "House Redistricting Outlooks for 1972 Elections." *Congressional Quarterly Weekly Report* 29 (Mar. 26, 1971): 647-681.

4794. "House Seats Will Reflect Shifting Population." *Congressional Quarterly Weekly Report* 18 (May 20, 1960): 881–892.

4795. Kearns, Doris H. "Prayer and Reapportionment: An Analysis of the Court." Ph.D. dissertation, Harvard University, 1968.

4796. Lader, Rose. "The Joint Resolution as a Method of Redistricting States." *St. John's Law Review* 7 (Dec. 1932): 114-118.

4797. Lambert, Louis E. *The Congressional District System in Indiana.* Bloomington: Institute of Politics, Department of Political Science, Indiana University, 1943.

4798. Lehne, Richard. "Suburban Foundations of the New Congress." *American Academy of Political and Social Science, Annals* 422 (Nov. 1975): 141-151.

4799. Loeb, Isidor. "Recent Controversies Regarding Congressional Districts." *St. Louis Law Review* 17 (April 1932): 211-220.

4800. "Majority of States Redistrict U.S. House Seats." *Congressional Quarterly Weekly Report* 24 (April 15, 1966): 812-817.

4801. Mason, Bruce B. *Congressional Redistricting in Arizona.* Tempe: Bureau of Government Research, Arizona State University, 1961.

4802. Miller, G. C. "Congressional Reapportionment." *Overland and Out West* 89 (Jan. 1931): 7-8.

4803. Noragon, Jack L. "Congressional Redistricting and Population Composition: 1964-1970." *American Journal of Political Science* 16 (May 1972): 295-302.

4804. Noragon, Jack L. "Representation and Redistricting: The Political Effects of Population Equality in Congressional Districting." Ph.D. dissertation, Ohio State University, 1968.

4805. Oliphant, J. Orin. "Congressional and Legislative Redistricting in Washington." *National Municipal Review* 21 (May 1932): 340-341.

4806. O'Rourke, Timothy G. *The Impact of Reapportionment.* New Brunswick, N.J.: Transaction Books, 1980.

4807. Orr, Douglas M. *Congressional Redistricting: The North Carolina Experience.* Chapel Hill: Department of Geography, University of North Carolina, 1970.

4808. Page, Thomas. *Legislative Apportionment in Kansas.* Lawrence: Bureau of Government Research, University of Kansas, 1952.

4809. Parsons, Stanley B., Beach, William W., and Hermann, Dan. *United States Congressional Districts, 1788-1841.* Westport, Conn.: Greenwood Press, 1978.

4810. Paschal, Joel F. "House of Representatives: 'Grand Depository of the Democratic Principle'?" *Law and Contemporary Problems* 17 (Spring 1952): 276-289.

4811. Pate, James E. "Redistricting for the Purpose of Representation." *Kentucky Law Journal* 23 (Mar. 1935): 470-489.

4812. "Populations of Congressional Districts Still Uneven." *Congressional Quarterly Weekly Report* 28 (Oct. 28, 1970): 2693-2697.

4813. "Reapportionment." *Congressional Quarterly Weekly Report* 13 (July 8, 1955): 797-799.

4814. "Redistricting Battles Will Shape House for Decade." *Congressional Quarterly Weekly Report* 28 (Nov. 20, 1970): 2820-2822.

4815. Reock, Ernest C. "Unequal Congressmen." *National Civic Review* 52 (June 1963): 308-312.

4816. Rosenbaum, Betty B. "The Urban–Rural Conflict as Evidenced in the Reapportionment Situation." *Social Forces* 12 (Mar. 1934): 421-426.

4817. Sauer, C. O. "Geography and the Gerrymander." *American Political Science Review* 12 (Aug. 1918): 403-426.

4818. Schwab, Larry M. "The Effects of the Court-Ordered Redistricting and the 1970 Reappointment and Redistricting on the U.S. House of Representatives." Ph.D. dissertation, Case Western Reserve University, 1975.

4819. Schwab, Larry M. "The Impact of Equal-Population Redistricting on the House of Representatives: A District, State and Regional Analysis." *Capitol Studies* 4 (Fall 1976): 67-83.

4820. Short, Lloyd M. "Congressional Redistricting in Missouri." *American Political Science Review* 25 (Aug. 1931): 634-649.

4821. Snowiss, Leo M. "Chicago and Congress: A Study of Metropolitan Representation." Ph.D. dissertation, University of Chicago, 1965.

4822. Tanner, Eugene O. "Congressional Reapportionment, 1910–1930." Ph.D. dissertation' University of Texas at Austin, 1937.

4823. Theobald, H. Rupert. "Equal Representation in Wisconsin: A Study of Legislative and Congressional Apportionment." Ph.D. dissertation, University of Wisconsin, 1972.

4824. "Threatened Representatives: Redistricting to Blame." *Congressional Quarterly Weekly Report* 30 (Oct. 28, 1972): 2782-2787.

4825. "Unequal Representation in Congress." *Law Notes* 24 (Oct. 1920): 124-126.

4826. Williams, Henry N. "Congressional Apportionment in Tennessee, 1796-1941." *Journal of Politics* 4 (Nov. 1942): 507-521.

XIII. The Members of Congress

Studies of Congressmen

General Studies

4827. Alpert, Harry. "Congressmen, Social Scientists, and Attitudes Toward Federal Support of Social Science Research." *American Sociological Review* 23 (Dec. 1958): 682-686.

4828. Broder, David S. "Portrait of a Typical Congressman." *New York Times Magazine,* 7 Oct. 1962, pp. 31, 97-99.

4829. Buchanan, William, Eulau, Heinz, Ferguson, Leroy C., and Wahlke, John C. "The Legislator as Specialist." *Western Political Quarterly* 13 (Sept. 1960): 636-651.

4830. Buys, Christian J., Word, Edwin D., Brisiel, Lawrence C., and Campbell, Jo. "Environmental Attitudes of United States Representatives: Ecology, Industry and Wildlife." *Psychological Reports* 42 (June 1978): 699-702.

4831. Capell, Frank A. "The Left: Collectivitists in the Congress." *American Opinion* 17 (July-Aug. 1974): 49-72.

4832. "Characteristics of Members of the 94th Congress." *Congressional Quarterly Weekly Report* 33 (Jan. 18, 1975): 120-130.

4833. "Characteristics of Members of the 92nd Congress." *Congressional Quarterly Weekly Report* 29 (Jan. 15, 1971): 126-133.

4834. Cohen, Richard E. "Are the Senate's Liberal Democrats Becoming an Endangered Species?" *National Journal* 11 (July 14, 1979): 1152-1155.

4835. Cohen, Richard E. "The New Breed of Southern Members Is Not Much Different from the Old." *National Journal* 10 (July 1, 1978): 1040-1044.

4836. Congressional Quarterly. *Members of Congress Since 1789,* Washington: Congressional Quarterly, 1977.

4837. Congressional Research Service. "Tax Laws Affecting Members of Congress." In *Senators: Offices, Ethics and Pressures: A Compilation of Papers,* pp. 84-85. Washington: GPO, 1976.

4838. Davenport, Frederick M. "Changing Character of Congress." *Boston University Law Review* 14 (April 1934): 299-312.

4839. Davidson, Roger H. "Public Prescriptions for the Job of Congressman." *Midwest Journal of Political Science* 14 (Nov. 1970): 648-666.

4840. Davidson, Roger H. and Parker, Glenn R. "Positive Support for Political Institutions: The Case of Congress." *Western Political Quarterly* 25 (Dec. 1972): 600-612.

4841. DeMott, Benjmain. "Looking for Intelligence in Washington." *Commentary* 30 (Oct. 1960): 291-300.

4842. Evans, Medford. "The Congress: Why Are the Intellectuals Cheering?" *American Opinion* 17 (June 1974): 33-48.

4843. Fiorina, Morris P. "Big Government: A Congressman's Best Friend." *Washington Monthly* 9 (Mar. 1977): 55-61.

4844. Froman, Lewis A. "Organization Theory and the Explanation of Important Characteristics of Congress." *American Political Science Review* 62 (June 1968): 518-526.

4845. Horn, Jack. "What Scholars, Strippers and Congressmen Share." *Psychology Today* 9 (May 1976): 34-35.

4846. Jenrette, John W. "Care and Feeding of a U.S. Congressman." *Trial* 13 (April 1977): 27-28.

4847. Jones, Charles O. "Notes on Interviewing Members of the House of Representatives." *Public Opinion Quarterly* 23 (Fall 1959): 404-406.

4848. Kempton, Murray. "Adult Congressman." *New Republic* 148 (April 6, 1963): 11-13.

4849. Lloyd, Raymond G. "Technique of Political Persuasion Used by Certain Congressmen from Selected States, 1921-1946." Ph.D. dissertation, New York University, 1946.

4850. McClellan, Larry D. "An Investigation of the Opinions of the Members of the Ninety-First Congress Toward Industrial Arts." Ph.D. dissertation, University of Northern Colorado, 1971.

4851. McKinney, Madge M. "The Personnel of the Seventy-Seventh Congress." *American Political Science Review* 36 (Feb. 1942): 67-75.

4852. McMurray, Carl D. and Parsons, Malcolm B. "Public Attitudes Toward the Representational Rules of Legislators and Judges." *Midwest Journal of Political Science* 9 (May 1965): 167-185.

4853. Malbin, Michael J. "There'll Be New Faces in the 95th But Not Just Because of the Election." *National Journal* 8 (Oct. 23, 1976): 1498-1505.

4854. Matthews, Donald R. "United States Senators: A Collective Portrait." *International Social Science Journal* 13 (1961): 620-634.

4855. Melsheimer, John T. *Standing of Members of Congress to Sue.* Washington: Congressional Research Service, 1977.

4856. Nocera, Joseph. "How to Make the Front Page: A Do-It-Yourself Guide for Congressmen." *Washington Monthly* 10 (Oct. 1978): 12-23.

4857. Nutting, Charles B. "Political Scientists Look at the Congress." *American Bar Association Journal* 50 (Jan. 1964): 90-91.

4858. Olson, Edwin L. "Federal Public Service Orientation of United States Congressmen." Ph.D. dissertation, American University, 1967.

4859. Robinson, James A. "The Social Scientist and Congress." In *International Conflict and Behavioral Science* ed. Roger Fisher, pp. 266-271.
New York: Basic Books, 1964.

4860. Robinson, James A. "Survey Interviewing Among Members of Congress." *Public Opinion Quarterly* 24 (Spring 1960): 127-138.

4861. Shull, Charles W. "The Tenure of Michigan in the Congress of the United States." *Michigan History* 49 (June 1965): 166-175.

4862. Smith, Robert E. "Colorado's Progressive Senators and Representatives." *Colorado Magazine* 45 (Winter 1968): 27-41.

4863. "Standing to Sue for Members of Congress." *Yale Law Journal* 83 (July 1974): 1665-1688.

4864. Stang, Alan. "The Right: Conservatives in the Congress." *American Opinion* 17 (July-Aug. 1974): 31-48.

4865. Welch, June R. *The Texas Senator.* Dallas, Tex.: G.L.A. Press, 1978.

Socioeconomic Background

4866. Aberback, Joel D. and Rockman, Bert A. "The Overlapping Worlds of American Federal Executives and Congressmen." *British Journal of Political Science* 7 (Jan. 1977): 23-47.

4867. Blaustein, Albert P. "Lawyers in the House of R&presentatives: 81st Congress Has Had Intensive Legal Training." *American Bar Association Journal* 35 (Oct. 1949): 825-826.

4868. Blaustein, Albert P. "Lawyers in the Senate: They Predominate in 81st Congress." *American Bar Association Journal* 35 (Feb. 1949): 108-109.

4869. Cater, Douglass. "Lonely Men on Capitol Hill." *Reporter* 21 (Oct. 15, 1959): 23-26.

4870. Chauhan, D. S. and Chopra, S. L. "Socio-economic Background of Legislators in Great Britain, India and United States of America." *Journal of Constitutional and Parliamentary Studies* 3 (Jan-Mar. 1969): 120-125.

4871. "College Training of Members of Congress, 1915-1916." *Journal of Education* 83 (Mar. 1916): 301.

4872. Dunn, Edward S. "Catholics in the 80th Congress." *American Catholic Sociological Review* 9 (Dec. 1948): 254-258.

4873. Dunn, Edward S. "Catholics in the Seventy-Ninth Congress." *American Catholic Sociological Review* 7 (Dec. 1946): 259-266.

4974. Fletcher, Ralph and Fletcher, Mildred. "Labor Turnover of the United States Congress." *Social Forces* 7 (Sept. 1928): 129-132.

4875. McKinney, Madge M. "Religion and Elections: Religious Affiliation of Members of the 78th Congress." *Public Opinion Quarterly* 8 (Spring 1944): 110-114.

4876. Mason, John B. "Lawyers in the 71st to 75th Congress: Their Legal Education and Experience." *Rocky Mountain Law Review* 10 (Dec. 1937): 43-52.

4877. Mason, John B. "Lawyers in the 74th Congress: Their Legal Education and Experience." *Rocky Mountain Law Review* 8 (Dec. 1935): 58-64.

4878. Matthews, Donald R. *The Social Background of Political Decision-Makers.* Garden City, N.Y.: Doubleday, 1954.

4879. Mitchell, William C. "The Ambivalent Social Status of the American Politician." *Western Political Quarterly* 12 (Sept. 1959): 683-698.

4880. "Our House of Lords." *North American Review* (May 1886): 454-465.

4881. Smith, Mapheus. "Rural and Urban Origins of Members of the American Congress." *Journal of Applied Psychology* 20 (Dec. 1936): 664-671.

4882. Steiwer, Frederick E. "The Lawyer in Congress." *Oregon Law Review* 10 (Dec. 1930): 30-38.

4883. Zweigenhaft, Richard. "Who Represents America?" *Insurgent Sociologist* 5 (Spring 1975): 119-130.

Ethnic Background

4884. Green, Dom M. "Services of the Polish-American Congressmen." *Polish American Studies* 21 (Jan.-June 1964): 28-31.

4885. Kardas, Tadeus J. "Sidelights on the Polish-American Congressmen." *Polish American Studies* 21 (Jan.-June 1964): 31-33.

4886. Lawson, Murray G. "Foreign-Born in Congress, 1789-1949: A Statistical Summary." *American Political Science Review* 51 (Dec. 1957): 1183-1189.

4887. Ludwicki, Raymond. "Background of Polish-American Congressmen." *Polish American Studies* 21 (Jan.-June 1964): 23-26.

4888. Rouhan, Dom J. "Sources of the Polish-American Congressmen." *Polish American Studies* 21 (Jan.-June 1964): 26-28.

4889. Stone, Amy and Szonyi, David. "Jews in Congress." *Moment 1 (May-June 1976): 27-32.*

4890. Szonyi, David. "What Does Your Jewish Congressperson Know About the Middle East?" *Interchange* 1 (Feb. 1976): 1, 6.

4891. William, Dom M. "Profile of the Typical Polish-American Congressman." *Polish American Studies* 21 (Jan.-June 1964): 34-35.

Career Patterns

4892. Bailey, Gil. "Why Congressmen Are Quitting: Red Eyes and Broken Marriages." *California Journal* 5 (May 1974): 161-166.

4893. Barber, James D. *The Lawmakers: Recruitment and Adaptation to Legislative Life.* New Haven, Conn.: Yale University Press, 1967.

4894. Brockway, Marian L. "A Study of the Geographical, Occupational and Political Characteristics of Congressmen, 1800-1919." Master's thesis, University of Kansas, 1938.

4895. Bullock, Charles S. "House Careerists: Changing Patterns of Longevity and Attrition." *American Political Science Review* 66 (Dec. 1972): 1295-1300.

4896. Clubok, Alfred B., Wilensky, Norman M., and Berghorn, Forrest J. "Family Relationships, Congressional Recruitment, and Political Modernization." *Journal of Politics* 31 (Nov. 1969): 1035-1062.

4897. Cohen, Richard E. "Retiring from Congess: The Job Ain't What It Used to Be." *National Journal* 10 (Mar. 11, 1978): 391-393.

4898. "Congress Is Getting Younger All the Time." *Congressional Quarterly Weekly Report* 37 (Jan. 27, 1979): 154.

4899. "Ex-Members of Congress: Some Go Home, Many Don't." *Congressional Quarterly Weekly Report* 35 (Sept. 17, 1977): 1969-1972.

4900. Frantzich, Stephen E. "De-Recruitment: The Other Side of the Congressional Equation." *Western Political Quarterly* 31 (Mar. 1978): 105-126.

4901. Frantzich, Stephen E. "Opting Out: Retirement from the House of Representatives, 1966-1974." *American Politics Quarterly* 6 (July 1978): 251-273.

4902. Kernell, Samuel. "Toward Understanding 19th Century Congressional Careers, Ambition, Competition, and Rotation." *American Journal of Political Science* 21 (Nov. 1977): 669-693.

4903. "Longevity of Members of Congress." *Metropolitan Life Statistical Bulletin* 51 (Dec. 1970): 2-5.

4904. Mezey, Michael L. "Ambition Theory and the Office of Congressman." *Journal of Politics* 32 (Aug. 1970): 563-579.

4905. Mitchell, R. Judson and Spink, George. "Presidential Support and Length of Service in the House of Representatives: An Exploratory Analysis: *Research Reports in the Social Sciences:* 1 (Fall 1967): 40-49.

4906. Oleszek, Walter J. "Congressional Career Patterns, 1910–1960." Ph.D. dissertation, State University of New York at Albany, 1968.

4907. Price, Hugh D. "The Congressional Career: Then and Now." In *Congressional Behavior,* ed. N. W. Polsby, pp. 14-27. New York: Random House, 1971.

4908. Rohde, David W. "Risk-Bearing and Progressive Ambition: The Case of Members of the United States House of Representatives." *American Journal of Political Science* 23 (Feb. 1979): 1-26.

4909. Smith, Mapheus and Brockway, Marian L. "Mobility of American Congressmen." *Sociology and Social Research* 24 (July-Aug. 1940): 511-525.

4910. Smith, Mapheus and Brockway, Marian L. "Some Political Characteristics of American Congressmen, 1800-1919." *Southwestern Social Science Quarterly* 22 (Dec. 1941): 209-222.

4911. Smoller, Frederic. "Patterns of Congressional Careers in the U.S. House." Master's thesis, University of Texas at Austin, 1977.

4912. Snowiss, Leo M. "Congressional Recruitment and Representation." *American Political Science Review* 60 (Sept. 1966): 627-639.

4913. Treas, Judith. "A Life Table for Postwar Senate Careers: A Research Note." *Social Forces* 56 (Sept. 1977): 202-207.

Congressional Ethics

Standards of Conduct

4914. Association of the Bar of the City of New York. Special Committee on Congressional Ethics. *Congress and the Public Trust: A Report.* Atheneum, 1970.

4915. Baker, Richard T. "Ethics in Washington." *Christianity and Crisis,* 2 Oct. 1967, pp. 214-215.

4916. Beard, Edmund and Horn, Stephen. *Congressional Ethics: The View from the House.* Washington: Brookings Institution,1975.

4917. Bennett, Charles E. "Congressional Ethics." In *Congress and Conscience,* ed. John B. Anderson, pp. 97–126. Philadelphia, Pa.: J. B. Lippincott, 1970.

4918. Cantor, Joseph. *Public Officials Integrity Act of 1977: Omnibus Watergate Reform.* Washington: Congressional Research Service, 1978.

4919. Case, Clifford P. "Congress, Too, Has Conflicts of Interest." *New York Times Magazine,* 19 May 1963, pp. 12, 114-115.

4920. Clapper, Raymond. *Racketeering in Washington.* Boston: L. C. Page, 1933.

4921. Clark, Joseph S. "Some Ethical Problems of Congress." *American Academy of Political and Social Science, Annals* 363 (Jan. 1966): 12-22.

4922. Clark, Marion and Maxa, Rudy. *Public Trust, Private Lust: Sex, Power, and Corruption on Capitol Hill.* New York: Morrow, 1977.

4923. Cohen, Richard E. "Having Dethroned a President, Congress Investigates Its Own." *National Journal* 9 (Sept. 10, 1977): 1400-1405.

4924. Committee for Economic Development. *Restoring Confidence in the Political Process: A Statement by the Program Committee of the Committee for Economic Development.* Washington: 1974.

4925. "Congressional Ethics: Need for Stricter Regulation." *Congressional Quarterly Weekly Report* 30 (May 27, 1972): 1181-1182.

4926. Congressional Quarterly. *Congressional Ethics.* Washington: Congressional Quarterly, 1977.

4927. Donner, Frank J. "Is There an Ethic in the House?" *Nation,* 23 Sept. 1968, pp. 270-280, 282.

4928. Douglas, Paul H. *Ethics in Government.* Cambridge, Mass.: Harvard University Press, 1952.

4929. Durbin, Thomas M. *Provisions in the United States Constitution, Federal Statutes and Rules of the House and Senate Governing the Conduct and Activities of Members of Congress and Their Staff—With Appropriate Annotations of Cases.* Washington: Congressional Research Service, 1976.

4930. "An Ethical Guide Sought for Congressional Behavior." *Congressional Quarterly Weekly Report* 21 (June 7, 1963): 897-905.

4931. Getz, Robert S. *Congressional Ethics: The Conflict of Interest Issue.* Princeton, N.J.: Van Nostrand, 1967.

4932. Getz, Robert S. "*Ex Parte* Communications: A Study in Legislative Reluctance." *Western Political Quarterly* 19 (Mar. 1966): 31-36.

4933. Goldwater, Barry M. "The Politics of Morality." In *Congress and Conscience,* ed. ed. John B. Anderson, pp. 73-95. Philadelphia, Pa.: J. B. Lippincott, 1970.

4934. Graham, George A. *Morality in American Politics.* New York: Random House, 1952.

4935. Hamer, John. "Ethics in Government." *Editorial Research Reports,* 16 May 1973, pp. 375-396.

4936. Humphrey, Hubert H. "Ethical Standards in American Legislative Chambers." *American Academy of Political and Social Science, Annals* 280 (Mar. 1952): 51-59.

4937. King, Larry L. "Dear Congressman: 'Is Doddism Dead;' " *New York Times Magazine,* 16 April 1967, pp. 26-27, 134, 140.

4938. Krasnow, Erwin and Lankford, Richard. "Congressional Conflicts of Interest: Who Watches the Watchers?" *Federal Bar Journal* 24 (Summer 1964): 264-285.

4939. Lee, Linda K. "Conflict of Interest: One Aspect of Congress' Problems." *George Washington Law Review* 32 (June 1964): 954-982.

4940. Lehmann, Mildred L. *Congressional Ethics.* Washington: Congressional Research Service, 1979.

4941. Lehmann, Mildred L. "Legislative Conflicts of Interest: Typologies, Practices, and Proposed Remedies." In *Senators: Offices, Ethics and Pressures: A Compilation of Papers,* pp. 61-79. Washington: GPO, 1976.

4942. McCarthy, Eugene J. "Congressional Ethics." In *The Senate Institution,* ed. Nathaniel S. Preston, pp. 147–158. New York: Van Nostrand Reinhold, 1969.

4943. May, John D. "The Congressional 'Watergate' Case." *Australian Ouarterly* 46 (Mar. 1974): 54-58.

4944. Mondale, Walter F. "There Can Be Morality in Poltitics." *Today's Health* 32 (Sept. 1972): 16, 18-20.

4945. Murphy, Thomas P. "Political Ethics in a Coattails Congress." *Ethics* 77 (July 1967): 291-296.

4946. Noggle, Burl. *Teapot Dome: Oil and Politics in the 1920s.* Baton Rouge: Louisiana State University Press, 1962.

4947. Pauls, Frederick H.; rev. by Mildred L. Lehmann. *The House Committee on Standards of Official Conduct: A History of Its Establishment and Jurisdiction.* Washington: Congressional Rssearch Service, 1978.

4948. Pearson, Drew and Anderson, Jack. *The Case Against Congress: A Compelling Indictment of Corruption on Capitol Hill.* New York: Simon and Schuster, 1968.

4949. Pincus, Walter. "House of Ill Repute." *Tne New Republic,* 8 Mar. 1975, pp. 16-18.

4950. Pincus, Walter. "The Scandalous Senate." *The New Republic,* 22 Feb. 1975, pp. 16-19.

4951. Rhodes, Robert M. "Enforcement of Legislative Ethics: Conflict Within the Conflictof Interest Laws." *Harvard Journal on Legislation* 10 (April 1973): 373-406.

4952. Rienow, Robert and Rienow, Leona T. *Of Snuff, Sin, and the Senate.* Chicago: Follett Pub. Co., 1965.

4953. Rieselbach, Leroy N. "Congress: After Watergate, What?" In his *People vs. Government: The Responsiveness of American Institutions,* pp. 61-118. Bloomington: Indiana University Press, 1975.

4954. Sasser, Jim. "Learning from the Past: The Senate Code of Conduct in Historical Perspective." *Cumberland Law Review* 9 (Fall 1977): 357-384.

4955. Southwick, Thomas P. "House Task Force Urges Strict Ethics Code." *Congressional Quarterly Weekly Report* 35 (Feb. 5, 1977): 198-200.

4956. Southwick, Thomas P. "Senate Adopts New Code of Ethics." *Congressional Quarterly Weekly Report* 35 (April 2, 1977): 591-599.

4957. U.S. Congress. House. Standards of Official Conduct Committee. *Ethics Manual for Members and Employees of the U.S. House of Representatives.* 96th Cong., 1st sess. Washington: GPO, 1979.

4958. "Watergate: Vital Work Ahead for Senate Committee." *Congressional Quarterly Weekly Report* 31 (Nov. 24, 1973): 3063-3069.

4959. Wilson, Bob. "Congressional Ethics." In *We Propose: A Modern Congress,* ed. Mary McInnis, pp. 253-259. New York: McGraw-Hill, 1966.

4960. Wilson, Harper H. *Congress: Corruption and Compromise.* New York: Rinehart, 1951.

4961. Wilson, Harper H. "Congressional Standards and 4961 Disciplinary Procedures." Ph.D. dissertation, University of Wisconsin, 1948.

4962. Yadlosky, Elizabeth and Ehlke, Richard C. *Provisions in the United States Code Prohibiting Conflicts of Interest by Members of Congress and by United States Government Officials and Employees.* Washington: Congressional Research Service, 1973.

Financial Disclosure

4963. Bagdikian, Ben H. and Oberdorfer, Don. "Conflict of Interest: Can Congress Crack Down on Its Own." *Saturday Evening Post,* 17 Nov. 1962, pp. 21-29.

4964. "Bank Ties of Senator and Representative Questioned." *Congressional Quarterly Weekly Report* 29 (June 25, 1971): 1389.

4965. "Business Interests Reported by 274 Representatives." *Congressional Quarterly Weekly Report* 27 (May 23, 1969): 755-757.

4966. "Business Interests Reported by 268 Representatives." *Congressional Quarterly Weekly Report* 28 (May 29, 1970): 1388-1394.

4967. Case, Clifford P. "Congress and Its Double Standard." *Federal Bar Journal* 24 (Summer 1964): 257-63.

4968. "Conflicts of Interest and the Changing Concept of Marriage: The Congressional Compromise." *Michigan Law Review* 75 (Aug. 1977): 1647-1680.

4969. Felton, John. "Outside Income Limit: Can It Be Evaded?" *Congressional Quarterly Weekly Report* 36 (Sept. 16, 1978): 2519-2520.

4970. Felton, John. "The Wealth of Congress." *Congressional Quarterly Weekly Report* 36 (Sept. 2, 1978): 2311-2366.

4971. "Financial Disclosure: New Rules Will Have Impact." *Congressional Weekly Report* 35 (July 23, 1977): 1507-1517.

4972. "Financial Interests Reported by House Members." *Congressional Quarterly Weekly Report* 27 (May 23, 1969): 767-794.

4973. "Financial Interests Reported by House Members." *Congressional Quarterly Weekly Report* 28 (May 29, 1970): 1395-1423.

4974. Gilson, Lawrence. *Money and Secrecy: A Citizen's Guide to Reforming State and Federal Practices.* New York: Praeger, 1972.

4975. Glass, Andrew J. "Senate Leaders Keep Ethics Panel Cool to Financial Disclosure Law." *National Journal* 2 (April 25, 1970): 900-905.

4976. Halloran, Richard. "Keeping the Lid on the Korean Scandal: The House Ethics Committee Won't Name the Names of Fellow Congressmen." *Inquiry Magazine* 1 (Feb. 1978): 10-15.

4977. Havemann, Joel. "Financial Disclosure Reports Show Fewer Conflicts of Interest." *National Journal* 7 (July 19,1975): 1041-1048.

4978. Helm, William P. *Washington Swindle Sheet.* New York: A. and C. Bonni, 1932.

4979. Martin, Ethyl E. "A Bribery Episode in the First Election of United States Senators in Iowa." *Iowa Journal of History* 7 (Oct. 1909): 483-502.

4980. Maskell, Jack. *Financial Disclosure by Officers and Employees of the Legislative Branch.* Washington: Congressional Research Service, 1978.

4981. Polk, James. R. "On the Take: The Secret Fringe Benefits Enjoyed by Congress." *New Republic,* 13 Sept. 1975, pp. 10, 14-18.

4982. "Some Members Avoid Income Limit Rule." *Congressional Quarterly Weekly Report* 37 (Sept. 1, 1979): 1841-1843.

4983. Southwick, Thomas P. "Senators Seek Court Test of New Senate Ethics Code: Foreign Travel Rule Studied." *Congressional Quarterly Weekly Report* 35 (July 16, 1977): 1445-1446.

4984. U.S. Congress. House Commission on Administrative Review. *Financial Ethics.* 95th Cong., 1st sess. Washington: GPO, 1977.

4985. U.S. Congress. House. Rules Committee. *Financial Ethics.* Washington: GPO, 1977.

4986. Watzman, Sanford. *Conflict of Interest, Politics and the Money Game.* Chicago: Cowles Boom Co., 1971.

Discipline and Seating

4987. Bowman, Dorian and Bowman, Judith F. "Article I, Section 5: Congress' Power to Expel—An Exercise in Self-Restraint." *Syracuse Law Review* 29 (Fall 1978): 1071-1108.

4988. Curtis, Thomas B. "Power of the House of Representatives to Judge the Qualifications of Its Members." *Texas Law Review* 45 (July 1967): 1199-1204.

4989. Dempsey, John T. "Control by Congress over the Seating and Disciplining of Members." Ph.D. dissertation, University of Michigan, 1956.

4990. Durbin, Thomas M. *Qualifications and Eligibility of Members of Congress.* Washington: Congressional Research Service, 1977.

4991. Edwards, G. Thomas. "Benjamin Stark, the U.S. Senate and the 1862 Membership Issues." *Oregon Historical Quarterly* 72 (Dec. 1971): 315-338; 73 (Mar. 1972): 31-59.

4992. Fleishman, Neill. "Power of Congress to Exclude Persons Duly Elected." *North Carolina Law Review* 48 (April 1970): 655-666.

4993. McGuire, O. R. "The Right of the Senate to Exclude or Expel a Senator." *Georgetown Law Journal* 15 (May 1927): 382-401.

4994. McLaughlin, Gerald T. "Congressional Self-Discipline: The Power to Expel, to Exclude and to Punish." *Fordham Law Review* 41 (Oct. 1972): 43-66.

4995. Meskin, Sanford A. "Qualifications for Members of Congress: Not Subject to State Control." *Maryland Law Review* 19 (Spring 1959): 163-165.

4996. Momsen, Reuben. "Right of the Senate to Exclude a Senator-Elect." *Notre Dame Lawyer* 4 (Sept.-Oct. 1928): 3-21.

4997. Sykes, Conwell S. "Has the Senate of the United States the Constitutional Right to Refuse to Seat a Senator Who Presents Proper Credentials from State Authorities Showing His Due Election to the United States Senate?" *Mississippi Law Journal* 1 (Oct. 1938): 211-212.

4998. Wulsin, Lucien. "Right of Congress to Exclude Its Members." *Virginia Law Review* 33 (May 1947): 322-336.

Freshmen Congressmen

4999. Asher, Herbert B. "The Changing Status of the Freshman Representative." In *Congress in Change: Evolution and Reform,* ed. Norman J. Ornstein, pp.216–239. New York: Praeger, 1975.

5000. Asher, Herbert B. *Freshman Representatives and the Learning of Voting Cues.* Beverly Hills, Calif.: Sage Publications, 1973.

5001. Asher, Herbert B. "The Freshman Congressman: A Deveopmental Analysis." Ph.D dissertation, University of Michigan, 1970.

5002. Bullock, Charles S. "The Committee Assignments of Freshmen in the House of Representatives, 1947-1967." Ph.D. dissertation, University of Washington, 1968.

5003. Bullock, Charles S. "Freshman Committee Assignments and Reelection in the United States House of Representatives." *American Political Science Review* 66 (Sept. 1972): 996-1007.

5004. Bullock, Charles S. "Motivations for U.S. Congressional Committee Preferences: Freshmen of the 92nd Congress." *Legislative Studies Quarterly* 1 (May 1976): 201-212.

5005. Cohen, Richard E. "Freshmen in the Senate Being Seen—And Heard." *National Journal* 11 (Mar. 17, 1979): 439-443.

5006. Dennis, James R. "Roll-Call Votes and National Security: Focusing in on the Freshmen." *Orbis* 22 (Fall 1978): 713-735.

5007. Elstein, Paul D. "A Longitudinal Analysis of the Legislative Behavior of Freshman United States Senators." Ph.D. dissertation, University of Maryland, 1973.

5008. Emmert, J. Richard. "Freshmen Congressmen and the Apprenticeship Norms." *Capitol Studies* 2 (Spring 1973): 49-64.

5009. Emmert, J. Richard. "Freshmen Congressmen: Variations in Support for Presidential Legislation, 1953-1968." Ph.D. dissertation, Brown University, 1970.

5010. Fenno, Richard F. "The Freshman Congressman: His View of the House." In *Congressional Behavior,* ed. Nelson W. Polsby, pp. 129-135. New York: Random House, 1971.

5011. "Freshman House Democrats' 1977 Voting Record More Conservice Than '74 Class." *Congressional Quarterly Weekly Report* 36 (Jan. 21, 1977): 116-117.

5012. "Freshman Members Go to School." *Congressional Quarterly Weekly Report* 17 (Jan. 23, 1959): 113-114.

5013. Long, Clarence D. "Observations of a Freshman in Congress." *New York Times Magazine,* 1 Dec. 1963, pp. 34, 70, 73, 75, 78.

5014. Malbin, Michael J. "A Year Older and Wiser, Freshmen Reassess Their Role." *National Journal* 8 (Feb. 14, 1976): 189-195.

5015. Mishler, William, Lee, James, and Thorpe, Alan. "Determinants of Institutional Continuity: Freshman Cue-Taking in the House of Representatives." In *Legislatures in Comparative Perspective,* ed. Allan Kornberg, pp. 363-397. New York: McKay, 1973.

5016. Murphy, Thomas P. "Extraordinary Power of Freshmen in Congress." *Trans-Action* 5 (Mar. 1968): 33-39.

5017. Pinkus, Matt and Reed, Bruce F. "Freshmen in the House: A Sobering Six Months." *Congressional Quarterly Weekly Report* 33 (Aug. 2, 1975): 1674-1677.

5018. Rapoport, Daniel. "A New Old Guard Has Come Forward in the House." *National Journal* 9 (Aug. 13, 1917): 1264-1269.

5019. Sturges, Gerald D. "The Freshman Faces Congress." In *To Be A Congressman: The Promise and the Power,* eds. Sven Groenning and Jonathan P. Hawley, pp. 23-36. Washington: Acropolis Books, 1973.

5020. Urich, Theodore. "The Voting Behavior of Freshman Congressmen." *Southwestern Social Science Quarterly* 39 (Mar. 1959): 337-341.

Minority Groups

Blacks

5021. Adair, August. "Black Legislative Influence in Federal Policy Decisions: The Congressional Black Caucus, 1971-1975." Ph.D. dissertation, Johns Hopkins University, 1976.

5022. Barnett, Marguerite R. "Congressional Black Caucus." *Academy of Political Science, Proceedings* 32 (1975): 34-50.

5023. Christopher, Maurice. *Black Americans in Congress5023*. rev. and expanded ed. New York: Crowell, 1976.

5024. Colburn, Kenneth S. *The Congressional Black Caucus and Joint Center for Political Studies Guide to Participation in the Delegate Selection Process for the Democratic & Republican National Party Conventions in 1976.* Washington: The Caucus, 1975.

5025. Elmore, Joseph E. "North Carolina Negro Congressmen, 1875-1901." Master's thesis, University of North Carolina, Chapel Hill, 1964.

5026. Henry, Charles P. "Legitimizing Race in Congressional Politics." *American Politics Quarterly* 5 (April 1977): 149-176.

5027. Hosmer, John and Fineman, Joseph. "Black Congressmen in Reconstruction Historiography." *Phylon* 29 (June 1978): 97-107.

5028. Jarrett, Calvin D. "Black Congressmen, 1869-1901." *Black World* 17 (Feb. 1968): 16-25.

5029. Levy, Arthur B. and Stoudinger, Susan. "Black Caucus in the 92nd Congress: Gauging Its Success." *Phylon* 39 (Dec. 1978): 322-332.

5030. Levy, Arthur B. and Stoudinger, Susan. "Sources of Voting Cues for the Congressional Black Caucus." *Journal of Black Studies* 7 (Sept. 1976): 29-45.

5031. Meyer, Mary. "Black Congressmen and How They Grew: One Hundred Years in Congress." *Black Politician* 1 (April 1970): 3-11.

5032. Miller, Jake C. "Black Legislators and African-American Relations, 1970-1975." *Journal of Black Studies* 10 (Dec. 1979): 245-261.

5033. "Negroes in Congress 1868-1895." *Negro History Bulletin* 31 (Nov. 1968): 12-13.

5034. O'Loughlin, John. "Black Representation Growth and Seat-Vote Relationship." *Social Science Quarterly* 60 (June 1979): 72-86.

5035. Perry, Robert T. *Black Legislators.* San Francisco: R & E Research Associates, 1976

5036. Smith, Samuel D. *The Negro in Congress, 1870-1901.* Chapel Hill: University of North Carolina Press, 1940.

5037. Sokolow, Alvin D. "Black Member, White Legislature." *Black Politician* 3 (Oct. 1971): 23-39.

5038. Taylor, Alrutheus A. "Negro Congressmen a Generation After." *Journal of Negro History* 7 (April 1922): 121-176.

5039. U.S. Congress. House. *Black Americans in Congress, 1870–1977.* House Doc. 95-208. Washington: GPO, 1977.

5040. Work, Monroe N. "Some Negro Members of Reconstruction Conventions and Legislatures and of Congress." *Journal of Negro History* 5 (Jan. 1920): 63-119.

Women

5041. Buchanan, Christopher. "Why Aren't There More Women in Congress." *Congressional Quarterly Weekly Report* 36 (Aug. 12, 1978): 2108-2110.

5042. Bullock, Charles S. and Heys, Patricia F. "Recruitment of Women for Congress: A Research Note." *Western Political Quarterly* 25 (Sept. 1972): 416-423.

5043. Caraway, Hattie W. "Women in Congress." *State Government* 10 (Oct. 1937): 203-204.

5044. Chamberlin, Hope. *A Minority of Members: Women in the U.S. Congress.* New York: Praeger, 1973.

5045. Darcy, Robert and Schramm, Sarah "When Women Run Against Men." *Public Opinion Quarterly* 41 (Spring 1977): 1-12.

5046. Douglas, Helen G. "How I Conceive the Congress: Women's Role During the Next Two Years." *Free World* 8 (Nov. 1944): 425-427.

5047. Englebarts, Rudolph. *Women in the United States Congress, 1917-1972: Their Accomplishments, with Bibliographies.* Littleton, Colo.: Libraries Unlimited, 1974.

5048. Fails, Eleanor V. "The American Congresswoman from 1950-1970: A Study in Role-Perception." Ph.D. dissertation, Loyola University of Chicago, 1974.

5049. Foote, Frieda L. "Role Stress and Cultural Resources: A Study of the Role of the Woman Member of Congress." Ph.D. dissertation, Michigan State University, 1967.

5050. Frakovic, Kathleen A. "Sex and Voting in the U.S. House of Representatives: 1961-1975." *American Politics Quarterly* 5 (July 1977): 315-330.

5051. Fulenwider, Claire K. "Feminist Ideology and the Political Attitudes and Participation of White and Minority Women." *Western Political Quarterly* 34 (Mar. 1981): 17-30.

5052. Gehlen, Frieda L. "Legislative Role Performance of Female Legislators." *Sex Roles* 3(Feb. 1977): 1-18.

5053. Gehlen, Frieda L. "Women in Congress: Their Power and Influence in a Man's World." *Trans-Action* 6 (Oct. 1969): 36-40.

5054. Gelb, Joyce and Palley, Marian L. "Women and Interest Group Politics: A Comparative Analysis of Federal Decision-Making." *Journal of Politics* 41 (May 1979): 362-392.

5055. Gertzog, Irwin.N. "Changing Patterns of Female Recruitment to the U.S. House of Representatives." *Legislative Studies Quarterly* 4 (Aug. 1979): 429-445.

5056. Holcomb, Morrigene. *Women in the United States Congress.* rev. ed. Washington: Congressional Research Service, 1975.

5057. "Increase in Female House Members in 1971 Expected." *Congressional Quarterly Weekly Report* 28 (July 10, 1970): 1745-1748.

5058. Kempfer, Katherine. "Congresswomen in Action." *Women Lawyers Journal* 34 (Winter 1948): 33, 37.

5059. Kempfer, Katherine. "Our Congresswomen in Action." *Women Lawyers Journal* 33 (April 1947): 49-50.

5060. Kincaid, Diane D. "Over His Dead Body: A Positive Perspective on Widows in the U.S. Congress." *Western Political Quarterly* 31 (Mar. 1978): 96-104.

5061. McQuatters, Geneva F. "Women in the 82nd Congress." *Independent Woman* 30 (Jan. 1951): 2-4.

5062. Meisol, Patricia. "Women in Politics: Increasing in Numbers, But Not on the Hill." *National Journal* 10 (July 15, 1978): 1128-1131.

5063. Paxton, Annabel. *Women in Congress.* Richmond, Va.: Dietz Press, 1945.

5064. Porter, Amy. "Ladies of Congress." *Colliers* 112 (Aug. 1943): 22-23.

5065. Rainey, Henry T., Mrs. "The Women's Congressional Club." *New England Magazine* 40 (May 1909): 265-271.

5066. "Salute to the Women of the 89th Congress." *National Business Woman* 44 (Jan. 1965): 25-28.

5067. Thompson, Joan H. "Career Patterns and Role Perceptions of United States Congresswomen Since 1916." Ph.D. dissertation, Johns Hopkins University, 1978.

5068. Thompson, Joan H. "Role Perceptions of Women in the Ninety-Fourth Congress." *Political Science Quarterly* 95 (Spring 1980): 71-82.

5069. Tolchin, Susan. *Women in Congress: 1917-1976*. Washington: GPO, 1976.

5070. "Tribute to Our Women in Congress." *Independent Woman* 34 (Feb. 1955): 48-50.

5071. U.S. Department of Labor. Women's Bureau. *Women of the 80th-90th Congress, 1946-67*. Washington: GPO, 1967.

5072. Van Helden, Morrigene. *Women in the United States Congress*. Washington: Congressional Research Service, 1971.

5073. Werner, Emmy E. "Women in Congress: 1917-1964." *Western Political Quarterly* 19 (Mar. 1966): 16-30.

5074. Werner, Emmy E. and Bachtold, Louise M. "Personality Characteristics of Women in American Politics and Congress." In *Women in Politics,* ed. Jane Jacquette, pp. 75-84. New York: Wiley, 1974.

5075. "Women Candidates: Many More Predicted for 1974." *Congressional Quarterly Weekly Report* 32 (April 13, 1974): 941-944.

5076. "Women in the 84th Congress." *Independent Woman* 29 (Jan. 1955): 20-23.

XIV. Support and Housing of Congress

Pay and Perquisites

General Studies

5077. Capps, Frank L. "Senate Vehicle Parking Report and Recommendations." In *Senate Administration: A Compilation of Papers Prepared for the Commission on the Operation of the Senate,* pp. 98-108. Washington: GPO, 1976.

5078. Cohen, Richard E. "Congressional Allowances Are Really Perking Up." *National Journal* 10 (Feb. 4, 1978): 180-183.

5079. "Congressional Mail: What Is Official Business?" *Congressional Quarterly Weekly Report* 31 (April 28, 1973): 1024-1026.

5080. "Congressional Patronage Dwindles into Headaches." *Congressional Quarterly Weekly Report* 28 (April 10, 1970): 966-969.

5081. "Cost of Congress: More Than Doubles in Five Years." *Congressional Quarterly Weekly Report* 27 (Aug. 19, 1972): 2063-2066.

5082. Cranor, John D. "Congress at the Grassroots: Congressional District Offices and Federal—Local Relations." Ph.D. dissertation, University of Missouri at Columbia, 1977.

5083. "Legislative Branch Costs Up 4.7 Percent in Year." *Congressional Quarterly Weekly Report* 27 (Sept. 5, 1969): 1654-1657.

5084. Nathanson, Iric and Ornstein, Norman J. "The Space Race." *Washington Monthly* 6 (Jan. 1975): 33-36.

5085. Ridley, Richard.'Space Use Problems in the Senate and Suggested Short-Range Improvements." In *Senate Administration: A Compilation of Papers Prepared for the Commission on the Operation of the Senate,* pp. 29-57. Washington: GPO, 1976.

5086. Sellers, Dorothy. "Legal Services for Congress." *American Bar Association Journal* 63 (Dec. 1977): 1728-1731.

5087. Southwick, Thomas P. "Legislative Funds Cleared: Total Kept Under $1 Billion." *Congressional Ouarterly Weekly Report* 35 (July 30, 1977): 1957-1958.

5088. Tax Foundation. *The Legislative Branch: The Next Bill Dollar Bureaucracy.* New York: Tax Foundation, 1976.

5089. U.S. General Services Administration. *Services Available to Members of Congress.* Washington: GPO, 1978.

5090. U.S. Congress. House. Ways and Means Committee. *Business Expenses of Legislators.* 96th Cong., 1st sess. Washington, GPO, 1979.

5091. U.S. Congress. House. Commission on Administrative Review. *Background Information on Administrative Units, Members' Offices, and Committees and Leadership Offices.* 95th Cong., 1st sess. Washington: GPO, 1977.

Salary and Income

5092. Armstrong, William L. "The Imperial Congress." In *Can You Afford This House?,* ed. by David Treen, pp. 15-22. Ottawa, Ill.: Green Hill Books, 1978.

5093. "Congressional Pay: Awkward Situation for Congress." *Congressional Quarterly Weekly Report* 31 (Sept. 1, 1973): 2374.

5094. "Congressional Pay Supplemented by Healthy Benefits." *Congressional Quarterly Weekly Report* 32 (Feb. 23, 1974): 496-498.

5095. Dwyer, Paul E. "Comparison of Salaries and Specified Benefits Available too Senators, Senate Employees and Civil Service Employees." In *Senators: Offices, Ethics and Pressures: A Compilation of Papers,* pp. 86-87. Washington: GPO, 1976.

5096. Dwyer, Paul E. *Salaries, Allowances and Retirement Benefits for the President, Vice President, Senators, Representatives, Justices of the Supreme Court, and Cabinet, Foreign Service and Other Federal Officers.* Washington: Congressional Research Service, 1977.

5097. Gressle, Sharon. "Commission on Executive, Legislative, and Judicial Salaries." In *Senators: Offices, Ethics and Pressures: A Compilation of Papers,* pp. 80-83. Washington: GPO, 1976.

5098. "House Income Limit Rule Under Attack." *Congressional Quarterly Weekly Report* 36 (April 15, 1978): 867-868.

5099. "One in Three Members Have Other Jobs." *Congressional Quarterly Weekly Report* 37 (Sept. 1, 1979): 1844-1848.

5100. "Outside Earnings Swell Wealth of Congress." *Congressional Quarterly Weekly Report* 37 (Sept. 1, 1979): 1823-1836.

5101. "Outside Income: Senate Fees Down, House Interests Up." *Congressional Quarterly Weekly Report* 31 (June 30, 1973): 1635-1645.

5102. "Outside Income: Senate Fees Up: House Lawyers Down." *Congressional Quarterly Weekly Report* 30 (June 17, 1972): 1379-1439.

5103. Phillips, A. Cabell. "The High Cost of Our Low-Paid Congress." *New York Times Magazine,* 24 Feb. 1952, pp. 7, 41-42, 44.

5104. Rhyne, Charles S. "Need for Increases in Judicial and Congressional Salaries." *Journal of the Bar Association of the District of Columbia* 22 (Mar. 1955): 119-124.

5105. Segal, Bernard G. "Udall-Broyhill Bill Gives New Hope for Judicial and Congressional Salary Reform." *American Bar Association Journal* 49 (Nov. 1963): 1055-1059.

5106. "'75 Senators Report $640,662 in Honoraria." *Congressional Quarterly Weekly Report* 28 (May 29, 1970): 1376-1387.

5107. Shaffer, Helen B. "Pay of Congress." *Editorial Research Reports* (July 1953): 445-461.

Franking

5108. Benton, W. Duane. "Congressional Perquisites and Fair Elections: The Case of the Franking Privilege." *Yale Law Journal* 83 (April 1974): 1055-1099.

5109. "Congressional Junk Mail: Abuse of a Privilege." *The Nation* 222, 10 Mar. 1976, pp. 339-340.

5110. DeMeter, Robert F. "Franking Privilege: A Threat to the Electoral Process." *American University Law Review* 23 (Summer 1974): 883-921.

5111. Freed, Bruce F. "House Allowances: More Mailings Expected." *Congressional Quarterly Weekly Report* 33 (June 21, 1975): 1291-1293.

5112. Porro, Alfred A. and Ascher, Stuart A. "Case for Congressional Franking Privilege." *University of Toledo Law Review* 5 (Winter 1974): 259-281.

5113. Shore, Benjamin. "The Congressional Franking Privileges: An Abuse Whose Time Is Up." *Harper's Magazine* 246 (April 1973): 102, 105-106.

5114. U.S. Congress. Senate. Post Office and Civil Service Committee. *Congressional Franking Reform: A Compilation of Legislative History.* Washington: GPO, 1974.

5115. Wasmund, H. Andrew. "Use and Abuse of the Congressional Franking Privilege." *Loyola University Law Review* 5 (Jan. 1972): 52-86.

5116. Yadlosky, Elizabeth and Carr, Richard P. *The Congressional Frank: Statutory Provisions, Legislative History, Judicial Construction and Some Proposals for Amending the Law.* Washington: Congressional Research Service, 1976.

Travel

5117. "Are Congressional Trips Worth the Cost." *Congressional Ouarterly Weekly Report* 13 (Nov. 4, 1955): 1175-1178.

5118. Carnahan, A. S. J. "Congressional Travel Abroad and Reports." *American Academy of Political and Social Science, Annals* 289 (Sept. 1953): 120-126.

5119. "Congress Sets New Record for Foreign Travel." *Congressional Quarterly Weekly Report* 37 (Sept. 8, 1979): 1921-1946.

5120. "Congressional Members Took Fewer Trips in 1969." *Congressional Quarterly Weekly Report* 29 (July 10, 1970): 1754-1757.

5121. "Congressional Travel Unusually Heavy." *Congressional Quarterly Weekly Report* 17 (May 22, 1959): 717-719.

5122. "Controls Placed on Senate and House Travel Funds." *Congressional Quarterly Weekly Report* 18 (Aug. 5, 1960): 1386-1388.

5123. "Cost Remains High for Congressional Tours." *Congressional Quarterly Weekly Report* 15 (Jan. 4, 1957): 22-23.

5124. "Election Year Cuts into Junketing." *Congressional Quarterly Weekly Report* 17 (Feb. 20, 1959): 297-306.

5125. "Foreign Travel: Congress Puts Lid on Public Disclosure." *Congressional Quarterly Weekly Report* 32 (May 18, 1974): 1289-1292.

5126. "Foreign Travel: Congress Spent $995,820 in 1972." *Congressional Quarterly Weekly Report* 21 (Aug. 18, 1973): 2253-2267.

5127. "Foreign Travel: Congress Spent $1 Million in 1971." *Congressional Quarterly Weekly Report* 27 (Aug. 5, 1972): 1931-1947.

5128. "Foreign Travel: Congressional Trips Cost $825,118." *Congressional Quarterly Weekly Report* 29 (June 25, 1971): 1383-1388.

5129. "$403,859 in Counterpart Funds Spent for Junkets in 1959." *Congressional Quarterly Weekly Report* 18 (June 10, 1960): 1017-1019.

5130. Gruenberg, Mark. "Congress Sets New Travel Spending Record." *Congressional Quarterly Weekly Report* 36 (Sept. 30, 1978): 2647-2672.

5131. Gruenberg, Mark. "1976 Foreign Travel: $2.4 Million Spent." *Congressional Quarterly Weekly Report* 35 (Aug. 20, 1977): 1753-1760.

5132. "Nearly Half of Congress Takes U.S.-Paid Trips." *Congressional Quarterly Weekly Report* 24 (Mar. 4, 1966): 505-520.

5133. "1976 Foreign Travel by Members of Congress." *Congressional Quarterly Weekly Report* 35 (Aug. 20, 1977): 1760-1772.

5134. "190 Congressmen Traveled Outside U.S. in 1959." *Congressional Quarterly Weekly Report* 18 (Feb. 26, 1960): 298-307.

5135. "318 Government-Paid Trips Made by Members in 1968." *Congressional Quarterly Weekly Report* 27 (May 9, 1969): 681-695.

5136. "306 Government-Paid Trips Made by Members in 1967." *Congressional Quarterly Weekly Report* 26 (July 12, 1968): 1737-1751.

5137. "337 Government-Paid Trips Made by Members in 1966." *Congressional Quarterly Weekly Report* 25 (May 12, 1967): 796-812.

5138. "Which Members of Congress Went Where in 1957?" *Congressional Quarterly Weekly Report* 16 (Jan. 24, 1958): 85-95.

Support Agencies

General Studies

5139. *Congressional Support Agencies: A Compilation of Papers Prepared for the Commission on the Operation of the Senate.* Washington: GPO, 1976.

5140. Frye, Alton. "The Congressional Resource Problem." In *Congress and Arms Control,* eds. Alan Platt and Lawrence D. Weiler, pp. 19-41. Boulder, Colo.: Westview Press, 1978.

5141. Griffith, Ernest S. "Four Agency Comparative Study." In *Congressional Support Agencies: A Compilation of Papers Prepared for the Commission on the Operation of the Senate,* pp. 95-148. Washington: GPO, 1976.

5142. Roback, Herbert. "Program Evaluation by and for the Congress." *Bureaucrat* 5 (April 1976): 11-36.

5143. Steiner, Oscar H. *The Case for the George Washington Congressional Institute.* Cleveland, Ohio: George Washington Memorial Foundation, 1976.

5144. Stringham, Raymond B. *The Congress Reserve.* New Milford, Conn.: J. J. Little and Ives, 1943.

5145. U.S. Congress. Joint Committee on Congressional Operations. *Congressional Research Support and Information Service.* 93rd Cong., 2nd sess. Washington: GPO, 1974.

Congressional Research Service

5146. Beckman, Norman. "Congressional Research Service: Resources for Oversight and Evaluation." In *Legislative Oversight and Program Evaluation: A Seminar Sponsored by the Congressional Research Service,* pp. 71-89. 94th Cong., 2d sess. Washington: GPO, 1976.

5147. Beckman, Norman. "Use of a Staff Agency by the Congress: Experiences of the Congressional Research Service Under the Legislative Reorganization Act of 1970." In *Comparative Legislative Reforms and Innovations,* eds. Abdo I. Baaklini and James J. Heaphey, pp. 91-122. Albany: Comparative Development Studies Center, Graduate School of Public Affairs, State University of New York, 1977.

5148. Beckman, Norman. "Use of a Staff Agency by the Congress: The Congressional Research Service." *Bureaucrat* 3 (Jan. 1975): 401-415.

5149. Chartrand, Robert L "Redimensioning Congressional Information Support." *Jurimetrics Journal* 11 (June 1971): 165-178.

5150. Galloway, George B. "The Legislative Reference Service of Congress." *Parliamentary Affairs* 8 (Spring 1955): 261-265.

5151. Goodrum, Charles A. "Congress and Congressional Research Service." *Special Libraries* 65 (July 1974): 253-258.

5152. Goodrum, Charles A. *The Congressional Research Service of the United States Congress.* Washington: Congressional Research Service, 1976.

5153. Goodrum, Charles A. "The Legislative Reference Service of the United States Congress." In *Library Services to the Legislature: A Symposium.* Sydney: New South Wales Parliament, 1965.

5154. Goodrum, Charles A., rev. by Kaldahl, S. John. *Automation and the Congressional Research Service.* Washington: Congressional Research Service, 1978.

5155. Graves, W. Brooke. "Legislative Reference Service for the Congress of the United States." *American Political Science Review* 41 (April 1947): 289-293.

5156. Gushee, David E. "The Service's Responsibilites for Emerging Issues and Terminating Programs." In *Legislative Oversight and Program Evaluation: A Seminar Sponsored by the Congressional Research Service, pp. 90-93. 94th Cong., 2d sess. Washington: GPO, 1976.*

5157. Jayson, Lester S. "The Legislative Reference Service: Research Arm of the Congress." *Parliamentarian* 50 (July 1969): 177-186.

5158. Kravitz, Walter. *The Congressional Research Service and the Legislative Reorganization Act of 1970.* Washington: Congressional Research Service, 1971.

5159. McBride, Margarete. "Reference Service for Congress Before 1915." Master's thesis, Drexel Institute of Technology, 1955.

5160. Malbin, Michael J. "CRS: The Congressional Agency That Just Can't Say 'No.'" *National1 Journal* 9 (Feb. 19, 1977): 284-289.

5161. Meller, Norman. *Institutional Adaptability: Legislative Reference in Japan and the United States.* Beverly Hills, Calif.: Sage Publications, 1974.

5162. Putnam, Herbert. "Legislative Reference for Congress." *American Political Science Review* 9 (Aug. 1915): 542-549.

5163. Stern, Robert J. "When the Experts Disagree." *Bulletin of the Atomic Scientists* 31 (Feb.1975): 29-31.

5164. U.S. Congress. House. Commission on Information and Facilities. *Organizational Effectiveness of the Congressional Research Service.* 95th Cong., 1st sess. Washington: GPO, 1977.

General Accounting Office

5165. Bowlin, Samuel W. "Look at the Congressional Fellowship Program." *GAO Review* (Winter 1973): 12-18.

5166. Brady, Bernard A. "In the Backyard of Congress." *GAO Review* (Spring 1974): 59-69.

5167. Brown, Richard E. "The GAO: Untapped Source of Congressional Power." Ph.D. dissertation, Harvard University, 1968.

5168. Civilian Personnel Group. Office of the General Counsel. "Determination of Legislative Intent." *GAO Review* (Summer 1974): 62-71.

5169. "Comptroller General's Authority to Examine the Private Business Records of Government Contractors." *Harvard Law Review* 92 (Mar. 1979): 1148-1159.

5170. Desanti, Vincent M. and Vellucci, Matthew J. "New Information for the Congress: The Congressional Sourcebook." *GAO Review* 10 (Fall 1976): 63-68.

5171. Donham, Philip and Fahey, Robert J. *Congress Needs Help.* New York: Random House; 1966.

5172. Fitzgerald, Martin J. "The Expanded Role of the General Accounting Office in Support of a Strengthened Congress." *Bureaucrat* 3 (Jan. 1975): 383-400.

5173. Hall, Robert B. "Being Responsive to the Congress." *GAO Review* 13 (Winter 1978): 38-43.

5174. Kloman, Erasmus H., ed. *Cases in Accountability: The Work of the GAO.* Boulder, Colo.: Westview Press, 1979.

5175. Knoll, Erwin. "The Half-Hearted GAO: The Congress Gets What It Wants." *Progressive* 35 (May 1971): 19-23.

5176. MacDonald, Scot. "Reorganization Along Function Lines Makes Congress' GAO More Responsive." *Government Executive* 4 (June 1972): 54-57.

5177. Marvin, Keith E. "Current Evaluation Activities in the General Accounting Office." In *Legislative Oversight and Program Evaluation: A Seminar Sponsored by the Congressional Research Service*, pp. 227-287. 94th Cong., 2d sess. Washington: GPO, 1976.

5178. Marvin, Keith E. "Status and Potential of Program Evaluation for the Congress." In *Techniques and Procedures for Analysis and Evaluation: A Compilation of Papers Prepared for the Commission on the Operation of the Senate*, pp. 106-120. 94th Cong., 2d sess. Washington: GPO, 1977.

5179. Marvin, Keith E. and Hedrick, James L. "GAO Helps Congress Evaluate Programs." *Public Administration Review* 34 (July/Aug. 1974): 327-333.

5180. Masterson, James E. "Legislative Reporting in the United States General Accounting Office." Master's thesis, American University, 1963.

5181. Morgan, Thomas D. "The General Accounting Office: One Hope for Congress to Gain Parity with the President." *North Carolina Law Review* 51 (Oct. 1973): 1279-1368.

5182. Mosher, Frederick D. *The GAO: The Quest for Accountability in American Government.* Boulder, Colo.: Westview Press, 1979.

5183. Oliver, James P. "The General Accounting Office's Responsibilities for Oversight and Evaluation in Reference to the Congressional Budget and Impoundment Act." In *Legislative Oversight and Program Evaluation: A Seminar Sponsored by the Congressional Research Service*, pp. *105-113. 94th Cong., 2d sess. Washington: GPO, 1976.*

5184. Pearce, John M. "Senate Seeks to Expand GAO's Watchdog Capabilities." *National Journal* 3 (Feb. 6, 1971): 273-279.

5185. Pois, Joseph. "The General Accounting Office as a Congressional Resource." In *Congressional Support Agencies: A Compilation of Papers Prepared for the Commission on the Operation of the Senate*, pp. 31-54. Washington: GPO, 1976.

5186. Pois, Joseph. "Trends in General Accounting Office Audits." In *The New Political Economy: The Public Use of the Private Sector,* ed. Bruce L. R. Smith, pp. 245-277.. London: Macmillan, 1975.

5187. Pois, Joseph. *Watchdog on the Potomac: A Study of the Comptroller General of the United States.* Washington University Press of America, 1979.

5188. Rourke, John T. "The GAO: An Evolving Role." *Public Administration Review* 38 (Sept. 1978): 453-457.

5189. Rubin, Harold H. "The Role of the GAO in the Seventies and What the GAO Is Doing to Prepare for It." *GAO Review* (Winter 1971): 45-52.

5190. Singer, James W. "When the Evaluators Are Evaluated, the GAO Often Gets Low Marks." *National Journal* 11 (Nov. 10, 1979): 1889-1892.

5191. Smith, Darrell H. *The General Accounting Office: Its History, Activities, and Organization.* Baltimore, Md: Johns Hopkins University Press, 1927.

5192. Staats, Elmer B. "The GAO: Government Watchdog, Analyst, Critic." *GAO Review* (Fall 1972): 1-10.

5193. Staats, Elmer B. "GAO, Evaluation and the Legislative Process." *GAO Review* 13 (Fall 1978): 24-29.

5194. Staats, Elmer B. "GAO: Present and Future." *Public Administration Review* 28 (Sept. 1968): 461-465.

5195. Staats, Elmer B. *General Accounting Office: Support of Committee Oversight. Working Papers on House Committee Organization and Operation. Presented to House Select Committee on Committees.* 93rd Cong. Washington: GPO, 1973.

5196. Staats, Elmer B. "Improving Congressional Control over the Federal Budget." *GAO Review* (Summer 1973): 1-13.

5197. Staats, Elmer B. "Objective Information Is Essential to the Congress and the Public." *GAO Review* (Winter 1975): 1-6.

5198. Staats, Elmer B. "The Use of Social Science in the Changing Role of the GAO." *Policy Studies Journal* 7 (Summer 1979): 820-826.

Congressional Budget Office

5199. Capron, William M. "The Congressional Budget Office.'.' In *Congressional Support Agencies: A Compilation of Papers Prepared for the Commission on the Operation of the Senate*, pp. 75-94. Washington: GPO, 1976.

5200. Havemann, Joel. "After Two Years, CBO Gets High Marks from Congress." *National Journal* 9 (Aug. 13, 1977): 1256-1260.

5201. Havemann, Joel. "Budget Report CBO Proceeds with Work While Taking Heat on Staff Size." *National Journal* 7 (Nov. 15, 1975): 1575-1577.

5202. Havemann, Joel. "Alice Rivlin Named Chief of Congressional Budget Office." *National Journal* 7 (Mar. 1, 1975): 332.

5203. Hederman, William F. and Nelson, T. A. *A Review of Selected Congressional Cost Analyses*. Santa Monica, Calif.: Rand, 1978.

5204. Kimery, Bruce F. "Federal Budgetary Process Changing." *Army Logistician* 7 (Jan.-Feb. 1975):6-9.

5205. Schick, Allen. "Battle of the Budget." *Academy of Political Science, Proceedings* 32 (1975): 51-70.

5206. Smith, Donald. "Congressional Budget Office: Under Fire." *Congressional Quarterly Weekly Report* 34 (June 5, 1976): 1430-1432.

5207. U.S. Congress. House. Commission on Information and Facilities. *Congressional Budget Office: A Study of Its Organizational Effectiveness*. 93rd Cong. Washington: GPO, 1977.

5208. U.S. Congress. House. Committee on the Budget. *Congressional Budget Office Oversight, Hearing Before the Task Force on Budget Process, June 2, 1977*. 95th Cong., 1st sess. Washington: GPO, 1977.

5209. U.S. Congress. Senate. Committee on the Budget. *Congressional Budget Office Oversight, Hearings, October 6, 1975*. 94th Cong., 1st sess. Washington: GPO, 1975.

5210. U.S. Congressional Budget Office. *Responsibilities and Organization*. Washington: GPO, 1976.

5211. Williams, Walter. *The Congressional Budget Office: A Critical Link in Budget Reform*. Seattle: University of Washington, 1974.

Office of Technology Assessment

5212. Burns, Stephen G. "Congress and the Office of Technology Assessment." *George Washington Law Review* 45 (Aug. 1977): 1123-1150.

5213. Casper, Barry M. "The Rhetoric and Reality of Congressional Technology Assessment." *Bulletin of the Atomic Scientists* 34 (Feb. 1978): 20-31.

5214. Daddario, Emilio Q. "Technology Assessment Legislation." *Harvard Journal on Legislation* 7 (May 1970): 507-532.

5215. Gaganidze, Theodore P. "Energy Policy Formation in the Ninety-Fourth Congress: The Role of the Office of Technological Assessment." Ph.D. dissertation, University of California at Los Angeles, 1977.

5216. O'Neill, Hugh V. "Policy Analysis, Technology, and the Congress." *Bureaucrat* 3 (Jan. 1975): 416-428.

5217. Peterson, Russell W. "Whither the Office of Technology Assessment." *Research Management* 12 (Jan. 1979): 6-11.

5218. Rich, Robert F. "Systems of Analysis, Technology Assessment, and Bureaucratic Power." *American Behavioral Scientists* 22 (Jan./Feb. 1979): 393-416.

5219. Skolnikoff, E. B. "The Office of Technology Assessment." In *Congressional Support Agencies: A Compilation of Papers Prepared for the Commission on the Operation of the Senate,* pp. 55-74. Washington: GPO, 1976.

5220. "Technology Assessment: A New Tool for Congress." *Congressional Quarterly Weekly Report* 31 (April 7, 1973): 772–775.

5221. Thomas, Gary. "The Office of Technology Assessment: A Description of the Office's Objectives and Activities." In *Legislative Oversight and Program Evaluation: A Seminar Sponsored by the Congressional Research Service,* pp. 114-145. 94th Cong., 2d sess. Washington: GPO, 1976.

5222. U.S. Congress. House. Science and Technology Committee. *Review of the Office of Technology Assessment and Its Organic Act.* 95th Cong., 2d sess. Washington: GPO, 1978.

Library of Congress

5223. Ashley, Frederick W. "Three Eras in the Library of Congress." In *Essays Offered to Herbert Putnam by His Colleagues and Friends on His Thirtieth Anniversary as Librarian of Congress, 5 April 1929,* eds. William W. Bishop and Andrew Keogh, pp. 57-67. New Haven, Conn.: Yale University Press, 1929.

5224. Bay, J. Christian. "Herbert Putnam, 1861-1955." *Libri* 6 (1957): 200-207.

5225. Benco, Nancy L. "Archibald MacLeish: The Poet Librarian." *Quarterly Journal of the Library of Congress* 33 (July 1976): 233-249.

5226. Berkeley, Edmund and Berkeley, Dorothy S. *John Beckley: Zelous Partisan in a Nation Divided.* Philadelphia, Pa.: American Philosophical Society, 1973.

5227. Berkeley, Edmund and Berkeley, Dorothy S. "The First Librarian of Congress: John Beckley." *Quarterly Journal of the Library of Congress* 32 (April 1975): 83-110.

5228. Bishop, William W. *Library of Congress.* Chicago: American Library Association Publishing Board, 1911.

5229. Bishop, William W. "Thirty Years of the Library of Congress, 1899 to 1929." *Library Journal* 54 (May 1, 1929): 379-382.

5230. Bishop, William W. and Keogh, Andrew, eds. *Essays Offered to Herbert Putnam by His Colleagues and Friends on His Thirtieth Anniversary as Librarian of Congress, 5 April.1929.* New Haven, Conn.: Yale University Press, 1929.

5231. Clapp, Verner W. "The Library of Congress and the Other Scholarly Libraries of the Nation (1800-1947)." *College and Research Libraries* 9 (April 1948): 116-125.

5232. Cole, John Y. "Ainsworth Spofford and the Copyright Law of 1870." *Journal of Library History* 6 (Jan. 1971): 34-40.

5233. Cole, John Y. "Ainsworth Spofford and the National Library." Ph.D. dissertation, George Washington University, 1971.

5234. Cole, John Y., ed. *Ainsworth Rand Spofford: Bookman and Librarian.* Littleton, Colo.: Libraries Unlimited, 1975.

5235. Cole, John Y. "Ainsworth Rand Spofford: The Valiant and Persistent Librarian of Congress." *Quarterly Journal of the Library of Congress* 33 (April 1976): 93-115.

5236. Cole, John Y. *For Congress and the Nation: A Chronological History of the Library of Congress.* Washington: GPO, 1979.

5237. Cole, John Y. "For Congress and the Nation: The Dual Nature of the Library of Congress." *Quarterly Journal of the Library of Congress* 32 (April 1975): 118-138.

5238. Cole, John Y. "The Library of Congress in the Nineteenth Century: An Informal Account." *Journal of Library History* 9 (July 1974): 222-240.

5239. Cole, John Y. "The National Monument for a National Library: Ainsworth Rand Spofford and the New Library of Congress, 1871-1897." *Records of the Columbia Historical Society* 48 (1971-1972): 468-507.

5240. Cole, John Y. "Smithmeyer and Plez: Embattled Architects of the Library of Congress." *Quarterly Journal of the Library of Congress* 29 (Oct. 1972): 282-307.

5241. Colket, Meredith B. and Preston, Edward H. "Local History and Genealogical Reference Section, Library of Congress." *American Genealogist* 17 (1940): 65-68.

5242. Cunningham, Noble E. "John Beckley: Early American Party Manager." *William and Mary Quarterly* 13 (1956): 40-52.

5243. Dickinson, Asa D. "Recollections of Herbert Putnam." *Wilson Library Bulletin* 30 (Dec. 1955): 311-315.

5244. Evans, Luther H. "The Strength by Which We Live." *Bulletin of the American Library Association* 44 (Oct. 1950): 339-345.

5245. Gabriel, Ralph H. "The Library of Congress and American Scholarship." *Bulletin of the American Library Association* 44 (Oct. 1950): 349-351.

5246. Goff, Frederick R. "Early Library of Congress Bookplates." *Quarterly Journal of the Library of Congress* 26 (Jan. 1969): 55-61.

5247. Goff, Frederick R. "Oldest Library in Washington: The Rare Book Division of the Library of Congress." *Records of the Columbia Historical Society* 47 (1969-1970): 332-345.

5248. Goldschmidt, Eva. "Archibald MacLeish, Librarian of Congress." *College and Research Libraries* 30 (Jan. 1969): 12-24.

5249. Goodrum, Charles A. *The Library of Congress.* New York: Praeger, 1974.

5250. Gordon, Martin K. "Patrick Magruder: Citizen, Congressman, Librarian of Congress." *Quarterly Journal of the Library of Congress* 32 (July 1975): 154-171.

5251. Green, Bernard R. "The Building for the Library of Congress." *Annual Reports of the Board of the Regents of the Smithsonian Institution.* (Jan.-July 1897): 625-632.

5252. Grisso, Karl M. "Ainsworth R. Spofford and the American Library Movement, 1861-1908." Master's thesis, Indiana University, 1966.

5253. Gropp, Arthur E. "The Library of Congress and the Hispanic American Field." *Bulletin of the American Library Association* 44 (Oct. 1950): 358-359.

5254. Hampton, William. "The Facilities of the Library of Congress." In *The Reform of Parliament,* ed. Bernard Crick; pp. 218-226. London: Weidenfeld and Nicolson, 1964.

5255. Johnston, William D. *The History of the Library of Congress. Volume I, 1800-1864.* Washington: GPO, 1904.

5256. Kaula, N. "175 Years of the Library of Congress." *Herald of Library Science* 14 (Oct. 1975): 244-246.

5257. Krieg, Cynthia J. "Herbert Putnam's Philosophy of Librarianship." Master's thesis, Long Island University, 1970.

5258. Lacy, Dan. "The Library of Congress: A Sesquicentenary Review 1800-1950.". *Library Quarterly* 20 (July 1950): 157-179; (Oct. 1950): 235-258.

5259. LaMontagne, Leo E. "Jefferson and the Library of Congress." In his *American Library Classification: With Special Reference to the Library of Congress,* pp. 27-62. Hamden, Conn.: Shoestring Press, 1961.

5260. Lord, Milton E. "The Library of Congress." *Bulletin of the American Library Association* 44 (Oct. 1950): 346-348.

5261. McDonough, John. "John Silva Meehan: A Gentleman of Amiable Manners." *Quarterly Journal of the Library of Congress* 33 (Jan. 1976): 3-28.

5262. McDonough, John. "Justin Smith Morrill and the Library of Congress." *Vermont History* 35 (1967): 141-150.

5263. MacLeish, Archibald. *Champion of a Cause: Essays and Addresses on Librarianship.* Chicago: American Library Association, 1971.

5264. MacLeish, Archibald. "The Reorganization of the Library of Congress, 1939-44." *Library Quarterly* 14 (Oct. 1977): 277-315.

5265. Marley, S. Branson. "Newspapers and the Library of Congress." *Quarterly Journal of the Library of Congress* 32 (July 1975): 207-237.

5266. Marsh, Philip M. "John Beckley: Mystery Man of Early Jeffersonians." *Pennsylvania Magazine of History and Biography* 72 (Jan. 1948): 54-69.

5267. Mearns, David C. "Ainsworth the Unforgettable." *Quarterly Journal of the Library of Congress* 25 (Jan. 1968): 1-5.

5268. Mearns, David C. "Herbert Putnam and His Responsible Eye." In *Herbert Putnam, 1861-1955: A Memorial Tribute*, pp. 1-52. Washington: Library of Congress, 1956.

5269. Mearns, David C. "Herbert Putnam: Librarian of the United States." *D.C. Libraries* 26 (Jan. 1955): 1-24.

5270. Mearns, David C. "Herbert Putnam, Librarian of the United States: The Minneapolis Years." *Wilson Library Bulletin* 29 (Sept. 1954): 59-63.

5271. Mearns, David C. "The Library of Congress." *Parliamentary Affairs* 2 (Summer 1949): 222-228.

5272. Mearns, David C. *The Story Up to Now: The Library of Congress 1800-1946.* Washington: GPO, 1947.

5273. Mearns, David C. "Virginia in the History of the Library of Congress, or Mr. Jefferson's Other Seedlings." *Vermont Library Bulletin* 16 (1951): 1-4.

5274. Metcalf, Keyes D. "The Library of Congress as a Bibliographic Center." *Bulletin of the American Library Association* 44 (Oct. 1950): 352-354.

5275. Miller, C. H. "Ainsworth Rand Spofford, 1825-1908." Master's thesis, George Washington University, 1938.

5276. Mood, Fulmer. "The Continental Congress and the Plan for a Library of Congress in 1782-1783: An Episode in American Cultural History." *Pennsylvania Magazine of History and Biography* 72 (Jan. 1948): 3-24.

5277. Mugridge, Donald H. "Thomas Jefferson and the Library of Congress." *Wilson Library Bulletin* 18 (April 1944): 608-611.

5278. Mumford, L. Quincy. "Bibliographic Developments at the Library of Congress." *Libri* 17 (1967): 294-304.

5279. Powell, Benjamin E. "Lawrence Quincy Mumford: Twenty Years of Progress." *Quarterly Journal of the Library of Congress* 33 (July 1976): 269-287.

5280. Putnam, Herbert. "Ainsworth Rand Spofford: A Librarian Past." *The Independent* 65 (Nov. 1908): 1149-1155.

5281. Ranganathan, S. R. "The Library of Congress Among National Libraries." *Bulletin of the American Library Association* 44 (Oct. 1950): 355-357.

5282. Rogers, Rutherford D. "LQM of LC." *Bulletin of Bibliography* 25 (Sept.-Dec. 1968): 161-165.

5283. Salamanca, Lucy. *Fortress of Freedom: The Story of the Library of Congress.* Philadelphia: Lippincott, 1942.

5284. Schubach, B. W. "Ainsworth Rand Spofford and the Library of the United States." Master's thesis, Northern Illinois University, 1965.

5285. Solberg, Thorvald. "A Chapter in the Unwritten History of the Library of Congress from January 17–April 5, 1899: The Appointment of Herbert Putnam as Librarian." *Library Quarterly* 9 (July 1939): 285-298.

5286. Spofford, Ainsworth R., et al. "Relations Between the Smithsonian Institution and the Library of Congress." In *The Smithsonian Institution, 1846-1896: The History of Its First Half Century,* ed. George B. Goode, pp. 823-830. Washington: 1897.

5287. Vance, John T. "The Centennial of the Law Library of Congress." *American Bar Association Journal* 18 (Sept. 1932): 597-599.

5288. Waters, Edward N. "Herbert Putnam: The Tallest Little Man in the World." *Quarterly Journal of the Library of Congress* 33 (April 1976): 151-175.

Congress and Information

Resources and Communications

5289. Aines, Andrew A. "Integration of Public and Private Archives for Government Decision Makers." In *Information Support, Program Budgeting and the Congress,* eds. Robert L. Chartrand, Kenneth Janda and Michael Hugo, pp. 127-142. New York: Spartan Books, 1968.

5290. Anderson, Clinton P. "Scientific Advice for Congress." *Science* 144 (April 1964): 29-32.

5291. Anderson, Mark W. "The Institutionalization of Futures Research in the U.S. Congress." *Technological Forecasting and Social Change* 11 (April 1978): 287-296.

5292. Beckman, Norman, rev. by Stevens, Arthur G. *Congressional Information Processes for Coordinating National Policies.* Washington: Congressional Research Service, 1975.

5293. Beckman, Norman. "Congressional Information Processes for National Policy." *American Academy of Political and Social Science, Annals* 394 (Mar. 1971): 84-99.

5294. Bezold, Clement. "Congress and the Future." *Futurist* 9 (June 1975): 132-142.

5295. Bezold, Clement and Renfro, William L. "Citizens and Legislative Foresight." In *Anticipatory Democracy: People in the Politics of the Future,* ed. Clement Bezold, pp. 114-133. New York: Random House, 1978.

5296. Bolling, Richard. "The Management of Congress." *Public Administration Review* 35 (Sept. 1975): 490-495.

5297. Brademas, John. "Congress in the Year 2000." In *The Future of the United States Government,* ed. Harvey Perloff, pp. 309-323. New York: George Braziller, 1971.

5298. Chaples, Ernest A. "Congress Gets New Ideas from Outside Experts." In *To Be A Congressman: The Promise and the Power,* eds. Sven Groenning and Jonathan P. Hawley, pp. 169-183. Washington: Acropolis Books, 1973.

5299. Chartrand, Robert L. "The Congressional Milieu: Information Requirements and Current Capabilities." In *Information Support, Program Budgeting and the Congress,* eds. Robert L. Chartrand, Kenneth Janda and Michael Hugo, pp. 1-8. New York: Spartan Books, 1968.

5300. Chartrand, Robert L. *The Legislator as Information User. Working Papers on House Committee Organization and Operation.* Presented to House Select Committee on Commitees. 93rd Cong. Washington: GPO, 1973.

5301. Cheatham, Anne W. "Helping Congress Cope with Tomorrow." *Futurist* 12 (April 1978): 113-115.

5302. Cohen, Richard E. "Information Gap Plagues Attempt to Grapple with Growing Executive Strength." *National Journal* 5 (Mar. 17, 1973): 379-388

5303. Cote, Alfred J. "Who Tells Congress About Technology." *Industrial Research* 9 (Sept. 1967): 78-82.

5304. Dechert, Charles R. "Availability of Information for Congress Operations." In *Twelve Studies of the Organization of Congress,* ed. Alfred de Grazia, pp. 167-211. Washington: American Enterprise Institute for Public Policy Research, 1966.

5305. Dreyfus, Daniel A. "Where We Are and Where We're Heading, Limitations of Policy Research in Congressional Decision-making." *Policy Studies Journal* 4 (Spring 1976): 269-274.

5306. Etzioni, Amitai. "How May Congress Learn?" *Science* 159 (Jan. 1968): 170-172.

5307. Ferkiss, Victor C. *The Shape of the Future, Working Papers on House Committee Organization and Operation. Presented to House Select Committee on Committees.* 93rd Cong. Washington: GPO, 1973.

5308. Hahn, Walter A. *Committee Information: Some Comments on Selected Sources. Working Papers on House Committee Organization and Operation. Presented to House Select Committee on Committees.* 93rd Cong. Washington: GPO, 1973.

5309. Hattery, Lowell H. and Hofheimer, Susan. "The Legislators' Source of Expert Information." *Public Opinion Quarterly* 18 (Fall 1954): 300-303.

5310. Hirsch, Sharlene P. "Congressmen's Use of Scholars as Advisors on Education Policy." Ph.D. dissertation, Harvard University, 1969.

5311. Janda, Kenneth. "Information Systems for Congress." In *Twelve Studies of the Organization of Congress,* ed. Alfred de Grazia, pp. 415-456. Washington: American Enterprise Institute for Public Policy Research, 1966.

5312. Jarass, Hans D. *Executive Information Systems and Congress.* Berlin: Schweitzer, 1974.

5313. Knox, William T. "External Sources of Information for Congress: The Executive Branch and the Private Sector." In *Information Support,Program Budgeting and the Congress,* eds. Robert L. Chartrand, Kenneth Janda and Michael Hugo, pp. 9-24. New York: Spartan Books, 1968.

5314. Lewis, E. Raymond. "The House Library." *Capitol Studies* 3 (Fall 1975): 107-128.

5315. Long, Richard W. "Legislative Operating Information." In *Committees and Senate Procedures: A Compilation of Papers prepared for the Commission on the Operation of the Senate,* pp. 169-190. Washington: GPO, 1977.

5316. MacNeil, Neil. "Congress and the Intellectual Community." In *The Congress and America's Future,* pp. 17-24. George Washington University American Assembly Report, 1965.

5317. Moles, Oliver C. "The Social Science Information Service." *Policy Studies Journal* 5 (Winter 1976): 228-234.

5318. Ornstein, Norman J. "Information, Resources and Legislative Decision Making: Some Comparative Perspectives on the United States Congress." Ph.D. dissertation, University of Michigan, 1972.

5319. Ornstein, Norman J. and Rohde, David W. "Resource Usage, Information and Policymaking in the Senate." In *Senators: Offices, Ethics and Pressures: A Compilation of Papers,* pp. 37-46. Washington: GPO, 1976.

5320. Porter, H. Owen. "Legislative Experts and Outsiders: The Two-Step Flow of Communication." *Journal of Politics* 36 (Aug. 1974): 703-730.

5321. Renfro, Ren. "How Congress Is Exploring the Future." *Futurist* 12 (April 1978): 105-112.

5322. Riddick, Floyd M. "What Congress Needs: Non-Partisan Experts as Consultants." *South Atlantic Ouarterly* 42 (April 1943): 185-191.

5323. Rose, Charles. "Building a Futures Network in Congress." In *Anticipatory Democracy: People in the Politics of the Future,* ed. Clement Bezold, pp. 105-113. New York: Random House, 1978.

5324. Schick, Allen. *The Supply and Demand for Analysis on Capitol Hill.* Washington: Congressional Research Service, 1975.

5325. Schick, Allen. "The Supply and Demand for Analysis on Capitol Hill." *Policy Analysis* 2 (Spring 1976): 215-234.

5326. Schneier, Edward V. "The Intelligence of Congress: Information and Public-Policy Patterns." *American Academy of Political and Social Science, Annals* 388 (Mar. 1970): 14-24.

5327. Schwengel, Frederic D. "Information Handling: 'For a Vast Future Also.'" In *We Propose: A Modern Congress,* ed. Mary McInnis, pp. 303-317. New York: McGraw-Hill, 1966.

5328. Schwengel, Frederic D. "Problems of Inadequate Information and Staff Resources in Congress." In *Information and Staff Resources in Congress." In Information Support, Program Budgeting and the Congress,* eds. Robert L. Chartrand, Kenneth Janda and Michael Hugo, pp. 97–108. New York: Spartan Books, 1968.

5329. Smith, H. Alexander. "Information and Intelligence for Congress." *American Academy of Political and Social Science, Annals* 289 (Sept. 1953): 114-119.

5330. Staats, Elmer B. "Social Indicators and Congressional Needs for Information." *American Academy of Political and Social Science, Annals* 435 (Jan. 1978): 277-285.

5331. Symmes, Harrison M. "The Information Interrelationship Between Congress and the Academic World." *Bulletin of the American Society for Information Science* 1 (April 1975): 16.

5332. U.S. Congress. Senate. Judiciary Committee. *Congressional Access to and Control and Release of Sensitive Government Information, Hearings.* Washington: GPO, 1977.

5333. Walker, Harvey. "Communication in the Legislative Assembly." *American Academy of Political and Social Science, Annals* 250 (Mar. 1947): 59-69.

5334. Zwier, Robert. "The Search for Information: Specialists and Nonspecialists in the U.S. House of Representatives." *Legislative Studies Ouarterly* 4 (Feb. 1979): 31-42.

Information Technology

5335. Bortnick, Jane, Wallace, Paul, Shampansky, Jay R., Perkins, Kathleen, and Fiori, Patricia. *The Use of Computers by House Members and Their Staff for Official and Campaign Purposes: Legal and Ethical Issues.* Washington: Congressional Research Service, 1978.

5336. Brademas, John. "Prognostications Regarding the Growth and Diversification of the Computers in the Service of Society: The Congressional Role." In *Computers in the Service of Society,* ed. Robert L. Chartrand, pp. 150-159. New York: Pergamon Press, 1972.

5337. Capron, William M. "Development of Cost-Effectiveness Systems in the Federal Government." In *Information Support, Program Budgeting and the Congress,* eds. Robert L. Chartrand, Kenneth Janda, and Michael Hugo, pp. 145-152. New York: Spartan Books, 1968.

5338. Chartrand, Robert L. "Computer Support for Congress." *Journal of Systems Management* 21 (July 1970): 8-11.

5339. Chartrand, Robert L. *Computers for Congress*. Washington: Congressional Research Service, 1969.

5340. Chartrand, Robert L. "Congress, Computers and the Cognitive Process." In *Planning and Politics: Uneasy Partnership*, eds. Thad L. Boyle and George Lathrop, pp. 167-187. New York: Odyssey Press, 1970.

5341. Chartrand, Robert L. *The Legislator as User of Information Technology*. Washington: Congressional Research Service, 1977.

5342. Chartrand, Robert L. "The Potential for Legislative Utilization of Systems Technology." *Journal of Constitutional and Parliamentary Studies* 3 (1969): 51-65.

5343. Chartrand, Robert L. "Providing Congress with Information: The Role of Technology." *News for Teachers of Political Science* 21 (Spring 1979): 12-13.

5344. Chartrand, Robert L. and Emard, Jean P. "Legislating Responsive Information Services." *Bulletin of the American Society for Information Science* 1 (April 1975): 18-19.

5345. Chartrand, Robert L., Janda, Kenneth, and Hugo, Michael, eds. *Information Support, Program Budgeting and the Congress*. New York: Spartan Books, 1968.

5346. Courtot, Marilyn E. "A Look at Senate Data Processing." *Law and Computer Technology* 9 (1976): 49-67.

5347. Croley, John D. *The Congressional Guide to Computers*. Washington: Congressional Management Corporation, 1977.

5348. Frantzich, Stephen E. "Computerized Information Technology in the U.S. House of Representatives." *Legislative Studies Quarterly* 4 (May 1979): 255-280.

5349. Frantzich, Stephen E. "Congress by Computer." *Social Policy* 8 (Jan. 1978): 42-45.

5350. Frantzich, Stephen E. "Technological Innovation Among Congressmen." *Social Forces* 57 (Mar. 1979): 968-974.

5351. Frantzich, Stephen E. "Technological Innovation Among Members of the House of Representatives." *Polity* 12 (Winter 1979): 333-348.

5352. Gude, Gilbert. "Providing Information to Congress." In *Information Technology Serving Society*, eds. Robert L. Chartrand and James W. Morentz, pp. 55-59. Elmsford, N.Y.: Pergamon Press, 1979.

5353. Janda, Kenneth. "Future Improvements in Congressional Information Support." In *Information Support, Program Budgeting and the Congress*, eds. Robert L. Chartrand, Kenneth Janda, and Michael Hugo, pp. 45-96. New York: Spartan Books, 1968.

5354. Janda, Kenneth. "Providing Information to Congressmen." In his *Information Retrieval: Application to Political Science*, pp. 184-220. Indianapolis, Ind.: Bobbs-Merrill, 1968.

5355. Janda, Kenneth. *Information Systems for Congress—Revisited. Working Papers on House Committee Organization and Operation*. Presented to House Select Committee on Committees. 93rd Cong. Washington: GPO, 1973.

5356. McClory, Robert. "Automatic Data Processing as a Major Informational Tool." In *Information Support, Program Budgeting and the Congress*, eds. Robert L. Chartrand, Kenneth Janda, and Michael Hugo, pp. 25-30. New York: Spartan Books, 1968.

5357. Meadows, Charles T. "Pros and Cons of Computer-Oriented Systems." in *Information Support, Program Budgeting and the Congress*, eds. Robert L. Chartrand, Kenneth Janda, and Michael Hugo, pp. 109-126. New York: Spartan Books, 1968.

5358. Rose, Charles. "Legislative Information Needs: Dreams and Realities." In *Information Technology Serving Society,* eds. Robert L. Chartrand and James W. Morentz, pp. 107-112. Elmsford, N.Y.: Pergamon Press, 1979.

5359. Ryan, Frank. *Information Systems Support to the U.S. House of Representatives. Working Papers on House Committee Organization and Operation. Presented to House Select Committee on Committees.* 93rd Cong. Washington: GPO, 1973.

5360. Southwick, Thomas P. "Computers Aid Congress in Work, Politics." *Congressional Quarterly Weekly Report* 35 (May 28, 1977): 1045-1051.

5361. Staenberg, Jane B. "Information Tools for the 95th Congress." *Bulletin of the American Society for Information Science* 3 (April 1977): 26-27.

5362. U.S. Congress. House. Committee on House Administration. *The Legislative Information and Status System for the United States House of Representatives.* Washington: GPO, 1979.

5363. U.S. Congress. House. Commission on Information and Facilities. *Automated Information Resources for the U.S. House of Representatives: A Report of the House Commission on Information and Facilities.* Washington: GPO, 1976.

5364. U.S. Congress. House. Commission on Information and Facilities. *Inventory of Information Resources and Services Available to the U.S. House of Representatives.* Washington: GPO, 1976.

5365. U.S. Congress. Committee on Rules and Administration. *Information Support for the U.S. Senate: A Survey of Computerized Resources and Services.* Washington: GPO, 1977.

5366. U.S. Congress. House. Select Committee on Committees. *The Congress and Information Technology: Staff Report.* 93rd Cong., 2d sess. Washington: GPO, 1974.

Supporting Organizations

Congressional Staff

5367. Albright, Joseph. "The Pact of the Two Henrys." *New York Times Magazine,* 5 Jan. 1975, pp. 16-17, 20, 24, 26, 28-31, 34.

5368. Allsbrook, John W. "Role of Congressional Staffs in Weapons System Acquisition." *Defense Systems Management Review* 1 (Spring 1977): 34-42.

5369. Balch, Stephen H. and Davis, David H. "The Political Science Education of the U.S. Senate Staff: Did We Win Their Hearts and Minds." *Teaching Political Science* 5 (Jan. 1978): 193-198.

5370. Beaach, Bennet. "Staff Infection." *Washington Monthly* 6 (Jan. 1975): 24-25.

5371. Brown, Eugene. "In the Shadows: Jobs on Capitol Hill." *Democratic Review* 1 (April-May 1975): 52-57.

5372. Broyhill, Joel T. "Reforms Needed in House Personnel Procedures." In *We Propose: A Modern Congress,* ed. Mary McInnis, pp. 191-198. New York: McGraw-Hill, 1966.

5373. Butler, Warren H. "Administering Congress: The Role of the Staff." *Public Administration Review* 26 (Mar. 1966): 3-13.

5374. Cavanagh, Thomas E. "Rational Allocation of Congressional Resources: Member Time and Staff Use in the House." In *Public Policy and Public Choice,* eds. by Douglas W. Rae and Theodore J. Eismeier, pp. 209–248. Beverly Hills, Calif.: Sage Publications, 1979.

5375. Claiborne, William L. "The Results of Role-Played Political Interviews on Congressional Staff." *Journal of Applied Social Psychology* 3 (April 1973): 144-149.

5376. Cohen, Richard E. "The Kennedy Staff: Putting the Senator Ahead." *National Journal* 9 (Dec. 3, 1977): 1880-1883.

5377. Cranor, John D. "Congress at the Grassroots: Congressional District Offices and Federal–Local Relations." Ph.D. dissertation, University of Missouri, 1977.

5378. Evans, Rowland. "The Invisibile Men Who Run Congress." *Saturday Evening Post,* 8 June 1963, pp. 13-17.

5379. Fox, Harrison W. "Personal Professional Staffs of United States Senators." Ph.D. dissertation, American University, 1972.

5380. Fox, Harrison W. and Hammond, Susan W. *Congressional Staffs: The Invisible Force in American Lawmaking.* New York: Free Press, 1977.

5381. Fox, Harrison W. and Hammond, Susan W. "Growth of Congressional Staffs." *The Academy of Political Science, Proceedings* 32 (1975): 112-124.

5382. Gwirtzman, Milton S. "The Bloated Branch." *New York Times Magazine,* 10 Nov. 1974, pp. 30-31, 98, 100–102.

5383. Hammond, Susan W. "Congressional Change and Reform: Staffing the Congress." In *Legislative Reform: The Policy Impact,* ed. Leroy N. Rieselbach, pp. 183-193. Lexington, Mass.: Lexington Books, 1978.

5384. Hammond, Susan W. "The Operation of Senators' Offices." In *Senators: Offices, Ethics and Pressures: A Compilation of Papers,* pp. 4-18. Washington: GPO, 1976.

5385. Hammond, Susan W. "Personal Staffs of Members of the United States House of Representatives." Ph.D. dissertation, Johns Hopkins University, 1973.

5386. Heaphey, James J. and Balutis, Alan P., eds. *Legislative Staffing: A Comparative Perspective.* New York: Wiley, 1975.

5387. Hogan, James J. "Increasing Executive and Congressional Staff Capabilities in the National Security Arena." In *The Changing World of the American Military,* ed. Franklin D. Margiotta, pp. 103–118. Boulder, Colo.: Westview Press, 1978.

5388. "House and Senate Staffs List Outside Interests." *Congressional Quarterly Weekly Report* 27 (July 4, 1969): 1171-1180.

5389. Jones, Rochelle and Woll, Peter. "The Tail and the Dog: How the Staff Wags Congress." *Washington Monthly* 11 (Oct. 1979): 30-38.

5390. Kampelman, Max M. "The Legislative Bureaucracy: Its Response to Political Change." *Journal of Politics* 16 (Aug. 1954): 539-550.

5391. King, Larry L. "Washington's Second Banana Politicians." *Harper's Magazine* 230 (Jan. 1965): 41-47.

5392. Kofmehl, Kenneth. *Professional Staffs of Congress.* 4th ed. West Lafayette, Ind.: Purdue University Press, 1962.

5393. Krasnow, Erwin G. and Kurzman, Stephen. "Lawyers for the Lawmakers." *American Bar Association Journal* 51 (Dec. 1965): 1191-1193.

5394. Loomis, Burdett A. "The Congressional Office as a Small (?) Business: New Members Set Up Shop." *Publius* 9 (Summer 1979): 35-55.

5395. McCartney, John D. "Political Staffing: A View from the District." Ph.D. dissertation, University of California, Los Angeles, 1975.

5396. Malbin, Michael.J. "Congressional Staffs: Growing Fast, But in Different Directions." *National Journal* 8 (July 10, 1976): 958-965.

5397. Malbin, Michael J. *Unelected Representatives: A New Role for Congressional Staffs.* New York: Basic Books, 1980.

5398. Meller, Norman. "Legislative Staff Services: Toxin, Specific, or Placebo for the Legislature's Ills." *Western Political Quarterly* 20 (June 1967): 381-389.

5399. Reveles, Robert A. and Maldonado, Daniel. "The Role of the Spanish Speaking Aide on the Hill." *Bureaucrat* 2 (Summer 1973): 173-177.

5400. Rogers, Lindsay. "Staffing of Congress." *Political Science Quarterly* 56 (Mar. 1941): 1-22.

5401. Rumsefeld, Donald. "The Operation of the Congressional Office." In *We Propose: A Modern Congress,* ed. mary McInnis, pp. 281-299. New York: McGraw-Hill, 1966.

5402. Saloma, John S. *Proposals for Meeting Congressional Staff Needs. Working Papers on House Committee Organization and Operation. Presented to House Select Committee on Committees.* 93rd Cong. Washington: GPO, 1973.

5403. Schlossberg, Kenneth. "The Ablest Men in Congress." *Washingtonian* 3 (Aug. 1968): 61-63, 72-75.

5404. Scully, Michael A. "Reflections of a Senate Aid." *Public Interest* 47 (Spring 1977): 41-48.

5405. Toynbee, Polly. "Living Through the Boss: A Day in the Life of a Senator's A.A." *Washington Monthly* 5 (June 1973): 46-60.

5406. U.S. Congress. House. House Administration Committee. *Studies Dealing with Budgetary, Staffing and Administrative Activities of the U.S. House of Representatives 1946-1978.* 95th Cong., 2d sess. Washington: GPO, 1978.

5407. Walker, David. "Legislative Underlabourers." *Political Quarterly* 50 (Oct.-Dec. 1979): 482-492.

5408. Woll, Peter. *American Bureaucracy.* 2nd ed. New York: Norton, 1977.

5409. Wolman, Harold L. and Wolman, Dianne M. "The Role of the U.S. Senate Staff in the Opinion Linkage Process: Population Policy." *Legislative Studies Quarterly* 2 (Aug. 1977): 281-293.

5410. Yacker, Marc D. *Casework and the Role of a Caseworker in a Congressional Office.* Washington: Congressional Research Service, 1977.

5411. Yacker, Marc D. *Closing a Congressional Office: A Brief Overview.* Washington: Congressional Research Service, 1978.

Supporting Personnel

5412. Alton, Edmund. *Among the Law-Makers.* New York: Charles Scribner's Sons, 1892.

5413. Arthur D. Little, Inc. *Management Study of the U.S. Congress.* Cambridge, Mass.: Arthur D. Little, 1965.

5414. Bogar, Carl F. "View from the Other Side via the Congressional Fellowship Program." *GAO Review (Summer 1974): 78-83.*

5415. Bowling, Kenneth R. "Good-by 'Charlies': The Lee-Adams Interest and the Political Demise of Charles Thomson, Secretary of Congress, 1774-1789." *Pennsylvania Magazine of History and Biography* 100 (July 1976): 314-335.

5416. "Congressional Costs Continue to Rise." *Congressional Quarterly Weekly Report* 17 (June 3, 1959): 757.

5417. "Cost of Congress Has Doubled in 10 Years." *Congressional Quarterly Weekly Report* 13 (May 13, 1955): 535.

5418. "Costs of Conqress Rise 82.1% in Four Years." *Congressional Quarterly Weekly Report* 15 (July 26, 1957): 891-892.

5419. Eckoff, Christian F. *Memoirs of a Senate Page (1855–1859).* New York: Broadway Publishing Co., 1909.

5420. Edmunds, Albert J. "Charles Thomson's New Testament." *Pennsylvania Magazine of History and Biography* 15 (1891): 327-335.

5421. Gleason, James P. "Legislative Counsel in Congress." *Georgetown Law Journal* 38 (Jan. 1950): 277-284.

5422. Hastings, George E. "Jacob Duche, First Chaplain of Congress." *South Atlantic Quarterly* 31 (Oct. 1932): 386-400.

5423. Henricks, J. Edwin. *Charles Thomson and the Making of a New Nation, 1729-1824.* Cranbury, N.J.: Fairleigh Dickinson University Press, 1979.

5424. Kneedler, Harry L. "Charles Thomson." Master's thesis, Temple University, 1940.

5425. Long, Richard W. "The Senate Page System." In *Senate Administration: A Compilation of Papers Prepared for the Commission on the Operation of the Senate,* pp. 109-110. Washington: GPO, 1976.

5426. Lyons, John F. "Thomson's Bible." *Journal of the Presbyterian Historical Society* 15 (1938-1939): 211-220.

5427. Madison, Frank. *A View from the Floor: Journal of a U.S. Senate Page Boy.* Englewood Cliffs, N.J.: Prentice-Hall, 1967.

5428. Miller, William. *Fishbait: The Memoirs of the Congressional Doorkeeper.* Englewood Cliffs, N.J.: Prentice-Hall, 1977.

5429. Parton, James. "The Small Sins of Congress." *Atlantic Monthly* 24 (Nov. 1869): 517-533.

5430. Rolater, Frederick S. "Charles Thomson, Secretary of the Continental Congress." Master's thesis, University of Southern California, 1965.

5431. Smith, Paul H. "Charles Thomson on Unity in the American Revolution." *Quarterly Journal of the Library of Congress* 28 (July 1971): 158-172.

5432. Springer, William L. "Congressional Pages: Their Work and Schooling." In *We Propose: A Modern Congress,* ed. Mary McInnis, pp. 181-188. New York: McGraw-Hill, 1966.

5433. Zimmerman, John J. "Charles Thomson: 'The Sam Adams of Philadelphia.'" *Mississippi Valley Historical Review* 45 (Dec. 1958): 464-480.

Discrimination

5434. Capitol Hill Women's Political Caucus. *Sexists in the Senate: A Study of Differences in Salary by Sex Among Employees of the U.S. Senate.* Washington: The Caucus, 1975.

5435. Cleveland, James C. "The Need for Increased Minority Staffing." In *We Propose: A Modern Congress,* ed. Mary McInnis, pp. 5-19. New York: Mc-Graw Hill, 1966.

5436. Cooper, Ann. "Hill Workers Push for Job Protections Congress Denied by Labor Exemptions." *Congressional Quarterly Weekly Report* 36 (Feb. 11, 1978): 337-346.

5437. Cooper, Ann. "Senate Job Discrimination Plan Reported, But Faces More Committee Study." *Congressional Quarterly Weekly Report* 36 (April 15, 1978): 877.

5438. Dale, Charles. *Legal Analysis of Various Questions with Regard to a Draft Resolution to Implement Senate Standing Rule L Which Prohibits Employment Discrimination with the Senate.* Washington: Congressional Research Service, 1978.

5439. Greenburg, Barbara C. "A Member of Congress is Liable for Damages Arising from His Sex-Based Dismissal of a Staff Member, But May Assert a Qualified Immunity Defense to Such Action." *George Washington Law Review* 46 (Nov. 1977): 137-155.

5440. House Republican Task Force on Congressional Reform and Minority Staffing. *We Propose: A Modern Congress.* New York: McGraw-Hill, 1966.

5441. "Last Plantation: Will Employment Reform Come to Capitol Hill?" *Catholic University Law Review* 28 (Winter 1979): 271-311.

5442. North, J. "Congress: The Last Plantation." *Barrister* 5 (Fall 1978): 46-50.

5443. Rapoport, Daniel. "'The Imperial Congress': Living Above the Law." *national Journal* 11 (June 2, 1979): 911-915.

Congressional Record

5444. Beard, Charles A. "Suggested Economy for Congress." *National Municipal Review* 10 (Nov. 1921): 542-542.

5445. "Blacklisting Through the Official Publication of Congressional Reports." *Yale Law Journal* 81 (Dec. 1971): 188-230.

5446. Cain, Earl R. "Obstacles to Early Congressional Reporting." *Southern Speech Communication Journal* 27 (Spring 1962): 239-247.

5447. "Congressional Record Not Always the Record." *Congressional Quarterly Weekly Report* 32 (Aug. 3, 1974): 2382-2383.

5448. Grau, Craig H. "What Publications Are Most Frequently Quoted in the *Congressional Record*." *Journalism Quarterly* 53 (Winter 1976): 716-719.

5449. McPherson, Elizabeth G. "The History of Reporting the Debates and Proceedings of Congress." Ph.D. dissertation, University of North Carolina at Chapel Hill, 1940.

5450. Mantel, Howard N. "Congressional Record: Fact or Fiction of the Legislative Process." *Western Political Quarterly* 12 (Dec. 1959): 981-995.

5451. Neuberger, Richard L. "The Congressional Record Is Not a Record." *New York Times Magazine,* 20 April 1958, pp. 14, 94-95.

5452. "The Record: Stirring Speeches in Absentia." *Congressional Quarterly Weekly Report* 33 (Mar. 15, 1975): 527-529.

5453. Schmeckebier, Laurence F. *The Government Printing Office: Its History, Activities and Organization.* Baltimore, Md.: Johns Hopkins University Press, 1925.

5454. U.S. Congress. Advisory Committee on Automation and Standardization of Congressional Publications. *Current Procedures and Production Processes of the Congressional Record.* Washington: GPO, 1978.

5455. U.S. General Accounting Office. *Government Printing Operation Improvements Since 1974.* Washington: General Accounting Office, 1977.

Legislative Drafting

5456. Cummings, Frank. *Capitol Hill Manual.* Washington: Bureau of National Affairs, 1976.

5457. Dickerson, Reed, ed. *Professional Legislative Drafting: The Federal Experience.* Chicago: American Bar Association, 1973.

5458. Dickerson, Reed. "Professionalizing Legislative Drafting: A Realistic Goal?" *American Bar Association Journal* 60 (May 1974): 562-564.

5459. Jones, Harry W. "The Drafting of Legislation in the Light of Congressional Responsibility for Constitutionality." *American Bar Association Journal* (Nov. 1948):. 594-595.

5460. Lee, Frederic P. "Office of the Legislative Counsel." *Columbia Law Review* 29 (April 1929): 381-403.

5461. Riddick, Floyd M. "Congressional Characteristics Affecting Legislation." *South Atlantic Quarterly* 43 (April 1944): 199-208.

5462. U.S. Congress. House. Commission on Information and Facilities. *Staff Requirements of the House Legislative Counsel.* 94th Cong., 1st sess. Washington: GPO, 1975.

Capitol

Building and History

5463. Aikman, Lonnelle. "Under the Dome of Freedom." *National Geographic Magazine* 125 (Jan. 1964): 4-59.

5464. Aikman, Lonnelle. "U.S. Capitol, Citadel of Democracy." *National Geographic Magazine* 102 (Aug. 1952): 143-192.

5465. Aikman, Lonnelle. *We, The People: The Story of the United Stated Capitol, Its Past and Its promise.* 7th ed. Washington: United States Capitol Historical Society, 1970.

5466. Anderson, Mary F. "The Old Brick Capitol, Washington D.C." *Americana* 23 (April 1929): 162-168.

5467. Arnold, James R. 'The Battle of Bladensburg." *Records of the Columbia Historical Society* 37-38 (1937): 145-168.

5468. Brown, Glenn. *History of the United States Capitol.* Washington: GPO, 1900.

5469. Brown, Glenn. "The United States Capitol in 1800." *Records of the Columbia Historical Society* 4 (1901): 128-134.

5470. Cammerer, H. Paul. "The Sesquicentennial of the Laying of the Cornerstone of the United States Capitol by George Washington." *Records of the Columbia Historical Society* 44-45 (1944): 161-189.

5471. Campioli, Mario E. "The Capitol's Old Senate, House, and Supreme Court Chambers." *Capitol Dome* 4 (April 1969): 2-4.

5472. Campioli, Mario E. "An Historic Review and Current Proposals for the Nation's Capitol." *Journal of the American Institute of Architects* 39 (Jan. 1963): 49-53.

5473. "The Capitol." *Life,* 2 July 1951, pp. 48-59.

5474. "The Capitol at Washington." *Building News and Engineering Journal* 16 (1869): 83-84.

5475. "The Capitol at Washington." *Burton's . Gentleman's Magazine* 5 (Nov. 1839): 231-235.

5476. "The Capitol at Washington." *United States Magazine* 3 (July 1856): 1-18.

5477. "The Capitol at Washington, No. 2." *United States Magazine* 3 (Aug. 1856): 97-109.

5478. *Centennial Anniversary of the Laying of the Corner Stone of the National Capitol.* Washington: Capitol Centennial Committee, 1893.

5479. Cox, Henry B. "The Nine Capitols of the United States." *Capitol Dome* 5 (April 1970): 2-4.

5480. *Documentary History of the Construction and Development of the United States Capitol Building and Grounds.* 58th Cong., 2d sess. H. Rept. 646, Washington: GPO, 1904.

5481. Downs, Joseph. "The Capitol." *Metropolitan Museum of Art Bulletin* 1 (Jan. 1943): 171-174.

5482. Drummond, William. *Our National Capitol: An Architect Proposes Minor Additions to Capitol and Extensive Changes Within Its Environing Area.* Chicago: National Capitol Publishers, 1946.

5483. Duhamel, James F. "Tiber Creek." *Records of the Columbia Historical Society* 28 (1926): 203-225.

5484. "The Emperor of Capitol Hill." *Architectural Forum* 129 (Sept. 1968): 81-85.

5485. Feeley, Stephen V. *The Story of the Capitol.* 2d ed. New York: Henry Stewart, 1969.

5486. Fortenbaugh, Robert. *The Nine Capitols of the United States.* York, Pa.: Maple Press Co., 1948.

5487. Frary, Ina T. *They Built the Capitol.* Richmond: Garrett and Massie, 1940.

5488. Grosvenor, Gilbert. "The Capitol, Wonder Building of the World." *National Geographic Magazine* 43 (June 1923): 603-638.

5489. Herron, Paul. *The Story of Capitol Hill.* New York: Coward-McCann, 1963.

5490. Holisher, Deside and Beckel, Graham. *Capitol Hill: The Story of Congress.* New York: H. Schuman, 1952.

5491. Morse, F. P. "The Completion of the Capitol." *Munsey's Magazine* 32 (Mar. 1905): 899-901.

5492. Osborne, John B. "The Removal of the Government to Washington." *Records of the Columbia Historical Society* 3 (1900): 136-160.

5493. Page, William T. and Lord, Frank B. *The Story of the Nation's Capitol.* Alexandria, Va.: Washington-Mt. Vernon Memorial Book Corporation, 1932.

5494. Poor, Benjmain P. "The Capitol at Washington." *Century Magazine* 25 (April 1883): 803-819.

5495. Robertson, James I. "Old Capitol: Eminence to Infamy." *Capitol Dome* 4 (Oct. 1969): 2-4.

5496. Schwengel, Frederick D. "The United States Capitol Building." *Records of the Columbia Historical Society* (1963–1965): 49-59.

5497. Spofford, Harriet P. "A Public Building." *Harper's New Monthly Magazine* 38 (Jan. 1869): 204-210.

5498. Swayne, Wager. "The Site of the National Capitol." *Harper's New Monthly Magazine* 40 (Jan. 1870): 181–92.

5499. Thornton, Willis. "The Day They Burned the Capitol." *American Heritage* 6 (Dec. 1954): 48-53.

5500. "The United States Capitol Building." *Architecture and Building* 27 (1897): 200-204.

5501. Van Doren Stern, Philip. "The Capitol." *Records of the Columbia Historical Society* (1969-1970): 178-189.

Capitol Architects

5502. Abbot, Henry L. "Memoir of Montgonery C. Meigs, 1816–1892." *National Academy of Sciences Biographical Memoirs* 3 (1895): 311-326.

5503. "The Architects of the Capitol." *Architecture and Building* 27 (1897): 197-204.

5504. Ashton, Eugene. "The Latrobe Corn-Stalk Columns in the Capitol at Washington." *Magazine of American History* 18 (Aug. 1887): 128-129.

5505. Brown, Glenn. "Dr. William Thornton." *Architectural Record* 6 (July-Sept. 1896): 53-70.

5506. Cammerer, H. Paul. "Architects of the United States Capitol." *Records of the Columbia Historical Society* 48–49 (1949): 1-28.

5507. Campioli, Mari E. "Thomas U. Walter, Edward Clark, and the United States Capitol." *Journal of the Society of Architectural Historians* 23 (Dec. 1964): 210-213.

5508. "Charles Bulfinch, Architect." *Brochure Series of Architectural Illustration* 9 (1903): 122-133.

5509. Clark, Allen. C. "Doctor and Mrs. Thornton." *Records of the Columbia Historical Society* 18 (1915): 144–208.

5510. "The First Architect in America, Benjamin Henry Latrobe: Noted and Letters on the Erection of the Capitol at Washington." *Appleton's Booklovers Magazine* (Sept. 1905): 345-355.

5511. "From William Thornton to Benjmain Latrobe to Thomas Walter: The Capitol Building Emerges." *Journal of the American Institute of Architects* 42 (Dec. 1964): 43-46.

5512. Gallagher, H. M. Pierce. *Robert Mills, Architect of the Washington Monument, 1781-1855.* New York: Columbia University Press, 1935.

5513. Gallagher, H. M. Pierce. "Robert Mills, Architect and Engineer." *Architectural Record* 40 (Dec. 1916): 584-588.

5514. Gallagher, H. M. Pierce. "Robert Mills, 1781-1885: America's First Native Architect. *Architectural Record* 65 (April-May 1929): 387-393; 478-484; 66 (July 1929): 67-72.

5515. Hamlin, Talbot F. *Benjamin Henry Latrobe.* New York: Oxford University Press, 1955.

5516. Hamlin, Talbot F. "Benjamin Henry Latrobe: The Man and the Architect." *Maryland Historical Magazine* 37 (Dec. 1942): 339-360.

5517. Hamlin, Talbot F. "Benjamin Henry Latrobe, 1764-1820." *Magazine of Art* 41 (Mar. 1948): 89-95.

5518. Howard, James Q. "The Architects of the American Capitol." *International Review* 1 (Nov. 1874): 736-753.

5519. Howells, John M. "Charles Bulfinch, Architect." *American Architect and Building News* 93 (June 1908): 194-200.

5520. Hunsberger, George S. "The Architectural Career of George Hadfield." *Records of the Columbia Historical Society* 51-52 (1951-1952): 46-65.

5521. Keller, George. "A Plea for the Recognition of Charles Frederick Anderson as the Designer of the Wings of the National Capitol." *Journal of the American Institute of Architects* 7 (July 1919): 329-330.

5522. Kimball, Fiske and Wells, Bennett. "William Thornton and the Design of the United States Capitol." *Art Studies vol. 1: Medieval, Renaissance and Modern*, ed. F.J. Maather, pp. 76-92. Cambridge, Mass.: Harvard University Press, 1923-1931.

5523. Langely, S. P. "Montgomery Cunningham Meigs." *Bulletin of the Philosophical Society of Washington* 12 (1892-1894): 471-476.

5524. Latrobe, Ferdinand C. "Benjmain Henry Latrobe: Descent and Works." *Maryland Historical Magazine* 33 (Sept. 1938): 247-261.

5525. Mason, George C. "Thomas Ustick Walter." *Journal of the American Institute of Architects* 8 (Nov. 1947): 225-230.

5526. Moore, Charles. *Daniel Burnham, Architect, Planner of Cities.* Boston: Houghton Mifflin, 1921. 2 vols.

5527. Morgan, J. Dudley. "L'Enfant's Idea as to How the Capitol Building Should Face." *Records of the Columbia Historical Society* 7 (1904): 107-113.

5528. Newcomb, Rexford. "Benjamin Henry Latrobe: Early American Architect." *The Architect* 9 (1927): 173-177.

5529. Newcomb, Rexford. "Doctor William Thornton, Early American Architect." *The Architect* 9 (1928): 559-563.

5530. Newcomb, Rexford. "Robert Mills, American Greek Revivalist." *The Architect* 9 (1928): 697-699.

5531. Newcomb, Rexford. "Thomas Ustick Walter." *The Architect* 10 (1928): 585-589.

5532. Norton, Paul. "Latrobe's Ceiling for the Hall of Representatives." *Journal of the Society of Architectural Historians* 10 (May 1951): 5-10.

5533. Owen, Frederick D. "First Government Architect: James Hoban, of Charleston, S.C." *Architectural Record* 11 (Oct. 1901): 581-589.

5534. Place, Charles A. *Charles Bulfinch, Architect and Citizen.* New YorK: Houghton Mifflin, 1925.

5535. Rosenberger, Homer T. "Thomas Ustick Walter and the Completion of the United States Capitol." *Records of the Columbia Historical Society* 50 (1948-1950): 273-322.

5536. Rusk, William S. "Thomas U. Walter and His Works." *Americana* 33 (1939): 151-179.

5537. Rusk, William S. "William Thornton, Architect." *Pennsylvania History* 2 (April 1935): 86-98.

5538. Semmes, John E. *John H. B. Latrobe and His Times, 1803–1891.* Baltimore, Md.: Norman, Remington Co., 1917.

5539. Shannon, Martha A. S. "The Architecture of Charles Bulfinch." *American Magazine of Art* 16 (Aug. 1925): 431-437.

5540. Skramstad, Harold K. "The Engineer as Architect in Washington: The Contribution of Montgomery Meigs." *Records of the Columbia Historical Society* (1969-1970): 266-284.

5541. Weigley, Russel F. "M. C. Meigs, Buildinger of the Capitol and Lincoln's Quartermaster General: A Biography." Ph.D. dissertation, University of Pennsylvania, 1956.

Art Works

5542. Allison, LeRoy W. "A Monument to Cast Iron." *Iron Age* 136 (Nov. 1936): 44-45.

5543. Bache, Rene. "Congress as a Landlord." *Harper's Weekly* 31 (Aug. 1907): 1282-1273.

5544. Baker, Abby G. "The Art Treasures of the United States Capitol." *Munsey's Magazine* 38 (Feb. 1908): 571-584.

5545. Bannister, Turpin C. "The Genealogy of the Dome of the United States Capitol." *Journal of the Society of Architectural Historians* 7 (Jan.-June 1948): 1-31.

5546. Bartlett, Paul W. "Unveiling of the Pediment Group of the House Wing of the National Capitol." *Art and Archaeology* 4 (1916): 178-184.

5547. Brown, Joan S. "William Adams and the Mace of the United States House of Representatives." *Antiques* 108 (July 1975): 76-77.

5548. Burns, John F. "Clocks of the White House and Capitol." *Bulletin of the National Association of Watch and Clock Collectors* 6 (1955): 421-423.

5549. Carroll, Mitchell. "Paul Bartlett's Pediment Group for the House Wing of the National Capitol." *Art and Archaeology* 1 (Jan. 1915): 163-173.

5550. "A Description of the Representatives' Hall at Washington." *American Register of General Depository of History, Politics, and Science* 5 (1809): 372-373.

5551. Fawcett, Waldon. "The Painting of the Capitol Dome." *American Inventor* 1 (July 1903): 3-4.

5552. Hazelton, George C. *The National Capitol, Its Architecture, Art and History.* New York: J. F. Taylor, 1902.

5553. Klapthor, Margaret B. "Furniture in the Capitol: Desks and Chairs Used in the Chamber of the House of Representatives, 1819-1857." *Records of the Columbia Historical Society* 47 (1969-1970): 190-211.

5554. Murdock, Myrtle C. *National Statuary Hall in the Nation's Capitol.* Washington: Monumental Press, 1955.

5555. "Proposed Changes in the Hall of the House of Representatives." *Engineering Record* 39 (1899): 382-383.

5556. Rand, Marguerite C. "Our Doors of Congress: The First to Be Cast in the United States." *Daughters of the American Revolution Magazine* 70 (Jan. 1936): 10-12.

5557. Schuyler, Montgomery. "The Old 'Greek Revival—Part I.' " *American Architect* 98 (1910): 121-128.

5558. Schuyler, Montgomery. "The Old 'Greek Revival—Part II.' " *American Architect* 98 (1910) 201-208.

5559. Sharpe, C. Melvin. "Brief Outline of the History of Electric Illumination in the District of Columbia." *Records of the Columbia Historical Society* 48 (1946–1947): 191-207.

5560. Starnes, Lucy G. "Sanctuary in the Capitol." *American Mercury* 85 (July 1957): 86-88.

5561. Sutherland, Harvey. "The American Westminster Abbey." *Munsey's Magazine* 28 (Mar. 1903): 831-842.

5562. U.S. Congress. House. *The Mace of the House of Representatives of the United States.* Washington: GPO, 1955.

5563. U.S. Congress. Senate. Commission on Art and Antiquities. *The Senate Chamber 1810-1859.* Washington: GPO, 1978.

Remodeling

5564. Brinton, Christian. "The Proposed Changes in the National Capitol." *Century Magazine* 70 (Sept. 1905): 693-702.

5565. Campioli, Mario E. "The Proposed Extension of the West Central Front of the Capitol." *Records of the Columbia Historical Society* 47 (1969-1970): 212-236.

5566. "Cooler Air and Longer Sessions: Air Conditioning Keeps Congress on Job." *Heating, Piping and Air Conditioning* 18 (Oct. 1946): 76-77.

5567. DeWitt, Roscoe P. "Extension of the East Front of the Capitol." *Journal of the American Institute of Architects* 29 (June 1958): 268-277.

5568. Doeleman, Herman F. "Investigations for Roofs of U.S. Capitol: After Ninety Years Trusses Need Replacement, Temporary Repairs Made." *Civil Engineering* 11 (June 1941): 327-330.

5569. Greenburg, Leonard and Bloomfield, J. J. "The New Ventilation Systems of the Senate and House Chambers of the Capitol, Washington, D.C." *Public Health Reports* 48 (Feb. 1933): 138-151.

5570. Gregson, Wilfred J. "Extending the Capitol's West Front: A Move Toward Safety." *Capitol Dome* 4 (July 1961): 2-4.

5571. Holland, Leicester B. "Wings over the Capitol." *Octagon* 9 (May 1937): 23-27.

5572. Hughes, William D. *The Capitol and Its Grounds: Their Defects: Plans for Improvement.* Washington: R. Beresford, 1876.

5573. Lewis, L. L. and Stacey, A. E. "Air-Conditioning the Halls of Congress." *Heating, Piping and Air Conditioning* 1 (1929): 665-671.

5574. McLaughlin, Charles C. "The Capitol in Peril? The West Front Controversy from Walter to Stewart." *Records of the Columbia Historical Society* 47 (1969-1970): 237-265.

5575. "New Strength and Beauty Built into Capitol." *Engineering News-Record* 147 (Aug. 1951): 30-32.

5576. Rodda, William H. "Physical Hazards of Capitol, White House." *Weekly Underwriter and the Insurance Press* 18 (Jan. 1930): 162-163.

5577. Sabine, Paul E. "The Acoustics of the Remodeled House and Senate Chambers of the National Capitol." *Journal of the Acoustical Society of America* 24 (Mar. 1952): 121-124.

5578. Smithmeyer, John L. *An Essay on the Heating and Ventilation of Public Buildings, with Special Reference to the Senate and House of Representatives of the United States.* Washington: R.O. Polkinhorn and Sons, 1886.

5579. Swartwout, Egerton. "The Extension of the East Front of the Capitol." *Octagon* 9 (May 1937): 16-22.

5580. Thompson, Nelson S. "Ventilation of the Capitol, Washington, D.C.: A Case of Faulty Distribution with an Up-Draft System." *Heating and Ventilating Magazine* 8 (Mar. 1911): 15-19.

Addendum

5581. Abramowitz, Alan I. "A Comparison of Voting for U.S. Senator and Representative in 1978." *American Political Science Review* 74 (Sept. 1980): 633-640.

5582. Abramowitz, Alan I. "Is the Revolt Fading? A Note on Party Loyalty Among Southern Democratic Congressmen." *Journal of Politics* 42 (May 1980): 568-576.

5583. Bledsoe, Robert L. and Handberg, Roger. "Changing Times: Congress and Defense." *Armed Forces and Society* 6 (Spring 1980): 415-429.

5584. Brady, David W. and Bullock, Charles S. "Is There a Conservative Coalition in the House?" *Journal of Politics* 42 (May 1980): 549-559.

5585. Chelimsky, Eleanor. "Evaluation Research Credibility and the Congress." *Policy Studies Journal* 8 (1980): 1177-1184.

5586. Clark, Timothy B. "The New Budgetary Discipline: Can Congress Really Make It Stick?" *National Journal* 12 (May 31, 1980): 898-902.

5587. Cohen, Richard E. "The 'Numbers Crunchers' at the CBO Try to Steer Clear of Policy Disputes." *National Journal* 12 (July 7, 1980): 938-941.

5588. Cronin, Thomas E. "A Resurgent Congress and the Imperial Presidency." *Political Science Quarterly* 95 (Summer 1980): 209-238.

5589. Davidson, Roger H. and Oleszek, Walter J. *Congress and Its Members.* Washington: Congressional Quarterly, 1981.

5590. Dodd, Lawrence C. and Oppenheimer, Bruce I. *Congress Reconsidered.* 2d ed. Washington: Congressional Quarterly, 1981.

5591. Draper, Frank D. and Pitsuada, Bernard T. "Congress and Executive Branch Budget Reform: The House Appropriations Committee and Zero-Base Budgeting." *International Journal of Public Administration* 2 (1980): 331-375.

5592. Enelow, James M. and Koehler, David H. "The Amendment in Legislative Strategy: Sophisticated Voting in the U.S. Congress." *Journal of Politics* 42 (May 1980): 396-413.

5593. Erikson, Robert S. and Wright, Gerald C. "Policy Representation of Constituency Interests." *Political Behavior* 2 (1980): 91-106.

5594. Feig, Douglas G. "The Stability of Congressional Committees: A Formal Analysis." *Political Methodology* 6 (1979): 311-341.

5595. Fisher, Louis. *The Politics of Shared Power: Congress and the Executive.* Washington: Congressional Quarterly, 1981.

5596. Gertzog, Irwin N. "The Matrimonial Connection: The Nomination of Congressmen's Widows for the House of Representatives." *Journal of Politics* 42 (Aug. 1980): 820-833.

5597. Goldenberg, Edie N. and Traugott, Michael W. "Congressional Campaign Effects on Candidate Recognition and Evaluation." *Political Behavior* 2 (1980): 61-90.

5598. Greenberg, Sarah B. "Constitutional Law—Separation of Powers—Congressional Employment Practices Involving Discrimination Are Reviewable by the Courts Under the Fifth Amendment. (Case Note) Davis V. Passman 99 S. Ct. 2264 (1929)." *Creighton Law Review* 13 (Spring 1980): 991-1003.

5599. Hinckley, Barbara. "The American Voter in Congressional Elections." *American Political Science Review* 74 (Sept. 1980): 641-650.

5600. Hoadley, John F. "The Emergence of Political Parties in Congress, 1789-1803." *American Political Science Review* 74 (Sept. 1980): 757-779.

5601. Huddleston, Mark W. "Assessing Congressional Budget Reform: The Impact on Appropriations." *Policy Studies Journal* 9 (Autumn 1980): 81-86.

5602. Hughes, G. Philip. "Congressional Influence in Weapons Procurement: The Case of Lightweight Fighter Commonality." *Public Policy* 28 (Fall 1980): 415-450.

5603. Kohn, Walter S. G. *Women in National Legislatures: A Comparative Study of Six Countries.* New York: Praeger, 1980.

5604. LeLoup, Lance T. *The Fiscal Congress: Legislative Control of the Budget.* Westport, Conn.: Greenwood Press, 1980.

5605. Lewis, Frederick P. *The Dilemma in the Congressional Power to Enforce the Fourteenth Amendment.* Washington: University Press of America, 1980.

5606. Mann, Thomas E. and Wolfinger, Raymond E. "Candidates and Parties in Congressional Elections." *American Political Science Review* 74 (Sept. 1980): 617-632.

5607. Nivola, Pietro S. "Energy Policy and the Congress: The Politics of the Natural Gas Policy Act of 1976." *Public Policy* 28 (Fall 1980): 491-543.

5608. Oliver, Covey T. "Getting the Senators to Accept the Reference of Treaties to Both Houses for Approval by Simple Majorities." *American Journal of International Law* 74 (Jan. 1980): 124-144.

5609. Owens, John R. and Olson, Edward C. "Economic Fluctuations and Congressional Elections." *American Journal of Political Science* 24 (Aug. 1980): 469-493.

5610. Parker, Glenn R. "Cycles in Congressional District Attention." *Journal of Politics* 42 (May 1980): 540-548.

5611. Parnell, Archie. *Congress and the IRS: Improving the Relationship.* Washington: Fund for Public Policy Research, 1980.

5612. Pastor, Robert A. *Congress and the Politics of U.S. Foreign Economic Policy, 1926-1976.* Berkeley: University of California Press, 1980.

5613. Peters, John G. and Welch, Susan. "The Effects of Charges of Corruption on Voting Behavior in Congressional Elections." *American Political Science Review* 74 (Sept. 1980): 697-708.

5614. Ratliff, Richard L. and Benedict, Bob. "A Businessman's Guide to the Non-legislative Powers of a Congressman." *Sloan Management Review* 21 (Spring 1980): 67-76.

5615. Ray, Bruce A. "Congressional Losers in the U.S. Federal Spending Process." *Legislative Studies Quarterly* 5 (Aug. 1980): 359-372.

5616. Ray, Bruce A. "Federal Spending and the Selection of Committee Assignments in the U.S. House of Representatives." *American Journal of Political Science* 24 (Aug. 1980): 495-510.

5617. Rourke, John T. "Congress, the Executive and Foreign Policy: A Proportional Analysis." *Presidential Studies Quarterly* 10 (Spring 1980): 179-193.

5618. Schick, Allen. *Congress and Money: Budgeting, Spending and Taxing.* Washington: Urban Institute, 1980.

5619. Schwarz, John E., Barton, Fenmore, and Volgy, Thomas J. "Liberal and Conservative Voting in the House of Representatives: A National Model of Representation." *British Journal of Political Science* 10 (July 1980): 317-340.

5620. Sulfridge, Wayne. "Ideology as a Factor in Senate Considerations of Supreme Court Nominations." *Journal of Politics* 42 (May 1980): 560-567.

SUBJECT INDEX

AUTHOR INDEX

Subject Index

Author Index